Seventh Edition

Management of
Cybersecurity

Michael E. Whitman

Herbert J. Mattord

Australia • Brazil • Canada • Mexico • Singapore • United Kingdom • United States

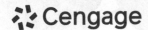

Management of Cybersecurity, 7th Edition
Michael E. Whitman, Herbert J. Mattord

SVP, Product Management: Cheryl Costantini

VP, Product Management: Mark Santee

Portfolio Product Director: Rita Lombard

Portfolio Product Manager: Natalie Onderdonk

Product Assistant: Anh Nguyen

Learning Designer: Carolyn Mako, Mary Convertino

Senior Content Manager: Michelle Ruelos Cannistraci

Content Project Manager: Geetha Dhandapani

Digital Project Manager: Jim Vaughey

Developmental Editor: Dan Seiter

Senior Manager, Product Marketing: Neena Bali

Senior Product Marketing Manager: Cybele Beckham

Content Acquisition Analyst: Nichole Nalenz

Production Service: Straive

Designer: Erin Griffin

Cover Image Source: iStockPhoto.com/ ValeryBrozhinsky

For product information and technology assistance, contact us at
**Cengage Customer & Sales Support, 1-800-354-9706
or support.cengage.com.**

For permission to use material from this text or product, submit all requests online at **www.copyright.com**.

Library of Congress Control Number: 2024948731

ISBN: 979-8-214-01173-8
Looseleaf ISBN: 979-8-214-01174-5

Cengage
5191 Natorp Boulevard
Mason, OH 45040
USA

Cengage is a leading provider of customized learning solutions. Our employees reside in nearly 40 different countries and serve digital learners in 165 countries around the world. Find your local representative at: **www.cengage.com**.

To learn more about Cengage platforms and services, register or access your online learning solution, or purchase materials for your course, visit **www.cengage.com**.

Notice to the Reader

Publisher does not warrant or guarantee any of the products described herein or perform any independent analysis in connection with any of the product information contained herein. Publisher does not assume, and expressly disclaims, any obligation to obtain and include information other than that provided to it by the manufacturer. The reader is expressly warned to consider and adopt all safety precautions that might be indicated by the activities described herein and to avoid all potential hazards. By following the instructions contained herein, the reader willingly assumes all risks in connection with such instructions. The publisher makes no representations or warranties of any kind, including but not limited to, the warranties of fitness for particular purpose or merchantability, nor are any such representations implied with respect to the material set forth herein, and the publisher takes no responsibility with respect to such material. The publisher shall not be liable for any special, consequential, or exemplary damages resulting, in whole or part, from the readers' use of, or reliance upon, this material.

Printed at CLDPC, USA, 12-24

Brief Contents

Contents

Chapter 4

Risk Management: Treating Risk 125

Chapter 5

Compliance: Law and Ethics 157

Chapter 9

Cybersecurity Management Practices   324

Chapter 10

Planning for Contingencies   354

Foreword

By David Rowan, Retired Senior Vice President and Director, Technology Risk and Compliance, Sun Trust Banks, Inc.

If you're reading this, I want to extend my gratitude. Your interest in this text signals a commitment to a career in cybersecurity or perhaps marks the beginning of such a journey. This is significant because we all—every one of us—need your expertise and dedication.

We live in a world where technology is not just a convenience; it is the very foundation of our daily lives. Much of what we take for granted—from the devices we hold in our hands to the systems that operate unseen—is the result of technological advancements. Consider, for instance, the smart thermostat in my home, which adjusts to my preferences without my direct involvement. I could monitor it via an app or wait for a notification, but I don't. I simply trust that it's doing its job, just as I trust the technology that delivers my news feed.

In essence, we inhabit two worlds: one driven by our intentions and actions, and another where services seem to function autonomously. Both are integral to our way of life, continually expanding and evolving. But the success of these worlds hinges on one critical element: trust.

We trust our phones to connect us, electricity to power our lives, our streaming services to deliver content, and our financial transactions to be secure and accurate. I trust that my home will be at the perfect temperature when I walk through the door. This trust in technology brings immeasurable benefits, enabling us to delegate tasks, share resources, exchange ideas, and engage in commerce with ease. It is a foundation worth protecting.

Yet, this trust is not invulnerable. There are those who seek to exploit it to disrupt, divert, or even destroy the benefits that technology and the free flow of information provide. Their motives may vary, but the responsibility to safeguard our technological trust falls on us. That's why your interest in this field is so crucial. We need vigilant guardians who will protect the trust that underpins our digital world.

With more than 35 years in the financial industry, the latter half focused on cybersecurity, I have witnessed the evolution of technology risk management from a niche back-office function to a critical board-level concern with global implications. Today, the intertwined nature of commerce, infrastructure, utilities, safety, and culture makes security a strategic priority. It's not just about the tools we use, but about how we use them. As the old saying goes, it's not the tools that make the carpenter but the skill with which they are used.

This edition of *Management of Cybersecurity* serves as a cornerstone, offering the latest insights into planning, governing, implementing, and managing a robust cybersecurity program. It is both holistic and comprehensive, addressing every facet of cybersecurity and integrating it into the systems we rely on daily. The text offers strategic guidance on policy development, risk identification, personnel management, organizational structure, and legal considerations, all within the context of our broader ecosystem.

Furthermore, as artificial intelligence becomes increasingly pervasive, the need for rigorous cybersecurity education and forward-thinking governance is more urgent than ever. This updated edition is not just a guide; it is a springboard for the next generation of cybersecurity leaders.

Strategy and management are not just components of cybersecurity; they are its very essence. This text will inform you of the what, why, and how of this critical discipline. *Management of Cybersecurity* is an indispensable resource for anyone dedicated to safeguarding our modern world. I encourage you to join this vital community of protectors.

—David Rowan, August 2024

Preface

As global use of the Internet continues to expand, the demand for and reliance on Internet-based information creates an increasing expectation of access. Global commerce relies on the Internet, which creates an increasing threat of attacks on information assets and a need for greater numbers of professionals capable of protecting those assets. With billions of Internet users capable of accessing and attacking online information from anywhere at any time, the threat of an attack grows daily.

To secure commerce and information assets from ever-increasing threats, organizations demand a breadth and depth of expertise from the next generation of cybersecurity practitioners. These professionals are expected to have an optimal mix of skills and experience to secure diverse information environments. Students of technology must learn to recognize the threats and vulnerabilities present in existing systems. They must also learn how to manage the use of information assets securely and support the goals and objectives of their organizations through effective cybersecurity governance, risk management, and regulatory compliance.

This textbook strives to fulfill the need for a high-quality academic textbook in cybersecurity management. While there are dozens of good publications on cybersecurity and its assurance for practitioners, few textbooks provide students with an in-depth study of cybersecurity management. Therefore, this book provides a managerial approach to cybersecurity and a thorough treatment of the secure administration of information assets. It can be used to support cybersecurity coursework for a variety of technology students as well as courses aimed at business students.

The authors are Certified Information Systems Security Professionals (CISSP) and Certified Information Security Managers (CISM), so these knowledge domains have had an influence on the design of this textbook. With the influence of the extensive library of information available from the Special Publications collection at the National Institute of Standards and Technology (NIST, at *csrc.nist.gov*), the authors have also tapped into government and industry standards for cybersecurity management. Although this textbook is by no means a certification study guide, much of the Common Bodies of Knowledge for the dominant industry certifications, especially in the management of cybersecurity, have been integrated into the text.

Intended Audience

This course is designed for those learning how to manage the use of information assets securely and support the goals and objectives of their organizations through effective cybersecurity governance, risk management, and regulatory compliance. The underlying tenet of this course is that cybersecurity in the modern organization is a management problem and not one that technology alone can answer; it is a problem that has important economic consequences and one for which management is accountable. Students must learn to recognize the threats and vulnerabilities present in existing systems. Those in disciplines such as cybersecurity, information systems, information technology, computer science, criminal justice, political science, and accounting information systems must understand the foundations of the management of cybersecurity and the development of managerial strategy for cybersecurity.

Chapter Descriptions

Chapter 1, "Introduction to the Management of Cybersecurity," establishes the foundation for understanding the field of cybersecurity by explaining the importance of information and identifying who is responsible for protecting an organization's information assets. Students learn the definition and key characteristics of cybersecurity as well as the differences between cybersecurity management and general management.

Chapter 2, "Governance and Strategic Planning for Cybersecurity," explains the importance of executive oversight of cybersecurity programs. The chapter further examines organizational planning and describes its principal components. It also explores the role of cybersecurity governance and strategic planning within the organizational context.

Chapter 3, "Risk Management: Assessing Risk," defines risk management and its role in the organization. The chapter demonstrates how to use risk management techniques to identify and prioritize risk factors for information assets. The risk management model presented assesses risk based on the likelihood of adverse events and the impact on information assets when adverse events occur. This chapter concludes with a brief discussion of how to document the results of the risk assessment process.

Chapter 4, "Risk Management: Treating Risk," presents essential risk mitigation strategy options and opens the discussion on controlling risk. Students learn to classify risk, use existing conceptual frameworks to evaluate risk controls, and formulate a cost-benefit analysis. They also learn how to maintain and perpetuate continuous improvement of risk controls.

Chapter 5, "Compliance: Law and Ethics," explains the legal and regulatory environment and its relationship to cybersecurity. This chapter describes the major national and international laws that affect the practice of cybersecurity as well as the role of culture in ethics as it applies to cybersecurity professionals.

Chapter 6, "Cybersecurity Policy," defines cybersecurity policy and describes its central role in a successful cybersecurity program. Industry and government best practices promote three major types of cybersecurity policy; this chapter explains what goes into each type and demonstrates how to develop, implement, and maintain various types of cybersecurity policies.

Chapter 7, "Developing the Cybersecurity Program," explores the various organizational approaches to cybersecurity and explains the functional components of a cybersecurity program. Students learn the complexities of planning and staffing for an organization's cybersecurity department based on the size of the organization and other factors, and they learn how to evaluate the internal and external factors that influence the activities and organization of a cybersecurity program. This chapter also identifies and describes the typical job titles and functions performed in the cybersecurity program and concludes with an exploration of the creation and management of a security education, training, and awareness program. This chapter concludes with an overview of project management, a necessary skill in any technology or business professional's portfolio.

Chapter 8, "Cybersecurity Management Models," describes the components of the dominant cybersecurity management models, including U.S. government and internationally sanctioned models, and discusses how to customize them for a specific organization's needs. Students learn how to implement the fundamental elements of key cybersecurity management practices. Models include NIST, ISO, and a host of specialized cybersecurity research models that help students understand confidentiality and integrity applications in modern systems.

Chapter 9, "Cybersecurity Management Practices," describes the fundamentals and emerging trends in cybersecurity management practices and explains how these practices help organizations meet U.S. and international compliance standards. The chapter contains an expanded section on security performance measurement and covers concepts of certification and accreditation of IT systems.

Chapter 10, "Planning for Contingencies," describes and explores the major components of contingency planning and the need for them in an organization. The chapter illustrates the planning and development of contingency plans, beginning with the business impact analysis and continuing through implementing and testing incident response, disaster recovery, business continuity, and crisis management contingency plans.

Chapter 11, "Cybersecurity Maintenance," describes the ongoing technical and administrative evaluation of the cybersecurity program that an organization must perform to maintain the security of its information systems. This chapter explores considerations needed for the varieties of vulnerability analysis in modern organizations, from Internet penetration testing to wireless network risk assessment, and relates them to the risk management process.

Chapter 12, "Cybersecurity Protection Mechanisms," introduces students to the domain of technical controls by exploring access control approaches, including authentication, authorization, and biometric access controls as well as firewalls and the common approaches to firewall implementation. It also covers the technical control approaches for intrusion detection and prevention systems and cryptography.

Features

This book contains the following features in each chapter.

- **Chapter objectives**—Chapters begin with a detailed list of concepts to be mastered. This list provides a quick reference to the contents of the chapter as well as a useful study aid.

- **Case Opener and Closing Case scenarios**—Each chapter opens with a short vignette that follows the same fictional company as it encounters various cybersecurity issues. The final part of each chapter is a conclusion to the scenario that also offers questions to stimulate in-class discussion. These questions give students and the instructor an opportunity to explore the issues that underlie the content.

- **View Point features**—An essay from a cybersecurity practitioner or academic is included in each chapter. These sections provide a range of commentary that illustrate real-world topics or share personal opinions, giving students a wider, applied view on the topics in the text.

- **Hands-on learning**—At the end of each chapter, students will find a chapter Summary and Review Questions as well as Exercises and Closing Case exercises, which give them the opportunity to examine the cybersecurity arena from an experiential perspective. Using the Exercises, students can research, analyze, and write to reinforce learning objectives and deepen their understanding of the text. The Closing Case exercises require that students use professional judgment, powers of observation, and elementary research to create solutions for simple cybersecurity scenarios.

- **Glossary**—Key terms are highlighted in context throughout the text and defined in a glossary at the end of the book.

- **Endnotes**—Citations at the end of the book list references for each chapter.

New to This Edition

Reflecting the latest advancements in the field, this edition presents the most current information on NIST, ISO, security governance, and other relevant changes related to today's cybersecurity.

The book includes the following revisions and enhancements from the previous edition:

- The sequence of chapters was reorganized to achieve a needed focus on risk management, governance, and compliance from a "top-down" perspective—from strategic to tactical cybersecurity operations.
- All content was updated and refreshed to maintain currency with industry and government guidance.
- Additional resources were included on the current state of cybersecurity employment to aid those entering the career field.

- Management topics on performance measures were expanded and enhanced.
- Chapter 1 contains expanded discussions and increased coverage of the latest threats and trends.
- Chapter 4 has been enhanced and expanded.
- Chapter 5 includes coverage of new and critical laws, including breach laws.
- Chapter 6 was reorganized and refreshed to reflect the evolution in industry practices.
- Chapter 8 now emphasizes cybersecurity management models.
- Chapter 9 has been expanded to cover personnel security issues.
- Chapter 12 includes expanded coverage in managing new technologies.

Text and Graphic Conventions

Wherever appropriate, additional information and exercises have been added to this text to help explain the topic at hand. The following labels are used throughout the text to alert readers to additional materials:

Note | Notes draw attention to helpful material related to the subject being described and offer expanded insights to enrich understanding.

View Point

An essay from a cybersecurity practitioner or academic is included in each chapter. These sections provide commentary that illustrate interesting topics or share personal opinions.

Self-Check

To complete the learning cycle, these self-check questions help students practice recalling the information they have read. With answers and extensive explanations provided at the end of each chapter, this low-stakes practice testing helps students assess how well they're learning and what material they might need to review before completing graded work.

Instructor Materials

Additional instructor resources for this product are available online. Instructor assets include an Instructor's Manual, an Educator's Guide, PowerPoint® slides, and a test bank powered by Cognero®. Sign up or sign in at www.cengage.com to search for and access this product and its online resources.

Instructor's Manual. The Instructor's Manual that accompanies this course provides additional instructional material to assist in class preparation, including suggestions for classroom activities, discussion topics, and additional projects.

Solution and Answer Guide. The instructor's resources include solutions to all end-of-chapter material, including review questions and exercises.

PowerPoint presentations. This course comes with Microsoft PowerPoint slides for each chapter. These are included as a teaching aid for classroom presentations, to make available to students on the network for chapter review, or to be printed for classroom distribution. Instructors, please feel at liberty to add your own slides for additional topics you introduce to the class.

Cengage testing powered by Cognero. This flexible online system allows instructors to do the following:

- Author, edit, and manage test bank content from multiple Cengage solutions.
- Create multiple test versions in an instant.
- Deliver tests from their learning management system, classroom, or wherever they want.

MindTap

MindTap for *Management of Cybersecurity, Seventh Edition*, is an online learning solution designed to help students hone the skills they need in today's workforce. Research shows that employers need critical thinkers, troubleshooters, and creative problem solvers to stay relevant in our fast-paced, technology-driven world. MindTap can help students achieve this with assignments and activities that provide hands-on practice, real-life relevance, and certification test prep. MindTap guides students through assignments that help them progress from basic knowledge and understanding to more challenging problems. MindTap activities and assignments are tied to industry certifications and standards. MindTap features include the following:

- **Live Virtual Machine labs** allow students to practice, explore, and try different solutions in a safe sandbox environment. Each chapter provides an opportunity to complete an in-depth project hosted in a live virtual machine environment. Students implement the skills and knowledge gained in the chapter through real design and configuration scenarios.
- **Pre- and Post-Assessments** assess students' understanding of key concepts at the beginning and end of the course and emulate the text.
- **Security for Life** assignments encourage students to stay current with what's happening in the field of cybersecurity.
- **Reflection** activities encourage classroom and online discussion of key issues covered in the chapters.

Instructors, MindTap is designed around learning objectives and provides analytics and reporting so you can easily see where the class stands in terms of progress, engagement, and completion rates. Use the content and learning path as is or pick and choose how your materials will integrate with the learning path. You control what students see and when they see it. Learn more at cengage.com/mindtap/.

Instant Access Code: (ISBN: 9798214011790)
Printed Access Code: (ISBN: 9798214011806)

About the Authors

Michael E. Whitman, Ph.D., CISM, CISSP is the director of the Center for Cybersecurity Education and Professor of Cybersecurity in the Michael J. Coles College of Business at Kennesaw State University (KSU). In 2004, 2007, 2012, 2015, and 2022 under Dr. Whitman's direction, the Center spearheaded KSU's successful bid for the prestigious National Center of Academic Excellence recognitions (CAE/IAE and CAE/CDE) awarded by the National Security Agency. Dr. Whitman is also the editor-in-chief of the *Journal of Cybersecurity Education, Research, and Practice*. Dr. Whitman is an active researcher and author in cybersecurity risk management, policy, threats, curriculum development, and ethical computing. He currently teaches graduate and undergraduate courses in cybersecurity. Dr. Whitman has several security textbooks currently in print, including *Principles of Information Security, Principles of Incident Response and Disaster Recovery*, and *Management of Cybersecurity*. He has published articles in *Information Systems Research, Communications of the ACM*, the *Journal of International Business Studies, Information and Management*, and the *Journal of Computer Information Systems*. Dr. Whitman is a member of the Information Systems Security Association, ISACA, and the Association for Information Systems. Previously, Dr. Whitman served the U.S. Army as an armored cavalry officer with additional duties as his unit's automated data processing system security officer.

Herbert J. Mattord, Ph.D., CISM, CISSP completed 24 years of IT industry experience as an application developer, database administrator, project manager, and cybersecurity practitioner before joining the faculty at KSU, where he is a professor of cybersecurity. Dr. Mattord currently teaches graduate and undergraduate courses. He is also a senior editor of the *Journal of Cybersecurity Education, Research, and Practice*. He and Dr. Michael Whitman have authored *Principles of Information Security*, *Principles of Incident Response and Disaster Recovery*, *Management of Cybersecurity*, and other books. Dr. Mattord is an active researcher, author, and consultant in cybersecurity management and related topics. He has published articles in the *Information Resources Management Journal*, the *Journal of Information Security Education*, the *Journal of Executive Education*, and the *International Journal of Interdisciplinary Telecommunications and Networking*. Dr. Mattord is a member of the Information Systems Security Association, ISACA, and the Association for Information Systems. During his career as an IT practitioner, Dr. Mattord was an adjunct professor at Kennesaw State University, Southern Polytechnic State University, Austin Community College, and Texas State University: San Marcos. He was formerly the manager of corporate information technology security at Georgia-Pacific Corporation.

Acknowledgments

The authors would like to thank their families for their support and understanding for the many hours dedicated to this project—hours taken, in many cases, from family activities.

Reviewers

The authors are indebted to the following individuals for their contributions of perceptive feedback on the initial proposal, the project outline, and the chapter-by-chapter reviews of the text:

- Paul D. Witman, Ph.D., Professor Emeritus, Information Technology Management, California Lutheran University, School of Management, Thousand Oaks, CA
- Rajiv Malkan, Ph.D., Professor, Business and Computer Science, Lone Star College, Houston, TX

Special Thanks

The authors want to thank the editorial and production teams at Cengage. Their diligent and professional efforts greatly enhanced the final product:

- Carolyn Mako and Mary Convertino, Learning Designers
- Dan Seiter, Developmental Editor
- Natalie Onderdonk, Portfolio Product Manager
- Michelle Ruelos Cannistraci, Senior Content Manager
- Geetha Dhandapani, Content Project Manager

In addition, several professional and commercial organizations and individuals have aided the development of this textbook by providing information and inspiration, and the authors want to acknowledge their contributions:

- David Rowan
- Charles Cresson Wood
- Clearwater Compliance

The authors also thank the authors of the View Point features: Henry Bonin, Lee Imrey, Bob Hayes and Kathleen Kotwica, David Lineman, Paul D. Witman and Scott Mackelprang, Alison Gunnels, George V. Hulme, Tim Callahan, Mark Reardon, Martin Lee, Karen Scarfone, Donald "Mac" McCarthy, and Todd E. Tucker.

Our Commitment

The authors are committed to serving the needs of the adopters and readers. We would be pleased and honored to receive feedback on the textbook and its supporting materials. You can contact us at cybercenter@kennesaw.edu.

Introduction to the Management of Cybersecurity

Chapter Objectives

After reading this chapter and completing the exercises, you should be able to:

1 Summarize the key characteristics of cybersecurity.

2 Outline the 12 dominant categories of threats to cybersecurity.

3 Discuss the key characteristics of leadership and management.

4 Differentiate types of management and their role in securing information assets.

> Management is, above all, a practice where art, science, and craft meet.
>
> —Henry Mintzberg

Case Opener

One month into her new position at Random Widget Works, Inc. (RWW), Iris Majwubu left her office early one afternoon to attend a meeting of the local chapter of the Information Systems Security Association (ISSA). She had recently been promoted from her previous assignment at RWW as manager of information risk to become the first chief cybersecurity officer named at the company.

This occasion marked Iris's first ISSA meeting. With a growing stack of pressing matters on her cluttered desk, Iris wasn't exactly certain why she was making it a priority to attend this professional society meeting. She sighed. Since her early-morning wake-up, she had spent many hours in business meetings, followed by long hours at her desk working toward defining her new position at the company.

At the ISSA meeting, Iris saw Charlie Moody, her supervisor from Sequential Label and Supply (SLS), the company she used to work for. Charlie was promoted to chief information officer of SLS almost three years ago.

"Hi, Charlie," she said.

"Hello, Iris," Charlie said, shaking her hand. "Congratulations on your promotion. How are things going in your new position?"

"So far," she replied, "things are going well—I think."

Charlie noticed Iris's hesitancy. "You think?" he said. "Okay, tell me what's going on."

"Well, I'm struggling to get a consensus from the senior management team about the problems we have," Iris explained. "I'm told that cybersecurity is a priority, but everything is in disarray. Any ideas that I bring up are ripped apart before they're even taken up by my leadership team. There's no established policy covering our cybersecurity needs, and it seems that we have little hope of getting one approved anytime soon. The cybersecurity budget covers my salary plus a little bit of funding that goes toward part of one position for a technician in the network department. The IT managers act like I'm wasting their time, and they don't seem to take our security issues as seriously as I do. It's like trying to drive a herd of cats; it's impossible!"

Charlie thought for a moment and then said, "I've got some ideas that may help. We should talk more, but not now; the meeting is about to start. Here's my number—call me tomorrow and we'll get together for coffee or lunch."

Introduction to Cybersecurity

In today's global markets, business operations are enabled by technology. From the boardroom to the mailroom, businesses buy and sell goods and services, track client accounts, and maintain inventory on company **assets**, all through the implementation of information technology (IT) systems. An asset is any resource that is being protected. IT enables the storage and transportation of information—often a company's most valuable resource—from one business unit to another. But what happens if the vehicle breaks down, even for a little while? Business deals fall through, shipments are lost, and company assets become more vulnerable to threats from both inside and outside the organization. In the past, the business manager's response to this problem was to proclaim, "We have technology people to handle technology problems." This statement might have been valid in the days when technology was confined to the climate-controlled rooms of the data center and when information processing was centralized. In the last few decades, however, technology has moved out from the data center to permeate every facet of the business environment. The business place is no longer static; it moves whenever employees travel from office to office, from city to city, or even from office to home. As businesses became more fluid, computer security evolved into information security (InfoSec) and then into cybersecurity. Cybersecurity covers a broader range of issues, from the protection of computer-based data to the protection of human knowledge. Cybersecurity is no longer the sole responsibility of a small, dedicated group of professionals in the company, or even of the IT department. It is now the responsibility of all employees, especially managers.

Astute managers increasingly recognize the critical nature of cybersecurity as the vehicle by which the organization's information assets are protected. In response to this growing awareness, businesses are creating new positions to solve these challenges. The emergence of executive-level cybersecurity managers—like Iris in the opening scenario of this chapter—allows for the creation of professionally managed cybersecurity teams that have a primary objective to protect information assets, wherever and whatever they may be. The focus of cybersecurity, then, is protecting **information assets**—digital resources that have value to the organization, specifically information and the systems that store, process, and transmit information.

Organizations must realize that cybersecurity planning and funding decisions involve more than managers of information, the members of the cybersecurity team, or the managers of IT. Altogether, they must involve the entire organization, as represented by three distinct groups of managers and professionals, or communities of interest:

- Those in the field of cybersecurity
- Those in the field of IT
- Those from the rest of the organization

These three groups should engage in a constructive effort to reach consensus on an overall plan to protect the organization's information assets.

The communities of interest and the roles they fulfill include the following:

- The cybersecurity community protects the organization's information assets from the many threats they face.
- The IT community supports the business objectives of the organization by supplying and supporting IT that is appropriate to the organization's needs.
- The general business community articulates and communicates organizational policy and objectives and allocates resources to the other groups.

Working together, these communities of interest make recommendations to executive management about how to secure an organization's information assets most effectively. As the discussion between Iris and Charlie in this chapter's opening scenario suggests, managing a successful cybersecurity program takes time, resources, and a lot of effort by all three communities within an organization. Each community of interest must understand that cybersecurity is about identifying, measuring, and mitigating—or at least understanding and documenting—the risk associated with operating information assets in a modern business environment. It is up to the leadership of the various communities of interest to identify and support initiatives for controlling the risks faced by the organization's information assets. To make sound business decisions concerning the security of information assets, managers must understand the concept of cybersecurity, the roles professionals play within that field, and the issues organizations face in a fluid, global business environment.

To understand the varied aspects of cybersecurity, you must know the definitions of certain key cybersecurity terms and concepts. This knowledge enables you to communicate effectively with, and within, the IT and cybersecurity communities.

Cybersecurity is based on the fundamental concept of security, the state of being secure and free from danger or harm, or the actions taken to make someone or something secure. Security is often achieved by means of multiple strategies undertaken simultaneously or used in combination with one another. Many of those strategies focus on specific areas of security, but they also have many elements in common. It is the role of management to ensure that each strategy is properly planned, organized, staffed, directed, and controlled. National security, for example, is a system of multilayered processes that protects the sovereignty of a state—its assets, resources, and people.

The dominant areas of security include:

- Cybersecurity—The protection of the confidentiality, integrity, and availability of information assets, whether in storage, processing, or transmission, via the application of policy, education, training and awareness, and technology; this area overlaps with all other security areas
- Computer security—The protection of computerized information processing systems and the data they contain and process
- Communications security—The protection of all communications media, technology, and content
- Network security—A subset of communications security; the protection of voice and data networking components, connections, and content
- Operations security—The protection of the details of an organization's operations and activities
- Physical security—The protection of physical items, objects, or areas from unauthorized access and misuse; known in the industry as corporate security

The efforts in each of these areas contribute to the cybersecurity program as a whole.

Note 1 | This text's definition of cybersecurity is derived in part from the standards published by the National Institute of Standards and Technology (NIST; see csrc.nist.gov), specifically NIST Special Publication 800-12, Revision 1 (https://nvlpubs.nist.gov/nistpubs/SpecialPublications/NIST.SP.800-12r1.pdf).

As described in the definitions above, cybersecurity focuses on the protection of information and the characteristics that give it value, such as confidentiality, integrity, and availability, and includes the systems and technologies that house and transfer that information through a variety of protection mechanisms, such as policy, training and awareness programs, and technology. Figure 1-1 shows that cybersecurity includes the broad areas of cybersecurity management, the topic of this text: computer security, data security, and network security. This figure also illustrates that policy is the space where these components overlap.

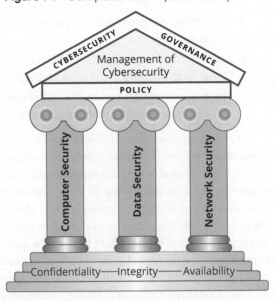

Figure 1-1   Components of cybersecurity

The Value of Information and the C.I.A. Triad

To better understand the management of cybersecurity, you must become familiar with the key characteristics of information that make it valuable to an organization, as expressed in the C.I.A. triad, the industry standard for computer-based security based on three characteristics that describe the utility of information: confidentiality, integrity, and availability (see Figure 1-2). However, present-day needs have rendered these characteristics inadequate on their own to conceptualize cybersecurity because they are limited in scope and cannot encompass today's constantly changing information environment, which calls for a more robust model. The C.I.A. triad, therefore, has been expanded into a more comprehensive list of critical characteristics, including privacy, authenticity, possession, and utility. To regulate access to information assets, systems use access control processes like identification, authentication, authorization, and accountability to ensure that only authorized individuals have access to the information. Information characteristics and access control processes are explained in more detail in the sections that follow.

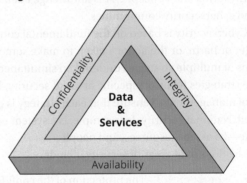

Figure 1-2   The C.I.A. triad

Confidentiality

Confidentiality, an attribute of information that describes how data is protected from disclosure or exposure to unauthorized individuals or systems, means limiting access to information only to those who need it and preventing access by those who do not. When unauthorized individuals or systems can view information, confidentiality is breached. To protect the confidentiality of information, several measures can be used, including:

- Information classification
- Secure document and data storage
- Application of general security policies
- Education, training, and awareness of information custodians and end users
- Cryptography (encryption)

Confidentiality is closely related to privacy, another key characteristic of information that is discussed later in this chapter. The complex relationship between these two characteristics is examined in detail in later chapters. In an organization, confidentiality of information is especially important for personal information about employees, customers, or patients. People expect organizations to closely guard such information. Whether the organization is a government agency, a commercial enterprise, or a nonprofit organization, problems arise when they disclose confidential information. Disclosure, the exposure of information assets to unauthorized parties, can occur either deliberately or by mistake. For example, confidential information could be mistakenly emailed to someone outside the organization rather than the intended person inside the organization. Or, perhaps an employee discards rather than destroys a document containing critical information. Maybe a hacker successfully breaks into an organization's internal systems and steals a database containing sensitive information about clients, such as names, addresses, or credit card information. Related to confidentiality is the concept of possession, an attribute of information that describes how the data's ownership or control is legitimate or authorized. Theft of information results in a loss of possession but may not result in a breach of confidentiality. For example, if an encrypted file is stolen, the organization has lost possession, but not necessarily confidentiality.

In the new world of Internet-connected systems, even organizations we would expect to be diligent and to take suitable precautions can find themselves holding the bag after a massive data spill. While U.S. federal agencies have had lapses that resulted in unwanted data disclosures, an event in July 2015 eclipsed all previous similar lapses. The loss of 21.5 million federal background-check files rocked the Office of Personnel Management, which had to disclose that names, addresses, financial records, health data, and other private information had fallen into the hands of what were believed to be Chinese hackers.[1]

This event followed the widely reported Sony data spill, illustrating again that the impact from massive data breaches spans every sector of modern society. Since then, there have been a steady flood of announcements of various data-loss events, such as the Yahoo email breach that occurred between 2013 and 2016, resulting in over 3 million user accounts being exposed. In January 2021, an estimated 60,000 Microsoft Exchange email servers were compromised, exposing billions of internal and external confidential messages. In May 2019, First American Financial Corporation had over 885 million file records leaked when a vulnerability in its websites allowed data to be viewed by anyone without authentication.[2]

Integrity

Information's integrity—an attribute of information that describes how data is whole, complete, and uncorrupted—is threatened when it is exposed to corruption, damage, destruction, or other disruption of its authentic state. Corruption can occur while information is being entered, stored, or transmitted. Many computer viruses and worms, for example, are designed to corrupt data. For this reason, the key method for detecting whether a virus or worm has caused an integrity failure to a file system is to look for changes in the file's state, as indicated by the file's size. In a more advanced operating system, its hash value or checksum is examined, as discussed later in this book.

File corruption is not always the result of deliberate attacks. Data can lose its integrity in a transmission channel or medium due to faulty programming or even noise, which is additional, disruptive signals in network communications or electrical power delivery. For example, a voltage lag in a signal carrying a digital bit (a 1 or 0) can cause the receiving system to record the data incorrectly.

To compensate for internal and external threats to the integrity of information, systems employ a variety of error-control techniques, including the use of redundancy bits and check bits. During each transmission, algorithms, hash values, and error-correcting codes ensure the integrity of the information. Data that has not been verified in this manner is retransmitted or otherwise recovered. Because information is of little or no value or use if its integrity cannot be verified, information integrity is a cornerstone of cybersecurity.

Related to the concept of information integrity is the concept of authenticity, an attribute of information that describes how data is genuine or original rather than reproduced or fabricated. While integrity focuses more on corruption, the authenticity of information focuses on whether it has been modified without authorization.

Availability

Availability, the attribute of information that describes how data is accessible and correctly formatted for use without interference or obstruction, means that users, either people or other systems, have access to it in a usable format. Availability does not imply that the information is accessible to any user; rather, it means information can be accessed when needed by authorized users.

To understand this concept more fully, consider the contents of a library—in particular, research libraries that require identification for access to the facility as a whole or to certain collections. Library patrons must present the required identification before accessing the collection. Once they are granted access, patrons expect to be able to locate and access their needed references in an appropriate language and format.

Privacy

Information that is collected, used, and stored by an organization should be used only for the purposes stated by the data owner at the time it was collected. This practice protects privacy, the right of individuals or groups to protect themselves and their information from unauthorized access, providing confidentiality.

In this context, privacy does not mean freedom from observation (the meaning usually associated with the word); it means that the information will be used only in ways approved by the person who provided it. Many organizations collect, swap, and sell personal information as a commodity. Today, it is possible to collect and combine nonprivate personal information from several different sources, a practice known as information aggregation, possibly resulting in information that violates privacy. This aggregation has resulted in databases that could be used in ways the original data owner has not agreed to or even knows about. The public has become aware of these practices and is looking to the government to protect their information's privacy.

Identification

In addition to the special characteristics that give information value and make it important to protect, there are characteristics of access control the organization should follow. To protect the confidentiality, integrity, and availability of information, only authorized individuals with a "need to know" should be able to access it. These characteristics include identification, authentication, authorization, and accountability.

An information system possesses the characteristic of identification when it can recognize individual users. Identification, the access control mechanism whereby unverified entities who seek access to a resource provide a credential by which they are known to the system, is the first step in gaining access to secured information, and it serves as the foundation for subsequent authentication and authorization. Identification and authentication are essential to establishing the level of access or authorization that an individual is granted. Identification is typically performed by means of a credential like a username or other recognition value.

Identification is the first element of the IAAA security framework, which includes identification, authentication, authorization, and accountability. This architectural framework is used to allow access to computer resources, enforce policies, and facilitate audits. It is essential for network and computer management and security. This process is mainly used so that network and software application resources are accessible to specific and legitimate users.

Authentication

Authentication, the access control mechanism that requires the validation and verification of an entity's asserted identity, is the process by which a control establishes whether a user (or system) is the entity it claims to be. Examples include the use of cryptographic certificates to establish Secure Sockets Layer (SSL) connections as well as the use of cryptographic hardware devices—for example, hardware tokens such as RSA's SecurID. Individual users may disclose a personal identification number (PIN), a password, or a passphrase to authenticate their identities to a computer system. The use of multiple authentication mechanisms is referred to as strong authentication or multifactor authentication (MFA). An example would be a bank requesting validation of login credentials (username and password) by sending a text message to the phone number associated with the account. The individual logging in must enter the code in the message before being granted access.

Authorization

After the identity of a user is authenticated, a process called authorization occurs. Authorization is the access control mechanism that represents the matching of an authenticated entity to a list of information assets and their corresponding access levels. It defines what the user (whether a person or computer system) has been specifically and explicitly authorized by the proper authority to do, such as access, modify, or delete the contents of an information asset. An example of authorization is the activation and use of access control lists and authorization groups in a networking environment. Another example is a database authorization scheme to verify that the user of an application is authorized for specific functions, such as reading, writing, creating, and deleting.

Accountability

Accountability of information, also known as auditability, is the access control mechanism that ensures all actions on a system, whether authorized or unauthorized, can be attributed to an authenticated identity. The most common tool for accountability is system logs, also known as audit logs. When users access or perform actions on a system, the logs record user activity, providing accountability.

Self-Check

1. Cybersecurity is now considered the sole responsibility of the IT department within an organization.

   a. True   **b.** False

2. Confidentiality in cybersecurity means limiting access to information only to those who need it and preventing access by those who do not.

   a. True   **b.** False

3. Identification in cybersecurity is the process by which a control establishes whether a user is the entity it claims to be.

   a. True   **b.** False

□ Check your answers at the end of this chapter.

Key Concepts of Cybersecurity: Threats and Attacks

Around 500 BC, the Chinese general Sun Tzu Wu wrote *The Art of War*, a military treatise that emphasizes the importance of knowing yourself as well as the threats you face.

> "One who knows the enemy and knows himself will not be in danger in a hundred battles.
>
> One who does not know the enemy but knows himself will sometimes win, sometimes lose.
>
> One who does not know the enemy and does not know himself will be in danger in every battle."[3]

To protect your organization's information, you must: (1) know yourself—that is, be familiar with the information assets to be protected, their inherent flaws and vulnerabilities, and the systems, mechanisms, and methods used to store, transport, process, and protect them—and (2) know the threats you face as well as their attack methods, characteristics, and potential outcomes. To make sound decisions about cybersecurity, management must be informed about the various threats to an organization's people, applications, data, and information systems. As illustrated in Figure 1-3, a **threat** represents a *potential* risk to an information asset, whereas an **attack**—sometimes called a **threat event**—represents an ongoing act against the asset that could result in a loss. A threat is defined as any event or circumstance that has the potential to adversely affect operations and assets; an attack is an intentional or unintentional act that can damage or otherwise compromise information and the systems that support it. A **threat agent** or **threat source**, a specific instance or component of a threat, attempts to damage or steal an organization's information or physical assets by using an **exploit**, a technique used to compromise a system to take advantage of a **vulnerability**. A vulnerability is a potential weakness in an asset or its defensive control systems where controls are not present or no longer effective. The word "exploit" could be used as a verb or a noun; threat agents may attempt to exploit a system or may use an exploit on a system. Unlike threats, which are always present, attacks exist only when a specific act may cause a loss. For example, the *threat* of damage from a thunderstorm is present throughout the summer in many places, but an *attack* and its associated risk of loss exist only for the duration of the actual storm. Loss is a single instance of an information asset that suffers damage or destruction, unintended or unauthorized modification or disclosure, or denial of use. The following sections discuss each of the major types of threats and corresponding attacks facing modern information assets.

To investigate the wide range of threats that pervade the interconnected world, many researchers have collected information on threats and attacks from practicing cybersecurity personnel and their organizations. While the categorizations may vary, threats are relatively well researched and fairly well understood.

Figure 1-3   Key concepts in cybersecurity

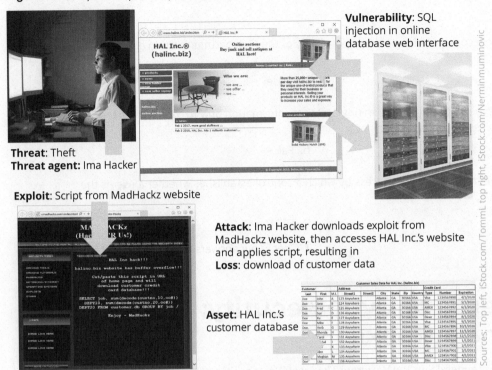

Vulnerability: SQL injection in online database web interface

Threat: Theft
Threat agent: Ima Hacker

Exploit: Script from MadHackz website

Attack: Ima Hacker downloads exploit from MadHackz website, then accesses HAL Inc.'s website and applies script, resulting in
Loss: download of customer data

Asset: HAL Inc.'s customer database

There is wide agreement that the threat from external sources increases when an organization connects to the Internet. The number of Internet users continues to grow. Over two-thirds (67.9 percent) of the world's 7.93 billion people had some form of Internet access as of mid-2023.[4] Therefore, a typical organization with an online connection to its systems and information faces more than 3.7 billion potential hackers.

Note 2 | For more information on world Internet use, visit the Internet World Stats: Usage and Population Statistics site at www.internetworldstats.com/stats.htm.

The 12 Categories of Threats

Table 1-1 shows the 12 general categories of threats that represent a clear and present danger to an organization's people, information, and systems. Each organization must prioritize the threats it faces based on the particular security situation in which it operates, its organizational strategy regarding risk, and the exposure levels of its assets. You may notice that many of the attack examples in the table could be listed in more than one category. For example, theft performed by a hacker falls into the category of "theft," but it can also be preceded by "espionage or trespass" as the hacker illegally accesses the information. The theft may also be accompanied by defacement actions to delay discovery, qualifying it for the category of "sabotage or vandalism."

Deviations in Services

An organization's IT systems depend on the successful operation of many interdependent support systems, including power grids, data and telecommunications networks, parts suppliers, service vendors, and even custodial staff and sanitation vendors. Any of these support systems can be interrupted by severe weather, employee illnesses, civil disruptions, or other unforeseen events—like a global pandemic. Deviations in services can result from such incidents as a backhoe taking out an Internet service provider's (ISP) buried cable.

Table 1-1 The 12 categories of threats to cybersecurity[5]

Category of Threat	Examples
Deviations in services	Utility service problems (Internet, phone, power, water, etc.)
Espionage or trespass	Unauthorized access and/or data disclosure
Forces of nature	Fire, floods, earthquakes, lightning, etc.
Human error or failure	Social engineering, accidents, or employee mistakes
Information extortion	Blackmail threatening information denial or disclosure
Intellectual property compromises	Piracy, copyright infringement, research and development (R&D) disclosure
Sabotage or vandalism	Unauthorized modification or destruction of systems or information
Software attacks	Malware, website spoofing, or denial of service
Technical hardware failures or errors	Equipment failure
Technical software failures or errors	Bugs or code problems
Technological obsolescence	Antiquated or outdated technologies
Theft	Illegal confiscation of equipment or information

If the organization has a backup provider, they may be online and in service but only able to supply a fraction of the bandwidth the organization needs for full service. This degradation of service is a form of availability disruption, an interruption in services that causes an adverse event within the organization. Irregularities in Internet service, communications, and power can dramatically affect the availability of information and systems. This category includes Internet service and a host of other services.

In organizations that rely heavily on the Internet and the web to support continued operations, ISP failures can considerably undermine the availability of information and their customers' ability to do business with the organization. Many organizations have employees working at remote locations, whether from home or while traveling, as was the case during the COVID-19 pandemic. When offsite employees cannot contact the host systems, they may not be able to conduct operations. When an organization places its web or e-commerce sites in the care of a web hosting provider, that provider assumes responsibility for all Internet services and for the hardware and operating system used to run the website. Almost all services are provided with a service level agreement (SLA), a document that specifies the expected level of service from a service provider and usually contains provisions for minimum acceptable availability and penalties or remediation procedures for downtime. When a service provider fails to meet the terms of the SLA, the provider may accrue fines, reimburse service payments, or provide service credits to cover any losses incurred by the client, but these payments seldom cover the losses generated by the outage.

Irregularities from power utilities are common and can lead to fluctuations such as power excesses, power shortages, and power losses. These fluctuations can pose problems for organizations that provide inadequately conditioned power for their information systems equipment. In the United States, residential users are supplied 120-volt, 60-cycle power, usually through 15- and 20-amp circuits. Commercial buildings may have 240-volt service and specialized power distribution infrastructure. When power voltage levels vary from normal, expected levels, an organization's sensitive electronic equipment can be easily damaged or destroyed. This is especially true for computing and network equipment.

The following is a list of power-related irregularities, most of which can be protected against by uninterruptible power supplies (UPSs), at least for a short time. Longer durations will require redundant power provisions like organizational generators.

- Blackout—A long-term interruption (outage) in electrical power availability
- Brownout—A long-term decrease in the quality of electrical power availability

- Fault—A short-term interruption in electrical power availability
- Sag—A short-term decrease in electrical power availability
- Spike—A short-term increase in electrical power availability, also known as a swell
- Surge—A long-term increase in electrical power availability

Other utility services can affect organizations as well. Among these are telephone, water, wastewater, trash pickup, natural or propane gas, and custodial services. The loss of these services can impair the ability of an organization to function. For instance, most facilities require water service to operate heating, ventilation, and air-conditioning (HVAC) systems. Without functioning HVAC, data centers would overheat—even in Minnesota in winter. If a wastewater system fails, an organization might be prevented from allowing employees into the building. While there are websites that compare service providers' pricing, few provide a comparative analysis of availability or downtime.

Espionage or Trespass

Espionage or trespass is a well-known and broad category of electronic and human activities that can breach the confidentiality of information. When an unauthorized person gains access to information an organization is trying to protect, the act is categorized as espionage or trespass. Attackers can use many different methods to access the information stored in an information system. Some information-gathering techniques are legal—for example, using a web browser to perform market research—and are collectively called competitive intelligence, the collection and analysis of information about an organization's business competitors through legal and ethical means to gain business intelligence and competitive advantage. This is often referred to by the acronym OSINT (open-source intelligence), the process of collecting and analyzing information from publicly available sources to be used in an intelligence context. The sources for OSINT can include public data available on the Internet, government reports, professional and academic publications, and other publicly accessible data. When information gatherers employ techniques that cross a legal or ethical threshold, they are conducting industrial espionage—the collection and analysis of information about an organization's business competitors, often through illegal or unethical means, to gain an unfair competitive advantage. Industrial espionage is also known as corporate spying and should be distinguished from espionage for national security reasons, although the two may overlap when industrial espionage is performed by a foreign nation. Many countries that are considered allies of the United States engage in industrial espionage against American organizations. When foreign governments are involved, these activities are considered a threat to national security.

Some forms of espionage are relatively low tech. One example is called shoulder surfing, the direct, covert observation of individual information or system use. It is done in public or semipublic settings when people gather information they are not authorized to have. Instances of shoulder surfing occur at computer terminals, desks, and ATMs. It also occurs on buses, airplanes, and subways, where people use smartphones and tablet PCs, and in any other public place where employees may access confidential information away from the office. Shoulder surfing defies the unwritten etiquette regarding technology use in public: If you can see another person entering personal or private information into a system, look away as the information is entered. Failure to do so constitutes not only a breach of etiquette but also an affront to privacy and a threat to the security of confidential information.

Hackers   Acts of trespass—unauthorized entry into the real or virtual property of another party—can lead to unauthorized actions that enable information gatherers to enter premises or systems without permission. Controls sometimes mark the boundaries of an organization's virtual territory. These boundaries give notice to trespassers that they are encroaching on the organization's cyberspace. Sound principles of authentication and authorization can help organizations protect valuable information and systems. These control methods and technologies employ multiple layers or factors to protect against unauthorized access and trespass.

The classic perpetrator of espionage or trespass is the hacker, a person who accesses systems and information without authorization and often illegally. Hackers are frequently glamorized in fictional accounts as people who stealthily manipulate a maze of computer networks, systems, and data to find information that solves the mystery and heroically saves the day. However, the true life of the hacker is far more mundane. In the real world, a hacker frequently spends long hours examining the types and structures of targeted systems and uses skill, guile, and fraud to attempt to bypass controls placed on information owned by someone else.

Hackers possess a wide range of skill levels, as with most technology users. However, most hackers are grouped into two general categories: expert and novice hackers. The expert hacker uses extensive knowledge of the inner workings of computer hardware and software to gain unauthorized access to systems and information. Expert hackers, also known as elite hackers, often create automated exploits, scripts, and tools used by other hackers. Typically, the expert hacker is a master of several programming languages, networking protocols, and operating systems and exhibits a mastery of the technical environment of the chosen targeted system. Once an expert hacker chooses a target system, the likelihood is high that they will successfully enter the system. Fortunately for poorly protected organizations in the world, there are substantially fewer expert hackers than novice hackers. The most notorious (individual) hacker to date is Kevin Mitnick, who was considered an expert hacker by most, yet he often used social engineering rather than technical skills to collect information for his attacks.

A new category of expert hackers has emerged. The professional hacker conducts attacks for personal financial benefit, for a crime organization, or for a foreign government (see the discussion on cyberterrorism later in this chapter), and should not be confused with the penetration tester, a cybersecurity professional with authorization to attempt to gain system access in an effort to identify and recommend resolutions for vulnerabilities in those systems. A penetration tester has authorization from an organization to test its information systems and network defense, and is expected to provide detailed reports of the findings. The primary differences between professional hackers and penetration testers are the authorization provided and the ethical professionalism displayed. These two groups may in fact use the same tools to perform their intrusions.

There has been a recent emergence of precisely targeted attacks against organizations or individuals called an advanced persistent threat (APT), a collection of processes typically directed by a human threat agent. These attacks are usually a combination of social engineering, spear phishing, and customized malware generated by organizations that sponsor nation-states or sophisticated criminal organizations. In many cases, these attacks seek to infiltrate high-value information for economic espionage or attacks against national security.

The novice hacker—a relatively unskilled hacker who uses the work of expert hackers to perform attacks—is also known as a neophyte, n00b, or newbie. This category of hackers includes individuals with little or no real expertise of their own, but who rely upon the prowess of expert hackers who have become dissatisfied with attacking systems directly and have turned their attention to writing exploits. These exploits are automated scripts and programs that allow a novice hacker to act as a script kiddie (also known as a skid, skiddie, or script bunny), using the program to attack a system. Other novice hackers known as packet monkeys use automated exploits to engage in denial-of-service attacks for no obvious reason.

The good news is that if an expert hacker can post a script tool where a script kiddie or a packet monkey can find it, then IT and cybersecurity professionals can find it, too. The developers of protection software and hardware and the service providers who keep defensive systems up to date also stay informed about the latest in exploit scripts. As a result of preparation and continued vigilance, attacks conducted by scripts are usually predictable and can be adequately defended against.

Once an attacker gains access to a system, the next step is to increase what they can access through privilege escalation, the unauthorized modification of an authorized or unauthorized system user account to gain advanced access and control over system resources. While most accounts associated with a system have only rudimentary "use" permissions and capabilities, an attacker wants administrative or "root" privileges. These privileges allow attackers to modify a system to view all information in it and to hide their activities by modifying system logs. The escalation of privileges is a skill set in and of itself. However, just as novice hackers can use available tools to gain access, they can use tools to escalate privileges.

A common example of privilege escalation is jailbreaking, which is used to gain administrator-level control over a smartphone operating system. A second example is rooting: escalating privileges to gain administrator-level control over a computer system. Owners of certain smartphones can download and use special tools to gain control over system functions, often against the intentions of their designers. The term "jailbreaking" is more commonly associated with Apple's iOS systems, while rooting is more common with Linux- and Android-based systems.

Other terms for system rule breakers may be less familiar. The term cracker—a hacker who intentionally removes or avoids software copyright protection—is commonly associated with copyright bypassing and password decryption. With the removal of copyright protection, software can be easily distributed and installed. With the decryption of user passwords from stolen system files, user accounts can be illegally accessed. In modern usage, the terms "hacker" and "cracker" both denote criminal intent.

Password Attacks   Password attacks fall under the category of espionage or trespass just as lock-picking falls under breaking and entering. Cracking is an attempt to reverse-engineer, remove, or bypass a password or other access control protection, such as the copyright protection on software. There are several alternative approaches to password cracking:

- The brute-force password attack is an effort to guess a password by attempting every possible combination of characters and numbers in it. This attack is rarely successful against systems that have adopted the manufacturer's recommended security practices. A system policy that limits the number of unsuccessful access attempts within a certain time is very effective against brute-force attacks. The same is true of a policy that prevents reuse of passwords, as it prevents users from using the same passwords over and over and having older, compromised passwords used in systems. The strength of a password is a combination of its length and complexity, which helps determine its ability to withstand a brute-force attack. Using best-practice policies for passwords can greatly enhance their strength; use passwords of at least 10 characters and at least one uppercase and lowercase letter, one number, and one special character. Also, use systems that allow case-sensitive passwords. Finally, protection against brute-force attacks is a good reason to always change the default administrator password assigned by the manufacturer.

- The dictionary password attack, or simply dictionary attack, is a variation of the brute-force password attack that attempts to narrow the range of possible passwords guessed by using a dictionary of common passwords and possibly including attempts based on the target's personal information. This information includes the names of relatives or pets and familiar numbers such as phone numbers, addresses, and even Social Security numbers. Organizations can use similar dictionaries to disallow certain passwords during the reset process and thus guard against passwords that are easy to guess. In addition, rules requiring numbers and special characters in passwords make the dictionary attack less effective.

- A far more sophisticated and potentially much faster password attack is possible if the attacker can gain access to a password file, such as the Security Account Manager (SAM) data file. These password files contain hashed representations of users' passwords rather than the actual passwords; the password is converted to a so-called hash value using a mathematical algorithm to conceal the plaintext value of the password. However, the attacker can cross-reference the hashed password against a rainbow table, a database of hash values and their corresponding plaintext values that can be used to look up passwords.

- While social engineering is discussed in detail later in the section called "Human Error or Failure," it is worth mentioning here as a mechanism to gain password information. For example, attackers may attempt to gain access to systems information by contacting low-level employees and offering to help with their computer issues. After all, what employee does not have issues with computers? By posing as a friendly and helpful helpdesk or repair technician, the attacker asks employees for their usernames and passwords, then uses the information to gain access to organizational systems. Some will ask the user to install a back door or rootkit, allowing the attacker to directly access the system. Some will even go so far as to resolve the user's issues. Social engineering password attacks are much easier than hacking servers for password files.

Forces of Nature

Forces of nature, sometimes called natural disasters, can present some of the most dangerous threats because they usually occur with little warning and are beyond the control of the organization. These threats, which include events such as fires, floods, earthquakes, lightning strikes, and volcanic eruptions, can disrupt not only people's lives but also business operations and the storage, transmission, and use of information. Another term you may encounter, *force majeure*, is roughly translated as "superior force" and includes forces of nature as well as civil disorder and acts of war. Because it is usually not possible to avoid threats from forces of nature, organizations must implement controls to limit damage and prepare contingency plans for continued operations, such as disaster recovery plans, business continuity plans, and incident response plans, as discussed later in this book.

Most forces of nature can only be mitigated through casualty or business interruption insurance, although careful design and placement of facilities can reduce the likelihood of damage to an organization's systems, buildings, or local infrastructure. Force of nature attacks include the following:

- Earthquake—A sudden movement of Earth's crust caused by volcanic activity, the movement of Earth's tectonic plates, or the release of stress accumulated along geologic faults.
- Excessive rainfall and snowfall—Too much of a good thing inevitably causes problems. Excessive rainfall can lead to flooding, while excessive snowfall can lead to whiteouts and impede movement. The 2014 "snowpocalypse" in Atlanta, Georgia, shut down public roads, resulted in power and communications outages, and threatened lives as people were trapped at home, school, work, and on the road without heat.
- Fire—The ignition of combustible material; damage can also be caused by smoke from fires or by water from sprinkler systems or firefighters.
- Flood—Water overflowing into an area that is normally dry, causing direct damage and subsequent indirect damage from high humidity and moisture.
- Hurricanes, typhoons, and tropical depressions—Severe tropical storms that commonly originate at sea and move to land, bringing excessive rainfall, flooding, and high winds.
- Landslide, mudslide, or avalanche—The movement of a mass of ice, snow, earth, or rock. These displacements also disrupt operations by interfering with access to buildings.
- Lightning—An abrupt, discontinuous natural electric discharge in the atmosphere, which can cause direct damage through an electrical surge or indirect damage from fires. Damage from lightning can usually be prevented with specialized lightning rods and by installing special electrical circuit protectors.
- Tornados or severe windstorms—Violent wind effects in which air moves at destructively high speeds, causing direct damage and indirect damage from thrown debris. A tornado is a rotating column of whirling air that can be more than a mile wide. Wind shear is a much smaller and linear wind effect, but it can have similar devastating consequences.
- Tsunami—A very large ocean wave caused by an underwater earthquake or volcanic eruption; it can reach miles inland as it crashes into land masses.

Two areas are not normally considered natural disasters but should be considered in this category:

- Dust contamination—Can dramatically reduce the effectiveness of cooling mechanisms and potentially cause components to overheat. Specialized optical technology, such as CD or DVD drives, can suffer failures due to excessive dust contamination inside systems.
- Electrostatic discharge (ESD)—Also known as static electricity, and usually little more than a nuisance. However, an employee walking across a carpet on a cool, dry day can generate up to 12,000 volts of electricity, and sensitive electronics can suffer damage from as little as 10 volts.[6]

Human Error or Failure

This category of threats includes acts performed without intent or malice, or in ignorance by an authorized user. When people are involved in any operation or process, especially with computers, mistakes happen. Similarly, errors happen when people fail to follow established policy. Inexperience, improper training, and incorrect assumptions are just a few things that can cause human error or failure. Regardless of the cause, even innocuous mistakes can produce extensive damage.

One of the greatest threats to an organization's information assets is its own employees, as they are the threat agents closest to the information. Because employees use data and information in everyday activities to conduct the organization's operations, their mistakes represent a serious threat to the confidentiality, integrity, and availability of data. Employee mistakes can easily lead to disclosure of classified data, entry of erroneous data, deletion or modification of data, storage of data in unprotected areas, and failure to effectively protect information. Leaving classified information in unprotected areas, such as on a desktop, on a website, or even in a trash can, is as much a threat as a person who seeks to exploit the information because carelessness can create a vulnerability and thus opportunity for an attacker. If someone damages or destroys data on purpose, however, the act belongs to a different threat category.

Human error or failure often can be prevented with training, ongoing awareness activities, and controls. These controls range from simple activities, like preventing a user from reusing a previous password, to more complex procedures, such as requiring a user to authenticate their login with a code or application on their phone. Many military applications have robust, dual-approval controls built in. Some systems that have a high potential for data loss or system outages use expert systems to monitor human actions and request confirmation of critical inputs. Some common types of human error include the following:

- **Social engineering.** In cybersecurity, social engineering is the process of using social skills to convince people to reveal access credentials or other valuable information to an attacker. This technique is used by attackers to gain system access or information that may lead to system access. There are several social engineering techniques, which usually involve a perpetrator posing as a fellow employee or offering money for seemingly minor assistance.

- **Advance-fee fraud (AFF).** AFF is a form of social engineering in which some third party offers an email recipient the promise of a large amount of money and requests a small advance fee or personal banking information to facilitate the transfer. AFF is internationally known as 4-1-9 fraud, and is named after a section of the Nigerian penal code. The perpetrators of 4-1-9 schemes often use the names of legitimate companies, such as the Nigerian National Petroleum Company. Alternatively, they may invent other entities, such as a bank, government agency, long-lost relative, lottery, or other nongovernmental organization.

- **Phishing.** Some attacks are sent by email and may consist of a notice that requires the recipient's urgent attention and response. These are known as phishing attacks, a form of social engineering in which the attacker provides what appears to be a legitimate communication, but it either contains hidden or embedded code that redirects the reply to a third-party site to extract personal or confidential information or asks the respondent to contact the sender directly. They may claim to represent a bank, business, government agency (especially the IRS), or charity the recipient may have done business with. While these attacks may seem crude to experienced users, the fact is that *many* email users have fallen for them. Phishing attacks use two primary techniques, often in combination with one another: URL manipulation and website forgery. In URL manipulation, attackers send an HTML-embedded email message or a hyperlink whose HTML code opens a forged website. In web forgery, the attacker copies the HTML code from a legitimate website and then modifies key elements. When victims type their banking ID and password, the attacker records that information and displays a message that the website is temporarily unavailable or offline.

- **Spear phishing.** While normal phishing attacks target as many recipients as possible, spear phishing is any highly targeted phishing attack. It involves an attacker sending a message custom-tailored to the recipient, often including their name or other personal information, which may have been taken from their workplace or social media presence. A spear phishing message may appear to be from a recipient's employer, a colleague, or other legitimate correspondent to a small group or even one person.

- **Pretexting.** Pretexting is a form of social engineering in which the attacker pretends to be an authority figure who needs information to confirm the target's identity, when their intent is to trick the target into revealing confidential information. Pretexting is sometimes referred to as phone phishing; it is a pure social engineering attack in which the attacker calls a potential victim on the phone in order to gain access to private or confidential information, such as health, employment, or financial records. The difference between pretexting and phishing is that pretexting relies on trust, often from the workplace, and phishing relies on publicly acquired information, urgency, and fear to prompt the target to respond. A specific type of this attack is business email compromise (BEC), a social engineering attack directed toward an employee by an individual posing as their supervisor or an organizational executive. BEC attacks attempt to convince an employee to purchase gift cards, authorize the transfer of funds, or provide confidential information to the attacker.

Of particular concern to cybersecurity professionals is the recent development of generative artificial intelligence (AI) applications, such as ChatGPT. Traditionally, social engineering attacks were easily detected, often due to their poor spelling and grammar usage, as many were translated from foreign languages. Freely available generative AI tools (such as Microsoft CoPilot, which uses ChatGPT) can create fluent and accurate translations that will make detecting social engineering emails much more difficult.

Note 3 | For more information on the preceding forms of attack and other fraudulent cyberattacks, visit the FBI's high-tech (cyber) crimes website at www.fbi.gov/about-us/investigate/cyber.

Information Extortion

Information extortion, the theft of confidential information from an organization and subsequent demand for compensation for its return or for an agreement not to disclose it, is common in the theft of payment card information and customer databases. This type of theft is also known as cyberextortion. In 2010, Anthony Digati allegedly threatened to conduct a spam attack on the insurance company New York Life. He reportedly sent dozens of emails to company executives threatening to conduct a negative image campaign by sending over 6 million emails to people throughout the country. He then demanded approximately $200,000 to stop the attack, and then threatened to increase the demand to more than $3 million if the company ignored him. His arrest thwarted the spam attack.

In 2012, a programmer from Walachi Innovation Technologies allegedly broke into the organization's systems and changed the access passwords and codes, locking legitimate users out of the system. He then reportedly demanded $300,000 in exchange for the new codes. A court order eventually forced him to surrender the information to the organization. In Russia, a hacker created malware that installed inappropriate materials on an unsuspecting user's system, along with a banner threatening to notify the authorities if a bribe was not paid. At 500 rubles (about $17), victims in Russia and other countries were more willing to pay the bribe than to risk prosecution or at least public humiliation.[7]

Recent information extortion attacks have involved specialized forms of malware known as ransomware, which is specifically designed to identify and encrypt valuable information in a victim's system to extort payment for the key needed to unlock the encryption. This attack is usually implemented with malware that is run on the victim's system after phishing or spear-phishing attacks. (See the section on software attacks.) The result is that the user's data is encrypted. Paying the adversary a ransom in a digital currency may or may not result in the victim receiving the encryption key to recover the data. Waves of attacks over the last decade used ransomware variants such as WannaCry, Petya, and NotPetya. Loss events to victims of the CryptoWall ransomware attacks in 2014 and 2015 included ransom payments ranging from $200 to $10,000 per incident as well as the costs associated with lost productivity, legal fees, and other recovery expenses.[8]

The WannaCry attacks in May 2017 triggered a global event that unfolded in just a few hours. This malware variant targeted out-of-date Windows computers, demanding ransom payments in the bitcoin cryptocurrency. WannaCry is believed to have infected over 200,000 systems. Other ransomware variants continue to plague computer users around the world; some, like Petya, were updated and made even more virulent in later versions. The most recent Petya variant, NotPetya, used a novel means of propagation in the June 2017 outbreak in Ukraine. The malware is believed to have used a tax-preparation software product update to infect victims' machines.

According to a 2021 Cloudwards study, 37 percent of organizations that responded indicated they had been the victim of a ransomware attack in the past year. Ransomware is most likely to enter the organization through an email-based phishing attack that tries to convince the unsuspecting victim to click a web link or open an infected attachment, which installs the malware. Ransomware perpetrators usually ask for a few hundred dollars, although some targeted attacks have demanded ransoms for tens of thousands of dollars. In spite of this, most victims do pay the ransom. A 2021 IDC Ransomware study found that 7 percent of U.S. organizations and 37 percent of organizations worldwide were hit with ransomware in the last few years, but only 13 percent of those hit by an attack did not pay the ransom. The average payment was almost $250,000.[9] Of those that refused to pay, approximately one-quarter of the victims lost files in the attack. So, if you do not pay, you will probably lose some files. If you do pay, however, there is no guarantee your files will be decrypted.[10]

In late 2015, ransomware took on a new level of danger. Prior to that time, organizations could reasonably assume that systems attacked by ransomware could be safely restored from backups, losing only hours or, at worst, days of data. Around November 2015, a persistent and delayed ransomware attack was distributed that remained dormant longer than had been previously seen, allowing it to be backed up with the rest of the organizations' data. When the attack was triggered and the organizations' systems and data were locked up, recovery from backups only reinstalled the ransomware. The bigger issue is with organizations that do not regularly back up their data. Those that do perform frequent backups do not always test the backups regularly to ensure they are reliable.

In February 2016, a hospital's systems in Hollywood, California, were crippled by a ransomware attack. Not only was data encrypted, systems were impacted so severely that the staff had to go back to paper forms and data collection. After paying a ransom of 40 bitcoins (the most commonly demanded form of ransomware payment), a total of approximately $17,000, the hospital was able to recover its data. Others were not so lucky.

In May 2017, the Wana Decrypt0r (or WannaCry) ransomware worm attack was first detected; it infected hundreds of thousands of systems in almost 200 countries. The chief concern about this ransomware is that the U.S. National Security Agency apparently detected the Microsoft Windows EternalBlue exploit that the ransomware used and incorporated it into their own cyberwarfare operations rather than report it to Microsoft. Because some advanced ransomware attacks within the larger attack automated the ransom payment and crypto key recovery, many experts speculated that the attack was focused more on damage than money. For example, WannaCry required a manual key recovery process after payment verification. Most of the organizations affected by WannaCry that paid the requested ransom reported no response from the attacking entity and no recovery of encrypted data. Figure 1-4 shows the WannaCry encryption notification.

Figure 1-4   WannaCry encryption notification

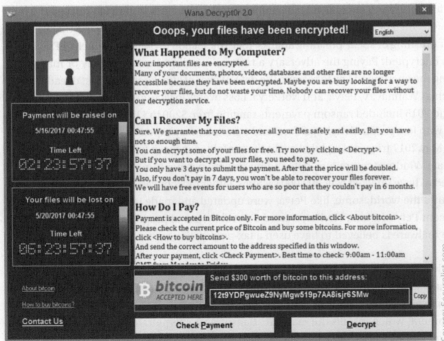

How do you react if you are the victim of ransomware? Cloud protection and information management specialists at the American software company Druva recommend the following:

1. Do not pay the ransom. There is no guarantee you will get your data back. Druva finds that one in three organizations affected pay the ransom, yet almost half do not get their data back.

2. Turn all devices off and disconnect from the network. Try to minimize the spread and damage from the infection. Shut down the Wi-Fi service and try to isolate infected systems so the damage does not spread further.

3. Find the source of the infection. Trying to determine how your systems were infected can assist you in preventing further spread by informing and educating users.

4. Alert all users. Let everyone know that a ransomware attack is in progress and how *not* to get infected. Do not just rely on email to send these alerts—you may want to activate your phone tree and spread the word that way.

5. Restore from a backup to a new device. Determine if your backups are infected by eliminating any chance that the infection was present on the computer to which you are restoring. Then, make sure the data is accessible before porting it to another system.

6. Reimage the infected systems. The only way to be sure ransomware is not lurking in a hidden file in the operating system, hard drive, or an application is to wipe the infected systems to their initial state and start over. Many organizations use standard images for their systems. Wiping all drives clean and reimaging provides a fresh start and some assurances that the systems will not be immediately reinfected once data is available.[11]

The struggle between users and attackers continues. In 2021 two hacker groups, REvil and Darkside, caused major disruptions. REvil is a criminal hacking ring and is projected to be the group behind the Kaseya IT solutions ransomware attack. That July 2021 attack included a demand for $70 million in Bitcoin. The company refused and cooperated with law enforcement, eventually obtaining a universal decryptor key to free its systems and those of its clients. In May 2021, however, a large meat supplier in the United States, the United Kingdom, and Australia paid an $11 million ransom in Bitcoin.

Also in May 2021, Darkside hit Colonial Pipeline's administrative offices. Even though the production systems were not directly affected, the company shut down their pipeline operations to ensure they weren't infected. The resulting impact on U.S. operations was staggering. The increased cost of gas due to unavailability not only affected individual drivers but also commercial transportation, impacting all aspects of the economy. Darkside also successfully attacked Brenntag, a German chemical company, which paid an estimated $4.4 million ransom. The list of affected companies goes on.[12]

Most recent ransomware attacks in the United States have targeted desktop systems, marking a shift in strategy by attackers. It is expected that attackers will continue to evolve the malware used in ransomware attacks, shifting their tools, techniques, and procedures to stay ahead of the defenders.

Intellectual Property Compromises

Many organizations support the development of intellectual property (IP)—the creation, ownership, and control of original ideas as well as the representation of those ideas—as part of their business operations. Intellectual property can be trade secrets, copyrights, trademarks, or patents. IP is protected by copyright laws and other regulations, carries the expectation of proper attribution or credit to its source, and potentially requires the acquisition of permission or payment for its use. For example, the use of a song in a movie or a photo in a publication may require a specific type of payment known as a royalty. The unauthorized use of IP constitutes a threat to cybersecurity. Employees may have access privileges to various types of IP, including purchased or developed software and organizational information such as research and development projects or production methods. Many employees typically need to use IP to conduct day-to-day business. This category focuses on the unauthorized use of copyrighted material beyond fair-use specifications, specifically software piracy and other copyright violations.

Organizations often purchase or lease the IP of other organizations and must abide by a purchase or licensing agreement for its fair and responsible use. The most common IP breach is the unauthorized duplication, installation, or distribution of copyrighted computer software, more commonly known as software piracy, which occurs when individuals and organizations do not purchase software as mandated by the owner's license agreements. Because software is licensed to a particular purchaser, its use is restricted to a specific number of users or to a designated organization. If a user installs the program more times than specified in the agreement without transferring an existing license or securing additional licenses, the user has violated the copyright. Software licenses are strictly enforced by federal and state agencies as well as regulatory and private organizations.

Software publishers have developed multiple control mechanisms over the years to prevent copyright infringement. Technical mechanisms, like digital watermarks, embedded code, copyright or activation codes, and even the intentional placement of bad sectors on software media, have been used to enforce copyright laws. The most common tool is a unique software registration code in combination with an end-user license agreement that usually pops up during the installation of new software, requiring users to indicate that they have legally purchased the software and agree to conditions of the software's use.

Another effort to combat piracy is online registration. Users who install software are often asked or even required to register their software to complete the installation, obtain technical support, or gain the use of all features. Some users believe that this process compromises personal privacy because they never know exactly what information is obtained from their computers and sent to the software manufacturer.

Intellectual property losses may result from the successful exploitation of vulnerabilities in asset protection controls. Many of the threats against these controls are described in this chapter.

Note 4 | For more information on software piracy and intellectual property protection, visit the Software and Information Industry Association (SIIA) website at www.siia.net and the Business Software Alliance website at www.bsa.org. SIIA is the organization formerly known as the Software Publishers Association.

Sabotage or Vandalism

This category of threat involves the deliberate sabotage of a computer system or business as well as acts of vandalism to destroy an asset, deny access to products or services, or damage the image of an organization. These acts can include petty vandalism by unhappy customers or by disgruntled employees who pose an insider threat, or they can rise to the level of organized sabotage against an organization.

Although they might not be financially devastating, attacks on the image of an organization are serious. Vandalism to a website (also known as website defacement) can erode consumer confidence, diminishing an organization's sales, net worth, and reputation. For example, in the early hours of July 13, 2001, a group known as Fluffi Bunni left its mark on the front page of the SANS Institute, a cybersecurity training organization providing security instruction and certification. The defacement read, "Would you really trust these guys to teach you security?"[13] At least one member of the group was subsequently arrested by British authorities.

In 2010, visitors to the website of the European Union president were redirected to a mock site that displayed an image of fictional character Mr. Bean instead of Spain's socialist leader Jose Zapatero. In 2013, websites of the U.S. Department of State and the U.S. Embassy were defaced by an Indonesian hacker.

Not all website defacement attacks involve hacking an organization's web servers. Some involve attacks on the DNS servers that direct users to the site (cross-site scripting attacks) and result in users being directed to sites other than the ones they want to view.

In general, the only real risk to an organization from website defacement is the loss of public trust in the organization's ability to protect its information assets. Defacement has become so common that most users tune it out when it occurs, like ignoring graffiti placed on buildings using spray paint.

Organizations can minimize their risk of website defacement by backing up their websites regularly, closely monitoring their websites, and minimizing the use of exploitable software such as scripts, plug-ins, and other application programming interfaces (APIs).

The use of the Internet and web has moved activism to the digital age:

- Online activism. There are innumerable reports of hackers accessing systems and damaging or destroying critical data. Hacked websites once made front-page news, as the perpetrators intended. The impact of these acts has lessened as the volume has increased. Today, security experts are noticing a rise in another form of online vandalism. Hacktivists (or cyberactivists) are attackers who seek to interfere with or disrupt systems to protest the operations, policies, or actions of an organization or government agency. For example, these activists might hack into a target's online resource, such as email or social media, and then release that information to the public.

- Cyberterrorism and cyberwarfare. A much more sinister form of hacking is cyberterrorism, the conduct of terrorist activities by online attackers. The United States and other governments are developing security measures intended to protect critical computing and communications networks as well as physical and power utility infrastructures. Some cyberterrorist attacks are perpetrated by individuals, organizations, or governments and are aimed at disrupting government agencies, while others seem designed to create mass havoc with civilian and commercial industry targets. However, the U.S. government conducts its own cyberwarfare (or information warfare), defined as formally sanctioned, offensive cybersecurity operations conducted by one government or nation-state against another. An example is targeting overseas efforts to develop nuclear enrichment plants by hacking into and destroying critical equipment.[14] In April 2015, the Pentagon announced a new strategy for cyberwarfare, identifying China, Russia, Iran, and North Korea as the countries that represent the greatest threat from cyberwarfare.[15] In 2020, vulnerabilities in the SolarWinds IT management software were suspected of being compromised by a group associated with Russian intelligence agencies, which installed malware on customer systems.[16]

- Positive online activism. Not all online activism is negative. Social media outlets, such as Facebook, Twitter, Reddit, Discord, Instagram, and YouTube, are commonly used to perform fundraising, raise awareness of social issues, gather support for legitimate causes, and promote involvement. Modern business organizations try to leverage social media and online activism to improve their public image and increase awareness of socially responsible actions.

Software Attacks

Deliberate software attacks occur when an individual or group designs and deploys software specifically to attack a system and steal, damage, or deny access to information. This type of attack is usually part of a campaign that integrates a variety of tactics, techniques, and procedures (TTP) to merge specially crafted software and social engineering methods that seek to trick users into installing computer code onto their systems. Once an infection occurs, the software leverages that foothold by attacking other systems that can be reached from the newly infected system. Attacking software agents usually try to spread to connected systems and then may attempt to steal information, become an agent of the attacker for other exploits (see the later discussion on bots and zombies), or encrypt users' data to be held for ransom (see the earlier discussion on ransomware).

There are several forms of software attacks, each of which is examined in the following sections:

- Malware, including viruses, worms, and Trojan horses
- Back doors, trap doors, and maintenance hooks
- Denial-of-service and distributed denial-of-service attacks
- Malicious email
- Communications interception attacks

Malware   The most common form of software attack is malware. Malware (malicious code or malicious software) is computer software specifically designed to perform malicious or unwanted actions. Malware attacks include the execution of viruses, worms, Trojan horses, and active web scripts to steal, damage, or deny access to information. The most state-of-the-art malicious code attack is the polymorphic worm, or multivector worm. These attack programs use up to six known attack vectors to exploit a variety of vulnerabilities in common information system devices.

- **Virus.** A computer virus, a type of malware that is attached to other executable programs, consists of code segments (programming instructions) that perform malicious actions. This code behaves much like a virus pathogen that attacks animals and plants, using the cell's own replication machinery to propagate the attack beyond the initial target. The code attaches itself to an existing program and takes control of the program's access to the targeted computer. The virus-controlled target program then carries out the virus plan by replicating itself into additional targeted systems. Often, users unwittingly help viruses get into a system. Opening infected email or some other seemingly trivial action, like clicking on a link, can cause anything from random messages appearing on a user's screen to the destruction of entire hard drives. Just as their namesakes are passed among living bodies, computer viruses are passed from machine to machine via physical media, email, or other forms of computer data transmission. When these viruses infect a machine, they may immediately scan it for email applications or even send themselves to every user in the email address book.

  Viruses can be classified by how they spread themselves. One of the most common types is the macro virus, which is written in a specific macro language to target applications that use the language. The virus is activated when the application's product is opened. A macro virus typically affects documents, slideshows, emails, or spreadsheets created by office suite applications. Another common virus is the boot virus (or boot-sector virus), which targets the boot sector or Master Boot Record (MBR) of a computer system's hard drive or removable storage media. Viruses can also be described by how their programming is stored and moved. Some are found as binary executables, including .exe or .com files; some are interpretable data files, such as command scripts or a specific application's document files; and other viruses are both.

  Alternatively, viruses may be classified as memory-resident viruses or non-memory-resident viruses, depending on whether they persist in a computer system's memory after they have been executed. Resident viruses are capable of reactivating when the computer is booted and continuing their actions until the system is shut down, only to restart the next time the system is booted.

- **Worms.** Named for the tapeworm in John Brunner's novel *The Shockwave Rider*, a worm is a type of malware that is capable of activation and replication without being attached to an existing program. It can continue replicating itself until it completely fills available resources, such as memory, hard drive space, and/or network bandwidth. The complex behavior of worms can be initiated with or without the user downloading or executing the file. Once the worm has infected a computer, it can redistribute itself to other systems connected to the compromised system using email directories and network links found on the infected system. Furthermore, a worm can deposit copies of itself onto all web servers that the infected system can reach; users who subsequently visit those sites become infected.

- **Trojan horses.** A Trojan horse is a malware program that hides its true nature and reveals its designed behavior only when activated. It may frequently be disguised as a helpful, interesting, or necessary piece of software, such as the readme.exe files often included with shareware or freeware packages. Like their namesake in Greek legend, once Trojan horses are brought into a system, they become activated and can wreak havoc on the unsuspecting user. One historical event occurred on January 20, 1999, when Internet email users began receiving messages with an attachment of a Trojan horse program named Happy99.exe. When the email attachment was opened, a brief multimedia program displayed fireworks and the message "Happy 1999." While the fireworks display was running, the Trojan horse program was installing itself into the user's system. The program continued to propagate itself by following up every email the user sent with a second email to the same recipient and with the same attack program attached. Most malware in use gains its initial foothold using this type of Trojan horse behavior, relying on system users to activate the initial infection with a mouse click or other means of implied approval.

- **Polymorphic threats.** One of the biggest challenges to fighting viruses and worms has been the emergence of polymorphic threats, malware that evolves over time by changing the way it appears to antivirus software programs and making itself undetectable by techniques that look for preconfigured signatures.

- Virus and worm hoaxes. As frustrating as viruses and worms are, perhaps more time and money are spent resolving virus hoaxes. Well-meaning people can disrupt the harmony and flow of an organization when they send group emails warning of supposedly dangerous viruses that do not exist. When people fail to follow virus-reporting procedures in response to a hoax, the network becomes overloaded and users waste time and energy forwarding the warning message to everyone they know, posting the message on bulletin boards, and trying to update their antivirus protection software.

Back Doors   Using a known or newly discovered access mechanism, an attacker can gain access to a system or network resource through a back door or trap door, a malware payload that provides access to a system by bypassing normal access controls. Viruses and worms can have a payload that installs a back-door component in a system, allowing the attacker to access the system at will with special privileges. Sometimes these doors are left behind by system designers or maintenance staff and are thus also referred to as maintenance hooks. More often, attackers place a back door into a system or network they have compromised, making their return to the system easier the next time. A trap door is hard to detect because the person or program that places it often makes the access exempt from the system's usual audit logging features and makes every attempt to keep the back door hidden from the system's legitimate owners.

Denial-of-Service and Distributed Denial-of-Service Attacks   A denial-of-service (DoS) attack attempts to overwhelm a computer target's ability to handle incoming communications, prohibiting legitimate users from accessing their systems by sending a large number of connection or information requests to a target (see Figure 1-5). So many requests are made that the target system becomes overloaded and cannot respond to legitimate requests for service. The system may crash or simply become unable to perform ordinary functions. In a distributed denial-of-service (DDoS) attack, a coordinated stream of requests is launched against a target from many locations at the same time using other compromised systems. Most DDoS attacks are preceded by a preparation phase in which many systems, perhaps thousands, are compromised. The compromised machines are turned into bots (an abbreviation of robots), automated software programs that execute certain commands when they receive a specific input from a system that is directed remotely by the attacker (usually via a transmitted command) to participate in the attack. A bot is also known as a zombie. DDoS attacks are more difficult to defend against, and currently there are no controls that any single organization can apply. To use a popular metaphor, DDoS is considered a weapon of mass destruction on the Internet.

Figure 1-5   Denial-of-service attack

In a denial-of-service attack, a hacker compromises a system and uses that system to attack the target computer, flooding it with more requests for services than the target can handle.

In a distributed denial-of-service attack, dozens or even hundreds of computers (known as zombies or bots) are compromised, loaded with DoS attack software, and then remotely activated by the hacker to conduct a coordinated attack.

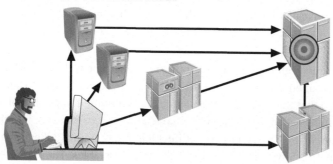

Any system connected to the Internet and providing TCP-based network services (such as a web server, FTP server, or mail server) is vulnerable to DoS attacks. DoS attacks can also be launched against routers or other network server systems if these hosts enable other TCP services, such as echo.

Email Attacks   Unwanted email, especially spam (unsolicited commercial email, typically advertising transmitted in bulk) is a common problem for email users. While many consider spam a trivial nuisance rather than an attack, it has been used as a means of enhancing malicious code attacks. Clicking on email attachments, whether in spam or as part of a phishing attack, and whether through inattention or because of the use of clickbait, has become a primary means of initial infection from malware.[17] Clickbait is content such as email attachments or embedded links crafted to convince unsuspecting users into clicking them, which results in more web traffic for the content provider or the installation of unwanted software or malware. The most significant consequence of spam, however, is the waste of computer and human resources. Many organizations attempt to cope with the flood of spam by using email filtering technologies. Other organizations simply tell users of the mail system to delete unwanted messages. The three most common forms of email attacks are wire fraud solicitations (see the earlier discussion of 4-1-9 scams), malware attachments, and clickbait.

A form of email attack that is also a DoS attack is called a mail bomb. This attack is designed to overwhelm the receiver with excessive quantities of email, and can be accomplished using traditional emailing techniques or by exploiting various technical flaws in the Simple Mail Transport Protocol (SMTP). The target of the attack receives an unmanageably large volume of unsolicited email. By sending large emails with forged header information, attackers can take advantage of poorly configured email systems on the Internet and trick them into sending many emails to an address of the attackers' choice. If many such systems are tricked into participating, the target email address is buried under thousands or even millions of unwanted emails.

Although phishing attacks occur via email, they are much more commonly associated with a method of social engineering designed to trick users to perform an action rather than simply making the user a target of a DoS email attack.

Communications Interception Attacks   Common software-based communications attacks include four subcategories designed to intercept and collect information in transit. These types of attacks include packet sniffers, spoofing, pharming, and man-in-the-middle attacks.

- Packet sniffer. A packet sniffer (or network sniffer) is a software program or hardware appliance that can intercept and interpret data traveling over a network. Sniffers can be used both for legitimate network management functions and for stealing information. Unauthorized sniffers can be extremely dangerous to a network's security because they are virtually impossible to detect and can be inserted almost anywhere. This feature makes them a favorite weapon in the hacker's arsenal. Sniffers add risk to networks because many systems and users send information on local networks in clear text. A sniffer program shows all the data going by, including plaintext usernames and passwords, file data such as word-processing documents, and potentially sensitive data from applications.

- IP spoofing. Some hackers engage in IP spoofing, a technique for gaining unauthorized access to computers using a forged or modified source IP address to give the perception that messages are coming from a trusted host. Hackers use a variety of techniques to obtain trusted IP addresses and then modify the packet headers to insert forged addresses. Newer routers and firewall arrangements can offer protection against IP spoofing. Other types of spoofing include phone spoofing, where the caller disguises or changes the number that appears on caller ID to convince the receiver that the communication is legitimate, and web spoofing, where the attacker sets up a fake website using content copied from a legitimate site to steal user credentials.

- Pharming. These attacks, which redirect legitimate user web traffic to illegitimate websites with the intent to collect personal information, often use Trojans, worms, or other virus technologies to attack an Internet browser's address bar so that the valid URL the user types is modified to be that of an illegitimate website. A form of pharming called Domain Name System (DNS) cache poisoning, the intentional hacking and modification of a DNS database to redirect legitimate traffic to illegitimate Internet locations, targets the Internet DNS system, corrupting legitimate data tables. The key difference between pharming and the phishing social engineering attack is that the latter requires the user to actively click a link or button to redirect to the illegitimate site, whereas pharming attacks modify the user's traffic without the user's knowledge or active participation.

- Man-in-the-middle attack. In this well-known attack, a person intercepts a communications stream and inserts themselves in the conversation to convince each of the legitimate parties that the attacker is the other communications partner. After the attacker monitors (or sniffs) packets from the network, the attacker modifies them and inserts them back into the network. In a TCP hijacking or session hijacking attack, a form of man-in-the-middle attack whereby the attacker inserts themselves into TCP/IP-based communications, the attacker uses address spoofing to impersonate other legitimate entities on the network. It allows the attacker to eavesdrop as well as to change, delete, reroute, add, forge, or divert data. A variant of TCP hijacking involves the interception of an encryption key exchange, which enables the hacker to eavesdrop on encrypted communications. You will learn more about encryption keys later in this book.

> **Note 5** | For more information on the preceding threats and other Internet threats, visit the website of Broadcom, the parent company of Symantec, and download their annual threat report at https://www.broadcom.com/support/security-center.

Technical Hardware Failures or Errors

Technical hardware failures or errors occur when a manufacturer distributes equipment containing a known or unknown flaw. These defects can cause the system to perform outside of expected parameters, resulting in unreliable service or lack of availability. Some errors are terminal—that is, they result in the unrecoverable loss of the equipment. Some errors are intermittent in that they only manifest themselves periodically, resulting in faults that are not easily repeated. Thus, equipment can sometimes stop working or work in unexpected ways. Murphy's Law (yes, there really was a Murphy) holds that if something can possibly go wrong, it will.[18] In other words, it is not a question *if* something will fail, but *when*.

Mean Time Between Failures   In hardware terms, failures are measured in mean time between failures (MTBF), the average amount of time between hardware failures, which is calculated as the total amount of operation time for a specified number of units divided by the total number of failures. A similar measurement, mean time to failure (MTTF), is the average amount of time until the next hardware failure is expected. While MTBF and MTTF are sometimes used interchangeably, MTBF presumes that the item can be repaired or returned to service, whereas MTTF presumes the item must be replaced. From a repair standpoint, MTBF = MTTF + MTTD + MTTR, where mean time to diagnose (MTTD) is the average amount of time a computer repair technician needs to determine the cause of a failure and mean time to repair (MTTR) is the average amount of time a computer repair technician needs to resolve the cause of a failure through replacement or repair of a faulty unit.[19] The most commonly failing piece of computer hardware is the hard drive, which currently has an average MTBF of approximately 500,000 hours. Hardware vendors are changing their reporting statistics to a new measure known as annualized failure rate (AFR), the probability of a failure of hardware based on the manufacturer's data of failures per year, which is calculated based on the manufacturer's product and warranty data. So, instead of a 500,000-hour MTBF, you might see an AFR of .05 percent, indicating that 1 in every 2000 devices typically fail each year.

Technical Software Failures or Errors

Large quantities of computer code are written, debugged, published, and sold before all their bugs are detected and resolved. Sometimes, combinations of certain software and hardware reveal new failures that range from bugs to untested failure conditions. Sometimes these bugs are not errors but purposeful shortcuts left by programmers for benign or malign reasons. Collectively, shortcut access routes into programs that bypass security checks are called trap doors, and they can cause serious security breaches.

Software bugs are so commonplace that an entire industry segment is dedicated to finding them. Bug tracking tools have become must-have applications for software developers and software assurance professionals. A simple web search will identify the "top bug tracking tools of this year." There are even lists of freeware and open-source tools, including entire projects on GitHub.

The Open Web Application Security Project (OWASP) was founded in 2001 as a nonprofit consortium dedicated to helping organizations create and operate software applications they could trust. Every three years or so, OWASP publishes a list of "The Ten Most Critical Web Application Security Risks" along with an

OWASP Developer's Guide. The OWASP Top 10 candidates for 2021, the most recent study as of this writing, are the following:

- Broken access control
- Cryptographic failures
- Injection
- Insecure design
- Security misconfiguration
- Vulnerable and outdated components
- Identification and authentication failures
- Software and data integrity failures
- Security logging and monitoring failures
- Server-side request forgery[20]

Many of these items are described in detail in the following section.

Some errors made during software development are so critical that they have been characterized as "deadly sins of software security" because they render the software vulnerable to exploitation in the hostile environment of the Internet.[21]

These "deadly sins" fall into the four broad categories of web application sins, implementation sins, cryptographic sins, and networking sins.

Web Application Sins   These sins are especially troublesome because in a very real sense, the web is "the Internet" to many users. Whether posting to social media, making a travel reservation, completing an online purchase, or managing finances, a web application is the intermediary that implements the desired functionality.

- SQL injection. Structured Query Language (SQL) injection occurs when developers fail to properly validate user input before passing it on to a relational database. The possible effects of an adversary's "injection" of SQL are not limited to improper access to information but may include damaging operations such as dropping the USERS table or perhaps shutting down the database.
- Web server-related vulnerabilities. These sins—cross-site scripting (XSS), cross-site request forgery (CSRF), and response splitting—are actually defects in web applications that exploit how the web server renders webpages to make it appear that an adversary's malicious content is actually coming from the website itself. Thus, the user "trusts" the malicious content to the same level as the website itself.
- Web client-related vulnerabilities (including XSS). Though like the previous sin, this malady is executed within the client's web browser and often makes use of gadgets or widgets (mini-applications such as a stock ticker or weather report). These mini-applications are often written to minimize footprint and maximize functionality without consideration for security.
- Use of magic URLs, predictable cookies, and hidden form fields. HTTP is a stateless protocol in which computer programs on either end of the communication channel cannot rely on a guaranteed delivery of any message. This makes it difficult for software developers to track a user's exchanges with a website over multiple interactions. Too often, sensitive state information is included in hidden form fields on the HTML page or simply included in a "magic" URL. (For example, the authentication ID is passed as a parameter in the URL for the exchanges that will follow.) If this information is stored as plaintext, an attacker can harvest the information from a magic URL as it travels across the network or use scripts on the client to modify information in hidden form fields. Depending on the structure of the application, the harvested or modified information can be used in spoofing or hijacking attacks or to change the way the application operates.[22]

Implementation Sins   These sins are classic programming errors that produce vulnerabilities in running software.

- Buffer overflow. Buffers are simply storage space in a program and are normally of some fixed size. When used to accept input from an external source (e.g., a form field on a webpage), the source may supply more information than the buffer was designed to hold and thus overwrite other areas in the program. This may cause the program to abort, or the adversary may specially craft the excess data to cause the program to perform unintended actions.

- Format string problems. Computer languages often are equipped with built-in capabilities to reformat data while they output it. The formatting instructions are usually written as a "format string." Unfortunately, some programmers may use data from untrusted sources as a format string.[23] An attacker may embed characters that are meaningful as formatting directives (such as %x, %d, %p, etc.) into malicious input. If this input is then interpreted by the program as formatting directives, the attacker may be able to access information or overwrite very targeted portions of the program's stack with data of the attacker's choosing.[24]

- Integer overflows. Although mathematical calculation theoretically can deal with numbers that contain an arbitrary number of digits, the binary representations used by computers are of a particular fixed length. The programmer must anticipate the size of the numbers to be calculated in any given part of the program. An integer bug can result when a programmer does not validate the inputs to a calculation to verify that the integers are of the expected size. Integer bugs "fall into four broad classes: overflows, underflows, truncations, and signedness errors. Even though integer bugs are often used to build a buffer overflow or other memory corruption attack, integer bugs are not just a special case of memory corruption bugs."[25]

- C++ catastrophes. C++ contains many features to simplify the process of writing software, but these features, such as classes, can be misused if the developer is not careful. For example, a class will often include virtual functions to provide functionality and encapsulate implementation. However, if the table that stores the virtual functions and their locations can be corrupted, the adversary can gain control of the program's execution, just as in other languages.

- Catching exceptions. Exception handling was introduced in modern programming languages to simplify the messy task of handling unexpected conditions. However, like any language feature, it is subject to misuse. Failures range from inappropriate handling (e.g., continuing execution when an abort is the appropriate action) to errors in the exception handling code itself (e.g., attempting to operate on an object whose creation failed and caused the current exception).

- Command injection. The problem of command injection is caused by a developer's failure to ensure that command input is validated before it is used in a program.

- Failure to handle errors correctly. What happens when a system or application encounters a scenario that it is not prepared to handle? Does it attempt to complete the operation (reading or writing data or performing calculations)? Does it issue a cryptic message that only a programmer could understand, or does it simply stop functioning? Failure to handle errors can cause a variety of unexpected system behaviors. Programmers are expected to anticipate problems and prepare their application code to handle them.

- Information leakage. One of the most common methods of obtaining inside and classified information is directly or indirectly from one person, usually an employee. A famous World War II military poster warned that "loose lips sink ships," emphasizing the risk to naval deployments from enemy attack if sailors, Marines, or their families disclosed the movements of U.S. vessels.

- Race conditions. A race condition is a failure of a program that occurs when an unexpected ordering of events in its execution results in a conflict over access to the same system resource. This conflict does not need to involve streams of code inside the program because current operating systems and processor technology automatically break a program into multiple threads that can be executed simultaneously. If the threads that result from this process share any resources, they may interfere with each other.

- Poor usability. Users prefer doing things the easy way. When faced with an "official way" of performing a task and an "unofficial way"—which is easier—they prefer the latter. The best solution to address this issue is to provide only one way—the secure way! Integrating security and usability, adding training and awareness, and ensuring solid controls all contribute to the security of information. Allowing users to choose easier solutions by default will inevitably lead to loss.

- Not updating easily. It is a given that software will need to be changed at some point during its life cycle, either to fix a problem, close a security vulnerability, or add new functionality. If the updating process is cryptic, users will probably not update their software, which may then be compromised due to a known and fixed vulnerability. As more computing capability is added to devices that do not look like computers, such as Internet of Things appliances, it becomes less obvious to know whether they need periodic updates. An equally important issue is to ensure that updates come from trusted sources. After all, if Alice Adversary can convince your user to install her malicious software as an "important security update," why should she spend the time to exploit a software vulnerability?

- Executing code with too much privilege. "Least privilege" is one of the core principles of cybersecurity, but it can be difficult to implement in the real world, as sometimes users do need to perform privileged operations. It is tempting for a developer always to run at the higher privilege level rather than provide a method for increasing privilege temporarily when it is needed. The risk is that when a program (or session) is compromised, malicious actions will be taken at the current privilege level.

- Failure to protect stored data. Storing and protecting data securely is a large enough issue to be the core subject of this entire text. Programmers are responsible for integrating access controls into programs and keeping secret information out of them. Access controls, the subject of later chapters, regulate who, what, when, where, and how users and systems interact with data. Failure to implement sufficiently strong access controls makes the data vulnerable. Overly strict access controls hinder business users in the performance of their duties, and as a result, the controls may be administratively removed or bypassed.

- The sins of mobile code. Mobile code is "code that is downloaded and executed on a user's computer, sometimes with little or no user consent."[26] It is responsible for the liveliness and interactivity of most web content but also can be a rich field for malicious activity. The core issue is that mobile code is often downloaded and executed automatically without the user being aware of it (e.g., the Adobe Flash object that plays an online video). If the code has vulnerabilities, they can be exploited to effect a compromise.

Cryptographic Sins   Cryptography is a valuable tool for securing information, but like any tool, it must be used correctly. When cryptography is misused, it often gives the illusion of security while leaving the user in worse condition than before.

- Use of weak password-based systems. Failure to require sufficient password strength and to control incorrect password entry is a serious security issue. Password policy can specify the acceptable number and type of characters, the frequency of mandatory changes, and even the reusability of old passwords. Similarly, a system administrator can regulate the permitted number of incorrect password entries that are submitted and further improve the level of protection. Systems that do not validate passwords, or that store passwords in easily accessible locations, are ripe for attack.

- Weak random numbers. Most modern cryptosystems, like many other computer systems, use random number generators. However, a decision support system that uses random and pseudo-random numbers for Monte Carlo method forecasting does not require the same degree of rigor and the same need for true randomness as a system that seeks to implement cryptographic procedures. These "random" number generators use a mathematical algorithm based on a seed value and another system component (such as the computer clock) to simulate a random number. Those who understand the workings of such a "random" number generator can predict specific values at specific times.

- Using the wrong cryptography. Many more people use cryptography than understand it, which leads to cryptographic implementations that fail to deliver their promised contribution to security. Examples of these sins include using a homegrown cryptographic algorithm rather than a professionally evaluated one, such as Advanced Encryption Standard (AES), and poor implementations of key generation methods that lead to predictable keys (as well as poor operational procedures for managing keys that may lead to key leakage or loss).

Networking Sins   The network is the piping that enables the worldwide flow of information and makes the Internet such an interesting place. However, because it is the medium for all that information flow, it is a rich target.

- Failure to protect network traffic. With the growing popularity of wireless networking comes a corresponding increase in the risk that wirelessly transmitted data will be intercepted. Most wireless networks are installed and operated with little or no protection for the information that is broadcast between the client and the network wireless access point. This is especially true of public networks found in coffee shops, bookstores, and hotels. Without appropriate encryption such as that afforded by Wi-Fi Protected Access (WPA), attackers can intercept and view your data.

- Improper use of PKI, especially SSL. Programmers use SSL to transfer sensitive data, such as credit card numbers and other personal information, between a client and server. While most programmers assume that using SSL guarantees security, it is easy to misapply this technology. SSL and its successor, Transport Layer Security (TLS), commonly use certificates for authenticating entities. Failure to validate a public key infrastructure (PKI) certificate and its issuing certificate authority or failure to check the certificate revocation list (CRL) can compromise the security of SSL traffic. You will learn much more about cryptographic controls later in this book.

- Trusting network name resolution. As described earlier, DNS is vulnerable to attack or "poisoning." DNS cache poisoning involves compromising a DNS server and then changing the valid IP address associated with a domain name into one the attacker chooses, usually a fake website designed to obtain personal information or one that accrues a benefit to the attacker—for example, redirecting shoppers from a competitor's website or to a fake "bank" site. Aside from a direct attack against a root DNS server, most attacks are made against primary and secondary DNS servers, which are local to an organization and part of the distributed DNS system. DNS relies on a process of automated updates that can be exploited. Attackers most commonly compromise segments of the DNS by attacking the name of the name server and substituting their own DNS primary name server, by incorrectly updating an individual record, or by responding before an actual DNS can.

Technological Obsolescence

Antiquated or outdated infrastructure can lead to unreliable and untrustworthy systems. Management must recognize that when technology becomes outdated, there is a risk of losing data integrity from attacks. Management's strategic planning should always include an analysis of the technology currently in use. Ideally, proper planning by management should prevent technology from becoming obsolete, but when obsolescence is clear, management must take immediate action. IT professionals play a large role in the identification of probable obsolescence.

Perhaps the most significant case of technology obsolescence in recent years is Microsoft operating systems. Microsoft XP, introduced in 2001, dominated the market for many years. XP evolved to be used in multiple variations such as XP Pro and XP Home, had feature and capability upgrades in three service packs, and even made the transition to new processors with a 64-bit edition. It was superseded in the corporation's lineup of desktop operating systems by Microsoft Vista in January 2007. As of April 2022, there were more Windows XP users than Windows 11 users worldwide; about 0.4 percent of all PCs in the world are still using Windows XP. More than 10 percent of the world's PCs are running Windows 7, which has also reached end-of-life (EOL) status.[27]

Microsoft discontinued support for Windows XP in April 2014 and for Windows 7 in January 2020. This removal of support was expected to cause concern and perhaps even disruptions in some business sectors, notably the utility industry. Many industries and organizations built critical elements of their business systems and even their infrastructure control systems on top of Windows XP and Windows 7, or they used it as an embedded operating system inside other systems, such as automated teller machines and power-generating and control systems.

Theft

The threat of theft, the illegal taking of another's property, whether physical, electronic, or intellectual, is a constant. The value of information is diminished when it is copied without the owner's knowledge. Physical theft can be controlled easily using a wide variety of measures, from locked doors to trained security personnel and the installation of alarm systems. Electronic theft, however, is a more complex problem to manage and control. When someone steals a physical object, the loss is easily detected; if it has any importance at all, its absence is noted. When electronic information is stolen, the crime is not always readily apparent. If thieves are clever and cover their tracks carefully, the crime may remain undiscovered until it is too late.

Theft is often an overlapping category with software attacks, espionage or trespass, information extortion, and compromises to intellectual property. A hacker or other individual threat agent could access a system and commit most of these offenses if they downloaded a company's information and then threatened to publish it if not paid.

Some or All of the Above

In today's complex attack environment, most threats do not manifest from only one of the categories listed in the previous sections. Rather, adversaries plan and execute sophisticated campaigns using all means of attack to achieve their ultimate objectives. The purpose of these categories is to provide a basis for understanding the threats, rather than to compartmentalize each threat or attack exclusively. The reality, as mentioned earlier, is much more complex. In this era of the advanced persistent threat, an attack may begin with a social engineering effort, leading to a spear phishing message that deploys a malware program designed to install a back door, which is then used by a hacker to conduct theft, espionage, data exfiltration, and/or information extortion. In spring 2015, Russian-based Kaspersky Lab, an antivirus and Internet security software company, detected an incident in its systems. Published summaries of the event indicated they had been subjected to a planned cyber-espionage attack. Based on indicators discovered in the subsequent investigation, they believed they were targeted by a nation-state as part of a broader campaign that leveraged the Duqu malware platform.

Duqu, a sophisticated suite of malware components, was discovered in 2011 and is thought by some to be related to the Stuxnet worm. The Laboratory of Cryptography and System Security of the Budapest University of Technology and Economics in Hungary discovered Duqu, and it was quickly confirmed by other organizations.[28] It is regarded as a toolset to implement back-door attacks and enable the theft of private information. Kaspersky Lab reported that the attackers believed they were undetectable. To preserve that illusion and to continue monitoring the attackers' actions, Kaspersky Lab tried to avoid exposing the ongoing attack while they controlled what information was revealed. This effort allowed Kaspersky Lab to see previously unknown methods of attack. The entire cyberattack protocol was extremely stealthy because it did not create, delete, or modify any files or settings.[29]

Noted security author Bruce Schneier wrote that the Duqu campaign was just one in a concerted effort by an undetermined nation-state to collect information on the Iran nuclear program talks conducted by China, France, Russia, the United Kingdom, and the United States, plus Germany (the so-called P5+1 countries). Many of the attacks by Duqu targeted hotels and conference centers that hosted the talks; the attacks occurred only three weeks prior to the talks.[30] The lesson learned is that some threats are now national security-level events and may even be concerted efforts to conduct international espionage. These threats combine the best (or worst) of each threat category to collect information for some unknown purpose and then to sneak out undetected or digitally destroy the systems to obfuscate the attacker's intent and actions.

Self-Check

4. A denial-of-service (DoS) attack is designed to overwhelm a target's ability to handle incoming communications, prohibiting legitimate users from accessing affected systems.

    a. True   b. False

5. In cybersecurity, social engineering refers to the physical manipulation of computer hardware to compromise security.

    a. True   b. False

6. Ransomware is a type of malware that encrypts the victim's files and demands a ransom for the decryption key.

    a. True   b. False

☐ Check your answers at the end of this chapter.

Management and Leadership

In order to understand what management of cybersecurity is, you must first understand what management is and how it can be used effectively. In its most basic form, management is the process of getting a job done and achieving other objectives by appropriately applying a given set of resources. A manager is a member of the organization assigned to request, organize, and administer resources, coordinate the completion of tasks, and handle the many roles necessary to complete the desired objectives. Managers have many roles to play within organizations, including the following:

- Informational role—Collecting, processing, and using information that can affect the completion of an objective
- Interpersonal role—Interacting with superiors, subordinates, outside stakeholders, and other parties that influence or are influenced by the completion of the task
- Decisional role—Selecting from among alternative approaches and resolving conflicts, dilemmas, or challenges

Note that there are differences between management and leadership, the ability to influence others to gain their willing cooperation and achieve an objective by providing purpose, direction, and motivation. A leader is more and does more than a manager. They are expected to lead by example and demonstrate personal traits that instill a desire in others to follow. By comparison, managers administer the resources they are assigned by the organization. They create budgets, authorize expenditures, and recruit, hire, evaluate, and terminate employees. This distinction between a leader and a manager is important because leaders do not always perform a managerial function, and managers are often assigned roles in which they are not responsible for personnel. However, *effective* managers can also be effective leaders.

Behavioral Types of Leaders

Among leaders, there are three basic behavioral types: autocratic, democratic, and laissez-faire. Autocratic leaders reserve all decision-making responsibility for themselves and are "do as I say" types. Such leaders typically issue an order to accomplish a task and do not usually seek or accept alternative viewpoints. Democratic leaders work in the opposite way, typically seeking input from all interested parties, requesting ideas and suggestions, and then formulating positions that can be supported by a majority.

Each of these two diametrically opposed approaches has its strengths and weaknesses. The autocratic leader may be more efficient and make quicker decisions, given that they are not constrained by the necessity to accommodate alternative viewpoints. The democratic leader may be less efficient because valuable time is spent in discussion and debate when planning for the task. On the other hand, the autocratic leader may be the least effective if their knowledge is insufficient for the task. The democratic leader may be more effective when dealing with very complex topics or those in which direct reports have strongly held opinions or expert knowledge.

The laissez-faire leader is also known as the "laid-back" leader. While both autocratic and democratic leaders tend to be action oriented, the laissez-faire leader often sits back and allows the process to develop as it goes, only making minimal decisions to avoid bringing the process to a complete halt.

Effective leaders function with a combination of these styles, shifting approaches as situations warrant. For example, depending on the circumstances, a leader may solicit input when the situation permits, make autocratic decisions when immediate action is required, and allow the operation to proceed with little direct intervention if it is progressing in an efficient and effective manner.

Note 6 | For more information on leadership, download the free white paper titled "Understanding Leadership" by W.C.H. Prentice, or other related articles on the topic from *Harvard Business Review* (https://hbr.org/2004/01/understanding-leadership).

Management Characteristics

The management of tasks requires certain basic skills. These skills are variously referred to as management functions or management principles. The two basic approaches to management are:

- Traditional management theory—This approach uses the core principles of planning, organizing, staffing, directing, and controlling (POSDC).
- Popular management theory—This approach uses the core principles of planning, organizing, leading, and controlling (POLC).

The traditional approach to management theory is often well covered in introductory business courses and will not be revisited here. Rather, we will focus on the POLC principles that managers employ when dealing with tasks. Figure 1-6 summarizes these principles and illustrates how they are conceptually related.

Figure 1-6   The planning-controlling link

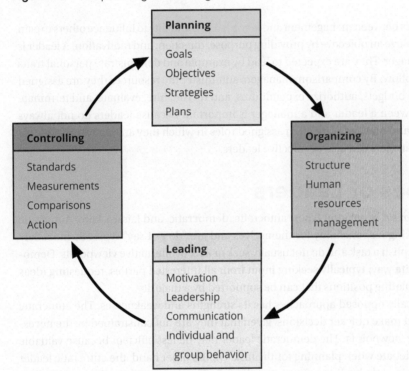

Planning

Several different approaches to planning—the process of creating designs or schemes for future efforts or performance—are examined more thoroughly in later chapters of this book. The three commonly used descriptors for levels of planning are:

- Strategic planning—Occurs at the highest levels of the organization and for a long period of time, usually five or more years
- Tactical planning—Focuses on production planning and integrates organizational resources at a level below the entire enterprise for an intermediate duration (such as one to five years)
- Operational planning—Focuses on the day-to-day operations of local resources and occurs in the present or the short term

There is also a category of planning used in non-normal business operations called contingency planning. Contingency planning and its components are discussed later in this book. Lack of planning can cause the kind of confusion and frustration among managers and staff that Iris describes in the opening scenario of this chapter.

The planning process begins with the creation of strategic plans for the entire organization. The resulting plan is then divided into planning elements relevant to each major business unit of the organization. These business units in turn create business plans that meet the requirements of the overall organizational strategy. The plans are communicated to midlevel managers so that they can create tactical plans with intermediate objectives that, if successful, would result in achievement of the strategic plan's goals. Supervisors use tactical plans to create operational plans that guide the day-to-day operations of the organization. To better understand its planning process, an organization must thoroughly define its goals and objectives. While the exact definition varies depending on context, the term "goal" refers to the result of a planning process—for example, increasing market share by 2 percent. The term "objective" refers to an intermediate point that allows you to measure progress toward the goal—for example, a growth in sales for each quarter. If you accomplish all objectives in a timely manner, then you are likely to accomplish your goal.

The management of the planning function within an organization encompasses an entire field of study. It requires an understanding of how to plan and a thorough understanding of project management. Project management is discussed later in this book.

Organizing

The organizing management function is the structuring of resources to maximize their efficiency and ease of use. It includes the structuring of departments and their associated staffs, the storage of raw materials to facilitate manufacturing, and the collection of information to aid in the accomplishment of tasks. Recent definitions of "organizing" include staffing because organizing people to maximize their productivity is not substantially different from organizing time, money, or equipment.

Leading

Leading, the application of leadership, encourages the implementation of the planning and organizing functions. It includes supervising employee behavior, performance, attendance, and attitude while ensuring the completion of the assigned tasks, goals, and objectives. Leadership generally addresses the direction and motivation of human resources.

Controlling

In general, controlling is the process of monitoring progress and making necessary adjustments to achieve desired goals or objectives. This process ensures the validity of the organization's plan. The manager reviews performance and ensures that sufficient progress is made, that impediments to the completion of the task are resolved, and that no additional resources are required. Should the plan be found invalid considering the operational reality of the organization, the manager takes corrective action.

The control function relies on the use of cybernetic control loops, often called negative feedback. These involve performance measurements, comparisons, and corrective actions, as shown in Figure 1-7. Here, the cybernetic control process begins with a measurement of actual performance, which is then compared to the expected standard of performance as determined by the planning process. If the standard is being met, the process is allowed to continue toward completion. If an acceptable level of performance is not being attained, either the process is corrected to achieve satisfactory results or the expected level of performance is redefined. This comparison is commonly referred to as a gap analysis, a comparison of actual versus planned or desired performance, outcomes, or achievements, with the "gap" being the difference between the two. Positive gap outcomes occur when the actual outcomes exceed expectations, while negative gap outcomes occur when they fall short.

Governance

As discussed later in the book, the very top of an organization includes a special level of management that involves planning, organizing, leading, and controlling the cybersecurity function. For most organizations that have such a governing body, it exists either at the board of directors' level or the senior executive level. This oversight by top management is referred to as governance, the set of responsibilities and practices exercised by the board and executive management with the goal of providing strategic direction, ensuring that

Figure 1-7   The control process

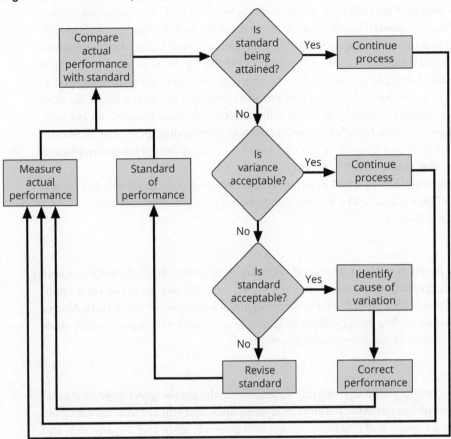

objectives are achieved, ascertaining that risks are managed appropriately, and verifying that the enterprise's resources are used responsibly.

Just as there are governance functions to manage the entire business side of the organization, there are special governance functions for IT and cybersecurity. Cybersecurity governance emphasizes escalating the importance of cybersecurity to the uppermost levels of the organization and providing it with an appropriate level of recognition and oversight. In more mature organizations that have long-established cybersecurity programs, governance structures provide oversight and increased attention to the various cybersecurity functions, specifically those addressing risk management, performance measures, and regulatory compliance. Risk management is made up of processes an organization implements to identify assets, assess risks to those assets, and reduce potential losses. Performance measures are identified evaluative criteria that an organization chooses to collect and evaluate to gain essential feedback on its quantitative and qualitative performance. Regulatory compliance is the set of actions an organization undertakes to assure evaluators that it complies with applicable laws, regulations, and standards. The term "Governance, Risk Management, and Compliance (GRC)," an amalgamation of the executive-level responsibilities for cybersecurity within an organization, is often used to describe this executive oversight.

Solving Problems

All managers encounter problems during the organization's day-to-day operation. Whether a problem has a low or high profile, the same basic process can be used to solve it. Time pressures often constrain decision making when problems arise, however. The process of gathering and evaluating the necessary facts may be beyond available capabilities. Nevertheless, the methodology described in the following steps can be used as a basic blueprint for resolving many operational problems.

Step 1: Recognize and Define the Problem

The most common flaw in problem solving is failing to completely define the problem. Begin by clearly identifying exactly which problem needs to be solved. For example, if Iris receives complaints at RWW about the receipt of a large number of unsolicited commercial emails (also known as spam), she must first determine whether the complaints are valid. Are employees in fact receiving unsolicited spam, or have they signed up for notifications and mailing lists?

Step 2: Gather Facts and Make Assumptions

To understand the background and events that shape the problem, a manager can gather facts about the organizational, cultural, technological, and behavioral factors that are at the root of the issue. The manager can then make assumptions about the methods that are available to solve the problem. For example, by interviewing several employees, Iris might determine that they are receiving a large quantity of unsolicited email. She might also determine that each of these employees has accessed approved vendor support sites, which require an email sign-in process. In such a case, Iris would suspect that the problem of excessive email is in fact the result of employees providing their company email addresses, which are being improperly used by the site owners.

Step 3: Develop Possible Solutions

The next step is to begin formulating possible solutions. Managers can use several methods to generate ideas. One of these is brainstorming, a process in which a group of individuals airs as many ideas as possible in a short time, without regard for their practicality. The group then reviews and filters the ideas to identify any feasible options. Problem solvers can also interview experts or perform research into solutions using the web, magazines, journals, or books. In any case, the goal is to develop as many solutions as possible. In the preceding example, once Iris locates the source of the spam emails, she can speak with the email server and firewall administrators and then turn to her professional reading list. She might contact several of her friends from the local ISSA module as well as spend time surfing security-related websites. After a few hours, Iris could have a significant collection of information that might be useful in solving this problem.

Step 4: Analyze and Compare Possible Solutions

Each proposed solution must be examined and ranked as to its likely success in solving the problem. This analysis may include reviewing economic, technological, behavioral, and operational feasibilities, which are described here:

- Economic feasibility—Comparing the costs and benefits of a possible solution with other possible solutions
- Technological feasibility—Assessing the organization's ability to acquire the technology needed to implement a particular solution
- Behavioral feasibility—Assessing the likelihood that subordinates will adopt and support a particular solution rather than resist it
- Operational feasibility—Assessing the organization's ability to integrate a particular solution into its current business processes

Using a feasibility analysis, you can compare various options. Using the spam example, Iris might immediately eliminate any overly expensive solutions, throw out some technical solutions incompatible with RWW's systems, and narrow the field to three alternatives: (1) do nothing, accepting the spam as a cost of doing business; (2) have the email administrator change the users' accounts; or (3) have the firewall administrator filter access to and traffic from the spam sites. Iris could then discuss these alternatives with all the involved administrators. Each solution is feasible, inexpensive, and does not negatively affect RWW's overall operations. After further analysis, the team may select one or more of the recommended solutions or reject them all in favor of a different solution.

Step 5: Select, Implement, and Evaluate

Once a solution is chosen and implemented, you must evaluate it to determine its effectiveness in solving the problem. It is important to monitor the chosen solution carefully so that if it proves ineffective, it can be canceled or altered quickly. In Iris's case, she might decide to implement the firewall filters to reduce the spam, as most of it comes from a few sources. She might also decide to require the affected employees to attend a training program for email security policies, where they can be reminded of the importance of controlling when and where they release company email addresses. In addition, these employees might be required to submit periodic reports about the status of the email problem.

> **Note 7** | For more information on problem solving and decision making, visit the Free Management Library and view the problem-solving section at http://managementhelp.org/personalproductivity/problem-solving.htm.

Self-Check

7. Leadership and management are interchangeable terms with no distinction between their roles and responsibilities.

    a. True

    b. False

8. Autocratic leaders typically involve subordinates in the decision-making process and value their input.

    a. True

    b. False

9. Operational feasibility involves assessing an organization's ability to integrate a particular solution into its current business processes.

    a. True

    b. False

□ Check your answers at the end of this chapter.

Principles of Cybersecurity Management

As part of the management team, the cybersecurity management team operates like all other management units by using the common characteristics of leadership and management discussed earlier in this chapter. However, the cybersecurity management team's goals and objectives differ from those of the IT and general management communities in that the cybersecurity management team is focused on the secure operation of the organization. In fact, some of the cybersecurity management team's goals and objectives may be contrary to or require resolution with the goals of the IT management team. The primary focus of the IT group is to ensure the effective and efficient processing of information, whereas the primary focus of the cybersecurity group is to ensure the confidentiality, integrity, and availability of information. Security, by its very nature, will slow down the information flow into, through, and out of an organization as information is validated, verified, and assessed against security criteria. Because the senior manager in charge of the cybersecurity management team most commonly reports directly to the chief information officer (CIO), who is responsible for the IT function, issues and prioritization conflicts can arise unless upper management intervenes. This issue and possible resolutions are discussed at length later in this text. Note that the title "chief cybersecurity officer (CCO/CCSO)" is not as common as "chief information security officer (CISO)" in industry or government, although it is rapidly emerging. The titles found for the senior cybersecurity officer vary radically between organizations. For this text, we will use the term "chief security officer (CSO)" as designation-neutral.

Because cybersecurity management oversees a specialized program, certain aspects of its managerial responsibility are unique. These unique functions, which are known as "the six Ps" (planning, policy, programs, protection, people, and project management), are discussed throughout this text and are briefly described in the following sections.

Planning

Planning in cybersecurity management is an extension of the basic planning model discussed earlier in this chapter. Included in the cybersecurity planning model are activities necessary to support the design, creation, and implementation of cybersecurity strategies within the planning environments of all organizational units, including IT. Because cybersecurity strategic plans must support not only the IT use and protection of information assets but also those of the entire organization, it is imperative that the CSO work closely with all senior managers in developing cybersecurity strategy.

Typically in organizations, the overall company strategy is translated into strategies for each subordinate unit, including IT. The strategies of each of these units, again with the IT strategy, are then used to develop the cybersecurity strategy. Just as the CIO uses the IT objectives gleaned from the business unit plans to create the organization's IT strategy, the CSO develops cybersecurity objectives from the IT and other business units to create the organization's cybersecurity strategy. The IT strategy and that of the other business units provides critical information used for cybersecurity planning as the CSO gets involved with the CIO and other executives to develop the strategy for the next level down.

The CSO then works with their subordinate security managers to develop operational security plans. These security managers consult with security technicians to develop tactical security plans. Each of these plans is usually coordinated across the business and IT functions of the enterprise and placed into a master schedule for implementation. The overall goal is to create plans that support long-term achievement of the overall organizational strategy. If all goes as expected, the entire collection of tactical plans accomplishes the operational goals and the entire collection of operational goals accomplishes the subordinate strategic goals; this helps to meet the strategic goals and objectives of the organization as a whole.

Several types of cybersecurity plans and planning functions exist to support normal and non-normal operations. These include incident response planning, business continuity planning, disaster recovery planning, policy planning, personnel planning, technology rollout planning, risk management planning, and security program planning, to name a few. Each of these plans has unique goals and objectives, yet each benefits from the same methodical approach. These planning areas are discussed in detail in later chapters of this book.

Another basic planning consideration unique to the establishment of the cybersecurity function in its inception is its location within the organization's reporting structure. This topic is discussed later in the book.

Note 8 | For more information on developing cybersecurity plans, read NIST Special Publication 800-18, Rev. 1 (https://csrc.nist.gov/publications/detail/sp/800-18/rev-1/final), which uses federal information systems as its focus but provides many excellent examples of general planning for cybersecurity.

Policy

In cybersecurity, there are three general categories of policy, managerial guidance that dictates certain behavior within the organization. Policy is discussed in greater detail later in this book.

- Program policy—Developed within the context of the organization's strategic plans, this policy sets the tone for the cybersecurity department and the cybersecurity climate across the organization. The CSO typically drafts the program policy, which is usually supported and signed by the CIO or the CEO.
- Issue-specific policies—Issue-specific policies include management rules that define acceptable behavior within a specific organizational resource, such as email or Internet usage.
- System-specific policies—A merger of technical and managerial intent, system-specific policies include both the managerial guidance for the implementation of a technology as well as the technical specifications for its configuration.

Programs

Cybersecurity operations that are specifically managed as separate entities are called programs. An example would be a security education, training, and awareness (SETA) program, a risk management program, or contingency programs such as incident response, disaster recovery, or business continuity. SETA programs provide critical information to employees to maintain or improve their current levels of security knowledge. Risk management programs include the identification, assessment, and control of risks to information assets. Contingency programs prepare the organization for non-normal business operations such as reacting to an incident or disaster, which may require the organization to relocate to an alternate site at least temporarily. Other programs that may emerge include a physical security program, complete with fire protection, physical access, gates, guards, and so on. Some organizations with specific regulations may have additional programs dedicated to client/customer privacy, awareness, and the like. Each organization will typically have several cybersecurity programs that must be managed.

Protection

The protection function is executed via a set of risk management activities as well as protection mechanisms, technologies, and tools. Most attacks originate from a people problem, like a social engineering attack or a phishing attack. Each of these mechanisms or safeguards represents some aspect of the management of specific controls in the overall cybersecurity plan.

People

People are the most critical link in the cybersecurity program. This area encompasses security personnel (the professional cybersecurity employees), the security of personnel (the protection of employees and their information), and aspects of the SETA program mentioned earlier.

Project Management

Whether a cybersecurity manager is asked to roll out a new security training program or select and implement a new firewall, it is important that the process be managed as a project. The final element for thorough cybersecurity management is the application of a project management discipline to all elements of the cybersecurity program. Project management involves identifying and controlling the resources applied to the project as well as measuring progress and adjusting the process as progress is made toward the goal.

View Point   Why Do I Have to Learn Management?

By Henry Bonin, business analyst and former faculty member at San Jose State University

This is the seventh edition of this textbook. That shows how much, how quickly, and how broadly the field has changed. Keeping up with the practice of cybersecurity and its management necessitates a new edition.

Most of you will start your career in some specific technical role. As you progress through your career, you may dive deeper into your original role to build your technical depth. Or, you may rotate into adjacent roles to build your breadth. Or, you may diversify into project management and develop new skills. Lastly, you may move into management of a technical staff.

Even if you do not move into management, an understanding of what a manager's role is will help make you a greater success in your role ... and help make your manager more successful.

So, what is management at its basic level? Imagine a manager as the director of an orchestra. The director keeps the beat so all the players stay together, moving in one direction toward a common goal. The director combines the sound and performance of each player into a wonderful experience for the listener.

The cybersecurity field will need many new, good managers. This textbook will prepare you for whatever relationship your career has with management. Cybersecurity is one of those rare fields where managers need to come from their own ranks. Good luck as you begin this challenging course.

Henry Bonin was a member of the faculty at San Jose State University in California. He taught a senior elective course on security management in the Information Management Systems Department of the School of Business. He also helped implement the Bank Secrecy Act for Anti-Money Laundering at Union Bank of California.

Note 9 | Read about the groundbreaking hacking attacks on Ukraine in December 2016 in Andy Greenberg's *Wired* article from June 20, 2017, "How an Entire Nation Became Russia's Test Lab for Cyberwar."

Self-Check

10. The primary focus of the IT management team and the cybersecurity management team are always aligned and never conflict.

   a. True   **b.** False

11. The CSO often reports directly to the CIO.

   a. True   **b.** False

12. In cybersecurity management, planning does not include the development of incident response or disaster recovery plans.

   a. True   **b.** False

☐ Check your answers at the end of this chapter.

Closing Case

Charlie and Iris met for a work lunch.

"First thing you need to do," Charlie told Iris, "is gain some consensus from your higher management to fund a new position for a security analyst. Then fill it by finding someone who has security skills but is primarily skilled in project management. Or find a strong security analyst and send them off for PM training."

"Why so?" Iris asked.

"A good project manager can help the entire team learn how to manage all the security projects to keep you from getting overwhelmed with deadlines and deliverables," Charlie said, smiling. "A good PM can make your operations proactive rather than reactive."

"That sounds good," Iris replied. "What else do I need to know?"

Case Discussion Questions

1. Based on your reading of the chapter and what you now know about the issues, list at least three other things Charlie could recommend to Iris.

2. What do you think is the most important piece of advice Charlie gave Iris? Why?

Case Ethical Decision Making

Assume that Charlie then tells Iris, "I have a friend who runs a placement service and can find you exactly the right person for this position. Once you have the job posted, you can have them help you fill it. If they find you a great candidate and the placement is made, I will split the finder's fee with you."

Iris knows that her company may pay as much as half a year's salary for the placement services needed for such a hire. Charlie's friend is likely to pay him a substantial finder's fee if Iris awards the placement contract to them and someone gets placed. If she can get a good employee and a little extra money on the side, everyone wins.

However, Iris is not comfortable with such an arrangement, and she is pretty sure it is against company policy.

If this comes to pass, is Charlie doing anything illegal? Is Iris? What is ethically wrong with Charlie's proposal?

Summary

In today's global markets, business operations are enabled by technology. IT enables the storage and transportation of information—often a company's most valuable resource—from one business unit to another. The focus of cybersecurity is protecting information assets.

Organizations know that cybersecurity involves more than managers of information, the members of the cybersecurity team, or the managers of IT. It must involve the entire organization, as represented by three communities of interest: those in the field of cybersecurity, those in the field of IT, and those from the rest of the organization.

Cybersecurity is based on the fundamental concept of security, the state of being secure and free from danger or harm. The dominant areas of security include cybersecurity, computer security, communications security, network security, operations security, and physical security.

Information has certain characteristics that make it valuable to an organization, including confidentiality, integrity, availability, privacy, identification, authentication, authorization, and accountability.

To protect your organization's information, you must know yourself and know the threats you face as well as their attack methods, characteristics, and potential outcomes. A threat is defined as any event or circumstance that has the potential to adversely affect operations and assets; an attack is an intentional or unintentional act that can damage or otherwise compromise information and the systems that support it. A threat agent or threat source, a specific instance or component of a threat, attempts to damage or steal an organization's information or physical assets by using an exploit, a technique used to compromise a system to take advantage of a vulnerability. A vulnerability is a potential weakness in an asset or its defensive control systems where controls are not present or no longer effective.

The 12 general categories of threats represent a clear and present danger to an organization's people, information, and systems. Each organization must prioritize the threats it faces based on the particular security situation in which it operates, its organizational strategy regarding risk, and the exposure levels of its assets.

In order to understand what management of cybersecurity is, you must first understand what management is. In its most basic form, management is the process of getting a job done and achieving other objectives by appropriately applying a given set of resources. Note that there are differences between management and leadership, the ability to influence others to gain their willing cooperation and achieve an objective by providing purpose, direction, and motivation. A leader is more and does more than a manager.

The management of tasks requires certain basic skills. These skills are variously referred to as management functions or management principles. The two basic approaches to management are traditional management theory and popular management theory.

The very top of an organization includes a special level of management that involves planning, organizing, leading, and controlling the cybersecurity function. For most organizations that have such a governing body, it exists either at the board of directors' level or the senior executive level. This oversight by top management is referred to as governance, the set of responsibilities and practices exercised by the board and executive management with the goal of providing strategic direction. The term "Governance, Risk Management, and Compliance (GRC)," an amalgamation of the executive-level responsibilities for cybersecurity within an organization, is often used to describe this executive oversight.

The cybersecurity management team's goals and objectives differ from those of the IT and general management communities in that the cybersecurity management team is focused on the secure operation of the organization.

Key Terms

4-1-9 fraud
accountability
advance-fee fraud (AFF)
advanced persistent threat (APT)
annualized failure rate (AFR)
asset
attack
authentication
authorization
availability
availability disruption
back door
blackout
boot-sector virus
boot virus
bot
brownout
brute-force password attack
business email compromise (BEC)
clickbait
communications security
competitive intelligence
computer security
confidentiality
controlling
cracker
cracking
cyberactivist
cybersecurity
cyberterrorism
cyberwarfare
denial-of-service (DoS) attack
dictionary attack
dictionary password attack
disclosure
distributed denial-of-service
   (DDoS) attack
Domain Name System (DNS)
   cache poisoning
elite hacker
expert hacker
exploit
fault

gap analysis
governance
hacker
hacktivist
IAAA security framework
identification
industrial espionage
information aggregation
information assets
information extortion
information warfare
integrity
intellectual property (IP)
IP spoofing
jailbreaking
leadership
leading
macro virus
mail bomb
maintenance hook
malicious code
malicious software
malware
man-in-the-middle attack
management
mean time between failures
   (MTBF)
mean time to diagnose
   (MTTD)
mean time to failure
   (MTTF)
mean time to repair
   (MTTR)
network security
network sniffer
noise
novice hacker
operations security
organizing
packet monkey
packet sniffer
penetration tester
pharming

phishing
physical security
planning
policy
polymorphic threat
possession
pretexting
privacy
privilege escalation
professional hacker
rainbow table
ransomware
rooting
sag
script kiddie
security
service level agreement
   (SLA)
session hijacking
shoulder surfing
social engineering
software piracy
spam
spear phishing
spike
surge
swell
tactics, techniques,
   and procedures
   (TTP)
TCP hijacking
theft
threat
threat agent
threat event
threat source
trap door
trespass
Trojan horse
virus
vulnerability
worm
zombie

Review Questions

1. What has caused cybersecurity to evolve beyond the responsibility of just the IT department?

2. How do organizations ensure that their cybersecurity planning and decisions involve the appropriate parties?

3. What are the key characteristics of information that make it valuable to an organization?

4. What measures can be used to protect the confidentiality of information?

5. How is the integrity of information protected against corruption and damage?

6. What role does authentication play in the access control mechanism of information systems?

7. How does knowing the threats faced by an organization assist in cybersecurity management?

8. What role does Internet connectivity play in the exposure of organizations to external threats?

9. How do DoS and DDoS attacks affect targeted systems?

10. What is the significance of implementing contingency plans for forces of nature in cybersecurity?

11. What role do human errors play in cybersecurity threats, and how can they be mitigated?

12. Why is technological obsolescence considered a cybersecurity threat, and how should organizations address it?

13. What is the fundamental difference between management and leadership?

14. What are the three basic behavioral types of leaders?

15. How does the POLC management theory framework differ from traditional management theory?

16. What is the role of contingency planning within the context of organizational management?

17. How can managers ensure the effectiveness of their chosen solution to a problem?

18. What factors should be considered in the analysis and comparison of possible solutions to a problem?

19. Describe a method for generating ideas during the problem-solving process.

20. What differentiates the goals of the cybersecurity management team from those of the IT management team?

21. What are the "six Ps" that constitute the unique functions of cybersecurity management?

22. How is the cybersecurity strategy developed within an organization?

23. What types of cybersecurity plans are necessary to support both normal and non-normal operations?

24. What are the three general categories of cybersecurity policy?

25. What role do people play in a cybersecurity program?

26. How does project management apply to cybersecurity management?

Exercises

1. Consider the information stored in your personal computer. Do you currently have information stored on your computer that is critical to your personal life? If that information became compromised or lost, what effect would it have on you?

2. Using the web, research the malware named Stuxnet. When was it discovered? What kind of systems does it target? Who created it and what is it used for?

3. Search the web for "The Official Phreaker's Manual." What information in this manual might help a security administrator protect a communications system?

4. The chapter discussed many threats and vulnerabilities to cybersecurity. Using the web, find at least two other sources of information about threats and vulnerabilities. Begin with www.securityfocus.com and use a keyword search on "threats."

5. Using the categories of threats mentioned in this chapter and the various attacks described, review several current media sources and identify examples of each threat.

Solutions to Self-Check Questions

Introduction to Cybersecurity

1. Cybersecurity is now considered the sole responsibility of the IT department within an organization.

    Answer: b. False.

    Explanation: Cybersecurity is the responsibility of all employees, especially managers, and not just the IT department.

2. Confidentiality in cybersecurity means limiting access to information only to those who need it and preventing access by those who do not.

    Answer: a. True.

    Explanation: Confidentiality involves protecting information from unauthorized access by limiting access to those who require it for their role.

3. Identification in cybersecurity is the process by which a control establishes whether a user is the entity it claims to be.

    Answer: b. False.

    Explanation: Identification is the access control mechanism whereby entities seeking access provide a credential by which they are known. Authentication is the process that validates and verifies an entity's asserted identity.

Key Concepts of Cybersecurity: Threats and Attacks

4. A denial-of-service (DoS) attack is designed to overwhelm a target's ability to handle incoming communications, prohibiting legitimate users from accessing affected systems.

    Answer: a. True.

    Explanation: A DoS attack aims to overload a system with excessive requests, making it unable to serve legitimate users.

5. In cybersecurity, social engineering refers to the physical manipulation of computer hardware to compromise security.

    Answer: b. False.

    Explanation: Social engineering is the use of social tactics to trick people into revealing access credentials or other valuable information to an attacker.

6. Ransomware is a type of malware that encrypts the victim's files and demands a ransom for the decryption key.

    Answer: a. True.

    Explanation: Ransomware encrypts data on the victim's system and demands payment for the decryption key to unlock it.

Management and Leadership

7. Leadership and management are interchangeable terms with no distinction between their roles and responsibilities.

    Answer: b. False.

    Explanation: Leadership involves influencing others to achieve an objective by providing purpose, direction, and motivation, whereas management involves administering resources and handling tasks to achieve desired objectives.

8. Autocratic leaders typically involve subordinates in the decision-making process and value their input.

   Answer: b. False.

   Explanation: Autocratic leaders reserve all decision-making responsibilities for themselves and do not usually seek or accept alternative viewpoints.

9. Operational feasibility involves assessing an organization's ability to integrate a particular solution into its current business processes.

   Answer: a. True.

   Explanation: Operational feasibility checks whether the organization can effectively implement a solution within its existing operations.

Principles of Cybersecurity Management

10. The primary focus of the IT management team and the cybersecurity management team are always aligned and never conflict.

    Answer: b. False.

    Explanation: The IT management team focuses on the effective and efficient processing of information, while the cybersecurity management team focuses on ensuring the confidentiality, integrity, and availability of information, which can sometimes lead to conflicts.

11. The CSO often reports directly to the CIO.

    Answer: a. True.

    Explanation: The senior manager in charge of the cybersecurity management team, commonly the CSO, most often reports directly to the CIO.

12. In cybersecurity management, planning does not include the development of incident response or disaster recovery plans.

    Answer: b. False.

    Explanation: Cybersecurity planning includes a variety of planning functions, including incident response planning, business continuity planning, disaster recovery planning, and more.

Governance and Strategic Planning for Cybersecurity

Chapter Objectives

After reading this chapter and completing the exercises, you should be able to:

1 Summarize the process, purpose, and impact of organizational planning.

2 Discuss the importance, process, and desired outcomes of cybersecurity governance.

3 Describe the principal components of cybersecurity system implementation planning.

> You got to be careful if you don't know where you're going, because you might not get there.
>
> —Yogi Berra

Case Opener

Iris was a little uneasy. While this wasn't her first meeting with Mike Edwards, RWW's chief information officer, it was her first strategic planning meeting. Around the table, information technology (IT) department heads were chatting and drinking their coffee. Iris stared at her notepad, where she had carefully written "Strategic Planning Meeting" and nothing else.

Mike entered the room, followed by his assistants. Stan, his lead executive assistant, was loaded down with stacks of copied documents, which he and the other assistants began handing out. Iris took her copy and scanned the title: Random Widget Works, Inc., Strategic Planning Document, Information Technology Division, FY 2026-2031.

"As you know, it's strategic planning time again," Mike began. "You just got your copies of the multiyear IT strategic plan. Last month, you each received your numbered copy of the company strategic plan." Iris remembered the half-inch-thick document she had carefully read and then locked in her filing cabinet.

Mike continued: "I'm going to go through the IT mission and vision statements and then cover the details of how the IT plan will allow us to meet the objectives articulated in the company's strategic plan. In 30 days, you'll submit your draft plans to me for review. Don't hesitate to come by to discuss any issues or questions."

Later that day, Iris dropped by Mike's office to discuss her planning responsibilities. This duty was not something he had briefed her about yet.

"I'm sorry, Iris," Mike said. "I meant to spend some time outlining your planning responsibilities as security manager in more detail. I'm afraid I can't do it this week; maybe we can start next week by reviewing some key points I want you to make sure are in your plan. In the meantime, I suggest you ask the other division heads for copies of their strategic plans and look for areas that don't overlap with IT's."

The next day, Iris had lunch with her mentor, Charlie Moody.

After they ordered, Iris said, "We just started on our strategic planning project, and I'm supposed to develop a security strategic plan. You know, I've never worked up one of these from the very beginning. Got any advice on where to start?"

"Sure," Charlie responded. "What you should start with is the previous cybersecurity strategic plan, if there is one."

Iris replied, "Well, I'm the first person to be assigned as an official CSO, so there's no separate plan for cybersecurity right now. However, I think there was some planning done by the CIO previously. I know there is a big section in the previous IT strategic plan that was designated for cybersecurity."

Charlie paused thoughtfully. "You know that can be an issue, right?"

Iris looked puzzled. "How so?"

Charlie sighed. "Cybersecurity has come a long way over the past few decades, but most organizations still assume it's just an IT function. As I hope you realize, your job is to support not just IT, but *all* business functions. And sometimes independently of IT's plans. That's what makes the strategic planning function in cybersecurity so important, and so challenging. The entire organization is your client, not just IT."

Iris smiled and said, "Well, that explains the stack of strategic plans I've been tasked to get."

Charlie laughed. "Good! That means your CIO understands the situation and can support rather than hinder your task. Speaking of which, I have something for you in my car that just might help."

After they finished lunch, the pair went out to the parking lot. Inside Charlie's trunk were two cardboard boxes marked "BOOKS." He opened one and rummaged around for a few seconds. "Here," he said, handing Iris a textbook.

She read the title out loud: "Strategic Planning."

"This one is from my MBA program," Charlie explained. "I was cleaning out some of my older books and planned to donate these to the library book sale. It's yours if you want it. It might help with your planning project."

Charlie closed the trunk and said, "Read over the first few chapters—that'll give you the basics. Then sit down with your current plans and any available prior plans from upper management, IT, and each of the other division heads. For each goal stated in these documents, think about what your department needs to do to support it. Write up how you think you and your cybersecurity department can support that objective. Then go back and identify the resources you'll need to make that happen."

"That's it?" Iris asked.

Charlie shook his head. "There's more to it than that, but this will get you started. Once you've got that done, I can share some of what I know about how to frame your plans and format them for use in the planning process."

The Role of Planning

It is difficult to overstate how essential planning is to organizational management and operations. In a setting where there are continual and ever-changing constraints on resources, both human and financial, effective planning enables an organization to make the most out of the materials at hand. While a chief security officer (CSO)—who may be called a chief cybersecurity officer (CCO or CCSO), chief information security officer (CISO), director of cybersecurity, or a host of other variations—and other cybersecurity managers can generate an urgent response to an immediate threat, they are well advised to utilize a portion of their routinely allocated resources in planning for the long-term viability of the cybersecurity program. However, some organizations spend too much time, money, and effort on planning with too little return to justify their investment. Each organization must balance the benefits of the planning effort against its costs.

In the previous chapter, we discussed cybersecurity management within the context of general management. The broader subject of planning encompasses general organizational planning as well as the specific processes involved in planning for cybersecurity. This chapter addresses organizational planning for routine operations—specifically, governance and strategic planning for cybersecurity. Later in this book, we cover cybersecurity planning for nonstandard operations, known as contingency planning, in greater detail.

Planning usually involves many organizational groups and processes. The groups involved in planning represent the three communities of interest that were introduced in the previous chapter. They may be internal or external to the organization and can include employees, management, customers, suppliers, contractors, and other outside stakeholders—people or organizations that have a vested interest in a particular aspect of the planning or operation of the organization. Among the other factors that affect planning are the organizational culture, the physical environment, the legal and regulatory environment, the competitive environment, and the technological environment.

When planning, members of the cybersecurity community of interest use the same processes and methodologies that general management and IT management use. Because cybersecurity seeks to support the protection of information assets throughout the entire organization, an effective cybersecurity planner should know how the entire organizational planning process works so that they can obtain the best possible outcome. Before you can explore the relationship between cybersecurity plans and the rest of an organization's planning processes, however, you must first understand organizational planning.

Planning is the dominant means of managing and allocating resources in organizations. It involves a formal sequence of actions intended to achieve specific goals during a defined period and then controlling the implementation of these steps. Planning provides direction for the organization's future. Without specific and detailed planning, organizational units would attempt to meet objectives independently, with each unit being guided by its own initiatives, priorities, and ideas. Such an uncoordinated effort would not only fail to meet objectives but also result in an inefficient use of resources. The purpose of the planning process is the creation of detailed plans—that is, systematic directions for how to meet the organization's target. This task is accomplished with a process that begins with the general and ends with the specific.

Organizational planning, when conducted by the appropriate segments of the organization, provides a coordinated and uniform script that increases efficiency and reduces waste and duplication of effort by each organizational unit. Organizational planning begins with the organization's leadership choosing the direction and initiatives that the entire organization should pursue. Initially, the organizational plan contains few details; instead, it outlines general desired outcomes. These general outcomes are commonly termed "goals," whereas intermediate checkpoints are termed "objectives," although the terms are sometimes used interchangeably. Each goal is broken into intermediate objectives, which, if all are met, will result in meeting the end goal.

Precursors to Planning

To implement effective planning, an organization's leaders usually begin with previously developed statements of the organization's ethical, entrepreneurial, and philosophical perspectives. In recent years, the critical nature of the first of these positions—the ethical perspective—has come sharply into focus. Widely publicized ethical lapses at such organizations as Enron, WorldCom, Fannie Mae, IBM, and HP illustrate the importance of solid and well-articulated ethical expectations. While ethical failures of this magnitude are (one hopes) exceptional, industry groups, governmental agencies, and legislatures have implemented standards and regulations that mandate an organization's compliance with legal requirements and industry regulations.

When an organization's stated philosophies do not match the demonstrated ethical, entrepreneurial, and philosophical actions of its management teams, the developmental plan—which is guided by the organization's mission, vision, values, and strategy—becomes unmanageable. Taken together, the mission, vision, and values statements provide the ethical and philosophical foundation for planning and guide the creation of the strategic plan.

Mission Statement

The mission statement explicitly declares the business of the organization and its intended areas of operations. It is, in a sense, the organization's identity. RWW's mission statement might take the following form:

> Random Widget Works designs and manufactures high-quality widgets and associated equipment and supplies to enable modern businesses to succeed.

Not the multipage sleeping pill you expected? A mission statement should be concise, reflect both internal and external operations, and be robust enough to remain valid for a period of several years. Simply put, the mission statement must explain what the organization does and for whom.

Many organizations encourage or require each division or major department—including the cybersecurity department—to generate its own mission statement. These mission statements can be as concise as the example provided, expressing a strong commitment to the confidentiality, integrity, and availability of information, or they can provide a more detailed description of the cybersecurity department's function, as shown in the following example. This mission statement is adapted from *Information Security Roles and Responsibilities Made Easy* by Charles Cresson Wood.

> The Cybersecurity Department is responsible for identifying, assessing, and appropriately managing risks to the organization's information and information systems. It evaluates the options for dealing with these risks and works with departments throughout the organization to decide upon and then implement controls that appropriately and proactively respond to these same risks. The department is also responsible for developing requirements that apply to the entire organization as well as external information systems in which the organization participates. These requirements include policies, standards, guidelines, and procedures. The focal point for all matters related to cybersecurity, this department is ultimately responsible for all endeavors within the organization that seek to prevent, detect, correct, or recover from threats to information or information systems.[1]

Vision Statement

The second cornerstone of organizational planning is the vision statement. The vision statement is an idealistic expression of what the organization wants to become; it works in tandem with the mission statement. The vision statement expresses where the organization wants to go, while the mission statement describes how it wants to get there.

Vision statements should therefore be ambitious; after all, they are meant to express the aspirations of the organization and to serve as a means for visualizing its future. In other words, the vision statement is the best-case scenario for the organization's future. Many organizations mix or combine the vision statement and the mission statement. RWW's vision statement might take the following form:

> Random Widget Works will be the preferred manufacturer of choice for every business's widget needs, with an RWW widget in every gizmo in use.

This is a very bold, ambitious vision statement. It may not seem very realistic, but vision statements are not meant to express the probable, only the possible.

Values Statement

Next, management must articulate the organization's values statement. The trust and confidence of customers and other stakeholders are important factors for any organization. By establishing a formal set of organizational principles and qualities in a values statement, as well as benchmarks for measuring behavior against these published values, an organization makes its conduct and performance standards clear to its employees and the public. The quality management movement of the 1980s and 1990s illustrated that organizations with strong values can earn greater loyalty from customers, employees, and other stakeholders.

RWW's values statement might take the following form:

> Random Widget Works values commitment, honesty, integrity, and social responsibility among its employees and is committed to providing its services in harmony with its corporate, social, legal, and natural environments.

The National Institute of Standards and Technology (NIST) has formal mission, vision, and values statements published on its website, as shown in Figure 2-1.

Figure 2-1 The NIST mission, vision, and values statement[2]

Strategic Planning

Strategic planning, the process of defining and specifying the long-term direction to be taken by an organization and the acquisition and allocation of resources needed to pursue this effort, guides organizational efforts and focuses resources toward specific, clearly defined goals amid an ever-changing environment. As applied, this form of planning usually makes use of a three-step process. First, an organization identifies a goal for an area of improvement or a need for a new capability (where do we want to go?). Next, it documents the current position of the organization relative to that goal (where are we now?). Finally, plans can be made for how to achieve that goal (how will we get there?).

A clearly directed strategy flows from top to bottom and requires a systematic approach to translate it into a process that can lead all members of the organization. As shown in the upper-left portion of Figure 2-2, strategic plans formed at the highest levels of the organization are used to create the overall corporate strategy. As lower levels of the organization are involved (moving down the hierarchy), these high-level plans are evolved into more detailed, more concrete planning. So, higher-level plans are translated into more specific plans for intermediate layers of management, and high-level goals are translated into lower-level goals (for each division) and objectives. That layer of strategic planning by function (shown as financial, IT, and operations strategies in the figure) is then converted into tactical planning for supervisory managers and eventually provides direction for the operational plans undertaken by nonmanagement members of the organization. This multilayered approach encompasses two key objectives: general strategy and overall strategic planning. First, general strategy is translated into specific strategy; then, overall strategic planning is translated into lower-level tactical and operational planning. Each of these steps is discussed in the following sections.

Figure 2-2 Top-down strategic planning

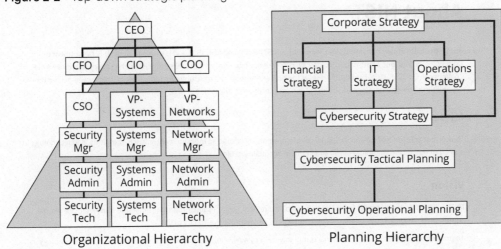

Organizational Hierarchy

Planning Hierarchy

Cybersecurity, like IT, must support more than its immediate parent in the organizational chart. As all organizational units use information, and not just IT-based information, the cybersecurity group must understand and support the strategic plans (strategies) of *all* business units. This role may at times conflict with that of the IT department, as IT's role is the efficient and effective delivery of information and administration of information resources, while cybersecurity's role is the protection of all information assets. For example, sometimes the natural downside of increased security is the decreased efficiency and speed of information delivery during a screening process, whether it involves a firewall allowing only authorized traffic, an antimalware application checking for embedded viruses, or increasingly complex credentials required for employees to log in securely to a computer system.

Creating a Strategic Plan

After an organization identifies its desired end goals, it must create an overall strategic plan to reach those goals. Subordinate managers then translate the organizational strategy into specific strategic plans for their divisions. Each level of each division translates those plans and goals into more specific plans and goals for the level below. For example, a chief executive officer (CEO) might develop the following general statement of strategy and goals:

Strategy: To provide the highest-quality, most cost-effective widgets in the industry.

Goals: To increase revenue by 10 percent annually.

             To increase market share by 5 percent annually.

             To decrease expenses by 5 percent annually.

To execute this broad strategy and turn the general statement into action, the executive team must first define individual responsibilities. This team is sometimes called the C-level or C-Suite of the organization, as in CEO, chief operations officer (COO), chief financial officer (CFO), chief information officer (CIO), and so on. For example, the CIO might respond to the CEO's statement with this IT-focused statement of strategy and its supporting goals:

Strategy: To provide high-level, cost-effective information service in support of the organization's operations.

Goals: To reduce IT-related expenses by 5 percent annually while maintaining systems, networks, and service capabilities to meet business needs.

To support corporate reduction in the cost of production through cost-effective systems development and implementation.

To recruit and retain highly competent IT professionals.

The COO might derive a different strategic statement and corresponding goals that focus more on the COO's own specific responsibilities:

Strategy: To provide the highest-quality, industry-leading widget development, manufacture, and delivery worldwide.

Goals: To reduce the cost of manufacture by 10 percent per year through the development of improved production methods.

To reduce the cost of distribution and inventory management by 10 percent per year through improved ordering methods with just-in-time delivery to our largest customers.

To improve the quality of products through research and development of better and more efficient product design and materials acquisition.

The CSO might interpret the CIO's and COO's statements and goals as follows:

Strategy: To protect the confidentiality, integrity, and availability of the organization's information assets, at a reasonable expense, in support of the organization's operations and information use.

Goals: To support reduced IT costs of new cybersecurity technologies and systems through the implementation of 20 percent use of open-source solutions.

To support improvements in all business units through improved security measures that support research and development without concern over the loss of intellectual property due to corporate espionage.

To maintain ongoing organizational efforts for the prevention of breaches and information disclosures.

To reduce costs associated with information breaches to near zero through improved security assessments and controls.

Note this is not a comprehensive list. An organization's security group may have a dozen or more such statements.

The conversion of strategic-level goals to the next lower level is more art than science. It relies on the executive's ability to understand and adapt the strategic goals of the entire organization, to understand the strategic and tactical abilities of each unit within the organization, and to negotiate with peers, superiors, and subordinates. This mix of skills helps to achieve the proper balance in articulating goals that fall within performance capabilities.

Planning Levels

Once the organization's overall strategic plan is translated into strategic goals for each major division or operation, the next step is to translate these strategic goals into objectives that are specific, measurable, achievable, relevant, and time bound, commonly referred to by the acronym SMART. Strategic plans are used to create tactical plans, which are in turn used to develop operational plans. Figure 2-3 illustrates the various planning levels discussed in this section.

Tactical planning has a shorter-term focus than strategic planning, usually a few years. It breaks down each applicable strategic goal into a series of incremental objectives. Each objective should be specific and ideally will have a delivery date within a year.

Figure 2-3   Strategic planning levels

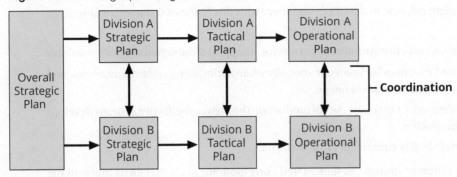

Budgeting, resource allocation, and personnel are critical components of the tactical plan. Although these components may be discussed in general terms at the strategic planning level, they are crucial at the tactical level because they must be in place before the tactical plan can be translated into the operational plan. Tactical plans often include project and resource acquisition planning documents such as product specifications, budgets, project reviews, and periodic reports (e.g., yearly, quarterly, monthly).

Because tactical plans are often created for specific projects, some organizations call this process project planning or intermediate planning. CSOs and their security managers use the tactical plan to organize, prioritize, and acquire resources necessary for the major projects and to provide support for the overall strategic plan.

Managers and employees use operational plans, which are derived from tactical plans, to organize the ongoing, day-to-day performance of tasks. An operational plan includes clearly identified coordination activities that span department boundaries, communications requirements, weekly meetings, summaries, progress reports, and associated tasks. These plans are carefully designed to reflect the organizational structure, with each subunit, department, or project team conducting its own operational planning and reporting components. Frequent communication and feedback from the teams to project managers and/or team leaders, and up to the various management levels, will make the planning process significantly more manageable and successful. For example, operational planning within cybersecurity may encompass such objectives as the selection, configuration, and deployment of a firewall or endpoint protection application; the selection, implementation, and conduct of a risk management program; or the design and implementation of a security education, training, and awareness (SETA) program. Each of these tasks needs effective tactical planning that covers its entire development life cycle.

Planning and the CSO

The first priority of the CSO and the cybersecurity management team should be designing the structure of their strategic plan. While each organization may have its own format for the design and distribution of a strategic plan, the fundamental elements of planning are similar for all types of enterprises. There are several excellent references on strategic planning, and the serious cybersecurity professional is encouraged to explore this topic.

The basic components of a typical organizational-level strategic plan include:

1. Executive summary
2. Mission, vision, and values statements
3. Organizational profile and history
4. Strategic issues and challenges
5. Organizational goals and objectives
6. Major business unit (or product/service) goals and objectives
7. Appendices (as applicable, including market analyses, internal/external surveys, budgets, and research and development projections)

You may have already learned about some of these components. The areas not previously discussed are very straightforward, such as the organizational profile and history and the appendices. They originate in studies conducted by the organization or highlight information about the environment in which the organization operates. The appendices may help the organization identify new directions or eliminate directions that are less feasible than anticipated. Cybersecurity planners can consult studies such as internally prepared risk assessments to help identify trends of interest or relevance to the organization. These documents are key resources for identifying areas that should be addressed by the cybersecurity strategic plan.

Brian Ward, a principal with Affinity Consulting and founder of Management4M.com, offers the following tips for planning:

1. Articulate a comprehensive and meaningful vision statement that communicates what the organization strives to accomplish. It should attract like-minded individuals to join in the effort to achieve that goal.

2. Endeavor to bring a sense of logical analysis of the objectives and what has been accomplished. Many organizations use a model known as the "balanced scorecard," which measures four main aspects of a business—learning and growth, business processes, customers, and finance—to track outcomes against intentions and measure effects against prior actions.

3. Work from an overarching plan that has been developed with input from key stakeholders.

4. Strive for transparency in the planning process so that inevitable changes to plans are explained to stakeholders.

5. Make planning a process that engages all involved to work toward common objectives.

6. Stick with the process over time because results may not always be achieved as quickly as intended.

7. Develop consistent and repeatable methods of planning that are adopted as part of the organization's culture.

8. Explain what is being done so that stakeholders perceive the intentions of the process.

9. Use processes that fit the organization's culture.

10. Make the process as engaging as possible so that participants are not overwhelmed and feel put upon by the required actions.[3]

Self-Check

1. Planning is only beneficial for responding to immediate threats in cybersecurity management.

   a. True **b.** False

2. Strategic planning focuses only on the immediate future and short-term goals of an organization.

   a. True **b.** False

3. Cybersecurity strategic planning should support the strategic plans of all business units, not just IT.

   a. True **b.** False

☐ Check your answers at the end of this chapter.

Cybersecurity Governance

Strategic planning and corporate responsibility are best accomplished using an approach the industry refers to as Governance, Risk Management, and Compliance (GRC), as defined in Chapter 1. GRC seeks to integrate these three previously separate responsibilities into one holistic approach that can provide and ensure sound executive-level strategic planning and management of the cybersecurity function. Risk management and compliance with laws and regulations are covered in later chapters. The subjects themselves are neither new nor unique to cybersecurity; however, recognition of the need to integrate the three at the board or executive level is becoming increasingly important to organizations. Note that the management of risk is not limited to an organization's cybersecurity effort.

Governance is a set of responsibilities and practices exercised by the board and executive management with the goal of providing strategic direction, ensuring that objectives are achieved, ascertaining that risks are managed appropriately, and verifying that the enterprise's resources are used responsibly. Governance of the cybersecurity program is a strategic planning responsibility whose importance has grown rapidly over the past several years. Good cybersecurity practices combined with sound cybersecurity governance have become recognized as a crucial component of U.S. national security in the protection of critical infrastructure as well as in the private sector. Unfortunately, cybersecurity is all too often regarded as a technical issue when it is, in fact, a strategic management issue. This misconception was illustrated by noteworthy cybersecurity events such as the data breaches at Facebook in 2021, Marriott International in 2018, and Yahoo, Ashley Madison, and the U.S. Office of Personnel Management in 2015, all of which had impacts on the entire organization. To secure information assets, an organization's management must integrate cybersecurity practices into the fabric of the organization, expanding corporate governance expectations, policies, and controls to encompass the objectives of the cybersecurity program.

Note 1 | For more information on major data breaches that have occurred over the past several years and the extent of their losses, visit https://en.wikipedia.org/wiki/List_of_data_breaches.

Cybersecurity objectives must be addressed at the highest levels of an organization's management team to be effective and offer a sustainable approach. In organizations with formal boards of directors, the board should be the basis for governance review and oversight. For organizations that have a parent organization, executive management of the parent should be the basis. For those organizations that don't have either, this strategic oversight must stem from a formal governance board consisting of executive management from across the organization, including the CEO or president and their immediate subordinate executives.

When security programs are designed and managed as a technical specialty in the IT department, they are less likely to be effective. A broader view of cybersecurity encompasses all of an organization's information assets, including IT assets. These valuable commodities must be protected regardless of how the information is processed, stored, or transmitted, with a thorough understanding of the risks and benefits associated with these assets. Ensuring that senior management knows what cybersecurity is and understands the extent to which they are personally responsible for its effective operations and support—through governance—is the first step.

Industry Approaches to Cybersecurity Governance

In 1998, ISACA, the organization founded to support the development and certification of auditing programs in computer systems, created the Information Technology Governance Institute (ITGI) to address the recognized need for the intellectual development and advancement of Governance of Enterprise IT. This organization became a recognized authority on governance in IT and eventually in cybersecurity, as it collected and propagated an organized knowledge base and approach to the subject. While ITGI is no longer active, ISACA still promotes and distributes ITGI content.

According to the ITGI model, cybersecurity governance includes all the accountabilities and methods undertaken by the board of directors and executive management to provide strategic direction, the establishment of objectives, the measurement of progress toward those objectives, verification that risk management practices are appropriate, and validation that the organization's assets are used properly.[4]

The ITGI model recommends that boards of directors supervise strategic cybersecurity objectives by:

1. Creating and promoting a culture that recognizes the criticality of information and cybersecurity to the organization
2. Verifying that management's investment in cybersecurity is properly aligned with organizational strategies and the organization's risk environment

3. Mandating and ensuring that a comprehensive cybersecurity program is developed and implemented

4. Requiring reports from the various layers of management on the cybersecurity program's effectiveness and adequacy[5]

Desired Outcomes

Cybersecurity governance consists of leadership, organizational structures, and processes that safeguard information. Critical to the success of these structures and processes is effective communication among all parties, which requires constructive relationships, a common language, and shared commitment to addressing the issues. If done properly, this should result in five basic outcomes of cybersecurity governance:

- Strategic alignment of cybersecurity with business strategy to support organizational objectives
- Risk management by executing appropriate measures to manage and mitigate threats to information resources
- Resource management by utilizing cybersecurity knowledge and infrastructure efficiently and effectively
- Performance measurement by measuring, monitoring, and reporting cybersecurity governance metrics to ensure that organizational objectives are achieved
- Value delivery by optimizing cybersecurity investments in support of organizational objectives

The National Association of Corporate Directors (NACD), the leading membership organization for boards of directors in the United States, recommends four essential cybersecurity governance practices for boards of directors:

1. Place cybersecurity on the board's agenda.
2. Identify cybersecurity leaders, hold them accountable, and ensure support for them.
3. Ensure the effectiveness of the corporation's cybersecurity policy through review and approval.
4. Assign cybersecurity to a key committee and ensure adequate support for that committee.[6]

Benefits of Cybersecurity Governance

Cybersecurity governance, if properly implemented, can yield significant benefits, including:

- An increase in share value for organizations
- Increased predictability and reduced uncertainty of business operations by lowering information security risks to definable and acceptable levels
- Protection from the increasing potential for civil or legal liability as a result of information inaccuracy or the absence of due care
- Optimization of the allocation of limited security resources
- Assurance of effective cybersecurity policy and policy compliance
- A firm foundation for efficient and effective risk management, process improvement, and rapid incident response
- A level of assurance that critical decisions are not based on faulty information
- Accountability for safeguarding information during critical business activities, such as mergers and acquisitions, business process recovery, and regulatory response[7]

When developing a cybersecurity governance program, the designers should ensure that the program includes:

- A cybersecurity risk management methodology
- A comprehensive security strategy explicitly linked with business and IT objectives
- An effective security organizational structure
- A security strategy that addresses the value of information being protected and delivered
- Security policies that address each aspect of strategy, control, and regulation

- A complete set of security standards for each policy to ensure that procedures and guidelines comply with policy
- Institutionalized monitoring processes to ensure compliance and provide feedback on effectiveness and mitigation of risk
- A process to ensure continued evaluation and updating of security policies, standards, procedures, and risks

Industry Frameworks for Cybersecurity Governance

In 2004, the Corporate Governance Task Force (CGTF), an advisory group from the National Cyber Security Partnership, developed and published a framework for cybersecurity governance. This document, "Information Security Governance: A Call to Action," encouraged organizations in both the public and private sectors to build cybersecurity governance programs and integrate them into their existing corporate governance structures.

The report recommended that all organizations adopt and support this framework, including publishing their intent on their public websites. Specifically, the report called for the membership of the CGTF to adopt the framework and for members of other industry partnerships to follow suit, such as TechNet, the Business Software Alliance, and the Information Technology Association of America, among others. It further called for the Department of Homeland Security and the Committee of Sponsoring Organizations (COSO) of the Treadway Commission to endorse and recommend the framework and modify internal documents (such as COSO's Internal Controls-Integrated Framework) to specifically include recommendations for cybersecurity governance in general and this framework in particular.[8]

According to the CGTF report, an organization should engage in a core set of activities suited to its needs to guide the development and implementation of the cybersecurity governance program:

- Conduct an annual cybersecurity evaluation, the results of which the CEO should review with staff and then report to the board of directors.
- Conduct periodic risk assessments of information assets as part of a risk management program.
- Implement policies and procedures based on risk assessments to secure information assets.
- Establish a security management structure to assign explicit individual roles, responsibilities, authority, and accountability.
- Develop plans and initiate actions to provide adequate cybersecurity for networks, facilities, systems, and information.
- Treat cybersecurity as an integral part of the system life cycle.
- Provide security awareness, training, and education to personnel.
- Conduct periodic testing and evaluation of the effectiveness of cybersecurity policies and procedures.
- Create and execute a plan for remedial action to address any cybersecurity deficiencies.
- Develop and implement incident response procedures.
- Establish plans, procedures, and tests to provide continuity of operations.
- Use security best practices guidance, such as the ISO 27000 series, to measure cybersecurity performance.[9]

The CGTF framework applies the IDEAL model to cybersecurity governance. The IDEAL model was originally published in a 1996 report on software process improvement by Bob McFeeley for the Software Engineering Institute of Carnegie Mellon University. Due to the incredible flexibility of the IDEAL model, it has been adapted to a wide variety of process improvement methodologies, including security governance. The model includes five phases—initiating, diagnosing, establishing, acting, and learning—as shown in Figure 2-4.

The CGTF framework defines the responsibilities of the board of directors and trustees, the senior organizational executive (i.e., the CEO), executive team members, senior managers, and all employees and users. Figure 2-5 shows the various responsibilities of these functional roles. The CGTF report also outlines the requirements for a cybersecurity program, as explored in additional detail in a later chapter of this text, and provides recommendations for organizational unit reporting and program evaluation.

Figure 2-4   IDEAL model use as a general governance framework

I	Initiating	Lay the groundwork for a successful improvement effort.
D	Diagnosing	Determine where you are relative to where you want to be.
E	Establishing	Plan the specifics of how you will reach your destination.
A	Acting	Do the work according to the plan.
L	Learning	Learn from the experience and improve your ability to adopt new improvements in the future.

Figure 2-5   Cybersecurity governance responsibilities[10]

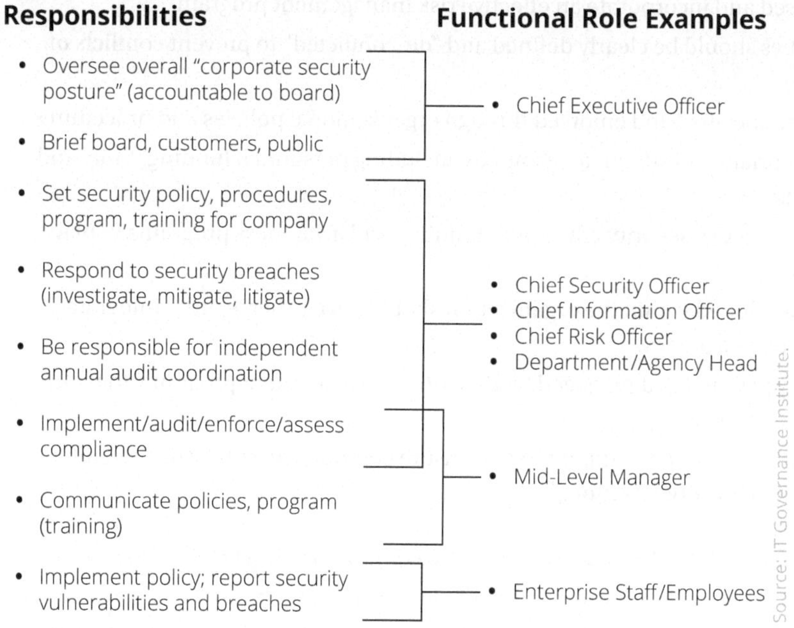

Responsibilities

- Oversee overall "corporate security posture" (accountable to board)
- Brief board, customers, public
- Set security policy, procedures, program, training for company
- Respond to security breaches (investigate, mitigate, litigate)
- Be responsible for independent annual audit coordination
- Implement/audit/enforce/assess compliance
- Communicate policies, program (training)
- Implement policy; report security vulnerabilities and breaches

Functional Role Examples

- Chief Executive Officer
- Chief Security Officer
- Chief Information Officer
- Chief Risk Officer
- Department/Agency Head
- Mid-Level Manager
- Enterprise Staff/Employees

Source: IT Governance Institute.

Note 2 | To download "Information Security Governance: A Call to Action," visit https://library.educause.edu/resources/2004/1/information-security-governance-a-call-to-action.

Governing for Enterprise Security Implementation

In 2007, the Computer Emergency Response Team (CERT) Division of Carnegie Mellon University's Software Engineering Institute (CMU/SEI) published and promoted an implementation guide for its trademarked Governing for Enterprise Security (GES) program. While no longer formally supported, the document still provides valuable insights into development and support for a cybersecurity governance program.

According to the GES, Enterprise Security Program (ESP) governance activities should be driven by a Board Risk Committee (BRC) in addition to the organization's executive management and select key stakeholders. The program should support and be supported by the organization's other ESP efforts, like the risk management program and organizational strategic planning components.[11]

The GES includes three supporting documents, referred to as Articles:

- Article 1: Characteristics of Effective Security Governance
- Article 2: Defining an Effective Enterprise Security Program
- Article 3: Enterprise Security Governance Activities

Article 1: Characteristics of Effective Security Governance

Article 1 focuses on answering the question "What is effective security governance?" by providing a list of 11 characteristics:

1. Cybersecurity is an organization-wide issue and affects everything within the organization.
2. Organizational leaders are accountable for cybersecurity, as well as for their stakeholders, their communities, and the business environment.
3. Cybersecurity should be viewed as a business requirement and aligned with the organization's strategic goals.
4. The ESP should be risk-based and incorporate an effective risk management program.
5. ESP roles and responsibilities should be clearly defined and "de-conflicted" to prevent conflicts of interest.
6. ESP requirements should be specified and enforced through organizational policies and procedures.
7. The ESP should have appropriate and adequate resources, including personnel, funding, time, and formal managerial support.
8. Organizations should have effective security education, training, and awareness programs in place and enforced.
9. All systems and software developed within the organization should have cybersecurity integrated throughout their development life cycles.
10. The ESP should be formally planned and managed, with defined measurement programs that are appropriately assessed and reviewed.
11. The BRC should periodically review and audit the ESP to ensure compliance with its desired intent and the goals and objectives of the organization.[12]

Article 2: Defining an Effective Enterprise Security Program

Article 2 provides a methodology for the specification and implementation of an ESP, both as an instructional tool for planners and an information role for an organization's senior leadership. This approach involves a hierarchy of programs with the risk management plan at the top, then the enterprise security strategy, then the enterprise security plan, and finally the various plans, policies, procedures, and architectures of the business units, as shown in Figure 2-6.

Figure 2-6 CERT GES hierarchy[13]

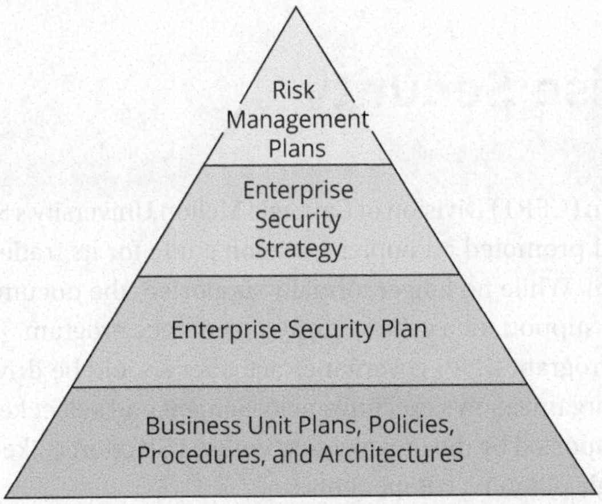

Source: Carnegie Mellon University, Software Engineering Institute, CERT.

Article 2 also specifies the composition and responsibilities of the BRC, recommending that it include a collection of high-level directors that report directly to the organization's board of directors. The BRC should be responsible for the following:

- Establishing the ESP governance structure for the organization
- Setting the "tone" for risk management, including privacy and security, through top-level policies and actions
- Ensuring qualified and capable personnel are hired or engaged for the development and sustainment of the ESP
- Defining roles and responsibilities and ensuring segregation of duties
- Obtaining board approval for the security budget
- Conducting risk assessments and reviews
- Developing, approving, and maintaining the organization's risk management program, enterprise security services, and enterprise security plan
- Categorizing assets by levels of risk and harm and approving security controls, key performance indicators, and metrics
- Steering the development, testing, and maintenance of plans for business continuity and disaster recovery, incident response, crisis communications, and relationships with vendors and other third parties
- Allocating sufficient financial resources for the development and sustainment of the program based on a security business case and return on investment
- Ensuring the ESP is implemented and personnel are effectively trained according to the implementation and training plan
- Conducting periodic (no less than annual) reviews of the ESP
- Ensuring material weaknesses in the ESP are rectified and the ESP is up to date[14]

The BRC should be the approval authority for the organization's security strategy and program and should be part of the approval process for the organization's risk management plan, which must also be approved by the organization's entire board of directors.[15]

Article 3: Enterprise Security Governance Activities

Article 3 continues the discussion, providing additional details on the GES and the ESP. Specifically, it describes the roles and responsibilities of the BRC and executive management. According to Article 3, this group is mandated to establish the governance structures, assign roles and responsibilities within this structure, including the reporting framework, and develop all needed high-level policies related to governance and the ESP.

The BRC group would then continue to ensure that the appropriate cybersecurity programs are integrated into ongoing operations, monitored and evaluated to ensure they meet expectations, and periodically reviewed for needed updates and improvement.[16]

Note 3 | For more information on the CERT CMU/SEI Governing for Enterprise Security Implementation Guide, visit the website at http://resources.sei.cmu.edu/library/asset-view.cfm?assetid=8251.

ISO/IEC 27014:2020 Governance of Information Security

The ISO 27000 series provides a set of international standards for the certification of an Information Security Management System. Note these are not documents designed to provide specific "how-to" instructions for designing, implementing, operating, and maintaining security systems but rather the specifications for certification, which allow the organization to assess whether its security program meets the expectations of the standard. If the organization decides to seek the certification, it may apply to be reviewed and assessed against these standards. In addition, there is value in reviewing the standards and determining what should be in place and functional prior to a certification visit; this exercise serves as a surrogate for an assessment of what makes an effective security program.

ISO 27014:2020, "Information security, cybersecurity and privacy protection—Governance of information security," is the ISO 27000 series standard for governance of cybersecurity. While brief, this document provides high-level recommendations for the assessment of a cybersecurity governance program. The standard specifies six "action-oriented" cybersecurity governance objectives:

1. Establish integrated, comprehensive, entity-wide information security.
2. Make decisions using a risk-based approach.
3. Set the direction of acquisition.
4. Ensure conformance with internal and external requirements.
5. Foster a security-positive culture.
6. Ensure security performance meets current and future requirements of the entity.[17]

The standard also promotes four governance processes, which should be adopted by the organization's executive management and its governing board. These processes are illustrated in Figure 2-7 and described in the following list.

- Evaluate—Review the status of current and projected progress toward organizational cybersecurity objectives and decide whether modifications of the program or its strategy are needed to keep on track with strategic goals.
- Direct—Provide instruction for developing or implementing changes to the security program. This could include modification of available resources, structure of priorities of effort, adoption of policy, recommendations for the risk management program, or alteration to the organization's risk tolerance.
- Monitor—Review and assess organizational cybersecurity performance toward the goals and objectives set by the governing body. Monitoring is enabled by ongoing performance measurement.
- Communicate—Ensure effective communication between the governing body and external stakeholders on organizational cybersecurity efforts and recommendations for improvement.[18]

Figure 2-7   ISO/IEC 27014:2020 governance processes[19]

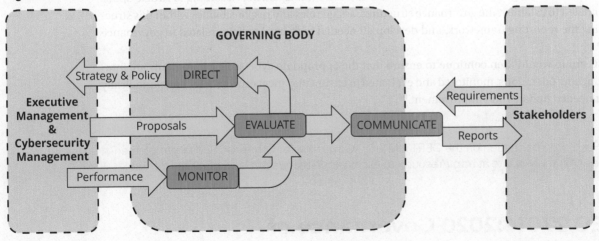

The information in this standard was adapted in part from ISO 38500, "Corporate Governance of IT," much as the ITGI adapted its Information Technology Governance approach for cybersecurity. There is some criticism in the cybersecurity community regarding the lack of detail in ISO standards and the need for more specificity in exactly how the organization should implement and obtain these principles and processes. Similar to other governance models, the overall goal of governance as assessed in ISO/IEC 27014:2020 is:

- Alignment of objectives and strategies between the cybersecurity program and the overall organization
- Increased value added to the organization, its executive management, and stakeholders
- Effective assignment of risk to the appropriate responsible party[20]

Achievement of the desired results from an efficient and effective information systems governance implementation includes improvements in:

- Visibility of the status of the cybersecurity program and efforts for executive management
- Decision making for risk management
- Quality of investments in cybersecurity
- Regulatory compliance to external requirements, contracts, and mandates[21]

GRC² or GRC Squared

A report by Verizon published in 2022 explored another approach to GRC known as the GRC² (GRC Squared) model. This approach couples two acronyms: "Goals, Requirements, and Constraints" and the more familiar "Governance, Risk Management, and Compliance."[22] This novel approach considers that GRC is an established process with 20 years of increasing use.

The scope of GRC extends beyond governance, risk management, and compliance to include assurance and performance management. Proper GRC implementation leads to better decision making, agility, cost reduction, sustained performance, and value delivery. Regulation is a significant driver for GRC, with a marked increase in demands for transparency from third-party stakeholders, including government agencies. The growth of the GRC tools industry has been noteworthy, but these technologies alone are not sufficient for an effective GRC program. Success in GRC will require a people-and-process perspective before considering technology. Issues and processes designed to integrate cybersecurity with human resources are presented later in the book.

The concept of GRC² applies a multiplier to each area of the acronym. Each element of governance, risk management, and compliance is evaluated in terms of its respective goals, requirements, and constraints. This offers an enhanced approach to the design, implementation, management, and evaluation of GRC in an organization.

G Squared: The Goals, Requirements, and Constraints of Governance

Governance in GRC ensures an organization is directed and controlled toward achieving its goals by setting directions through strategy and policy, monitoring performance and controls, and evaluating outcomes. It entails the combination of processes established, executed, and supported at all management levels, and is designed to facilitate decision making and communicate control mechanisms. These processes aim to provide ongoing support for governance functions, ensuring that management receives critical, relevant, and accurate information in a timely manner for clear visibility.

R Squared: The Goals, Requirements, and Constraints of Risk Management

Risk management involves anticipating potential risks that may harm or impede an organization's ability to meet its goals. It focuses on the swift identification, analysis, and control of risks that threaten the attainment of strategic objectives. This area encompasses the processes of risk identification and classification, assessment, communication, mitigation, and reporting on risk containment.

C Squared: The Goals, Requirements, and Constraints of Compliance

Compliance involves a well-defined process and consistent accounting of an organization's practices to ensure adherence to policies, standards, and guidelines. It encompasses measures and controls to meet both internal and external requirements, setting measurable standards for policies, procedures, and behaviors to align with the expectations of stakeholders, including third-party contractual obligations and external regulations like PCI security. The process entails documenting compliance components, assessing the organization's compliance state, and conducting cost–benefit analyses of noncompliance, documentation processes, identification and documentation of controls, assessment of control effectiveness, remediation of issues, and disclosure and certification of compliance activities.

Security Convergence

The convergence of security-related governance in organizations has been debated since the broad deployment of information systems began in the 1970s and 1980s. For years, industry media have discussed the issues surrounding this merging of management accountability in the areas of corporate (physical) security, corporate risk management, computer security, network security, and cybersecurity. More formal discussion has also occurred, including the landmark industry report titled "Convergence of Enterprise Security Organizations," which the consulting firm Booz Allen Hamilton issued in conjunction with the professional organizations ASIS, ISACA, and ISSA.[23] That report looked at industry practices in the areas of security convergence at U.S.-based global organizations. It also identified key drivers toward increased convergence, including how organizations seek to reduce costs and gain improved results as they reduce their reliance on physical assets and make increased use of logical assets. This is occurring as organizations face increasing compliance and regulatory requirements as well as ongoing pressures to reduce costs. The report concluded that while convergence is a driving force, the real value remains in aligning security functions (whether converged or diverged) with the business mission.

A later report prepared by the consulting firm Deloitte, commissioned by the Alliance for Enterprise Security Risk Management, further explored the topic of convergence and identified enterprise risk management (ERM) as a valuable approach that can better align security functions with the business mission while offering opportunities to lower costs. While that report limited its perspective to the two traditional facets of ERM control elements (specifically cybersecurity and physical security), it did identify the key approaches organizations are using to achieve unified ERM, including:

- Combining physical security and cybersecurity under one leader as one business function
- Using separate business functions (each with a separate budget and autonomy) that report to a common senior executive
- Using a risk council approach to provide a collaborative method for risk management, where representatives from across the organization work collectively to set policy regarding risk to the organization

The Deloitte report proposed the risk council approach as the preferred mechanism and went on to explore what makes effective ERM and how risk councils can be used to best effect.[24]

The Open Compliance and Ethics Group, a global, industry-spanning think tank, commissioned a report to explore some of the complexities of GRC and how these critical functions might best be executed.[25] The key finding of this report was that GRC functions (including those defined as part of ERM) are often fragmented and often not integrated to the degree needed for streamlined operations. The report also identified the benefits of increased levels of ERM along with integration and convergence of governance and compliance business functions.

Currently, accepted industry practices focus on achieving a synthesis of these approaches to reap the benefits of ERM. This could refer to the degree to which an organization integrates managerial command and control over its multiple risk control facilities to address the business mission requirements to manage risk and conform to compliance objectives.

A 2015 study of cybersecurity management practices found that most larger organizations (2,500 employees or more) still keep physical and cybersecurity efforts segregated even with significant collaboration, while full integration is much more common in smaller organizations (less than 1,000 employees).[26] This is illustrated in Figure 2-8.

Figure 2-8 Security convergence in organizations

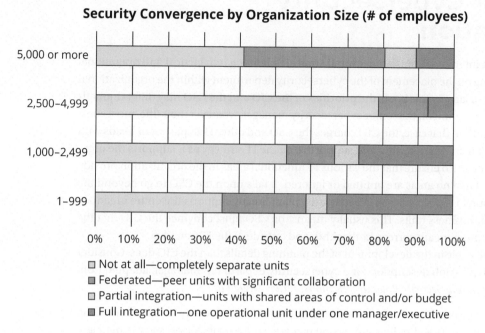

A more recent study from 2023 reported the following:

> In organizations, the evolution to a more optimized security structure, either merged
> or partnered, was traditionally due to unplanned or unforeseen events; e.g., a spin-off/
> acquisition, new security leadership, or a negative security incident was the initiator.
> This is in contrast to a proactive management decision or a formal plan to change or
> enhance the security structure for reasons that include reducing costs of operations and/
> or improving outcomes to reduce operational risks.[27]

Today, security convergence still varies radically from organization to organization, with some seeking to optimize the degree of convergence suitable for their form of governance and others discounting it as an unnecessary complication. Even with published recognition of the value of security convergence, the trend toward integration seems to be slower than industry observers anticipated, especially in larger organizations. It would seem logical that larger organizations would have a much larger, more politically potent physical security division, which would be resistant to integration with the logical aspects of cybersecurity. It has been discovered, however, that organizational culture is the largest factor in whether an organization considers convergence worth considering.

Self-Check

4. Cybersecurity governance is solely a technical issue and not a strategic management issue.
   a. True   **b.** False

5. Cybersecurity objectives only need to be addressed at middle management levels to be effective.
   a. True   **b.** False

6. Cybersecurity governance can lead to an increase in share value for organizations and optimization of the allocation of limited security resources.
   a. True   **b.** False

☐ Check your answers at the end of this chapter.

Planning for Cybersecurity Implementation

The CIO and CSO play important roles in translating overall strategic planning into tactical and operational cybersecurity plans. Depending on the placement of the cybersecurity department within the organizational chart, a topic discussed in detail later in this book, the priorities of the CIO and the CSO may differ dramatically. In the current business environment, the senior cybersecurity manager, whatever their title, most commonly reports directly to the CIO. In that case, the CIO charges the CSO and other IT department heads with creating and adopting plans that are aligned with, and supportive of, the IT strategy as it supports the organizational strategy. The CIO must also ensure that the various IT functional areas in the organization provide broad support for the plan and that no areas are omitted or ignored. It falls upon the CSO to go beyond the plans and efforts of the IT group to ensure that the cybersecurity plan directly supports the entire organization and the strategies of other business units. This usually means the CSO must convince the CIO that the priorities of the cybersecurity program are correct, both within and outside of the IT function.

The CSO plays a more active role in the development of the planning details than the CIO does. Consider the following excerpt from a typical job description for a cybersecurity department manager, adapted from Charles Cresson Wood's *Information Security Roles and Responsibilities Made Easy*:

- Creates a strategic cybersecurity plan with a vision for the future of cybersecurity in the organization (utilizing evolving cybersecurity technology, this vision meets a variety of objectives such as management's fiduciary and legal responsibilities, customer expectations for secure modern business practices, and the competitive requirements of the marketplace).
- Understands the fundamental business activities performed by the organization and, based on this understanding, suggests appropriate cybersecurity solutions that uniquely protect these activities.
- Develops action plans, schedules, budgets, status reports, and other managerial communications intended to improve the status of cybersecurity in the organization.[28]

View Point A Brief Introduction to the Value of Corporate Security for Non-Security Professionals

By Bob Hayes, Managing Director, and Kathleen ("K2") Kotwica, Ph.D., Executive Vice President and Chief Knowledge Strategist, Security Executive Council

Have you ever wondered how companies prevent or respond to issues that could result in injured workers, employee deaths, damaged or lost assets, lawsuits, regulatory fines, or loss of important corporate information? Most *Fortune* 500 companies have experienced these types of incidents, and many have established a corporate security department to minimize the impact and losses from such issues.

Business activities that managers have overseen for years have recently become more complex and potentially damaging. Examples include:

- Employee disagreements with other employees or managers can become visible to customers, damage the image of the organization, and lead to conflict and potential lawsuits.
- Corporate travel to new countries to buy materials or consider selling products there may expose the company to new risks.
- Controlling intellectual property has become more challenging. This control includes keeping others from stealing new innovations, secrets to operating success, or even customer lists.
- Compliance with government regulations and requirements has become more widespread and onerous. These activities often carry significant penalties for things such as failing to protect employees, products, property, and computer systems, which can take significant time and resources and can result in unwanted costs and publicity.

Depending on a company's size and industry, corporate security can mean different things. For example, the Security Leadership Research Institute has identified 20 different responsibilities that fall under a corporate security department.

Some companies have elevated the security manager position to the executive level by creating a CSO position. While a typical CSO position does not exist in corporate America, there are areas of security that different CSOs at different companies will be responsible for (see Figure 2-9), depending on the industry or sector and what risks and threats are perceived to be important to address.

It is essential that the CSO works closely with other executive-level functions and leaders, such as Opera-

Figure 2-9   Collective knowledge: Realm of security responsibilities

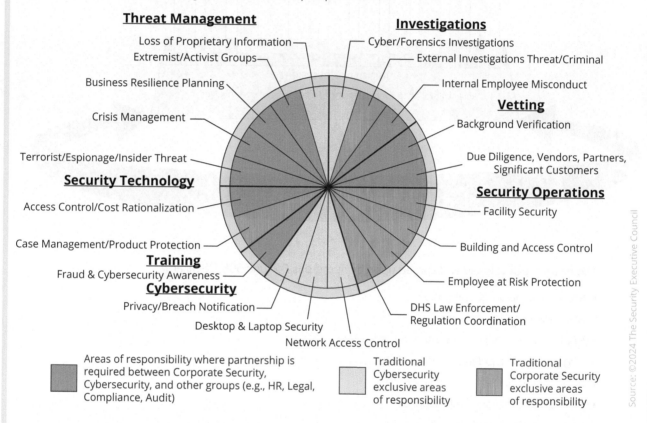

tions, Human Resources, Legal, IT, Finance, and other business units. This has recently become more critical than ever to help effectively reduce security risks to the organization. Figure 2-10 creates a visualization of Unified Risk Oversight, where all the company's organizations and leaders work in concert to reduce or eliminate security risks.

The foundational elements of a corporate security program are listed and defined in *Adding Business Value by Managing Security Risks* (also known as *The Manager's Handbook for Business Security*). This publication was created at the urging of the federal government to provide a resource to help businesses combat the types of losses or damages discussed previously.

Figure 2-10   The Unified Risk Oversight model

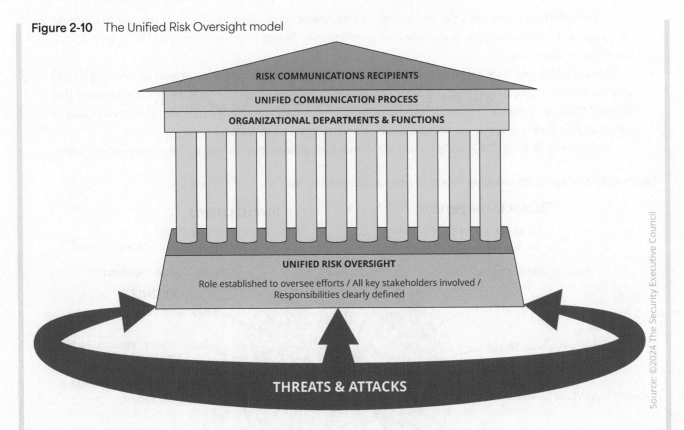

The elements developed and agreed upon by numerous *Fortune* 500 CSOs are:

- Risk assessment and mitigation
- Strategic security planning
- Marketing the security program to the business
- Organizational models for the security department
- Regulations, guidelines, and standards
- Physical security and first response
- Security training and education
- Communication and awareness programs
- Safe and secure workplaces
- Business conduct and ethics
- Business resiliency
- Securing the supply chain
- Measures and metrics
- Continuous learning: addressing risk with after-action reviews

Additional research has identified five key elements in corporate security success that need to be taken into consideration and managed when implementing or upgrading a program.

- Corporate-level/organizational readiness for security—The company's view of what cybersecurity means to them and its purpose considering the company's business goals
- Security leadership capability—The right fit for current expectations and a vision of what could be
- Security department maturity status—Knowing the state of the security program helps to develop a roadmap to a desired end state

- Corporate culture—Understanding the corporate culture and tailoring strategies and tactics within that framework
- Regulatory requirements—The requirements for a particular company or industry

Once a security function is in place, the real work begins in identifying vendors and service providers, managing the various information based on risks, and recruiting experienced and talented people. Finally, the best security departments work with executive management to add more value to the business, enable the business to operate where and how it needs to, and provide employees a resource for safety and security concerns.

The Security Executive Council (SEC) is the leading research and advisory firm that specializes in security risk mitigation. They offer experience-based solutions, program decision assurance, and targeted information to ensure that security initiatives are on target and cost effective. The SEC has experience in all realms of security, including physical security, information, and compliance, as well as experience in all industries and sectors.

Once the organization's overall strategic plan has been translated into IT departmental objectives by the CIO and translated into strategic, tactical, and operational plans by the CSO, the implementation of cybersecurity can begin. Historically, its implementation in an organization originated in one of two ways: bottom-up or top-down. These two basic approaches are illustrated in Figure 2-11.

Figure 2-11 Approaches to cybersecurity program development

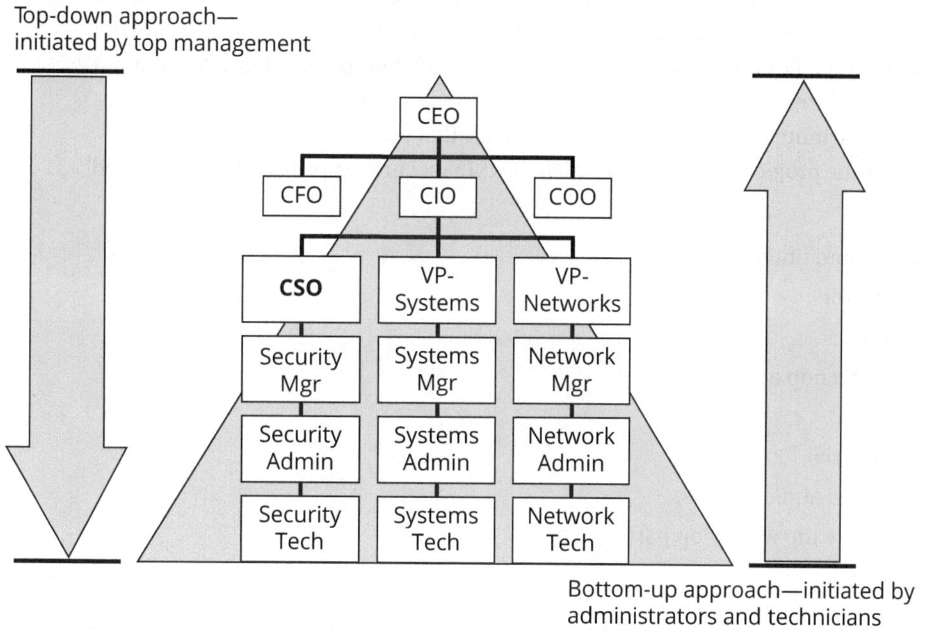

Top-down approach—
initiated by top management

Bottom-up approach—initiated by
administrators and technicians

Cybersecurity programs that evolve from the bottom-up approach might begin as a grassroots effort in which systems and network administrators (or admins) attempt to improve the security of their systems. As these administrators begin exchanging information and requesting additional support and resources, the need for an integrated approach could be recognized by lower-level supervisors and managers, until the entire effort gains enough traction to be recognized and supported as a formal strategy by upper management. The key advantage of this approach is that it utilizes the technical expertise of the individual administrators who work with the information systems daily. System and network administrators possess in-depth knowledge that can greatly enhance the state of cybersecurity in the organization. These professionals know and understand many of the threats to their systems and the mechanisms needed to protect them successfully. Unfortunately, this approach seldom works in the long term, as it lacks critical features such as coordinated planning from upper management, coordination between departments, and the provision of sufficient resources. The program becomes fractured and poorly supported if individual administrators become more concerned with the security of "their" systems than with an integrated approach to security in the organization.

When security programs are developed using the top-down approach, they benefit from strong upper-management support, a dedicated champion, dedicated funding, a clear planning and implementation process, and the ability to influence organizational culture. In this approach, cybersecurity begins as a formal program, proposed and coordinated by high-level managers with executive management support to provide resources, give direction, issue policies, procedures, and processes, dictate the goals and expected outcomes of the project, and determine who is accountable for each of the required actions. As the program is designed to support the entire organization in a holistic effort, all technical and nontechnical stakeholders are involved in the implementation of security, and there are few gaps in the resulting program.

For any top-down approach to succeed, high-level management must buy into the effort and provide its full support to all departments. Such an initiative must have a champion, a high-level executive who will provide support and influence for the project. Ideally, the champion is an executive with sufficient influence to move the project forward, ensure that it is properly managed, and push for its acceptance throughout the organization. For cybersecurity programs, this is usually the CIO. Without this high-level support, many mid-level administrators fail to dedicate enough resources to the project or dismiss it as a lower priority than the multitude of other tasks and projects before them.

Involvement and support of end users is also critical to the success of this type of effort. Because the process and outcome of the initiative most directly affect these individuals, they must be included in the cybersecurity planning process. Key end users should be assigned to planning and design teams like the joint application design teams used in systems development. These teams meet periodically to formulate and organize the *requirements* for a successful and effective cybersecurity program, rather than to create the program.

A successful cybersecurity program design team must be able to survive employee turnover; it should not be vulnerable to changes in personnel. For this reason, the processes and procedures must be documented and integrated into organizational culture. They must be endorsed, promoted, and supported by the organization's upper management. These attributes are seldom found in projects that begin as bottom-up initiatives. For this approach to be successful, the project workshops in which the cybersecurity specifications are created should include the following:

1. Identify project objectives and limitations.
2. Identify critical success factors.
3. Define project deliverables.
4. Define the schedule of workshop activities.
5. Select participants.
6. Prepare the workshop material.
7. Organize workshop activities and exercises.
8. Prepare, inform, and educate the workshop participants.
9. Coordinate workshop logistics.

To maximize success, a number of guidelines or critical success factors are recommended, based on research and experience in conducting program design sessions:

- Use experienced and skilled facilitators. Facilitators are the individuals who lead the structured workshops to ensure the sessions stay on track.
- Obtain executive sponsorship (i.e., the champion) to provide needed commitment and support.
- Involve the appropriate stakeholders as participants and clearly define their roles and responsibilities before the start of the workshops.
- Establish goals and objectives that are well defined, understood, and obtainable.
- Develop a detailed agenda and ensure it is followed.

- Specify the needed and expected deliverables early in the process.
- Try to minimize technical jargon; use language that all users can follow.
- Make every effort to create the final report (design specification) as soon as possible upon completion of the workshop sessions.

The success of cybersecurity plans can be enhanced using the processes of system analysis and design, a discipline that is an integral part of most academic curricula in the field of IT. The following sections offer a brief overview of this topic but do not replace a more detailed study of the discipline.

Implementing the Security Program Using an SDLC Approach

When developing any major program, the organization must identify a model or blueprint it wants to implement, as described later in the book. However, to implement that model, the organization will need to identify a formal methodology to provide guidance. A methodology is a formal approach to solving a problem based on a structured sequence of procedures, the use of which ensures a rigorous process and increases the likelihood of achieving the desired final objective. Organizations often implement information systems by using an approach based on the systems development life cycle (SDLC), a methodology for design and implementation that generally contains phases addressing the investigation, analysis, design, implementation, and maintenance of the system. This tried-and-true approach is combined with sound project management practices to develop key project milestones, allocate resources, select personnel, and perform the tasks needed to accomplish a project's objectives. The SDLC approach can be scaled up to support the design, implementation, and maintenance of an entire cybersecurity program.

Alternatively, many organizations choose implementation methodologies based on more agile practices. These methodologies include methods and practices to gather requirements and develop solutions through a collaborative effort of self-organizing and cross-functional teams consisting of customers and end users. The cybersecurity program should leverage its expertise and experience by partnering with information systems developers within the organization.

Once a cybersecurity program is implemented, it should be supported with a continuous improvement program (CIP). A CIP ensures that the entire program is reviewed on a periodic basis and refined so that, as the name suggests, it continually improves its ability to protect the organization's information assets. While many CIP models are available, one of the more popular is the IDEAL model, which you saw applied to cybersecurity governance earlier in this chapter. As you have learned, the IDEAL model is flexible and can be applied to any program, process, or function to support continuous improvement.

System projects may be initiated in response to specific conditions or combinations of conditions. The impetus to begin an SDLC-based project may be *event*-driven—that is, a response to some event in the business community, inside the organization, or within the ranks of employees, customers, or other stakeholders. Alternatively, it could be *plan*-driven—that is, the result of a carefully developed planning strategy. Either way, once an organization recognizes the need for a project, the use of a methodology ensures that development proceeds in an orderly, comprehensive fashion. At the end of each phase, a structured review takes place, during which the team and management-level reviewers decide whether the project should be continued, discontinued, outsourced, or postponed until additional expertise or organizational knowledge is acquired.

Several popular SDLC methodologies can be used to support cybersecurity program development and implementation. The model selected for this discussion is based on an older, more simplistic approach known as the waterfall model. The term "waterfall model" indicates that the work products of each phase fall into the next phase to serve as its starting point. The adapted SDLC process involves the identification of specific threats and the risks that they represent as well as the subsequent design and implementation of specific controls to counter those threats and manage the risk. The process turns cybersecurity into a coherent program rather than a series of responses to individual threats and attacks. Figure 2-12 shows the phases in the adapted cybersecurity program SDLC.

Figure 2-12 SDLC waterfall methodology

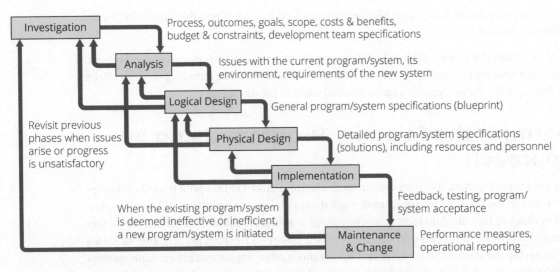

Deliverables:

Investigation → Process, outcomes, goals, scope, costs & benefits, budget & constraints, development team specifications

Analysis → Issues with the current program/system, its environment, requirements of the new system

Logical Design → General program/system specifications (blueprint)

Physical Design → Detailed program/system specifications (solutions), including resources and personnel

Implementation → Feedback, testing, program/system acceptance

Maintenance & Change → Performance measures, operational reporting

Revisit previous phases when issues arise or progress is unsatisfactory

When the existing program/system is deemed ineffective or inefficient, a new program/system is initiated

The recommended approach is to use a methodology that has a specific set of stages, like the waterfall model, which also requires periodic review of previous efforts. As illustrated in Figure 2-12, each stage in the waterfall model allows some degree of rework, revisiting previous stages when issues arise or when progress is unsatisfactory. The entire process can become recursive during the final stages if the developed approach is deemed ineffective or inefficient and restarting the entire project is preferred. The waterfall model is not intended as the definitive approach, nor is it represented as the only approach. Here, the waterfall approach is intended to facilitate understanding of the use of a methodology-based approach to develop and implement new cybersecurity programs.

Investigation in the SDLC

The investigation phase of the SDLC begins with a directive from upper management specifying the process, outcomes, and goals of the project as well as its budget and other constraints. Frequently, this phase begins with the affirmation or creation of security policies on which the organization's security program is or will be founded. Teams of managers, employees, and consultants are assembled to investigate problems, define their scope, specify goals and objectives, and identify any additional constraints not covered in the governing policy, like cybersecurity's program policy, as discussed in detail later in this book. Finally, an organizational feasibility analysis determines whether the organization has the resources and commitment to conduct the next stages—in this case, a successful cybersecurity analysis and design.

Unfortunately, many cybersecurity projects are initiated in response to a significant intrusion or breach within an organization. While these circumstances may not be the ideal conditions under which to begin work on an organization's cybersecurity posture, the SDLC team should emphasize that improvement is now underway.

Analysis in the SDLC

In the analysis phase, the team studies the documents from the investigation phase. The development team that was assembled during the investigation phase conducts a preliminary analysis of existing policies or programs. For cybersecurity programs, this includes the aforementioned policies, along with documented current threats and associated controls. This phase also includes an analysis of relevant legal issues that could affect the design of the solution. Increasingly, privacy laws are a major consideration when making decisions about information systems that manage personal information.

For cybersecurity programs, the risk management task also begins in this stage. Risk management is the process of identifying, assessing, and evaluating the levels of risk an organization faces—specifically, the threats to the organization's security and to the information stored and processed by the organization, as you learned in the previous chapter. Cybersecurity program analysis begins by getting to know your adversary.

In cybersecurity, the adversary is the entire set of threats and attacks that your systems face as they provide services to your organization and its customers.

The next task in the cybersecurity program analysis phase is to assess the relative risk for each information asset via a process called risk assessment. Risk assessment assigns a comparative risk rating or score to each information asset. While this number does not mean anything in absolute terms, it is useful in gauging the relative risk introduced by each vulnerable information asset and allows you to make comparative ratings later in the risk control process. Risk assessment is covered in detail later in this book.

Design in the SDLC

The SDLC design phase consists of two distinct phases: the logical design and the physical design. In the logical design phase, team members create and develop the blueprint for the desired solution, and they examine and implement key policies that influence later decisions. For the cybersecurity program, critical contingency plans for incident response are developed at this stage. Next, a feasibility analysis determines whether the project should continue in-house or be outsourced.

In the physical design phase, team members evaluate the technology needed to support the solution (in this case, the cybersecurity blueprint), generate alternative solutions, and agree on a final design. The cybersecurity blueprint may be revisited to keep it synchronized with the changes needed when the physical design is completed. Criteria for determining the definition of successful solutions are also prepared during this phase, as are designs for physically securing the technological solutions. At the end of this phase, a feasibility study should determine the readiness of the organization for the proposed project, and then the champion and users should be presented with the design. At that point, the interested parties have a chance to approve or request additional revisions to the project before implementation begins.

During the cybersecurity program's logical and physical design phases, the team may decide to use an established cybersecurity model to guide the design process. Cybersecurity models provide frameworks for ensuring that all areas of security are addressed. Organizations can adapt or adopt a framework to meet their own cybersecurity needs. Several cybersecurity frameworks have been published, and a few are discussed in detail in later chapters.

One of the design elements (or, in some projects, redesign elements) of the cybersecurity program is the organization's cybersecurity policy. The meaning of the term "security policy" differs depending on the context in which it is used. Governmental agencies, for example, discuss security policy in terms of national security and interaction with foreign states. In another context, a security policy can be part of a credit card agency's method of processing credit card numbers. In general, a security policy consists of a set of rules that protect an organization's assets. A cybersecurity policy provides guidance and requirements for protecting the information assets of an organization. As stated previously, the task of the cybersecurity program is to protect the confidentiality, integrity, and availability of information and information systems, whether in transit, storage, or processing, using policy, SETA programs, and technology.

Another integral part of the cybersecurity program is the SETA program, which is discussed in detail later in this book. Part of the CSO's responsibilities, the SETA program is a control measure designed to reduce accidental security breaches by employees. As mentioned earlier, employee errors represent one of the top threats to information assets; for this reason, it is well worth expending resources to develop programs to combat this problem. SETA programs are designed to supplement the general cybersecurity education and training programs that are already in place. Good practice dictates that the SDLC includes user training during the implementation phase to ensure that all employees are trained properly.

The design phase continues with the formulation of controls and safeguards, which are security mechanisms, policies, or procedures that can successfully counter attacks, reduce risk, resolve vulnerabilities, and otherwise improve security within an organization to protect information from attacks by threats. The terms "control" and "safeguard" are often used interchangeably. According to NIST, there are three categories of controls: managerial controls, operational controls, and technical controls.

Managerial controls cover security processes that are designed by the strategic planners and executed by the security administration of the organization. They set the direction and scope of the security process and provide detailed instructions for its conduct. Managerial controls address the design and implementation of the security planning process and security program management. They also address risk management and security control reviews (discussed in later chapters). Management controls further describe the necessity and scope of legal compliance and the maintenance of the entire security system's life cycle.

Operational controls deal with the operational functionality of security in the organization. They cover management functions and lower-level planning, such as disaster recovery and incident response planning. In addition, these controls address personnel security, physical security, and the protection of production inputs and outputs. Operational controls also provide structure to the development of education, training, and awareness programs for users, administrators, and management. Finally, they address hardware and software systems maintenance and the integrity of data.

Technical controls address technical approaches used to implement security in the organization. Operational controls address specific operational issues, such as control development and integration into business functions, whereas cybersecurity technical controls must be selected, acquired (made or bought), and integrated into the organization's IT structure. Technical controls include access controls, such as those used for identification, authentication, authorization, and accountability.

Another element of the design phase is the creation of essential preparedness documents. Managers in the IT and cybersecurity communities engage in strategic planning to ensure the continuous availability of the organization's information systems. In addition, managers of the organization must be ready to respond when an attack occurs. The various plans for handling attacks, disasters, or other types of incidents include business continuity plans (BC plans), disaster recovery plans (DR plans), and incident response plans (IR plans). These are often known collectively as contingency plans, which are part of the contingency planning (CP) process. In large, complex organizations, each of these named plans may represent separate but related planning functions, differing in scope, applicability, and design. In a small organization, the security administrator (or systems administrator) may have one simple plan, which consists of a straightforward set of media backup and recovery strategies and a few service agreements from the company's service providers. The sad reality is that many organizations have a level of response planning that is woefully deficient. Some industry observers noted that the Target data breach in December 2013, as significant as it was, appeared even worse because the scope of the breach seemed to expand with each successive announcement, implying that the company was either lying about the facts or incompetent to resolve the issue. Similarly, the Colonial Pipeline ransomware attack in 2021 resulted in a reaction by the organization that impacted the petroleum supply to the southeast United States. The ransomware attack never threatened the pipeline itself, but it was shut down by management after ransomware affected corporate systems responsible for billing customers.

Incident response, disaster recovery, business continuity, and crisis management are all components of CP. CP is the overall planning conducted by the organization to prepare for, react to, and recover from events that threaten the security of information assets in the organization, and to provide for the subsequent restoration to normal business operations. Organizations need to develop DR plans, IR plans, and BC plans as subsets of the overall CP. IR planning is the process associated with the identification, classification, response, and recovery from an incident. DR planning is the process associated with the preparation for and recovery from a disaster, whether originating from natural or human sources. BC planning is the process associated with ensuring that critical business functions continue if a catastrophic incident or disaster occurs. These critical building blocks of response planning are presented later in this book.

The cybersecurity program's design phase next addresses physical security, which requires the design, implementation, and maintenance of countermeasures to protect the physical resources of an organization. Physical resources include people, hardware, and the supporting system elements and resources associated with the management of information in all its states: transmission, storage, and processing. Many technology-based cybersecurity controls can be circumvented if an attacker gains physical access to the devices being controlled. For example, when employees fail to secure a server console, the operating system running on that computer becomes vulnerable to attack. Because it is easier to steal information by stealing the hard drives that contain it, physical security should receive as much attention as logical security in the SDLC.

Implementation in the SDLC

During the cybersecurity program's SDLC implementation phase, cybersecurity solutions are acquired (made or bought), tested, implemented, and retested. Personnel issues are evaluated and specific training and education programs are conducted. Finally, the entire tested package is presented to upper management for final approval.

The cybersecurity systems and software selection process is not appreciably different from that for general IT needs. Vendors should be given detailed specifications and then provide detailed information about products and costs. As in IT system implementation, it is essential to establish clear specifications and rigorous test plans to ensure a high-quality implementation.

Perhaps the most important element of the cybersecurity program's implementation phase is the management of the project plan. Project management, as described in a later chapter, is the process that underlies all phases of an SDLC. The execution of the project plan proceeds in three steps:

1. Planning the project
2. Supervising the tasks and action steps within the project plan
3. Wrapping up the project plan

A project plan can be developed in any number of ways. Each organization must determine its own project management methodology for IT and cybersecurity projects. Whenever possible, cybersecurity projects should follow the organizational practices of project management. For organizations that have not established clearly defined project management practices, the following pages supply general guidelines on recommended practices.

Cybersecurity is a field with a vast array of technical and nontechnical requirements. For this reason, the project team should include individuals who are experienced in one or more requirements of both the technical and nontechnical areas. Many of the same skills needed to manage and implement security are needed to design it. Members of the development team fill the following roles:

- Champion—A senior executive who promotes the project and ensures its support, both financially and administratively, at the highest levels of the organization.
- Team leader—A project manager (perhaps a departmental line manager or staff unit manager) who understands project management, personnel management, and cybersecurity technical requirements.
- Cybersecurity policy developers—Individuals who understand the organizational culture, existing policies, and requirements for developing and implementing successful policies.
- Risk assessment specialists—Individuals who understand financial risk assessment techniques, the value of organizational assets, and the security methods to be used.
- Cybersecurity professionals—Dedicated, trained, and well-educated specialists in all aspects of cybersecurity from both technical and nontechnical standpoints.
- IT systems administrators—Individuals with the primary responsibility for administering the systems that house the organization's information.
- End users—The individuals whom the new system will most directly affect; ideally, a disparate group of users from various departments and levels, and with varying degrees of technical knowledge, to assist the team in applying realistic controls in ways that do not disrupt the essential business activities they seek to safeguard.

Just as each potential employee and employer look for the best fit during the hiring process, each organization should thoroughly examine its options when staffing the cybersecurity function. When implementing cybersecurity in an organization, many human resource issues must be addressed. First, the organization must decide how to position and name the security function within the organization. Second, the cybersecurity community of interest must plan for the proper staffing for the cybersecurity function. Third, the IT community of interest must understand how cybersecurity affects every role in the IT function and adjust job descriptions and documented practices accordingly. Finally, the general management community of interest must work with the cybersecurity professionals to integrate solid cybersecurity concepts into the personnel management practices of the organization as a whole.

It takes a variety of professionals to support a diverse cybersecurity program. Because a good cybersecurity plan is initiated from the top down, senior management is the key component and vital force driving the successful implementation of a cybersecurity program. To develop and execute specific cybersecurity policies and procedures, additional administrative support may be required. Finally, technical expertise is necessary to implement the details of the security operation. Here are more precise descriptions of the various roles involved in cybersecurity:

- Chief information officer—The senior technology officer responsible for aligning the strategic efforts of the organization and integrating them into action plans for the information systems or data-processing division.
- Chief security officer—The individual responsible for the cybersecurity program, including the assessment, management, and implementation of information-protection activities in the organization.
- Cybersecurity managers—The individuals accountable for ensuring the day-to-day operation of the cybersecurity program, accomplishing the objectives identified by the CSO, and resolving issues identified by technicians.
- Cybersecurity technicians—Technically qualified individuals who are tasked with configuring firewalls and intrusion detection and prevention systems, implementing cybersecurity software, diagnosing and troubleshooting problems, and coordinating with systems and network administrators to ensure that cybersecurity technology is properly implemented.
- Data trustees—The executive management group that is generally responsible for the collection, storage, use, and management of the data by the organization's business units that report directly to them; most "C-level" executives are data trustees of their respective business units, with one or more data owners reporting to them.
- Data owners—Individuals who control, and are therefore responsible for, the protection and use of a particular set of information; data owners may rely on custodians for the practical aspects of protecting their information and specifying which users are authorized to access it, but they are ultimately responsible for it.
- Data custodians—Individuals who work directly with data owners and are responsible for storage, maintenance, and protection of the information; the IT and cybersecurity groups are the most common data custodians.
- Data users—Internal and external stakeholders, including customers, suppliers, and employees, who interact with the information in support of their organization's planning and operations.

Many organizations seek employees or contractors who have professional certifications so that they can more easily identify these individuals' proficiency. A thorough discussion of cybersecurity industry certification is also provided later in the book.

Maintenance in the SDLC

The maintenance and change phase of the cybersecurity program, though last, is perhaps the most important, given the flexibility and persistence of many of the threats facing modern organizations. Today's cybersecurity systems need constant monitoring, testing, modifying, updating, and repairing. Traditional application systems that are developed under an SDLC are not designed to anticipate a vicious attack that requires some degree of application reconstruction as a normal course of operation. In cybersecurity, the battle for stable, reliable systems is a defensive one. As new threats emerge and old threats evolve, the cybersecurity profile of an organization requires constant adaptation to prevent threats from successfully penetrating sensitive data.

Once the cybersecurity program is implemented, it must be operated, managed, and continuously improved by means of established procedures. If the program is not adjusting adequately to changes in the internal or external environment, it may be necessary to begin the SDLC cycle again. The CSO determines whether the cybersecurity group can adapt adequately and maintain the cybersecurity profile of the organization or whether the macroscopic process of the SDLC must start anew to redevelop a fundamentally different cybersecurity profile. It is less expensive and more effective when a cybersecurity program is able to deal with change. Even when a cybersecurity program is adapting and growing, those processes of maintenance and change mirror the overall process of the SDLC, differing only in scope. As deficiencies are found and vulnerabilities pinpointed, projects to maintain, extend, or enhance the program follow the SDLC steps. Therefore, the organization should establish formal security maintenance, as described in greater detail in a later chapter. Whereas a systems management model is designed to manage and operate systems, a maintenance model is intended to complement a systems management model and focus ongoing maintenance efforts needed to keep systems usable and secure.

Note 4 | If you would like to learn more about the role of ethics in governance, we recommend *A Companion to Ethics* by Peter Singer, published by Wiley-Blackwell (1993).

Self-Check

7. The senior cybersecurity manager most commonly reports directly to the chief information officer.
    a. True   b. False

8. A project champion is a low-level executive who provides minor administrative support for the cybersecurity project.
    a. True   b. False

9. Involvement and support of end users are not necessary for the success of cybersecurity planning and implementation.
    a. True   b. False

□ Check your answers at the end of this chapter.

Closing Case

Mike and Iris met to discuss the strategic plan that would be presented at the upcoming company-wide strategic planning workshop. Mike had given Iris the IT division's list of strategic goals. She had already seen RWW's most recent set of corporate strategic goals.

"Mike, I see that you have kept a one-to-one alignment of your goals to the company goals," Iris said. "Do you think it's necessary for cybersecurity's goals to have the same arrangement?"

"I've found that by keeping the alignment in place, it helps those higher up to stay focused on what IT will be doing to help them execute their important priorities," Mike replied. "But you'll notice that there are in fact a lot of differences."

Mike then pointed to a section of the plan. "Notice here that corporate goal number three is an overall reduction in operating costs as a percentage of revenue," Mike explained. "I have the IT plan element in support still as goal number three, but it now has four parts listed within it. Each of those is a specific IT-related goal to reduce costs.

"Now look at corporate goal one, which really just says we need to increase revenue," Mike continued. "Because RWW doesn't really have any profit centers in the IT parts of the company, I just wrote a short section on how we will assist the revenue-producing parts of the company in doing more of that. Even though the IT goal isn't very concrete, taking it out may be confusing if someone is trying to identify alignment."

Iris nodded.

"So, alignment is about making sure that what the lower-level business unit can do supports the higher-level unit's objectives," she said.

"Exactly right," Mike said, also nodding.

"So do you want the cybersecurity goals to be subordinate to the corporate goals or just subordinate to the IT goals?" Iris asked.

"Well, I think either approach will come to about the same thing," Mike responded. "But for this cycle, you can work from the draft IT planning goals in this version as long as you keep up the alignment in the numbering. Because you're new to this, that might make it a little easier. In the long run, however, you will need to make sure that being subordinate to IT goals doesn't negate your responsibility to support other business units. As you know, all the information you must protect isn't in the IT department."

Case Discussion Questions

1. Few cybersecurity business units can generate revenue. Do you think Iris should word her plans to coordinate with IT efforts to support revenue-generating business units, or should she adopt Mike's goal and seek to support the company's profit centers directly? Why is the second choice better for Iris and the cybersecurity unit?
2. What options will Iris have if she finds an IT strategic objective that she thinks would reduce the security of RWW's information assets?

Case Ethical Decision Making

Suppose Iris discovers an element of the IT strategic plan stating that IT will reduce costs by implementing a specific new technology. Suppose also that Iris knows this new technology may introduce unexpected vulnerabilities into RWW's systems. Should Iris challenge Mike on this issue, or should she leave that subject alone? Is she ethically obligated to raise this issue with higher management?

Summary

Planning is essential to organizational management and operations and involves many organizational groups and processes known as stakeholders. Because cybersecurity seeks to support the protection of information assets throughout the entire organization, an effective cybersecurity planner should know how the entire organizational planning process works so that they can obtain the best possible outcome.

Planning is the dominant means of managing and allocating resources in organizations. It involves a formal sequence of actions intended to achieve specific goals during a defined period and then controlling the implementation of these steps.

To implement effective planning and guide the creation of the strategic plan, an organization's leaders usually begin with previously developed statements of the organization's ethical, entrepreneurial, and philosophical perspectives guided by the organization's mission, vision, values, and strategy.

The mission statement explicitly declares the business of the organization and its intended areas of operations. The vision statement is an idealistic expression of what the organization wants to become; it works in tandem with the mission statement. The values statement articulates a formal set of organizational principles and qualities.

Strategic planning is the process of defining and specifying the long-term direction to be taken by an organization and the acquisition and allocation of resources needed to pursue this effort. Strategic planning guides organizational efforts and focuses resources toward specific, clearly defined goals amid an ever-changing environment.

Once the organization's overall strategic plan is translated into strategic goals for each major division or operation, the next step is to translate these strategic goals into objectives that are specific, measurable, achievable, relevant, and time-bound. This information is used to create tactical plans, which are in turn used to develop operational plans. Tactical planning has a shorter-term focus than strategic planning, usually a few years. Operational plans organize the ongoing, day-to-day performance of tasks.

Strategic planning and corporate responsibility are best accomplished using an approach the industry refers to as Governance, Risk Management, and Compliance (GRC). GRC seeks to integrate these three previously separate responsibilities into one holistic approach that can provide and ensure sound executive-level strategic planning and management of the cybersecurity function. The subjects themselves are neither new nor unique to cybersecurity; however, recognition of the need to integrate the three at the board or executive level is becoming increasingly important to organizations. Note that the management of risk is not limited to an organization's cybersecurity effort.

Governance is a set of responsibilities and practices exercised by the board and executive management with the goal of providing strategic direction, ensuring that objectives are achieved, ascertaining that risks are managed appropriately, and verifying that the enterprise's resources are used responsibly.

The implementation of cybersecurity in an organization originated in one of two ways: bottom-up or top-down. Cybersecurity programs that evolved from the bottom-up approach might have begun as a grassroots effort. When security programs are developed using the top-down approach, they benefit from strong upper-management support, a dedicated champion, dedicated funding, a clear planning and implementation process, and the ability to influence organizational culture.

When developing any major program, the organization must identify a model or blueprint it wants to implement. Organizations often implement information systems by using an approach based on the systems development life cycle. Once a cybersecurity program is implemented, it should be supported with a continuous improvement program.

Key Terms

champion
controls and safeguards
methodology

stakeholders
strategic planning

systems development life cycle
(SDLC)

Review Questions

1. What is the primary goal of planning within organizations?

2. How does planning benefit cybersecurity management?

3. What role does the chief security officer play in planning?

4. Why is an ethical perspective important in organizational planning?

5. How does a mission statement influence an organization?

6. What is the function of a vision statement in planning?

7. Describe the importance of values statements in organizations.

8. What are the key components of strategic planning?

9. How is cybersecurity integrated into strategic planning?

10. What are tactical plans and how do they relate to strategic plans?

11. Explain the relationship between operational and tactical planning.

12. Why is cybersecurity governance crucial for organizations?

13. What outcomes are expected from effective cybersecurity governance?

14. How does the ISO/IEC 27014:2020 standard contribute to cybersecurity governance?

15. What challenges does security convergence aim to address?

16. What are the benefits of a top-down approach to cybersecurity implementation?

17. Why is the involvement of end users important in cybersecurity planning?

18. What factors influence corporate readiness for cybersecurity?

19. How does understanding the security department's maturity status aid planning?

20. Why are regulatory requirements important in cybersecurity planning?

21. What is the role of continuous learning in cybersecurity?

22. What key elements should a strategic cybersecurity plan include?

23. How do cybersecurity programs evolve from a bottom-up approach?

24. What advantages do integrating physical and cybersecurity efforts offer?

25. Why is a champion necessary for the success of top-down cybersecurity initiatives?

26. How can cybersecurity governance increase an organization's share value?

27. Describe the role of continuous learning in cybersecurity management.

Exercises

1. Using a web search engine, find an article from a reputable source, published within the past six months, that reports on the risk coming from inside the organization compared to the risk coming from outside. If the article notes that this relative risk is changing, how is it changing, and to what is the change attributed?

2. Using a web search engine, find five examples of values, vision, and mission statements as well as public declarations of organizational strategy. Do these examples express concern for the security of corporate information?

3. Search your institution's published documents (or another organization's), including its webpages. Locate its values, vision, and/or mission statement, as well as strategic goals. Identify any references to cybersecurity. Also, look for any planning documents related to cybersecurity.

4. Use a web search engine to find a general encyclopedic article on agile approaches to an SDLC. You might use a search phrase of "agile SDLC wiki." Read the article. What differentiates agile development from traditional development?

5. Use a web search engine to explore converged approaches to enterprise risk management. You should use the search phrases "converged enterprise risk management" and "all hazard risk management." Read at least three posts you find for each search term.

6. Next, find and read the article at https://www.securityexecutivecouncil.com/spotlight/?sid=30603. How does an "ordinary" approach to governing the security process in a company differ from the converged models you read about in Exercise 5?

Solutions to Self-Check Questions

The Role of Planning

1. Planning is only beneficial for responding to immediate threats in cybersecurity management.
   Answer: b. False.
   Explanation: While planning allows for an urgent response to immediate threats, it is also essential for the long-term viability of the cybersecurity program, enabling effective and proactive use of resources.

2. Strategic planning focuses only on the immediate future and short-term goals of an organization.
   Answer: b. False.
   Explanation: Strategic planning defines the long-term direction to be taken by an organization and involves acquiring and allocating resources to pursue this effort.

3. Cybersecurity strategic planning should support the strategic plans of all business units, not just IT.
   Answer: a. True.
   Explanation: The cybersecurity group must understand and support the strategic plans of all business units because all organizational units use information. This necessitates a role that may sometimes conflict with that of the IT department.

Cybersecurity Governance

4. Cybersecurity governance is solely a technical issue and not a strategic management issue.
   Answer: b. False.
   Explanation: Cybersecurity governance is a strategic management issue, not just a technical issue. It requires integration into the fabric of the organization, expanding corporate governance to include the objectives of the cybersecurity program.

5. Cybersecurity objectives only need to be addressed at middle management levels to be effective.

   Answer: b. False.

   Explanation: Cybersecurity objectives must be addressed at the highest levels of an organization's management team to be effective and provide a sustainable approach.

6. Cybersecurity governance can lead to an increase in share value for organizations and optimization of the allocation of limited security resources.

   Answer: a. True.

   Explanation: Properly implemented cybersecurity governance can yield significant benefits, including an increase in share value and optimization of the allocation of limited security resources.

Planning for Cybersecurity Implementation

7. The senior cybersecurity manager most commonly reports directly to the chief information officer.

   Answer: a. True.

   Explanation: In the current business environment, the senior cybersecurity manager, regardless of their title, most commonly reports directly to the CIO.

8. A project champion is a low-level executive who provides minor administrative support for the cybersecurity project.

   Answer: b. False.

   Explanation: A project champion is a senior executive who promotes the project and ensures its support both financially and administratively at the highest levels of the organization.

9. Involvement and support of end users are not necessary for the success of cybersecurity planning and implementation.

   Answer: b. False.

   Explanation: Involvement and support of end users are critical to the success of cybersecurity planning and implementation. Key end users should be assigned to planning and design teams to ensure the program effectively meets organizational needs without disrupting essential business activities.

Risk Management: Assessing Risk

Chapter Objectives

After reading this chapter and completing the exercises, you should be able to:

1 Define risk management and its role in the organization.

2 Prioritize risk factors for information assets using the risk management process.

> Once we know our weaknesses, they cease to do us any harm.
>
> —G. C. (Georg Christoph) Lichtenberg (1742-1799), German physicist and philosopher

Case Opener

Iris Majwubu and Mike Edwards sat side by side on the short flight to the nearby city where the Random Widget Works board of directors' audit committee was meeting that afternoon. The two had been invited to present RWW's IT risk management program to the committee. The board's concerns stemmed from a recent briefing by the National Association of Corporate Directors, which focused on trends affecting the potential liability of board members in the areas of cybersecurity in general and risk management in particular.

After the plane leveled off, Mike pulled out his copy of the presentation he planned to give that afternoon. He and Iris had been working on it for the past two weeks, and each knew the slides by heart. Iris was along to assist with the question-and-answer period that would follow Mike's presentation.

"They're not going to be happy when you're done," Iris said.

"No, they're not," Mike said. "The CEO is worried about how they'll respond and about what might come up at the full board meeting next month. I'm afraid the disconnect between IT and Internal Audit may have some unexpected consequences."

Iris considered what she knew about the weaknesses of the Internal Audit Department's approach to the company's non-IT assets. Where Mike and Iris had built a sound, fact-based approach to estimating and controlling cybersecurity risk, some of the other company divisions used less established and reliable methods.

"I think we should come out of this okay," Iris told Mike. "After all, the main concern of the audit committee members is the new perception of their liability for cybersecurity and the impact that risk has on the issues surrounding privacy. We have a solid risk management plan in place that's working well, in my opinion."

Mike looked up from his notes and said, "It's not us I'm worried about. I'm afraid we may create some discomfort and unwanted attention for our peers after the board sees the wide variety of risk management approaches used in other divisions."

Introduction to the Management of Risk in Cybersecurity

Chinese general Sun Tzu's observation, made more than 2,400 years ago, continues to have direct relevance to the philosophy of cybersecurity today:

> Therefore I say: One who knows the enemy and knows himself will not be in danger in a hundred battles.
>
> One who does not know the enemy but knows himself will sometimes win, sometimes lose.
>
> One who does not know the enemy and does not know himself will be in danger in every battle.[1]

Cybersecurity strategy and tactics are similar in some ways to those employed in conventional warfare, with the obvious exception that the law prohibits offensive operations on the part of a targeted organization, outside of official military and governmental cyberwarfare operations. Cybersecurity managers and technicians are the defenders of information. They constantly face a myriad of threats to the organization's information assets. A layered defense is the foundation of any cybersecurity program. So, as Sun Tzu recommends, to reduce risk, an organization must know itself and know its enemy. This means that managers from all three communities of interest must locate the weaknesses of their organization's information operations, understand how the organization's information is processed, stored, and transmitted, and identify what resources are available. Only then can they develop a strategic plan for defense.

Knowing Yourself and Knowing the Enemy

When operating any kind of organization, a certain amount of risk is always involved. Risk is inherent in personnel management, the creation and delivery of products and services, and even in the location where the organization resides and operates. Risk finds its way into the daily operations of every organization, and if it is not properly managed, it can cause operational failures and even lead to the organization going out of business.

For an organization to manage its cybersecurity risk properly, managers should understand how and where information is collected, processed, stored, and transmitted. Knowing yourself in this context requires identifying which information assets are valuable to the organization, categorizing and classifying those assets, and understanding how they are currently being protected. Armed with this knowledge, the organization can then initiate an in-depth risk management (RM) program. Note that the mere existence of an RM program is not sufficient. Frequently, RM mechanisms are implemented but not maintained or monitored. Risk management is a process, which means the control strategies that are devised and implemented are not "install-and-forget" occurrences; rather, they require time and attention to remain effective.

Once an organization becomes fully aware of itself—as in knowing its information assets and how they're being protected—managers can take up Sun Tzu's second dictum: Know the enemy. This means identifying, examining, and understanding the threats facing the organization's information assets. Managers must be fully prepared to identify threats that pose risks to the organization and the security of its information assets, as discussed earlier in this book.

Knowing your enemy implies that you must assess the motivations for each of the adversaries you face. Each class of adversary has differing motivations and capabilities. Some adversaries want to steal money or data with value; others want to steal your data or systems capabilities. Others are motivated by ideology or hatred for your organization or executive team and want to inflict damage or pain. Still others are competitors who want to generate noise that distracts you from your primary focus. Some are just playing with Internet attack toolkits to see what happens. These motivations and capabilities are all different, and some defenses may work against all of them, but others will need a more specialized response.

The Cybersecurity Risk Management Framework

Risk exists in every environment. From an organization's perspective, the evaluation and reaction to this risk, including financial risk, competitive risk, and economic risk, is commonly referred to as enterprise risk management (ERM), the evaluation and reaction to risk for the entire organization, not just the risk facing information assets. For the purposes of this discussion, the risk to information assets is of the most concern to the cybersecurity function and its personnel. The aspect directly related to cybersecurity is commonly referred to as cybersecurity risk management, or IT risk management. This discussion uses the term cybersecurity risk management, the application of safeguards or controls to reduce the risks to an organization's information assets to an acceptable level. Elsewhere in this textbook, the term used is simply risk management.

Risk management is the process of discovering and assessing the risks to an organization's operations and determining how those risks can be controlled or mitigated. This process involves discovering and understanding answers to some key questions regarding the risk associated with an organization's information assets:

1. Where and what is the risk (risk identification)?
2. How significant is the current level of risk (risk analysis)?
3. Is the current level of risk acceptable (risk evaluation)?
4. What do I need to do to bring the risk to an acceptable level (risk treatment)?

The term "risk assessment" is commonly used to describe the entire set of activities associated with the first three questions, while risk treatment (or risk control)—the reduction of risk, including cybersecurity risk, to an acceptable level—describes the fourth. Risk treatment is discussed in a later chapter. Here, we examine these activities individually to ensure that the distinctions between these stages are clear.

Cybersecurity in an organization exists primarily to manage the risk to information assets stemming from their use by the organization's employees and other stakeholders. Managing risk is a key responsibility for every manager within an organization. Well-developed RM programs rely on formal and repeatable processes that are continuously reviewed and improved. The coverage of RM in this text was developed based on an extensive assessment of best practices in industry, government, and formal standards. The formal standard most closely aligned with the findings of this assessment, ISO 31000 – Risk management, was selected and adapted to facilitate ease of presentation and discussion.

Risk management is a complex operation that requires a formal methodology, much like the systems development life cycle (SDLC) discussed in an earlier chapter. Figure 3-1 explores the entire approach to RM, which involves two key areas: the RM framework, which is the overall structure of the strategic planning and design for the entirety of the organization's RM efforts; and the RM process, which is the identification, analysis, evaluation, and treatment of risk to information assets, as specified in the RM framework. The RM framework (planning) guides the RM process (doing), which conducts the processes of risk assessment and risk treatment. The RM framework assesses the RM process, which in turn assesses risk in the organization's information assets.

The RM framework and the RM process are both continuous improvement activities. This means they are ongoing, repetitive, and designed to continually assess current performance to improve future RM results. The RM framework repeatedly assesses and improves not only how the RM process is evaluating and reacting to risk, it continuously assesses and improves how well the planning and review activities are being performed within the framework itself. As an example, in a manufacturing plant, executives oversee the measurement of product quality and manufacturing productivity (the results and the equivalent of the RM process) while also assessing the effectiveness of the management processes used to structure manufacturing (the equivalent of the RM framework).

The left side of Figure 3-1 illustrates the major activities associated with the RM framework. As you have seen with other major cybersecurity initiatives, this framework is developed and reviewed by an executive team led by a champion and organized using effective project management methods. Organizations that have existing RM programs may be able to adapt their operations to the methodology shown here, with

Figure 3-1 The risk management framework and process

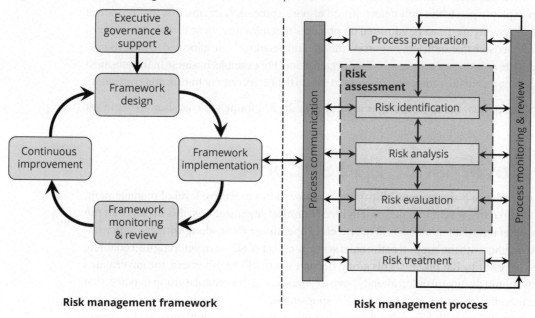

minimum impact on their current efforts. Organizations that do not have formal RM programs, or have programs that are unsuccessful, inefficient, or ineffective, need to begin the process from scratch. The RM framework consists of five key stages:

1. Executive governance and support
2. Framework design
3. Framework implementation
4. Framework monitoring and review
5. Continuous improvement

If the entire process looks familiar, perhaps like the SDLC discussed earlier, there's a reason. Most project-oriented work usually benefits from following similar methodologies. While this framework is provided as an example of how to perform RM in an organization, it is not by any means the only way to do so. Each organization must decide for itself what works best from the options available. The model shown here is adapted to be in alignment with an International Organization for Standardization (ISO) standard, while others are based on industry standards or proprietary models. It would not be difficult for an organization to take the general recommendations of this RM framework and process and adapt it to fit the details of another methodology. Only those involved in the process know what's best for their organizations.

Roles of Communities of Interest in Managing Risk

Each community of interest in an organization shares the responsibility for the management of risk. The executive management of the organization is ultimately accountable for the RM program that is implemented. Of the three communities of interest directly linked to managing the risks to information assets, each has a particular strategic role to play:

- Cybersecurity—Because members of the cybersecurity community best understand the threats and attacks that introduce risk to information assets, they often take a leadership role in addressing risk.
- IT—This group is responsible for building secure systems and ensuring their safe operation, in cooperation with the cybersecurity community. For example, IT builds and operates information systems that are mindful of operational risks and have proper controls implemented to reduce risk.

- General management and users—When properly trained and kept aware of the threats faced by the organization, this group plays a part in the early detection and response process. Users must be made aware of threats to data and systems and must be educated on practices that minimize those threats. Members of this community also ensure that sufficient resources (money and personnel) are allocated to the cybersecurity and IT groups to meet the security needs of the organization. For example, business managers must ensure that supporting records for orders remain intact in case of data entry error or transaction corruption.

The following sections discuss the specific stages identified in the RM framework, as shown on the left side of Figure 3-1.

Executive Governance and Support

As you have learned, governance is the responsibility of the organization's executive level of management, typically at the board of directors or senior management level. For most organizations, this means that the chief executive officer, chief information officer (CIO), and chief operating officer, along with any other relevant executives, work together with the support of the chief security officer (CSO) in developing and enabling the RM framework and its resulting RM process. This group becomes, formally or otherwise, the governance group for the RM effort. Should the organization already have a cybersecurity governance group in place, that group may simply add this effort to its existing portfolio of responsibilities.

The entire RM program begins with a formal acknowledgment by the organization's governance group that RM is invaluable and critical to the organization's long-term sustainability and viability. After acknowledging this strategic worth, the group formally commissions the development and eventual implementation of the RM project.

Prior to the actual design of the framework, the governance group must demonstrate its commitment to the RM effort by notifying the entire organization. The key elements of that communication are:

- A major RM project is underway
- The project is of the utmost importance to the strategic future of the organization
- The participation and cooperation of all aspects of the organization are mandated and are crucial to the project's success

As the RM effort moves forward, the governance group will need to periodically reinforce its commitment, especially when the RM teams meet resistance to the project. True commitment is demonstrated only when the group continues its support throughout the project, rather than simply distributing a memo at its outset.

Additional tasks are performed by the governance group during the framework design phase in cooperation with the RM framework team (sometimes labeled as the RM planning team). These tasks include:

- Ensuring compliance with all legal and regulatory statutes and mandates
- Guiding the development of, and formally approving, the RM policy
- Recommending performance measures for the RM effort and ensuring that they are compatible with other performance measures in the organization
- Assigning roles and responsibilities
- Ensuring that the selected goals and objectives are appropriate and in alignment with the organization's strategic goals and objectives
- Providing needed resources

Legal and Regulatory Compliance

Organizations seldom operate in a vacuum. There is a wide body of laws, regulations, and industry standards with which they are required to comply. It is the governance group's responsibility to ensure that the RM process is in complete compliance with all applicable requirements. This is commonly done by assigning a member of the organization's legal team (when there is one) to the RM framework team or by requiring that all work products from the team are reviewed and approved by designated legal counsel. With the continuing development of federal and state laws for breach notification, privacy protection, and the like, organizations must continually scan the legal environment to ensure they are prepared for mandated compliance in cybersecurity and privacy. Similarly, the expectations of other industry regulations, such as PCI-DSS, also could negatively impact the organization if the RM process results in changes that fall short of regulatory requirements.

The RM Policy

Policy communicates management's intent for the outcome of an organization's effort or the use of its resources. For RM program development and implementation, the project leader, in cooperation with the governance group, drafts a **risk management policy**, the managerial directive designed to regulate organizational efforts related to the identification, assessment, and treatment of risk to information assets. This policy converts the instructions and perspectives provided to the RM framework team by the governance group into cohesive guidance that structures and directs all subsequent RM efforts within the organization.

The RM policy, much like the organization's cybersecurity program policy, is a strategic document that formalizes much of the intent of the governance group. While no two policies are identical, most include the following:

- Purpose and scope—What is this policy for and to whom does it apply?
- RM intent and objectives—What is the general view of RM by the governance group and how will that be translated into RM goals and objectives for the entire organization?
- Roles and responsibilities—A list of the assignments and expectations for each constituent responsible for the RM program. These lists should specify who will be involved (usually by position or group) and what their involvement is:
  - Oversight and governance group
  - RM framework team, responsible for the development and implementation of the RM framework and the development of the RM process
  - RM process implementation team (if different from the framework team)
  - Business units
  - IT department
  - Cybersecurity group

  For example, the chief cybersecurity officer will serve as project team leader for the RM framework development team and is responsible for ensuring completion of the framework and implementation of the process within the timelines, budgets, and other constraints specified.
- Resource requirements—A list of the resources allocated to the support of RM as a program and to the framework and process teams. The resource list should be compatible with the roles and responsibilities specified earlier.
- Risk appetite and tolerances—A summary of the expectations and preferences of executive management regarding the level of risk the organization is willing to tolerate.
- RM program development guidelines—Organization-specific instructions to guide the development and implementation of the RM effort. These could include a need to comply with specific regulations, to follow a particular methodology (which could either be incorporated into this RM project or in place of it), and any other special considerations the governance team wants to make known.
- Special instructions and revision information—Guidelines for the planned review and revision of the policy document, including information on "who," "how," and "when."
- References to other key policies, plans, standards, and guidelines—A list of key documents (internal or external) that the organization should remain cognizant of during the development and implementation of the RM program.

Assigning Key Responsibilities

As the organization moves forward with RM development efforts, key responsibilities must be specified by the governance group. Who will be the leader of the RM framework team, and who will be the project manager? Who will be assigned to the framework team? Who will be assigned to the process team? Who will manage each of these teams? While the governance group will be periodically briefed on the progress and successes of RM framework development and implementation, it will not actually do the work of designing, implementing, and operating the RM framework and process. It is up to the governance group to specify who will perform which tasks, based on the recommendation of the organization's IT and cybersecurity leaders. In most organizations, either the CIO, CSO, or their equivalent leads the RM effort. In certain industries, like the financial sector, this may fall under the responsibility of an executive-level chief risk officer (or VP of enterprise risk) who handles both financial risk and information risk, as the two are closely related. Most organizations have one of the two technology leaders guide the overall RM project. In many instances, the CIO serves as the champion while the CSO serves as the project manager. Like every other major organizational effort, all managers have a vested interest in the success of the RM process and should support it:

- Cybersecurity management must lead the way with skill, professionalism, flexibility, and subject expertise because it works with the other communities of interest to coordinate the project, balancing the constant trade-offs between the organization's need to use information and its responsibility to protect it.
- IT management must appoint representatives who understand how IT supports the needs of the broader organization and how IT interacts with cybersecurity to protect information assets.
- General management must support the RM function by providing representatives who understand how the business areas of the organization use information, how cybersecurity is critical to the effective use of that information, and how those areas are impacted by the RM project.

Developing Priorities and Objectives

Once the members of the RM framework team have been identified, the governance group should communicate its intent, priorities, and desired outcomes for the overall RM program. The project leader will then translate this intent into a set of goals and objectives for the RM effort. These goals and objectives are then used to create the RM policy and eventually the RM plan.

The goals and objectives could include the following:

- Develop a common understanding of risk across multiple functions and business units to manage risk cost-effectively on an enterprise-wide basis.
- Achieve a better understanding of risk for competitive advantage.
- Build safeguards against earnings-related surprises.
- Build and improve capabilities to respond effectively to low-probability, critical, catastrophic risks.
- Achieve cost savings through better management of internal resources.
- Allocate capital more efficiently.[2]
- Complete initial RM framework development by a defined date.
- Report RM program progress to the governance group on a defined periodic basis.

Some goals and objectives could also be directed toward the RM project itself:

- Complete RM process implementation by a defined date.
- Implement the entire RM framework and process based on a defined, allocated budget.
- Complete the initial RM process cycle by a defined date.
- Report RM process findings to the governance group on a defined periodic basis.

Providing Resources

Once a policy has been developed, or concurrently with development of that policy, the governance group must allocate the resources needed to support RM program development and implementation. This is usually a multiphase effort, beginning with the allocation of enough resources to support the framework design. Once the framework design is approved by the governance group, supplemental resources are allocated to support the framework implementation, followed by another review phase, and then resources are allocated for RM process implementation and execution. While an organization may simply choose to allocate enough resources for the entire project, most are more comfortable with understanding what is needed in the next stage before committing the time, money, personnel, and other resources.

Framework Design

In this stage, the framework team begins designing the RM process by which the organization will understand its current levels of risk and determine what, if anything, it needs to do to bring them down to acceptable levels in alignment with the risk appetite specified earlier in the process. Designing the RM program means not only defining and specifying the detailed tasks to be performed by the framework team but also those to be performed by the process team. Once the framework itself has been designed and implemented, most of the work of the framework team involves oversight of the process.

As mentioned previously, a wide variety of methodologies are available for conducting RM. At this stage, the organization may simply select an "off-the-shelf" implementation of such a methodology, which it can adapt to its needs. The organization may even decide to develop its own methodology or hire a consultant to design one for them. Whatever it chooses, this is the phase of the RM framework in which the entire RM program is designed and the corresponding details are specified. In addition to coordinating with the governance group on the tasks outlined in the previous section, the framework team must formally document and define the organization's risk appetite and draft the RM plan.

Defining the Organization's Risk Tolerance and Risk Appetite

As the governance group communicates its intent to the RM framework development team, it also needs to communicate its general perspective on what level of risk is acceptable and what risk must be reduced or resolved in some fashion (treated). In other words, the RM framework team needs to understand and be able to determine whether the level of controls identified at the end of the risk process results in a level of risk that management can accept. The amount of risk that remains after information assets have undergone risk treatment is called residual risk. The organization may very well reach this point in the RM process, examine the documented residual risk, simply state, "Yes, we can live with that," and then document everything for the next RM review cycle.

The difficulty lies in the process of formalizing exactly what the organization "can live with." This process is the heart of risk appetite, the quantity and nature of risk that organizations are willing to accept as they evaluate the trade-offs between perfect cybersecurity and unlimited accessibility. Documenting risk appetite as part of the RM framework development effort is often a vague and poorly understood proposition. Selecting responses informed by risk appetite will involve trade-offs. Choosing to address one risk may have impacts on other risks, so risk-driven decisions require careful consideration of the impact of various choices.

According to KPMG, a global network of professional firms providing audit, tax, and advisory services:

A well-defined risk appetite should have the following characteristics:

- Reflective of strategy, including organizational objectives, business plans, and stakeholder expectations
- Reflective of all key aspects of the business
- Acknowledges a willingness and capacity to take on risk
- Is documented as a formal risk appetite statement
- Considers the skills, resources, and technology required to manage and monitor risk exposures in the context of risk appetite
- Is inclusive of a tolerance for loss or negative events that can be reasonably quantified
- Is periodically reviewed and reconsidered with reference to evolving industry and market conditions
- Has been approved by the board[3]

The KPMG approach to defining risk appetite involves understanding the organization's strategic objectives, defining risk profiles for each major current organizational activity and future strategic plan, and defining a risk tolerance (or risk threshold)—the assessment of the amount of risk an organization is willing to accept for a particular information asset or set of assets, typically synthesized into the organization's overall risk appetite for each profile. This is shown in a risk appetite statement, a formal document developed by the organization that specifies its overall willingness to accept risk to its information assets, based on a synthesis of individual risk tolerances.

Risk tolerance works closely with risk appetite, as it more clearly defines the range of acceptable risk for each initiative, plan, or activity. If an administrator is asked what level of attack success and loss they are willing to accept for a particular system, the answer should provide insight into the risk threshold for that system, as well as that for the data it stores and processes. If the answer to the question is "absolutely none," the administrator has a zero tolerance risk exposure—an extreme level of risk acceptance whereby the organization is unwilling to allow any successful attacks or suffer any loss to an information asset—which will require the highest (and perhaps unavailable or unreasonably expensive) level of protection. A realistic tolerance usually falls somewhere between "sporadic hardware/software issues" and "total destruction." The reality is that zero risk is not achievable when system services must be delivered.

The synthesis of risk thresholds becomes the risk appetite for the organization. Risk thresholds are more tactical or operational in nature, and the risk appetite is more strategic. The final result of risk assessment is the formalization of risk appetite in the risk appetite statement, which is included in the RM framework policy.

The Risk Management Plan

The risk management plan, a document that contains specifications for the implementation and conduct of RM efforts, includes not only the specifications of the RM process but also the RM framework. The plan conducts the RM process and is used in conjunction with the RM policy to guide the collection and evaluation of risk information. What is in the RM plan? It contains a detailed set of the steps to perform in the conduct of both the RM framework and the RM process, along with supporting information on who performs each step and how. Whereas the RM policy focuses on the "why" of RM, the plan is focused on the "how," although both will address the "who" for their respective parts. Some organizations may combine the two into a single cohesive document; however, they should be kept separate to better support maintenance and review. The organization typically refers to the developed framework as "the plan" because it represents the formal documentation of the framework's concepts.

Framework Implementation

Once the framework team has finished designing the RM program, including both the framework and the process, it begins implementing the program. As with any major project, this involves specifying both the leader and the project manager for the process and laying out the detailed implementation methodology. The RM process, which is specified in the right half of Figure 3-1, provides general steps to follow in the conduct of risk evaluation and remediation and is designed to be intentionally vague so it can be easily adapted.

The implementation of the RM plan, specifically including the RM process, could be based on several traditional IT implementation methods, typically after the organization has distributed the plan to all managers affected by the program for a "desk check" prior to deployment.

- The organization could pilot-test it in a small area to gauge initial issues and success prior to deployment across the entire organization.
- The organization may use a phased approach in which only a portion of the RM program is initially implemented, such as initial meetings with key managers or initial inventory of information assets.
- The bold organization may simply choose a direct cutover (also known as a cold-turkey conversion) in which the new RM project is launched across the entire organization.

Whatever rollout method is selected, it is important for the RM framework team to carefully monitor, communicate, and review the implementation so it can detect and address issues before they become threatening to the viability of the program, as discussed in the next section.

Framework Monitoring and Review

After the initial implementation and as the RM effort proceeds, the framework team continues to monitor the conduct of the RM process while simultaneously reviewing the utility and relative success of the framework planning function itself. In the first few iterations, the framework team will examine how successful it was in designing and implementing the RM framework, plan, and RM process, and what issues required adjustments of each. The framework itself only exists as a methodology to design and implement the process, so once the framework is documented in the RM plan, the success of the process becomes the greatest concern. Failures in the framework's planning process may be relatively simple to resolve if addressed early, but issues downstream in the actual RM process may require redesign all the way back up to the framework and then modification of the RM plan. Performance measures, which are described in detail in a later chapter, are often used to collect data about the RM process and determine its relative success or failure. The results of these assessments are used in the continuous improvement stage, which is described next.

Once the RM process is implemented and operating, the framework team is primarily concerned with the monitoring and review of the overall RM process cycle. However, until the framework and plan are implemented and operational, the framework team is also concerned with oversight of the RM framework and plan. The governance group also expects regular feedback on the entire RM program, including information about the relative success and progress of both the framework and process activities.

Continuous Improvement

Continuous improvement, as you will learn in greater detail in a later chapter, is a maintenance process that implements a formal program designed to continuously review and improve any type of organizational effort. Using the methodologies described in Figure 3-1, the organization formalizes its commitment to review the RM plan (both the framework and process) on a regular, recurring basis, to continuously compare outcomes from past and current performance against the desired outcomes, and to make any needed changes to keep the project working toward those desired outcomes. The difference between current outcomes and the ideal outcomes envisioned is commonly referred to as the gap; the assessment between the two is known as a gap analysis.

The performance measures implemented in the RM process provide the data used to assess the performance outcome of the overall RM effort. As the team continues to assess the performance of the RM effort, it can adjust the plans for future RM cycles to improve past performance and increase the probability of success of future iterations.

Self-Check

1. Sun Tzu's philosophy implies that knowing both the enemy and oneself is crucial for cybersecurity RM.

    a. True   **b.** False

2. A cybersecurity RM program's existence alone is sufficient for effective RM.

    a. True   **b.** False

3. Every organization should adopt the same RM framework and process.

    a. True   **b.** False

□ Check your answers at the end of this chapter.

The Risk Management Process

During the implementation phase of the RM framework, the RM plan guides the implementation of the RM process, in which risk evaluation and remediation of key assets are conducted. The three communities of interest must work together to address every level of risk, ranging from full-scale disasters to the smallest mistake made by an employee. To do so, representatives from each community collaborate to be actively involved in RM process activities. This process uses the specific knowledge and perspective of the team to complete the following tasks:

- Establishing the context, which includes understanding both the organization's internal and external operating environments and other factors that could impact the RM process

- Identifying risk, which includes:
  - Creating an inventory of information assets
  - Classifying and organizing those assets meaningfully
  - Assigning a value to each information asset
  - Identifying threats to the valued and cataloged assets
  - Pinpointing vulnerabilities in specific assets from specific threats
- Analyzing risk, which includes:
  - Determining the likelihood that vulnerable systems will be attacked by specific threats
  - Estimating the probable impact or consequences of an attack on each information asset
  - Assessing the relative risk facing the organization's information assets, so that RM and control activities can focus on assets that require the most urgent and immediate attention
  - Calculating the risks to which assets are exposed in their current setting as a function of the probability and consequences of an attack
  - Looking in a general way at controls that might come into play for identified vulnerabilities and ways to control the risks that the assets face
  - Documenting and reporting the findings of risk identification and assessment
- Evaluating the risk to the organization's key assets and comparing identified uncontrolled risks against its risk appetite:
  - Identifying individual risk tolerances for each information asset
  - Combining or synthesizing these individual risk tolerances into a coherent risk appetite statement
- Treating the unacceptable risk:
  - Determining which treatment/control strategy is best considering the value of the information asset and which control options are cost-effective, and generating acceptable trade-offs, if applicable
  - Acquiring or installing the appropriate controls
  - Overseeing processes to ensure that the controls remain effective
- Summarizing the findings, which involves stating the conclusions of the identification, analysis, and evaluation stages of risk assessment in preparation for moving into the stage of controlling risk by exploring methods to further mitigate risk where applicable or desired

RM Process Preparation: Establishing the Context

As the RM process team convenes, it is initially briefed by representatives of the framework team and possibly by the governance group. Representatives of the framework team usually serve on the process team, at least initially, to provide ongoing guidance and information. Both the framework team and the governance group seek to provide executive guidance for the work to be performed by the RM process team, and to ensure that the team's efforts are in alignment with managerial intent, as documented in the RM policy and plan. The group is briefed on its responsibilities and set to its work. The plan is reviewed and individual assignments given.

The context in this phase is the understanding of the external and internal environments the RM team will be interacting with as it conducts the RM process. It also means understanding the RM process as defined by the framework team and having the internal knowledge and expertise to implement it. Finally, it means ensuring that all members of the RM process team understand the organization's risk appetite statement and can use the risk appetite to translate that statement into the appropriate risk treatment when the time comes.

The National Institute of Standards and Technology's (NIST) Special Publication 800-30, Revision 1, "Guide for Conducting Risk Assessments," recommends preparing for the risk process by performing the following tasks:

- Identify the purpose of the assessment.
- Identify the scope of the assessment.

- Identify the assumptions and constraints associated with the assessment.
- Identify the sources of information to be used as inputs to the assessment.
- Identify the risk model and analytic approaches (i.e., assessment and analysis approaches) to be employed during the assessment.[4]

External Context

Understanding the external context means understanding the impact the following external factors could have on the RM process, its goals, and its objectives:

- The business environment—Customers, suppliers, competitors
- The legal/regulatory/compliance environment—Laws, regulations, industry standards
- The threat environment—Threats, known vulnerabilities, attack vectors
- The support environment—Government agencies like NIST and the Cybersecurity and Infrastructure Security Agency (CISA), professional associations like the Information Systems Security Association, and service agencies such as Equifax or third-party cybersecurity consulting firms
- Other groups as appropriate

These factors should influence the organization's conduct of the RM process, its assessment methods, its findings, and most importantly, its decisions when treating risk.

Internal Context

The internal context is the understanding of the internal factors that could impact or influence the RM process:

- The organization's governance structure (or lack thereof)
- The organization's internal stakeholders
- The organization's culture
- The maturity of the organization's cybersecurity program
- The organization's experience in policy, planning, and RM in general

Self-Check

4. The RM process involves only the cybersecurity team in risk evaluation and remediation activities.
   a. True
   b. False

5. Identifying risks includes creating an inventory of information assets and assigning value to each asset.
   a. True
   b. False

6. The RM process does not require understanding both the organization's internal and external operating environments.
   a. True
   b. False

☐ Check your answers at the end of this chapter.

Risk Assessment: Risk Identification

The first operational phase of the RM process is the identification of risk. Risk identification—the recognition, enumeration, and documentation of risks to an organization's information assets—begins with the process of self-examination. As Sun Tzu stated, the organization must know itself to understand the risk to its information assets and where that risk resides. At this stage, managers must (1) identify the organization's information assets, (2) classify them, (3) categorize them into useful groups, and (4) prioritize them by overall importance. This can be a daunting task, but it must be done to identify weaknesses and the threats they present.

The RM process team must initially confirm or define the categories and classifications to be used for the information assets, once identified. Some organizations prefer to collect the inventory first and then see what natural categories and classifications emerge; those areas are discussed later in this book. Once the RM team has its organization formalized, it begins with the first major task of risk identification.

Identification of Information Assets

The risk identification process begins with the identification and cataloging of information assets, including people, procedures, data, software, hardware, and networking elements. This step should be performed without prejudging the value of each asset; values will be assigned later in the process. One of the toughest challenges in the RM process is identifying information assets with precision for the purposes of RM. In the most general sense, an information asset is any asset that collects, stores, processes, or transmits information, or any collection, set, or database of information that is of value to the organization. For these purposes, the terms "data" and "information" are commonly used interchangeably. In some RM efforts, information and its supporting technologies—hardware, software, data, networking, and personnel—are defined separately, and the decision whether to include a specific category or component is made by the RM process team.

Some commercial RM applications simplify the decision by separating information assets from **information media** (or **system components**), which are system elements such as hardware, operating systems, applications, and utilities that collect, store, process, and transmit information. In this context, media are ignored, leaving only the data and applications containing internal data storage as information assets for the purposes of RM. When an application interfaces with an external database, data set, or data file, the data is treated as an information asset while the application is treated as media. When an application has data that is integral to its operations, it is treated as an information asset. By separating components that are much easier to replace (hardware, operating systems, and applications) from the information assets that are in some cases almost irreplaceable, the RM effort becomes much more straightforward. After all, what is the organization most concerned with? Is it the physical server used to host a critical application, or is it the information? Servers, switches, routers, and most host technologies are easy to replace. If a server dies, the organization simply purchases a new one or re-tasks an existing one and then loads the applications and data that give that server purpose in the organization. If an application dies, the organization can reinstall it or restore it from backup. Lost data is not so easily recovered. This is not to insinuate that these assets don't have value to the organization, but that they are not necessarily integral to an RM program. If an application has been internally developed or heavily customized, replacement may be much more complicated than simply reinstalling off-the-shelf software, and the application may be defined as an information asset for that reason.

Some organizations choose to focus narrowly during their initial RM process, then add more information assets in later iterations. They may begin with data and core applications, then add communications software, operating systems, and supporting utilities, and finally add physical assets. This approach may be best for organizations just starting out in RM. The bottom line is that the RM process team should decide and define exactly what constitutes an information asset for the purposes of the RM effort so it can effectively and efficiently manage the scope and focus of the effort.

Table 3-1 shows a model outline of some information assets the organization may choose to include or exclude in its RM effort. These assets are categorized as follows:

- The people asset can be divided into internal personnel (employees) and external personnel (non-employees). Insiders can be further divided into employees who hold trusted roles and therefore have correspondingly greater authority and accountability, and regular staff members who do not have any special privileges. Outsiders consist of other users who have access to the organization's information assets; some are trusted and some are not.

Table 3-1   Organizational assets used in systems

Information System Components	Risk Management Components	Example Risk Management Components
People	Internal personnel External personnel	Trusted employees Other staff members People trusted outside the organization Strangers
Procedures	Procedures	IT and business standard procedures IT and business-sensitive procedures
Data	Data/information	Transmission Processing Storage
Software	Software	Applications Operating systems Utilities Security components
Hardware	Hardware	Systems and peripherals Mobile devices Personal devices connected to organizational networks Security devices Network-attached process control devices and other embedded systems (Internet of Things)
Networking	Networking	Local area network components Intranet components Internet or extranet components Cloud-based components

- Procedures can be information assets because they are used to create value for the organization. They can be divided into IT and business standard procedures and IT and business-sensitive procedures. Sensitive procedures have the potential to enable an attack or to otherwise introduce risk to the organization. For example, the procedures used by a telecommunications company to activate new circuits pose special risks because they reveal aspects of the inner workings of a critical process, which can be subverted by outsiders for the purpose of obtaining unbilled, illicit services.

- The data asset includes information in all states: transmission, processing, and storage. This is an expanded use of the term "data," which is usually associated with data sets and databases as well as the full range of information used by modern organizations.

- Software can be divided into applications, operating systems, utilities, and cybersecurity components. Software that provides cybersecurity controls may fall into the operating systems or applications category but is differentiated by the fact that it is part of the cybersecurity control environment and must therefore be protected more thoroughly than other systems components.

- Hardware can be divided into the usual systems devices and their peripherals and the devices that are part of cybersecurity control systems. The latter must be protected more thoroughly than the former.

- Networking components can include networking devices (such as firewalls, routers, and switches) and the systems software within them, which is often the focal point of attacks, with successful attacks continuing against systems connected to the networks. Of course, most of today's computer systems include networking elements. You will have to determine whether a device is primarily a computer or primarily a networking device. A server computer that is used exclusively as a firewall or a proxy server may be classified as a networking component, while an identical server configured as a database server may be classified as hardware. For this reason, networking devices should be considered separately rather than combined with general hardware and software components.

In some approaches to RM, this list may be simplified into three groups: People, Processes, and Technology. Regardless of which approach is used in the development of the RM process, an organization should ensure that all its information resources are properly identified, assessed, and managed for risk.

Identifying Hardware, Software, and Network Assets

Many organizations use asset inventory applications to keep track of their hardware, network, and software components. Numerous packages are available, and it is up to the CSO or the CIO to determine which package best serves the needs of the organization. Organizations that do not use a packaged inventory system must create an equivalent manual or automated process. Note that the number of items and large quantity of data per item can quickly overwhelm any manual system and might stress poorly designed automated inventory systems.

Whether automated or manual, the inventory process requires a certain amount of planning. Most importantly, you must determine which attributes of each of these information assets should be tracked. That determination will depend on the needs of the organization and its RM efforts as well as the preferences and needs of the cybersecurity and IT communities. When deciding which attributes to track for each information asset, consider the following list of potential attributes:

- Name—Some organizations may have several names for the same product, and each of them should be cross-referenced in the inventory. This redundancy rationalizes the usage across the organization. No matter how many names you track or how you select a name, always provide a definition of the asset in question. A recommended practice is to adopt naming standards that do not convey critical information to potential system attackers. For instance, a server named CUSTOMER_DB or HQ_FINANCE may entice attackers.

- Asset tag—This is used to facilitate the tracking of physical assets. Asset tags are unique numbers assigned to assets and permanently affixed to tangible assets during the acquisition process.

- Internet Protocol (IP) address—This attribute may be useful for network devices and servers at some organizations, but it rarely applies to software. This practice is limited when the organization uses the Dynamic Host Configuration Protocol within TCP/IP, which reassigns IP numbers to devices as needed. In such cases, there is no value in using IP numbers as part of the asset-identification process.

- Media access control (MAC) address—As per the TCP/IP standard, all network-interface hardware devices have a unique number called the MAC address (also called an electronic serial number or a hardware address). The network operating system uses this number to identify specific network devices. The client's network software uses it to recognize traffic that it needs to process. In most settings, MAC addresses can be a useful way to track connectivity, but they can be spoofed by some hardware/software combinations. Note that some devices may have multiple network interfaces, each with their own MAC address, and others may have configurable MAC addresses, making them even less useful as a unique identifier. Given the possibility of MAC address spoofing, many organizations have stopped using them as a reliable identifier.

- Asset type—This attribute describes the function of each asset. For hardware assets, a list of possible asset types that includes servers, desktops, networking devices, and test equipment should be developed. For software assets, a list that includes operating systems, custom applications by type (accounting, human resources, or payroll, to name a few), and packaged applications and/or specialty applications (such as firewall programs) should be developed. The degree of specificity is determined by the needs of the organization. Asset types can be recorded at two or more levels of specificity by first recording one attribute that classifies the asset at a high level and then adding attributes for more detail. For example, one server might be listed as follows:

- DeviceClass = S (Server)
- DeviceOS = Win22 (Windows 2022)
- DeviceCapacity = AS (Advanced Server)

- Serial number—This is a number that uniquely identifies a specific device. Some software vendors also assign a software serial number to each instance of the program licensed by an organization.

- Manufacturer name—This attribute can be useful for analyzing threat outbreaks when specific manufacturers announce specific vulnerabilities.

- Manufacturer's model or part number—This number identifies exactly what the asset is; it can be very useful in the later analysis of vulnerabilities because some threats apply only to specific models of certain devices and/or software components.

- Software version, update revision, or FCO number—This attribute includes information about software and firmware versions and, for hardware devices, the current field change order number. A field change order (FCO) occurs when a manufacturer performs an upgrade to a hardware component at the customer's premises. Tracking this information is particularly important when inventorying networking devices that function mainly through the software running on them. For example, a firewall device may have three version numbers associated with it: a Basic Input/Output System (BIOS) firmware version, the running operating system version, and the firewall appliance application software version. Each organization will have to determine which of these version numbers will be tracked or if they want to track all three.

- Software licensing data—The nature and number of an organization's software licenses, as well as where they are deployed, can be a critically important asset. Because licenses for software products are often tied to specific version numbers, geographic locations, or even specific users, this data may require specialized efforts to track.

- Physical location—This attribute does not apply to software elements. Nevertheless, some organizations may have license terms that indicate where software can be used. This may include systems leased at remote locations (so-called "co-lo equipment"), often described as being "in the cloud."

- Logical location—This attribute specifies where an asset can be found on the organization's network. The logical location is most applicable to networking devices and indicates the logical network segment (including virtual local area networks) that houses the device.

- Controlling entity—This refers to the organizational unit that controls the asset. In some organizations, a remote location's onsite staff could be placed in control of network devices; in other organizations, a central corporate group might control all the network devices. The inventory should determine which group controls each asset because the controlling group will want a voice in determining how much risk that device can tolerate and how much expense can be sustained to add controls.

Identifying People, Procedures, and Data Assets

Personnel, documentation, and data information assets are not as readily identified and documented as hardware and software, if for no other reason than they are not under the direct control and authority of the IT department. Responsibility for identifying, describing, and evaluating these information assets should be assigned to managers who possess the necessary knowledge, experience, and judgment. As these assets are identified, they should be recorded via a reliable data-handling process like the one used for hardware and software.

The record-keeping system should be flexible, allowing you to link assets to attributes based on the nature of the information asset being tracked. Basic attributes for various classes of assets include the following:

People

- Position name/number/ID—Avoid names; use position titles, roles, or functions
- Supervisor name/number/ID—Avoid names; use position titles, roles, or functions
- Security clearance level
- Special skills

Procedures

- Description
- Intended purpose
- Software/hardware/networking elements to which the procedure is tied
- Location where procedure documents are stored for reference
- Location where documents are stored for update purposes

Data

- Classification
- Owner/creator/manager
- Size of data structure
- Data organization used (e.g., hierarchical, sequential, or relational)
- Online or offline; if online, whether accessible from outside the organization or not
- Physical location
- Media access method (e.g., through user client desktops, laptops, mobile media, etc.)
- Backup procedures, timeline, and backup storage locations

Consider carefully what should be tracked for specific assets. Larger organizations often find that they can effectively track only a few valuable facts about the most critical information assets. For instance, a company may track only an IP address, server name, and device type for its mission-critical servers. The organization might forgo additional attribute tracking on all devices and completely omit the tracking of the applications on desktop or laptop systems. As you will learn later in the text, several commercial applications can assist with the collection, organization, and management of these inventories. As shown in Figure 3-2, the Clearwater IRM|Analysis application has detailed fields in its asset inventory list to assist in the inventory and description of information assets, once that information has been collected.

Classifying and Categorizing Information Assets

Once the initial inventory is assembled, you must determine whether its asset categories are meaningful to the organization's RM program. Such a review may cause managers to further subdivide the categories presented in Table 3-1 or create new categories that better meet the needs of the RM program. For example, if the category "Internet Components" is deemed too general, it could be further divided into subcategories of servers, networking devices (routers, hubs, switches), protection devices (firewalls, proxies), and cabling.

The inventory should also reflect the sensitivity and cybersecurity priority assigned to each information asset. A data classification scheme—the assignment of levels of confidentiality to information assets as part of an access control methodology, designed to restrict the number of people who can access it—should be developed (or reviewed, if already in place). This scheme also can assist in categorizing information assets based on their sensitivity and cybersecurity needs. A typical organization may not need a complex classification scheme and may be able to operate with only three levels, such as confidential, internal-use only, and

Figure 3-2   Clearwater IRM|Analysis information asset description

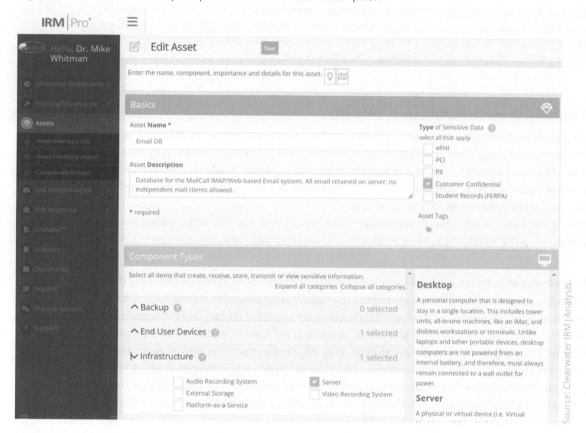

public. Each of these classification levels influences the amount of protection needed for a particular information asset. Classification categories must be comprehensive and mutually exclusive. "Comprehensive" means that all inventoried assets fit into a category; "mutually exclusive" means that each asset is found in only one category.

Some asset types, such as personnel, require an alternative classification scheme that identifies the level of information the individual may access. This scheme is called a security clearance, or clearance level, which specifies the maximum classification of information the individual is authorized to access. For example, one employee might be given a "confidential" clearance while another only receives an "internal use only" clearance. Keep in mind that having a clearance doesn't automatically grant the individual the ability to access information. It is further restricted by their position requirements and need to know.

As you would expect, organizations that need higher levels of cybersecurity, including government agencies, will have very complex data classification schemes. The degree of cybersecurity will depend on a number of factors, primarily whether the information is determined to be National Security Information (NSI) or not (Non-NSI). A number of presidential executive orders have defined the security classifications within these two categories; in 2009, Executive Order 13526 affirmed the use of "Top Secret," "Secret," and "Confidential" as the primary classifications for NSI information.[5] Previous administrations used a relatively simple structure of "For Official Use Only (FOUO)," "Sensitive But Unclassified (SBU)," and "Law Enforcement Sensitive (LES)" categories for Non-NSI information, but the structure has evolved into a rather complex collection of specialized categories, each with multiple subcategories, in spite of the executive order's declaration that it was simplifying and standardizing the process. For most organizations, there is no need for such a complex approach, and the simple public-internal-confidential model described previously is sufficient. For organizations that need higher levels of cybersecurity for very sensitive data, such as research and development (R&D), additional levels can be added above "classified."

Note 1 | For more information on governmental cybersecurity classifications, read Executive Order 13526 (for NSI) at www.federalregister.gov/documents/2010/01/05/E9-31418/classified-national-security-information or Executive Order 13556 for Non-NSI (www.federalregister.gov/documents/2010/11/09/2010-28360/controlled-unclassified-information).

Assessing the Value of Information Assets

As each information asset is identified, categorized, and classified, a relative value must be assigned to it. Relative values are comparative judgments intended to ensure that the most valuable information assets are given the highest priority when managing risk. It is practically impossible to know in advance—in absolute economic terms—what losses will be incurred if an asset is compromised; however, a relative assessment helps to ensure that the higher-value assets are protected first.

As each information asset is assigned to its proper category, posing the following basic questions can help you develop the weighting criteria to be used for information asset valuation or impact determination.

- Which information asset is the most critical to the success of the organization? When determining the relative importance of each information asset, refer to the organization's mission statement or statement of objectives. From this source, determine which assets are essential for meeting the organization's objectives, which assets support the objectives, and which are merely adjuncts. For example, a manufacturing company that makes aircraft engines may decide the process control systems that control the machine tools on the assembly line are the first order of importance. Although shipping and receiving data entry consoles are important to those functions, they may be less critical if alternatives are available or can be easily arranged. Another example is an online organization such as Amazon.com. Web e-commerce servers that advertise the company's products and receive its orders 24 hours a day are essential, whereas the desktop systems used by the customer service department to answer emails from clients are less critical.

- Which information asset contributes the most to revenue generation? The relative value of an information asset depends on its impact on organizational revenue—or, in the case of a nonprofit organization, how it impacts the delivery of services. Some organizations have different systems in place for each line of business or service they offer. Which of these assets plays the biggest role in generating revenue or delivering services?

- Which information asset contributes the most to profitability? Managers should evaluate how much profit depends on a particular asset. For instance, at Amazon.com, some servers support the book sales operations, others support the auction process, and still others support the customer book review database. Which of these servers contributes the most to profitability? Although important, the review database server does not directly contribute to profit generation. Note the distinction between revenues and profits: Organizations may have different product or service lines. When comparing multiple systems that all support revenue generation, which systems support the most profitable products? In nonprofit organizations, you can determine what percentage of the agency's clientele receives services from the information asset being evaluated.

- Which information asset is the most expensive to maintain or replace? Sometimes an information asset acquires special value because it is unique. Other assets may require specialized, and expensive, maintenance expertise. If an enterprise still uses a Model-129 keypunch machine to create special punch-card entries for a critical batch run, for example, that machine may be worth more than its cost, because spare parts or repair personnel may no longer be available. Another example is a specialty device with a long delivery time frame because of manufacturing or transportation requirements. Organizations must control the risk of loss or damage to such unique assets—for example, by buying and storing a backup device or seeking to train personnel in-house to support maintenance.

- Which information asset is the most expensive to protect? Some assets are by their nature difficult to protect, and formulating a complete answer to this question may not be possible until the risk identification phase is complete because the costs of controls cannot be computed until the controls are identified. However, you can still make a preliminary assessment of the relative difficulty of establishing controls for each asset.

- Which information asset's loss or compromise would cause the greatest liability or be the most embarrassing? Almost every organization is aware of its image in the local, national, and international spheres. Loss or exposure of some assets would prove especially embarrassing. Lifelock, a company that sells identity theft protection, is famous for its CEO publishing his Social Security number. In 2007, a thief used that number at a check cashing company to get a $500 loan. The company was also in the news in 2011 for failing to comply with Federal Trade Commission orders to resolve their own protection methods.[6] The company made the news again in 2018 when a third-party website that managed Lifelock's email subscriptions had a vulnerability that allowed thieves to extract customer account numbers and their email addresses.[7]

As you can see, most of these questions can be answered relatively by comparing a group of assets rather than by determining a specific financial worth. If the organization desires more specific, quantitative values, there are additional questions in the next chapter. You can use a worksheet, such as the one shown in Figure 3-3, to collect the answers to the preceding list of questions for later analysis. You may also need to identify and add other institution-specific questions to the evaluation process.

Throughout this chapter, numbers are assigned to example assets to illustrate the concepts being discussed. This highlights one of the challenging issues in RM. While other industries use actuarially derived sources to make estimates, cybersecurity RM lacks such data. Many organizations use a variety of estimating methods to assess values. Some in the industry question the use of "guesstimated" values in calculations with other estimated values, claiming this degree of uncertainty undermines the entire RM endeavor. Research in this field is ongoing, and you are encouraged to study the sections in the next chapter that discuss alternative

Figure 3-3   Sample asset classification scheme

System Name: ___SLS E-Commerce_____
Date Evaluated: ___February 2024_____
Evaluated By: ___D. Jones_____

Information assets	Data classification	Impact to profitability
Information Transmitted:		
EDI Document Set 1 — Logistics BOL to outsourcer (outbound)	Confidential	High
EDI Document Set 2 — Supplier orders (outbound)	Confidential	High
EDI Document Set 2 — Supplier fulfillment advice (inbound)	Confidential	Medium
Customer order via SSL (inbound)	Confidential	Critical
Customer service Request via e-mail (inbound)	Private	Medium
DMZ Assets:		
Edge Router	Public	Critical
Web server #1 — home page and core site	Public	Critical
Web server #2 — Application server	Private	Critical

Notes: BOL: Bill of Lading
DMZ: Demilitarized Zone
EDI: Electronic Data Interchange
SSL: Secure Sockets Layer

techniques for qualitative RM. Figure 3-4 illustrates a simplistic method that can be used to value an information asset by determining its "importance," as used in Clearwater IRM|Analysis.

Figure 3-4   Clearwater IRM|Analysis information asset importance

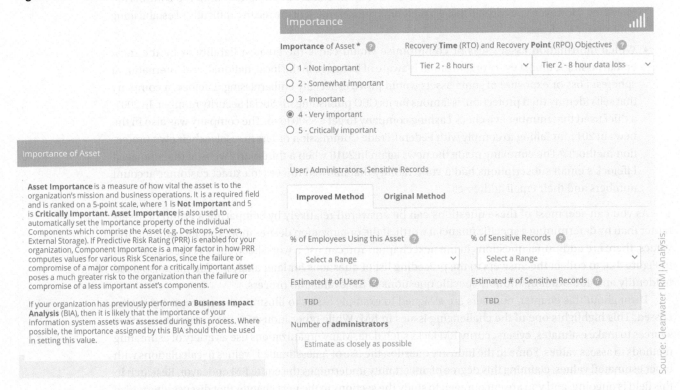

Prioritizing (Rank Ordering) Information Assets

The final step in the risk identification process is to prioritize, or rank order, the assets. This goal can be achieved by using a weighted table analysis, also known as a decision matrix, like the one shown in Table 3-2. In this process, each information asset is listed in the first column. Next, the relevant criteria that the organization wants to use to value the assets are listed in the top row. Next, each criterion is assigned a weight or value that typically sums to 100 (as in 100 percent), or some other value that is easy to sum. The use of these weights is what gives this analysis its name. Next, the organization assigns a value to each asset, again using a scale of 0–1.0, 5, 10, or 100, based on the specified value criteria. Table 3-2 uses values from 1 (unimportant) to 5 (critical). Finally, each information asset's cell values are multiplied by the criteria weights and then summed to create the weighted score for that information asset. Sorting the table by the weighted scores results in a prioritized list of information assets. Such tables can be used as a method of valuing information assets by ranking them based on criteria specified by the organization. This method may prove to be much more straightforward than a raw estimation based on some other more ambiguous criteria.

A quick review of Table 3-2 shows that "Customer order via SSL (inbound)" is the most important asset on this worksheet, and that "EDI Document Set 2—Supplier fulfillment advice (inbound)" is the least critical asset.

Associating Information Assets with Media

For organizations that distinguish between information assets and the media used to access that information, it is important to specify that access. Several applications provide an assessment of the general vulnerabilities that may arise from using various media in association with information assets. There are methods to identify unique and specific vulnerabilities using techniques described in the next section and later in the book. Figure 3-5 illustrates the use of Clearwater IRM|Analysis to associate assets with media.

Table 3-2 Example of a weighted factor analysis worksheet

Information Asset	Criterion 1: Impact on Revenue (weight 30%)	Criterion 2: Impact on Profitability (weight 40%)	Criterion 3: Impact on Public Image (weight 30%)	Weighted Score
Customer order via SSL (inbound)	5	5	5	5
EDI Document Set 2–Supplier orders (outbound)	4	3	3	3.3
EDI Document Set 1–Logistics bill of lading to outsourcer (outbound)	3	4	2	3.1
Customer service request via email (inbound)	2	2	4	2.6
EDI Document Set 2–Supplier fulfillment advice (inbound)	2	3	2	2.4

Scale: 5 = Critical to 1 = Unimportant; 0 = Not Applicable

Note: In the table, EDI is electronic data interchange and SSL is Secure Sockets Layer.

Figure 3-5 Clearwater IRM|Analysis information asset/component grouping

Source: Clearwater IRM | Analysis.

Threat Assessment

As mentioned at the beginning of this chapter, one of the primary goals of risk identification is to assess the circumstances and setting of each information asset to reveal any vulnerabilities. Armed with a properly classified inventory, you can assess potential weaknesses in each information asset and identify any attackers that could take advantage of those weaknesses, a process known as **threat assessment**. This evaluation of threats to information assets includes a determination of their likelihood of occurrence and potential impact of an attack.

Every organization faces a wide variety of threats. If you assume that every threat can and will attack every information asset, then the project scope becomes too complex and unwieldy. To improve the process, each step in threat identification and vulnerability identification is managed separately and then coordinated at the end. At every step, the manager is called on to leverage their judgment and experience to make the process function smoothly.

Identifying Threats

Earlier in this book you learned about the 12 categories of threats to information assets, which are repeated in Table 3-3. Each of these threats presents a unique challenge to cybersecurity and must be handled with specific controls that directly address the specific threat and its typical attack strategy. Before threats can be assessed in the risk identification process, however, each threat must be further examined to determine its potential to affect the targeted information asset. This is the primary focus of a threat assessment.

Table 3-3   The 12 categories of threats to cybersecurity

Category of Threat	Examples
Deviations in services	Utility service problems (Internet, phone, power, water, etc.)
Espionage or trespass	Unauthorized access and/or data disclosure
Forces of nature	Fire, floods, earthquakes, lightning, etc.
Human error or failure	Social engineering, accidents, or employee mistakes
Information extortion	Blackmail threatening information denial or disclosure
Intellectual property compromises	Piracy, copyright infringement, R&D disclosure
Sabotage or vandalism	Unauthorized modification or destruction of systems or information
Software attacks	Malware, website spoofing, or denial of service
Technical hardware failures or errors	Equipment failure
Technical software failures or errors	Bugs or code problems
Technological obsolescence	Antiquated or outdated technologies
Theft	Illegal confiscation of equipment or information

Source: *Communications of the ACM.*

Assessing Threats

Not all threats endanger every information asset, of course. Examine each of the categories in Table 3-3 and eliminate any that do not apply to your organization or your assets. It is unlikely that an organization can eliminate an entire category of threats, but even eliminating a few speeds up the threat assessment process. The following section, "Threats to Cybersecurity: Industry Surveys," describes the threats that some CIOs of major companies identified for their organizations. Although the section directly addresses only cybersecurity, note that a weighted ranking of threats should be compiled for any information asset that is at risk.

The amount of danger posed by a threat is sometimes difficult to assess. It may be tied to the probability that the threat will attack the organization, or it may reflect the amount of damage that the threat could create or the frequency with which the attack may occur. The big question every organization wants to answer is, "Which threats represent the greatest danger to our information assets in its current environment?" Posing the following questions can help you find an answer by understanding the various threats the organization faces and their potential effects on an information asset:

- Which threats represent an actual danger to our information assets? If there is no possibility a threat can attack an asset, it can be safely ignored. For example, the odds of certain natural disasters vary greatly based on an organization's geographic locations. An organization located on the plains of Oklahoma shouldn't worry about tidal waves, mudslides, or other events that are extremely uncommon in that region. Similarly, an organization that doesn't use a particular software or hardware package doesn't need to worry about threats to vulnerabilities in those items.

- Which threats are internal, and which are external? Some threat environments require different approaches, while some defenses address threats from multiple environments. Understanding the potential source of a threat helps to prioritize it.

- Which threats have the highest probability of success? A threat with a low probability of success is of less concern than one with a high probability of success. Some of the attacks conducted by threats require extremely complicated attack exploits or highly sophisticated attack skills. The more complicated the exploit or the more expert the attacker must be for the attack to occur, the less the organization should worry about it. This question essentially asks, "If attacked, would this threat be able to access my information assets?" The probability or likelihood of a successful attack is one of the variables in the calculation of risk.

- Which threats could result in the greatest loss if successful? Of equal concern is understanding what damage could result from a successful attack by a threat. A threat with a high probability of success that would cause little or no impact is of less concern than a threat with a lower chance of success that would create a much greater loss to an organization. For example, threats that would result in website defacement are typically of less concern to an organization than threats that seek to steal customer information. The impact or consequences of a successful attack is another variable in the calculation of risk.

- Which threats is the organization least prepared to handle? If the organization is ill-prepared to handle an attack from a specific threat, it should give priority to that threat in its preparations and planning. This issue becomes increasingly important when rolling out new technologies, starting new business ventures, or making any other change in the organization in which the cybersecurity function finds itself in new competitive and threat environments.

- Which threats cost the most to protect against? Another factor that affects the danger posed by a particular threat is the amount it would cost to protect against that threat. Some threats carry a nominal cost to protect against (e.g., malicious code), while others are very expensive, as in protection from forces of nature. Especially in small to medium-sized businesses, the budget may be insufficient to cover all the defensive strategies the organization would like to implement; as a result, some threat prioritization may boil down simply to available funds. Here again, the manager ranks, rates, or attempts to quantify the level of danger associated with protecting against a particular threat by using the same techniques as for calculating recovery costs. (See the following section to examine what issues executives focus their efforts on financially.)

- Which threats cost the most to recover from? One of the calculations that guides corporate spending on controls is the cost of recovery operations if an attack occurs and is successful. At this preliminary phase, it is not necessary to conduct a detailed assessment of the costs associated with recovering from a particular attack. An estimate or scaled approach will work, as the goal at this phase is to provide a rough assessment of the cost to recover normal business operations if the attack interrupts them.

As you will discover in the next chapter, you can use quantitative and/or qualitative measures to rank values. The preceding questions can be used as categories in a weighted table analysis of threats, like the asset analysis described earlier in this chapter. Because information in this case is preliminary, an organization may simply want to identify threats that top the list for each question.

The preceding list of questions may not cover everything that affects risk assessment. An organization's specific guidelines or policies should influence the process and will inevitably require that some additional questions be answered.

Threats to Cybersecurity: Industry Surveys

What are the threats to cybersecurity according to top computing executives?

Table 3-4 presents data collected in a study published in the *Journal of Information Systems Security* and based on a previous study published in the *Communications of the ACM* that asked that very question. Based

Table 3-4   Weighted ranks of threats to cybersecurity[8,9]

Categories of Threats	2003 Rank	2012 Rank
Espionage or trespass	4	1
Software attacks	1	2
Human error or failure	3	3
Theft	7	4
Intellectual property compromises	9	5
Sabotage or vandalism	5	6
Technical software failures or errors	2	7
Technical hardware failures or errors	6	8
Forces of nature	8	9
Deviations in services	10	10
Technological obsolescence	11	11
Information extortion	12	12

Sources: *Journal of Information Systems Security* and *Communications of the ACM.*

on the categories of threats presented earlier, more than 1,000 top computing executives were asked to rate each threat category.

In 2024, the commercial insurance organization Embroker provided their ranking of the top 10 cybersecurity threats, as listed in Table 3-5.

While the threats shown in Table 3-5 differ from the categories discussed in Table 3-4 and elsewhere in this text, three key points arise. First, regardless of how you label threats, they are still prevalent and of great concern to an organization. Second, the top threat of social engineering indicates that an organization's stakeholders, especially its employees, are still one of the greatest threats to its information. Most of the rest of the threats have a basis in human errors or failures—mistakes, failures to configure, patch, and update, and exposures from working remotely. Finally, the COVID-19 pandemic set cybersecurity back significantly as employees worked from home on unsecured systems and often over insecure networks. Attackers took advantage of these weaknesses and increased their efforts to breach and disrupt organizations.

Another survey of computing executives asked the following question: "In your organization's RM efforts, what basis do you use to assess threats?" Multiple responses were allowed. The percentages of respondents who selected each option are shown in Table 3-6.

Prioritizing Threats

Just as it did with information assets, the organization should conduct a weighted table analysis with threats. The organization should list the categories of threats it faces and then select categories that correspond to the questions of interest described earlier. Next, it assigns a weighted value to each question category, and finally it assigns a value to each threat with respect to each question category. The result is a prioritized list of threats the organization can use to determine the relative severity of each threat facing its assets. In extreme cases, the organization may want to perform such an assessment of each threat by asset, if the severity of each threat is different depending on the nature of the information asset under evaluation.

Vulnerability Assessment

Once the organization has identified and prioritized both its information assets and the threats facing those assets, it can begin to compare information assets to threats. This review leads to the creation of a list of vulnerabilities that remain potential risks to the organization. Vulnerabilities represent specific avenues that

Table 3-5   Top 10 cybersecurity threats of 2024[10]

1. Social engineering	According to Verizon, an estimated 85 percent of all data breaches involve human interaction.[11]
2. Third-party exposure	According to an FBI report, the dramatic shift to work-from-home employees associated with the COVID-19 pandemic has resulted in a 300 percent increase in attacks. This level of remote work makes it easier for criminals to exploit systems.
3. Configuration mistakes	Rapid7 reports that 80 percent of its penetration tests found an exploitable misconfiguration.[12]
4. Poor cyber hygiene	**Cyber hygiene**, the individual decisions made and practices used when interacting with computing technology, addresses things like password storage, changes, reuse, and use of unsecured networks (e.g., public Wi-Fi). Our cyber hygiene habits have significant room for improvement.
5. Cloud vulnerabilities	Cloud computing and storage is the fastest-growing computing market segment, yet in 2021 Verizon found that 90 percent of the breaches identified in its analysis of over 29,000 successful attacks were the result of web application compromises.[13]
6. Mobile device vulnerabilities	The pandemic also resulted in a dramatic increase in the use of personal mobile devices for work. Check Point Software found that, in 2021, 46 percent of organizations had a cybersecurity incident that involved an employee downloading a malicious mobile application (malware).[14]
7. Internet of Things (IoT)	Both home and office are now populated with smart devices, ranging from voice-activated, AI-controlled infrastructure to Wi-Fi-enabled appliances. Between January and June 2021, over 1.5 billion breaches were successfully executed against IoT devices, according to Kaspersky.[15]
8. Ransomware	A Cybereason study on ransomware found 66 percent of respondents reported their organization had to deal with a ransomware attack. On average, there is a ransomware attack on an organization every 11 seconds.[16]
9. Poor data management	Organizations collect massive amounts of data. Data management is just as much about what you store as how you store it. Failing to protect sensitive data (e.g., healthcare, personal data, and financial data) can have direct impacts on the organization, usually from fines or lawsuits.
10. Inadequate post-attack procedures	During the time immediately after an attack, an organization is the most vulnerable. Attackers share their successes, and other attackers want to test the speed at which organizations recover. In 2021, Cybereason found that 80 percent of organizations hit with a ransomware attack were hit with additional attacks soon after.[17]

Table 3-6   Means to assess threats

Answer Options	Response Percentage
Probability of occurrence	85.4%
Reputation loss if successful	77.1%
Financial loss if successful	72.9%
Cost to protect against	64.6%
Cost to recover from successful attack	64.6%
Frequency of attack	52.1%
Competitive advantage loss if successful	35.4%
None of these	6.3%

Source: Security Executive Council.

threat agents can exploit to attack an information asset. In other words, they are chinks in the asset's armor—a flaw or weakness in an information asset, cybersecurity procedure, design, or control that can be exploited accidentally or on purpose to breach the asset, resulting in a loss. Such loss includes damage, theft, destruction, and denial of use. For example, Table 3-7 analyzes the threats to a demilitarized zone (DMZ) router and its possible vulnerabilities.

Table 3-7   Vulnerability assessment of a DMZ router

Threat	Possible Vulnerabilities
Deviations in services	Unless suitable electrical power conditioning is provided, failure is probable over time.
Espionage or trespass	The router has little intrinsic value, but other assets protected by this device could be attacked if it is compromised.
Forces of nature	All information assets in the organization are subject to forces of nature unless suitable controls are provided.
Human error or failure	Employees or contractors may cause an outage if configuration errors are made.
Information extortion	The router has little intrinsic value, but other assets protected by this device could be attacked if it is compromised.
Intellectual property compromises	The router has little intrinsic value, but other assets protected by this device could be attacked if it is compromised.
Sabotage or vandalism	IP is vulnerable to denial-of-service attacks. The device may be subject to defacement or cache poisoning.
Software attacks	IP is vulnerable to denial-of-service attacks. Outsider IP fingerprinting activities can reveal sensitive information unless suitable controls are implemented.
Technical hardware failures or errors	Hardware could fail and cause an outage. Power system failures are always possible.
Technical software failures or errors	Vendor-supplied routing software could fail and cause an outage.
Technological obsolescence	If it is not reviewed and periodically updated, a device may fall too far behind its vendor support model to be kept in service.
Theft	The router has little intrinsic value, but other assets protected by this device could be attacked if it is stolen.

A list like the one in Table 3-7 should be created for each information asset to document its vulnerability to each possible or likely attack. This list is usually long and shows all the vulnerabilities of the information asset. Some threats manifest themselves in multiple ways, yielding multiple vulnerabilities for the asset–threat pair. By necessity, the process of listing vulnerabilities is somewhat subjective and is based on the experience and knowledge of the people who create the list. Therefore, the process works best when groups of people with diverse backgrounds work together in a series of brainstorming sessions. For instance, the team that reviews the vulnerabilities for networking equipment should include networking specialists, the systems management team that operates the network, cybersecurity risk specialists, and even technically proficient users of the system.

Example Breaches

The following are some examples of noteworthy breaches.

Equifax   Sometimes, a big news event can be used to reinforce what we know about cybersecurity and provide a real-life example of the importance of RM. One such event was the Equifax data breach in 2017.

The Equifax breach was first publicly reported on September 7, 2017. A press release by the firm observed that the breach was first suspected a few weeks earlier, on July 29. Outside forensic analysis revealed that data loss began in May for as many as 143 million Americans, credit card numbers were compromised for up to 209,000 U.S. consumers, and other critical personal information was compromised for up to 182,000 additional U.S. consumers. Almost 11 million U.S. consumers had details of their drivers' licenses compromised. The latest figures indicate that as many as 145.5 million people had at least some personal information compromised.

The root cause of the breach appears to have been a cybersecurity vulnerability in a tool called Apache Struts, which is used to create web applications. Equifax was reportedly aware of the widely known vulnerability for several months before the breach was discovered.

The fallout from this event included the resignation of several senior executives at Equifax, including CEO Richard Smith, the chief information officer, and the chief information security officer.

Colonial Pipeline   In May 2021, Colonial Pipeline, which moves oil from the Gulf of Mexico to states along the U.S. East Coast, was shut down for several days. Once the pipeline was restored, it was determined that the organization had suffered a ransomware attack on some of its systems. However, the attack did not directly affect the pipeline's operational technology control systems; the pipeline was shut down by management to prevent the ransomware from spreading to those systems. Even though Colonial Pipeline brought in the security investigation organization Mandiant and notified federal agencies, including the Department of Homeland Security, the Department of Energy, the FBI, and the National Security Agency's CISA, the systems were recovered in the end by paying $4.4 million in bitcoin to attackers from the Russian-based cybercriminal organization DarkSide. The FBI eventually recovered $2.3 million of the ransom by seizing the group's digital wallet. Shortly thereafter, DarkSide issued a statement indicating that they did not realize the attack would affect critical infrastructure: "We are apolitical, we do not participate in geopolitics. . . . Our goal is to make money and not creating problems for society."[18] DarkSide later reported they were shutting down operations due to increased international attention and the loss of its funds and payment server.[19]

The TVA Worksheet

At the end of the risk identification process, an organization should have a prioritized list of assets and a prioritized list of threats facing those assets. Prioritized lists should be developed using a technique like the weighted table analysis discussed earlier.

The organization should also have a working knowledge of the vulnerabilities that exist between each threat and each asset. These lists serve as the starting point for the next step in the RM process: risk assessment. The prioritized lists of assets and threats can be combined into a Threats–Vulnerabilities–Assets (TVA) worksheet, in preparation for the addition of vulnerability and control information during risk assessment. Along one axis lies the prioritized set of assets. Table 3-8 shows the placement of assets along the horizontal axis, with the most important asset at the left. The prioritized list of threats is placed along the vertical axis, with the most important or most dangerous threat listed at the top. The resulting grid provides a convenient method of examining the "exposure" of assets, allowing a simple vulnerability assessment. We now have a starting point for our risk assessment, along with the other documents and forms.

Before you begin the risk analysis process, it may be helpful to create a list of the TVA "triplets" to facilitate your examination of the severity of vulnerabilities. For example, between Threat 1 and Asset 1, there may or may not be a vulnerability. After all, not all threats pose risks to all assets. If a pharmaceutical company's most important asset is its research and development database and it resides on a stand-alone network (i.e., one that is not connected to the Internet), then there may be no vulnerability to external hackers. If the intersection of T1 and A1 has no vulnerability, then the risk assessment team simply crosses out that box. It is much more likely, however, that one or more vulnerabilities exist between the two; as these vulnerabilities are identified, they are categorized as follows:

- T1V1A1—Vulnerability 1 that exists between Threat 1 and Asset 1
- T1V2A1—Vulnerability 2 that exists between Threat 1 and Asset 1
- T2V1A1—Vulnerability 1 that exists between Threat 2 and Asset 1 . . . and so on

Table 3-8   The TVA worksheet

	Asset 1	Asset 2	Asset 3	...	...	...	...	...	...	Asset n
Threat 1	T1V1A1 T1V2A1 T1V3A1 ...	T1V1A2 T1V2A2 ...	T1V1A3 ...	T1V1A4 ...						
Threat 2	T2V1A1 T2V2A1 ...	T2V1A2 ...	T2V1A3 ...							
Threat 3	T3V1A1 ...	T3V1A2 ...								
Threat 4	T4V1A1 ...									
Threat 5										
Threat 6										
...										
...										
Threat n										
Priority of effort	1	2	3	4	5	6	7	8	...	

These bands of controls should be continued through all asset–threat pairs.

Because some vulnerabilities may impact multiple threat–asset pairs, once this table is complete, the organization may rewrite the list of identified vulnerabilities as follows:

- Vulnerability[1,2] is a vulnerability that affects Threat 1 and Asset 2.
- Vulnerability [1,2/2,3/2,4] is a vulnerability that affects Threat 1 and Asset 2, Threat 2 and Asset 3, and Threat 2 and Asset 4.

This provides the security group with a list of vulnerabilities that affect multiple assets and allows prioritization based on widest impact.

In the risk analysis phase discussed in the next section, the assessment team examines the identified vulnerabilities and analyzes any existing controls that protect the asset from the threat or mitigate the losses that may occur. Cataloging and categorizing these controls is the next step in the risk identification process.

There is a key delineator here between risk identification and risk analysis: in developing the TVA spreadsheet, the organization is performing risk identification simply by determining whether an asset is at risk from a threat and identifying any vulnerabilities that exist. Determining or calculating the level of the asset's risk falls under risk analysis. The fine line between the two is part of the reason that many organizations follow the methodology outlined in Figure 3-1 described earlier in this chapter, then merge risk identification, risk analysis, and risk evaluation into one logical process and just call it risk assessment.

| View Point | Getting at Risk |

By George V. Hulme, an independent business and technology journalist who has covered cybersecurity for more than 20 years for such publications as *InformationWeek* and *Information Security*

The risks that organizations face have never been higher. More systems are interconnected today than ever before, and there is only one constant to those systems: change. Aside from hackers, disgruntled employees, and corporate spies, a growing number of laws and regulations (such as Sarbanes-Oxley, Gramm-Leach-Bliley, and the Health Information Portability and Accountability Act) have forever changed the role of the cybersecurity professional as the gatekeeper of information and the manager of risk.

The role of the cybersecurity professional is to help the organization manage risks poised against the confidentiality, integrity, and availability of its information assets. The foundation of all cybersecurity programs begins and forever lives with the process of risk assessment. Risk is not static. Rather, risk is fluid and evolves over time. A risk assessment conducted on the first day of the month can be quite different from the same assessment conducted several weeks later. The levels of risks for particular information systems can change as quickly as IT systems change. Events such as war, economic changes, new employee hires, layoffs, and the steady introduction of new technologies all work to change the amount of risk faced by an organization.

The first task in risk assessment is to identify, assess, classify, and then decide on the value of digital assets and systems. Many believe that the most difficult aspect of risk assessment is uncovering the myriad system and configuration vulnerabilities that place systems at risk, but that is not so; an abundance of tools are available that can help automate that task. It is really deciding, organization-wide, the value of information and intellectual property that poses one of the most daunting challenges for the cybersecurity professional.

How much is the research and development data worth? How much will it cost the organization if it loses access to the accounting or customer relationship management systems for a day? Without knowing the value of information and the systems that ensure its flow, it is impossible to make reasonable decisions about how much can reasonably be spent protecting that information. It makes little sense to spend $200,000 annually to protect information that would not cost an organization more than $25,000 if exposed or lost. In a perfect world, with unlimited budgets and resources in hand, everything could be protected all the time. But we do not live in a perfect world, and tough decisions need to be made. That means bringing together management, legal, human resources, physical cybersecurity, and other groups in the organization. In assessing risk, you must decide what needs to be protected and how much the information is worth. Only then can reasonable decisions be made for how to mitigate risk by implementing defensive measures and sound policy.

During the risk assessment process, vulnerabilities to systems will inevitably be uncovered. The challenge here is to determine which ones pose the greatest threats to protected assets. It is a challenge that cybersecurity professionals face every day. Does a low-risk vulnerability (something unlikely to be exploited) on a system holding highly valuable corporate information need to be remediated more quickly than a high-risk vulnerability (one that is likely to be exploited) on a system holding information of little value? Maybe. It all depends. And each situation is different.

Risk can never be entirely eliminated; it can only be managed to levels that an organization can tolerate. The best way to keep risk low is to remain eternally vigilant by following a four-step process: (1) identify new assets, vulnerabilities, and threats; (2) assess and classify assets, vulnerabilities, and threats; (3) remediate and defend; and (4) return to Step 1.

Self-Check

7. In the risk identification process, the value of each information asset should be predetermined before cataloging.

   a. True   **b.** False

8. All information assets, including data and applications, are always treated as information assets for the purposes of RM.

   a. True   **b.** False

9. Organizations should use a single approach to classifying and categorizing information assets and should not adjust or redefine categories.

   a. True   **b.** False

☐ Check your answers at the end of this chapter.

Risk Assessment: Risk Analysis

Understanding the risk facing each asset's vulnerabilities is accomplished via a process called risk analysis, a determination of the extent to which an organization's information assets are exposed to risk. Risk analysis assigns a risk rating, value, or score to each specific vulnerability. While this number may not mean anything in absolute terms, it enables the organization to gauge the relative risk associated with each vulnerable information asset, and it facilitates the creation of comparative ratings later in the risk treatment process.

Estimating risk is not an exact science. Some practitioners use calculated values for risk estimation, whereas others rely on broader methods of estimation. The NIST approach to assessing risk is shown in Figure 3-6 and illustrates how the components discussed in this section work together to provide overall risk assessment activities based on the NIST RM framework. While very similar to the risk framework discussed in this chapter, there are variations in the NIST model that should prove relatively easy to adapt either to this model or vice versa. This section discusses the understanding of risk analysis. Pay close attention to the NIST model because it illustrates the integration of the analysis with the understanding of the threats discussed previously.

The goal of risk analysis is to develop a repeatable method to evaluate the relative risk of each asset's vulnerability that has been identified and added to the list. Later in this book, a method will be described for

Figure 3-6   NIST generic risk model with key risk factors

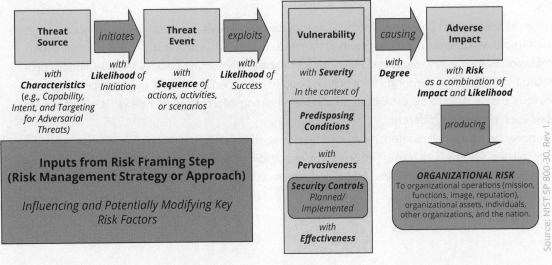

Source: NIST SP 800-30, Rev 1.

determining more precise costs that may be incurred from vulnerabilities that lead to losses as well as projected expenses for the controls that reduce the risks. The model used by Clearwater IRM|Analysis to evaluate risk is based on the NIST approach, as shown in Figure 3-7. The next section describes the factors used to calculate the relative risk for each vulnerability, based on existing controls, and the likelihood and impact of a threat event. Figure 3-7 also illustrates the Clearwater IRM|Analysis approach to risk determination (their term for risk analysis), which uses a series of risk questionnaires to examine the threats and vulnerabilities facing each information asset. At the top of this figure is the listed information asset (backup media/HRIS), which was cataloged previously. This is followed by a list of recommended generic control implementations.

Figure 3-7 Clearwater IRM|Analysis risk questionnaire form

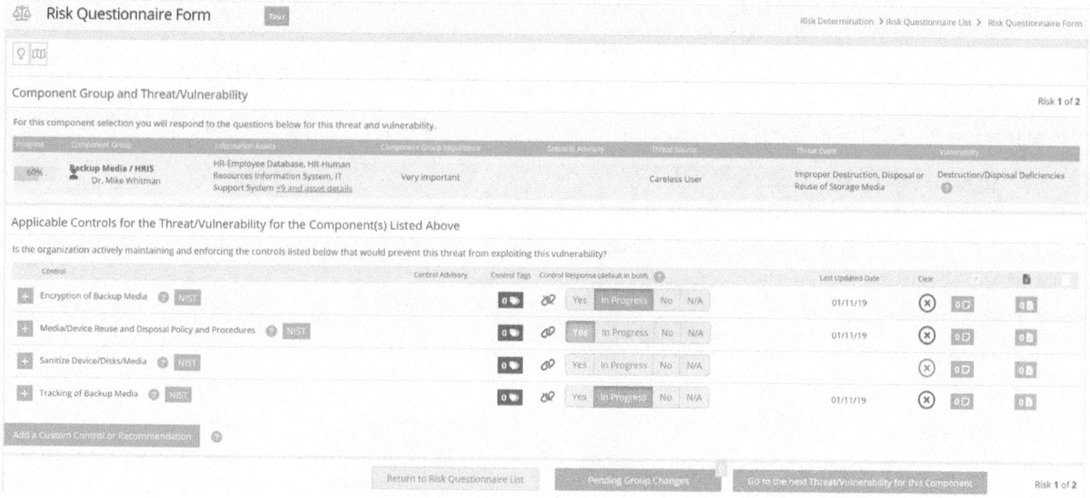

Mitigation of Applicable Controls

If a vulnerability is fully managed by an existing control, it can be set aside. If it is partially controlled, you can estimate what percentage of the vulnerability has been controlled. A simplistic approach involves determining what recommended controls have been implemented as part of the cybersecurity program and describing the current level of implementation, as shown in Figure 3-8. The figure displays controls from NIST Special Publication 800-53, Revision 5: "Security and Privacy Controls for Information Systems and Organizations," which are used to determine whether the information asset's general vulnerabilities have been sufficiently protected by existing applied controls. Note that this information does not include application-specific vulnerabilities, such as those inherent in a computer system's operating system. The organization must research those vulnerabilities independently of the NIST recommendations to ensure a complete investigation.

Note 2 │ For more information on general controls and their use in protecting against general vulnerabilities, download NIST Special Publication 800-53, Revision 5: "Security and Privacy Controls for Information Systems and Organizations," from https://csrc.nist.gov/publications/sp.

Determining the Likelihood of a Threat Event

In cybersecurity RM, risk can be calculated based on two variables, starting with likelihood: the probability of the successful exploitation of a specific asset's vulnerability by a threat. This exploitation is commonly referred to as a threat event, as described earlier in the book. According to NIST's SP 800-30, Rev. 1:

> The likelihood of occurrence is a weighted risk factor based on an analysis of the probability that a given threat is capable of exploiting a given vulnerability (or set of vulnerabilities). The likelihood risk factor combines an estimate of the likelihood that

Figure 3-8   Clearwater IRM|Analysis rating of risk likelihood

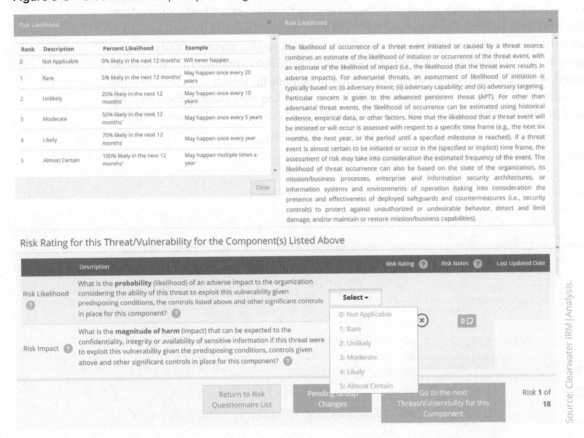

Source: Clearwater IRM|Analysis.

the threat event will be initiated with an estimate of the likelihood of impact (i.e., the likelihood that the threat event results in adverse impacts). For adversarial threats, an assessment of likelihood of occurrence is typically based on: (i) adversary intent; (ii) adversary capability; and (iii) adversary targeting. For other than adversarial threat events, the likelihood of occurrence is estimated using historical evidence, empirical data, or other factors.[20]

A simple method of assessing risk likelihood is to score the event on a rating scale, like the one shown in Table 3-9 and in the Clearwater IRM|Analysis software in Figure 3-8.

Table 3-9   Risk likelihood

Value	Description	Percent Likelihood	Example
0	Not Applicable	0% likely in the next 12 months	Will never happen
1	Rare	5% likely in the next 12 months	May happen once every 20 years
2	Unlikely	25% likely in the next 12 months	May happen once every 10 years
3	Moderate	50% likely in the next 12 months	May happen once every 5 years
4	Likely	75% likely in the next 12 months	May happen once every year
5	Almost Certain	100% likely in the next 12 months	May happen multiple times a year

Source: Clearwater IRM|Analysis.

Using this scale, the likelihood of a system being damaged by a water leak could be rated as 1, while the likelihood of receiving at least one email that contains a virus or worm in the next year would be rated as 5. You could choose to use a different number scale, such as 1 to 10 or 1 to 100, depending on the granularity needed by the organization's process. Whatever rating system you employ for assigning likelihood, use the professional experience and best judgment of the organization to determine the rating—and use it consistently. Whenever possible, use external references for likelihood values after reviewing and adjusting them for your specific circumstances. For many asset/vulnerability combinations, existing sources have already determined their likelihood. For example, the following information may be available from outside references, such as insurance, cybersecurity, and academic sources:

- The likelihood of damage from a fire or other natural disaster for each type of structure, depending on location
- The likelihood that an email will contain a virus or worm
- The number of network attacks based on how many external network addresses the organization has been assigned

Assessing Potential Impact on Asset Value

Once the probability of an attack by a threat has been evaluated, the organization typically looks at the attack's possible impact (or consequence), the potential outcome of the successful exploitation of a specific asset's vulnerability by a threat. One feared impact is the loss of asset value. As mentioned in the section on assessing threats, the impact of an attack (most often as a loss in asset value) is of significant concern to the organization in determining where to focus its protection efforts. The weighted tables used in risk identification can help organizations better understand the magnitude of a potential breach. Another good source of information is via popular media venues that report on successful attacks in other organizations.

> The level of impact from a threat event is the magnitude of harm that can be expected to result from the consequences of unauthorized disclosure of information, unauthorized modification of information, unauthorized destruction of information, or loss of information or information system availability. Such harm can be experienced by a variety of organizational and non-organizational stakeholders, including, for example, heads of agencies, mission and business owners, information owners/stewards, mission/business process owners, information system owners, or individuals/groups in the public or private sectors relying on the organization—in essence, anyone with a vested interest in the organization's operations, assets, or individuals, including other organizations in partnership with the organization, or the Nation. Organizations make explicit: (i) the process used to conduct impact determinations; (ii) assumptions related to impact determinations; (iii) sources and methods for obtaining impact information; and (iv) the rationale for conclusions reached with regard to impact determinations.[21]

Organizations can create scenarios to better understand the potential impact of a successful attack. Using a "worst case/most likely" approach is common, in which organizations speculate on the worst possible outcome of a successful attack by a particular threat, given the organization's current protection mechanisms. Once the organization frames this worst-case scenario, it moves on to determine the most likely outcome. The organization can use this approach in most of its risk planning and assessment activities.

The use of a risk impact value like the one used for risk likelihood, on a scale ranging from 0 to 5, is shown in Table 3-10 and in the Clearwater IRM|Analysis application in Figure 3-9.

Once the risk impact has been documented for all TVA triplets, it is useful for organizations to retain this information because it can also be used during contingency planning, as you will learn later in the book. Attack scenarios play a key role in understanding how the organization needs to react to a successful attack, particularly in its plans for incident response, disaster recovery, and business continuity. Crafting this information at the assessment stage and forwarding it to the contingency planning team saves the organization time and effort.

Table 3-10   Risk impact

Value	Description	Example	# of Records	Productivity Hours Lost	Financial Impact
0	Not applicable threat	No impact	N/A	N/A	N/A
1	Insignificant	No interruption, no exposed data	0	0	0
2	Minor	Multi-minute interruption, no exposed data	0	2	$20,000
3	Moderate	Multi-hour interruption, minor exposure of data	499	4	$175,000
4	Major	One-day interruption, exposure of data	5,000	8	$2,000,000
5	Severe	Multi-day interruption, major exposure of sensitive data	50,000	24	$20,000,000

Source: Clearwater IRM|Analysis.

Figure 3-9   Clearwater IRM|Analysis rating of risk impact

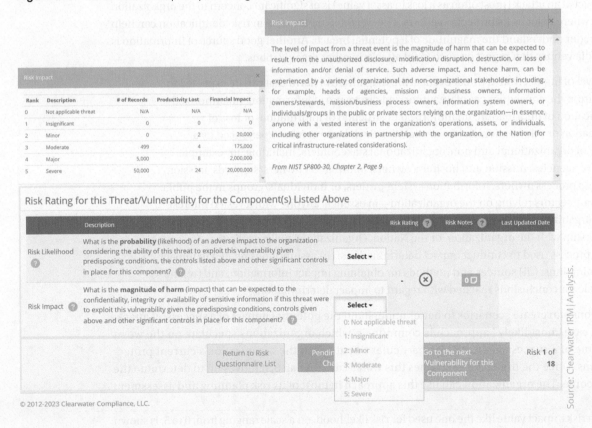

Source: Clearwater IRM | Analysis.

Risk Aggregation

If the RM process begins to overwhelm an organization, the RM team can use a process known as **risk aggregation**, the merging or combining of groups of assets, threats, and their associated risks into more general categories to simplify risk assessment. As described in NIST 800-30, Rev. 1:

> Organizations may use risk aggregation to roll up several discrete or lower-level risks into a more general or higher-level risk. Organizations may also use risk aggregation to

efficiently manage the scope and scale of risk assessments involving multiple information systems and multiple mission/business processes with specified relationships and dependencies among those systems and processes. . . . In general, for discrete risks (e.g., the risk associated with a single information system supporting a well-defined mission/business process), the worst-case impact establishes an upper bound for the overall risk to organizational operations, assets, and individuals.[22]

Risk aggregation is one tool to assist in the RM process, combining assets and threats into groups or categories. Others include using simpler methodologies (although the method shown here is relatively simplistic) with more qualitative approaches or purchasing applications that guide the organization through the entire process.

Uncertainty

It is not possible to know everything about every vulnerability, such as the likelihood of an attack against an asset or how great an impact a successful attack would have on the organization. The degree to which a current control can reduce risk is also subject to estimation error. A factor that accounts for uncertainty—the state of having limited or imperfect knowledge of a situation, making it less likely that organizations can successfully anticipate future events or outcomes—must always be considered; it consists of an estimate made by the manager using good judgment and experience.

Uncertainty is inherent in the evaluation of risk, due to such considerations as: (i) limitations on the extent to which the future will resemble the past; (ii) imperfect or incomplete knowledge of the threat (e.g., characteristics of adversaries, including tactics, techniques, and procedures); (iii) undiscovered vulnerabilities in technologies or products; and (iv) unrecognized dependencies, which can lead to unforeseen impacts. Uncertainty about the value of specific risk factors can also be due to the step in the RMF or phase in the system development life cycle at which a risk assessment is performed. For example, at early phases in the system development life cycle, the presence and effectiveness of cybersecurity controls may be unknown, while at later phases in the life cycle, the cost of evaluating control effectiveness may outweigh the benefits in terms of more fully informed decision making. Finally, uncertainty can be due to incomplete knowledge of the risks associated with other information systems, mission/business processes, services, common infrastructures, and/or organizations. The degree of uncertainty in risk assessment results, due to these different reasons, can be communicated in the form of the results (e.g., by expressing results qualitatively, by providing ranges of values rather than single values for identified risks, or by using visual representations of fuzzy regions rather than points).[23]

Risk Determination

Once the likelihood and impact are known, the organization can perform risk determination, the calculation of risk associated with a TVA triplet using a formula based on the methodology employed that seeks to quantify certain risk elements. In the approach used here, risk equals likelihood of a successful threat event (attack) occurrence multiplied by the attack's impact (or consequence), plus or minus an element of uncertainty. The result is a risk rating factor, the quantification of risk present in a TVA triplet, as derived in risk determination. To see how this equation works, consider the following scenario:

- Information asset 1 faced with threat 1 is at risk with general vulnerability 1. The risk rating for A1V1T1 (or T1V1A1 if you prefer) has been assigned a Likelihood value of 3 and an Impact value of 5. You estimate that assumptions and data are 90 percent accurate (uncertainty of ± 10 percent). The resulting risk rating is 15 ± 1.5, so your risk rating range is 13.5 to 16.5 on a 25-point scale.
- Information asset 2 faced with threat 2 is at risk with general vulnerabilities 2 and 3. The risk rating for A2V2T2 has a Likelihood rating of 4 and an Impact rating of 4. The risk rating for A2V3T2 has a

Likelihood rating of 3 and an Impact rating of 2. You estimate that assumptions and data are 80 percent accurate. The resulting risk rating for A2V2T2 is 16 ± 3.2 (range of 12.8–19.2). The risk rating for A2V3T2 is 6 ± 1.2 (range of 4.8–7.2).

Most organizations simply accept the uncertainty factor and go with the simpler formula of Likelihood $\times$ Impact. The results provide a range of risk ratings from 1 to 25, as shown in Figure 3-10. Use of the value of zero in either estimation means the likelihood or impact is not applicable or so insignificant as to preclude inclusion.

Figure 3-10   Clearwater IRM|Analysis risk rating matrix

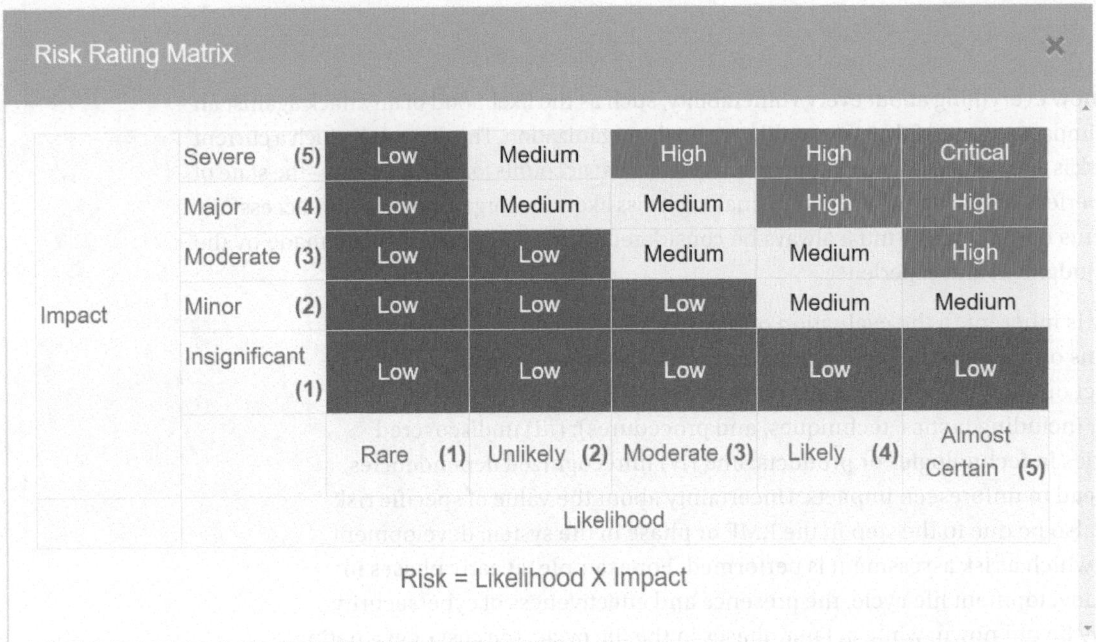

Source: Clearwater IRM|Analysis.

The results of this analysis can be summarized in a **risk rating worksheet**, an extension of the TVA spreadsheet that only includes assets and relevant vulnerabilities along with the risk determination, as shown in Table 3-11. A review of this worksheet reveals similarities to the weighted factor analysis worksheet depicted earlier in Table 3-2. Table 3-11 illustrates the use of a weighted spreadsheet to calculate risk vulnerability for a few information assets, using the simpler model of ignoring uncertainty. The columns in the worksheet are used as follows:

- Asset—List each vulnerable asset.
- Vulnerability—List each uncontrolled vulnerability.
- Likelihood—State the likelihood of the realization of the vulnerability by a threat agent, as indicated in the vulnerability analysis step. (In our example, the potential values range from 0 to 5.)
- Impact—Show the results for this asset from the weighted factor analysis worksheet. (In our example, this value is also a number from 0 to 5.)
- Risk rating factor—Enter the figure calculated by multiplying the asset impact and its likelihood. (In our example, the calculation yields a number ranging from 0 to 25.)

Looking at Table 3-11, you may be surprised that the most pressing risk requires making the web server or servers more robust and ensuring that the organization is contracting with a reliable Internet service provider with high availability. The high likelihood and severe impact of such an exploit make the risk to this specific information asset/vulnerability pair the most severe of those shown in the table. Figure 3-11 illustrates the same information, as developed in the Clearwater IRM|Analysis application for each set of media, assets, threats, and vulnerabilities. This information illustrates the intent of the entire process of identifying assets,

Table 3-11 **Risk rating worksheet (sorted by risk rating factor)**

Asset	Vulnerability	Likelihood	Impact	Risk Rating Factor
Customer order via SSL (inbound)	Lost orders due to web server or ISP service failure	4	5	20
Customer service request via email (inbound)	Email disruption due to software failure	4	3	12
Customer order via SSL (inbound)	Lost orders due to web server hardware failure	2	5	10
Customer order via SSL (inbound)	Lost orders due to web server software failure	2	5	10
Customer service request via email (inbound)	Email disruption due to hardware failure	3	3	9
Customer service request via email (inbound)	Email disruption due to power failure	3	3	9
Customer service request via email (inbound)	Email disruption due to ISP service failure	2	3	6
Customer order via SSL (inbound)	Lost orders due to web server denial-of-service attack	1	5	5
Customer order via SSL (inbound)	Lost orders due to web server buffer overrun attack	1	5	5
Customer service request via email (inbound)	Email disruption due to SMTP mail relay attack	1	3	3

Note: In the table, ISP is Internet service provider, SMTP is Simple Mail Transfer Protocol, and SSL is Secure Sockets Layer.

Figure 3-11 Clearwater IRM|Analysis risk ratings

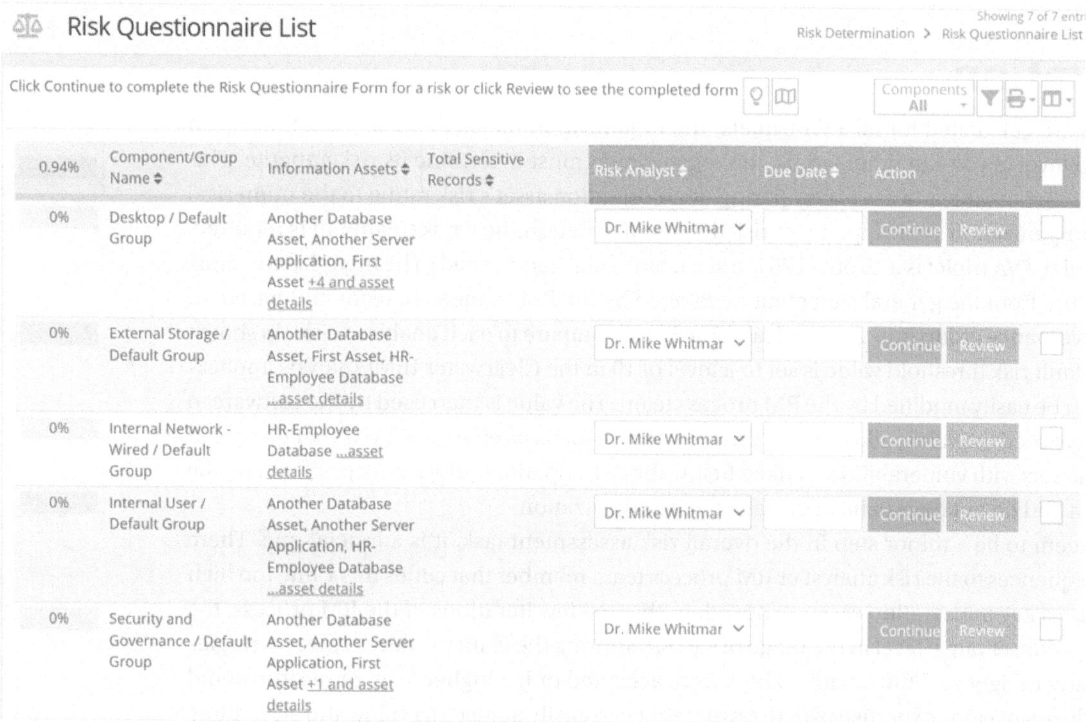

Source: Clearwater IRM | Analysis.

matching them to vulnerabilities, and assessing the relative risks for each pair. Once the most pressing pair is identified, it becomes the pair that would most benefit the organization to remedy.

The biggest problem in using more complex quantitative approaches in risk determination is the massive amount of "guesstimation" that must occur to develop discrete values. Very few concrete examples exist to provide the likelihood for a particular threat attack on a more granular scale (say, from 1 to 100), and even fewer examples allow the organization to determine the exact impact on an asset's value from a successful attack (again on a 1–100 scale). For the most part, professionals will tell you "It depends." When a method like this is employed in a *consistent* fashion, it allows making decisions on a *relative* basis, even when precise values are unknowable.

Any time a calculation is based on pure quantitative numbers of this caliber, the value of the outcome is immediately suspect because the numbers used in the calculations are most likely general estimates. As a result, more and more organizations are turning to qualitative or semi-qualitative assessments, as illustrated in the RM framework and process discussed in this chapter.

Self-Check

10. Risk analysis assigns an absolute value or score to each specific vulnerability to precisely quantify its risk.

    a. True   b. False

11. The NIST approach to assessing risk is fundamentally different and incompatible with the risk framework discussed in the chapter.

    a. True   b. False

12. The likelihood of a threat event is solely based on historical evidence and does not consider adversary intent or capability.

    a. True   b. False

□ Check your answers at the end of this chapter.

Risk Evaluation

Once the risk ratings are calculated for all TVA triplets, the organization needs to decide whether it can live with the analyzed level of risk—in other words, the organization must determine its risk appetite. This stage is called risk evaluation, the process of comparing an information asset's risk rating to the numerical representation of the organization's risk appetite or risk threshold to determine if risk treatment is required. Knowing that a particular TVA triplet is a 16 out of 25 is a start, but is that good or bad? The organization must translate its risk appetite from the general statement developed by the RM framework team and based on guidance from the governance group into a numerical value it can compare to each analyzed risk. As shown in Figure 3-12, the default risk threshold value is set to a level of 10 in the Clearwater IRM|Analysis application, but that value can be easily modified by the RM process team. The value is then used by the software to filter TVAs that do not exceed the value, allowing the process team to focus its efforts on TVAs that *do* exceed the value. Therefore, assets with vulnerabilities ranked below the risk appetite settings are not shown on the Risk Treatment screen and do not have to be addressed by the organization.

While this may seem to be a minor step in the overall risk assessment task, it is a crucial one. There could be severe consequences to the risk analyst or RM process team member that codes this value too high and consequently leaves key information assets exposed. In the first few iterations of the RM process, the value should be set to a conservative level in the range of 6 to 8, requiring the team to address the risk ratings of assets it might otherwise ignore if the default values were accepted or if a higher level of risk threshold were selected. After the team gains expertise with the process, it can easily adjust this value and streamline

Figure 3-12   Clearwater IRM|Analysis risk threshold

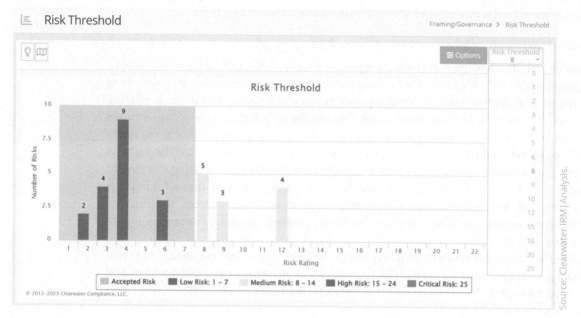

the process, with fewer TVAs to review throughout the cycle. The average information asset has more than 50 general vulnerabilities to review in the current Clearwater IRM|Analysis application, so the fewer TVAs the team must review, the faster it can address those rated as having insufficient levels of current controls.

Once the general vulnerabilities have been addressed, the organization may want to revisit the list of hardware- and OS-specific vulnerabilities, such as those available at Mitre's CVE site (https://cve.mitre.org/), Homeland Security's CISA site (https://www.cisa.gov/), and the sites of the manufacturers. When these general risks are included, the organization can then evaluate the previous risk ratings developed by the RM process team to address vulnerabilities that may not have been on the internally developed list and that were made known to them from the general list posted by NIST.

Documenting the Results of Risk Assessment

The efforts to compile risks into a comprehensive list allow the organization to make informed choices from the best available information. It is also of value for future iterations of the process to document the results in a reusable form. As these efforts to compile and assess risk are completed, the results of these steps are documented for current and future use in the list of deliverables, as shown in Table 3-12.

Table 3-12   Risk assessment deliverables

Deliverable	Purpose
Information asset and classification worksheet	Assembles information about information assets, their sensitivity levels, and their value to the organization
Information asset value weighted table analysis	Rank-orders each information asset according to criteria developed by the organization
Threat severity weighted table analysis	Rank-orders each threat to the organization's information assets according to criteria developed by the organization
TVA controls worksheet	Combines the output from the information asset identification and prioritization with the threat identification and prioritization, identifies potential vulnerabilities in the "triplets," and incorporates extant and planned controls
Risk ranking worksheet	Assigns a risk rating ranked value to each TVA triplet, incorporating likelihood, impact, and possibly a measure of uncertainty

While the organization may require additional deliverables, the table lists the minimum required to fully document the operations of the RM process team to provide continuity for future iterations.

Evaluating Risk

Once the risk has been identified and its relative severity against the value of the information asset has been evaluated, the organization must decide whether the current level of risk is acceptable or whether something must be done to reduce it. If the RM process team completes its analysis and shares its findings with the governance group and the executive decision makers state, "We can live with that," then the process moves on to the monitoring and review function, where the organization keeps an eye on the assets, the threat environment, and known vulnerabilities list for a trigger to restart the RM process anew. If the decision makers indicate that they are not comfortable with the current level of risk, then the next stage of the RM process—risk treatment—proceeds. In most organizations, this is not a simple decision. Instead, it requires extensive input from the RM process team, along with recommendations and cost estimates. This decision process typically requires a formal presentation in which the RM process team provides multiple options to reduce the current level of risk.

Even the decision for whether the current level of risk is acceptable is not a clear-cut choice. Although the governance team provides guidance for general risk appetite, it seldom comes to a simple mathematical comparison, as in "Our risk appetite is level 10, and the current level of risk in this particular information asset is a 9, so we recommend 'live with it.'"

Another factor that makes this process even more challenging is that the solution for one information asset may positively or negatively affect the level of risk in other information assets. If the simple solution to protect a critical asset is to upgrade the organization's firewall or hire additional firewall administrators, that decision could prove substantially expensive but could very positively impact many other information assets. On the other hand, if the recommendation is to reduce the potential effectiveness of a control—for example, replacing an overly complex firewall implementation with a simpler alternative that is easier to manage—other information assets could be negatively impacted. The bottom line is that once the risk is known, it requires extensive deliberation and understanding before the "yea or nay" decision is made.

Another step performed during risk evaluation is the prioritization of effort for the treatment of risk, which occurs in the next step of the RM process and is addressed in the next chapter. The organization can use the asset weighted table analysis performed earlier in the process to make this prioritization, or it can delay the ranking until it has a better understanding of the expected costs and benefits of the various treatment options. Many organizations choose to do a two-pronged approach, developing a draft listing of treatment priorities and then confirming or adjusting that list once the expected costs and benefits are understood. There is also the chance that the organization may think it does not have enough information to decide whether to treat the residual risk in a particular information asset, and may need to request additional information. If this decision is reached by the RM process team, the framework team, or the governance group, then the conduct of additional investigation falls under the risk evaluation phase.

Risk Treatment/Risk Control

Risk treatment, also known as risk control, is the process of doing something about risk once the organization has identified the risk, assessed it, evaluated it, and then determined that the current level of remaining risk—the residual risk—is unacceptable. A variety of options are open to organizations, including removing the information asset from harm's way, modifying how it is currently protected, and passing the responsibility for its administration and/or protection to third parties. Risk treatment is discussed in full detail in the next chapter.

Process Communications, Monitoring, and Review

As the process team works through the various RM activities, it needs to continually provide feedback to the framework team about the relative success and challenges of its RM activities. This feedback is used to improve not only the process but the framework as well. It is critical that the process team have one or more individuals designated to collect and provide this feedback, as well as a formal mechanism to submit it to the framework team. **Process communications**—the necessary information flow within and among the governance group, RM framework team, and RM process team during the implementation of RM—facilitates the actions in the **process monitoring and review**, the data collection and feedback associated with performance measures used during the conduct of the process. The former involves requesting and providing information as direct feedback about issues that arise in the implementation and operation of each stage of the process. The latter involves establishing and collecting formal performance measures and assessment methods to determine the relative success of the RM program. Performance measures are discussed in additional detail later in the book.

Note 3 | An informative and interesting book that lays the groundwork for RM is *Against the Gods: The Remarkable Story of Risk* by Peter L. Bernstein, published by John Wiley & Sons.

Self-Check

13. Risk evaluation is the stage where the organization decides if the analyzed level of risk is within its risk appetite.
    a. True   **b.** False

14. Documenting the results of the risk assessment process is unnecessary for future iterations of the process.
    a. True   **b.** False

15. Feedback during the RM activities is only beneficial for the process team and does not influence the framework team.
    a. True   **b.** False

☐ Check your answers at the end of this chapter.

Closing Case

Mike and Iris were flying home from the meeting. The audit committee's reaction had not been what they expected.

"I'm glad they understood the situation," Mike said. "I'd like you to start revising our risk management documentation to make it a little more general. It sounds like the board will want to take our approach company-wide soon."

Iris nodded and pulled out her notepad to make a to-do list.

Case Discussion Questions

1. What will Iris have on her to-do list?
2. What resources can Iris call on to assist her?

Case Ethical Decision Making

Suppose that after Mike and Iris returned to the office, Mike was called to a private meeting with a senior executive from another division of the firm. During the discussion, Mike felt he was being subtly threatened with nonspecific but obviously devastating consequences to his career prospects at RWW as well as long-term damage to his professional reputation if he did not back off on his efforts to improve company-wide risk management at RWW. The other executive was adamant that the costs of improving the risk management process would hurt the firm without gaining any real improvement.

Was this executive simply expressing disagreement with Mike's approach, or has some ethical line been crossed? Should Mike take any overt actions based on this conversation or inform others about the perceived threats? What could Mike do that would not embarrass the other executive and still offer some protection in this situation?

Summary

Risk management examines and documents an organization's information assets.

Management is responsible for identifying and controlling the risks that an organization encounters. In the modern organization, the cybersecurity group often plays a leadership role in RM.

A key component of an RM strategy is the identification, classification, and prioritization of the organization's information assets.

Assessment is the identification of assets, including all the elements of an organization's system: people, procedures, data, software, hardware, and networking elements.

The human resources, documentation, and data information assets of an organization are not as easily identified and documented as tangible assets, such as hardware and software. These more elusive assets should be identified and described using knowledge, experience, and judgment.

You can use the answers to the following questions to develop weighting criteria for information assets:

- Which information asset is the most critical to the success of the organization?
- Which information asset generates the most revenue?
- Which information asset generates the highest profitability?
- Which information asset is the most expensive to replace?
- Which information asset is the most expensive to protect?
- Which information asset's loss or compromise would be the most embarrassing or cause the greatest liability?

After identifying and performing a preliminary classification of information assets, the threats facing an organization should be examined. There are 12 general categories of threats to cybersecurity.

Each threat must be examined during a threat assessment process that addresses the following questions: Which of these threats exist in this organization's environment? Which are the most dangerous to the organization's information? Which requires the greatest expenditure for recovery? Which requires the greatest expenditure for protection?

Each information asset is evaluated for each threat it faces; the resulting information is used to create a list of the vulnerabilities that pose risks to the organization. This process results in an information asset and vulnerability list, which serves as the starting point for risk assessment.

A Threats–Vulnerabilities–Assets (TVA) worksheet lists the assets in priority order along one axis and the threats in priority order along the other axis. The resulting grid provides a convenient method of examining the "exposure" of assets, allowing a simple vulnerability assessment.

The goal of risk assessment is the assignment of a risk rating or score that represents the relative risk for a specific vulnerability of a specific information asset.

If any specific vulnerability is completely managed by an existing control, it no longer needs to be considered for additional controls.

The risk identification process should designate what function the resulting reports serve, who is responsible for preparing them, and who reviews them. The TVA worksheet and the ranked vulnerability risk worksheet are the initial working documents for the next step in the RM process: assessing and controlling risk.

Key Terms

consequence

cyber hygiene

cybersecurity risk management

data classification scheme

enterprise risk management (ERM)

impact

information media

likelihood

process communications

process monitoring and review

residual risk

risk aggregation

risk analysis

risk appetite

risk appetite statement

risk control

risk determination

risk evaluation

risk identification

risk management

risk management plan

risk management policy

risk rating factor

risk rating worksheet

risk threshold

risk tolerance

risk treatment

RM framework

RM process

system components

threat assessment

uncertainty

zero tolerance risk exposure

Review Questions

1. What is the foundational philosophy of cybersecurity strategy as suggested by Sun Tzu's observations?

2. What are the four key components of the cybersecurity RM process?

3. How does the chapter suggest organizations should approach the adoption of an RM framework and process?

4. What role does continuous improvement play in the RM framework?

5. What is the significance of risk tolerance and risk appetite in the RM process?

6. What steps are involved in the implementation of the RM plan?

7. What are the main tasks involved in establishing the context within the RM process?

8. How does the RM process approach the identification of risks?

9. What does analyzing risk in the RM process entail?

10. How is the evaluation of risk to the organization's key assets conducted in the RM process?

11. What steps are involved in treating unacceptable risks in the RM process?

12. What is the primary goal of risk identification in the context of RM?

13. How does the process of identifying information assets begin?

14. What is a challenge in the RM process?

15. How does an organization approach the classification and categorization of information assets?

16. What criteria are suggested for assessing the value of information assets?

17. How should an organization prioritize information assets?

18. What is the significance of the Threats–Vulnerabilities–Assets (TVA) worksheet as described?

19. What is the purpose of risk analysis in the context of RM?

20. How is the likelihood of a threat event determined according to NIST?

21. What factors are considered in assessing the potential impact of a threat event on asset value?

22. What is risk aggregation, and how does it simplify the risk assessment process?

23. How does uncertainty factor into the risk determination process?

24. What is risk evaluation in the context of RM?

25. Why is it important to document the results of risk assessment?

26. What factors contribute to the decision-making process when evaluating if the current level of risk is acceptable?

27. How can the treatment of risk in one information asset affect other information assets?

28. What are the options available to an organization during risk treatment?

29. What role does feedback play in the RM process?

Exercises

1. If an organization has three information assets to evaluate for RM purposes, as shown in the following list, which vulnerability should be evaluated for additional controls first? Which vulnerability should be evaluated last?

   - Switch L47 connects a network to the Internet. It has two vulnerabilities: (1) susceptibility to hardware failure, with a likelihood of 2, and (2) susceptibility to an SNMP buffer overflow attack, with a likelihood of 1. There is a 75 percent certainty of the assumptions and data.
   - Server WebSrv6 hosts a company website and performs e-commerce transactions. It has web server software that is vulnerable to attack via invalid Unicode values. The likelihood of such an attack is estimated at 3. The server has been assigned an impact value of 5. There is an 80 percent certainty of the assumptions and data.
   - Operators use the MGMT45 control console to monitor operations in the server room. It has no passwords and is susceptible to unlogged misuse

   by the operators. Estimates show the likelihood of misuse is 2. There are no controls in place on this asset, which has an impact rating of 4. There is a 90 percent certainty of the assumptions and data.

2. Using the web, search for at least three tools to automate risk assessment. Collect information on automated risk assessment tools. What do they cost? What features do they provide? What are the advantages and disadvantages of each one?

3. Using a data classification scheme, identify and classify the information contained in your personal computer or personal digital assistant. Based on the potential for misuse or embarrassment, what information is confidential, sensitive but unclassified, and suitable for public release?

4. Using the asset valuation method presented in this chapter, conduct a preliminary risk assessment on the information contained in your home. Answer each of the valuation questions listed in this chapter. What would it cost if you lost all your data?

Solutions to Self-Check Questions

Introduction to the Management of Risk in Cybersecurity

1. Sun Tzu's philosophy implies that knowing both the enemy and oneself is crucial for cybersecurity RM.
   Answer: a. True.
   Explanation: The relevance of Sun Tzu's observations to cybersecurity indicates the importance of knowing both the enemy and oneself to reduce risk.

2. A cybersecurity RM program's existence alone is sufficient for effective RM.
   Answer: b. False.
   Explanation: Merely having an RM program is not enough; it needs to be maintained and monitored continuously.

3. Every organization should adopt the same RM framework and process.
   Answer: b. False.
   Explanation: Each organization must decide for itself what works best, indicating that the framework and process can be adapted to fit different organizational needs.

RM Process Preparation: Establishing the Context

4. The RM process involves only the cybersecurity team in risk evaluation and remediation activities.
   Answer: b. False.
   Explanation: The three communities of interest must work together in the RM process, indicating involvement beyond just the cybersecurity team.

5. Identifying risks includes creating an inventory of information assets and assigning value to each asset.

   Answer: a. True.

   Explanation: Identifying risk involves creating an inventory of information assets and assigning a value to each, among other tasks.

6. The RM process does not require understanding both the organization's internal and external operating environments.

   Answer: b. False.

   Explanation: Establishing the context, a part of the RM process, includes understanding both the organization's internal and external operating environments.

Risk Assessment: Risk Identification

7. In the risk identification process, the value of each information asset should be predetermined before cataloging.

   Answer: b. False.

   Explanation: The step of identifying and cataloging information assets should be performed without prejudging the value of each asset; values will be assigned later in the process.

8. All information assets, including data and applications, are always treated as information assets for the purposes of RM.

   Answer: b. False.

   Explanation: In some RM efforts, information and its supporting technologies are defined separately, where applications interfacing with external databases are treated as media and only the data is treated as an information asset.

9. Organizations should use a single approach to classifying and categorizing information assets and should not adjust or redefine categories.

   Answer: b. False.

   Explanation: Once the initial inventory is assembled, organizations may need to review and possibly redefine the categories to ensure they are meaningful to the organization's RM program, indicating flexibility in approach.

Risk Assessment: Risk Analysis

10. Risk analysis assigns an absolute value or score to each specific vulnerability to precisely quantify its risk.

    Answer: b. False.

    Explanation: Risk analysis assigns a risk rating, value, or score to each specific vulnerability, which does not represent an absolute value but enables the organization to gauge the relative risk associated with each vulnerable information asset.

11. The NIST approach to assessing risk is fundamentally different and incompatible with the risk framework discussed in the chapter.

    Answer: b. False.

    Explanation: The NIST approach to assessing risk is very similar to the risk framework discussed in the chapter. Either one should prove relatively easy to adapt to the other.

12. The likelihood of a threat event is solely based on historical evidence and does not consider adversary intent or capability.

    Answer: b. False.

    Explanation: The likelihood of a threat event's occurrence considers not only historical evidence but also adversary intent, adversary capability, and adversary targeting.

Risk Evaluation

13. Risk evaluation is the stage where the organization decides if the analyzed level of risk is within its risk appetite.

    Answer: a. True.

    Explanation: Risk evaluation involves comparing an information asset's risk rating against the organization's risk appetite to determine if risk treatment is required and if the level of risk is acceptable.

14. Documenting the results of the risk assessment process is unnecessary for future iterations of the process.

    Answer: b. False.

    Explanation: Documenting the results of the risk assessment is important for making informed decisions and provides continuity for future iterations of the RM process.

15. Feedback during the RM activities is only beneficial for the process team and does not influence the framework team.

    Answer: b. False.

    Explanation: Feedback during the RM activities is critical for both the process team and the framework team. It is used to improve the process and the framework based on the challenges and successes encountered.

Risk Management: Treating Risk

Chapter Objectives

After reading this chapter and completing the exercises, you should be able to:

1 Contextualize risk treatment strategies.

2 Implement popular methodologies used in the industry to manage risk.

3 Summarize alternative approaches to risk management.

> Weakness is a better teacher than strength. Weakness must learn to understand the obstacles that strength brushes aside.
>
> —Mason Cooley, U.S. aphorist (1927-2002)

Case Opener

Iris went into the manager's lounge to get a soda. As she was leaving, she saw Jane Harris—the accounting supervisor at Random Widget Works (RWW)—at a table, poring over a spreadsheet that Iris recognized.

"Hi, Jane," Iris said. "Can I join you?"

"Sure, Iris," Jane said. "Perhaps you can help me with this form Mike wants us to fill out."

Jane was working on the asset valuation worksheet that Iris had designed to be completed by all RWW managers. The worksheet listed all the information assets in Jane's department. Mike Edwards had asked each manager to provide three values for each item: its total cost of ownership (including creation and maintenance costs), its estimated replacement value, and its ranked criticality to the company's mission, with the most important item being ranked highest. Mike hoped that Iris and the rest of the risk management team could use the data to build a consensus about the relative importance of various assets.

"What's the problem?" Iris asked.

"I understand these first two columns. But how am I supposed to decide what's the most important?"

"Well," Iris began, "with your accounting background, you could base your answers on some of the data you collect about each of these information assets. For this quarter, what's more important to senior management—revenue or profitability?"

"Profitability is almost always more important," Jane replied. "We have some projects that generate lots of revenue but operate at a loss."

"Well, there you go," Iris said. "Why not calculate the profitability margin for each listed item and use that to rate and rank them?"

"Okay, Iris. Thanks for the idea," Jane said. She then started making notes on her copy of the form.

Introduction to Risk Treatment

After the risk management (RM) process team has identified, analyzed, and evaluated the level of risk currently inherent in its information assets as part of risk assessment, it then must treat the risk that is deemed unacceptable—in other words, when it exceeds the organization's risk appetite. This process of risk treatment is also known as risk response or risk control.

Treating risk begins with an understanding of what risk treatment strategies are and how to formulate them. The chosen strategy may include discontinuing or updating existing controls or applying additional or newer controls to some or all the assets and vulnerabilities found in the tables prepared in the preceding chapter.

As shown in Figure 4-1, after the RM process team has completed its risk assessment, it must treat the risk that exceeds its risk appetite or the risk associated with critical assets, as mandated by law, regulation, or policy. As risk treatment begins, the organization has a list of information assets with currently unacceptable levels of risk; it must select the appropriate strategy and then apply the strategy to each asset. In this chapter, you will learn how to assess risk treatment strategies, estimate costs, weigh the relative merits of the available alternatives, and gauge the benefits of various treatment approaches.

Once the RM team has identified the information assets with unacceptable levels of risk, they must choose one of four basic strategies to treat the risks for those assets:

Figure 4-1 The risk management process: risk treatment

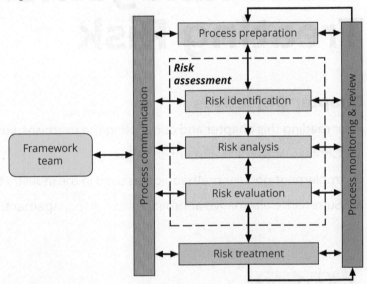

- Mitigation—Applying controls and safeguards that eliminate or reduce the remaining uncontrolled risk
- Transference—Shifting risks to other areas or to outside entities
- Acceptance—Understanding the consequences of choosing to leave an information asset's vulnerability facing the current level of risk, but only after a formal evaluation and intentional acknowledgment of this decision
- Termination—Removing or discontinuing the information asset from the organization's operating environment

Some methodologies use different terminology or a different number of strategies. Some approaches merge acceptance and termination, or don't list termination as a strategy; they just remove the asset when no longer supported. Therefore, it's important to understand your organization's terminology before using a particular methodology.

Risk Mitigation

The **mitigation risk treatment strategy**—which attempts to eliminate or reduce risk through the application of additional controls and safeguards—is sometimes referred to as the **defense risk treatment strategy**, or simply **risk mitigation**. This is the preferred approach to risk treatment, and it is accomplished by means of countering threats, removing vulnerabilities in assets, limiting access to assets, and adding or improving protective safeguards. In essence, the organization is attempting to improve the security of an information asset by reducing the likelihood or probability of a successful attack.

There are three common approaches to implement the mitigation risk treatment strategy:

- Application of policy—As discussed in the previous chapter, the application of policy allows all levels of management to mandate that certain procedures are always followed. For example, if the organization needs to control password use more tightly, it can implement a policy requiring passwords on all information technology (IT) systems. However, policy alone may not be enough. Effective management always couples changes in policy with the training and education of employees, application of technology, or both.

- Application of security education, training, and awareness (SETA) programs—Simply communicating new or revised policy to employees may not be adequate to ensure compliance. Awareness, training, and education are essential to creating a safer and more controlled organizational environment and to achieving the necessary changes in end-user behavior.

- Application of technology—In the everyday world of cybersecurity, technical controls and safeguards are frequently required to effectively reduce risk. For example, firewall administrators can deploy new firewall and intrusion detection and prevention system (IDPS) technologies where and how policy requires them, and where administrators are both aware of the requirements and trained to implement them.

Risks can be mitigated by countering the threats facing an asset or by minimizing the exposure of a particular asset. Eliminating all risk posed by a threat is virtually impossible, but it is possible to reduce the residual risk to an acceptable level in alignment with the organization's documented risk appetite.

Risk Transference

The transference risk treatment strategy—which attempts to shift risk to other assets, processes, or organizations—is sometimes known as risk sharing or simply risk transfer. For example, it might attempt to shift risk to another entity like a managed security services provider. This may be accomplished by rethinking how services are offered, revising deployment models, outsourcing to other organizations, purchasing insurance, or implementing service contracts with providers.

In their best-selling book *In Search of Excellence*, management consultants Thomas Peters and Robert Waterman presented case studies of high-performing corporations. One of the eight characteristics of excellent organizations the authors describe is that they "stick to their knitting." In other words, "They stay reasonably close to the business they know."[1] What does this mean? It means that Nabisco focuses on the manufacture and distribution of snack foods, while General Motors focuses on the design and manufacture of cars and trucks. Neither company spends strategic energy on the technology for securing websites. They focus energy and resources on what they do best while relying on consultants or contractors for other types of expertise.

Organizations should consider this point whenever they begin to expand their operations, including information management, systems management, and even cybersecurity. When an organization does not have adequate cybersecurity management and administration experience, it should consider hiring individuals or organizations that provide expertise in those areas. For example, many organizations want web services, including web presences, domain name registration, and domain and web hosting. Rather than implementing their own servers and hiring their own web developers, web systems administrators, and even specialized web security experts, savvy organizations hire web services organizations. This approach allows them to transfer the risks associated with the management of these complex systems to other organizations with more experience in dealing with those risks.

The key to an effective transference risk treatment strategy is the implementation of an effective service level agreement (SLA). In some circumstances, an SLA is the only guarantee that an external organization will implement the level of security the client organization wants for valued information assets. According to the Federal Deposit Insurance Corporation (FDIC) in their document "Tools to Manage Technology Providers' Performance Risk: Service Level Agreements," a typical SLA should contain the following elements:

- Service category (e.g., system availability or response time)
- Acceptable range of service quality
- Definition of what is being measured
- Formula for calculating the measurement

- Relevant credits and penalties for achieving or failing to achieve performance targets
- Frequency and interval of measurement[2]

The FDIC also suggests that organizations use the following four steps to create a successful SLA. While originally written for financial institutions, these recommendations are equally applicable and easily adaptable to virtually any organization:

- Determining objectives—Reviewing the strategic business needs of the institution includes evaluating its day-to-day operating environment, risk factors, and market conditions. Consideration should be given to how the outsourced service fits into the organization's overall strategic plan.
- Defining requirements—Identifying the operational objectives, such as the need to improve operating efficiency, reduce costs, or enhance security, will help the institution define performance requirements. It will also help identify the levels of service the organization needs from the service provider to meet its strategic goals and objectives for the outsourced activity.
- Setting measurements—Clear and impartial performance measures, or metrics, can be developed once the strategic needs and operating objectives have been defined. The metrics are used to confirm that the necessary service levels have been achieved and the objectives and strategic intent have been met.
- Establishing accountability—It is useful to select, develop, adapt, and implement a framework that ensures accountability after the measures have been clearly defined. The service provider rarely has full accountability and responsibility for all tasks.

Establishing this accountability usually includes a clear statement of the outcome if the level of service is exceeded or if the expected service fails to meet the stated standard.[3]

Of course, outsourcing is not without its own risks. It is up to the owner of the information asset, IT management, and the cybersecurity team to ensure that the requirements of the outsourcing contract are sufficient and have been met before services are needed.

Risk Acceptance

As described earlier, mitigation is a treatment approach that attempts to reduce the effects of an exploited vulnerability by preparing to react if it occurs. In contrast, the acceptance risk treatment strategy indicates the organization is willing to accept the current level of residual risk; as a result, the organization makes a conscious decision to do nothing else to protect an information asset from risk and to "live with" the outcome from any resulting exploitation. This strategy, also known simply as risk acceptance, is the decision to do nothing beyond the current level of protection to shield an information asset from risk. While the selection of this treatment strategy may not be a conscious business decision in some organizations, the unconscious acceptance of risk is not an effective or successful approach to risk treatment.

Acceptance is recognized as a valid strategy only when the organization has:

- Determined the level of risk posed to the information asset
- Assessed the probability of attack and the likelihood of a successful exploitation of a vulnerability
- Estimated the potential impact (damage or loss) that could result from a successful attack
- Evaluated potential controls using each appropriate type of feasibility
- Performed a thorough risk assessment, including a financial analysis such as a cost–benefit analysis
- Determined that the costs to treat the risk to the function, service, collection of data, or information asset do not justify the cost of implementing and maintaining the controls

This strategy assumes that it is a prudent business decision to examine the alternatives and conclude that the cost of protecting an asset does not justify the security expenditure. For example, suppose an organization has an older web server that only provides information related to legacy products. All information on the server is considered public and is only provided for the benefit of legacy users. The information has no significant value and does not contain any information the organization has a legal obligation to protect. A risk assessment and an evaluation of treatment options determine that it would cost a substantial amount of money to update the security on this server. The management team is unwilling to remove it from operation but determines it is not feasible to upgrade the existing controls or add new controls. They may choose to make a conscious business decision to accept the current level of residual risk for this information asset, despite any identified vulnerabilities. Note, however, that risk in this scenario might involve damage to reputation if the server is breached and perhaps defaced. Under these circumstances, management may be satisfied with taking its chances and saving the money that would otherwise be spent on protecting this particular asset.

An organization that decides on acceptance as a strategy for every identified risk of loss may be unable to conduct proactive cybersecurity activities and may have an apathetic approach to cybersecurity in general. It is not acceptable for an organization to plead ignorance and thus abdicate its legal responsibility to protect employees' and customers' information. In general, unless the organization has formally reviewed an information asset and determined the current residual risk is at or below the organization's risk appetite, the risks far outweigh the benefits of this approach.

Risk Termination

Like acceptance, the termination risk treatment strategy—which eliminates all risk associated with an information asset by removing it from service—also known as risk avoidance or simply risk termination, is based on the organization's intentional choice not to protect an asset. Here, however, the organization does not want the information asset to remain at risk and removes it from the operating environment by shutting it down or disabling its connectivity to potential threats. Only completely shutting down and sanitizing an asset will provide complete protection because attackers will have no access. Simply disabling programmatic functions or disconnecting the host system from the network may not remove the data from exposure.

Sometimes, the cost of protecting an asset outweighs its value. In other words, it may be too difficult or expensive to protect an asset, compared to the value or advantage that asset offers the company. In any case, termination must be a conscious business decision, not simply the abandonment of an asset, which would technically qualify as acceptance.

Process Communications, Monitoring, and Review

As the process team works through the various RM activities, it needs to continually provide feedback to the framework team about the relative success and challenges of its RM activities. This feedback is used to improve not only the process but the framework as well. It is critical that the process team have one or more individuals designated to collect and provide this feedback, as well as a formal mechanism to submit it to the framework team. These process communications—the necessary information flow within and between the governance group, RM framework team, and RM process team during the implementation of RM—facilitate the actions in process monitoring and review, the data collection and feedback associated with performance measures used during the conduct of the process. The former involves requesting and providing information as direct feedback about issues that arise in the implementation and operation of each stage of the process. The latter involves establishing and collecting formal performance measures and assessment methods to determine the relative success of the RM program.

Mitigation and Risk

In previous editions of this text, we referred to a different form of mitigation that focused on planning and preparation to reduce the impact or potential consequences of an incident or disaster. This form of mitigation is part of contingency planning (CP), which you will learn about in a later chapter. Not to be confused with risk mitigation, CP mitigation derives value from its ability to detect, react, respond to, and recover from incidents and disasters as quickly as possible, thus minimizing the damage to an information asset. Table 4-1 summarizes the four types of CP mitigation plans, including descriptions and examples of each. Regardless of which risk treatment strategy the organization selects for a particular asset, it is important to ensure that CP mitigation plans are in effect if the risk treatment approach fails to stop an attack.

Table 4-1 Summary of mitigation plans

Plan	Description	Examples	When Deployed	Time Frame
Incident response (IR) plan	Actions an organization takes during incidents (attacks or accidental data loss)	• List of steps to be taken during an incident • Intelligence gathering • Information analysis	As an incident or disaster unfolds	Immediate and real-time reaction
Disaster recovery (DR) plan	• Preparations for recovery should a disaster occur • Strategies to limit losses before and during a disaster • Step-by-step instructions to regain normalcy	• Procedures for the recovery of lost data • Procedures for the reestablishment of lost technology infrastructure and services • Shutdown procedures to protect systems and data	Immediately after the incident is labeled a disaster	Short-term recovery
Business continuity (BC) plan	Steps to ensure continuation of the overall business when the scale of a disaster exceeds the DR plan's ability to quickly restore operations	• Preparation steps for activation of alternate data centers • Establishment of critical business functions in an alternate location	Immediately after the disaster is determined to affect the continued operations of the organization	Long-term organizational stability
Crisis management (CM) plan	Steps to ensure the safety and welfare of the people associated with an organization in the event of an incident or disaster	• Procedures for the notification of personnel in the event of an incident or disaster • Procedures for communication with associated emergency services • Procedures for reacting to and recovering from personnel safety threats	Immediately after the incident or disaster is deemed to threaten personnel safety	Both short-term safety and long-term personnel welfare

Self-Check

1. The RM process team must treat all identified risks, regardless of their level.

   a. True   **b.** False

2. Risk transference involves accepting the current level of risk without making changes.

   a. True   **b.** False

3. Risk acceptance means the organization has made a conscious decision to do nothing further to protect an information asset from risk.

   a. True   **b.** False

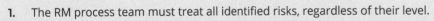

☐ Check your answers at the end of this chapter.

Managing Risk

As described in the previous chapter, risk appetite is the quantity and nature of risk that organizations are willing to accept as they evaluate the trade-offs between perfect cybersecurity and unlimited accessibility. For instance, a financial services company, regulated by government and conservative by nature, seeks to apply every reasonable control and even some invasive controls to protect its information assets. Other less closely regulated organizations may also be conservative and thus seek to avoid the negative publicity and perceived loss of integrity caused by the exploitation of a vulnerability. A business executive might direct the installation of a set of firewall rules that are far more stringent than necessary, simply because being hacked would jeopardize the organization's reputation in the market. Other executives may take on dangerous risks because of ignorance. The reasoned approach to risk is one that balances the expense (in terms of finance and the usability of information assets) against the possible losses, if exploited.

James Anderson, RM and cybersecurity expert consultant, believes that cybersecurity in today's enterprise should strive to be a well-informed sense of assurance that information risks and controls are in balance.[4] The key is for the organization to find balance in its decision-making processes and in its feasibility analyses, thereby assuring that its risk appetite is based on experience and facts, not on ignorance or wishful thinking.

When vulnerabilities have been controlled to the greatest extent possible, there will be remaining risk that has not been completely removed, shifted, or planned for—in other words, residual risk. Figure 4-2 illustrates how residual risk persists even after safeguards are implemented to reduce the levels of risk associated with threats, vulnerabilities, and information assets.

Figure 4-2   Residual risk

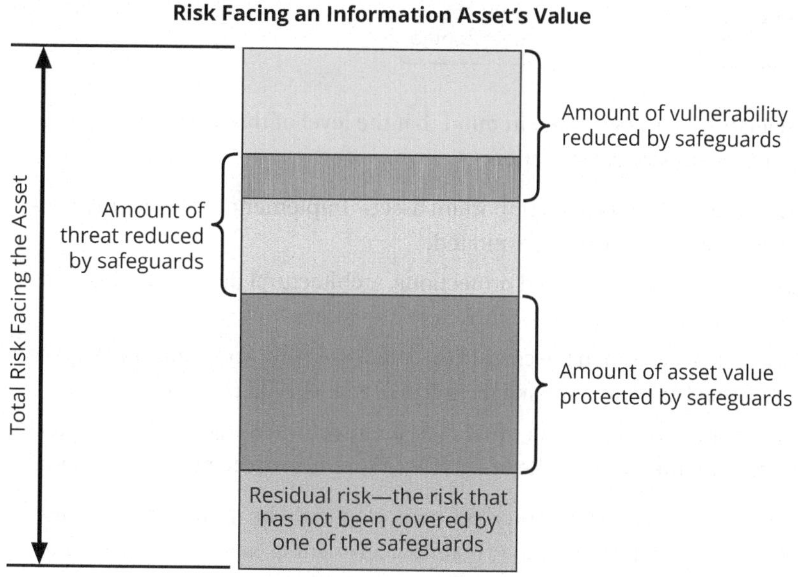

Risk Facing an Information Asset's Value

- Amount of vulnerability reduced by safeguards
- Amount of threat reduced by safeguards
- Amount of asset value protected by safeguards
- Residual risk—the risk that has not been covered by one of the safeguards
- Total Risk Facing the Asset

Although it might seem counterintuitive, the goal of cybersecurity is not to bring residual risk to zero, as that is virtually impossible if the asset is to continue providing value to the organization. Rather, the goal is to bring residual risk in line with an organization's risk appetite. If decision makers have been informed of uncontrolled risks and the organization's executive management decides to leave residual risk in place, then the cybersecurity program has accomplished its primary goal.

Figure 4-3 illustrates the process by which an organization chooses a risk treatment strategy. As shown in this diagram, after an information system is implemented, the RM team must determine whether the system has vulnerabilities that can be exploited. If a viable threat exists, they try to determine what an attacker will gain from a successful attack. Then, they estimate the expected loss the organization will incur if the vulnerability is successfully exploited. If this loss is within the range of losses the organization can absorb, or if the attacker's gain is less than the likely cost of executing the attack, the organization may choose to accept the risk. Otherwise, it must select one of the other treatment strategies.

Figure 4-3 Risk-handling action points

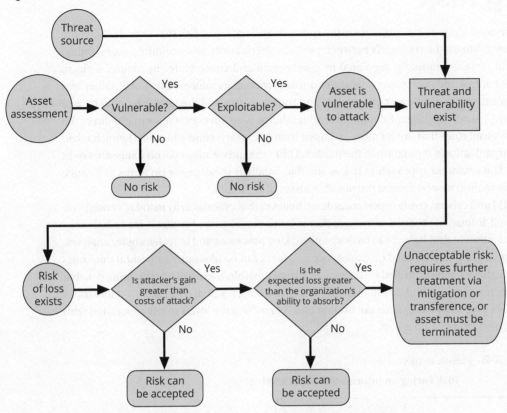

Here are some guidelines for selecting a strategy. Keep in mind that the level of threat and the value of the asset should play major roles in treatment strategy selection:

- When a vulnerability (flaw or weakness) exists in an important asset—Implement cybersecurity controls to reduce the likelihood of a vulnerability being exploited.
- When a vulnerability can be exploited—Apply layered protections, architectural designs, and administrative controls to minimize the risk or prevent the occurrence of an attack.
- When the attacker's potential gain is greater than the costs of the attack—Apply protections to increase the attacker's cost or reduce the attacker's gain by using technical or managerial controls.
- When the potential loss is substantial—Apply design principles, architectural designs, and technical and nontechnical protections to limit the extent of the attack, thereby reducing the potential for loss.[5]

Once a treatment strategy has been selected and implemented, controls should be monitored and measured on an ongoing basis to determine their effectiveness and to maintain an ongoing estimate of the remaining risk. Figure 4-4 shows how this cyclical process ensures that risks are controlled.

At a minimum, each information threat–vulnerability–asset (TVA) triplet developed in the risk assessment should have a documented treatment strategy that clearly identifies any residual risk remaining after the proposed strategy has been executed. This approach must articulate which of the fundamental risk-reducing strategies will be used and how multiple strategies might be combined. This process must justify the selection of treatment strategies by referencing the feasibility studies. Organizations should document the outcome of the treatment strategy selection for each TVA triplet in an action plan. This action plan includes concrete tasks, with accountability for each task being assigned to an organizational unit or an individual. It may include hardware and software requirements, budget estimates, and detailed timelines.

As shown in the Clearwater IRM|Analysis application in Figures 4-5 and 4-6, once the organization has decided on a risk treatment strategy, it must then reestimate the effect of the proposed strategy on the residual risk that would be present after the proposed treatment is implemented. For situations in which the organization has decided to adopt the mitigation risk treatment strategy, the software provides recommendations for

Figure 4-4   Risk treatment cycle

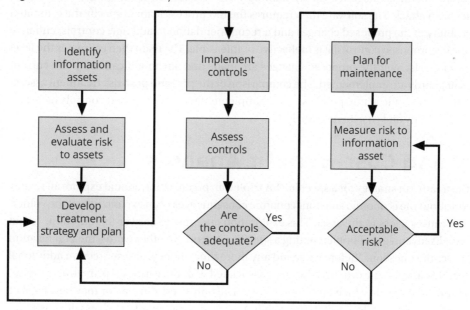

Figure 4-5   Clearwater IRM|Analysis: risk response (risk treatment)

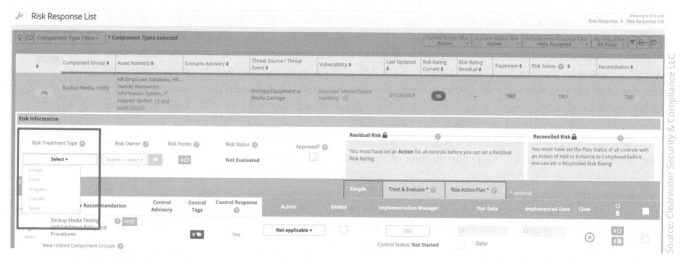

Figure 4-6   Clearwater IRM|Analysis: residual risk selection

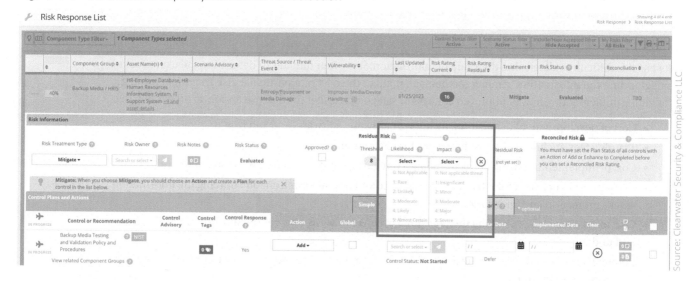

implementing general controls in all categories (policy, training and awareness, and technology) to reduce the likelihood and impact of an attack. The software then requires the RM process team to specify the estimated effectiveness and feasibility of the proposed changes and a recommendation to add new controls, enhance existing controls, or omit a proposed control if it is ineffective or infeasible. The team then estimates the level of residual risk that would exist after the proposed changes are made and any modifications to the current level of controls and safeguards are implemented. The comparison of the pre- and post-risk treatment assessments provides a foundation for the actual purchasing and implementation of proposed controls based on further assessment of feasibility and cost–benefit analysis.

Feasibility and Cost–Benefit Analysis

Before deciding on the treatment strategy for a specific TVA triplet, an organization should explore all readily accessible information about the economic and noneconomic consequences of an exploitation of the vulnerability when the threat causes a loss to the asset. This exploration attempts to answer the question, "What are the advantages and disadvantages of implementing a specific control?" In other words, the organization is simply trying to answer the question, "Before we spend any more time, money, or resources on additional mechanisms to protect this asset, is it worth it?" The costs associated with the various risk treatment strategies may help the organization decide which option to choose. The only overriding factor may be a legal or regulatory requirement to protect certain sensitive information, regardless of the cost, such as with customer financial information under the Gramm-Leach-Bliley Act or patient healthcare information under the Health Insurance Portability and Accountability Act (HIPAA).

While the advantages of a specific strategy can be identified in various ways, the primary way is to determine the value of the information assets it is designed to protect. There are also many ways to identify the disadvantages associated with specific risk treatment options. The following sections describe some of the more commonly used techniques for making these choices. Some of these techniques use dollar-denominated expenses and savings from economic **cost avoidance**—the financial savings from using the defense risk treatment strategy to implement a control and eliminate the financial ramifications of an incident—while others use noneconomic feasibility criteria.

The criterion most often used when evaluating a strategy to implement cybersecurity controls and safeguards is economic feasibility. While any number of alternatives may solve a particular problem, some are more expensive than others. Most organizations can spend only a reasonable amount of time and money on cybersecurity, although the definition of "reasonable" varies from organization to organization and even from manager to manager. Organizations can begin this type of economic feasibility analysis by valuing the information assets and determining the loss in value if those information assets are compromised. Common sense dictates that an organization should not spend more to protect an asset than it's worth. This decision-making process is called a **cost-benefit analysis (CBA)**, also known as an economic feasibility study: the formal assessment and presentation of the economic expenditures needed for a particular cybersecurity control, contrasted with its projected value to the organization.

Cost

Just as it is difficult to determine the value of information, it is often difficult to determine the exact cost of safeguarding the information. Among the items that affect the cost of a particular risk treatment strategy, including implementing new or improved controls or safeguards under the defense option, are the following:

- Cost of development or acquisition, including hardware, software, and services
- Training fees, including the cost to train or hire personnel
- Cost of implementation, including installing, configuring, and testing hardware, software, and services
- Service costs, such as vendor fees for maintenance and upgrades or from outsourcing the information asset's protection and/or insurance
- Cost of maintenance, including the personnel expense to verify and continually test, maintain, train, and update
- Potential cost from the loss of the asset, either from removal of service due to a termination decision or compromise by attack

Benefit

Benefit is the value to the organization of using controls to prevent losses associated with a specific vulnerability. It is usually determined by valuing the information asset or assets exposed by the vulnerability and then determining how much of that value is at risk and how much risk exists for the asset. This result can be expressed as the annualized loss expectancy (ALE), which is defined later in this chapter.

Asset Valuation

As you learned in the previous chapter, the value of information differs within and between organizations. Some argue that it is virtually impossible to accurately determine the true value of information and information-bearing assets, which is perhaps one reason insurance underwriters currently have no definitive valuation tables for information assets. Asset valuation—the process of assigning financial value or worth to each information asset—can draw on the assessment of information assets performed as part of the risk identification process you learned in the previous chapter.

Asset valuation involves the estimation of real or perceived costs associated with the design, development, installation, and maintenance of strategies to protect, recover from, and defend against loss or litigation. Some costs are easily determined, such as the cost of replacing a network switch or the cost of the hardware needed for a specific server. Other costs are almost impossible to determine, such as the dollar value of the loss in market share if information on a firm's new product offerings is released prematurely and the company loses market share as competitors counter the new product. A further complication is that, over time, some information assets acquire value that is beyond their intrinsic value. The higher acquired value is the more appropriate value in most cases.

Asset valuation is a complex process, and each organization must decide for itself how it wants to value its information assets. In addition to the qualitative questions provided in the previous chapter, more quantitative assessment questions commonly used in CBA include the following:

- Value retained from the cost of creating the information asset—Information is created or acquired at a cost, which can be calculated or estimated. For example, many organizations have developed extensive cost-accounting practices to capture the costs associated with collecting and processing data as well as the costs of developing and maintaining software. Software development costs include the efforts of the many people involved in the systems development life cycle for each application and system. Although this effort draws mainly on IT personnel, it also includes the user and general management communities and possibly cybersecurity staff. In today's marketplace, with high programmer salaries and even higher contractor expenses, the average cost to complete even a moderately sized application can quickly escalate.

- Value retained from past maintenance of the information asset—It is estimated that between 60 and 80 percent of the total cost of acquiring and operating an information asset is incurred in the maintenance phase. This typically means that for every dollar spent on developing an application or acquiring and processing data, another $4 to $5 will be spent after the software is in use. If actual costs have not been recorded, the cost can be estimated in terms of the human resources required to continually update, support, modify, and service the applications and systems.

- Value implied by the cost of replacing the information—The costs associated with replacing information should include the human and technical resources needed to reconstruct, restore, or regenerate the information from backups, independent transaction logs, or even hard copies of data sources. Most organizations rely on routine media or cloud backups to protect their information. When estimating recovery costs, keep in mind that you may have to hire contractors or pay employees overtime to carry out the workload that employees will be unable to perform during recovery efforts. To restore this information, the various information sources may have to be reconstructed, with the data reentered into the system and validated for accuracy.

- Value from providing the information—Separate from the cost of developing or maintaining the information is the cost of providing the information to users who need it. Such costs include the values associated with the delivery of the information through databases, networks, and hardware and software systems. They also include the cost of the infrastructure and related services necessary to provide access to and control of information.

- Value acquired from the cost of protecting the information—The value of an asset is based in part on the cost of protecting it, and the amount of money spent to protect an asset is based in part on the value of the asset. While this is a seemingly unending circle, estimating the value of protecting an information asset can help you better understand the expense associated with its potential loss. The values listed previously are easy to calculate with some precision. This value and those that follow are likely to be estimates of cost.

- Value to owners—How much is your Social Security number worth to you? Or your bank account number? Placing a value on information can be quite a daunting task. For example, a market researcher might collect data from a company's sales figures and determine that a new product offering has a strong potential market appeal to members of a certain age group. While the cost of creating this new information may be small, how much is the new information worth? It could be worth millions if it successfully captures a new market share. Although it may be impossible to estimate the value of information to an organization or what portion of revenue is directly attributable to that information, it is vital to understand the overall cost that could be a consequence of the information's loss to better realize its value. Here again, estimating value may be the only method possible.

- Value of intellectual property—The value of a new product or service to a customer may ultimately be unknowable. How much would a cancer patient pay for a cure? How much would a shopper pay for a new flavor of cheese? What is the value of a logo or advertising slogan? Related but separate are intellectual properties known as trade secrets. Intellectual information assets like research and development projects (or textbooks) are the primary assets of some organizations.

- Value to adversaries—How much is it worth to an organization to know what the competition is doing? Many organizations have established departments tasked with the assessment and estimation of the activities of their competition, known as competitive intelligence. Even organizations in traditionally nonprofit industries can benefit from knowing what is going on in political, business, and competitive organizations. Stories of industrial espionage abound, including the urban legend of Company A encouraging its employees to hire on as janitors at Company B. As custodial workers, the employees could snoop through open terminals, photograph and photocopy unsecured documents, and rifle through internal trash and recycling bins. Such legends support a widely accepted concept: Information can have extraordinary value to the right individuals. Similarly, stories are circulated of how disgruntled employees, soon to be terminated, steal information and present it to competing organizations to curry favor and obtain new employment. Those who hire such applicants to gain from their larceny should consider whether benefiting from such a tactic is wise. After all, such thieves could presumably repeat their activities after becoming disgruntled with their new employers.

- Loss of productivity while the information assets are unavailable—When a power failure occurs, effective use of uninterruptible power supply (UPS) equipment can prevent data loss, but users may not be able to create new information. Although this is not an example of an attack that damages information, it is an instance in which a threat (deviations in services) affects an organization's productivity. The hours of wasted employee time, the cost of using alternatives, and the general lack of productivity will incur costs and can severely set back a critical operation or process.

- Loss of revenue while information assets are unavailable—Have you ever been purchasing something at a retail store and the payment card terminal couldn't recognize your credit card? How many times did you reinsert or reswipe the card before the salesperson tried entering the numbers manually? How long did it take to enter the numbers manually, in contrast with the quick insert? What if the credit card verification process was offline? Did the organization have a manual process to validate or process credit card payments in the absence of the familiar approval system? If the payment card system goes down, most organizations would resort to cash-only sales or be forced to shut down completely. Imagine an online retailer such as Amazon.com suffering a power outage. The entire operation is instantly closed. Even if Amazon's offering system were operational, what if the payment systems were offline? Customers could make selections but could not complete their purchases. Most organizations would be unable to conduct business if certain pieces of information were unavailable. The Federal Emergency Management Agency (FEMA) estimates that 40 percent of businesses do not reopen after a disaster and another 25 percent fail within one year.[6]

- Total cost of ownership—Ultimately, the single value that best reflects all costs associated with an information asset is known as the total cost of ownership (TCO). This is the sum total of the elements of the previous categories, encompassing all expenses associated with acquiring, operating, and disposing of the asset. It is critical to the economics of project management to understand that the cost of a software application or data management project to an organization includes much more than the cost of the development and implementation of the project. TCO includes both direct and indirect costs, most of which have been described here. However, TCO becomes more complicated when you factor in the breadth of the indirect costs. For a new software application, the organization will need a server to run it on, possibly a separate database application to store and manage the data, networking hubs, cables, power conditioning and protection (UPS), electricity, heating and cooling equipment, lighting to view the console, perhaps a separate keyboard, video, and mouse (KVM) switch, space in a server cabinet, a location in a data storage closet, and insurance. In addition, costs include those from software programmers, network engineers, database developers, and project managers—all of whom have salary, benefits, training, and equipment requirements—unless the project will leverage cloud-based resources, thus trading off direct hardware and operating costs for the indirect costs of managed services. All of this is just to develop, install, and run the application. Users must be trained to use the application, so their salaries and benefits are part of TCO. Training facilities require space, power, heating and cooling, insurance, and networking. Once the application requires maintenance, updates, improvements, enhancements, and an entire host of cybersecurity expenses—like the development requirements—the web of indirect costs required to keep a software application becomes increasingly difficult to track. The true TCO may never be fully understood; what the organization must do is devise a method of estimating TCO that management can live with and that makes sense to them.

The traditional model of calculating quantitative CBAs involves comparing the sum of the costs of an item against its expected benefits. In RM, that process becomes more complex when the benefits are a reduction in risk. Once an organization has estimated the worth of various assets, it can begin to calculate the potential loss from the successful exploitation of a vulnerability; this calculation yields an estimate of potential loss per risk. The questions that must be asked at this stage include the following:

- What damage could occur, and what financial impact would it have?
- What would it cost to recover from the attack, in addition to the financial impact of damage?
- What is the single loss expectancy for each risk?

In a CBA, a single loss expectancy (SLE) is the calculated value associated with the most likely loss from an attack (impact). The SLE is the product of the asset's value and the exposure factor; it takes into account both the value of the asset and the expected percentage of loss that would occur from a particular attack. In other words:

$$\text{SLE} = \text{asset value (AV)} \times \text{exposure factor (EF)}$$

where the exposure factor (EF) is the percentage loss that would occur from a given vulnerability being exploited.

For example, an organization determines a website has an estimated value of $1 million as determined by asset valuation, and a sabotage or vandalism scenario shows that 10 percent of the website's value would be damaged or destroyed in such an attack (the EF). In this case, the SLE for the website would be $1,000,000 \times 0.10 = \$100,000$. This estimate is then used to calculate another value, annualized loss expectancy, which is discussed later in this section.

As difficult as it is to estimate the value of information, estimating the probability of a threat occurrence or attack (likelihood) is even more difficult. There are not always tables, books, or records that indicate the frequency or probability of any given attack, although some sources are available for certain asset/threat pairs. For instance, the likelihood of a tornado or thunderstorm destroying a building of a specific type of construction within a specified region of the country is available to insurance underwriters. In most cases, however, an organization can rely only on its internal information to calculate the security of its information assets. Even if the network, systems, and cybersecurity administrators have been actively and accurately tracking these threat occurrences, the organization's information will be sketchy at best. As a result, this information is usually estimated.

Usually, the probability of a threat occurring is depicted as a table that indicates how frequently an attack from each threat type is likely to occur within a given time frame (e.g., once every 10 years). This value is commonly referred to as the annualized rate of occurrence (ARO) in a CBA; it represents the probability or likelihood of an adverse event per year. For example, if a successful act of sabotage or vandalism occurs about once every two years, then the ARO would be 50 percent (0.5). A network attack that can occur multiple times per second might be successful once each month and would have an ARO of 12.

Once you determine the loss from a single attack and the likely frequency of successful attacks, you can calculate the overall loss potential per risk, expressed as an annualized loss expectancy (ALE). In a CBA, the ALE is the product of the annualized rate of occurrence and SLE.

$$ALE = SLE \times ARO$$

To use our previous example, if SLE = \$100,000 and ARO = 0.5, then

$$ALE = \$100,000 \times 0.5 = \$50,000$$

Thus, the organization could expect to lose \$50,000 per year unless it increases its web security. Now, armed with a figure to justify its expenditures for controls and safeguards, the cybersecurity design team can deliver a budgeted value for planning purposes. Sometimes, noneconomic factors are considered in this process, so even when ALE amounts are not large, control budgets can be justified.

CBA determines whether the benefit from a control alternative is worth the associated cost of implementing and maintaining the control. Such analyses may be performed before implementing a control or safeguard, or they can be performed after controls have been in place for a while. Observation over time adds precision to the evaluation of the safeguard's benefits and the determination of whether the safeguard is functioning as intended.

Although many CBA techniques exist, the easiest way to calculate it is by using the ALE from earlier assessments:

$$CBA = ALE(pre) - ALE(post) - ACS$$

where ALE(pre) is the ALE of the risk before the implementation of the control; ALE(post) is the ALE examined after the control has been in place for a period of time; and ACS is the annualized cost of the safeguard.

Once the controls are implemented, it is crucial to examine their benefits continually to determine when they must be upgraded, supplemented, or replaced. As Frederick Avolio states in his article "Best Practices in Network Security":

> Security is an investment, not an expense. Investing in computer and network security measures that meet changing business requirements and risks makes it possible to satisfy changing business requirements without hurting the business's viability.[7]

Qualitative and Hybrid Asset Valuation Measures

Approaches to asset valuation like CBA attempt to use actual values or estimates to create a quantitative assessment. In some cases, an organization might be unable to determine these values. Fortunately, risk assessment steps can be executed using estimates based on a qualitative assessment, as mentioned in the previous chapter. For example, instead of placing a value of once every 10 years for the ARO, the organization might list all possible attacks on a particular set of information and rate each in terms of its probability of occurrence—high, medium, or low. The qualitative approach uses labels to assess value rather than numbers.

A more granular approach is the hybrid asset valuation, which attempts to create a value for an information asset that reduces some of the ambiguity of qualitative measures without resorting to the unsubstantiated estimations used for quantitative measures. This is also known as the semi-qualitative asset valuation; it uses scales tied to ranges rather than specific estimates. For example, the qualitative scales discussed for likelihood and impact in the previous chapter use ordinal rankings from 0 (not applicable threat) to 5 (almost certain) for likelihood and 0 (not applicable) to 5 (severe) for impact. The key difference between hybrid and pure qualitative assessment is that the hybrid approach has scales tied to quantitative values, whereas purely qualitative scales use simple relative scale values. To illustrate, Figure 4-7 shows the risk likelihood and risk impact scales for the risk rating used by Clearwater. If an organization simply used the Insignificant to Severe scale for risk ratings and did not also provide additional detail about likelihood and impact, it would be a qualitative scale. However, by benchmarking the values to include values for likelihood and impact, the scale becomes hybrid. By saying a loss is severe, more qualitatively minded managers can associate it with a numerical loss they can better understand and plan for.

Figure 4-7 Clearwater IRM|Analysis likelihood and impact

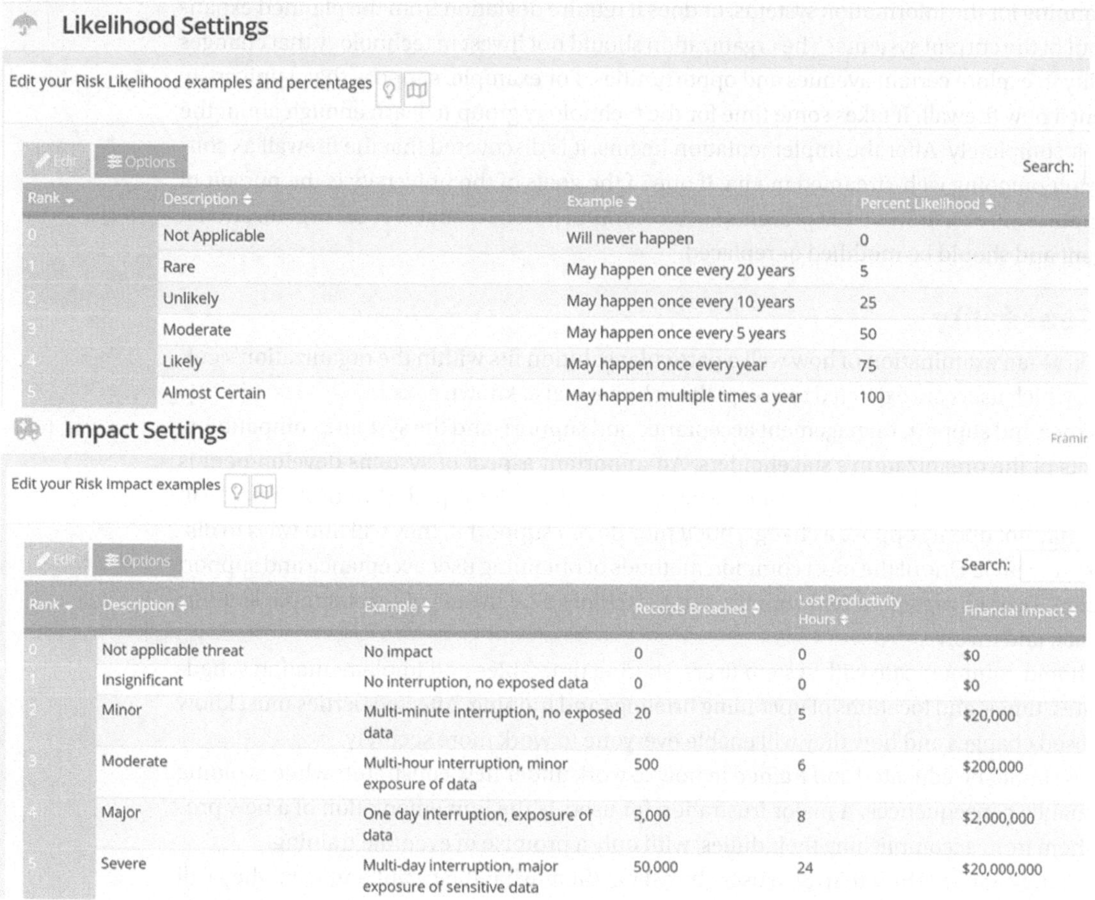
Likelihood Settings

Edit your Risk Likelihood examples and percentages

Edit | Options | Search:

Rank	Description	Example	Percent Likelihood
0	Not Applicable	Will never happen	0
1	Rare	May happen once every 20 years	5
2	Unlikely	May happen once every 10 years	25
3	Moderate	May happen once every 5 years	50
4	Likely	May happen once every year	75
5	Almost Certain	May happen multiple times a year	100

Impact Settings

Edit your Risk Impact examples

Edit | Options | Search:

Rank	Description	Example	Records Breached	Lost Productivity Hours	Financial Impact
0	Not applicable threat	No impact	0	0	$0
1	Insignificant	No interruption, no exposed data	0	0	$0
2	Minor	Multi-minute interruption, no exposed data	20	5	$20,000
3	Moderate	Multi-hour interruption, minor exposure of data	500	6	$200,000
4	Major	One day interruption, exposure of data	5,000	8	$2,000,000
5	Severe	Multi-day interruption, major exposure of sensitive data	50,000	24	$20,000,000

Source: Clearwater Security & Compliance LLC

Delphi Technique

How do you calculate the values and scales used in asset valuation and risk assessment? An individual can pull the information together based on personal experience, but as the saying goes, "Two heads are better than one"—and a team of heads is better than two. The Delphi technique, named for the oracle of Delphi who predicted the future in Greek mythology, is a process whereby a group rates or ranks a set of information. The individual responses are compiled and then returned to the group for another iteration. This process continues until the entire group is satisfied with the result. This technique can be applied to the development of scales, asset valuation, asset or threat ranking, or any scenario that can benefit from the input of more than one decision maker.

Other Influences on Risk Treatment Feasibility

Earlier in this chapter, the concept of economic feasibility was employed to justify proposals for cybersecurity controls. The next step in measuring an organization's readiness for these controls is to determine the potential organizational, operational, technical, and political feasibility of the proposal. These intangible feasibility studies may be useful in determining unexpected resistance to a proposal or other issues beyond economic feasibility.

Organizational Feasibility

Organizational feasibility—an examination of how well a particular solution fits within the organization's strategic planning objectives and goals—explores how proposed cybersecurity alternatives will contribute to the efficiency, effectiveness, and overall operation of an organization. Does the implementation align well with the strategic planning for the information systems, or does it require deviation from the planned expansion and management of the current systems? The organization should not invest in technology that changes its fundamental ability to explore certain avenues and opportunities. For example, suppose that a university decides to implement a new firewall. It takes some time for the technology group to learn enough about the firewall to configure it completely. After the implementation begins, it is discovered that the firewall as configured does not permit outgoing web-streamed media. If one of the goals of the university is the pursuit of distance-learning opportunities, a firewall that prevents such communication has not met the organizational feasibility requirement and should be modified or replaced.

Operational Feasibility

Operational feasibility—an examination of how well a particular solution fits within the organization's culture and the extent to which users are expected to accept the solution—also known as behavioral feasibility, refers to user acceptance and support, management acceptance and support, and the system's compatibility with the requirements of the organization's stakeholders. An important aspect of systems development is obtaining user buy-in on projects. If the users do not accept a new technology, policy, or program, it will inevitably fail. Users may not openly oppose a change, but if they do not support it, they will find ways to disable or otherwise circumvent it. One of the most common methods of obtaining user acceptance and support is via user engagement. User engagement and support can be achieved by means of three simple actions: communicate, educate, and involve.

Organizations should communicate with system users, sharing timetables and implementation schedules as well as the dates, times, and locations of upcoming briefings and training. Affected parties must know the purpose of proposed changes and how they will enable everyone to work more securely.

In addition, users should be educated and trained in how to work under new constraints while avoiding any negative performance consequences. A major frustration for users is the implementation of a new program that prevents them from accomplishing their duties, with only a promise of eventual training.

Finally, those making changes should involve users by asking them what they want and what they will tolerate from the new systems. One way to do this is to include representatives from the various constituencies in the development process.

Communication, education, and involvement can reduce resistance to change and build resilience for it—that ethereal quality that allows workers not only to tolerate constant change but also to understand it is a necessary part of the job.

Technical Feasibility

Unfortunately, many organizations rush to acquire new safeguards without thoroughly examining what is required to implement and use them effectively. Because the implementation of technological controls can be extremely complex, the project team must consider their technical feasibility—an examination of how well a particular solution can be supported given the organization's current technological infrastructure and resources, which include hardware, software, networking, and personnel. In other words, technical feasibility helps determine whether the organization already has or can acquire the technology necessary to implement and support its valuable resources. For example, does the organization have the hardware and software necessary to support a new firewall system? If not, can it be obtained?

Technical feasibility analysis also examines whether the organization has the technological expertise to manage the new technology. Does the staff include individuals who are qualified (and possibly certified) to install and manage the new firewall system? If not, can staff be spared from their current obligations to attend formal training and education programs to prepare them to administer the new systems, or must personnel be hired? In the current environment, how difficult is it to find qualified personnel?

Political Feasibility

Politics has been defined as the art of the possible. Political feasibility—an examination of how well a particular solution fits within the organization's political environment—considers what can and cannot occur based on the consensus and relationships among the communities of interest. The limits imposed by cybersecurity controls must fit within the realm of the possible before they can be effectively implemented, and that realm includes the availability of staff resources.

In some organizations, the cybersecurity community is assigned a budget, which they then allocate to activities and projects, making decisions about how to spend the money using their own judgment. In other organizations, resources are first allocated to the IT community of interest, and the cybersecurity team must compete for these resources. Sometimes, CBA and other forms of justification discussed in this chapter are used to make rational decisions about the relative merits of proposed activities and projects. Unfortunately, in other settings, these decisions are politically driven and do not focus on the pursuit of the greater organizational goals.

Another methodology for budget allocation requires the cybersecurity team to propose and justify use of resources for activities and projects in the context of the entire organization. This approach requires that arguments for cybersecurity spending articulate the benefit of the expense for the whole organization so that members of its communities of interest can understand and perceive their value.

Alternatives to Cost–Benefit Analysis

Rather than using CBA or some other feasibility reckoning to justify risk treatments, an organization might look to alternative models. These models will be discussed in detail in a later chapter. A short list of alternatives is provided here:

- Benchmarking is the comparison of organizational effectiveness, efficiency, and productivity against an established measure. External benchmarking is the process of seeking out and studying the practices used in other organizations that produce the results you desire in your organization. Internal benchmarking, also known as baselining, involves comparing measured past performance (the baseline) against actual performance for the assessed category. In both external and internal benchmarking, the comparison of the two performance states may reveal shortfalls in the organization's performance (known as the gap). A gap analysis allows the organization to create a plan for moving closer to the ideal level of performance. When benchmarking, an organization typically uses either metrics-based or process-based measures.

- Due care and due diligence describe an organization's actions when it adopts a certain minimum level of security—that is, what any prudent organization would do in similar circumstances.

- Best business practices are those thought to be among the best in the industry, balancing the need to access information with adequate protection.

- The gold standard is for ambitious organizations in which the best business practices are not sufficient. They aspire to set the standard for their industry and are thus said to be in pursuit of the gold standard.

- Government recommendations and best practices are useful for organizations that operate in industries regulated by governmental agencies. Government recommendations (in effect, requirements) can also serve as excellent sources for information about what some organizations are doing to control cybersecurity risks.

View Point   Cybersecurity and Cyber Risk Management

By Tim Callahan, Senior Vice President, Global Security and Global Chief Information Security Officer, Aflac, Inc.

There have been increasing conversations about the need for effective cyber risk management. This was evident recently when U.S. financial regulatory bodies released an advance notice of proposed rulemaking (ANPR) regarding enhanced cyber risk management standards for large and interconnected entities. For years, the cybersecurity profession has held responsibility for cybersecurity and at times wrestled with how risk management principles integrated with cybersecurity principles. This discussion explores the complementary nature of cybersecurity and risk management and suggests they are truly one and the same.

For the purpose of this discussion, the following is a working definition of each term. Cybersecurity involves protecting the confidentiality, integrity, and availability of information, which includes systems, hardware, and networks that process, store, and transmit the information. Risk management involves understanding "risk" and applying the appropriate controls commensurate with the mission and goals of the organization. Like cybersecurity, risk management involves governance, management, consideration of internal and external risks, and incident response.

At face value, we may see a paradox, or seeming contradiction, between the two concepts. One implies full protection with less regard for cost or mission, while the other implies knowledge, decision making, and judgment of controls appropriate for the mission. A cybersecurity purist may say we need to protect information at any cost, whereas a risk management mindset would look more at benefit, reward, and practicality of controls weighed against business objectives.

However, there is no contradiction. The cybersecurity profession has matured significantly in the last decade; it now encompasses aspects of cyber, physical, personal, data, communications, and network security. The cybersecurity professional now sees these disciplines as interconnected, where a weakness in one impacts the other. So, the inclination is to ensure all types of security are "bolted down." This premise is correct; they are all interconnected and should be locked down. However, over the course of the last few years, we have seen the reality of cost and benefit discussions as well as the proliferation of cybersecurity tools influence the practice. It is not practical to have one of every cybersecurity tool available. This reality has brought about the merging of risk management practices with cybersecurity practice.

Most cybersecurity professionals have embraced this concept, and many would argue the risk-based approach was always a part of the profession. There is truth to that; however, this merging has brought about a need for greater discipline in documenting risk practices. Solid risk management programs provide a formal process to understand risk, document risk, determine the organization's risk tolerance, and decide on the appropriate risk mitigation strategy.

Understanding risk begins with an "organizational" risk assessment. A good risk assessment will document the company profile—the purpose of the company, its mission and objectives, the risks found in the industry, risks particular to the company based on internal and external threats, and the risk tolerance of the organization. In doing the assessment, risk should be considered in terms of threat (criminal or otherwise), regulatory compliance, and reputation. These are generally industry-specific. A bank, for instance, would have concerns in all three areas. Being secure in one does not mean being secure in all. A company could be solid in addressing the threat but may not be regulatory-compliant. Another company could be solid in meeting the threat and all regulatory compliance but have a negative reputation with the public. All should be addressed.

Therefore, the risk assessment should define controls that may be in place to reduce or mitigate the risk. The assessment should also document the strategy for risk management in terms of elimination, acceptance, mitigation, or transference. Within cybersecurity, there are places where the strategy should be one of elimination. For instance, technology is employed that detects a threat and seeks to eliminate the threat. A simple example may be the elimination of all malware. In other instances, there could be a strategy of risk acceptance if the risk is deemed low or if the protection cost far outweighs the penalty.

You may be wondering, "Why should I go to all this trouble? I just want to secure the environment!" Well, the goal of a formal risk management program is to employ a governance framework that achieves a known and consistent state—a state that can be measured, discussed, and continuously improved in an organized manner over time. Additionally, a formal program provides an avenue to ensure that corporate governance entities such as corporate risk committees or the board of directors has sufficient awareness of risk and what the program is doing to address risk. One can then align the cybersecurity program to manage agreed-upon risk and help prioritize cybersecurity initiatives. The program, in essence, provides a form of corporate agreement on what the cybersecurity professional should be working toward. It is actually liberating in that sense.

In summary, the key to solid risk management is to understand your company objectives, risk tolerance, and risk profile, and then make risk-based decisions that meet the company's mission and objective. The most successful programs combine these concepts and principles into the cybersecurity program and operate as a risk management program.

Risk Treatment Practices

Assume that a risk assessment has determined it is necessary to protect a particular asset's vulnerabilities from a particular threat, at a cost of up to $50,000. Unfortunately, most budget authorities focus on the "up to"—they try to cut a percentage off the total figure to save the organization money. This tendency underlines the importance of developing strong justifications for specific action plans and of providing concrete estimates in those plans.

Then consider that each control or safeguard affects more than one TVA combination. If a new $50,000 firewall is installed to protect the Internet connection infrastructure from hackers launching port-scanning attacks, the same firewall will also protect other information assets from other threats and attacks. The final choice may call for a balanced mixture of controls that provides the greatest value for as many asset/threat pairs as possible. This example reveals another facet of the problem: cybersecurity professionals manage a dynamic matrix covering a broad range of threats, information assets, controls, and identified vulnerabilities. Each time a control is added to the matrix, it undoubtedly changes the ALE for the information asset's vulnerability, and it may also change the ALE for other information assets' vulnerabilities. To put it more simply, if you put in one safeguard, you may decrease the risk associated with all subsequent control evaluations. To complicate matters even further, the action of implementing a control may change the values assigned or calculated in a prior estimate.

Between the difficult task of valuing information assets and the dynamic nature of ALE calculations, it is no wonder that organizations typically look for a more straightforward method of implementing controls. This preference has prompted an ongoing search for ways to design cybersecurity architectures that go beyond the direct application of specific controls for specific information asset vulnerability. The following sections cover some of these alternatives.

Self-Check

4. The goal of cybersecurity is to bring residual risk down to zero.

   a. True   **b.** False

5. Once vulnerabilities have been controlled to the greatest extent possible, there is no residual risk remaining.

   a. True   **b.** False

6. The process of selecting a risk treatment strategy includes estimating the attacker's potential gain and the expected loss to the organization.

   a. True   **b.** False

☐ Check your answers at the end of this chapter.

Alternative Risk Management Methodologies

Until now, this chapter has presented a general treatment of RM, synthesizing methodologies from many sources to present the customary or usual approaches that organizations often employ to manage risk. The following sections present alternative approaches to RM, including international and national standards and methodologies from industry-leading organizations.

The OCTAVE Methods

The Operationally Critical Threat, Asset, and Vulnerability Evaluation (OCTAVE) method was a risk evaluation methodology promoted by Carnegie Mellon University's Software Engineering Institute (SEI) that allowed organizations to balance the protection of critical information assets against the costs of providing protective and detection controls. This process, illustrated in Figure 4-8, could enable an organization to measure itself against known or accepted good security practices and then establish an organization-wide protection strategy and risk mitigation plan. While no longer actively promoted by SEI, the methodology still provides valid insight into a viable alternate RM methodology. The OCTAVE process had three variations:

- The original OCTAVE method, which formed the basis for the OCTAVE body of knowledge, was designed for large organizations (300 or more users).
- OCTAVE-S was designed for smaller organizations of about 100 users.
- OCTAVE-Allegro was a streamlined approach for risk assessment.

Figure 4-8   OCTAVE overview

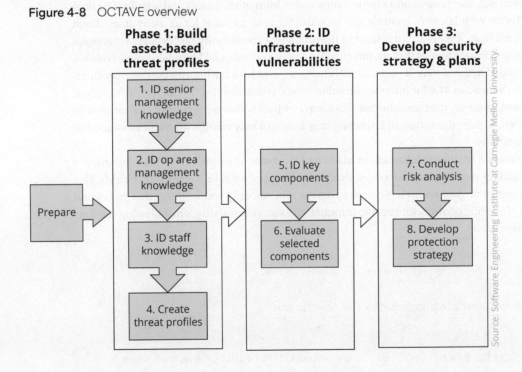

Even though the program is no longer actively promoted by SEI, the documents are still available as excellent references to an alternate approach to understanding RM (see https://resources.sei.cmu.edu/library/asset-view.cfm?assetid=309051).

FAIR

Factor Analysis of Information Risk (FAIR), an RM framework developed by Jack A. Jones, can also help organizations understand, analyze, and measure information risk. The reported outcomes include more cost-effective information RM, greater credibility for the cybersecurity profession, and a foundation from which to develop a scientific approach to information RM. The FAIR framework, as shown in Figure 4-9, includes the following:

- A taxonomy for information risk
- Standard nomenclature for information risk terms
- A framework for establishing data collection criteria
- Measurement scales for risk factors
- A computational engine for calculating risk
- A modeling construct for analyzing complex risk scenarios

Basic FAIR analysis comprises 10 steps in four stages:

Stage 1—Identify Scenario Components

1. Identify the asset at risk.
2. Identify the threat community under consideration.

Stage 2—Evaluate Loss Event Frequency (LEF)

3. Estimate the probable threat event frequency (TEF).
4. Estimate the threat capability (TCap).
5. Estimate control strength (CS).
6. Derive vulnerability (Vuln).
7. Derive LEF.

Stage 3—Evaluate Probable Loss Magnitude (PLM)

8. Estimate worst-case loss.
9. Estimate probable loss.

Stage 4—Derive and Articulate Risk

10. Derive and articulate risk.

Figure 4-9   Factor Analysis of Information Risk

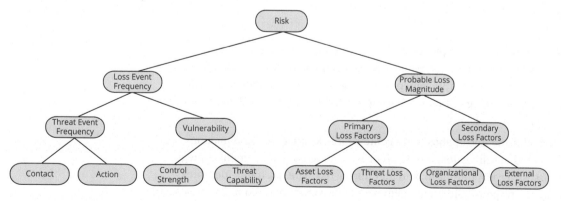

In 2011, FAIR became the cornerstone of a commercial consulting venture, CXOWARE, which built FAIR into an analytical software suite called RiskCalibrator. In 2014, FAIR was adopted by the Open Group as an international standard for RM and rebranded as Open FAIR™. Shortly thereafter, publicly viewable information on the FAIR Wiki site was taken down and all web links to the archival material were redirected to the

FAIR Institute website or the Open Group Standards e-commerce site. In 2015, CXOWARE was rebranded as RiskLens, and the FAIR Institute was established.

ISO Standards for Risk Management

The International Organization for Standardization (ISO) has several standards related to cybersecurity and two that specifically focus on RM. These standards include ISO 27005 and ISO 31000. ISO 31000 was developed using the Australian/New Zealand standard AS/NZS 4360:2004 as a foundation. In 2018, both standards were updated to create a unified approach to RM, which the methodology in this text is based on. ISO 27005 was updated again in 2022, with minor changes.

Originally, there was a slight difference in the 27005 and 31000 approaches, as the 31000 approaches were more general in nature and focused on all types of RM, not just cybersecurity. With the recent updates, the standards have a common perspective as applicable to all. However, ISO 27005 focuses on the RM process aspect of the model, as shown in Figure 4-10, while ISO 31000 includes the framework and a set of guiding principles, as illustrated in Figure 4-11.

Other related standards include ISO Guide 73: 2009 Risk management—Vocabulary and ISO/IEC 31010:2019 Risk Management—Risk Assessment Techniques.

NIST Risk Management Framework

The National Institute of Standards and Technology (NIST) has modified its fundamental approach to systems management and certification/accreditation to one that follows the industry standard of effective RM. Two key documents describe the Risk Management Framework (RMF): SP 800-37 and SP 800-39. You can find both at https://csrc.nist.gov/publications/sp.

As discussed in SP 800-39:

> This NIST document describes a process that organizations can use to frame risk decisions, assess risk, respond to risk when identified, and then monitor risk for ongoing effectiveness and continuous improvement to the risk management process. The intent is to offer a complete and organization-wide approach that integrates risk management into all operations and decisions.
>
> Framing risk establishes the organization's context for risk-based decision making with the intent of establishing documented processes for a risk management strategy that enables assessing, responding to, and monitoring risk. The risk frame identifies boundaries for risk responsibilities and delineates key assumptions about the threats and vulnerabilities found in the organization's operating environment.
>
> Assessing risk within the context of the organizational risk frame requires the identification of threats, vulnerabilities, consequences of exploitation leading to losses, and the likelihood of such losses. Risk assessment relies on a variety of tools, techniques, and underlying factors. These factors include organizational assumptions about risk,

Figure 4-10   ISO 27005 Cybersecurity risk management process

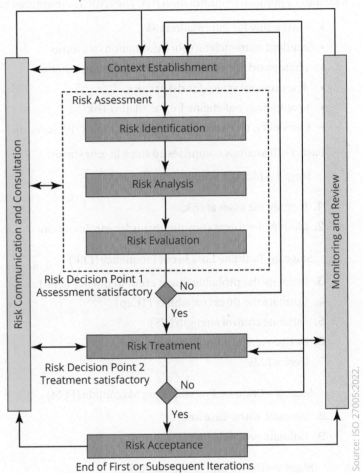

Source: ISO 27005:2022.

Figure 4-11   ISO 31000 Risk management principles, framework, and process

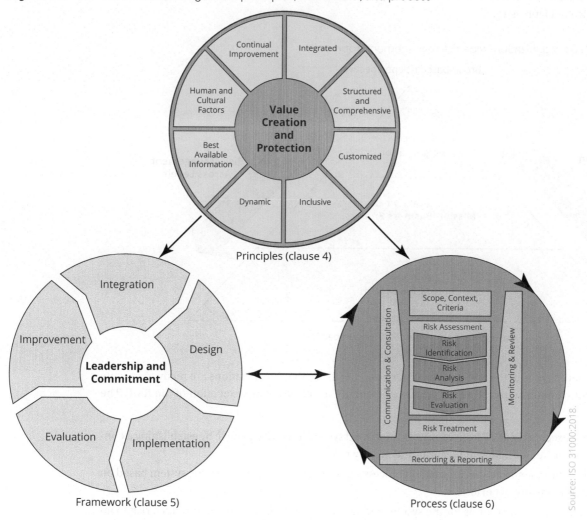

a variety of constraints within the organization and its environment, the roles and responsibilities of the organization's members, how and where risk information is collected and processed, the particular approach to risk assessment in the organization, and the frequency of periodic reassessments of risk.

Organizations will respond to risk once it is determined by risk assessments. Risk response should provide a consistent and organization-wide process based on developing alternative responses, evaluating those alternatives, selecting appropriate courses of action consistent with organizational risk appetites, and implementing the selected course(s) of action.

Risk monitoring over time requires the organization to verify that planned risk response measures are implemented and that the ongoing effectiveness of risk response measures has been achieved. In addition, organizations should describe how changes that may impact the ongoing effectiveness of risk responses are monitored.

NIST SP 800-37, Rev. 2 uses the framework level described in SP 800-39 and proposes processes for implementation using the RMF. Those processes emphasize the building of cybersecurity capabilities into information systems using managerial, operational, and technical security controls. The RMF promotes the concept of timely RM and robust continuous monitoring and encourages the use of automation to make cost-effective, risk-based decisions.

NIST's RMF follows a three-tiered approach. Most organizations work from the top down, focusing first on aspects that affect the entire organization, such as governance (level 1). Then, after the more strategic issues are addressed, they move toward more tactical issues around business processes (level 2). The most detailed aspects are addressed in level 3; they deal with information systems (and cybersecurity). This relationship is shown in Figure 4-12.

Figure 4-12   NIST organization-wide risk management approach

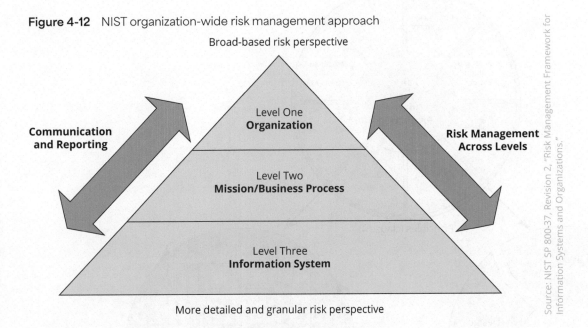

Source: NIST SP 800-37, Revision 2, "Risk Management Framework for Information Systems and Organizations."

There are seven steps in the RMF: a preparatory step to ensure that organizations are ready to execute the process and six main steps. All seven steps are essential for the successful execution of the RMF. The steps are:

- Prepare to execute the RMF from an organization- and system-level perspective by establishing a context and priorities for managing security and privacy risk.
- Categorize the system and the information processed, stored, and transmitted by the system based on an analysis of the impact of loss.
- Select an initial set of controls for the system and tailor the controls as needed to reduce risk to an acceptable level based on an assessment of risk.
- Implement the controls and describe how the controls are employed within the system and its environment of operation.
- Assess the controls to determine if the controls are implemented correctly, operating as intended, and producing the desired outcomes with respect to satisfying the security and privacy requirements.
- Authorize the system or common controls based on a determination that the risk to organizational operations and assets, individuals, other organizations, and the Nation is acceptable.
- Monitor the system and the associated controls on an ongoing basis to include assessing control effectiveness, documenting changes to the system and environment of operation, conducting risk assessments and impact analyses, and reporting the security and privacy posture of the system.

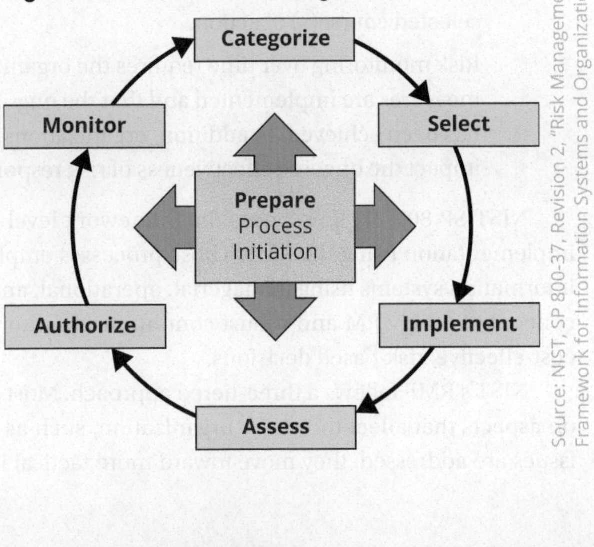

The seven steps of the RMF are shown in Figure 4-13.
According to NIST SP 800-37, Rev. 2, the RMF operates at all levels in the RM hierarchy illustrated in Figure 4-13.

Figure 4-13   NIST Risk Management Framework

Source: NIST, SP 800-37, Revision 2, "Risk Management Framework for Information Systems and Organizations."

While the RMF steps are listed in sequential order above . . . , the steps following the Prepare step can be carried out in a nonsequential order. After completing the tasks in the Prepare step, organizations executing the RMF for the first time for a system or set of common controls typically carry out the remaining steps in sequential order. However, there could be many points in the risk management process where there is a need to diverge from the sequential order due to the type of system, risk decisions made by senior leadership, or to allow for iterative cycles between tasks or revisiting of tasks (e.g., during agile development). Once the organization is in the Monitor step, events may dictate a nonsequential execution of steps. For example, changes in risk or in system functionality may necessitate revisiting one or more of the steps in the RMF to address the change.

Other Methods

The few methods described in this section so far are by no means all the available methods. In fact, many other organizations compare methods and provide recommendations for RM tools that the public can use. A few additional methods are listed here:

- MITRE—This nonprofit organization is designed to support research and development groups that have received federal funding. In its systems engineering guide, MITRE presents an RM plan that uses a four-step approach of (1) risk identification, (2) risk impact assessment, (3) risk prioritization analysis, and (4) risk mitigation planning, implementation, and progress monitoring. For more details, see www.mitre.org/publications/systems-engineering-guide/about-the-seg.

- European Network and Information Security Agency (ENISA)—This agency of the European Union ranks 12 tools using 22 different attributes. It also provides a utility on its website that enables users to compare RM methods or tools (www.enisa.europa.eu/activities/risk-management/current-risk/risk-management-inventory). The primary RM process promoted by ENISA is shown in Figure 4-14.

Figure 4-14 ENISA risk management process[8]

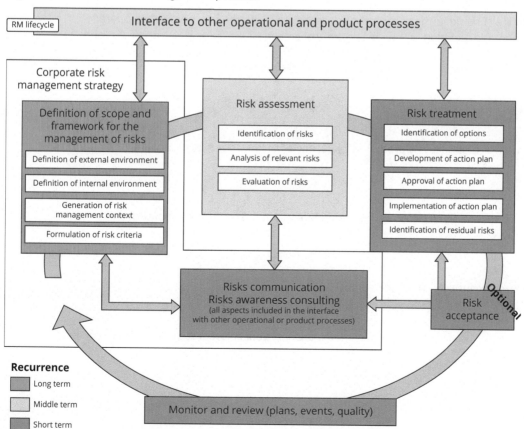

- New Zealand's IsecT Ltd.—An independent governance, RM, and compliance consultancy, IsecT maintains the ISO 27001 cybersecurity website at http://iso27001security.com. This website describes several RM methods (www.iso27001security.com/html/risk_mgmt.html).

Selecting the Best Risk Management Model

Most organizations already have a set of RM practices in place. The model followed is often an adaptation of a model mentioned earlier in this chapter. For organizations that have no RM process in place, starting such a process may be somewhat intimidating. A recommended approach is that the people assigned to implement an RM program should begin by studying the models presented earlier in this chapter and identifying what each offers to the envisioned process. Once the organization understands what each RM model offers, it can adopt and/or adapt one that is a good fit for the specific needs at hand.

Other organizations may hire a consulting firm to provide or even develop a proprietary model. Many of these firms have tried to adapt approaches based on popular RM models and have gained expertise in customizing them to suit specific organizations. This approach is most certainly not the least expensive option, but it guarantees that the organization can obtain a functional RM model as well as good advice and training for how to put it into use.

When faced with the daunting task of building a new RM program, it may be best to talk with other cybersecurity professionals, perhaps through cybersecurity organizations like the Information Systems Security Association, to find out how others in the field have approached this problem. Not only will you learn what models they prefer, you may also find out why they selected a particular model. While your peers may not disclose proprietary details about their models and how they use them, they may at least be able to point you in a direction. No two organizations are identical, so what works well for one organization may not work well for others. As organizations move forward with their RM efforts, keep this truism in mind: "The perfect is the enemy of the good." This can be translated into "Good security now is better than perfect security never."

Note 1 | To help define IT risk in terms of business risk associated with the use, ownership, operation, involvement, influence, and adoption of IT within an enterprise, see *COBIT 5 for Risk*, a book published by ISACA.

Self-Check

7. The OCTAVE method is still actively promoted by Carnegie Mellon University's Software Engineering Institute (SEI).

    a. True   **b.** False

8. FAIR was adopted by the Open Group as an international standard for RM and rebranded as Open FAIR™.

    a. True   **b.** False

9. ISO 31000 focuses exclusively on cybersecurity RM.

    a. True   **b.** False

☐ Check your answers at the end of this chapter.

Closing Case

Mike and Iris were reviewing the asset valuation worksheets that had been collected from all the company managers.

"Iris," Mike said after a few minutes, "the problem, as I see it, is that no two managers gave us answers that can be compared to each other's. Some gave only one value, and some didn't actually use a rank order for the last part. In fact, we don't know what criteria were used to assess the ranks or even where they got the cost or replacement values."

"I agree," Iris said, nodding. "These values and ranks are really inconsistent. This makes it a real challenge to create a useful, comprehensive list of information assets. We're going to have to visit all the managers and figure out where they got their values and how the assets were ranked."

Case Discussion Questions

1. If you could have spoken to Mike Edwards before he distributed the asset valuation worksheets, what advice would you have given him to make the consolidation process easier?
2. How would you advise Mike and Iris to proceed with the worksheets they already have in hand?

Case Ethical Decision Making

Suppose Mike and Iris decide to simply take the higher of each of the values without regard to how they were determined by the person who made the initial assessment. Then, they determine their own rankings among all of the compiled assets. When the list is later included in the planning process, they represent it as being authoritative because it came from "all of the managers."

Is this method, even if it is faster and easier, an ethical way to do business? Why or why not?

Summary

After the risk management (RM) process team has identified, analyzed, and evaluated the level of risk currently inherent in its information assets as part of risk assessment, it then must treat the risk that is deemed unacceptable.

Treating risk begins with an understanding of what risk treatment strategies are and how to formulate them. Once the RM team has identified the information assets with unacceptable levels of risk, they must choose one of four basic strategies to treat the risks for those assets:

- Mitigation—Applying controls and safeguards that eliminate or reduce the remaining uncontrolled risk
- Transference—Shifting risks to other areas or to outside entities
- Acceptance—Understanding the consequences of choosing to leave an information asset's vulnerability facing the current level of risk, but only after a formal evaluation and intentional acknowledgment of this decision
- Termination—Removing or discontinuing the information asset from the organization's operating environment

As the process team works through the various RM activities, it needs to continually provide feedback to the framework team about the relative success and challenges of its RM activities. The information flow within and between the governance group, RM framework team, and RM process team during the implementation of RM facilitates the RM activities.

Risk appetite is the quantity and nature of risk that organizations are willing to accept as they evaluate the trade-offs between perfect cybersecurity and unlimited accessibility.

Before deciding on specific treatment strategies, an organization should explore all readily accessible information about the economic and noneconomic consequences of an exploitation of the vulnerability.

Asset valuation is a complex process used to estimate the real or perceived costs or values associated with the operation of an asset.

Economic feasibility is often employed to justify proposals for cybersecurity controls. The next step in measuring an organization's readiness for these controls is to determine the potential organizational, operational, technical, and political feasibility of the proposal. These intangible feasibility studies may be useful in determining unexpected resistance to a proposal or other issues beyond economic feasibility.

Rather than using CBA or some other feasibility reckoning to justify risk treatments, an organization might look to alternative models such as benchmarking: the comparison of organizational effectiveness, efficiency, and productivity against an established measure. It might also try baselining measured past performance against actual performance. Due care and due diligence describe an organization's actions when it adopts a certain minimum level of security—that is, what any prudent organization would do in similar circumstances. Best business practices are those thought to be among the best in the industry, balancing the need to access information with adequate protection. The gold standard is for ambitious organizations in which the best business practices are not sufficient. They aspire to set the standard for their industry and are thus said to be in pursuit of the gold standard.

Key Terms

acceptance risk treatment strategy

annualized loss expectancy (ALE)

annualized rate of occurrence (ARO)

asset valuation

behavioral feasibility

cost avoidance

cost-benefit analysis (CBA)

defense risk treatment strategy

exposure factor (EF)

hybrid asset valuation

mitigation risk treatment strategy

operational feasibility

organizational feasibility

political feasibility

risk acceptance

risk avoidance

risk mitigation

risk sharing

risk termination

risk transfer

semi-qualitative asset valuation

single loss expectancy (SLE)

technical feasibility

termination risk treatment strategy

transference risk treatment strategy

Review Questions

1. What are the four basic strategies for treating risks identified by the risk management (RM) process team?

2. How does the risk mitigation strategy aim to reduce risk?

3. What is the purpose of the transference risk treatment strategy?

4. Under what circumstances might an organization choose the acceptance risk treatment strategy?

5. What actions are involved in the termination risk treatment strategy?

6. Why is continuous feedback important in the RM process?

7. What distinguishes risk mitigation from contingency planning (CP) mitigation?

8. How can organizations effectively implement the transference risk treatment strategy?

9. What is the significance of assessing risk treatment strategies in the context of an organization's risk appetite?

10. What is the primary goal of a cybersecurity program in the context of managing residual risk?

11. How does the concept of risk appetite influence an organization's decision making in cybersecurity?

12. What are some of the guidelines for selecting a risk treatment strategy?

13. What role does an action plan play in risk treatment strategy selection?

14. How is economic feasibility evaluated in the context of cybersecurity controls?

15. What are the challenges associated with determining the cost of safeguarding information?

16. How can the value of information assets and the benefit of using controls be determined?

17. What does the annualized loss expectancy (ALE) represent, and how is it calculated?

18. What alternative models to cost–benefit analysis might an organization consider for justifying risk treatments?

19. What is the OCTAVE method, and who promoted it?

20. What does FAIR stand for, and what is its purpose in RM?

21. How has the FAIR framework been institutionalized or adopted by organizations or standards?

22. What ISO standards are specifically focused on RM, and what updates were made in 2018?

23. What is the primary purpose of the NIST Risk Management Framework (RMF)?

24. Can you describe the seven steps of the RMF?

25. How does MITRE's approach to RM differ from other methodologies?

26. What role does the European Network and Information Security Agency (ENISA) play in comparing RM tools?

27. What considerations should an organization take into account when selecting an RM model?

Exercises

1. Using the following table, calculate the SLE, ARO, and ALE for each threat category listed.

XYZ Software Company (Asset value: $1,200,000 in projected revenues)

Threat Category	Cost per Incident	Frequency of Occurrence
Programmer mistakes	$5,000	1 per week
Loss of intellectual property	$75,000	1 per year
Software piracy	$500	1 per week
Theft of information (hacker)	$2,500	1 per quarter
Theft of information (employee)	$5,000	1 per 6 months
Web defacement	$500	1 per month
Theft of equipment	$5,000	1 per year
Viruses, worms, Trojan horses	$1,500	1 per week
Denial-of-service attack	$2,500	1 per quarter
Earthquake	$250,000	1 per 20 years
Flood	$250,000	1 per 10 years
Fire	$500,000	1 per 10 years

2. How do you think the XYZ Software Company arrived at the values shown in the table in Exercise 1? For each row in the table, describe how you might go about determining the cost per incident and the frequency of occurrence.

3. How could we determine an exposure factor (EF) if there is no percentage of exposure given? Which method is easier for determining the SLE: a percentage of value lost or cost per incident?

4. Assume a year has passed and XYZ has improved its cybersecurity. Using the following table, calculate the SLE, ARO, and ALE for each threat category listed here:

XYZ Software Company (Asset value: $1,200,000 in projected revenues)

Threat Category	Cost per Incident	Frequency of Occurrence	Cost of Controls	Type of Control
Programmer mistakes	$5,000	1 per month	$20,000	Training
Loss of intellectual property	$75,000	1 per 2 years	$15,000	Firewall/intrusion detection system (IDS)
Software piracy	$500	1 per month	$30,000	Firewall/IDS
Theft of information (hacker)	$2,500	1 per 6 months	$15,000	Firewall/IDS
Theft of information (employee)	$5,000	1 per year	$15,000	Physical security
Web defacement	$500	1 per quarter	$10,000	Firewall
Theft of equipment	$5,000	1 per 2 years	$15,000	Physical security
Viruses, worms, Trojan horses	$1,500	1 per month	$15,000	Antivirus
Denial-of-service attack	$2,500	1 per 6 months	$10,000	Firewall
Earthquake	$250,000	1 per 20 years	$5,000	Insurance/backups
Flood	$50,000	1 per 10 years	$10,000	Insurance/backups
Fire	$100,000	1 per 10 years	$10,000	Insurance/backups

5. In the table in Exercise 4, why have some values changed in the Cost per Incident and Frequency of Occurrence columns? How could a control affect one but not the other?

6. Assume that the costs of controls presented in the table in Exercise 4 are unique costs directly associated with protecting against that threat. In other words, do not worry about overlapping costs between threats. Calculate the CBA for each control. Are they worth the costs listed?

7. Using the web, research the costs associated with the following items when implemented by a firm with 1,000 employees and 100 servers:

- Managed antivirus software licenses (not open source) for 500 workstations
- Cisco commercial firewalls (other than residential models)
- Tripwire host-based IDS for 10 servers
- Java programming continuing education training program for 10 employees
- Check Point firewall solutions

Solutions to Self-Check Questions

Introduction to Risk Treatment

1. The RM process team must treat all identified risks, regardless of their level.
    Answer: b. False.
    Explanation: The RM process team must treat risks that are deemed unacceptable—in other words, when they exceed the organization's risk appetite.

2. Risk transference involves accepting the current level of risk without making changes.
    Answer: b. False.
    Explanation: Risk transference is defined as shifting risks to other areas or outside entities, not accepting the current level of risk.

3. Risk acceptance means the organization has made a conscious decision to do nothing further to protect an information asset from risk.
    Answer: a. True.
    Explanation: Risk acceptance occurs when the organization decides to accept the current level of residual risk and chooses to do nothing beyond the current level of protection.

Managing Risk

4. The goal of cybersecurity is to bring residual risk down to zero.
    Answer: b. False.
    Explanation: The goal of cybersecurity is not to bring residual risk to zero but to align it with an organization's risk appetite. It is virtually impossible to bring residual risk to zero while continuing to provide value to the organization, so the aim is to align residual risk with the organization's tolerance for risk.

5. Once vulnerabilities have been controlled to the greatest extent possible, there is no residual risk remaining.
    Answer: b. False.
    Explanation: Even after vulnerabilities have been controlled as much as possible, there is still residual risk that has not been completely removed or shifted. Residual risk persists even after implementing safeguards to reduce the levels of risk associated with threats, vulnerabilities, and information assets.

6. The process of selecting a risk treatment strategy includes estimating the attacker's potential gain and the expected loss to the organization.
    Answer: a. True.
    Explanation: The process involves estimating what an attacker will gain from a successful attack and the expected loss the organization will incur if the vulnerability is successfully exploited.

Alternative Risk Management Methodologies

7. The OCTAVE method is still actively promoted by Carnegie Mellon University's Software Engineering Institute (SEI).
    Answer: b. False.
    Explanation: The OCTAVE method is no longer actively promoted by SEI, but its documents remain available as references for an alternate approach to understanding RM. The OCTAVE method still provides valid insight into a viable alternative RM methodology.

8. FAIR was adopted by the Open Group as an international standard for RM and rebranded as Open FAIR™.

   Answer: a. True.

   Explanation: FAIR was adopted by the Open Group as an international standard for RM and subsequently rebranded as Open FAIR™.

9. ISO 31000 focuses exclusively on cybersecurity RM.

   Answer: b. False.

   Explanation: ISO 31000 is more general in nature and focuses on all types of RM, not exclusively on cybersecurity. Originally, ISO 31000 had a broader focus compared to ISO 27005, addressing general RM rather than being confined to cybersecurity.

Compliance: Law and Ethics

Chapter Objectives

After reading this chapter and completing the exercises, you should be able to:

1 Summarize the impact that law and ethics have on cybersecurity.

2 List the most prominent professional cybersecurity organizations and explain their codes of conduct.

3 Identify significant national and international laws that relate to cybersecurity.

4 Describe organizational liability and key law enforcement agencies.

> In law a man is guilty when he violates the rights of others. In ethics he is guilty if he only thinks of doing so.
>
> —Immanuel Kant
> (1724–1804)

Case Opener

Iris was just over halfway through her usual morning email ritual when she came to a message that caught her attention. Just a few weeks before, Random Widget Works (RWW) had set up a new customer feedback web server to facilitate open dialogue and unrestricted feedback. This system would allow anyone, anywhere to send anonymous emails to the company's executive management team. Apparently, someone had sent just such a message, and the CEO's executive assistant had relayed it to Iris. The email read as follows:

> To: Iris Majwubu
> From: Cassandra Wilmington, Special Assistant to the CEO
> Date: 2024-11-18 07:45 AM
> Subject: FW: Anonymous Ethics Report–2024-11-17 07:46 AM
> Iris, you better look at this. The attached message came in on the anonymous customer feedback system. I captured the text, encrypted it, and have attached it to this email. The boss has already seen it and asked me to distribute secure copies to you as well as Robin, Jerry, and Mike. He has asked me to set up a meeting with you four this morning at 10:00. A meeting invitation follows. . .

Iris opened her safe, retrieved and mounted her secure document drive, and then exported the attachment file to it. She opened the decryption program, entered her employee credentials, and validated the dual authentication on her company mobile phone to decrypt the message. The text appeared:

> To: RWW Anonymous Feedback Mailbox
> From: A Friend
> Date: 2024-11-14 02:46 AM
> Subject: RWW is for sale
> You might want to look at the everythingz4zale.com auction site at www.everythingz4zale.com/auctions/ref=19085769340

Iris opened her browser window and typed in the URL. She saw the following:

Item #19085769340

RWW, Inc. customer and key accounts list

Starting bid: 0.2 Bitcoin

Time left: 1 day 22 hours 50 mins 3-day listing

History: 0 bids

Iris picked up her phone and dialed RWW's legal affairs office. She knew it was going to be a busy day.

Introduction to Law and Ethics

This chapter covers fundamental cybersecurity professional ethics and relevant laws. Although the two topics are intertwined, the first part of this chapter discusses ethics as the foundation of law and its impact on the development of codes of ethics and conduct in cybersecurity-related organizations. The second part of this chapter discusses legislation and regulations concerning information management in an organization. You can use this chapter both as a reference guide to the legal aspects of cybersecurity and as an aid in planning professional development.

Within modern society, individuals elect to trade some aspects of personal freedom for social order. As Jean Jacques Rousseau explained in *The Social Contract, or Principles of Political Right*[1] (1762), laws are the rules that societies create to balance an individual's rights with the needs of the state. Laws are rules adopted and enforced by governments to codify expected behavior in modern society. They are largely drawn from the ethics of a culture, which define socially acceptable behaviors that conform to the widely held principles of the members of that society. The key difference between law and ethics is that law carries the sanction of a governing authority and ethics do not. Ethics are based on cultural mores, which are the relatively fixed moral attitudes or customs of a societal group. Some ethics are thought to be universal. For example, murder, theft, and assault are actions that deviate from ethical and legal codes in most, if not all, of the world's cultures.

The cybersecurity professional plays an important role in an organization's approach to controlling liability for privacy and security risks. In the modern litigious societies of the world, sometimes laws are enforced in civil courts, with plaintiffs awarded compensation for damages or to punish defendants. To minimize this potential liability, the cybersecurity practitioner must understand the current legal environment and keep up to date on new laws, regulations, and ethical issues as they emerge. By educating employees and management about their legal and ethical obligations and the proper use of information technology (IT) and cybersecurity, security professionals can keep organizations focused on their primary mission.

The cybersecurity professional has a unique position within the organization, as they are trusted with one of the most valuable assets the organization has: its information. Not only are cybersecurity professionals responsible for protecting the information, they are privy to the secrets and structures of the systems that store, transmit, use, and protect that information. Thus, they are individuals who must be beyond reproach, with the highest ethical standards. The Roman poet Juvenal, in his work *Satire VI*, asked "Quis custodiet ipsos custodies?", which is loosely translated as, "Who will watch the watchmen?" This expression has gained unique meaning within the cybersecurity community, as cybersecurity professionals, above all else, are expected to understand the need for accountability. Partly for this reason, it is unusual for organizations to hire new employees directly into cybersecurity positions, unless they have established experience at other organizations where they have proven their trustworthiness. While this standard may change in years to come, most organizations still expect new hires to prove themselves worthy of the responsibility associated with this high-trust role. Therefore, it is imperative for you to understand and take to heart this expectation of trust—the expectation of being beyond ethical reproach—as you continue your professional journey into cybersecurity.

Ethics in Cybersecurity

Ethics is the branch of philosophy that considers the nature, criteria, logic, and validity of moral judgment. Some define ethics as the organized study of how humans ought to act. Others define it as a set of rules we should live by. The student of cybersecurity is not expected to study ethics in a vacuum but within a larger framework. However, cybersecurity professionals are expected to be more informed about the topic than others in the organization, as they must often withstand a higher degree of scrutiny. When we add a qualitative assessment to the study of ethics, we are adding the dimension known as *morality*, which defines acceptable and unacceptable behavior within a group context.

View Point   Ethics in Cybersecurity

By Lee Imrey, CISO advisor, security architect, go-to-market specialist, and IANS Faculty member; formerly Chair of the ISSA International Ethics Committee and Instructor of Computer Law and Ethics for (ISC)[2]

It is easy to configure a router to share routing table updates with peer devices. It is simple to configure file and directory permissions in a distributed file system. With the right training, it is possible to test for and conclusively demonstrate the efficacy of each.

Ethical decisions are more complex. Ethics, in a general sense, is a common understanding of what constitutes appropriate behavior, or doing the right thing. But, as a common understanding, it lies somewhere between the belief of the individual and of the community. What constitutes right behavior varies with the values of each community. The community may be as small as a family unit, a social circle, or a village. This is why questions of ethical conduct may be brought to a parent, or village elders, in whom the ethical values of the community are vested. This can be seen in the U.S. legal system, as well as that of other countries, when people are judged by a jury of their peers. In other words, they are judged by members of the community with whom their ethics should be most aligned.

On the other hand, in some cases, the community defining ethical boundaries may be as large as a country or even larger. For instance, in cases of treason or crimes against humanity, people may be prosecuted for violation of laws that have been set up to codify ethical standards common across regional or national boundaries.

However, these are the easy cases. The real challenge in determining ethical behavior is in determining the community whose ethical values should be applied. In today's world, we see members of different communities in conflict and individuals acting according to the ethical values of their communities:

- Pharmaceutical companies developing medicines for the sick
- Animal rights activists protesting animal testing
- High-income nations trying to impose strict emission controls on factories
- Low-income nations driving economic prosperity through the use of cheap fuels
- Intellectual property owners (i.e., of copyrights, patents, etc.) trying to profit from their investments
- Nations trying to reap the benefit of scientific and cultural progress without paying cost-prohibitive fees

In these examples, proponents on both sides of each issue feel they are behaving ethically in the context of their own communities. The communities frame the ethical choices for their members.

Your ethical choices define who you are. If you want to be an activist, go be an activist. If your highest allegiance is to your country or a political cause, then follow your dreams and enlist or sign up for the cause you believe in.

If you want to be a cybersecurity professional, you need to align your ethical values, your choices, and your behavior with the growing community of cybersecurity professionals worldwide. Apply your efforts to building reliable information systems that businesses and consumers can trust, and that function according to their design and minimize the opportunity for misuse. A professional engineer building a bridge or road is expected to hold public safety paramount in the performance of their duties. Follow this model, keeping the safety of the public and their information as your highest obligation, and you will gain credibility as an ethical cybersecurity professional.

Traditional foundations and frameworks of ethics include the following:

- Normative ethics—The study of what makes actions right or wrong, also known as moral theory (i.e., how people should act)
- Meta-ethics—The study of the meaning of ethical judgments and properties (i.e., what is right)
- Descriptive ethics—The study of the choices that have been made by individuals in the past (i.e., what others think is right)
- Applied ethics—An approach that applies moral codes to actions drawn from realistic situations; it seeks to define how we might use ethics in practice
- Deontological ethics—The study of the rightness or wrongness of intentions and motives as opposed to the rightness or wrongness of the consequences (i.e., a person's ethical duty); also known as duty-based or obligation-based ethics

From these well-defined ethical frameworks come a series of ethical standards or approaches as follows:

- Utilitarian approach—Emphasizes that an ethical action is one that results in the most good or the least harm; this approach seeks to link consequences to choices.
- Rights approach—Suggests that the ethical action is the one that best protects and respects the moral rights of those affected by that action; it begins with a belief that humans have an innate dignity based on their ability to make choices. The list of moral rights is usually thought to include the right to make one's own choices about what kind of life to lead, the right to be told the truth, the right not to be injured, and the right to a degree of privacy. These rights imply certain duties—specifically, the duty to respect the rights of others. There are some that argue nonhumans have rights as well.
- Fairness or justice approach—Founded on the work of Aristotle and other Greek philosophers who contributed the idea that all people should be treated equally; today, this approach defines ethical actions as those with outcomes that regard all human beings equally, or that incorporate a degree of fairness based on some defensible standard. This is often described as a "level playing field."
- Common-good approach—Based on the work of the Greek philosophers, a notion that life in community yields a positive outcome for the individual, and therefore every individual should contribute to that community. This approach argues that the complex relationships found in a society are the basis of a process founded on ethical reasoning that respects and has compassion for all others, most particularly the most vulnerable members of a society. This approach tends to focus on the common welfare.
- Virtue approach—A very ancient ethical model postulating that ethical actions ought to be consistent with so-called ideal virtues; that is, those virtues that all of humanity finds most worthy and that, when present, indicate a fully developed humanity. In most virtue-driven ethical frameworks, the virtues include honesty, courage, compassion, generosity, tolerance, love, fidelity, integrity, fairness, self-control, and prudence. Virtue ethics asks everyone to consider if the outcome of any specific decision will reflect well on others' perceptions of them.

These ethical standards or approaches offer a set of tools for decision making in the era of computer technology. People remain responsible for the choices they make, whether a choice affects only themselves or many others as well.

Ethics in the Information Processing Professions

Ethics for professionals in information processing have two dimensions beyond those for many white-collar career categories. First, IT workers are often given access to sensitive information or encounter it as part of their assigned duties. This access can lead to situations in which they have added power and increased responsibilities. Second, systems professionals who design and implement automated system processes are working to institutionalize policy and practices that will guide how all members of the organization act and react as it conducts its operations. When systems are designed and implemented to lead to ethically valid outcomes and these practices become a requirement for operations, the process can lead to a more ethical workplace. When systems are deployed without such checks and balances, the system's users are free to make moral choices or not.

Often, professionals in information processing know how to perform the technical aspects of an assignment but may not understand how the misuse of information assets can lead to legal and ethical misconduct. Important questions about ownership of information and who can delegate access and control of it could create organizational lapses that lead to legal and public relations catastrophes. How many information processing professionals grasp that their daily decision making raises ethical issues?

Many of these issues involve privacy. For example, is it acceptable to browse through email messages on a mail server for which you are an administrator? Perhaps the task is an assigned role to enforce company policy, but only when system users have been informed of the policy. Is it permissible to use key loggers or network sniffers to record what users type into company systems? Again, the task may be part of an employee's assigned role, but only when enabled by the organization's policy. When an employee has network and system credentials that allow access privileges to the organization's information assets, perhaps even encrypted information, how the privileges are used is the essential point. Just because employees have a privilege does not mean they need to use it in every situation.

Many discussions of ethics include the concept of the slippery slope. This idea pertains to the ease with which a person can justify an action based on a previous justified action. For example, if one task of your job is to use a network sniffer to assess how firewall rules are processed by examining network traffic through the firewall, you might be justified in inspecting packet headers, and you could easily start reading packet payload data out of idle curiosity. Or, employees might be assigned to oversee a data exfiltration monitoring system and watch for systems misuse, but then they read an embarrassing email that provides an opportunity for personal amusement or revenge. In these cases, an employee can extend an authorized activity into unethical territory.

Sometimes, systems are deployed for reasons that are unethical at a higher level. Several books describe how governments have implemented information systems to commit acts of oppression or genocide. One of the most examined cases involved IBM Corporation and its business practices in the 1930s and 1940s with the German government. Journalist Edwin Black's book *IBM and the Holocaust: The Strategic Alliance between Nazi Germany and America's Most Powerful Corporation* documents how IBM's technology was abused to support the commission of genocide.

As organizations are increasingly required to comply with privacy and data management laws, they more often rely on their employees, contractors, and consultants to act accordingly. Knowing the ethical frameworks that support moral decision making makes appropriate and professional behavior more likely.

The Ten Commandments of Computer Ethics

To improve the visibility of ethical concepts in the minds of practicing professionals, one professional group has prepared a focused list of objectives that individuals and organizations can use to stay focused on ethical actions. The "Ten Commandments of Computer Ethics"[2] are:

1. Thou shalt not use a computer to harm other people.
2. Thou shalt not interfere with other people's computer work.
3. Thou shalt not snoop around in other people's computer files.
4. Thou shalt not use a computer to steal.

5. Thou shalt not use a computer to bear false witness.

6. Thou shalt not copy or use proprietary software for which you have not paid.

7. Thou shalt not use other people's computer resources without authorization or proper compensation.

8. Thou shalt not appropriate other people's intellectual output.

9. Thou shalt think about the social consequences of the program you are writing or the system you are designing.

10. Thou shalt always use a computer in ways that ensure consideration and respect for your fellow humans.

Source: "The Ten Commandments of Computer Ethics." Computer Professionals for Social Responsibility. cpsr.org/issues/ethics/cei.

Ethics and Education

Key studies reveal that the overriding factor in leveling ethical perceptions within a small population is education. Employees must be educated and kept up to date on cybersecurity topics, including the expected behavior of an ethical employee. This is especially important in areas of cybersecurity, as many employees may not have the formal technical knowledge to understand that their behavior is unethical or even illegal. One way to introduce employees and other stakeholders to thinking about ethics is to use scenarios based on practical situations where ethical choices must be made in the world of work and school, as shown in the following section. Proper ethical and legal education, training, and awareness are vital to creating an informed, well-prepared, and low-risk employee or other stakeholder.

The Use of Scenarios in Computer Ethics Studies

The following vignettes, originally developed by David Paradice and extended by Mike Whitman in their research, can be used in an open and frank discussion of computer ethics. Review each scenario carefully and then answer each question by choosing from the following list the degree of ethical behavior you believe the person has displayed: very ethical, ethical, neither ethical nor unethical, unethical, very unethical. If you use these scenarios for class assignments, be sure to justify your responses.

Ethical Decision Evaluation

1. A scientist developed a theory that required proof through the construction of a computer model. The scientist hired a computer programmer to build the model, and the theory was shown to be correct. The scientist won several awards for the development of the theory but never acknowledged the contribution of the computer programmer.

    The scientist's failure to acknowledge the computer programmer was _____.

2. The owner of a small business needed a customized inventory system. The owner identified various required inputs and outputs, showed the design to a computer programmer, and asked the programmer if they could build such a system. The programmer knew they could implement the system from having developed much more sophisticated systems in the past. In fact, the programmer felt the design was rather crude and would soon need several major revisions. However, they did not say anything about the design flaws because the business owner did not ask, and they thought they might be the one hired to implement the needed revisions later.

    The programmer's decision not to point out the design flaws was _____.

3. A student suspected and found a vulnerability in a university's computer system that allowed access to other students' records. The student told the system administrator about the vulnerability but continued to access other records until the problem was corrected two weeks later.

    The student's action in searching for the vulnerability was _____.

    The student's action in continuing to access others' records for two weeks was _____.

    The system administrator's failure to correct the problem sooner was _____.

4. An online customer ordered accounting software from a vendor's website. Upon receiving the order, the customer found that the store had accidentally sent a very expensive word-processing program as well as the accounting software. The invoice listed only the accounting software. The user decided to keep the word-processing program.

   The user's decision to keep the word-processing program was _____.

5. A systems administrator at a bank realized that they had accidentally overdrawn their checking account. The administrator made a small adjustment in the bank's accounting system to exclude the account from the normal balance audit so that the account would not have an additional service charge assessed. As soon as they deposited funds that made the balance positive again, they corrected the bank's accounting system.

   The programmer's modification of the accounting system was _____.

6. A programmer enjoys building apps to give to friends. The programmer would frequently go to the office on Saturday when no one was working and use company systems to develop these apps. The programmer did not hide the fact that they were going into the building; they had to sign a register at a security desk each time they entered.

   The programmer's use of the company systems was _____.

   If the programmer sold the apps, these actions would have been _____.

7. A student enrolled in a computer class was also employed at a local business part time. Frequently, class homework assignments involved using popular word-processing and spreadsheet packages. Occasionally, the student worked on the assignments using the office computer at the part-time job during coffee or meal breaks.

   The student's use of the company computer was _____.

   If the student had done their homework during "company time" (not during a break), the use of the company computer would have been _____.

8. A university student learned to use an expensive spreadsheet program in an accounting class. The student would go to the university computer lab and use the software to complete assignments. Signs were posted in the lab indicating that copying software was forbidden. One day, the student decided to copy the software anyway in order to complete work assignments at home.

   The student's action in copying the software was _____.

Deterring Unethical and Illegal Behavior

It is the responsibility of cybersecurity personnel to deter unethical and illegal acts using policy, education and training, and technology as controls or safeguards to protect the organization's information and systems. Many security professionals understand technological means of protection, but many underestimate the value of policy.

There are three general categories of unethical behavior that organizations and society should seek to eliminate:

- Ignorance. Ignorance of the law is no excuse, but ignorance of policies and procedures is. The first method of deterrence is the security education, training, and awareness (SETA) program. Organizations must design, publish, and disseminate organizational policies and relevant laws, and employees must explicitly agree to abide by them. Reminders and training and awareness programs support retention and compliance.

- Accidents. Individuals with authorization and privileges to manage information within the organization have the greatest opportunity to cause harm or damage by accident. Careful placement of controls can help prevent accidental modification or damage to systems and data.

- Intent. Criminal or unethical intent refers to the state of mind of the individual committing the infraction. A legal defense can be built on whether the accused acted out of ignorance, by accident, or with the intent to cause harm or damage. Deterring those with criminal intent is best done by means of technical controls and investigations, followed by prosecution. Intent is only one of several factors to consider when determining whether a computer-related crime has occurred.

Deterrence is the act of attempting to prevent an unwanted action by threatening punishment or retaliation toward the instigator if they perform the action. It is the best method for preventing an illegal or unethical activity. Laws, policies, and technical controls are all examples of deterrents. However, laws and policies and their associated penalties only deter if three conditions are present:

1. Expectation of being caught. Potential perpetrators must have an expectation that if they perform an illegal or unethical act, they will be caught. If the organization does not have an established record of investigating these acts, there is little deterrence.

2. Fear of the penalty. Potential perpetrators must have a strong aversion to the penalties associated with getting caught performing an illegal or unethical act. If the organization's penalty for these acts is minor or inconsequential, there is little deterrence.

3. Expectation of penalty being administered. Potential perpetrators must have an expectation that if they are caught performing an illegal or unethical act, they will receive the penalty. If individuals caught performing these acts are let off with a warning or only minor penalties, there is little deterrence.

In the absence of any one of these criteria, employees will not respect or follow the policies. Many organizations write policies without explicit penalties, condemning them to irregular compliance and opening the organization to lawsuits should violators be penalized. Only through effective implementation of all three deterrence criteria can organizations expect compliance with established policy.

Self-Check

1. Ethics and laws are interchangeable in the context of cybersecurity.

   a. True   b. False

2. The cybersecurity professional is solely responsible for the technical aspects of cybersecurity and not the ethical implications.

   a. True   b. False

3. Ethical behavior in cybersecurity is intuitive and does not require formal education or training.

   a. True   b. False

☐ Check your answers at the end of this chapter.

Professional Organizations and Their Codes of Conduct

Many professional organizations have established codes of conduct and codes of ethics that members are expected to follow. Codes of ethics can have a positive effect on an individual's judgment for computer use.[3] Unfortunately, few employers encourage or require their employees to join these professional organizations, outside of professions that require licensing, like the medical and engineering fields. The loss of licensing or certification due to a violation of a code of conduct can be a deterrent, as it can dramatically reduce the individual's marketability and potential earning power.

In general, research has shown that some certifications have little impact on the long-term earning potential of practitioners, whereas other certifications, notably those in cybersecurity, have a lingering effect on the economic prospects of certificate holders.[4] The long-term value of a cybersecurity certification adds leverage to the certification-granting authority to exert influence over its members, including influence in matters of ethical responsibility.

It remains the individual responsibility of cybersecurity professionals to act ethically and according to the policies and procedures of their employers, their professional organizations, and the laws of society. It is likewise the organization's responsibility to develop, disseminate, and enforce its policies. The following sections describe several relevant professional associations.

Association for Computing Machinery (ACM)

ACM (www.acm.org), a well-respected professional society, was established in 1947 as the world's first educational and scientific computing society. It is one of the few organizations that strongly promotes education and provides discounted membership for students. The ACM's code of ethics requires members to perform their duties in a manner befitting an ethical computing professional. The code contains specific references to protecting the confidentiality of information, causing no harm (with specific references to malware), protecting the privacy of others, and respecting the intellectual property and copyrights of others.

Note 1 | The full ACM code of ethics can be viewed at www.acm.org/code-of-ethics.

International Information System Security Certification Consortium, Inc. (ISC)²

(ISC)² is a nonprofit organization that focuses on education and certification in cybersecurity. It manages a body of knowledge on cybersecurity and administers and evaluates examinations for cybersecurity certifications. The code of ethics put forth by (ISC)² is primarily designed for cybersecurity professionals who have earned one of their certifications.

This code includes four mandatory canons:

- Protect society, the common good, necessary public trust and confidence, and the infrastructure.
- Act honorably, honestly, justly, responsibly, and legally.
- Provide diligent and competent service to principals.
- Advance and protect the profession.[5]

Through this code, (ISC)² seeks to provide sound guidance that will enable reliance on the ethicality and trustworthiness of the cybersecurity professional as a guardian of information and systems.

Note 2 | The (ISC)² website is at www.isc2.org. Its full code of ethics can be viewed at www.isc2.org/ethics/default.aspx.

SANS

Founded in 1989, SANS (www.sans.org) is a professional research and education cooperative organization. The organization (officially the Escal Institute of Advanced Technologies) is dedicated to the training of IT and cybersecurity professionals. In 1999, SANS formed the independent entity Global Information Assurance Certification (GIAC) to manage certifications associated with SANS training. Individuals receiving these certifications must agree to comply with a supplemental code of ethics, which opens with the following:

Respect for the Public

- I will accept responsibility in making decisions with consideration for the security and welfare of the community.
- I will not engage in or be a party to unethical or unlawful acts that negatively affect the community, my professional reputation, or the cybersecurity discipline.

Respect for the Certification

- I will not share, disseminate, or otherwise distribute confidential or proprietary information pertaining to the GIAC certification process.
- I will not use my certification, or objects or information associated with my certification (such as certificates or logos), to represent any individual or entity other than myself as being certified by GIAC.

Respect for My Employer

- I will deliver capable service that is consistent with the expectations of my certification and position.
- I will protect confidential and proprietary information with which I come into contact.
- I will minimize risks to the confidentiality, integrity, or availability of an information technology solution, consistent with risk management practice.

Respect for Myself

- I will avoid conflicts of interest.
- I will not misuse any information or privileges I am afforded as part of my responsibilities.
- I will not misrepresent my abilities or my work to the community, my employer, or my peers.[6]

Note 3 | The GIAC code of ethics can be found at www.giac.org/policies/ethics/.

Information Systems Audit and Control Association (ISACA)

ISACA (www.isaca.org) is a professional association with a focus on auditing, control, and cybersecurity education and certification. Its membership comprises both technical and managerial professionals. ISACA also develops and provides IT control practices and standards. The organization offers the Certified Information Security Manager (CISM) and Certified Information Systems Auditor (CISA) certifications. While the CISA certification does not focus exclusively on cybersecurity, it does contain many cybersecurity components.

According to ISACA, its constituents must abide by the following code of ethics.

Members and ISACA certification holders shall:

1. Support the implementation of, and encourage compliance with, appropriate standards and procedures for the effective governance and management of enterprise information systems and technology, including audit, control, security, and risk management.
2. Perform their duties with objectivity, due diligence, and professional care, in accordance with professional standards.
3. Serve in the interest of stakeholders in a lawful manner while maintaining high standards of conduct and character, and not discrediting their profession or the Association.
4. Maintain the privacy and confidentiality of information obtained in the course of their activities unless disclosure is required by legal authority. Such information shall not be used for personal benefit or released to inappropriate parties.
5. Maintain competency in their respective fields and agree to undertake only those activities they can reasonably expect to complete with the necessary skills, knowledge, and competence.
6. Inform appropriate parties of the results of work performed, including the disclosure of all significant facts known to them that, if not disclosed, may distort the reporting of the results.
7. Support the professional education of stakeholders in enhancing their understanding of the governance and management of enterprise information systems and technology, including audit, control, security, and risk management.[7]

Note 4 | The full ISACA code of ethics can be found at www.isaca.org/credentialing/ code-of-professional-ethics.

Information Systems Security Association (ISSA)

ISSA (www.issa.org) is a nonprofit society of cybersecurity professionals. Its primary mission is to bring together qualified practitioners of cybersecurity for information exchange and educational development. ISSA conducts conferences and regional meetings and manages publications and information resources to promote cybersecurity awareness and education.[8] ISSA also supports a code of ethics, like the other organizations mentioned previously, for "promoting management practices that will ensure the confidentiality, integrity, and availability of organizational information resources."[9] ISSA expects its members to follow this pledge:

I have in the past and will in the future:

- Perform all professional activities and duties in accordance with all applicable laws and the highest ethical principles.
- Promote generally accepted information security current best practices and standards.
- Maintain appropriate confidentiality of proprietary or otherwise sensitive information encountered in the course of professional activities.
- Discharge professional responsibilities with diligence and honesty.
- Refrain from any activities that might constitute a conflict of interest or otherwise damage the reputation of or be detrimental to employers, the information security profession, or the Association.
- Not intentionally injure or impugn the professional reputation or practice of colleagues, clients, or employers.[10]

Note 5 | The full ISSA code of ethics can be found at www.issa.org/issa-code-of-ethics.

Self-Check

4. The (ISC)² code of ethics is only applicable to cybersecurity professionals who have not earned any of their certifications.

    a. True   b. False

5. SANS, founded in 1989, is dedicated solely to the certification of IT and cybersecurity professionals, without providing any training.

    a. True   b. False

6. ISSA's primary mission is to facilitate the exchange of cybersecurity information and the educational development of cybersecurity professionals.

    a. True   b. False

☐ Check your answers at the end of this chapter.

Cybersecurity and Law

Cybersecurity and IT professionals and managers must possess a rudimentary grasp of the legal framework within which their organizations operate. The legal environment influences behavior depending on the nature of the organization and the scale on which it operates. All managers, specifically cybersecurity professionals, are expected to act in compliance with legal and regulatory requirements when collecting, storing, and using information, especially sensitive information like personally identifiable information (PII), personal healthcare information (PHI), and financial data.

Types of Law

There are several ways to categorize laws within the United States. In addition to the hierarchical perspective of local, state, federal, and international laws, most U.S. laws can be categorized based on their origins:

- Constitutional law—Originates with the U.S. Constitution, a state constitution, or local constitution, bylaws, or charter
- Statutory law—Originates from a legislative branch specifically tasked with the creation and publication of laws and statutes
- Regulatory or administrative law—Originates from an executive branch or authorized regulatory agency and includes executive orders and regulations
- Common law, case law, and precedent—Originates from a judicial branch or oversight board and involves the interpretation of law based on the actions of a previous and/or higher court or board

Within statutory law, one can further divide laws into their association with individuals, groups, and the state:

- Civil law embodies a wide variety of laws pertaining to relationships between individuals and organizations. Civil law includes contract law, employment law, family law, and tort law. Tort law is the subset of civil law that allows individuals to seek redress in the event of personal, physical, or financial injury. Perceived damages within civil law are pursued in civil court and are not prosecuted by the state.
- Criminal law addresses violations harmful to society and is actively enforced and prosecuted by the state. Criminal law addresses statutes associated with traffic law, public order, property damage, and personal damage, where the state takes on the responsibility of seeking retribution on behalf of the plaintiff or injured party.

Yet another distinction addresses how legislation affects individuals in society and is categorized as private law or public law. Private law is considered a subset of civil law and regulates relationships among individuals as well as relationships between individuals and organizations, encompassing family law, commercial law, and labor law. Public law regulates the structure and administration of government agencies and their relationships with citizens, employees, and other governments, and includes criminal law, administrative law, and constitutional law.

Regardless of how you categorize laws, it is important to understand which laws and regulations are relevant to your organization and what it needs to do to comply.

Relevant U.S. Laws

The United States has led the development and implementation of cybersecurity legislation to prevent misuse and exploitation of information and IT. The development of cybersecurity legislation promotes the general welfare and creates a stable environment for a solid economy. In its capacity as a global leader, the United States has demonstrated a clear understanding of the problems facing the cybersecurity field and has specified penalties for individuals and organizations that fail to follow the requirements set forth in the U.S. civil statutes. Table 5-1 summarizes the U.S. laws relevant to cybersecurity. You can find more information about each of these laws by searching the web.

Table 5-1 Key U.S. laws of interest to cybersecurity professionals

Area	Act	Date	Description
Online commerce and information protection	Federal Trade Commission Act (FTCA)	1914	Recently used to challenge organizations with deceptive claims about the privacy and security of customers' personal information
Telecommunications	Communications Act (47 USC 151 et seq.)	1934	Includes amendments found in the Telecommunications Deregulation and Competition Act of 1996; this law regulates interstate and foreign telecommunications (amended 1996 and 2001)
Freedom of information	Freedom of Information Act (FOIA)	1966	Allows for the disclosure of previously unreleased information and documents controlled by the U.S. government
Protection of credit information	Fair Credit Reporting Act (FCRA)	1970	Regulates the collection and use of consumer credit information
Privacy	Federal Privacy Act	1974	Governs federal agency use of personal information
Privacy of student information	Family Educational Rights and Privacy Act (FERPA) (20 USC 1232g; 34 CFR Part 99)	1974	Also known as the Buckley Amendment; protects the privacy of student education records
Copyright	Copyright Act; update to U.S. Copyright Law (17 USC)	1976	Protects intellectual property, including publications and software
Cryptography	Electronic Communications Privacy Act (update to 18 USC)	1986	Regulates interception and disclosure of electronic information; also referred to as the Federal Wiretapping Act
Access to stored communications	Stored Communications Act (18 USC 2701)	1986	Provides penalties for illegally accessing communications (such as email and voice mail) stored by a service provider
Threats to computers	Computer Fraud and Abuse (CFA) Act; also known as Fraud and Related Activity in Connection with Computers (18 USC 1030)	1986	Defines and formalizes laws to counter threats from computer-related acts and offenses (amended 1996, 2001, and 2006)
Federal agency cybersecurity	Computer Security Act (CSA)	1987	Requires all federal computer systems that contain classified information to have security plans in place and requires periodic security training for all individuals who operate, design, or manage such systems
Trap and trace restrictions	General prohibition on pen register and trap-and-trace device use; exception (18 USC 3121 et seq.)	1993	Prohibits the use of electronic "pen registers" and trap-and-trace devices without a court order
Criminal intent	National Information Infrastructure Protection Act (update to 18 USC 1030)	1996	Categorizes crimes based on a defendant's authority to access a protected computer system and criminal intent
Trade secrets	Economic Espionage Act	1996	Prevents abuse of information gained while employed elsewhere

(Continues)

Table 5-1   Key U.S. laws of interest to cybersecurity professionals (*Continued*)

Area	Act	Date	Description
Personal health information protection	Health Insurance Portability and Accountability Act (HIPAA)	1996	Requires medical practices to ensure the privacy of personal medical information
Encryption and digital signatures	Security and Freedom Through Encryption Act	1997	Affirms the rights of people in the United States to use and sell products that include encryption and to relax export controls on such products
Intellectual property	No Electronic Theft Act amends 17 USC 506(a)–copyright infringement and 18 USC 2319–criminal infringement of copyright (Public Law 105-147)	1997	These parts of the U.S. Code amend copyright and criminal statutes to provide greater copyright protection and penalties for electronic copyright infringement
Electronic records	Part 11, Title 21 of the Code of Federal Regulations	1997	Establishes guidelines for the use and acceptance of electronic signatures and electronic records for all Food and Drug Administration (FDA) regulated industries
Copyright protection	Digital Millennium Copyright Act (DMCA); update to 17 USC 101	1998	Provides specific penalties for removing copyright protection from media
Identity theft	Identity Theft and Assumption Deterrence Act (18 USC 1028)	1998	Attempts to instigate specific penalties for identity theft by identifying the individual who loses their identity as the true victim, not just those commercial and financial credit entities who suffered losses
Child privacy protection	Children's Online Privacy Protection Act (COPPA)	1998	Provides requirements for online service and website providers to ensure that the privacy of children under age 13 is protected
Banking	Gramm-Leach-Bliley Act, also known as the Financial Services Modernization Act	1999	Repeals the restrictions on banks affiliating with insurance and securities firms; has significant impact on the privacy of personal information used by these industries
Accountability	Sarbanes-Oxley Act, also known as the Public Company Accounting Reform and Investor Protection Act	2002	Enforces accountability for executives at publicly traded companies; is having ripple effects throughout the accounting, IT, and related units of many organizations
General cybersecurity	Federal Information Security Management Act (FISMA; 44 USC 3541 et seq.)	2002	Requires each federal agency to develop, document, and implement an agency-wide program to provide cybersecurity for the information and information systems that support the operations and assets of the agency, including those provided or managed by another agency, contractor, or other source
Spam	Controlling the Assault of Non-Solicited Pornography and Marketing Act (15 USC 7701 et seq.)	2003	Sets the first national standards for regulating the distribution of commercial email, including mobile phone spam
Fraud with access devices	Fraud and Related Activity in Connection with Access Devices (18 USC 1029)	2004	Defines and formalizes law to counter threats from counterfeit access devices like ID cards, credit cards, telecom equipment, and mobile or electronic serial numbers, as well as the equipment that creates them

(*Continues*)

Table 5-1 Key U.S. laws of interest to cybersecurity professionals (*Continued*)

Area	Act	Date	Description
Terrorism and extreme drug trafficking	USA PATRIOT Improvement and Reauthorization Act (update to 18 USC 1030)	2006	Renews critical sections of the USA PATRIOT Act
Privacy of PHI	American Recovery and Reinvestment Act	2009	In the privacy and security area, requires new reporting requirements and penalties for breach of protected health information (PHI)
Privacy of PHI	Health Information Technology for Economic and Clinical Health (HITECH) Act, part of ARRA-2009	2009	Addresses privacy and security concerns associated with the electronic transmission of PHI through several provisions that strengthen HIPAA rules for civil and criminal enforcement
Defense information protection	International Traffic in Arms Regulations (ITAR) Act	2012	Restricts the exportation of technology and information related to defense and military-related services and materiel, including research and development information
National cyber infrastructure protection	National Cybersecurity Protection Act	2014	Updates the Homeland Security Act of 2002, which established the Department of Homeland Security (DHS), to include a national cybersecurity and communications integration center to share information and facilitate coordination between agencies and perform analysis of cybersecurity incidents and risks
Federal cybersecurity updates	Federal Information Security Modernization Act	2014	Updates many outdated federal cybersecurity practices, updating FISMA, providing a framework for ensuring effectiveness in cybersecurity controls over federal information systems, and centralizing cybersecurity management within DHS
National cybersecurity employee assessment	Cybersecurity Workforce Assessment Act	2014	Tasks DHS to perform an evaluation of the national cybersecurity employee workforce at least every three years and to develop a plan to improve recruiting and training of cybersecurity employees
Terrorist tracking	USA FREEDOM Act	2015	Updates the Foreign Intelligence Surveillance Act (FISA); transfers the requirement to collect and report communications to/from known terrorist phone numbers to selected federal agencies upon request
Information sharing	Cybersecurity Information Sharing Act	2015	Encourages private companies to share information on threats and vulnerabilities, with liability protection if they do; also requires government to set up information sharing agencies
Incident reporting for federal assistance	Cyber Incident Reporting for Critical Infrastructure Act of 2022 (CIRCIA)	2022	Requires the federal government to implement regulation requiring reporting of incidents and ransomware payments to the Cybersecurity and Infrastructure Security Agency (CISA); federal government will then respond with resources and assistance

General Computer Crime Laws

The Computer Fraud and Abuse (CFA) Act of 1986 is the cornerstone of many computer-related federal laws and enforcement efforts. The CFA formally criminalizes "accessing a computer without authorization or exceeding authorized access" for systems containing information of national interest as determined by the U.S. government. The CFA was amended in 1996 by the National Information Infrastructure Protection Act of 1996, which modified several sections of the previous act and increased the penalties for selected crimes. Punishment for offenses prosecuted under this statute varies from fines to imprisonment for up to 20 years or can include both. The penalty depends on the value of the information obtained and whether the offense is judged to have been committed for one of the following reasons:

- For purposes of commercial advantage
- For private financial gain
- In furtherance of a criminal act

The CFA Act was further modified by the USA PATRIOT Act of 2001 (the abbreviated name for "Uniting and Strengthening America by Providing Appropriate Tools Required to Intercept and Obstruct Terrorism Act of 2001"), which was enacted to investigate and respond to the 9/11 attacks on the World Trade Center in New York. The USA PATRIOT Act provides law enforcement agencies with broader latitude to combat terrorism-related activities. Some of the laws modified by the USA PATRIOT Act are among the earliest laws created to deal with electronic technology. Certain portions of the act were extended in 2006, 2010, and 2011.

In May 2015, the U.S. Senate failed to extend the act, resulting in its expiration on June 1, 2015. The controversy over Section 215, which allowed the National Security Agency (NSA) to collect metadata (the to: and from: information from phone records), initially resulted in an attempt to transfer the responsibility for collecting and reporting this information to the telecommunications companies involved as part of the USA FREEDOM Act, an abbreviation of "Uniting and Strengthening America by Fulfilling Rights and Ending Eavesdropping, Dragnet-collection and Online Monitoring Act." However, this act met with similar resistance, until the stalemate in Congress resulted in the sunset of key components of the USA PATRIOT Act. The complex issues within the political context of this law were eventually resolved and the USA FREEDOM Act was signed into law by President Barack Obama in June 2015.

> **Note 6** | The full text of the Computer Fraud and Abuse Act of 1986 (Section 1030, Chapter 47, Title 18 USC) can be found at https://www.justice.gov/jm/jm-9-48000-computer-fraud.

Another U.S. law of critical importance to cybersecurity professionals is the Computer Security Act (CSA) of 1987, which was designed to improve the security of federal information systems. This law charged the National Bureau of Standards, now the National Institute of Standards and Technology (NIST), with the development of standards, guidelines, and associated methods and techniques for computer systems, among other responsibilities. This legislation was one of the first attempts to protect federal computer systems by establishing minimum acceptable security practices. The CSA charges NIST, in cooperation with the NSA, with the development of:

- Standards, guidelines, and associated methods and techniques for computer systems
- Uniform standards and guidelines for most federal computer systems
- Technical, management, physical, and administrative standards and guidelines for the cost-effective security and privacy of sensitive information in federal computer systems
- Guidelines for use by operators of federal computer systems that contain sensitive information in training their employees in security awareness and accepted security practice
- Validation procedures for, and evaluation of the effectiveness of, standards and guidelines through research and liaison with other government and private agencies[11]

The CSA also established a Computer System Security and Privacy Advisory Board within the Department of Commerce. This board identifies emerging managerial, technical, administrative, and physical safety issues relative to computer systems security and privacy, and it advises NIST and the Secretary of Commerce on security and privacy issues pertaining to federal computer systems. The board reports to the Secretary of Commerce, the Director of the Office of Management and Budget, the Director of the NSA, and the appropriate committees of Congress.

The CSA also amended the Federal Property and Administrative Services Act of 1949. The amendments require the National Bureau of Standards to distribute standards and guidelines pertaining to federal computer systems. This act also permits the head of any federal agency to employ more stringent standards than those distributed.

Another provision of the CSA requires mandatory periodic training in computer security awareness and accepted computer security practice for all employees involved with the management, use, or operation of federal computer systems. This training is intended to enhance awareness of the threats to computer systems and encourage the use of good computer security practices. It also informs federal agencies who is responsible for computer systems security and privacy, requires the identification of systems that contain sensitive information, and outlines the requirements for formal security plans.

Privacy Laws

Many organizations collect, trade, and sell personal information as a commodity, and many people are becoming aware of these practices and asking governments to protect their privacy. In the past, it was not possible to create databases that contained personal information collected from multiple sources. Today, information aggregation from multiple sources permits unethical organizations to build databases with alarming quantities of personal information.

The number of statutes addressing individual privacy rights has grown. However, privacy in this context is not absolute freedom from observation; rather, it is defined as the state of being free from unsanctioned intrusion.[12] It is possible to track this concept of freedom from intrusion to the Fourth Amendment of the U.S. Constitution, which states the following:

> The right of the people to be secure in their persons, houses, papers, and effects, against
> unreasonable searches and seizures, shall not be violated, and no Warrants shall issue,
> but upon probable cause, supported by Oath or affirmation, and particularly describing
> the place to be searched, and the persons or things to be seized.[13]

The origins of this right can be traced to a 1772 document by Samuel Adams titled "The Rights of the Colonists and a List of Infringements and Violations of Rights." This document in turn had its roots in a 1604 ruling by a British court that upheld the rights of a man to refuse entry to the king's men without royal warrant, or at least to restrict the search to items listed in a warrant.[14] To better understand this rapidly evolving issue, some of the more relevant privacy laws and regulations are discussed in the following sections.

The Privacy of Customer Information provisions in section 222 of USC Title 47, Chapter 5, Subchapter II, Part I, which covers common carriers[15] (organizations that process or move data for hire), specifies that any proprietary information shall be used explicitly for providing services and not for marketing purposes. It also stipulates that carriers cannot disclose this information except when necessary to provide its services, or by customer request, and then the disclosure is restricted to that customer's information only.

The law does permit the use of aggregate information (which is created by combining nonprivate data elements) if the same information is provided to all common carriers and the carrier in question conducts business with fair competition. The use of aggregate information raises privacy concerns because an organization could assemble data from a variety of sources in ways that would allow correlation of seemingly innocuous information into something more intrusive. For example, the mapping of a government census database with telephone directory information, cross-indexed to bankruptcy court records, could be used to facilitate marketing efforts to people experiencing financial difficulties.

While the common carrier regulation controls public carriers' use of private data, the Privacy Act of 1974 regulates the official collection, storage, use, and dissemination of individual personal information contained in government records. In short, the Privacy Act ensures that federal agencies protect the privacy of such information. Also, the act holds those agencies responsible if any portion of the information is released without permission. The act states the following: "No agency shall disclose any record which is contained in a system of records by any means of communication to any person, or to another agency, except pursuant to a written request by, or with the prior written consent of, the individual to whom the record pertains...."[16] The following entities are exempt from some of the regulations so that they can perform their duties:

- Bureau of the Census
- National Archives and Records Administration
- U.S. Congress
- Comptroller General
- Certain court orders
- Credit agencies

In addition, individuals can access information controlled by others if they can demonstrate that it is necessary to protect their health or safety.

The **Electronic Communications Privacy Act (ECPA) of 1986**—a collection of U.S. statutes that regulate the interception of wire, electronic, and oral communications, commonly referred to as the "federal wiretapping acts"—addresses the following areas:[17]

- Interception and disclosure of wire, oral, or electronic communications
- Manufacture, distribution, possession, and advertising of wire, oral, or electronic communication intercepting devices
- Confiscation of wire, oral, or electronic communication intercepting devices
- Evidentiary use of intercepted wire or oral communications
- Authorization for interception of wire, oral, or electronic communications
- Authorization for disclosure and use of intercepted wire, oral, or electronic communications
- Procedure for interception of wire, oral, or electronic communications
- Reports concerning intercepted wire, oral, or electronic communications
- Injunction against illegal interception

Until 2015, the U.S. Federal Trade Commission (FTC) was responsible for the regulation of Internet service providers (ISPs). In March 2015, in its Open Internet Order (FCC 15-24), the Federal Communications Commission (FCC) removed the FTC's authority over ISPs, essentially deregulating them. In 2016, the FCC established Internet privacy rules, reportedly to give consumers better control over their personal data by requiring ISPs to get permission from users before sharing or selling the data (communications header, browsing, and other information) with third parties. In early 2017, Congress struck down this regulation before it could take effect. Most ISPs use such data for targeted advertising, but some activists are concerned it could lead to increased issues with information aggregation.

Note 7 | For more information on federal privacy programs, laws, and regulations, visit the U.S. General Services Administration website at www.gsa.gov/portal/category/21419.

Note 8 | For more information on the fight for electronic privacy, visit the Electronic Frontier Foundation's website at www.eff.org.

Note 9 | When you make an inadvertent cell-phone call, often called a "butt dial," you have no expectation of privacy if the called party listens in to the activities around you. In 2015, the courts ruled that an accidental call of this type made from a Kentucky public official did not lead to a violation of the official's privacy.[18]

Health Insurance Portability and Accountability Act

The Health Insurance Portability and Accountability Act (HIPAA) of 1996, also known as the Kennedy-Kassebaum Act, attempts to protect the confidentiality and security of healthcare data by establishing and enforcing standards and by standardizing electronic data interchange. This law affects all healthcare organizations, including small medical practices, health clinics, life insurers, and universities, as well as some organizations that have self-insured employee health programs. It provides significant penalties for organizations that fail to comply with the law, with fines up to $250,000 and/or 10 years imprisonment for knowingly misusing client information. Organizations were required to comply with the act as of April 2003.[19]

HIPAA affects the field of cybersecurity in many ways. It requires organizations that retain healthcare information to use cybersecurity mechanisms to protect this information, and it requires policies and procedures to maintain them. This is known as the HIPAA Security Rule. The purpose of the law is summarized by the U.S. Department of Health and Human Services (DHHS) as follows:

> The HIPAA Security Rule establishes national standards to protect individuals' electronic personal health information that is created, received, used, or maintained by a covered entity. The Security Rule, located at 45 CFR Part 160 and Subparts A and C of Part 164, requires appropriate administrative, physical, and technical safeguards to ensure the confidentiality, integrity, and security of electronic PHI.[20]

HIPAA also requires a comprehensive assessment of the organization's cybersecurity systems, policies, and procedures. HIPAA provides guidelines for the use of electronic signatures based on security standards, ensuring message integrity, user authentication, and nonrepudiation. There is no specification of particular security technologies for each of the security requirements, although the act states that security must be implemented to ensure the privacy of healthcare information.

The privacy standards of HIPAA severely restrict the dissemination and distribution of private health information without documented consent. This is known as the HIPAA Privacy Rule and is explained by DHHS as follows:

> The HIPAA Privacy Rule establishes national standards to protect individuals' medical records and other personal health information and applies to health plans, healthcare clearinghouses, and those healthcare providers that conduct certain healthcare transactions electronically. The Rule, located at 45 CFR Part 160 and Subparts A and E of Part 164, requires appropriate safeguards to protect the privacy of personal health information, and sets limits and conditions on the uses and disclosures that may be made of such information without patient authorization. The Rule also gives patients rights over their health information, including rights to examine and obtain a copy of their health records, and to request corrections.[21]

The Privacy Rule also restricts the use of health information to the minimum required for the healthcare services needed.

HIPAA has five fundamental privacy principles:

- Consumer control of medical information
- Boundaries on the use of medical information
- Accountability for the privacy of private information
- Balance of public responsibility for the use of medical information for the greater good measured against impact to the individual
- Security of health information

ARRA and HITECH

Enacted in 2009, the American Recovery and Reinvestment Act (ARRA) was designed to provide a response to the economic crisis in the United States. The act was specifically focused on providing tax cuts and funding for programs, federal contracts, grants, and loans. While the base act is important, of particular interest to the cybersecurity community was the inclusion of the Health Information Technology for Economic and Clinical Health (HITECH) Act. The U.S. Department of Health and Human Services explains HITECH as follows:

> HITECH amends Section 3002 of the Public Health Service Act to establish the Health IT Policy Committee to make policy recommendations to the National Coordinator around the implementation of a nationwide health information technology infrastructure. Section 3003 establishes the Health IT Standards Committee to make recommendations to the National Coordinator around standards, implementation specifications, and certification criteria for electronic exchange and use of health information.
>
> HITECH amends Sections 3004 and 3005 of the Public Health Service Act to describe the processes for evaluation, adoption, and implementation of endorsed standards, implementation specifications, and certification criteria for health IT.
>
> Sections 13400–13411 of HITECH describe HHS's work to improve privacy and security provisions for electronic exchange and use of health information.[22]

HIPAA and HITECH also require that covered entities notify information owners of breaches. DHHS explains the Breach Notification Rule as:

> The HIPAA Breach Notification Rule, 45 CFR 164.400-414, requires HIPAA covered entities and their business associates to provide notification following a breach of unsecured protected health information. Similar breach notification provisions implemented and enforced by the Federal Trade Commission (FTC) apply to vendors of personal health records and their third-party service providers, pursuant to section 13407 of the HITECH Act.[23]

Note 10 | To read more about health information privacy, including HIPAA and HITECH information, visit the U.S. Department of Health and Human Services website at www.hhs.gov/ocr/privacy/.

Federal Trade Commission Consumer Protection Laws

The FTC has several "rules"—essentially federal laws—that seek to prevent unfair business practices, fraud, and consumer abuse: "Whether combating telemarketing fraud, Internet scams, or price-fixing schemes, the FTC's mission is to protect consumers and promote competition. The FTC administers a wide variety of laws and regulations, including the Federal Trade Commission Act, Telemarketing Sale Rule, Identity Theft Act, Fair Credit Reporting Act, and Clayton Act."[24]

Gramm-Leach-Bliley Act of 1999

The Gramm-Leach-Bliley (GLB) Act, also known as the Financial Services Modernization Act of 1999, contains several provisions that affect banks, securities firms, and insurance companies. This act requires all financial institutions to disclose their privacy policies, describing how they share nonpublic personal information and how customers can request that their information not be shared with third parties. The act also ensures that the privacy policies in effect in an organization are fully disclosed when a customer initiates a business relationship and are distributed at least annually for the duration of the professional association.

Note 11 | For more information on financial privacy information, including GLB, visit the FTC's website at www.ftc.gov/business-guidance/privacy-security/gramm-leach-bliley-act.

Export and Espionage Laws

The need to protect national security, trade secrets, and a variety of other state and private assets has led to several laws affecting what information and information management and security resources may be exported from the United States. These laws attempt to stem the theft of information by establishing strong penalties for related crimes.

To protect intellectual property and competitive advantage, Congress passed the Economic Espionage Act (EEA) in 1996. According to the U.S. Department of Justice, this law attempts to protect trade secrets "from the foreign government that uses its classic espionage apparatus to spy on a company, to the two American companies that are attempting to uncover each other's bid proposals, or to the disgruntled former employee who walks out of his former company with a USB drive full of engineering schematics."[25]

The Security and Freedom Through Encryption (SAFE) Act of 1997 provides guidance on the use of encryption and institutes measures of public protection from government intervention. Specifically, the act:

- Reinforces an individual's right to use or sell encryption algorithms without concern for the impact of other regulations requiring some form of key registration. Using key registration, a cryptographic key (or its text equivalent) is stored with another party to be used to break the encryption of data under some circumstances. This is often called key escrow.
- Prohibits the federal government from requiring the use of encryption for contracts, grants, other official documents, and correspondence.
- States that the use of encryption is not probable cause to suspect criminal activity.
- Relaxes export restrictions by amending the Export Administration Act of 1979.
- Provides additional penalties for the use of encryption in the commission of a criminal act.

U.S. Copyright Law

U.S. copyright law extends protection to intellectual property, which includes works published in electronic formats. The doctrine of fair use allows material to be quoted for news reporting, teaching, scholarship, and other related activities as long as the purpose is educational and not for profit and the usage is not excessive. Proper acknowledgment must be provided to the author and/or copyright holder, including a description of the location of source materials by using a recognized form of citation.

Freedom of Information Act of 1966

All federal agencies are required under the Freedom of Information Act (FOIA) to disclose unclassified records requested in writing by any person. However, agencies may withhold information pursuant to nine exemptions and three exclusions contained in the statute. FOIA applies only to federal agencies and does not create a right of access to records held by Congress, the courts, or state or local government agencies. Each state has its own public access laws that should be consulted for access to state and local records.

Sarbanes-Oxley Act of 2002

In the wake of the Enron and WorldCom financial scandals and the damage to financial markets from criminal violations of the federal securities laws, the U.S. Congress enacted the Sarbanes-Oxley (SOX) Act of 2002, which was designed to enforce accountability for the financial reporting and record keeping at publicly traded corporations. While this law would not seem to affect cybersecurity or even general IT functions, its effects are being felt throughout the organizations to which it applies.

The law requires that the chief executive officer (CEO) and chief financial officer (CFO) assume direct and personal accountability for the completeness and accuracy of a publicly traded organization's financial reporting and record-keeping systems. As these executives attempt to ensure that the integrity of reporting and recording systems is sound—often relying upon the expertise of the chief information officer (CIO) and chief security officer (CSO) to do so—they also must maintain the availability and confidentiality of information. The provisions include:

- Creation of the Public Company Accounting Oversight Board (PCAOB)
- A requirement that public companies evaluate and disclose the effectiveness of their internal controls as they relate to financial reporting and that independent auditors for such companies "attest to" (i.e., agree to or qualify) such disclosure

- Certification of financial reports by CEOs and CFOs
- Auditor independence, including outright bans on certain types of work for audit clients and precertification by the company's audit committee of all other non-audit work
- A requirement that companies listed on stock exchanges have fully independent audit committees that oversee the relationship between the company and its auditor
- A ban on most personal loans to any executive officer or director
- Accelerated reporting of trades by insiders
- Prohibition of insider trading during pension fund blackout periods
- Additional disclosure
- Enhanced criminal and civil penalties for violations of securities law
- Significantly longer maximum jail sentences and larger fines for corporate executives who knowingly and willfully misstate financial statements, although maximum sentences are largely irrelevant because judges generally follow the Federal Sentencing Guidelines in setting actual sentences
- Employee protections allowing corporate fraud whistleblowers who file complaints with the Occupational Safety and Health Administration within 90 days to win reinstatement, back pay and benefits, compensatory damages, abatement orders, and reasonable attorney fees and costs

CIOs are responsible for the security, accuracy, and reliability of the systems that manage and report financial data. Therefore, the financial reporting process, along with other important processes, must be assessed for compliance with the SOX Act. Although the act signals a fundamental change in business operations and financial reporting and places responsibility in corporate financial reporting on the CEO and CFO, the CIO plays a significant role in the approval of financial statements.[26]

Breach Laws

A more recently created area of law related to cybersecurity addresses breaches or data spills. A breach law requires organizations to notify affected parties when they have experienced a specified type of loss of information (the breach). This often includes specific forms of PII from various stakeholders. Most of these laws also require some form of after-breach support from the organization, such as free or discounted credit monitoring, progress reports, and a description of actions taken to rectify the incident and prevent reoccurrence.

Although the United States currently does not have a national breach law, several bills and proposals are being reviewed by the U.S. Congress. For details, see the next section on future laws. At the time of this writing, all 50 states, the District of Columbia, Guam, Puerto Rico, and the U.S. Virgin Islands have breach notification laws. While new legislation is still winding through Congress, the only currently established federal breach notification statutes are those within the FTC, the Gramm-Leach-Bliley Act, and HIPAA.

In February 2023, the discount prescription organization GoodRx was the first formal case in which the FTC ruled that a company's privacy practices violated the Health Breach Notification Rule, fining them $1.5 million. In violation of its own policies and federal law, GoodRx was sharing personal health and identification information with digital advertisers.[27]

Note 12 | For a list of state security breach notification laws, visit the National Conference of State Legislatures website at www.ncsl.org/technology-and-communication/security-breach-notification-laws.

The Future of U.S. Cybersecurity and Privacy Laws

A stream of cybersecurity-related bills are fighting their way through the U.S. Congress at any given time. However, because most bills never get approved or signed into law, it is important that cybersecurity professionals know how to monitor the legal horizon for laws that could impact their organization. Websites such as GovTrack (www.govtrack.us) report the status of bills as they proceed through Congress and have predefined categories of interest such as privacy rights (www.govtrack.us/congress/bills/subjects/right_of_privacy/5910); science, technology, and communications (www.govtrack.us/congress/bills/subjects/

science_technology_communications/6293); and crime and law enforcement (www.govtrack.us/congress/bills/subjects/crime_and_law_enforcement/5952). These categories could contain relevant bills that, if passed, might impact American organizations.

Security professionals should monitor the news in all forms—broadcast, print, and Internet. When a relevant bill makes news, security professionals should add the bill to a list of potential legislation they monitor. Once a bill is signed into law, cybersecurity professionals should refer to their organizations' legal departments or consultants for interpretation and compliance recommendations.

International Laws and Legal Bodies

IT professionals and cybersecurity practitioners must realize that when their organizations do business over the Internet, they may be doing business globally. Many domestic laws and customs do not apply to international trade, which is governed by international treaties and trade agreements. While it may seem obvious that a variety of laws and ethical practices exist in other parts of the world, this fact is often overlooked. Different international cybersecurity-related groups and laws are described in the following sections. Because of the political complexities of the relationships among nations and the inherent cultural differences, few international laws currently relate to privacy and cybersecurity. Therefore, these international security bodies and regulations are sometimes limited in scope and enforceability.

European Council Cybercrime Convention

In 2001, the Council of Europe drafted the European Council Cybercrime Convention, which empowers an international task force to oversee a range of Internet security functions and to standardize technology laws across international borders. It also attempts to improve the effectiveness of international investigations into breaches of technology law. This convention is well received by advocates of intellectual property rights because it provides for copyright infringement prosecution.

As with any complex international legislation, the Cybercrime Convention lacks any realistic provisions for enforcement. The goal of the convention is to simplify the acquisition of information for law enforcement agents in certain types of international crimes as well as during the extradition process. The convention has more than its share of skeptics who see it as an attempt by the European community to exert undue influence to control a complex problem. Critics of the convention say that it could create more problems than it resolves. As the product of multiple governments, the convention tends to favor the interests of national agencies over the rights of businesses, organizations, and individuals.

Until October 2015, many U.S. organizations that worked internationally with European Union (EU) countries and organizations had to comply with the EU-U.S. Safe Harbor Framework, a set of guidelines implemented between 1998 and 2000 and designed to facilitate data transfers between EU- and U.S.-regulated organizations. Differences in regulations between these two groups have created difficulties in transferring customer data, especially due to the EU's stricter privacy regulations.

In October 2015, the European Court of Justice (ECJ) overturned the Safe Harbor Framework, claiming the self-certification provisions were inadequate to protect customer privacy data. In 2016, a replacement framework known as the EU-U.S. Privacy Shield was developed between the United States and the EU; it allows for the transfer of personal data from the EU to the United States. A similar framework has also been developed for U.S. and Swiss business commerce.

In July 2020, the Court of Justice of the European Union issued a judgment declaring as "invalid" the European Commission's Decision (EU) 2016/1250 in July 2016 on the adequacy of the protection provided by the EU-U.S. Privacy Shield. As a result of that decision, the EU-U.S. Privacy Shield Framework is no longer a valid mechanism to comply with EU data protection requirements when transferring personal data from the EU to the United States. That decision does not relieve participants in the EU-U.S. Privacy Shield of their obligations under the EU-U.S. Privacy Shield Framework.[28] The Swiss-U.S. Privacy Shield Framework was similarly devalued in September 2020, leaving the status of the frameworks in question.

The General Data Protection Regulation (GDPR) is a set of laws enacted in the EU in May 2018. The GDPR has specific requirements regarding the transfer of data out of the EU. One of these requirements is that transfers can occur only to countries deemed to have adequate data protection laws. The Privacy Shield is designed to implement a program in which participating companies are deemed as having adequate protection, which facilitates the transfer of information.

Note 13 | Learn more about the GDPR at www.icaew.com/en/technical/information-technology/cyber-resource-centre/general-data-protection-regulations.

Digital Millennium Copyright Act

The Digital Millennium Copyright Act (DMCA) is the U.S.-based component of the international effort to reduce the impact of copyright, trademark, and privacy infringement, especially via the removal of technological copyright protection measures. The European Union equivalents of the DMCA are Directive 95/46/EC of the European Parliament and the report from the European Council of October 24, 1995, which increase individual rights to process and freely move personal data. The United Kingdom has already implemented a version of this directive called the Database Right.

Australian High-Tech Crime

High-tech crimes are defined and prosecuted in Australia under its Commonwealth legislation Part 10.7—Computer Offences of the Criminal Code Act 1995. The law specifically includes:

- Data system intrusions (such as hacking)
- Unauthorized destruction or modification of data
- Actions intended to deny service of computer systems to intended users, such as denial-of-service (DoS) attacks and distributed denial-of-service (DDoS) attacks using botnets
- Creation and distribution of malicious software (malware)

Each state and territory in Australia has also implemented laws for computer-related offenses that are similar to the national Commonwealth legislation.[29]

Note 14 | For a more comprehensive list of international privacy laws, visit Information Shield's website at https://informationshield.com/free-security-policy-tools/international-data-privacy-laws/.

State and Local Regulations

Each state or locality may have its own laws and regulations that affect the use of computer technology. It is the responsibility of cybersecurity professionals to understand state laws and regulations and ensure that their organization's security policies and procedures comply with the laws and regulations.

For example, the State of Georgia passed the Georgia Computer Systems Protection Act in 1991, which has various computer security provisions and establishes specific penalties for using computer technology to attack or exploit information systems in organizations. These laws do not affect people or entities outside the state unless they do business or have offices in the state.

The Georgia legislature also passed the Georgia Identity Theft Law in 1998 (Section 120 et seq., Chapter 9, Title 16, Official Code of Georgia Annotated). As explained by the State of Georgia, this law prohibits a business from discarding a record containing personal information unless it:

- Shreds the customer's record before discarding the record
- Erases the personal information contained in the customer's record before discarding the record
- Modifies the customer's record to make the personal information unreadable before discarding the record
- Takes actions that it reasonably believes will ensure that no unauthorized person will have access to the personal information contained in the customer's record for the period between the record's disposal and the record's destruction[30]

Personal information is defined as:

- Personally identifiable data about a customer's medical condition, if the data is not generally considered to be public knowledge
- Personally identifiable data that contains a customer's account or identification number, account balance, balance owing, credit balance, or credit limit, if the data relates to a customer's account or transaction with a business
- Personally identifiable data provided by a customer to a business upon opening an account or applying for a loan or credit
- Personally identifiable data about a customer's federal, state, or local income tax return[31]

Failure to properly dispose of customer information can result in a fine of $500 per instance up to a total of $10,000.

"Consumer victim" in the Georgia law means any individual whose personal identifying information has been obtained, compromised, used, or recorded in any manner without their permission.

"Identifying information" includes but is not limited to:

- Current or former names
- Social Security numbers
- Driver's license numbers
- Checking account numbers
- Savings account numbers
- Credit and other financial transaction card numbers
- Debit card numbers
- Personal identification numbers
- Electronic identification numbers
- Digital or electronic signatures
- Medical identification numbers
- Birth dates
- Mother's maiden name
- Tax identification numbers
- State identification card numbers
- Any numbers or information that can be used to access a person's or entity's resources

In 2017, the state of New York implemented new regulation that requires organizations—specifically, financial institutions, law firms, and tax-exempt organizations—to conduct periodic risk assessments of their information assets and systems. This requirement is an effort to bring to light the issues and vulnerabilities of an organization's information systems to its management team. This regulation also includes requirements to (1) establish and maintain a formal security program, (2) develop and implement written security policies, and (3) regulate user access privileges in accordance with the results of the risk assessment. The risk assessment must include at a minimum:

- Evaluation and categorization of identified cyber risks or threats facing the institution
- Assessment of the "confidentiality, integrity, security, and availability" of the institution's network and nonpublic information
- Requirements setting forth how the identified risks "will be mitigated or accepted based on the Risk Assessment" and how they are addressed by the cybersecurity program[32]

Note 15 | For a more complete list of state privacy and security laws, see the website for the National Conference of State Legislatures at www.ncsl.org/research/telecommunications-and-information-technology/privacy-and-security.aspx.

Standards versus Law

Several industry groups have created standards that offer guidance for how cybersecurity could or should be applied to industry segments or geographic areas. Some industries have security requirements defined at least in part by government regulations; banking, healthcare, and education come to mind, as well as their regulations' acronyms, such as FFIEC, HIPAA, FERPA, and SOX. Other industries impose binding requirements on themselves that include significant enforcement mechanisms—for example, the credit card processing requirements from the Payment Card Industry (PCI) Security Standards Council.

Payment Card Industry Data Security Standard

Critical to any organization that handles online payments, the Payment Card Industry Data Security Standard (PCI DSS) is a set of industry standards that are mandated for any organization that handles credit, debit, and specialty payment cards. This standard was created by the PCI Security Standards Council to reduce credit card fraud.

The current version of the standard, v4.0, was released in March 2022. The standard is presented by the PCI Security Standards Council as focusing on 12 requirements in six areas:

> Build and Maintain a Secure Network and Systems
>> Requirement 1: Install and Maintain Network Security Controls
>> Requirement 2: Apply Secure Configurations to All System Components
> Protect Account Data
>> Requirement 3: Protect Stored Account Data
>> Requirement 4: Protect Cardholder Data with Strong Cryptography During Transmission Over Open, Public Networks
> Maintain a Vulnerability Management Program
>> Requirement 5: Protect All Systems and Networks from Malicious Software
>> Requirement 6: Develop and Maintain Secure Systems and Software
> Implement Strong Access Control Measures
>> Requirement 7: Restrict Access to System Components and Cardholder Data by Business Need to Know
>> Requirement 8: Identify Users and Authenticate Access to System Components
>> Requirement 9: Restrict Physical Access to Cardholder Data
> Regularly Monitor and Test Networks
>> Requirement 10: Log and Monitor All Access to System Components and Cardholder Data
>> Requirement 11: Test Security of Systems and Networks Regularly
> Maintain an Information Security Policy
>> Requirement 12: Support Information Security with Organizational Policies and Programs[33]

In addition to the preceding requirements, a supplemental requirement (A.1) states that shared hosting providers must protect the cardholder data.[34]

According to the 2019 Verizon Payment Security Report, as of 2018, only about 36 percent of organizations surveyed achieved "full compliance" and actively maintained their PCI DSS programs. Figure 5-1 illustrates the rise and fall of PCI DSS compliance between 2012 and 2018. Approximately 18 percent of organizations did not have a formal PCI DSS program, and none had a program classified as "mature" or "optimized." The same study found that no organization that suffered a breach had 100 percent PCI DSS compliance. As shown in Figure 5-2, the percentages of "partially compliant" and "Not in place" vary dramatically among breached organizations for the 12 requirements of the PCI DSS standard listed previously.[35]

Despite its obvious value, PCI DSS is not law. It is mandated by many payment card issuers, including Visa, MasterCard, American Express, and Discover. If your organization plans to process those cards,

Figure 5-1 PCI DSS compliance by year, 2012-2018[36]

% Fully PCI DSS Compliant

Source: Verizon 2019 Payment Security Report: Percentage of surveyed organizations that were fully PCI DSS compliant.

- 2012: 11.1%
- 2013: 20.0%
- 2014: 37.1%
- 2015: 48.4%
- 2016: 55.4%
- 2017: 52.5%
- 2018: 36.7%

Figure 5-2 Breached organizations' PCI DSS control status[37]

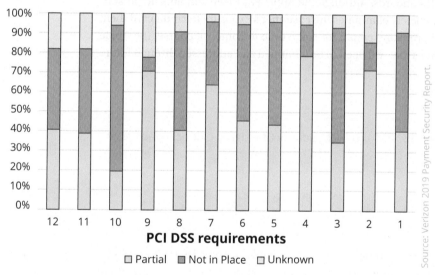

PCI DSS requirements

☐ Partial   ☐ Not in Place   ☐ Unknown

Source: Verizon 2019 Payment Security Report.

it is expected to comply. This standard does not apply to a retail store that accepts credit cards but more to organizations that provide payment acceptance and authorization systems, which are the credit/debit card machines seen in most retail stores. The benefits of PCI DSS compliance, as promoted by the PCI Security Standards Council, include:

- An assertion that systems processing payment cards are secure, promoting trust in customers
- Improved reputation with payment card issue and payment processing organizations
- Prevention of security breaches
- Assistance in complying with other security standards, such as HIPAA, SOX, and GLB
- Support for organizational security strategies
- Increased efficiency of the information infrastructure[38]

Note that the requirements listed earlier mirror generally accepted best security practices, as they were specifically designed to do. Organizations are expected to periodically review and validate their systems against these standards. Failure to do so can result in loss of ability to process payment information. Note again that these standards apply more to organizations that process credit card information than those that allow customers to use their cards in a retail setting.

Verizon offers eight "navigation points" to assist adopters of PCI DSS v4.0:

1. Do not delay.
2. Start strong—meet PCI DSS v.3.2.1.
3. Understand the PCI DSS v.4.0 requirements.
4. Choose your control design and compliance validation option wisely.
5. Take care when selecting a customized approach.
6. Use control design and management templates.
7. Do early validation of control designs.
8. Prepare for ongoing compliance.[39]

What is the future of PCI DSS? The recent increase in popularity of using embedded smart chips in cards still does not negate the requirements to protect cardholder data once it has been collected and processed at the point of sale. Even with the increasing popularity of tokenization—the use of digital equivalents of credit cards, such as Apple Pay, in lieu of the actual card—it is expected that such use will lead to little reduction in the expectation of compliance with PCI DSS standards. Although the Apple Pay token contains no personally identifiable information and almost completely eliminates the customer's exposure to credit card theft, the demand for traditional credit cards will probably remain for some time to come. Of course, the Apple Pay system might have unknown vulnerabilities that will need to be identified and addressed through future standards.

Note 16 | For more information on PCI DSS, visit the PCI Security Standards Council website at www.pcisecuritystandards.org/.

Policy versus Law

Most organizations develop and formalize policies as descriptions of acceptable and unacceptable employee behavior. Properly defined and enforced policies function in an organization the same way as laws do in society, complete with penalties, judicial practices, and sanctions. Because policies function like laws, they must be crafted with the same care as laws to ensure that the policies are complete, appropriate, and fairly applied to everyone in the workplace. The key difference between policy and law is that while ignorance of the law is not an excuse ("ignorantia juris non excusat"), ignorance of policy *is* a viable defense, and therefore policies must be:

- Distributed to all individuals who are expected to comply with them
- Read by all employees, with multilingual translations and translations for visually impaired or low-literacy employees
- Understood by all employees, with quizzes or other assessments for validation
- Acknowledged by the employee, usually by means of a signed consent form
- Uniformly enforced, with no special treatment for any group (for example, executives)

Only when all these conditions are met does the organization have the reasonable expectation that policy violations can be appropriately penalized without fear of legal retribution. You will learn more about policy later in this book.

Organizational Liability and the Key Law Enforcement Agencies

What if an organization does not require or even encourage ethical conduct on the part of its employees? What if an organization does not behave ethically? Even if there is no criminal conduct, there can be liability—an entity's legal obligation or responsibility. Liability can be applied to conduct even when no law or contract has been breached. Liability for a wrongful act includes the obligation to make payment or restitution, a legal requirement for compensation after a loss or injury. If an employee acting with or without authorization performs an illegal or unethical act, causing some degree of harm, the organization can be held financially liable for that action. An organization increases its liability if it refuses to exercise *due care*—measures that an organization takes to ensure every employee knows what is acceptable and what is not.

Due diligence—reasonable steps taken by people or organizations to meet the obligations imposed by laws or regulations—requires that an organization make a valid and ongoing effort to protect others. Due to the global nature of the Internet, it is possible that a person wronged by an organization's members could be anywhere around the world.

Under the U.S. legal system, any court can impose its authority over an individual or organization if it can establish jurisdiction, the area within which a court or law enforcement agency is empowered to make legal decisions. This is related to the concept of long-arm jurisdiction, the ability of a legal entity to exercise its influence beyond its normal boundaries by asserting a connection between an out-of-jurisdiction entity and a local legal case. The concept is so named because the long arm of the law reaches across a country or around the world, allowing an entity to bring an accused individual or organization into its own court systems. Trying a case in the injured party's home area usually favors that party, as it creates a "home court advantage."[40]

Key Law Enforcement Agencies

Sometimes, organizations need assistance from law enforcement. While local law enforcement may be the first point of contact and capable of handling physical security threats or employee problems, it is usually ill equipped to handle electronic crimes. In the United States, most states have their own law enforcement and investigation agencies. For example, the Georgia State Patrol and the Georgia Bureau of Investigation have separate structures and missions but work together with local law enforcement to assist organizations and individuals.

Several key federal agencies are charged with the protection of federal and nationwide information assets and the investigation of threats or attacks against these assets. Among them are the FBI InfraGard organization, the DHS's National Protection and Programs Directorate, the NSA, and the U.S. Secret Service.

The FBI's National Infrastructure Protection Center (NIPC) was established in 1998 and served as the U.S. government's focal point for threat assessment and the warning, investigation, and response to threats or attacks against critical U.S. infrastructures. The NIPC was folded into the DHS after the 2001 terrorist attacks to increase communications and focus the department's efforts on cybersecurity defense. It is now a part of DHS's National Protection and Programs Directorate, which seeks to secure U.S. physical and information system infrastructures.

The components of the National Protection and Programs Directorate include:

- Federal Protective Service (FPS)—FPS is an agency that provides integrated security and law enforcement services to federally owned and leased buildings, facilities, properties, and other assets.
- Office of Biometric Identity Management (OBIM)—OBIM provides biometric identity services to DHS and its mission partners that advance informed decision making by producing accurate, timely, and high-fidelity biometric identity information while protecting individuals' privacy and civil liberties.
- Office of Cyber and Infrastructure Analysis (OCIA)—OCIA provides consolidated all-hazards consequence analysis, ensuring there is an understanding and awareness of cyber and physical critical infrastructure interdependencies and the impact of a cyber threat or incident to the nation's critical infrastructure.
- Office of Cybersecurity and Communications (CS&C)—Its mission is to ensure the security, resiliency, and reliability of the nation's cyber and communications infrastructure.
- Office of Infrastructure Protection (IP)—IP leads the coordinated national effort to reduce risk to critical infrastructure posed by acts of terrorism. IP thus increases the nation's level of preparedness and the ability to respond and quickly recover in the event of an attack, natural disaster, or other emergency.[41]

Established in January 2001, InfraGard (www.infragard.org) is a U.S. association consisting of regional chapters of the Federal Bureau of Investigation (FBI) and affiliations of public, private, and academic organizations that cooperate to exchange information on the protection of critical national information resources. InfraGard began as a cooperative effort between the FBI's Cleveland field office and local technology professionals. The FBI sought assistance in establishing a more effective method of protecting critical national information resources. The resulting cooperative formed the first InfraGard chapters as a formal effort to combat both cyber and physical threats. Today, every FBI field office has established an InfraGard chapter and collaborates with local InfraGard Members Alliances (IMAs) like the InfraGard Atlanta Members Alliance (infragardatlanta.org), which represents public and private organizations and the academic community, and shares information about attacks, vulnerabilities, and threats. These local IMAs have combined into a formal national organization in recent years: the InfraGard National Members Alliance (INMA). The National InfraGard program serves its members using the following tools:

- Intrusion alert network using encrypted email
- Secure website for communication about suspicious activity or intrusions
- Local chapter activities
- Help desk for questions

InfraGard's primary contribution is the free exchange of information to and from the private sector in the subject areas of threats and attacks on information resources.[42]

Another key U.S. agency is the NSA. As the nation's key cryptologic organization, the NSA coordinates, directs, and performs highly specialized activities to protect U.S. information systems and produce foreign intelligence information. It is also one of the government's most important centers of foreign language analysis and research.[43]

The NSA is responsible for the security of communications and information systems at many federal government agencies associated with national security. The NSA's Information Assurance Directorate (IAD) provides cybersecurity "solutions including the technologies, specifications and criteria, products, product configurations, tools, standards, operational doctrine, and support activities needed to implement the protect, detect and report, and respond elements of cyber defense."[44] The IAD also develops and promotes an Information Assurance Framework Forum in cooperation with commercial organizations and academic researchers.

This framework provides strategic guidance as well as technical specifications for security solutions. IAD's Common Criteria are a set of standards designed to promote understanding of cybersecurity.

Prominent among the NSA's cybersecurity efforts and activities are its cybersecurity outreach programs. The NSA recognizes universities that offer cybersecurity education opportunities and that integrate cybersecurity philosophies and efforts into their internal operations. These recognized Centers of Academic Excellence in Cybersecurity (CAE-C), including emphases in cyber defense education (CAE-CDE), research (CAE-R), and cyber operations (CAE-CO), can display this recognition on their websites and in other materials, and are named on the NSA's website. Graduates of these programs receive certificates recognizing this designation.

Note 17 | For more information on the NSA/DHS Centers of Academic Excellence programs, go to www.nsa.gov/Academics/Centers-of-Academic-Excellence/.

In addition to its well-known mission to protect key members of the U.S. government, the U.S. Secret Service is charged with the detection and arrest of any person committing a federal offense relating to computer fraud or false identification crimes.[45] This is an extension of its original duty to protect U.S. currency. After all, the communications networks of the United States carry more funds, in the form of electronic data, than all the armored cars in the world combined. If you protect the networks and protect the data, you protect money, stocks, and other financial transactions.

The USA PATRIOT Act and subsequent PATRIOT Improvement and Reauthorization Act increased the Secret Service's role in investigating fraud and related activity in connection with computers. In addition, these acts authorized the director of the Secret Service to establish nationwide electronic crime task forces to assist law enforcement, the private sector, and academia in detecting and suppressing computer-based crime. The acts increase the statutory penalties for the manufacture, possession, dealing, and passing of counterfeit U.S. or foreign obligations, and they allow enforcement action to be taken to protect financial payment systems while combating transnational financial crimes.

The Secret Service was transferred from the Department of the Treasury to the DHS in 2003. Since that time, DHS has added the protection of the nation's cyber infrastructures to its critical infrastructure defense strategies. To directly support the public, DHS promotes individual emergency preparedness through its READY Campaign and Citizen Corps (www.ready.gov). This site has content dedicated to cyber incidents.

Note 18 | For more information about the DHS Ready.gov website on cybersecurity, visit www.ready.gov/cybersecurity.

Self-Check

10. The U.S. Secret Service's original duty was to protect U.S. currency; it has been extended to include the detection and arrest of any person committing a federal offense related to computer fraud.

    a. True   **b.** False

11. InfraGard is a U.S. association consisting of regional chapters of the FBI and affiliations of public, private, and academic organizations that cooperate to exchange information on the protection of critical national information resources.

    a. True   **b.** False

12. The Office of Infrastructure Protection leads the national effort to secure U.S. physical infrastructures against acts of terrorism, without concern for information system infrastructures.

    a. True   **b.** False

☐ Check your answers at the end of this chapter.

Closing Case

Iris was a little unsure of what to do next. She had just left the meeting with the other executives. At the meeting, they confirmed the need for action on the matter of the critical information offered for sale on a public auction site. That was the last point of agreement. This was a risk they had simply not planned for, and they were completely unprepared. Just before the meeting ended, they had made assignments to various people in the meeting. Robin, the CEO, was going to contact the members of the board of directors to brief them so that if the story became public, they would not be surprised. Jerry, the corporate counsel, was going to start an intensive effort to discover what peer companies had done in situations like this. Mike, the CIO, was assigned to contact the auction site to get the auction shut down and lay the groundwork for working with authorities on the criminal aspects of the case.

Iris was assigned to research which law enforcement agency should be involved in the investigation. She already knew that the auction site was hosted on a server owned by a company that was not in the United States, where RWW was located. She opened the professional networking app on her phone and began searching for her contacts in law enforcement.

Case Discussion Questions

1. Do you think the response of the company so far indicates any flaws in company policy or practices?
2. With which law enforcement agency do you think Iris should consult? On what factors do you base that recommendation?
3. What criminal acts might have occurred in this situation? Considering who the perpetrators might be, what do you think their relationship to RWW might be?

Case Ethical Decision Making

Suppose that Cassandra, the CEO's executive assistant, was involved in the criminal activity of selling company data. Also suppose that when the anonymous tip came in, she deleted the message without bringing it to anyone else's attention. One of Cassandra's tasks is to delete all messages deemed to be "noise" or a nuisance and then bring the remaining messages to the attention of the CEO.

By deleting the message that Iris would have received, is Cassandra's act unethical? Is it illegal?

Summary

Laws are formally adopted rules for acceptable behavior in modern society. Ethics are socially acceptable behaviors. The key difference between laws and ethics is that laws bear the sanction of a governing authority and ethics do not.

Deterrence can prevent an illegal or unethical activity from occurring. Successful deterrence requires the institution of severe penalties, the probability of apprehension, and an expectation that penalties will be enforced.

As part of an effort to sponsor positive ethics, a number of professional organizations have established codes of conduct and codes of ethics that their members are expected to follow.

Organizations formalize desired behaviors in documents called policies. Unlike laws, policies must be distributed, read, understood, explicitly agreed to by employees, and uniformly enforced before they are enforceable.

Civil law encompasses a wide variety of laws that regulate relationships between and among individuals and organizations. Criminal law addresses violations that harm society and that are prosecuted by the state. Tort law is a subset of civil law that deals with lawsuits brought by individuals rather than criminal prosecution by the state.

The desire to protect national security, trade secrets, and a variety of other state and private assets has led to several laws affecting what information and information management and security resources may be exported from the United States.

U.S. copyright law extends intellectual property rights to the published word, including electronic publication.

Several key U.S. agencies are charged with the protection of American information resources and the investigation of threats or attacks against these resources.

Key Terms

Computer Fraud and Abuse (CFA) Act of 1986

Computer Security Act (CSA) of 1987

deterrence

due diligence

Electronic Communications Privacy Act (ECPA) of 1986

ethics

Health Insurance Portability and Accountability Act (HIPAA) of 1996

InfraGard

jurisdiction

liability

long-arm jurisdiction

Privacy Act of 1974

restitution

Review Questions

1. How does Jean Jacques Rousseau's concept from *The Social Contract* relate to modern cybersecurity laws?

2. What distinguishes law from ethics in the context of cybersecurity?

3. Why are ethics particularly important for cybersecurity professionals?

4. Can you describe the different ethical frameworks that inform decision making in cybersecurity?

5. In what ways can the deployment of IT systems lead to ethical dilemmas?

6. What role do education and training play in promoting ethical behavior among cybersecurity professionals?

7. How can organizations deter unethical and illegal behavior in cybersecurity?

8. What impact do codes of ethics have on the judgment of individuals regarding computer use?

9. How can the loss of licensing or certification from a violation of a code of conduct affect a cybersecurity professional?

10. What long-term value does a cybersecurity certification provide to its holders?

11. What is the primary focus of (ISC)²?

12. How does SANS contribute to the cybersecurity profession?

13. What ethical principles does ISACA's code of ethics emphasize for its members and certification holders?

14. How does ISSA aim to promote cybersecurity awareness and education?

15. What is the primary reason for cybersecurity and IT professionals to understand the industry's legal framework?

16. How are laws within the United States categorized based on their origins?

17. What distinguishes civil law from criminal law in the United States?

18. Can you explain the distinction between private law and public law?

19. What is the significance of the Computer Fraud and Abuse (CFA) Act of 1986 in computer-related federal laws?

20. How does the Privacy Act of 1974 regulate the government's use of personal information?

21. What are the core objectives of the Health Insurance Portability and Accountability Act (HIPAA)?

22. How does the Sarbanes-Oxley (SOX) Act of 2002 impact cybersecurity practices within organizations?

23. What is the purpose of the Payment Card Industry Data Security Standard (PCI DSS)?

24. What constitutes organizational liability in the absence of criminal conduct?

25. What is the difference between due care and due diligence in organizational contexts?

26. How can jurisdiction impact the legal authority over an individual or organization?

27. What was the primary role of the FBI's National Infrastructure Protection Center established in 1998?

28. What are the components of the DHS's National Protection and Programs Directorate?

29. What is InfraGard, and how does it serve its members?

30. What is the main responsibility of the National Security Agency (NSA) in terms of cybersecurity?

31. How does the U.S. Secret Service contribute to cybersecurity?

Exercises

1. (ISC)² has several certifications. Use a web browser to read about (ISC)² certifications. What does CISSP stand for? Using the Internet, find out which continuing education is required for the holder of a CISSP to remain current and in good standing.

2. Use a web browser to explore the career options in cybersecurity at the U.S. National Security Agency. For what kinds of cybersecurity jobs does the NSA recruit? What qualifications do the jobs require?

3. Using the resources available in your library, find out what laws your state has passed to prosecute computer crimes.

4. Go to www.eff.org. What is this group's mission and what are its current top concerns?

5. Consider the ethical scenarios on computer use that were presented earlier in this chapter and note your responses. Bring your answers to class to compare them with those of your peers.

Solutions to Self-Check Questions

Introduction to Law and Ethics

1. Ethics and laws are interchangeable in the context of cybersecurity.
   Answer: b. False.
   Explanation: Ethics are based on cultural mores and do not carry the sanction of a governing authority, unlike laws, which are enforced by governments.

2. The cybersecurity professional is solely responsible for the technical aspects of cybersecurity and not the ethical implications.
   Answer: b. False.
   Explanation: Cybersecurity professionals are trusted with sensitive information and must adhere to the highest ethical standards, implying a responsibility beyond just technical aspects.

3. Ethical behavior in cybersecurity is intuitive and does not require formal education or training.
   Answer: b. False.
   Explanation: Key studies show that education is the overriding factor in leveling ethical perceptions, indicating that formal education and training are necessary for understanding and upholding ethical behavior in cybersecurity.

Professional Organizations and Their Codes of Conduct

4. The (ISC)² code of ethics is only applicable to cybersecurity professionals who have not earned any of their certifications.
   Answer: b. False.
   Explanation: The (ISC)² code of ethics is primarily designed for cybersecurity professionals who have earned one of their certifications.

5. SANS, founded in 1989, is dedicated solely to the certification of IT and cybersecurity professionals, without providing any training.

Answer: b. False.

Explanation: SANS is dedicated to the training of IT and cybersecurity professionals and manages certifications associated with SANS training.

6. ISSA's primary mission is to facilitate the exchange of cybersecurity information and the educational development of cybersecurity professionals.

Answer: a. True.

Explanation: ISSA's primary mission is indeed to bring together qualified practitioners of cybersecurity for information exchange and educational development.

Cybersecurity and Law

7. The Computer Fraud and Abuse (CFA) Act was amended by the National Information Infrastructure Protection Act of 1996 to increase penalties for selected computer-related crimes.

Answer: a. True.

Explanation: The CFA Act was amended in October 1996 by the National Information Infrastructure Protection Act, which modified several sections of the previous act and increased penalties for selected crimes.

8. The Privacy Act of 1974 applies only to the federal government and does not create a right of access to records held by state or local government agencies.

Answer: a. True.

Explanation: The Privacy Act of 1974 is a U.S. law that regulates the government's collection, storage, use, and dissemination of personal information. It does not apply to state or local government agencies.

9. HIPAA was designed to protect the confidentiality and security of healthcare data by establishing standards and standardizing electronic data interchange.

Answer: a. True.

Explanation: HIPAA was enacted to protect the confidentiality and security of healthcare information, and it includes provisions for standardizing electronic data interchange.

Organizational Liability and the Key Law Enforcement Agencies

10. The U.S. Secret Service's original duty was to protect U.S. currency; it has been extended to include the detection and arrest of any person committing a federal offense related to computer fraud.

Answer: a. True.

Explanation: The U.S. Secret Service, known for its mission to protect key members of the U.S. government, also has the duty of detecting and arresting individuals involved in computer fraud and false identification crimes, extending its original role of protecting U.S. currency.

11. InfraGard is a U.S. association consisting of regional chapters of the FBI and affiliations of public, private, and academic organizations that cooperate to exchange information on the protection of critical national information resources.

Answer: a. True.

Explanation: InfraGard was established as a cooperative effort between the FBI and local technology professionals to protect critical national information resources.

12. The Office of Infrastructure Protection leads the national effort to secure U.S. physical infrastructures against acts of terrorism, without concern for information system infrastructures.

Answer: b. False.

Explanation: The Office of Infrastructure Protection actually leads the coordinated national effort to reduce risk to both physical and information system infrastructures posed by acts of terrorism.

Cybersecurity Policy

Chapter Objectives

After reading this chapter and completing the exercises, you should be able to:

1 Explain cybersecurity policy and its central role in a successful cybersecurity program.

2 Outline cybersecurity program policy.

3 Discuss issue-specific cybersecurity policies.

4 Explain system-specific policies.

5 Discuss the process of developing, implementing, and maintaining various types of cybersecurity policies.

> Each problem that I solved became a rule which served afterwards to solve other problems.
>
> —René Descartes

Case Opener

Iris was returning from lunch when she ran into Susan Weinstein, one of RWW's senior account executives, who was accompanied by a man Iris didn't know. Susan introduced him as Bob Watson, a prospective client. As they were chatting, Iris noticed Bob's distracted demeanor and Susan's forced smile and formal manner.

Iris realized that RWW would not get the account.

A few minutes later, she saw why the meeting between RWW's account executive and the prospective client did not go well. In the cubicle across the hall from Susan's office, two programmers were having lunch. Tim had his feet propped up on his desk. In one hand was a half-eaten hamburger; in the other, he held several playing cards. John had made himself comfortable by taking off his shoes. Teetering over a laptop, tablet, and smartphone was a jumbo soft drink threatening a flood of sugary soda water that could inundate the desk.

Iris went into her office and pulled up the company's policy manual on the company's intranet. She was familiar with most of RWW's policies, but for the actions she had in mind, she needed specifics. RWW's policy and procedure manual did not contain policies about alerting employees to meetings with prospective clients, playing cards, or eating and drinking in the workplace. What was most disconcerting, though, was that it didn't even contain specifics about practices that supported data protection and other cybersecurity objectives.

Before Iris left that evening, she typed up her notes and scheduled an early-morning meeting with her boss, Mike Edwards. As she left for home, she wondered whether Tim and John playing cards and eating in their office may have cost RWW a new account. She made a mental note to suggest to Mike that they reconvene the policy review committee.

Why Policy?

In this chapter, you learn about cybersecurity policy: what it is, how to write it, how to implement it, and how to maintain it. The success of any cybersecurity program lies in policy development. In 1989, the National Institute of Standards and Technology (NIST) addressed this point in Special Publication (SP) 500-169, "Executive Guide to the Protection of Information Resources":

> The success of an information resources protection program depends on the policy generated, and on the attitude of management toward securing information on automated systems. You, the policy maker, set the tone and the emphasis on how important a role [cybersecurity] will have within your agency. Your primary responsibility is to set the information resource [cybersecurity] policy for the organization with the objectives of reduced risk, compliance with laws and regulations, and assurance of operational continuity, information integrity, and confidentiality.[1]

Policy is the essential foundation of an effective cybersecurity program. As stated by consultant Charles Cresson Wood in his book *Information Security Policies Made Easy*:

> The centrality of [cybersecurity] policies to virtually everything that happens in the information security field is increasingly evident. For example, system administrators cannot securely install a firewall unless they have received a set of clear [cybersecurity] policies. These policies will stipulate the type of transmission services that should be permitted, how to authenticate the identities of users, and how to log information security-relevant events. An effective security training and awareness effort cannot be initiated without writing [cybersecurity] policies because policies provide the essential content that can be utilized in training and awareness material.[2]

A high-quality cybersecurity program begins and ends with policy. A cybersecurity policy is a statement of managerial intent designed to direct and regulate employee and other stakeholder behavior regarding the authorized use of information assets and their technologies, including penalties for noncompliance. Such policy is designed to provide structure and to create a productive and effective work environment, free from unnecessary distractions and inappropriate actions. In information technology (IT), policy may refer to a computer configuration specification used to standardize system and user behavior.

Properly developed and implemented policies enable and support the efficient and effective function of the cybersecurity program. Although cybersecurity policies are one of the least expensive means of control, they are often the most difficult to properly implement and guarantee compliance. Policy controls cost only the time and effort that the management team spends to create, approve, and communicate them, along with the time and effort that employees spend learning the policies and integrating them into their daily activities. Even when the management team hires an outside consultant to assist in the development of policy, the costs are minimal compared to those of other controls, especially expensive technical components like enterprise-level firewalls.

Why is policy so important? Among the other reasons listed here, policy may be one of the very few controls or safeguards protecting certain information. Consider Figure 6-1, which depicts the levels and layers of protection the organization can place between information and those with access to it. As shown on the left side, to access information from outside the organization, people must traverse the Internet and go through the organization's perimeter defense (gateway, firewalls, and routers), across the organization's network, into the organization's computer systems, and finally onto the drives physically storing that information. This gives the organization several defense points, attack axes, or avenues of approach (however you wish to describe them) that it can use to place defensive control safeguards.

Figure 6-1   Spheres of cybersecurity

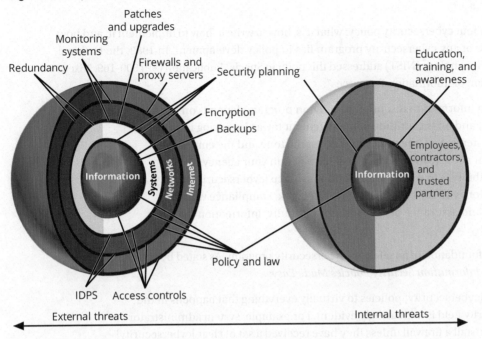

The right side of the sphere shows that people within the organization have much less restricted access to information, especially when it is in physical form. Some access is a direct function of people's job requirements, and other forms are an indirect result of physical access to internal locations, such as meeting rooms, supervisors' offices, and administrative support facilities like the workroom and mailroom. A long-standing adage states that "physical access trumps logical security." In other words, if you can touch it, you can take it. This means that for personnel inside the organization, especially employees, the organization must make a more concerted effort to properly protect information from unauthorized access and misuse. While an employee who is intent on abuse may be much more difficult to control, accidental loss and damage to information can be greatly reduced with effective education and training programs, mitigation planning, and *policy*.

Some basic rules must be followed when developing a policy:

- Policy should never conflict with the law.
- Policy must be able to stand up in court if challenged.
- Policy must be properly supported and administered.

Consider some of the facts that were revealed during the Enron scandal in 2001. The management team at Enron Energy Corporation was found to have lied about the organization's financial records, specifically about reported profits. The management team was also accused of a host of dubious business practices, including concealing financial losses and debts. The depth and breadth of the fraud was so great that tens of thousands of investors lost significant amounts of money and one executive died by suicide rather than face criminal charges. One of the company's accounting firms, Arthur Andersen, contributed to the problem by shredding literally tons of financial documents. Andersen's auditors and IT consultants claimed that this shredding of working papers was in accordance with Andersen's established policy. The chief auditor from Andersen was fired after an internal probe revealed that the company shredded the documents and deleted email messages related to Enron, with the intent to conceal facts from investigators. The auditor pleaded guilty to obstruction of justice, which carries a maximum sentence of 10 years in prison. Although the Supreme Court overturned the conviction and the charges were subsequently dropped, the lesson remains valid: An organization must conform to its own policy and that policy must be consistently applied.

In the Enron/Andersen scandal, managers, employees, and others affiliated with the two companies claimed they were simply following policy. In this case, because the policy as written did not violate any laws, they might have been able to use that claim as a defense, but they would need to have been *consistently* following that policy prior to the incidents in question. Andersen's document-retention policy originally stated that staff must keep working papers for six years before destroying them. On the other hand, client-related files, such as correspondence or other records, were to be kept only until they were no longer useful. Managers and partners keeping such material in client folders or other files were supposed to destroy the documents once they were no longer needed, according to the policy.

In cases of threatened litigation, the policy dictated that Andersen staff should not destroy information related to the potential case. However, a subsequent change to the document-retention policy at Andersen was interpreted as a mandate to shred all but the most essential working papers as soon as possible unless destruction was precluded by an order for legal discovery. The Enron-related shredding began right after Andersen management found out that Enron was to be investigated for fraudulent business practices, which implied an intent to cover the firm's tracks and those of its business partners. The shredding policy was a problem because it was not consistently applied—Andersen staff assigned to the Enron project did not follow the policy routinely, but only when it enabled them to shred incriminating documents.

Policy can be difficult to implement effectively. According to Bergeron and Bérubé, the following guidelines can help in the formulation of cybersecurity policy:

- All policies must contribute to the success of the organization.
- Management must ensure the adequate sharing of responsibility for proper use of information systems.
- End users of information systems should be involved in the steps of policy formulation.[3]

Policy must be tailored to the specific needs of the organization. It makes little sense to have policies that are not well aligned with the organization. Organizations that handle sensitive information should not have relaxed cybersecurity policies. Likewise, organizations that don't handle sensitive information would be poorly served with a stringent policy environment. While policies should be complete and comprehensive, the existence of too many policies or policies that are too complex can cause confusion and possibly demoralize employees. One implementation model that emphasizes the role of policy in a cybersecurity program is the bull's-eye model. Because it provides a proven mechanism for prioritizing complex changes, the bull's-eye model has become widely accepted among cybersecurity professionals. In this model, issues are addressed by moving from the general to the specific, always starting with policy. That is, the focus is on systemic solutions instead of individual problems. Figure 6-2 illustrates the four layers of the bull's-eye model, which are as follows:

Figure 6-2   Bull's-eye model

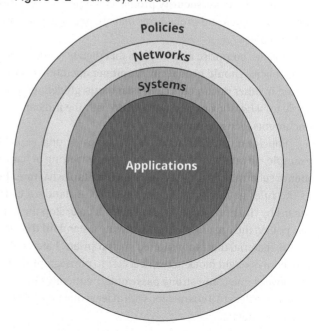

1. Policies—This is the outer layer in the bull's-eye diagram, reflecting that it is the initial viewpoint most users have for interacting with cybersecurity. It is available from published documents that express the will of management and seeks to guide user behavior.

2. Networks—This is the environment where threats from public networks meet the organization's networking infrastructure. In the past, most cybersecurity efforts focused on networks. Until recently, in fact, cybersecurity was often thought to be synonymous with network cybersecurity.

3. Systems—These are the collections of hardware and software being used as servers or desktop computers as well as systems used for process control and manufacturing.

4. Applications—These are the programs that support the organization's operations, ranging from packaged applications, such as office productivity and email

programs, to high-end enterprise resource planning (ERP) packages and custom software or process control applications developed by the organization.

Whether via the use of the bull's-eye model or any other methodology, until sound and usable cybersecurity policy is developed, communicated, and enforced by an organization, no additional resources should be spent on controls.

In *Information Security Policies Made Easy*, Wood summarizes the need for policy as follows:

> [P]olicies are important reference documents for internal audits and for the resolution of legal disputes about management's due diligence, [and] policy documents can act as a clear statement of management's intent.[4]

However, policy isn't just a management tool to meet legal requirements. It is necessary to protect the organization and the jobs of its employees. Consider this scenario: An employee behaves inappropriately in the workplace, perhaps by viewing inappropriate websites or reading another employee's email. Another employee is offended by this behavior and, claiming a hostile workplace, sues the company. The company does not have a policy that prohibits the behavior, so any direct action against the offending employee risks further litigation. The lawsuit is settled in the disgruntled employee's favor, and the resulting judgment awarding large financial damages puts the organization into bankruptcy. Once the organization goes out of business, the rest of the employees lose their jobs—all because the company did not have effective policies in place that would have enabled it to terminate the misbehaving employee without risking additional litigation. Consider a variation of the same scenario, where a manager fires the employee who was behaving inappropriately. That employee then sues the organization for wrongful termination. After all, there was no policy in place that prohibited the employee from the actions that led to dismissal. The courts would likely rule for the aggrieved and wrongfully terminated employee, and again, the company could lose money and go out of business. In either example, an effective policy could have saved the organization.

Policy, Standards, Guidelines, and Practices

Policy represents a formal statement of the organization's managerial philosophy—in our case, the organization's cybersecurity philosophy. The communities of interest described in previous chapters use policy to express their views about the cybersecurity environment of the organization and the stakeholders' use of information assets. This policy then becomes the basis for planning, management, and maintenance of the cybersecurity profile. Once policies are designed, created, approved, and implemented, the technologies and procedures that are necessary to implement them can be designed, developed, and put into place.

Policies comprise a set of rules that dictate acceptable and unacceptable behavior within an organization. Policies should not specify the proper operation of equipment or software—this information should be placed in other documents called standards, guidelines, practices, and procedures. Policies define *who* they apply to, *what* they can do and not do with the indicated topic, and *when* and *where* they can do it. Other documents focus on the *how*.

Policies must also specify the penalties for unacceptable behavior and define an appeals process. For example, an organization that prohibits the viewing of inappropriate websites in the workplace must implement a set of standards—detailed statements of what must be done to comply with policy, sometimes viewed as the rules governing policy compliance. A standard clarifies and defines exactly what the organization means by "inappropriate" and what it will do to stop the behavior. In the implementation of an appropriate-use policy, the organization might create a standard that all inappropriate content will be blocked and then list the material that is considered inappropriate. Later in the process, technical controls and their associated procedures might block network access to pornographic websites. As another example, if a policy states that employees must "use strong passwords, frequently changed," the standard might specify that the password "must be at least 10 characters, with at least one number, one uppercase letter, one lowercase letter, and one special character."

Guidelines are nonmandatory recommendations the employee may use as a reference in complying with a policy. They complete the document set, providing recommendations the employee can use to meet the intent of policy. If the policy states to "use strong passwords," the guidelines might recommend that "you don't use family or pet names, or parts of your Social Security number, employee number, or phone number in your password."

Practices are examples of actions that illustrate compliance with policies. If the policy states to "use approved technologies to store passwords," the practices might advise that "according to ACME security software, the following applications provide effective and secure password management."

Procedures are step-by-step instructions designed to assist employees in following policies, standards, and practices; they provide the means to comply with the policy. If the policy states to "change passwords every six months," the procedure might advise that "in order to change your password, first click on the Windows Start button, then . . . ."

Figure 6-3 illustrates the relationship among policies, standards, guidelines, practices, and procedures.

Figure 6-3 Policies, standards, guidelines, practices, and procedures

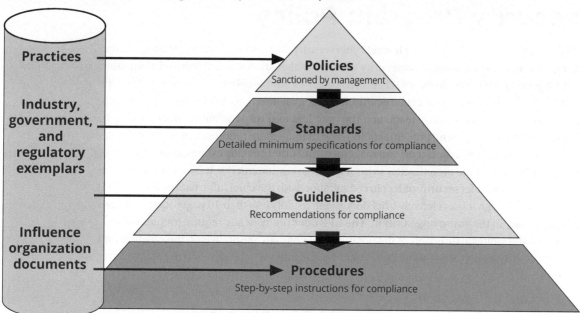

To produce a complete cybersecurity policy portfolio, management must define three types of cybersecurity policies. These are based on NIST's SP 800-12, Revision 1, which outlines what is required of managers when writing cybersecurity policy. The three types of cybersecurity policy are as follows:

- Cybersecurity program policy (CPP)
- Issue-specific policy
- System-specific policy

Each of these cybersecurity policy types is found in most organizations. The usual procedure is to create the CPP first—the highest level of cybersecurity policy. After that, general policy needs are met by developing issue-specific and system-specific policies. The three types of cybersecurity policy are described in detail in the following sections.

Note 1 | For more information on NIST SP 800-12's approach to cybersecurity policy, visit NIST's website at https://csrc.nist.gov/publications/sp and download the publication.

Self-Check

1. Organizations that handle sensitive information should have relaxed cybersecurity policies.

   a. True   b. False

2. In the implementation of an appropriate-use policy, all inappropriate content should be blocked.

   a. True   b. False

3. Cybersecurity policies are expensive to implement compared to other controls.

   a. True   b. False

□ Check your answers at the end of this chapter.

Cybersecurity Program Policy

The **cybersecurity program policy (CPP)**—a high-level cybersecurity directive that sets the strategic direction, scope, and tone for an organization's cybersecurity efforts—is also known as enterprise information security policy (EISP), general cybersecurity policy, IT security policy, or simply cybersecurity policy. The CPP assigns responsibilities for the various areas of cybersecurity, including maintenance of cybersecurity policies, roles and responsibilities of the cybersecurity team, and the practices and responsibilities of end users. In particular, the CPP guides the development, implementation, and management requirements of the cybersecurity program, which must be met by cybersecurity management and other specific cybersecurity functions.

The CPP must directly support the organization's vision and mission statements. It is an executive-level document, usually drafted by the chief security officer in consultation with the chief information officer (CIO) and other executives. Even though it is a relatively brief document, usually less than 10 pages long, it shapes the cybersecurity philosophy in the entire organization. The CPP does not typically require frequent or routine modification unless the strategic direction of the organization changes. Nonetheless, the creation and management of cybersecurity policy is not static but should be considered dynamic, as the cybersecurity landscape does experience a high rate of change compared with other business processes.

Integrating an Organization's Mission and Objectives into the CPP

The CPP plays several vital roles, not the least of which is to state the importance of cybersecurity to the organization's mission and objectives. As demonstrated in the organizational and cybersecurity planning processes discussed earlier, cybersecurity strategic planning derives from other organizational strategic policies, such as the IT strategic plans and key business unit strategic plans, which are in turn derived from the organization's strategic planning. Unless the CPP directly reflects this association, the policy will likely become confusing and counterproductive.

How can the CPP be crafted to reflect the organization's mission and objectives? Suppose that an academic institution's mission statement promotes academic freedom, independent research, and the relatively unrestricted pursuit of knowledge. This institution's CPP should reflect great tolerance in the use of organizational technology, a commitment to protecting the intellectual property of the faculty, and a degree of freedom for study that delves into what could be described as specialized or sensitive areas. The CPP should not contradict the organization's mission statement. For example, if the academic institution's mission statement supports the unrestricted pursuit of knowledge, then the CPP should not restrict access to legal but potentially objectionable websites or specify penalties for such access. Such a policy would directly contradict the academic institution's mission statement. However, it would be prudent for that institution to have policies that govern such access and ensure that it does not interfere with other employees or create a hostile work environment for them. For example, the institution could require that an employee who researches potentially objectionable material take steps to ensure that others are not exposed to the material.

CPP Elements

Although the specifics of CPPs vary from organization to organization, CPP documents should include the following elements:

- An overview of the corporate philosophy on cybersecurity
- Information on the structure of the cybersecurity organization and individuals who fulfill the cybersecurity role
- Fully articulated responsibilities for cybersecurity that are shared by all members of the organization (employees, contractors, consultants, partners, and visitors)
- Fully articulated responsibilities for cybersecurity that are unique to each role within the organization

The components of an effective CPP are shown in Table 6-1.

Table 6-1   Components of the CPP

Component	Description
Purpose	Answers the question, "What is this policy for?" Provides a framework that helps the reader to understand the intent of the document. Can include text such as the following, which is adapted from Washington University in St. Louis: "This document will: - Identify the elements of a good cybersecurity policy. - Explain the need for cybersecurity. - Specify the various categories of cybersecurity. - Identify the cybersecurity responsibilities and roles. - Identify appropriate levels of cybersecurity. - Reference supporting standards and guidelines. This document establishes an overarching cybersecurity policy and direction for our company. Individual departments are expected to establish standards, guidelines, and operating procedures that adhere to and reference this policy while addressing their specific and individual needs."[5]
Elements	Defines the whole topic of cybersecurity within the organization as well as its critical components. For example, the policy may define the elements of cybersecurity as "protecting the confidentiality, integrity, and availability of information while in processing, transmission, and storage, through the use of policy, education and training, and technology" and then identify where and how the elements are used. This section can also lay out cybersecurity definitions or philosophies to clarify the policy.
Need	Justifies the need for the organization to have a program for cybersecurity. This is done by providing information on the importance of cybersecurity in the organization and the obligation (legal and ethical) to protect critical information, whether regarding customers, employees, or markets.
Roles and responsibilities	Defines the staffing structure designed to support cybersecurity within the organization. It will likely describe the placement of the governance elements for cybersecurity as well as the categories of individuals with responsibility for cybersecurity (IT department, management, users) and their cybersecurity responsibilities, including maintenance of this document.
References	Lists other standards that influence and are influenced by this policy document, including relevant federal and state laws and other policies.

Example CPP Elements

In *Information Security Policies Made Easy*, Wood includes several sample high-level cybersecurity policy statements or elements. Table 6-2 shows some of these statements; when integrated into the framework described in Table 6-1, they provide detailed directives to include in an organization-specific CPP. As mentioned earlier, a policy document usually contains many individual policy statements, or statements of compliance. In his book, Wood also provides justification for each policy statement and the target audience, information that would not typically be included in the policy document itself. Note that the policy statements provided in Table 6-2 are designed to be worked into a CPP and are not intended to represent a stand-alone CPP framework.

Table 6-2   Sample CPP policy statements

1. Protection of Information	
Policy:	Information must be protected in a manner commensurate with its sensitivity, value, and criticality.
Commentary:	This policy applies regardless of the media on which information is stored, the locations where the information is stored, the systems technology used to process the information, or the people who handle the information. This policy encourages examining the ways information flows through an organization. The policy also points to the scope of cybersecurity management's work throughout, and often even outside, an organization.
Audience:	Technical staff

2. Use of Information	
Policy:	Company X information must be used only for the business purposes expressly authorized by management.
Commentary:	This policy states that all nonapproved uses of Company X information are prohibited.
Audience:	All

3. Information Handling, Access, and Usage	
Policy:	Information is a vital asset and all accesses to, uses of, and processing of Company X information must be consistent with policies and standards.
Commentary:	This policy sets the context for a number of other cybersecurity policies. Such a statement is frequently incorporated into the first set of policies and summary material oriented toward users and members of the top management team. It is necessary for these people to appreciate how information has become a critical factor of production in business. This policy motivates the need for cybersecurity measures and to create a new understanding of the importance of information systems in organizations.
Audience:	All

4. Data and Program Damage Disclaimers	
Policy:	Company X disclaims any responsibility for loss or damage to data or software that results from its efforts to protect the confidentiality, integrity, and viability of the information handled by computers and communications systems.
Commentary:	This policy notifies users that they cannot hold Company X liable for damages associated with management's attempts to secure its system.
Audience:	End users

(Continues)

Table 6-2   Sample CPP policy statements (*Continued*)

5. Legal Conflicts	
Policy:	Company X cybersecurity policies were drafted to meet or exceed the protections found in existing laws and regulations, and any Company X cybersecurity policy believed to be in conflict with existing laws or regulations must be promptly reported to cybersecurity management.
Commentary:	This policy creates a context for the requirements specified in a cybersecurity policy document. Sound policies go beyond laws and regulations, or at least ensure that an organization will meet the requirements specified by laws and regulations. This policy acknowledges support for laws and regulations and expresses an intention to stay in compliance with existing laws and regulations. The policy is suitable both for internal cybersecurity policies and those made available to the public.
Audience:	End users
6. Exceptions to Policies	
Policy:	Exceptions to cybersecurity policies exist in rare instances where a risk assessment examining the implications of being out of compliance has been performed, where a standard risk acceptance form has been prepared by the data owner or management, and where this form has been approved by both cybersecurity management and internal audit management.
Commentary:	Management will be called upon to approve certain exceptions to policies. This policy clarifies that exceptions will be granted only after a risk acceptance form has been completed, signed, and approved. The form should include a statement in which the data owner or management takes responsibility for any losses occurring from the out-of-compliance situation. The existence of such a form provides an escape valve that can be used to address situations in which users insist on being out of compliance with policies. All out-of-compliance situations should be made known and documented so that if a loss occurred as a result, management could demonstrate to a judge or jury that it was aware of the situation, examined the risks, and decided to waive the relevant policy or standard.
Audience:	End users
7. Policy Nonenforcement	
Policy:	Management's nonenforcement of any policy requirement does not constitute its consent.
Commentary:	This policy notifies policy statement readers that they should not expect out-of-compliance conditions to be continued only because management has not yet enforced the policy. This policy eliminates any claim that local management may state that an out-of-compliance condition should remain as it is because the condition has been in existence for a considerable period of time.
Audience:	End users
8. Violation of Law	
Policy:	Company X management must seriously consider prosecution for all known violations of the law.
Commentary:	This policy encourages the prosecution of abusive and criminal acts. While a decision to prosecute will be contingent on the specifics of the case, management should not dismiss prosecution without review. This policy may be important in terms of communicating to would-be perpetrators of abusive or criminal acts. Many computer crimes are not prosecuted and perpetrators often know this, expecting victim organizations to terminate them and suppress the entire affair.
Audience:	Management

(*Continues*)

Table 6-2   Sample CPP policy statements (*Continued*)

9. Revocation of Access Privileges	
Policy:	Company X reserves the right to revoke a user's information technology privileges at any time.
Commentary:	This policy notifies users that they jeopardize their status as authorized users if they engage in activities that interfere with the normal and proper operation of Company X information systems, that adversely affect the ability of others to use these information systems, or that are harmful or offensive to others. For example, crashing the system could be expected to be harmful to other users and would subject the perpetrator to disciplinary action including privilege revocation. The policy attempts to broadly describe an ethic for computing. Rather than specifying all of the adverse things that people could do, such as crashing a system, this policy is discreet and at a high level. This policy may give management latitude when it comes to deciding about privilege revocation.
Audience:	End users
10. Industry-Specific Cybersecurity Standards	
Policy:	Company X information systems must employ industry-specific cybersecurity standards.
Commentary:	This policy requires systems designers and other technical staff to employ industry-standard controls. For example, in banking, encryption systems should use industry-specific systems for key management. Other industry-specific controls are relevant to the medical services industry, the aerospace and defense community, and other industry groups.
Audience:	Technical staff
11. Use of Cybersecurity Policies and Procedures	
Policy:	All Company X cybersecurity documentation, including but not limited to policies, standards, and procedures, must be classified as "Internal Use Only" unless expressly created for external business processes or partners.
Commentary:	This policy prevents workers from disclosing to outsiders the specifics of how Company X secures its information and systems; such details could be used to compromise Company X information and systems.
Audience:	All
12. Cybersecurity Controls Enforceability	
Policy:	All cybersecurity controls must be enforceable prior to being adopted as a part of standard operating procedure.
Commentary:	Controls that are not enforced tend to become useless. For example, if management has a "clean desk" policy about locking up all sensitive materials after work and it is not enforced, then employees quickly learn to ignore the policy. This policy is intended to require management to review the enforcement of controls, an issue that may not occur before adopting a control. A definition of the word "enforceable" may be advisable in some instances. For a control to be enforceable, it must be possible for management to clearly determine whether staff is in compliance with the control and whether the control is effectively doing its intended job. The policy is purposefully vague about what constitutes standard operating procedure. This permits the policy to apply to a wide variety of circumstances, regardless of whether the control is documented, specific to a certain department, or used in an experimental way. In some instances, this policy may require the control designers to add a monitoring mechanism that reports on the status of the control. For example, encryption boxes from some vendors have lights indicating that they are working as they should.
Audience:	Management and technical staff

Source: Charles Cresson Wood, *Information Security Policies Made Easy*, 12th ed. Information Shield. Used with permission.

The formulation of the CPP establishes the overall cybersecurity environment. As noted earlier, any number of specific issues may require policy guidance beyond what can be offered in the CPP. The next level of policy document, the issue-specific policy, delivers this needed specificity.

Self-Check

4. Cybersecurity policies should only be revised to correct errors or in response to changes in the organization's strategic direction.
   a. True   b. False

5. A policy of "Information must be protected in a manner commensurate with its sensitivity" applies only to electronic data.
   a. True   b. False

6. Cybersecurity policy enforcement is the sole responsibility of the IT department.
   a. True   b. False

☐ Check your answers at the end of this chapter.

Issue-Specific Policy

An issue-specific policy is an organizational directive that provides detailed, targeted instructions for all members of the organization to regulate the appropriate use of an issue or resource. It is also referred to as an issue-specific security policy (ISSP) or fair and responsible use policy.

An issue-specific policy should begin by introducing the organization's fundamental resource-use philosophy. It should assure members that its purpose is not to establish a foundation for administrative enforcement or legal prosecution but to provide a common understanding of the purposes for which an employee can and cannot use the resource. Once this understanding is established, employees are free to use the resource without seeking approval for each type of use. This type of policy serves to protect both the employee and the organization from inefficiency and ambiguity. The issue-specific policy can sometimes become confusing. Its structure allows for more detailed elements than those found in higher-level policy documents like the CPP. The intent of the issue-specific policy is to act as a readily accessible standard for compliance with the more broadly defined policies established in the CPP.

An effective issue-specific policy accomplishes the following:

- It articulates the organization's expectations about how its technology-based resources should be used.
- It documents how the technology-based resource is controlled and identifies the processes and authorities that provide this control.
- It indemnifies the organization against liability for an employee's inappropriate or illegal use of the resource.

An effective issue-specific policy is a binding agreement between parties (the organization and its employees and stakeholders) and shows that the organization has made a good-faith effort to ensure that its resources will not be used in an inappropriate manner. Every organization's issue-specific policy has three characteristics:

- It addresses specific technology-based resources.
- It requires frequent updates.
- It contains a statement explaining the organization's position on the approved use of a particular issue.[6]

What are the areas for which an issue-specific policy may be used? The following are areas in the organization that typically require an issue-specific policy. Note that this list is designed to be exemplary, not comprehensive:

- Use of email, instant messaging (IM), and other electronic communications applications
- Use of the Internet, the web, and company networks by company equipment
- Malware protection requirements (such as anti-malware implementation)
- Installation and use of externally issued software or hardware on the organization's assets, such as personal computing devices or Internet of Things (IoT) appliances
- Processing and/or storage of organizational information on externally owned computers, such as cloud computing providers
- Prohibitions against hacking or testing the organization's cybersecurity controls or attempting to modify or escalate access control privileges
- Personal and/or home use of company-owned computer equipment
- Removal of organizational equipment from the organization's property
- Use of personal equipment on company networks, such as "BYOD" (bring your own device)
- Use of personal technology during work hours (mobile phones, tablets, etc.)
- Use of organizational telecommunications technologies and networks (fax, phone, mobile phone, intercom)
- Use of photocopying and scanning equipment
- Requirements for storage and access to company information while outside company facilities (e.g., encryption)
- Specifications for the methods, scheduling, conduct, and testing of data backups
- Requirements for the collection, use, and destruction of information assets (commonly referred to as a data retention policy)
- Requirements and permissions for storage of access control credentials by users
- Sharing and distribution of organizational information on social media (both personal and organizational)
- Other topics listed in NIST 800-12, Rev. 1

While many other issue-specific policies in the organization, such as those described in the chapter's opening scenario, may fall outside the responsibility of cybersecurity, representatives of the cybersecurity unit can serve on policy committees and advise other departments on the creation and management of their policies.

Elements of the Issue-Specific Policy

Table 6-3 lists typical elements that go into an issue-specific policy. Each of these is discussed in the sections that follow. The specific situation of each organization dictates the exact wording of the supporting cybersecurity procedures as well as issues not covered within these general directives.

Statement of Purpose

The issue-specific policy should begin with a clear statement of purpose that outlines the scope and applicability of the policy. This statement should clarify where, how, when, to whom, and to what a policy applies, including:

- What purpose does this policy serve?
- Who is responsible and accountable for policy implementation?
- What technologies and issues does the policy document address?
- Under what circumstances (when and where) does the policy apply?

Table 6-3   Elements of a typical issue-specific policy

1. Statement of Purpose
   a. Scope and Applicability
   b. Definition of Technology Addressed
   c. Responsibilities

2. Authorized Uses
   a. User Access
   b. Fair and Responsible Use
   c. Protection of Privacy

3. Prohibited Uses
   a. Disruptive Use or Misuse
   b. Criminal Use
   c. Offensive or Harassing Materials
   d. Copyrighted, Licensed, or Other Intellectual Property
   e. Other Restrictions

4. Systems Management
   a. Management of Stored Materials
   b. Employer Monitoring
   c. Virus Protection
   d. Physical Cybersecurity
   e. Encryption

5. Violations of Policy
   a. Procedures for Reporting Violations
   b. Penalties for Violations

6. Policy Review and Modification
   a. Scheduled Review of Policy
   b. Procedures for Modification

7. Limitations of Liability
   a. Statements of Liability
   b. Other Disclaimers

Source: Communications of the ACM. Reprinted with permission.

Authorized Uses

This section of the policy provides a statement of the organization's position, explaining who can use the resources governed by the policy and for what purposes. Recall that an organization's IT systems are the exclusive property of the organization and users have no rights of use. Each technology and process is provided explicitly to support organizational operations. This section defines "fair and responsible use" of equipment and other organizational assets, and it addresses key legal issues, such as protection of personal information and privacy. Any use for any purpose that is not explicitly identified is considered a misuse of equipment according to the policy. When it is management's intention to allow some selective, extra-organizational uses, such as using company systems and networks for personal email, apps, or web access, such use must be specifically allowed for and defined in the policy.

Prohibited Uses

While the previous section specifies what the issue or technology *can* be used for, this section outlines what it *cannot* be used for. Unless a particular use is clearly prohibited, the organization cannot penalize employees for it. For example, the following actions might be prohibited: personal use; disruptive use or misuse; criminal use; use of offensive or harassing materials; and infringement of copyrighted, licensed, or other intellectual property. In some organizations, that which is not permitted is prohibited; in others, that which is not prohibited is permitted. In either case, be sure to clearly state the assumptions and then the exceptions. The organization's stance will make a difference in how the topic of usage is addressed. Some organizations use the approach given in the preceding list, which explicitly states what is allowed and prohibited. Other organizations might want to be less explicit and combine the Authorized Uses and Prohibited Uses sections into a single section titled "Appropriate Uses." This provides direction under the rule of: "Here is what you can do, and here is what you can't. If your actions aren't addressed by one of these lists, ask permission." The organizational philosophy, which is discussed later in this chapter in the section on policy design, may guide the organization to choose either appropriate uses or prohibited uses as the sole section.

Systems Management

This section focuses on the users' relationships to systems management. This section is optional and may be omitted if the issue being discussed doesn't have a "systems" perspective. A company may want to issue specific rules regarding the use of email and electronic documents and storage of those documents, as well as directives regarding authorized employer monitoring and the physical and electronic cybersecurity of email and other electronic documents. If an organization has established policies on data management, including data backup and retention policies, they should be summarized and/or referenced here. This section should address management of physical systems as well as electronic systems. The systems management section should specify users' and systems administrators' responsibilities so that all parties know what they are accountable for.

Violations of Policy

This section specifies the penalties and repercussions of violating the usage and systems management policies. Penalties should be laid out for each violation. This section should also provide instructions on how to report observed or suspected violations, both openly and anonymously, as some employees may fear retaliation from powerful individuals in the organization against a whistleblower. Anonymous submissions, perhaps using a web form on the company intranet, are often the only way to convince individual users to report the unauthorized activities of other, more influential employees. When anonymous submission is used, it should be reviewed by the organization's legal department, if one exists, or by a committee of representatives from throughout the organization to ensure that no one individual can corrupt the process.

Policy Review and Modification

Every policy should contain procedures and a timetable for periodic review. This section should outline a specific methodology for the review and modification of the issue-specific policy, including who is responsible for reviewing and modifying the policy as well as specifying the process by which the policy may be modified and specifying the schedule for such review. Furthermore, it should document a mechanism for collecting feedback from those affected by the policy. This will ensure that users always have directives that reflect the organization's current technologies and needs. The mechanism used to collect feedback for this process could be combined with the mechanism used for reporting violations.

Limitations of Liability

The final section offers a general statement of liability or a set of disclaimers. If an individual employee is caught conducting illicit or illegal activities with organizational equipment or assets, management does not want the organization to be held liable. In other words, if employees violate a company policy or any law using company technologies, the company will not protect them and the company is not liable for their actions, assuming that the violation is not known or sanctioned by management. Many statements designed to limit liability also indicate that if an employee violates policy and commits a crime in doing so, not only will the organization not provide legal support for the employee, it will also actively aid in their prosecution.

Implementing the Issue-Specific Policy

There are many approaches for creating and managing issue-specific policies. Three of the most common are:

- Create independent issue-specific policy documents, each tailored to a specific issue.
- Create a single, comprehensive issue-specific policy document that covers all issues.
- Create a modular issue-specific policy document that unifies policy creation and administration while maintaining each specific issue's requirements.

Table 6-4 describes the advantages and disadvantages of each approach. The recommended approach is the modular policy, as it results in a document that relies on sections (modules), each with a standard template for structure and appearance, in which certain aspects are standardized while others—including much of the content—are customized for each issue. The end result is several independent issue-specific policy documents, all derived from a common template, that are well managed and easy to use. This approach offers a balance between ease of policy development and effectiveness for policy management. The policies generated via this approach are individual modules, each created and updated by the individuals who are responsible for a specific issue. These individuals report to a central policy administration group that incorporates the specific issues into an overall policy set.

Table 6-4   Issue-specific policy document approaches

Approach	Advantages	Disadvantages
Individual Policy	• Clear assignment to a responsible department • Written by those with superior subject-matter expertise for technology-specific systems	• Typically yields a scattershot result that fails to cover all of the necessary issues • Can suffer from poor policy dissemination, enforcement, and review
Comprehensive Policy	• Well controlled by centrally managed procedures ensuring complete topic coverage • Often provides better formal procedures than when policies are individually formulated • Usually identifies processes for dissemination, enforcement, and review	• May overgeneralize the issues and skip over vulnerabilities • May be written by those with less complete subject-matter expertise
Modular Policy	• Often considered an optimal balance between the individual issue-specific policy and the comprehensive policy approach • Well controlled by centrally managed procedures, ensuring complete topic coverage • Clear assignment to a responsible department • Written by those with superior subject-matter expertise for technology-specific systems	• May be more expensive than other alternatives • Implementation can be difficult to manage

Cybersecurity Policies: The Contract with Employees, Customers, and Partners

By David Lineman, President, Information Shield

Cybersecurity policies used to be a group of arcane documents that most people didn't read or understand. Cybersecurity was for the technical folks, so the documents often stayed locked in paper binders or virtual binders on the corporate intranet.

But the world has changed. Today, written cybersecurity policies are a key way to communicate your cybersecurity program with the outside world.

One of the growing trends in risk management is the requirement to validate the cybersecurity risk of vendors. A single vendor with a laptop full of customer information can cost an organization millions of dollars. In many industries, including financial services and healthcare, regulations require organizations to validate the cybersecurity programs of their vendors. In every case, examples of written policies are a key piece of evidence.

Cybersecurity policies can have three primary audiences. First, policies are used to inform employees and contractors about the proper and secure use of information. Second, policies are used to communicate the cybersecurity posture of the organization to senior management, including the board of directors. Finally, cybersecurity policies are used to communicate with customers and business partners.

While I use the term "contract" loosely as a way to formalize an agreement between parties, policies are increasingly considered real contracts when cybersecurity ends up in court. For example, organizations that suffer a data breach must often produce written policies to document that they were making best efforts to protect customer information. In cases where employees have been terminated for violating cybersecurity policies, the written policy is a key piece of evidence supporting the organization. Outdated or nonexistent policies send a message that the organization was lax in both intent and enforcement. Customers view privacy policies as a contract for handling their personal information. Groups of customers have been known to sue an organization for having a misleading privacy policy.

If your organization still considers cybersecurity policies unimportant or not relevant to modern business, you might think again. Today, you must have written policies to document your compliance posture to concerned parties. In the not-too-distant future, it will be impossible to earn business without them. Sooner or later, someone with a gavel or a purchase order will come knocking on your door, asking to see your written cybersecurity policies.

Self-Check

7. An issue-specific policy begins with a clear statement of purpose that outlines the scope and applicability of the policy.

   a. True   **b.** False

8. Unauthorized uses of IT systems in an organization are generally permitted unless explicitly prohibited.

   a. True   **b.** False

9. Having a single, comprehensive issue-specific policy document is always the best approach for managing these types of policies.

   a. True   **b.** False

☐ Check your answers at the end of this chapter.

System-Specific Policy

While a CPP is a high-level policy and an issue-specific policy is a document that focuses on use of specific issues, both are formalized as written documents easily identifiable as policy. System-specific policies—organizational directives that function as standards or procedures to be used when configuring or maintaining systems—can be separated into two general groups: managerial guidance and technical specifications. System-specific policies may be written as a single unified document and may have a different appearance than the other types of policies; they can seem more like informal procedures to some. Such documents should include a statement of managerial intent; guidance to network engineers on selecting, configuring, and operating the system; configuration rule specifications; and an access control list (discussed in detail later) that defines levels of access for each authorized user. Note that the policy framework ensures that the creation and use of an issue-specific policy or system-specific policy is enabled by the CPP position on those topic areas.

Managerial Guidance System-Specific Policies

A managerial guidance system-specific policy is created by management to guide the implementation and configuration of a piece of technology and to address the behavior of people in the organization in ways that support cybersecurity. These system-specific policies are targeted at the technologists responsible for implementation and/or configuration to ensure continuity of intent between management and IT. For example, while the specific configuration of a firewall belongs in a technical specification system-specific policy, the process of constructing and implementing the firewall must follow directives established by management. Why? In the absence of this guidance, a firewall administrator may configure the firewall as they see fit, which may or may not align with the organization's intent. For example, suppose the new firewall administrator for Boom! Technologies, a Department of Defense contractor for explosives development, implements a new firewall using a set of rules identical to those used on the firewall at their previous employer, Free Thinking University. These rules, ideal for an institution that promotes the free and open flow of knowledge but most likely not sufficiently stringent for the defense contractor, could allow a hacker to steal information about the company's research and development projects. Firewalls are not the only systems that may require system-specific policies. Any technology that affects the confidentiality, integrity, or availability of information must be assessed to evaluate the trade-off between improved cybersecurity and restrictions that may impede the organization's operations.

System-specific policies are typically developed independently of issue-specific policies but are usually prepared in advance of their related issue-specific policies. Before management can craft a policy informing users what they can do with the technology and how they may do it, it might be necessary for systems administrators to configure and operate the system. It may be best for organizations to develop issue-specific policies and system-specific policies in tandem, so that operational procedures and user directives are created almost simultaneously. However, this then requires implementing the technology according to the system-specific policy, before users receive the issue-specific policy, to ensure it is operational and ready for users to integrate into their operations.

Technical Specification System-Specific Policies

While a manager may work with a systems administrator to create managerial policy, as described in the previous section, the systems administrator may need a different type of policy to document the implementation of the technology. For example, an issue-specific policy may require that user passwords be changed quarterly; a systems administrator can implement a technical control within a specific application to enforce this policy. So, while the manager is primarily responsible for the creation of the managerial specifications version of the system-specific policy, systems administrators may be the primary authors or architects of the technical specifications version. In many cases, simply creating a document with the final configuration of the cybersecurity technology may meet the criteria for a technical specification system-specific policy; when filed with the managerial version of the specification, it would meet the need for a well-documented and managed system-specific policy. This provides clear documentation for future administrators and managers of the technology to understand the reasons and methods behind the current implementation, which better supports future maintenance and use.

Figure 6-4 illustrates some of the Local Security Policy settings from the Windows 10 Professional operating system, which is virtually identical to the Windows 11 version. There are two general methods of implementing such technical controls: access control lists and configuration rules.

Figure 6-4   Windows local security policy settings

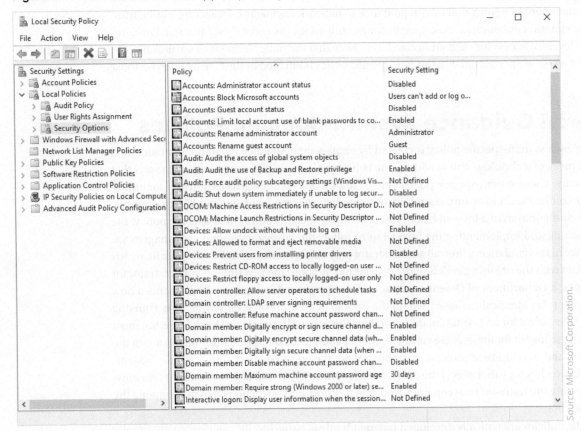

Source: Microsoft Corporation.

Access control lists (ACLs)—specifications of authorization that govern the rights and privileges of users to a particular information asset—include user access lists, matrices, and capability tables. ACLs can control access to file storage systems, object brokers, or other network communications devices. A capability table specifies which subjects and objects users or groups can access; in some systems, capability tables are called "user profiles" or "user policies." These specifications frequently take the form of access control matrices in which assets are listed along the column headers while users are listed along the row headers. The resulting matrix would then contain ACLs in columns for a particular device or asset, while a row would represent the capability table for a particular user.

Most modern server operating systems translate ACLs into configuration sets that administrators can use to control access to their systems. The level of detail and specificity (often called granularity) may vary from system to system, but in general, ACLs enable administrators to restrict access according to user, computer, time, duration, or even a particular file. This range gives a great deal of control to the administrator. In general, ACLs regulate the following aspects of access:

- Who can use the system
- What authorized users can access
- When authorized users can access the system
- Where authorized users can access the system from
- How authorized users can access the system

Restricting who can use the system requires no explanation. To restrict what a specific user can access—for example, which printers, files, communications, and applications—administrators assign user privileges (also known as permissions) such as Read, Write, Execute, and Delete. This list is not exhaustive, but it contains some key ACL privilege types. To make the management of privileges more convenient, the operating system allows for *users* of the system to be clustered into privilege *groups*. Figures 6-5 and 6-6 show how the ACL group cybersecurity model has been implemented in various operating systems. The top window in Figure 6-5 lists the groups that have been defined on the system shown. Clicking one of the groups would show the lower window, which would display the privilege set for each member of that group and allow those privileges to be changed as well.

Figure 6-5 Windows ACLs

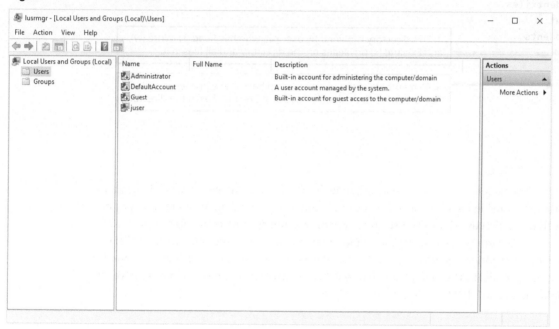

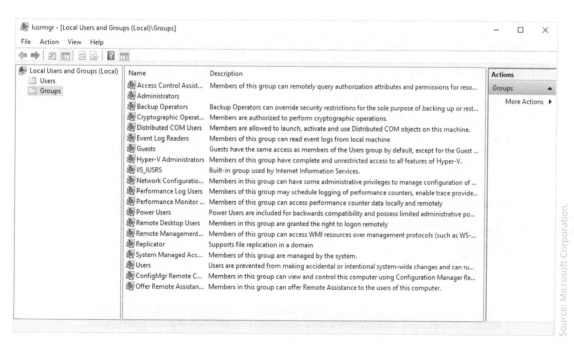

Figure 6-6   Linux ACL

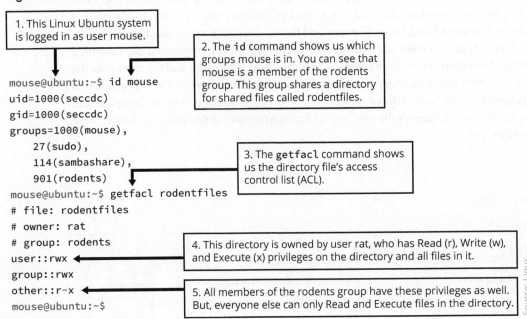

1. This Linux Ubuntu system is logged in as user mouse.

2. The `id` command shows us which groups mouse is in. You can see that mouse is a member of the rodents group. This group shares a directory for shared files called rodentfiles.

3. The `getfacl` command shows us the directory file's access control list (ACL).

```
mouse@ubuntu:~$ id mouse
uid=1000(seccdc)
gid=1000(seccdc)
groups=1000(mouse),
    27(sudo),
    114(sambashare),
    901(rodents)
mouse@ubuntu:~$ getfacl rodentfiles
# file: rodentfiles
# owner: rat
# group: rodents
user::rwx
group::rwx
other::r-x
mouse@ubuntu:~$
```

4. This directory is owned by user rat, who has Read (r), Write (w), and Execute (x) privileges on the directory and all files in it.

5. All members of the rodents group have these privileges as well. But, everyone else can only Read and Execute files in the directory.

Source: Linux.

Configuration Rules

Configuration rules—instructional codes or scripts that guide the execution of the system when information is passing through it—are considered more specific to the operation of a system than ACLs are, and they may or may not deal with users directly. Many cybersecurity systems require specific configuration scripts that dictate which actions to perform on each set of information they process. Examples include firewalls, host intrusion detection and prevention systems (HIDPSs), other IDPSs, and proxy servers. Figures 6-7 and 6-8 show how a cybersecurity model has been implemented by Palo Alto in a firewall rule set and by Ionx Verisys (File Integrity Monitoring) in an HIDPS set of rules, respectively.

Figure 6-7   Sample Palo Alto firewall configuration rules

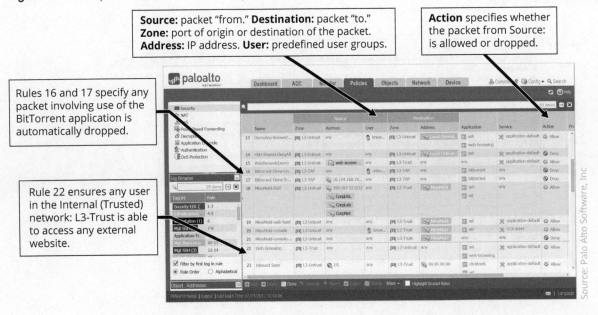

Source: packet "from." **Destination:** packet "to." **Zone:** port of origin or destination of the packet. **Address:** IP address. **User:** predefined user groups.

Action specifies whether the packet from Source: is allowed or dropped.

Rules 16 and 17 specify any packet involving use of the BitTorrent application is automatically dropped.

Rule 22 ensures any user in the Internal (Trusted) network: L3-Trust is able to access any external website.

Source: Palo Alto Software, Inc

Figure 6-8   Ionx Verisys (File Integrity Monitoring) use of rules

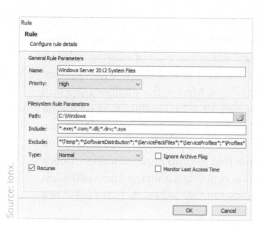

Source: Ionx.

Self-Check

10. Managerial guidance system-specific policies are solely targeted at nontechnological staff within an organization.

    a. True   b. False

11. Access control lists (ACLs) can be used to control access to file storage systems and network communication devices.

    a. True   b. False

12. A system-specific policy for configuring and operating a firewall will include only the technical specifications.

    a. True   b. False

☐ Check your answers at the end of this chapter.

Guidelines for Effective Policy Development and Implementation

How policy is developed and implemented can help or hinder its usefulness to an organization. If an organization acts on a policy, any individuals affected may sue the organization, depending on how it implemented the penalties or other actions defined in the policy. Employees terminated for violating poorly designed and implemented policies could sue their organization for wrongful termination and win both compensatory and punitive damages. In general, policy is only enforceable and legally defensible if it is properly designed, developed, and implemented using a process that ensures verifiable and repeatable results.

A recommended and effective approach to policy implementation has six stages: development (writing and approving), dissemination (distribution), review (reading), comprehension (understanding), compliance (agreement), and uniform enforcement. Thus, for policies to be effective and legally defensible, they must be properly:

- Developed using industry-accepted practices and formally approved by management
- Distributed using all appropriate methods
- Read by all employees
- Understood by all employees
- Formally agreed to by act or affirmation
- Uniformly applied and enforced

We examine each of these stages in the sections that follow. However, before beginning an explanation about developing policy, you should realize that almost every organization has a set of existing policies, standards, procedures, guidelines, and practices. This installed base of directives may not always have been prepared using an approach that delivers consistent or even usable results. Most of the situations you find yourself in will involve policy maintenance more than policy development. When maintaining policy, all the complexity of the process described here may not be needed. However, when the policy maintenance project becomes sufficiently large and complex, it might best be considered as policy redevelopment, and then most of the process described here can come into use. Also note that prior to implementation, policy should be reviewed by the organization's legal counsel to ensure it is acceptable within the limits of the law and that implementation of the policy and its corresponding penalties would be defensible in the event of a legal dispute.

Developing Cybersecurity Policy

It is often useful to view policy development as a three-part project. In the first part of the project, a policy is designed and written (or, in the case of an outdated policy, redesigned and rewritten). In the second part, a senior manager or executive at the appropriate level and the organization's legal counsel review and formally approve the policy. In the third part, management processes are established to perpetuate the policy within the organization. The first part is an exercise in project management, whereas the latter two parts require adherence to good business practices and legal regulation.

Writing a policy is not always as easy as it seems. However, the prudent cybersecurity manager always scours available resources (including the web) for examples that may be adapted to the organization. Seldom will the manager find the perfect policy, ready to be used in their organization. Some online sites sell policies or policy templates that you can customize to your organization. In any event, it is important that the organization respects the intellectual property of others when developing policy. If parts of another organization's policy are adapted, appropriate attribution must be made. Most policies contain a reference section where the author may list any policies used in the development of the current document. Even policies that are purchased from policy vendors or developed from a book on writing policies may require some level of annotation or attribution. It is recommended that any policies adapted from outside sources are thoroughly rewritten but referenced to prevent the need for direct quotations, which can detract from the message the policy is attempting to convey—that "our organization" wants employees to be effective and efficient without undue distractions.

Policy Distribution

While it might seem straightforward, getting the policy document into the hands of employees can require a substantial investment by the organization. The most common options are hard-copy distribution and electronic distribution. Hard-copy distribution involves either directly giving a printout of the policy to the employee or posting it in a public location. Posting a policy on a bulletin board or in another public area may be insufficient unless another policy requires the employees to read policies posted there on a specified schedule (daily, weekly, etc.). Distribution by mail may still not guarantee that the individual receives the document. Unless the organization can prove that the policy reached the end users, it cannot be enforced. Unlike in civil or criminal law, ignorance of policy, where policy is inadequately distributed, is considered an acceptable excuse. Distribution of classified policies—those containing confidential internal information—requires additional levels of controls in the labeling of the document, in the dissemination and storage of new policy, and in the collection and destruction of older versions to ensure the confidentiality of the information contained within the policy documents themselves. Earlier, we discussed data classification and management approaches, which should be applied to all policies.

Another common method of dissemination is by electronic means: email, newsletter, intranet, or document management systems. Perhaps the easiest way is to post current and archived versions of policies on a secure intranet. The organization must still enable a mechanism to prove distribution, such as an auditing log for tracking when users access the documents. As an alternative delivery mechanism, email has advantages and disadvantages. While it is easy to send a document to an employee and even track when the employee opens the email, email tracking may not be sufficient as proof that the employee downloaded and actually read any attached policies. The email can also get lost in an avalanche of business emails, spam, and phishing attacks. Perhaps the best method is to use electronic policy management software, which is described in the section on automated tools. Electronic policy management software not only assists in the distribution of policy documents but supports policy development and the assessment of comprehension.[7]

Policy Reading

Barriers to employees' reading of policies can arise from literacy or language issues. A surprisingly large percentage of the workforce is considered functionally illiterate. The National Center for Education Statistics, a federal agency that works in concert with the U.S. Department of Education, conducted the Program for the International Assessment of Adult Competencies (PIAAC), which found that in 2017, 19 percent of Americans between the ages of 16 and 65 scored "below basic" in literacy.[8] Although many jobs do not require literacy skills, workers in these positions can still pose risks to cybersecurity, so they must be made familiar with policy even if it must be provided to them in alternate forms. Visually impaired employees may also require additional assistance through documents that are compliant with the Americans with Disabilities Act.

Of the adults identified as illiterate in the PIAAC survey, 8 million could not answer simple test questions due to pure reading deficiencies and 11 million could not take the test because of language barriers.[9] The number of non-English-speaking residents in the United States continues to climb. However, language challenges are not restricted to organizations with locations in the United States. Multinational organizations also must deal with the challenges of gauging reading levels of foreign citizens. Simple translations of policy documents, while a minimum requirement, necessitate careful monitoring. Translation issues have long created challenges for organizations. For example, a translation error by the Nike Corporation resulted in an advertisement showing a Samburu tribesman speaking in his native language, ostensibly echoing the company's slogan. What he really said was, "I don't want these. Give me big shoes."[10]

Policy Comprehension

A quote attributed to Confucius states: "Tell me and I forget; show me and I remember; let me do and I understand." In the policy arena, this means simply making certain that a copy of the policy gets to employees in a form they can review may not ensure they truly understand what the policy requires of them. Comprehension means the employees can grasp the meaning of management's intent and fully understand the permissions, restrictions, and penalties for noncompliance with the policy.

To be certain that employees understand the policy, the document must be written at a reasonable reading level, with minimal technical jargon and management terminology. According to JD Supra in the article "Can Your Employees Understand Your Policies?", the author states that if the organization doesn't ensure the readability of a policy is below an eight-grade level, employees may simply be saying "Huh?"[11] The readability statistics supplied by most productivity suite applications such as Microsoft Word can help determine the current reading level of a policy. Figure 6-9 shows the readability statistics rendered by Microsoft Word for a sample of text taken from this chapter.

Figure 6-9   Readability statistics

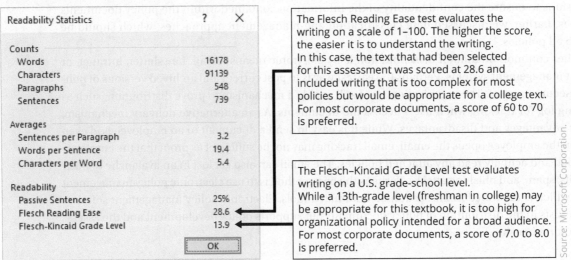

The Flesch Reading Ease test evaluates the writing on a scale of 1–100. The higher the score, the easier it is to understand the writing. In this case, the text that had been selected for this assessment was scored at 28.6 and included writing that is too complex for most policies but would be appropriate for a college text. For most corporate documents, a score of 60 to 70 is preferred.

The Flesch–Kincaid Grade Level test evaluates writing on a U.S. grade-school level. While a 13th-grade level (freshman in college) may be appropriate for this textbook, it is too high for organizational policy intended for a broad audience. For most corporate documents, a score of 7.0 to 8.0 is preferred.

Source: Microsoft Corporation.

The next step is to use some form of assessment to gauge how well employees understand the policy's underlying message. Quizzes and other forms of examination can be employed to assess quantitatively which employees understand the policy by earning a minimum score (e.g., 70 percent) and which employees require additional training and awareness efforts before the policy can be enforced. Quizzes can be conducted in either hard-copy or electronic format. The electronic policy management systems mentioned elsewhere in this chapter can assist in the assessment of employee performance on policy comprehension.[12]

Policy Compliance

Policy compliance means the employee must agree to the policy. According to Whitman in "Security Policy: From Design to Maintenance":

> Policies must be agreed to by act or affirmation. Agreement by act occurs when the employee performs an action, which requires them to acknowledge understanding of the policy, prior to use of a technology or organizational resource. Network banners, end-user license agreements, and posted warnings can serve to meet this burden of proof. However, these in and of themselves may not be sufficient. Only through direct collection of a signature or the equivalent digital alternative can the organization prove that it has obtained an agreement to comply with policy, which also demonstrates that the previous conditions have been met.[13]

What if an employee refuses explicitly to agree to comply with policy? Can the organization deny access to information that the employee needs to do their job? While this situation has not yet been adjudicated in the legal system, it seems clear that failure to agree to a policy is tantamount to refusing to work and thus may be grounds for termination. Organizations can avoid this dilemma by incorporating policy confirmation statements into employment contracts, annual evaluations, or other documents necessary for the individual's continued employment.

Policy Enforcement

The final component of the design and implementation of effective policies is uniform and impartial enforcement. As in law enforcement, policy enforcement must be able to withstand external scrutiny. Because this scrutiny may occur during legal proceedings—for example, in a civil suit contending wrongful termination—organizations must establish high standards of due care regarding policy management. For instance, if policy mandates that all employees wear identification badges in a clearly visible location and select members of management decide they are not required to follow this policy, any actions taken against other employees will not withstand legal challenges. If an employee is punished, censured, or dismissed because of a refusal to follow policy and is subsequently able to demonstrate that the policies are not uniformly applied or enforced, the organization may find itself facing punitive as well as compensatory damages.

One forward-thinking organization found a way to enlist employees in the enforcement of policy. After the organization had just issued a new ID badge policy, the manager responsible for the policy was seen without their ID. An employee chided the manager in jest, saying, "You must be a visitor here, since you don't have an ID. Can I help you?" The manager smiled and promptly produced the ID, along with a $20 bill for the employee as a reward for vigilant policy enforcement. Soon, the entire staff was routinely challenging anyone without a badge.[14]

Policy Development and Implementation Using the SDLC

Like any major project, a policy development or revision project should be well planned, properly funded, and aggressively managed to ensure that it is completed on time and within budget. One way to accomplish this goal is to use a systems development life cycle (SDLC). The following discussion expands the use of a typical SDLC model by describing the tasks that could be included in each phase of the SDLC during a policy development project.

Investigation Phase

During the investigation phase, the policy development team or committee should attain the following:

- Support from senior management because any project without it has a reduced chance of success. Only with the support of top management will a specific policy receive the attention it deserves from the intermediate-level managers who must implement it and from the users who must comply with it.
- Support and active involvement of IT management, specifically the CIO. Only with the CIO's active support will technology-area managers be motivated to participate in policy development and support the implementation efforts to deploy it once created.
- Clear articulation of goals. Without a detailed and succinct expression of the goals and objectives of the policy, broken into distinct expectations, the policy will lack the structure it needs to obtain full implementation.
- Participation of the correct individuals from the communities of interest affected by the recommended policies. Assembling the right team by ensuring the participation of the proper representatives from the groups that will be affected by the new policies is very important. The team must include representatives from the legal department, the human resources department, and end users of the various IT systems covered by the policies, as well as a project champion with sufficient stature and prestige

to accomplish the goals of the project and a capable project manager to see the project through to completion.

- A detailed outline of the scope of the policy development project and sound estimates for the cost and scheduling of the project.

Analysis Phase

The analysis phase should produce the following:

- A new or recent risk assessment or IT audit documenting the current cybersecurity needs of the organization. This risk assessment should include any loss history as well as past lawsuits, grievances, or other records of negative outcomes from cybersecurity areas.
- The gathering of key reference materials, including any existing policies. Sometimes policy documents that affect cybersecurity will be housed in the human resources department as well as the accounting, finance, legal, or corporate cybersecurity departments.

According to Wood's *Information Security Policies Made Easy*:

> To identify the policy areas needing further attention, copies of all other relevant and current organizational policy documents should be collected. Relevant policies include application systems development policies, computer operations policies, computer equipment acquisition policies, human resources policies, information systems quality control policies, and physical security policies. If they are obtainable, policies from other organizations in the same industry can also provide useful background information. If the organization is a subsidiary or affiliate of another organization, then the parent organization's policies should be obtained and used as reference material. If the organization is a participant in an extranet, an electronic data interchange, value added network, a multi-organizational Internet commerce arrangement, or any other multi-organizational networks, the policies of these networks should be obtained and reviewed. The information security policies of various information systems-related service providers, such as an Internet service provider or a data center outsourcing firm, should also be obtained.
>
> Some who are facing significant time or resource constraints will be tempted to skip the above-mentioned data-gathering processes. Whenever data gathering is significantly abbreviated, the likelihood that management will reject the resulting document increases. It is through this data-gathering process that management's view of information security can be identified, [as well as] the policies that already exist, the policies that need to be added or changed, how management enforces policies, the unique vulnerabilities that the organization faces, and other essential background information. If serious consideration has not been given to this background information, it is unlikely that a newly written information security policy will be responsive to the true needs of the organization.[15]

As part of the analysis phase, the policy development committee must determine the fundamental philosophy of the organization when it comes to policy. This will dictate the general development of all policies, in particular the format to be used in the crafting of all issue-specific policies. This philosophy typically falls into one of two groups:

- "That which is not permitted is prohibited." Also known as the "whitelist" approach, it is the more restrictive of the two and focuses on creating a situation where specific authorization is provided for various actions and behaviors, and all other actions and behaviors (and uses) are prohibited or at least require specific permissions. This approach can impede normal business operations if appropriate options emerge but cannot be incorporated into policy until subsequent revisions are made.
- "That which is not prohibited is permitted." Also known as the "blacklist" approach, this alternative specifies what actions, behaviors, and uses are prohibited and then allows all others by default. While easier to implement, this approach can result in issues, as more and more areas that should be prohibited are discovered by users.

Design Phase

The first task in the design phase is the drafting of the actual policy document. While this task can be done by a committee, it is commonly done by a single author. This document should incorporate all the specifications and restrictions from the investigation and analysis phases. This can be a challenging process, but you do not have to come up with a good policy document from scratch, as many resources are available:

- The web—You can search for other similar policies. The point here is not to advocate wholesale copying of these policies but to encourage you to look for ideas for what should be contained in your policy. For example, hundreds of policies available on the web describe fair and responsible use of various technologies. What you may not find, however, are policies that relate to sensitive internal documents or processes. The SANS site at www.sans.org/information-security-policy/ also contains security policy templates.

- Government sites—Sites such as http://csrc.nist.gov have sample policies and policy support documents, such as NIST SP 800-100, "Information Security Handbook: A Guide for Managers," and NIST SP 800-12, Rev. 1, "An Introduction to Information Security." Even policies that are written primarily for government agencies or other public organizations may be adaptable to meet your organization's needs.

- Professional literature—Several authors have published books on the subject. Of particular note is Wood's *Information Security Policies Made Easy* series, now promoted by Information Shield (https://informationshield.com/security-policies/), which not only provides more than 1,000 pages of policies but makes them available in electronic format, complete with permission to use them in internal documents. Exercise caution when using such resources, however; it is extremely easy to take large sections of policy and end up with a massive document that is neither efficient nor effective.

- Peer networks—Other cybersecurity professionals must write similar policies and implement similar plans. Attend meetings like those offered by the Information Systems Security Association (www.issa.org) or the Information Systems Audit and Control Association (www.isaca.org) and ask your peers.

- Professional consultants—Policy is one area of cybersecurity that can certainly be developed in-house. However, if your organization does not have the requisite expertise, or even if your team simply cannot find the time to develop your own policy, then hiring an outside consultant may be your best option. Keep in mind that no consultant can know your organization as thoroughly as you do; you may decide to have the consultant design generic policies that you can then adapt to your specific needs.

Next, the development team or committee reviews the work of the primary author and makes recommendations about its revision. Once the committee approves the document, it goes to the appropriate manager or executive and possibly the legal team for approval. If any issues are identified by the approval authority, the document goes back to the committee for revision. This cycle is repeated until the approving manager or executive and legal team sign off on the policy.

Implementation Phase

In the implementation phase, the team must create a plan to distribute the policy and verify its distribution. Members of the organization must explicitly acknowledge that they have received and read the policy (compliance). Otherwise, an employee can claim never to have seen a policy, and unless the manager can produce strong evidence to the contrary, any enforcement action, such as dismissal for inappropriate use of the web, can be overturned and punitive damages might be awarded to the former employee. The simplest way to document acknowledgment of a written policy is to attach a cover sheet that states, "I have received, read, understood, and agreed to this policy." The employee's signature and date provide evidence of their receipt of the policy.

Some situations preclude a formal documentation process. Take, for instance, student use of campus computer labs. Most universities have stringent policies on what students can and cannot do in a computer lab. These policies are usually posted on the web, in the student handbook, in course catalogs, and in several other locations, including bulletin boards in the labs. For the policies to be enforceable, however, some mechanism must be established that records the student's acknowledgment of the policy. This is frequently accomplished with a banner screen that displays a brief statement warning the user that the policy is in place and that use of the system constitutes acceptance of the policy. The user must then click an OK button or press a key to get past the screen. However, this method can be ineffective if the acknowledgment screen does not require any unusual action to move past it; such a screen is often called a "blow-by" screen, as users can skip past it without even seeing it.

Commonly, companies use banners or pop-up windows to display end-user license agreements (EULAs). A EULA, which is usually presented on a screen to the user during software installation, spells out fair and responsible use of the software being installed. At one time, EULAs were typically presented on blow-by screens, with an instruction like "Press any key to accept." Users could then install the software simply by pressing the Enter key without explicitly reviewing and acknowledging the restrictions on software use, thus potentially negating the software company's legal claim. Today, most EULA screens require that the user click a specific button, press a function key, or type text to agree to the terms of the EULA. Some even require the user to scroll down to the bottom of the EULA screen before the "I accept" button is activated or viewable. Similar methods are used on network and computer logins to reinforce acknowledgement of the system use policy. Figure 6-10 provides an example of a EULA screen that requires specific user input.

Figure 6-10   Sample end-user license agreement

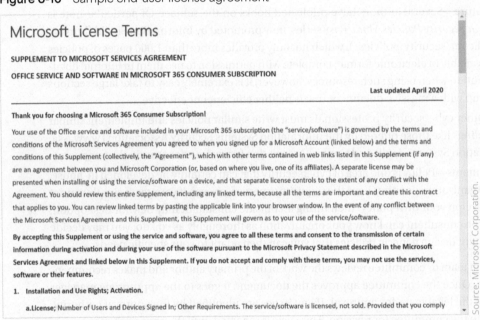

A stronger mechanism to document and ensure comprehension is a compliance assessment, such as a short quiz, to make sure that users both read the policy and understand it. A minimum score is commonly established before the employee is certified to be in compliance. Coupled with a short training video, the compliance quiz is the current industry best practice for policy implementation and compliance. The design should also include specifications for any automated tool used for the creation and management of policy documents, as well as revisions to feasibility analysis reports based on improved costs and benefits as the design is clarified.

During the implementation phase, the policy development team ensures that the policy is properly distributed, read, understood, and agreed to by those to whom it applies, and that their understanding and acceptance of the policy are documented, as described in later sections of this chapter.

Maintenance Phase

During the maintenance phase, the policy development team monitors, maintains, and modifies the policy as needed to ensure that it remains effective as a tool to meet changing threats. The policy should have a built-in mechanism through which users can report problems, preferably anonymously through a web form monitored either by the organization's legal team or a committee assigned to collect and review such content. It is in this phase that the last component of effective policy development—uniform enforcement—comes into play. The organization should make sure that everyone is required to follow the policy equally and that policies are not implemented differently in different areas or hierarchies of the organization.

Software Support for Policy Administration

The need for effective policy management has led to the emergence of a class of software tools that supports policy development, implementation, and maintenance. One such tool, which couples policy publishing and tracking with training videos and compliance quizzes, is Compliance Shield by Information Shield. As shown in Figure 6-11, the software integrates the content from *Information Security Policies Made Easy*, allowing seamless and explicitly permitted integration of existing policy components, and even sample policies, into the organization's portfolio. Once developed, the policies can be approved by management and then published for users to review. The organization can then add links to its training material and create and administer compliance quizzes. All material is electronic, meaning there is no need for hard-copy documents because the site is hosted on the web and not a company's intranet. In the event of an incident or disaster that disables internal computing infrastructure, critical policies can still be accessed as the organization works to recover.

Figure 6-11   Compliance Shield

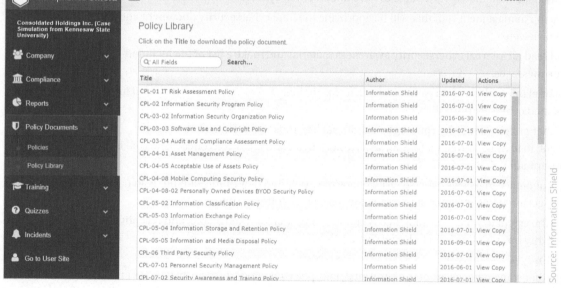

When policies are created and distributed in hard-copy form, it is often not clear where the policies originated and which manager approved them, unless the organization enforces a process to include such notations in the policy document. However, with tools like Compliance Shield, the primary manager responsible for the policy has their name associated with it, along with the date of approval. This identification can make managers reluctant to implement policies using automated software tools because it can associate a particular manager with new restrictions or rules. This hesitancy is a difficult hurdle to overcome, but it can be addressed by evaluating managerial job performance on achieved objectives—in this case, an effective policy process—rather than on the basis that "an unobserved failure is a success."

Note 2 | For a listing of policy management software, visit www.capterra.com/sem-compare/policy-management-software/ or www.softwareadvice.com/policy-management/.

Other Approaches to Cybersecurity Policy Development

There are several other approaches to developing cybersecurity policy. The following section, adapted from Wood's *Information Security Policies Made Easy* and used with permission, provides a checklist to follow during policy development.

Checklist of Steps in the Policy Development Process

This checklist is intended to provide a quick overview of the major steps associated with the development, refinement, and approval of an internal cybersecurity policy document. [. . .] Many of the following steps can be pursued simultaneously or in an order different than the following:

1. Perform a risk assessment or information technology audit to determine your organization's unique cybersecurity needs. These needs must be addressed in a policy document.

2. Clarify what the word "policy" means within your organization so that you are not preparing a "standard," "procedure," or some other related material.

3. Ensure that roles and responsibilities related to cybersecurity are clarified, including responsibility for issuing and maintaining policies.

4. Convince management that it is advisable to have documented cybersecurity policies.

5. Identify the top management staff that will be approving the final cybersecurity document and all influential reviewers.

6. Collect and read all internal cybersecurity awareness material and make a list of the included bottom-line messages.

7. Conduct a brief internal survey to gather ideas that stakeholders believe should be included in a new or updated cybersecurity policy.

8. Examine other policies issued by your organization, such as those from Human Resources management, to identify prevailing format, style, tone, length, and cross-references. The goal is to produce information that conforms to previous efforts.

9. Identify the audience to receive cybersecurity policy materials and determine whether [each person will] get a separate document or a separate page on an intranet site.

10. Determine the extent to which the audience is literate, computer knowledgeable, and receptive to cybersecurity messages. This includes understanding the corporate culture surrounding cybersecurity.

11. Decide whether some other awareness efforts must take place before cybersecurity policies are issued. For example, one effort might show that information itself has become a critical factor of production.

12. Using ideas from the risk assessment, prepare a list of absolutely essential policy messages that must be communicated. Consult the policy statements as well as the sample policies found in this book.

13. If there is more than one audience, match the audiences with the bottom-line messages to be communicated through a coverage matrix. [. . .]

14. Determine how the policy material will be disseminated, noting the constraints and implications of each medium of communication. An intranet site is recommended. [. . .]

15. Review the compliance checking process, disciplinary process, and enforcement process to ensure that they all can work smoothly with the new policy document.

16. Determine whether the number of messages is too large to be handled all at one time, and if so, identify different categories of material that will be issued at different times.

17. Have an outline of topics to be included in the first document reviewed by several stakeholders. A cybersecurity management committee is the ideal review board.

18. Based on comments from the stakeholders, revise the initial outline and prepare a first draft. [. . .]

19. Have the first draft document reviewed by the stakeholders for initial reactions, presentation suggestions, and implementation ideas.

20. Revise the draft in response to comments from stakeholders. Expect this step to [be repeated] several times.

21. Request top management approval of the policy. Changes may be necessary, in which case this step may [be repeated] several times.

22. Prepare extracts of the policy document for selected purposes—for example, for a form signed by users receiving new or renewed user IDs and passwords.

23. Develop an awareness plan that uses the policy document as a source of ideas and requirements.

24. Create a working papers memo indicating the disposition of all comments received from reviewers, even if no changes were made.

25. Write a memo about the project, what you learned, and what needs to be fixed so that the next version of the policy document can be prepared more efficiently, better received by the readers, and more responsive to the unique circumstances facing your organization.

26. Prepare a list of next steps that will be needed to implement the requirements specified in the policy document. [These steps] can include the development of a cybersecurity architecture, manual procedures documents, technical cybersecurity standards, acquisition of new products, hiring new technical staff, and other matters.

Next Steps

There are many paths available after a cybersecurity policy has been approved. [. . .] There will typically be many other projects that are initiated as a result of preparing a cybersecurity policy document. For example, a policy preparation effort may have illuminated the fact that an existing cybersecurity requirement is obsolete. [. . .][16]

NIST's SP 800-18, Rev. 1 reinforces a business process–centered approach to policy management. Although this document is targeted at U.S. federal agencies, it puts forward a very practical approach to cybersecurity planning that many other organizations may be able to use. While larger organizations may be able to mine this guide for practical advice on structuring a complete cybersecurity program, smaller organizations may find that the guide's planning approaches are more complex than needed or that the proposed controls are not suitable for a small-business setting.

Because policies are living documents that constantly change and grow, organizations cannot simply create such an important set of documents and then shelve them. Instead, these documents must be properly disseminated (distributed, read, understood, and agreed to) and managed. Good management practices for policy development and maintenance make for a more resilient organization. For example, all policies, including cybersecurity policies, undergo tremendous stress when corporate mergers and divestitures occur. In these situations, changes happen quickly, and employees suffer uncertainty and are faced with many distractions; these stresses can reveal weaknesses in the management of cybersecurity policies. When two companies come together as one but still have separate policies, it can be very difficult to implement cybersecurity controls. Likewise, when one company with unified policies splits in two, the policy needs of both spin-offs change and must be accommodated. To keep policies current and viable, an individual must be responsible for scheduling reviews, defining review practices and procedures, and ensuring that policy and revision dates are present.

Note 3 | For more information on NIST policy guidelines, read the "Information Security Handbook: A Guide for Managers" at www.nist.gov/publications/information-security-handbook-guide-managers.

Self-Check

13. Distributing policy documents by email guarantees that the policy has reached the end users.

   a. True   **b.** False

14. A measurable percentage of the workforce in the United States is considered functionally illiterate, which affects their ability to understand cybersecurity policies.

   a. True   **b.** False

15. The policy development process should skip the data-gathering phase to speed up the creation of the document.

   a. True   **b.** False

☐ Check your answers at the end of this chapter.

A Final Note on Policy

As mentioned earlier, while policies can help organizations avoid litigation, their first and foremost function is to inform employees of what is and is not acceptable behavior in the organization. Policy development is meant to improve employee productivity and prevent potentially embarrassing situations and legal issues. There are three general causes of unethical and illegal behavior, such as an employee failing to follow policy:

- Ignorance—Ignorance of the law is no excuse; however, ignorance of policy and procedures is. The first method of deterrence is education, which is accomplished by designing, publishing, and disseminating an organization's policies and relevant laws and obtaining agreement to comply with these policies and laws from all members of the organization. Reminders, training, and awareness programs keep policy information in front of employees to support retention and compliance. Fair and impartial enforcement will ensure that employees do not dismiss policies as arbitrary and unimportant.
- Accident—People who have authorization and privileges to manage information within the organization are most likely to cause harm or damage by accident. Careful planning and control help prevent accidental modifications to systems and data.
- Intent—Criminal or unethical intent goes to the state of mind of the person or organization performing the act; it is often necessary to establish criminal intent to successfully prosecute offenders. Protecting a system against those with intent to cause harm or damage is best accomplished by means of technical controls and vigorous application of appropriate penalties or litigation if these controls fail.

Whatever the cause of illegal, immoral, or unethical behavior, one thing is certain: Cybersecurity personnel must do everything in their power to deter these acts and to use policy, education and training, and technology to protect information and systems. Many cybersecurity professionals understand the technological aspect of protection but underestimate the value of policy. However, laws, policies, and their associated penalties only provide deterrence if three conditions are present, as illustrated in Figure 6-12:

- Fear of the penalty—Potential offenders must fear the penalty. Threats of informal reprimand or verbal warnings do not have the same impact as the threat of termination, imprisonment, or forfeiture of pay.
- Probability of being apprehended—Potential offenders must believe there is a strong possibility of being caught by management or reported by a coworker.
- Probability of penalty being applied—Potential offenders must believe that if they are caught, the penalty will be administered and they will not simply be "let off with a warning" or given a reduced penalty.

Figure 6-12 Deterrents to illegal or unethical behavior

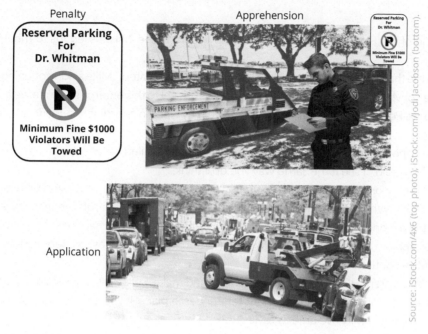

In reality, most employees inherently want to do what is right. If properly educated on what is acceptable and what is not, they will choose to follow the rules for acceptable behavior. Most people prefer systems that provide fair treatment. If they know the penalties for failure to comply, no outrage will arise when someone is caught misbehaving and the penalties are applied. Knowing what is prohibited, what the penalties are, and how penalties will be enforced is a preventive measure that should free employees to focus on the business at hand.

Note 4 | You can gain additional insight into practical aspects of policy creation with these texts:

- *Writing Information Security Policies* by Scott Barman, published by New Riders and Sams (2001, 2002).
- *Information Security Policies, Procedures, and Standards: A Practitioner's Reference* by Douglas J. Landoll, published by CRC Press (2016).

Self-Check

16. The primary function of policies in organizations is to avoid litigation.

   a. True   **b.** False

17. Ignorance of policy and procedures is an excuse for not following them.

   a. True   **b.** False

18. Cybersecurity personnel are only responsible for the technological aspects of information protection.

   a. True   **b.** False

☐ Check your answers at the end of this chapter.

Closing Case

Prior to the first meeting of the RWW Enterprise Policy Review Committee, Mike asked Iris to meet him in his office.

"You've convinced me that IT and cybersecurity policy are tightly integrated," Mike said, motioning for Iris to sit down. "And you've convinced me that cybersecurity policy is critical to this enterprise. Since we are each members of the Enterprise Policy Review Committee, I think we may want to coordinate our efforts when we bring issues up in that group. You agree?"

Iris, who knew how important policy was to her program's success, smiled.

"Sure, no problem," she said. "I see it the same way you do, I think."

"Good," Mike said. "We'll work together to make sure the CPP you've drafted is integrated with the other top-level enterprise policies. What we need to watch out for now is all the cross-references between the top-level policies and the second- and third-tier policies. The entire issue of internal consistency between supporting policies is a problem, especially with getting the HR department policies to integrate fully."

Iris nodded while Mike continued.

"I want you to take the current HR policy document binder and make a wish list of possible changes," he said. "You should focus on making sure we get the right references in place. If you can send me the change plan by the end of the weekend, I will have time to review it."

Iris smiled. "Will do, Mike!" she said. "But I can tell you, the first thing I'll recommend is that we toss these antique binders and look into an intranet policy administration application so we can move RWW into the 21st century!"

Case Discussion Questions

1. If the Enterprise Policy Review Committee is not open to the approach that Mike and Iris want to use for structuring cybersecurity policies into three tiers, how should Mike and Iris proceed?
2. Should the chief information security officer (Iris) be assessing HR policies? Why or why not?

Case Ethical Decision Making

Suppose that Iris sends Mike her detailed plan for a CPP along with a draft of a fully revised enterprise IT policy, with all of the necessary changes in the supporting policies. Suppose further that, during the Enterprise Policy Review Committee meeting, Mike submits the revised CPP exactly as Iris has revised it but does not include any reference to the work that Iris did. In fact, Mike presents the enhanced CPP as his own work. Has Mike broken any laws in representing Iris' policy work as his own? Has Mike committed an ethical lapse in doing so, or is he just being inconsiderate?

Summary

A high-quality cybersecurity program begins and ends with policy. Policy drives the performance of personnel in ways that enhance the cybersecurity of an organization's information assets.

Developing proper guidelines for a cybersecurity program is a management problem, not a technical one. The technical aspect of a cybersecurity program is merely one part of the entire program and should be dealt with only after management has created relevant policies.

Although cybersecurity policies are the least expensive means of control, they are often the most difficult to implement. Policy controls cost only the time and effort that the management team spends to create, approve, and communicate them, along with the time employees spend to integrate the policies into their daily activities.

The cybersecurity policy must satisfy several criteria:

- Policy should never conflict with law.
- Policy must stand up in court when it is challenged.
- Policy must be properly supported and administered.

Guidelines for the formulation of cybersecurity policy are as follows:

- Policy must contribute to the success of the organization.
- Management must ensure the adequate sharing of responsibility.
- End users should be involved in the policy development process.

A policy is a statement of the organization's position that is intended to influence and determine decisions and actions. It is used to control the actions of people and the development of procedures.

A policy may be viewed as a set of rules that dictate acceptable and unacceptable behavior within an organization. It must contain information about what is required and what is prohibited, the penalties for violating policy, and the appeals process.

Supporting guidance for policy comes from standards, practices, procedures, and guidelines.

Management must define three types of cybersecurity policies:

- Cybersecurity program policy (CPP), which sets the strategic direction, scope, and tone for all cybersecurity efforts; the CPP must be based on and support the organization's vision and mission statements.
- Issue-specific cybersecurity policies, which provide guidance to all members of an organization about the use of IT.
- System-specific cybersecurity policies, which guide the management and technical specifications of particular technologies and systems.

Developing cybersecurity policy usually follows a process in which policy is designed, written, formally approved, and finally integrated into ongoing management processes. The organization must make sure the policy is properly distributed, read, and understood, and that each employee agrees to comply. Management must also ensure that policy is uniformly and impartially enforced.

Policy is often developed using a project management approach much like that of the SDLC, meaning it should be planned, properly funded, and aggressively managed to ensure that it is completed on time and within budget. This effort should include an investigation phase to gain support from senior management and achieve a clear articulation of goals as well as an analysis phase to gather key reference materials, including any existing policies. In the design phase, the actual policy document is created. In the implementation phase, the organization must distribute and gain acknowledgment of the policy. Once deployed, policy enters a maintenance phase in which the focus shifts to keeping the policy effective as a tool to meet changing threats.

Policy management can be achieved with software tools that support policy development, implementation, and maintenance.

Other approaches to developing cybersecurity policy include the approach described in *Information Security Policies Made Easy* and NIST SP 800-18.

Three general causes lead to unethical and illegal behavior: ignorance, accident, and intent.

Deterrence can be created when three conditions are present: fear of penalty, probability of being apprehended, and probability of the penalty being applied.

Key Terms

access control lists (ACLs)

configuration rules

cybersecurity policy

cybersecurity program policy (CPP)

guidelines

issue-specific policy

practices

procedures

standards

system-specific policies

Review Questions

1. What is the purpose of cybersecurity policies in an organization?

2. How do policies, standards, procedures, and guidelines differ in terms of their function within an organization?

3. What is the bull's-eye model in cybersecurity, and how is it used?

4. Why is it important for policies to be aligned with the organization's needs?

5. What are the potential consequences of not having effective cybersecurity policies?

6. How can cybersecurity policies impact the success of a cybersecurity program?

7. What steps should be taken to develop sound cybersecurity policies?

8. What role do cybersecurity policies play in legal disputes regarding management's due diligence?

9. What are the key elements that should be included in a comprehensive cybersecurity program policy?

10. Why is it important for a cybersecurity program policy to include specific cybersecurity roles and responsibilities?

11. What justifies the need for an organization to have a robust cybersecurity program?

12. How should an organization handle the enforcement of its cybersecurity policies?

13. What actions should be considered if a violation of law is discovered within an organization?

14. Under what circumstances can an organization revoke a user's IT privileges?

15. What specific measures should be taken when integrating cybersecurity standards into industry-specific systems?

16. What is the purpose of issue-specific policies in an organization?

17. What are some examples of technologies that an issue-specific policy might cover?

18. What constitutes a misuse of an organization's resources?

19. How does an organization manage violations of policies?

20. What are the procedures for modifying an issue-specific policy?

21. How does an organization limit its liability in the event of policy violations by employees?

22. What are the benefits and drawbacks of modular policy document organization?

23. What are system-specific policies and how are they typically developed?

24. Why are managerial guidance system-specific policies important in an organization?

25. How do access control lists function within an organization's technology systems?

26. What are some typical components of a system-specific policy?

27. Can a system-specific policy serve as a stand-alone document, and if so, how?

28. What role does technology play in the execution of system-specific policies?

29. How do issue-specific policies differ from system-specific policies in terms of development and focus?

30. What could be the consequences of not adhering to system-specific policies within an organization?

31. How might system-specific policies evolve over time in a typical organization?

32. What are the initial steps recommended when developing a cybersecurity policy?

33. How should the cybersecurity policy's audience be assessed before disseminating policy materials?

34. What factors should be considered when matching cybersecurity messages to different audiences?

35. What are the challenges associated with policy dissemination and how can they be addressed?

36. What are some methods to ensure employees understand and comply with cybersecurity policies?

37. How should the compliance of cybersecurity policies be monitored and enforced?

38. What steps should be taken if the number of policy messages is too large to communicate at once?

39. How can the effectiveness of a cybersecurity policy be enhanced after initial approval and implementation?

40. What role does top management play in cybersecurity policy development?

41. What are the three general causes of unethical and illegal behavior?

42. Why is ignorance of policy and procedures considered excusable?

43. What is necessary to successfully prosecute offenders with criminal or unethical intent?

44. What three conditions must be present to provide deterrence through policies and penalties?

45. Why do threats of informal reprimand or verbal warnings not have the same impact as more severe penalties?

46. How can knowing the penalties and enforcement procedures for policies help employees focus on their work?

Exercises

1. Go to the International Information System Security Certification Consortium (ISC)² website at www.isc2.org and look for the information security common body of knowledge (CBK). When you review the list of areas in the CBK, is policy listed? Why do you think this is so?

2. Search your institution's intranet or website for its cybersecurity policies (perhaps listed as information security policies). Do you find an enterprise cybersecurity policy? What issue-specific cybersecurity policies can you locate? Are all of these policies issued or coordinated by the same individual or office, or are they scattered throughout the institution?

3. Using the framework presented in this chapter, evaluate the comprehensiveness of each policy you located in Exercise 2. Which areas are missing?

4. Using the framework presented in this chapter, draft a sample issue-specific policy for an organization. At the beginning of your document, describe the organization for which you are creating the policy and then complete the policy using the framework.

5. Search for sample cybersecurity policies on the web. Identify five cybersecurity program policies and five issue-specific policies and bring them to class. Compare these with the framework presented in this chapter and comment on the policies' comprehensiveness.

Solutions to Self-Check Questions

Why Policy?

1. Organizations that handle sensitive information should have relaxed cybersecurity policies.
Answer: b. False.
Explanation: Organizations dealing with sensitive information require stringent cybersecurity policies to ensure proper protection.

2. In the implementation of an appropriate-use policy, all inappropriate content should be blocked.
Answer: a. True.
Explanation: The enforcement of an appropriate-use policy requires that standards be set to block all content deemed inappropriate.

3. Cybersecurity policies are expensive to implement compared to other controls.
Answer: b. False.
Explanation: Cybersecurity policies are one of the least expensive means of control, mainly requiring time and effort for their development, approval, and communication.

Cybersecurity Program Policy

4. Cybersecurity policies should only be revised to correct errors or in response to changes in the organization's strategic direction.
Answer: a. True.
Explanation: Cybersecurity policy documents typically do not require frequent modifications unless there is a change in the strategic direction of the organization.

5. A policy of "Information must be protected in a manner commensurate with its sensitivity" applies only to electronic data.

   Answer: b. False.

   Explanation: Information must be protected irrespective of the media on which it is stored, including electronic and nonelectronic formats.

6. Cybersecurity policy enforcement is the sole responsibility of the IT department.

   Answer: b. False.

   Explanation: The responsibilities for cybersecurity are shared by various groups within the organization, not just the IT department, indicating a joint responsibility among management, users, and the cybersecurity team.

Issue-Specific Policy

7. An issue-specific policy begins with a clear statement of purpose that outlines the scope and applicability of the policy.

   Answer: a. True.

   Explanation: Each issue-specific policy should start with a statement of purpose that defines the scope, applicability, responsibilities, and technologies addressed by the policy.

8. Unauthorized uses of IT systems in an organization are generally permitted unless explicitly prohibited.

   Answer: b. False.

   Explanation: Generally, any use not explicitly identified as authorized is considered a misuse of equipment, implying that unauthorized uses are not permitted unless explicitly allowed.

9. Having a single, comprehensive issue-specific policy document is always the best approach for managing these types of policies.

   Answer: b. False.

   Explanation: The recommended approach for issue-specific policies is a modular policy approach, which balances ease of policy development with effective policy management, rather than creating a single comprehensive document.

System-Specific Policy

10. Managerial guidance system-specific policies are solely targeted at nontechnological staff within an organization.

    Answer: b. False.

    Explanation: Managerial guidance system-specific policies are created to guide both the implementation and configuration of technology and to address the behavior of people in the organization, including the technologists responsible for implementation and configuration.

11. Access control lists (ACLs) can be used to control access to file storage systems and network communication devices.

    Answer: a. True.

    Explanation: ACLs can control access to various systems, including file storage systems, object brokers, and other network communication devices, among others.

12. A system-specific policy for configuring and operating a firewall will include only the technical specifications.

    Answer: b. False.

    Explanation: A system-specific policy can include managerial intent and guidance on configuring and operating firewalls, not just technical specifications. This guidance ensures continuity of intent between management and the IT staff.

Guidelines for Effective Policy Development and Implementation

13. Distributing policy documents by email guarantees that the policy has reached the end users.

    Answer: b. False.

    Explanation: Distribution by email does not guarantee that an individual has received or read the policy, as emails can get lost among other business communications or face other delivery issues.

14. A measurable percentage of the workforce in the United States is considered functionally illiterate, which affects their ability to understand cybersecurity policies.

    Answer: a. True.

    Explanation: A significant portion of the workforce, particularly in the United States, is considered functionally illiterate, which impacts their capacity to comprehend and follow cybersecurity policies.

15. The policy development process should skip the data-gathering phase to speed up the creation of the document.

    Answer: b. False.

    Explanation: The document emphasizes the importance of not skipping the data-gathering process in policy development, as it is crucial for understanding the needs and context of the organization; skipping it increases the likelihood of management rejection.

A Final Note on Policy

16. The primary function of policies in organizations is to avoid litigation.

    Answer: b. False.

    Explanation: The primary function of policies is to inform employees about acceptable and unacceptable behaviors, aiming to improve productivity and prevent embarrassing or legal issues.

17. Ignorance of policy and procedures is an excuse for not following them.

    Answer: a. True.

    Explanation: The ignorance of policy and procedures is considered an excuse, unlike ignorance of the law, which is not.

18. Cybersecurity personnel are only responsible for the technological aspects of information protection.

    Answer: b. False.

    Explanation: Cybersecurity personnel must also use policy, education, training, and technology to protect information and systems.

7

Developing the Cybersecurity Program

Chapter Objectives

After reading this chapter and completing the exercises, you should be able to:

1 Outline the functional components of a cybersecurity program.

2 Summarize how to plan and staff an organization's cybersecurity program.

3 Explain the internal and external factors that influence the development and structure of a cybersecurity program.

4 Summarize the development and maintenance needed for a security education, training, and awareness program.

5 Discuss the role of project management in cybersecurity.

> We trained hard ... but every time we formed up teams we would be reorganized. I was to learn that we meet any new situation by reorganizing. And a wonderful method it can be for creating the illusion of progress while producing confusion, inefficiency, and demoralization.
>
> —Petronius Arbiter, Roman writer and satirist, 210 B.C.

Case Opener

Iris was looking over the freshly printed first issue of her company's cybersecurity newsletter, *The Guardian*, when Mike Edwards walked into her office.

"What's new, Iris?" he asked.

"See for yourself!" Iris replied with a grin, handing Mike her latest completed project.

"Very nice," he commented. "How close are you to publication?"

"We've just put it on the intranet, and we're going to run off a few dozen hard copies for our office. That's your copy."

"Thanks!" Mike said while scanning the cover article. "What is this disclosure situation all about?"

Mike was referring to the recent state law that mandated very specific requirements for reporting information breaches, including disclosure of numbers of records breached. The new law also mandated notification of affected parties and the offering of identity theft support for individual customers. What had caught Mike's attention was the clause that defined penalties for failure to report breaches of personally identifiable information in a timely manner. The penalties ranged from fines based on the number of records disclosed up to several years in prison.

"We need to talk about this issue at the senior staff meeting," Mike said. "We should get the other departments involved to make sure we don't have any problems complying with this law."

Iris nodded and said, "Maybe someone from corporate legal should be there, too."

"Good idea," Mike said while looking at the newsletter's listing of cybersecurity training sessions.

"Where did you get the training staff?" he asked Iris.

"I've been meaning to talk to you about that," she said. "I'll teach the classes until my cybersecurity manager, Tom, can take over. But we should ask the corporate training office about getting some of their staff up to speed on our topics."

"Sounds good," Mike said. "I'll get with Jerry tomorrow after the staff meeting."

Organizing for Cybersecurity

Some organizations use the term "security program" to describe the set of personnel, plans, policies, and initiatives related to cybersecurity. Others use the term "cybersecurity" to refer to the broader context of corporate or physical cybersecurity along with areas usually associated with computer, network, or data cybersecurity. The term cybersecurity program—the entire set of activities, resources, personnel, and technologies used by an organization to manage the risks to its information assets—is used in this book to describe the structure and organization of cybersecurity efforts. There is an old joke about management that goes something like this:

> Two new executives arrive at their new company for work and are shown to their offices. On both office desks is a letter from the new executive's predecessor and three sealed, numbered envelopes. Each letter congratulates the executive on the new position; the predecessor expresses regret for being unable to assist with the transition. However, the outgoing executives note that they have provided the newcomers with three pieces of advice in case of problems. Each of these nuggets is stored in one of the three numbered envelopes, which should be opened in order and only when advice is truly needed. The new executives scoff at the idea that they need any help.

> The first executive is a natural fit with the company; the other one struggles. Weeks go by until one day a major problem emerges that the new executive cannot solve. Frustrated and desperate, the executive remembers the three envelopes and opens the first one. Inside, the note states, "Blame everything on me." The new executive calls in all division subordinates, declares that the problems facing them are due to the departed predecessor, and that the division will now turn in a new direction. This buys the executive some time.

> A few months later, the next major problem emerges. The executive opens the second envelope to discover a message that reads, "Reorganize everything." The executive promptly calls a meeting and declares that the current situation is a result of poor organization; to resolve it, they must restructure the entire division. It is a very busy time, and everyone is occupied with the rigors of reorganization for quite a while. Eventually, however, the next major problem presents itself to the executive, who confidently reaches for the third envelope. The message this time: "Fill out three new envelopes."

Sometimes, the problems faced by executives must be answered head-on, without attempts to place the blame on others or the organizational structure. In some cases, data breaches occur and executives are held accountable. The most significant information breach to date is the 2013 Yahoo data breach, which affected over 3 billion consumer records, including customer names, email addresses, phone numbers, and dates of birth. The breach resulted in a loss of $350 million to the value of the organization, as it was in negotiation to be purchased by Verizon. This event underscores the value of the cybersecurity program within an organization's culture.

Among the variables that determine how an organization chooses to structure its cybersecurity program are organizational culture, size, cybersecurity personnel budget, and cybersecurity technology budget. The first and most influential of these variables is the organizational culture. If upper management believes that cybersecurity is a waste of time and resources, or is simply unimportant, the cybersecurity program will remain small and poorly supported. The efforts of the cybersecurity team will be viewed as contrary to the organization's mission and detrimental to its productivity. Conversely, where there is a strong, positive view of cybersecurity, the cybersecurity program is likely to be larger and well supported, both financially and otherwise. An alignment is needed between the cybersecurity program in place and the culture of the organization. Without it, conflicts may result in the program being less effective.

An organization's size and available resources also directly affect the size and structure of its cybersecurity program. Organizations with complex information technology (IT) infrastructures and sophisticated system users will require more cybersecurity support. In fact, large, complex organizations may have entire divisions dedicated to cybersecurity, including a chief security officer (CSO), with teams of cybersecurity managers, administrators, and technicians. Such divisions might have specialized staff focusing on specific areas—for example, policy, planning, firewalls, and intrusion detection and prevention systems (IDPSs). By contrast, smaller organizations may only have a single cybersecurity administrator, or they may assign cybersecurity responsibilities to a systems or network administrator or a manager within the IT department.

Another variable is the budget for the cybersecurity program. The size of the cybersecurity budget typically corresponds to the size of the organization; in many cases, it may be a fraction of the IT budget. Although no standard exists for the size of the cybersecurity budget or the number of cybersecurity personnel an organization has, industry averages are available. These numbers vary widely and may be expressed in terms of cybersecurity budget per unit of revenue, cybersecurity staff per number of total employees, or cybersecurity budget as a percentage of IT budget. Determining the industry average in any given case may be a challenge, but regardless of this average, the organization's executive management has the most influence over budgets, for better or worse. In general, cybersecurity programs are understaffed and undersupported in terms of resources for the tasks they are faced with. Top cybersecurity managers must constantly struggle to create policies and plans, manage personnel issues, develop training, and keep the administrative and support staff focused on their assigned responsibilities and tasks.

Organizational Culture

What is organizational culture? Simply put, it is the way the values of an organization's management and employees are turned into everyday activities and recurring practices. Also known as "corporate culture," organizational culture may be reflected in the values statement of the organization; however, in many organizations, it is represented by the collective consciousness the organization manifests when interacting with its stakeholders and other constituents. An organization's culture is often a reflection of how management interacts with employees and outsiders, such as suppliers and customers. People who have worked for multiple organizations often report unique cultures in each organization, beyond the conduct of business functions and processes. Organizational culture is as much about attitude and perspective as it is about skills and capabilities or products and services. In most cases, organizational culture is undocumented and learned through observation and interaction with others.

BusinessDictionary.com explains that organizational culture manifests itself in "(1) how the organization conducts its business, [and] treats its employees, customers, and the wider community, (2) the extent to which autonomy and freedom is allowed in decision making, developing new ideas, and personal expression, (3) how power and information flow through the organizational hierarchy, and (4) the employees' commitment to collective objectives."[1] A strong and positive organizational culture often supports and empowers employees in having effective interactions with one another, with management, and with business partners and customers. A weak or negative organizational culture can impede an organization's ability to function, perhaps to the level of making it dysfunctional. Improving destructive or dysfunctional organizational culture is an extreme challenge.

According to Andrew Briney and Frank Prince, authors of the article "Does Size Matter?":

> As organizations get larger in size, their cybersecurity departments are not keeping up with the demands of increasingly complex organizational infrastructures. Cybersecurity spending per user and per machine declines exponentially as organizations grow, leaving most handcuffed when it comes to implementing effective cybersecurity procedures.[2]

Office politics, the economy, and budget forecasts are just some of the factors that cause upper management to juggle staffing issues. In today's environment, many organizational cybersecurity programs still do not receive the support they need to function properly. That situation continues to change, however, because the current political climate and the many reported cybersecurity breaches, ransomware attacks, and other incidents are rapidly forcing organizations to realign their perspective of cybersecurity as a critical function.

Another important variable is the portion of the capital and expense budget for physical resources that is dedicated to cybersecurity. This budget includes allocation of offices, computer labs, and support facilities as well as the general cybersecurity expense budget. Because the cybersecurity staff handles confidential information about cybersecurity plans, policies, structures, designs, and a host of other items, it is prudent to provide this group with its own secured physical resources, including office space.

Although the size of an organization dictates the makeup of its cybersecurity program, certain basic functions should occur in every organization, so these functions should be included in any budget allocation. Table 7-1 outlines the functions that should be funded and implemented for a successful cybersecurity program. They are not necessarily performed within the cybersecurity department, but they must be performed somewhere within the organization.

Table 7-1 Cybersecurity program critical success functions

Function	Description	Comments
Risk assessment	Identifies and evaluates the risk present in IT initiatives and systems	This function includes identifying the sources of risk and may include offering advice on controls that can reduce risk.
Risk management	Implements or oversees use of controls to reduce risk	This function is often paired with risk assessment.
Systems testing	Evaluates patches used to close software vulnerabilities and acceptance testing of new systems to ensure compliance with policy and effectiveness	This function is usually part of the incident response and risk management functions.
Policy	Maintains and promotes cybersecurity policy across the organization	This function must be coordinated with organization-wide policy processes.
Legal assessment	Maintains awareness of planned and actual laws and their impact, and coordinates with outside legal counsel and law enforcement agencies	This function is almost always external to the cybersecurity and IT departments.
Incident response	Handles the initial response to potential incidents, manages escalation of actual incidents, and coordinates the earliest responses to incidents and disasters	This function often spans other functions and is drawn from multiple departments. It should include middle management to manage escalation processes.
Planning	Researches, creates, maintains, and promotes cybersecurity plans; often takes a project management approach to planning as contrasted with strategic planning for the whole organization	This function must coordinate with organization-wide policy processes.

(Continues)

Table 7-1   Cybersecurity program critical success functions (*Continued*)

Function	Description	Comments
Measurement	Uses existing control systems and perhaps specialized data collection systems to measure all aspects of the cybersecurity environment	Managers rely on timely and accurate statistics to make informed decisions.
Compliance	Verifies that system and network administrators repair identified vulnerabilities promptly and correctly	This function poses problems for good customer service because it is difficult to be customer focused and enforce compliance at the same time.
Centralized authentication	Manages the granting and revocation of network and system credentials for all members of the organization	This function is often delegated to the help desk or staffed in conjunction (and co-located) with the help-desk function.
Systems cybersecurity administration	Administers the configuration of computer systems, which are often organized into groups by the operating system they run	Many organizations may have originally assigned some cybersecurity functions to groups outside of the cybersecurity function. This can be a source of conflict when organizations update their cybersecurity programs.
Training	Trains general staff in cybersecurity topics, IT staff in specialized technical controls, and internal cybersecurity staff in specialized areas of cybersecurity, including both technical and managerial topics	Some or all of this function may be carried out in conjunction with the corporate training department.
Network security administration	Administers configuration of computer networks; often organized into groups by geographic location or logical network area, such as a wide area network, local area network, or demilitarized zone (DMZ)	Many organizations may have originally assigned some cybersecurity functions to groups outside of the cybersecurity function, which may require close coordination or reassignment.
Vulnerability assessment (VA)	Locates exposure within information assets so vulnerabilities can be repaired before weaknesses are exploited	VA is sometimes performed by a penetration testing team or ethical hacking unit. This function is often outsourced to specialists hired as consultants that test systems controls to find weak spots. They are sometimes known as "red teams" or "tiger teams."

Security in Large Organizations

Organizations that have more than 1,000 devices are likely to be staffed and funded at a level that enables them to accomplish most of the cybersecurity functions identified in Table 7-1. Large organizations often create an internal entity to deal with the specific cybersecurity challenges they face. For example, they often operate in multiple legal jurisdictions and must act accordingly. Not surprisingly, the cybersecurity functions and organizational approaches implemented by larger organizations are as diverse as the organizations themselves. Cybersecurity divisions in such organizations tend to form and reform internal teams to meet long-term challenges even as they handle day-to-day cybersecurity operations. Thus, functions are likely to be split into groups in larger organizations; in contrast, smaller organizations typically create fewer teams, perhaps only having one general team representing the whole department.

One recommended approach is to separate the functions into four areas:

1. Functions performed by nontechnology business units outside the IT area of management control, such as:
   - Legal
   - Training

2. Functions performed by IT groups outside the cybersecurity area of management control, such as:
   - Systems security administration
   - Network security administration
   - Centralized authentication

3. Functions performed within the cybersecurity division as a customer service to the organization and its external partners, such as:
   - Risk assessment
   - Systems testing
   - Incident response planning
   - Disaster recovery planning
   - Performance measurement
   - Vulnerability assessment

4. Functions performed within the cybersecurity division as a compliance enforcement obligation, such as:
   - Policy
   - Compliance/audit
   - Risk management

It remains the CSO's responsibility to see that cybersecurity functions are adequately performed somewhere within the organization. As indicated in Figures 7-1 and 7-2, large and very large organizations typically have dedicated staffs to support the cybersecurity program. The deployment of full-time cybersecurity personnel depends on many factors, including sensitivity of the information to be protected, industry regulations for fields such as finance and healthcare, and general profitability. The more resources the company can dedicate to its personnel budget, the more likely it is to maintain a large cybersecurity staff. As shown in Figure 7-1, a typical large organization has an average of one to two full-time cybersecurity managers, three to four full-time administrators/technicians, and as many as 16 part-time staff members who have cybersecurity duties in addition to their duties in other areas. For example, a systems administrator of a Windows 2022 server may be responsible for maintaining both the server and the cybersecurity applications running on it. A very large organization, as illustrated in Figure 7-2, may have more than 20 full-time cybersecurity personnel and 40 or more individuals with part-time responsibilities.

Figure 7-1   Cybersecurity staffing example for a large organization

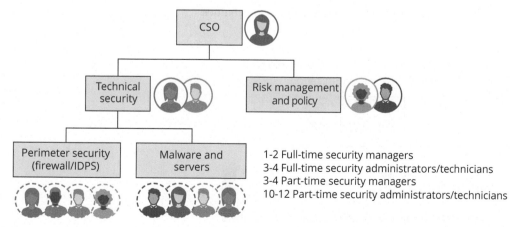

1-2 Full-time security managers
3-4 Full-time security administrators/technicians
3-4 Part-time security managers
10-12 Part-time security administrators/technicians

Figure 7-2 Cybersecurity staffing example for a very large organization

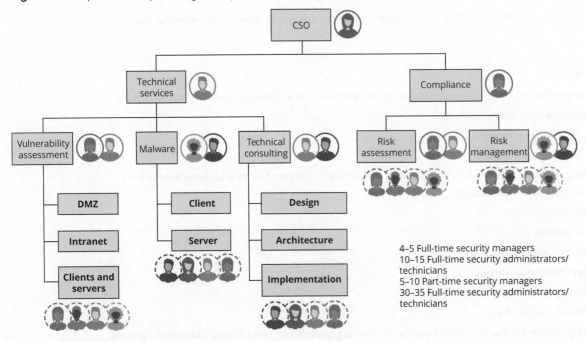

4–5 Full-time security managers
10–15 Full-time security administrators/
technicians
5–10 Part-time security managers
30–35 Full-time security administrators/
technicians

Security in Medium-Sized Organizations

Medium-sized organizations have between 100 and 1,000 computers requiring cybersecurity management. These organizations may still be large enough to implement the multitiered approach to cybersecurity described earlier for large organizations, though perhaps with fewer dedicated groups and more functions assigned to each group. In a medium-sized organization, more of the functional areas from Table 7-1 are assigned to other departments within IT but outside the cybersecurity department. Also, the central authentication function is often handed off to systems administration personnel within the IT department.

Medium-sized organizations tend to ignore some of the functions from Table 7-1—in particular, when the cybersecurity department cannot staff a certain function and IT or another department is not encouraged or required to perform that function in its stead. In these cases, the CSO must improve the collaboration among these groups and provide leadership in advocating decisions that stretch the capabilities of the entire organization. This is an example of the inherent difference between the focus of the chief information officer (CIO) and the CSO. As organizations get larger, CSOs will increasingly widen their perspectives beyond the IT scope of an issue and consider the impact across the whole organization.

As illustrated in Figure 7-3, the full-time and part-time staff of a medium-sized organization is dramatically smaller than that of its larger counterparts. This organization may only have one full-time cybersecurity person, with perhaps three individuals with part-time cybersecurity responsibilities.

Figure 7-3 Cybersecurity staffing example for a
medium-sized organization

1 Full-time manager and partial-support staff members

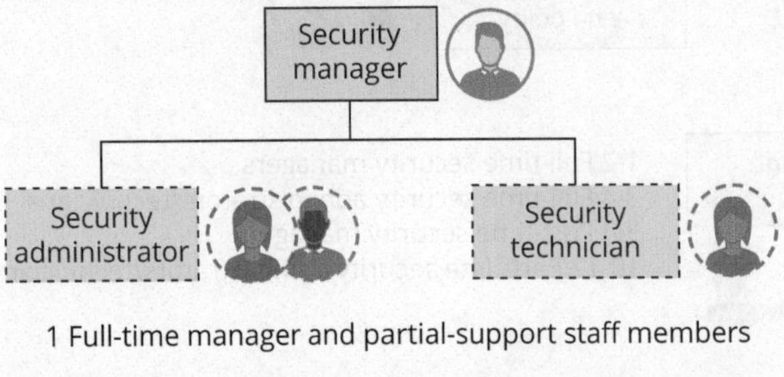

Security in Small Organizations

Smaller organizations—those with fewer than 100 systems to supervise—face unique challenges. In a small organization, cybersecurity often becomes the responsibility of a jack-of-all-trades, a single cybersecurity manager or administrator with perhaps one or two assistants for managing the technical components. It is not uncommon in smaller organizations to have IT administrators perform these roles. Such organizations frequently have little in the way of formal policy, planning, or cybersecurity measures, and they usually outsource their web presence or e-commerce operations. As a result, the cybersecurity administrator most often deals with issues involving desktop management, virus protection, and local area network cybersecurity.

Because resources are often limited in smaller organizations, the cybersecurity manager frequently turns to freeware or open-source software to lower the costs of assessing and implementing cybersecurity. As you will learn in later chapters, these tools can be quite effective both in providing access to otherwise unavailable utilities and lowering the total cost of cybersecurity. Cybersecurity training and awareness is usually conducted on a one-on-one basis, with the cybersecurity manager providing advice to users as needed. Any published policies are likely to be issue-specific—for example, policies on web and Internet use and fair and responsible use of office equipment. Formal planning, when it happens, is usually part of the IT planning conducted by the CIO or IT manager.

Some observers feel that small organizations avoid certain threats precisely because of their small size. The thinking is that hacktivists, hackers, and other threat agents may be less likely to go after smaller companies, opting instead to attack larger, more prestigious targets. This questionable strategy has not been proven, and it is not wise to gamble the future of the organization on its staying unnoticed. As the saying goes, "There is no security in obscurity." Threats from insiders are also less likely in an environment where every employee knows every other employee. In general, the less anonymity an employee has, the less likely they feel able to get away with abuse or misuse of company assets. The lack of resources available to a smaller organization's cybersecurity team is somewhat offset by the lower risk of becoming a target. Figure 7-4 illustrates the limited staffing found in smaller organizations, which typically have either one individual with full-time duties in cybersecurity or, more likely, one individual who manages or conducts cybersecurity duties in addition to those of other functional areas (probably IT). This individual may have partial supervision or the support of just one or two administrators or technicians.

Figure 7-4   Cybersecurity staffing example for a small organization

1 Full-time/part-time manager and part-time support staff members

Does Size Matter?

While many IT professionals may think they will have better careers with more rapid advancement or higher salaries in the big IT departments of nationally renowned organizations, they may be better off at a smaller organization. Big organizations have large staffs, full-time and part-time cybersecurity professionals, and more problems than the typical smaller organization. Here, we define small, medium-sized, large, and very large organizations, and we describe the problems inherent in each and how the organizations are staffed to deal with them.

- The small organization has 10 to 100 computers. Most small organizations have a simple, centralized IT organizational model and spend disproportionately more on cybersecurity, averaging almost 20 percent of the total IT budget. The typical cybersecurity staff in this organization is usually only one person (the Lone Ranger!), if in fact there is a full-time cybersecurity professional. Much more frequently, cybersecurity is an additional duty of one of the IT staffers. However, small organizations, including ones with the smallest budgets, spend more per user than medium-sized and large organizations.[3]

- The medium-sized organization has 100 to 1,000 computers and has a smaller budget (averaging about 11 percent of the total IT budget), about the same cybersecurity staff, and a larger need for cybersecurity than the small organization. Cybersecurity staff in the medium-sized organization must rely on help from IT staff to carry out cybersecurity plans and practices. "Their ability to set policy, handle incidents in a regular manner, and effectively allocate resources are, overall, worse than any other group. Considering their size, the number of incidents they recognize is skyrocketing."[4]

- The large organization has 1,000 to 10,000 computers. Organizations of this size have generally integrated planning and policy into the organizational culture; "eight in ten organizations say at least some of their cybersecurity decisions are guided by them."[5] Unfortunately, the large organization tends to spend substantially less on cybersecurity (an average of only about 5 percent of the total IT budget), creating issues across the organization, especially in the "people" areas.

- The very large organization has more than 10,000 computer systems and large cybersecurity budgets, which grow faster than IT budgets. However, in these multimillion-dollar cybersecurity budgets, the average amount per user is still less than in any other type of organization. "Where small organizations spend more than $5,000 per user on cybersecurity, very large organizations spend about one-eighteenth of that, roughly $300 per user," or approximately six percent of the total IT budget. The very large organization does a better job in the policy and resource management areas.[6]

Self-Check

1. The term "cybersecurity program" refers specifically to the activities, resources, personnel, and technologies used by an organization to manage its information security risks.

   a. True   b. False

2. A strong organizational culture for cybersecurity often results in a smaller, less supported cybersecurity program.

   a. True   b. False

3. Large organizations spend a greater percentage of their IT budget on cybersecurity compared to smaller organizations.

   a. True   b. False

☐ Check your answers at the end of this chapter.

Placing Cybersecurity within an Organization

In large organizations, cybersecurity is often located within an IT division and headed by the CSO, who reports directly to the CIO. Such a structure implies that the goals and objectives of the CSO and CIO are closely aligned. In reality, this is not always the case. By its nature, a cybersecurity program that is subordinate to IT may sometimes find itself at odds with IT's goals and objectives. On the one hand, the CIO, as the executive in charge of the organization's technology, tries to maximize the efficiency in processing and accessing the organization's information. Anything that limits access or slows information processing directly contradicts the CIO's mission. On the other hand, the CSO functions more like an internal auditor, with the cybersecurity department examining existing systems to discover cybersecurity faults and flaws in technology, software, and employees' activities and processes. In addition, new cybersecurity technologies designed to ensure that only authorized users access information may result in slower and more complex login procedures. At times, these activities may disrupt or delay access and use of the organization's information. Because the goals and objectives of the CIO and the CSO may come into conflict, cybersecurity ideally should be separate from IT rather than subordinate to it.

The vision of separate IT and cybersecurity functions is shared by many executives. A survey conducted by Meta Group found that only 3 percent of the consulting firm's clients positioned the cybersecurity department outside IT; the same clients viewed this positioning as what a forward-thinking organization should have. An article in *InformationWeek* titled "Where the Chief Security Officer Belongs" states this idea more succinctly: "The people who do and the people who watch shouldn't report to a common manager."[7] This perspective is shared by others, including consultant and columnist Dejan Kosutic:

> The security manager should not work in the IT department, although since this is very difficult to achieve in smaller organizations, it is usually tolerated; however, for larger organizations such conflict of interest is not allowed, and some industries are heavily regulated in this respect.[8]

The challenge is to design a reporting structure for cybersecurity that balances the competing needs of the communities of interest. In many cases, the unit that executes the cybersecurity program is forced into the organizational chart in a way that reflects its marginal status, and it may be shuffled from place to place within the organization with little attention paid to how such moves hinder its effectiveness. Organizations searching for a rational compromise will attempt to find a place for the cybersecurity program that allows it to balance risk assessment and policy enforcement with education, training, awareness, and customer service needs. This approach can help make cybersecurity a positive aspect of the organization's culture.

There are many ways to position the cybersecurity program within an organization. Kosutic asserts there should be three options for placing the CSO and the cybersecurity team in the organization. These options are generally driven by the organization's size:

- In a separate group reporting directly to the chief executive officer (CEO)/president—In this option, the CSO and cybersecurity team would be independent and equally represented in the top executive's strategic C-level council. This is most commonly seen in larger and more mature organizations.
- Under a division/department with no conflict of interest—Here, the CSO and cybersecurity team are placed into a larger division for administrative purposes and selected to ensure there are no conflicts like those described with IT earlier. This is most commonly seen in medium-sized to large organizations.
- As an additional duty for an existing manager/executive—This option is most commonly seen in smaller organizations; here, the CSO or simply the "cybersecurity manager" may also *be* the IT manager.[9]

In his book *Information Security Roles and Responsibilities Made Easy*, Charles Cresson Wood compiled many of the best practices on cybersecurity program positioning from a variety of industry groups. His module covering this topic, titled "Reporting Relationships," has been condensed and adapted here with permission.

Reporting Relationships

This section covers the generally accepted and frequently encountered reporting relationships for a cybersecurity department. The pros and cons of 12 options and five reporting relationships are explored. Because cybersecurity could occupy one of many places in the organizational hierarchy, you should review the list of pros and cons for each option and consider what is most important in your organization. You should then summarize these considerations in a memo; afterward, you will most likely be leaning in the direction of one of these reporting relationships. At that point, a clear and well-justified proposal for a cybersecurity department reporting relationship can be formulated.

In these successful organizational structures, cybersecurity reports to an executive near the top of the organization's hierarchy. Reporting directly to top management is advisable for the cybersecurity manager or CSO because it fosters objectivity and the ability to perceive what's truly in the best interest of the organization, rather than what's in the best interest of a particular department (such as IT). A highly placed executive in charge of cybersecurity will also be more able to gain management's attention, increasing the likelihood that the cybersecurity department will obtain the necessary budget and staffing resources. A cybersecurity department that reports to a position near the top of the management ladder will also be more able to force compliance with certain requirements, such as a standard specifying consistent implementation of certain encryption technology.

In an increasing number of progressive organizations, being located high on the management ladder means that the cybersecurity manager is a senior vice president who reports directly to the CEO. This is, for example, the organizational structure now found at a well-known credit card company. Organizations that are less dependent on highly visible and impeccable cybersecurity typically have the cybersecurity manager reporting further down on the organizational ladder.

Nonetheless, in some organizations, having a cybersecurity manager who reports directly to the CEO may be appropriate for a short while until major improvements in the cybersecurity area have been made. This temporary reporting structure clearly communicates that cybersecurity is important and worthy of top management's attention. Such a direct reporting relationship with the CEO may exist appropriately for a year or two after a major cybersecurity incident to emphasize the importance of the function both to insiders and outsiders.

The ideal executive to whom the cybersecurity manager reports should in turn report directly to the CEO or a person as high in the organizational hierarchy as possible. This executive's organizational unit will also need a credible day-to-day relationship with the cybersecurity function, or at least a strategic tie-in. For example, a risk and insurance management department would have such a tie-in, but an assembly line operations department most often would not. Although the candidates are many, some common choices are the executive vice president for administrative services and the legal department manager (chief legal officer).

This section refers to several figures that illustrate some common options. These reporting relationships are explored in that sequence. Other options that are not as frequently encountered are discussed as well. The figures are illustrative of real-world organizations and are not meant to be hypothetical or normative. Throughout this section, the author has attempted to be descriptive rather than to propose a new paradigm; in that respect, because these options are based on real-world experience, you can be assured that any of these first five options could be effective within your organization. The figures are also meant to indicate good practice on which you can rely.

Option 1: Information Technology

In the organizational structure shown in Figure 7-5, the cybersecurity department reports to the IT department. The cybersecurity department manager reports directly to the CIO or the vice president of information systems. This option is the most common organizational structure and is usually selected because the manager to whom the cybersecurity manager reports generally has influence with top management and understands IT issues in broad and general terms. This option can also be advantageous because it involves only one manager between the cybersecurity manager and the CEO—generally the CIO. The option is additionally attractive and convenient because the cybersecurity department staff must spend a good deal of time with the IT division staff on a day-to-day basis.

Nonetheless, despite these advantages, this option is flawed because it includes an inherent conflict of interest. When confronted with resource allocation decisions or when required to make trade-offs, the CIO is likely to discriminate against the cybersecurity function. In these cases, other objectives such as cost minimization, enhanced user friendliness, or rapid time-to-market concerns with a new product or service will likely take precedence over cybersecurity. If cybersecurity is seen as just another technological specialty, it will be treated as a routine technical matter, like data administration and other IT subspecialties. Although being part of the IT division is common, it is not as desirable as some of the other options listed in this section and is therefore not recommended.

Note that in Figure 7-5, the cybersecurity function does not report to an intermediate manager who reports in turn to the CIO or the vice president of IT. Having an additional level of management increases the likelihood that messages sent from the cybersecurity department to the CEO will be corrupted in transit or reduced in emphasis (the "whisper down the lane" problem). Other reasons not to pursue this organizational structure are covered later in the "Other Options" section.

Figure 7-5 Wood's option 1: Cybersecurity reporting to an IT division

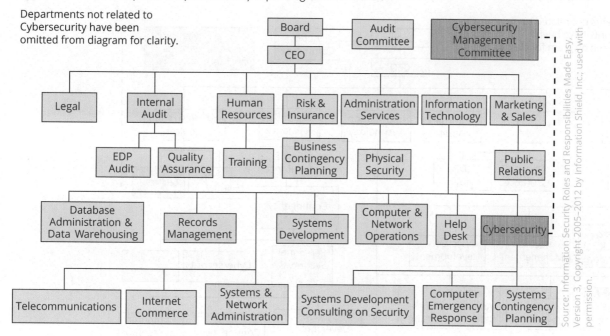

Departments not related to Cybersecurity have been omitted from diagram for clarity.

Source: Information Security Roles and Responsibilities Made Easy, Version 3, Copyright 2005–2012 by Information Shield, Inc.; used with permission.

In Figure 7-5, the cybersecurity manager also has a "dotted-line" reporting relationship with the cybersecurity management committee. A dotted line indicates that employees report to a secondary manager in addition to a primary manager. This secondary reporting line is often used for specific projects, functions, or tasks and typically represents a less formal, indirect structure than a solid-line reporting relationship. Although they are highly recommended, both this dotted-line relationship and the committee can be omitted for smaller organizations. A committee of this nature is a good idea because it provides a sounding board, a management direction-setting body, and a communication path with the rest of the organization. A drawback of such a committee is that it may take longer to get management approval for certain initiatives, but the approval that is obtained is likely to be more lasting and more widely distributed throughout the organization.

Option 2: Security

Another popular option, which again is not necessarily recommended, involves the cybersecurity department reporting to a security division. In this case, the cybersecurity function is perceived to be primarily protective in nature and therefore comparable to the physical security department as well as the personnel security and safety department. Where this organizational design prevails, you may occasionally find that the security division is referred to as the information protection division instead. Shown in Figure 7-6, this approach is desirable because it facilitates communication with others who have both a security perspective and related security responsibilities. This may help with incident investigations as well as reaching practical solutions to problems like laptop computer theft, which involves a combination of physical security and cybersecurity. This option is also desirable because it brings a longer-term preventive viewpoint to cybersecurity activities, which in turn is likely to lower overall cybersecurity costs.

Nonetheless, there are some problems with this structure. Although cybersecurity and physical security may at first seem philosophically aligned, there is a significant cultural difference between the two. For example, cybersecurity staff see themselves as IT professionals, while physical security staff see themselves as criminal justice professionals. These cultural differences may cause some cybersecurity specialists to feel that it is not appropriate to be managed by a specialist in physical security, which will most often be the background of the security division manager. Moreover, this option is undesirable because the budget for physical security at most firms has not increased much over the last few years, but the budget for cybersecurity has rapidly escalated; by combining these two departments under the security division umbrella, top management may underestimate the resources the cybersecurity function needs.

Figure 7-6 Wood's option 2: Cybersecurity reporting to a broadly defined security division

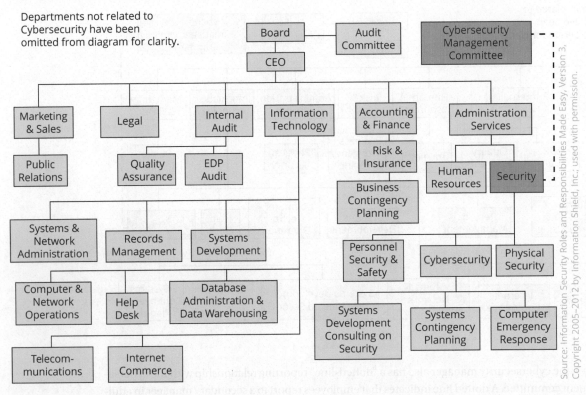

Departments not related to Cybersecurity have been omitted from diagram for clarity.

Option 2 is also undesirable because the security division manager will often lack an appreciation of IT and so may be a poor communicator with top management. In addition, this option involves two managers in the communication path between the security division manager and the CEO. To make it even less appealing, this option could indirectly communicate that the security division is a new type of police; this perspective will make it more difficult for cybersecurity staff to establish consultative relationships with other departments. On balance, this organizational structure is acceptable but not as desirable as some of the others described.

Option 3: Administrative Services

A significant improvement over both options 1 and 2 is shown in Figure 7-7. Here, the cybersecurity department reports to the administrative services division, which could also be called administrative support. In this case, the cybersecurity department manager reports to the administrative services division manager or the vice president of administration. This approach assumes that the cybersecurity department is advisory in nature (also called a staff function) and performs services for workers throughout the organization, much like the Human Resources department. This option is desirable because there is only one manager between the cybersecurity department manager and the CEO. The approach is also advisable because it acknowledges that information and IT are found everywhere throughout the organization and that employees are expected to work with the cybersecurity department. This option is also attractive because it supports efforts to secure information no matter what form it takes, rather than viewing the cybersecurity function as strictly a computer- and network-oriented activity.

In many cases, depending on who fills the position of administrative services vice president, this option suffers because the vice president does not know much about IT, which may hamper their efforts to communicate with the CEO about cybersecurity. This option may also be ill advised for organizations that could severely suffer or even go out of business if major cybersecurity problems were encountered. An Internet products or services organization fits this billing. For these firms, this option does not give cybersecurity the prominence it deserves, nor does it give the organization the strategic and long-term focus that cybersecurity requires. Thus, with this option, the cybersecurity department may be subject to more cost-cutting pressure from top management than it would with option 4 or 5. On balance, though, for organizations that are not highly information-intensive, such as a chain of restaurants, this is a desirable and recommended option.

Figure 7-7   Wood's option 3: Cybersecurity reporting to an administrative services division

Departments not related to Cybersecurity have been omitted from diagram for clarity.

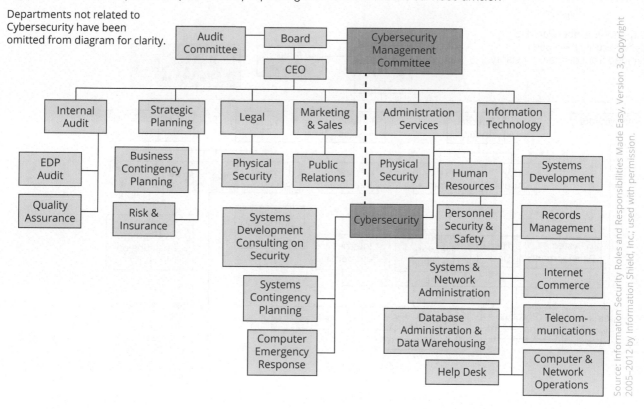

Option 4: Insurance and Risk Management

Figure 7-8 shows how the cybersecurity department can report to the insurance and risk management division. With this approach, the cybersecurity department manager would typically report to the chief risk manager (CRM) or the vice president of risk and insurance management. This option is desirable because it fosters what is often called an integrated risk management perspective. With this viewpoint, a centralized perspective prioritizes and compares all risks across the organization. The application of this idea typically involves assessing the extent of potential losses and the likelihood of losses across all functional departments, including cybersecurity, physical cybersecurity, legal, internal audit, customer relations, accounting, and finance. The intention is to see the big picture and be able to allocate resources to departments and risk management efforts that most need these resources. You are strongly urged to foster the integrated risk management viewpoint, even if the current or proposed organizational structure does not reflect it; cybersecurity is often shown to be a serious and largely unaddressed problem area deserving greater organizational resources and management attention. Beyond integrated risk management, this option is desirable because it involves only one manager between the cybersecurity department manager and the CEO.

The CRM is also likely to be prevention-oriented and to adopt a longer-term viewpoint. In addition, the CRM can engage the CEO in intelligent discussions about risk acceptance (doing nothing), risk mitigation (adding controls), and risk transfer (buying insurance). A CRM is also likely to be comfortable thinking about the future and generating scenarios that reflect several different possibilities, including cybersecurity scenarios such as a denial-of-service (DoS) attack. The CRM, however, is often not familiar with IT, and so may need some special coaching or extra background research from the cybersecurity department manager to make important points with the CEO. Another problem with this approach is that its focus is strategic, and the operational and administrative aspects of cybersecurity, such as changing privileges when people change jobs, may not get the attention they deserve from the CRM. Nonetheless, this is generally a desirable option and is recommended for organizations that are information-intensive, such as banks, stock brokerages, telephone companies, and research institutes.

Figure 7-8   Wood's option 4: Cybersecurity reporting to an insurance and risk management division

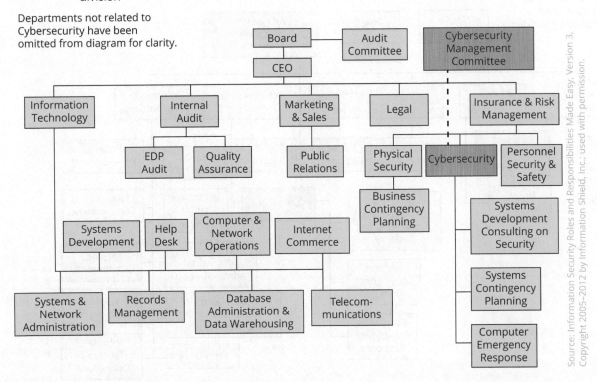

Departments not related to Cybersecurity have been omitted from diagram for clarity.

Source: Information Security Roles and Responsibilities Made Easy, Version 3, Copyright 2005–2012 by Information Shield, Inc.; used with permission.

Option 5: Strategy and Planning

Figure 7-9 illustrates still another possible organizational structure found in the real world. Here, the cybersecurity department reports to the strategy and planning division. In this case, the cybersecurity department manager reports directly to the vice president of strategy and planning. This option views the cybersecurity function as critical to the success of the organization. This option would be appropriate for an Internet products or services organization or a payment card company, both of which are critically dependent on the success of the cybersecurity function. This option is desirable because it involves only one manager between the cybersecurity department manager and the CEO. Thus, the position is just one step down from the option discussed at the beginning of this chapter, where the cybersecurity division manager reports directly to the CEO.

Option 5 is desirable because it underscores the need for documented cybersecurity requirements, such as policies, standards, and procedures, that apply to the entire organization. Like options 3 and 4, this reporting structure also acknowledges the multidepartmental and multidisciplinary nature of cybersecurity tasks such as risk analysis and incident investigations. This option is also advisable because the cybersecurity department works with others that share a scenario-oriented view of the world (they often ask "what if" questions). Another desirable aspect of this approach is that it implicitly communicates that cybersecurity is most importantly a management and people issue, not just a technological issue.

This same advantage can be a disadvantage if workers in the IT department consider the staff in the cybersecurity department to be management-oriented and out of touch when it comes to technology. Of course, the work of the cybersecurity department can clearly communicate that this is a misperception.

One problem with this approach is that the focus is strategic, and the operational and administrative aspects of cybersecurity—for example, changing privileges when people change jobs—may not get the attention that they deserve from the vice president of strategy and planning. On balance, though, this is an advisable reporting relationship for the cybersecurity function and should be something that the cybersecurity department manager is considering for the long run even if they are not proposing it today.

Figure 7-9 Wood's option 5: Cybersecurity reporting to a strategy and planning division

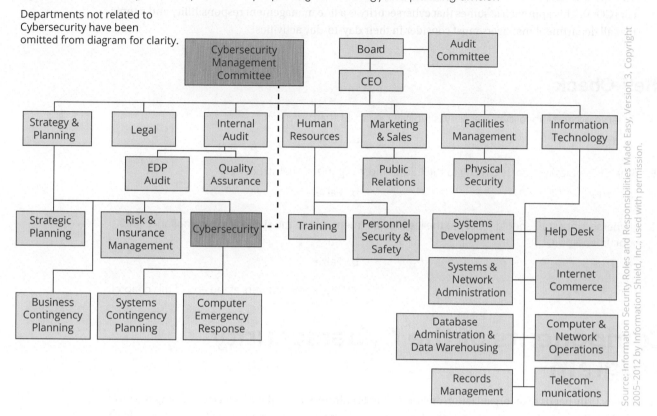

Departments not related to Cybersecurity have been omitted from diagram for clarity.

Source: Information Security Roles and Responsibilities Made Easy, Version 3, Copyright 2005–2012 by Information Shield, Inc.; used with permission.

Other Options

Other options from Wood for positioning the cybersecurity department include the following:

- In the legal division—This option emphasizes copyrights, patents, trademarks, and related mechanisms for intellectual property protection as well as compliance with laws, regulations, and ethical standards such as privacy. An advantage of this reporting structure is that members of the legal department spend a lot of time developing documentation such as policies and procedures; documentation showing that the organization complies with the cybersecurity standard of due care is increasingly important.

- In the internal auditing division, reporting directly to the division manager—Because this division is charged with reviewing the work done by other units, including the cybersecurity department, this reporting structure would yield a conflict of interest.

- Under the help desk—This option is not advised. The help desk is a lower-level technical group that does not get much attention or respect from top management. Also, the help desk does not command many resources, a scarcity that might be carried over into the cybersecurity department.

- Under the accounting and finance division, via the IT department—This option is undesirable because the cybersecurity department would be buried deep in the organizational hierarchy and would therefore not get the resources and top management attention it needs. Also, the needs of the cybersecurity department could be lost or overshadowed by the needs of the accounting and finance divisions.

- Under the human resources division—Both groups develop policies that must be followed by workers throughout the organization. However, this is generally considered an ill-advised position for the cybersecurity department because the human resources division manager often knows very little about information systems and is most often not a credible conduit for communications to top management.

- Reporting to the facilities management division (sometimes called Buildings and Grounds)—With this organizational structure, the cybersecurity department is seen by top management as an asset protection function, much like the physical security department.

- The operations approach—The cybersecurity department manager reports to the chief operating officer (COO). This approach assumes that cybersecurity is a line management responsibility and a topic that all department managers must consider in their day-to-day activities.

Self-Check

4. In large organizations, cybersecurity is typically a part of the IT division.
   a. True   b. False

5. The CSO typically reports directly to the CEO in most organizational structures.
   a. True   b. False

6. Cybersecurity staff should report to the legal department due to the synergies in compliance and documentation.
   a. True   b. False

☐ Check your answers at the end of this chapter.

Components of the Cybersecurity Program

The cybersecurity needs of an organization are unique to its culture, size, and budget. Determining the level at which the cybersecurity program operates depends on the organization's strategic plan, particularly its vision and mission statements. The CIO and CSO should use these two documents to formulate the mission statement for the cybersecurity program.

The National Institute of Standards and Technology (NIST)'s repository provides several documents with guidance for developing the cybersecurity program. An example is Special Publication (SP) 800-12, Rev. 1: "An Introduction to Information Security." Table 7-2 summarizes the essential program elements adapted from several NIST SPs. A related NIST publication, SP 800-100: "Information Security Handbook: A Guide for Managers," was designed to provide guidance for organizational managers in the development of their own cybersecurity programs. The document also covers a variety of topics related to the establishment of a cybersecurity program. These and other NIST resources could be used when reviewing the components of any specific cybersecurity program.

Table 7-2 Elements of a cybersecurity program

Primary Element	Components
Policy	Program policy, issue-specific policy, system-specific policy
Program management	Central cybersecurity program, system-level program
Risk management	Risk assessment, risk mitigation, uncertainty analysis
Life-cycle planning	Security plan, initiation phase, development/acquisition phase, implementation phase, operation/maintenance phase
Personnel/user issues	Staffing, user administration
Preparing for contingencies and disasters	Business plan, identifying resources, developing scenarios, developing strategies, testing and revising the plan

(Continues)

Table 7-2   Elements of a cybersecurity program (*Continued*)

Primary Element	Components
Computer cybersecurity incident handling	Incident detection, reaction, recovery, follow-up
Awareness and training	Security education, training, and awareness (SETA) plans, awareness projects, and policy and procedure training
Security considerations in computer support and operations	Help-desk integration, defending against social engineering, improving system administration
Physical and environmental cybersecurity	Guards, gates, locks and keys, alarms
Identification and authentication	Identification, authentication, passwords, advanced authentication
Logical access control	Access criteria, access control mechanisms
Audit trails	System logs, log review processes, log consolidation and management
Cryptography	Temporal key integrity, virtual private networks, key management, key recovery

Source: National Institute of Standards and Technology

Among the most critical of these components is personnel function and their expectations, roles, responsibilities, and credentials. Maintaining a secure environment requires that the cybersecurity department be carefully structured and staffed with appropriately skilled and screened personnel. It also requires that the proper procedures be integrated into all human resources activities, including hiring, training, promotion, and termination practices.

Note 1 | Many NIST special publications provide additional details and updated discussions of the topics discussed in this section. These documents can be found at https://csrc.nist.gov/publications/sp.

View Point   Building Your Cybersecurity Program from Inside and Outside

By Scott Mackelprang, MS, retired CSO, Asurion, and Paul D. Witman, PhD, Professor Emeritus, California Lutheran University School of Management

Like shoes, cybersecurity programs need to fit their owners, and they need to conform to the objectives and activities of the owners. Just as a ballerina cannot be effective while wearing lumberjack boots and a lumberjack can't be effective while wearing a banker's shoes, your cybersecurity program needs to fit your organization and conform to its activities. Good cybersecurity programs are composed of similar functional elements and employ similar commercial and open-source cybersecurity tools, but in order to be effective, they need to be shaped to reflect important characteristics of the organization they are intended to protect.

It is the cybersecurity leader's job to determine which of the organization's characteristics should be used to design an optimal cybersecurity program. An organization's size, its products and services, its regulatory obligations, and the funding for its cybersecurity function are important considerations in the decision.

Many organizations operate their cybersecurity programs in-house, while others choose to outsource parts of the program to third parties. Some organizations might not be large enough to invest sufficient specialization and expertise in cybersecurity, while other organizations might feel that third parties offer sufficient unique expertise to be worth the cost.

Some industries have cybersecurity requirements defined at least in part by government regulations. Industries such as banking, healthcare, and education come to mind, along with the multiple acronyms for their regulations, such as FFIEC, HIPAA, FERPA, and SOX. Other industries impose regulations on themselves—for example, the credit card processing requirements from the Payment Card Industry Security Standards Council.

If a company develops software to offer highly sensitive services like online banking or healthcare over the Internet, its cybersecurity program must include a focus on secure software development processes, tools, and training. Brick-and-mortar businesses without similar online offerings will likely lack such a focus.

Thinking about your organization's capabilities and its risk tolerance will contribute to discussions about insourcing/outsourcing, funding, and other topics. Insourcing provides greater control; outsourcing often provides access to more specialized resources and skills that may be otherwise unavailable. In addition, the cybersecurity program needs to address not only the explicit outsourcing of cybersecurity activities but the cybersecurity functions performed by all of the organization's suppliers. This includes not just suppliers of technology but also materials and services—supplier issues can manifest in supply chain disruption, indirect cyberattacks, and more.

Good cybersecurity programs have several common elements. They lay out the cybersecurity function's mission and scope of responsibilities. They make clear how the cybersecurity program supports the organization's strategic objectives. They describe the resources, tools, and processes that will be used to accomplish cybersecurity objectives. They openly acknowledge the importance of balancing costs of the program with the benefits of managing cybersecurity risk. They clearly describe the governance functions that ensure consistency of results over time and seek to provide recurring measures of the program's success to senior stakeholders.

Finally, core to every cybersecurity program is an overarching ethical obligation to act in the best interests of the organization's stakeholders, to protect their information and systems, and to manage the organization's risks. This inevitably involves making trade-offs; every decision comes with costs and benefits as well as risks and opportunities. The cybersecurity leader must consider all options for fulfilling the objectives of the cybersecurity program. The purpose must be to ensure the viability and ongoing operations of the organization and the value chain of which they are a part.

Staffing the Cybersecurity Function

Selecting an effective mix of cybersecurity personnel for your organization requires the consideration of several criteria. Some of these criteria are within the control of the organization; others are not, such as the supply and demand for various skills and experience levels. In general, when the demand for any commodity rises quickly, including personnel with critical cybersecurity technical or managerial skills, supply initially fails to meet it. As demand becomes known, new professionals enter the job market and existing professionals refocus to gain the required job skills, experience, and credentials to meet the new demand. Until this new supply can meet the demand, however, competition for the scarce resource will continue to drive up costs (as in salaries). Once the supply is level with or higher than demand, organizations can become more selective and no longer need to pay a premium for those skills. This process swings back and forth like a pendulum because the real economy, unlike an econometric model, is seldom in a state of equilibrium for very long. For example, there was excess demand for experienced enterprise resource planning (ERP) professionals in the 1990s and for experienced COBOL (Common Business-Oriented Language) programmers at the turn of the 21st century because of concerns about Y2K issues. At the time of this writing, the outlook is very good for experienced cybersecurity professionals, and most new entrants to the field find employment. However, funding priorities often prevent massive hiring to meet the demonstrated need for skilled cybersecurity professionals. Many economic forecasters expect hiring in the field to resume at a greater rate as organizations seek to meet the perceived demand for cybersecurity workers. The cold reality is that as long as there are hackers and other bad actors, there will be a need for competent cybersecurity professionals.

Many future jobs taken by students entering school now will have titles and descriptions that do not currently exist. Consider the rapidly evolving areas of the Internet of Things (IoT), generative artificial intelligence, and cloud-based services. These technical areas did not exist a few years ago; the roles that will evolve to protect these and other new technologies demand a flexible approach from future cybersecurity professionals.

The 2022 (ISC)[2] Cybersecurity Workforce Study found that even though almost 4.7 million people worldwide were employed in the field, there was still a gap of approximately 3.4 million workers. The study surveyed 11,779 professionals. The top reasons that organizations reported a shortfall were: (1) they can't find enough talent, (2) they're struggling with turnover or attrition, (3) they aren't paying a competitive wage, and (4) they don't have the budget.

Note 2 | To view the current supply and demand for cybersecurity jobs, nationally or by state, visit www.cyberseek.org/heatmap.html.

Despite this massive shortfall, employers are reporting an increasing expectation for experienced applicants. This has resulted in a severe drop in the number of entry-level jobs while dramatically increasing the number of "senior" positions. This may be the result of layoffs and business closings during the COVID-19 pandemic, a lack of funding for training, or a lack of experience in the organization's current cybersecurity staff to train new entry-level hires.[10]

Defining Qualifications and Requirements

The hiring teams in many organizations may still have questions about which qualifications competent cybersecurity personnel should have. In many cases, cybersecurity positions lack clearly defined roles and responsibilities. To move the cybersecurity discipline forward, organizations should take the following steps:

- The general management community of interest should learn more about the requirements and qualifications for both cybersecurity positions and related IT positions.
- Upper management should learn more about cybersecurity budgetary and personnel needs.
- The IT and general management communities of interest should grant the cybersecurity function—particularly the CSO—an appropriate level of influence and prestige, especially over cybersecurity hiring.

In most cases, organizations look for a technically qualified cybersecurity generalist with a solid understanding of how organizations operate. In many other fields, the more specialized professionals become, the more marketable they are. In cybersecurity, overspecialization may be a drawback, however; if recent trends are an indicator, specializations in vulnerability detection and analysis and other positions in the security operations center will continue to remain a priority for hiring.

Cybersecurity Positions

Standardizing job descriptions can increase the understanding of cybersecurity competencies as well as improve the consistency of roles and responsibilities among organizations. Organizations can find complete cybersecurity job descriptions in Charles Cresson Wood's book, *Information Security Roles and Responsibilities Made Easy, Version 3*. Excerpts from this book are provided later in this chapter.[11]

A study of cybersecurity positions by Schwartz, Erwin, Weafer, and Briney found that the positions can be classified into three types: those that *define*, those that *build*, and those that *administer*:

> Definers provide the policies, guidelines, and standards.[. . .] They're the people who
> do the consulting and the risk assessment, who develop the product and technical

architectures. These are senior people with a lot of broad knowledge, but often not a lot of depth. Then you have the builders. They're the real techies, who create and install cybersecurity solutions.[. . .] Finally, you have the people who operate and administer the cybersecurity tools, the cybersecurity monitoring function, and the people who continuously improve the processes.[. . .] What I find is we often try to use the same people for all of these roles. We use builders all the time.[. . .] If you break your cybersecurity professionals into these three groups, you can recruit them more efficiently, with the policy people being the more senior people, the builders being more technical, and the operating people being those you can train to do a specific task.[12]

A typical medium-sized or large organization will have a small team of dedicated individuals with cybersecurity responsibilities. While the titles used may be different from one organization to the next, most of the job functions fit into one of the following categories:

- CSO (CISO, CCO, or CCSO)
- Security managers
- Security administrators and analysts
- Security technicians and engineers
- Security staffers and watchstanders
- Security consultants
- Security officers and investigators
- Help-desk technicians

Chief Security Officer

Though not usually an executive-level position, the chief security officer (CSO) is the top cybersecurity manager in the organization. The CSO frequently reports directly to the chief information officer (CIO), who is typically the top IT executive in an organization. The CIO usually reports directly to the CEO. Remember that this text uses the title "CSO" to represent either a chief information security officer, chief cybersecurity officer, or other title for the top cybersecurity manager. Some organizations use the title "CSO" to describe an executive who oversees both physical (i.e., corporate) security and cybersecurity areas. Although CSOs are business managers first and technologists second, they must be conversant in all areas of cybersecurity, especially technology, planning, and policy. They are expected to draft or approve a range of cybersecurity policies. They also work with their CIOs and other executive managers on strategic planning, develop tactical plans, and work with cybersecurity managers on operational planning. Finally, they develop cybersecurity budgets based on available funding and make decisions or recommendations about purchasing, project and technology implementation and administration, and the recruiting, hiring, supervision, and firing of cybersecurity staff. Ultimately, the CSO is the spokesperson for the cybersecurity team and is responsible for the overall cybersecurity program.

Qualifications and Position Requirements   The most common qualifications for the CSO include experience working as a cybersecurity manager as well as experience or expertise in planning, policy, and budgets. The most common relevant certifications include the Certified Information Systems Security Professional (CISSP) and the Certified Information Security Manager (CISM), which are described later in this chapter. A bachelor's degree is almost always required and a graduate degree in business, technology, criminal justice, or another related field is common as well.

Employment as a senior cybersecurity professional comes with an expectation of seniority, experience, and skill. Most CSOs are hired from outside the organization based on their performance as a cybersecurity manager at another organization, although it is not uncommon for a CSO to rise through the ranks internally from a lower-level cybersecurity manager position. A lot of CSOs began in technical fields; however, even today there is no clear path from an entry-level position to CSO.

Wood's *Information Security Roles and Responsibilities Made Easy, Version 3* defines and describes the CSO position, which he calls the cybersecurity manager or cybersecurity department manager.

In addition to taking on these roles and responsibilities, CSOs should follow six key principles to shape their careers:

- Practice business engagement—It is important to build professional relationships with key stakeholders in the organization. These relationships become key to understanding the level of investment needed to support various areas of the organization that are outside the CSO's areas of expertise.

- Focus initiatives on what is learned—The knowledge gained from business engagement becomes a tool in developing and prioritizing efforts for the cybersecurity department. Cybersecurity initiatives and strategies will naturally follow the needs of the organization and increase support from stakeholders.

- Align, target, and time initiatives—Once the priority of effort is developed, along with stakeholder buy-in, it is important to convey resource availability and constraints to the organization to maintain organizational support and confidence. This information, along with an understanding of the requirements of the department for both planned and unplanned cybersecurity efforts, will help manage expectations.

- Deliver services—Maintaining a professional "service-oriented" perspective for the organization will enhance the organization's opinion of the cybersecurity department's value. The CSO should focus on communicating with business stakeholders and executive management using appropriate nontechnical language, and emphasize the value-added, return-on-investment contribution of the cybersecurity department.

- Establish and maintain credibility—A CSO should promote the value of the cybersecurity department, highlighting its skill, expertise, and quality of efforts. The CSO should seek to elevate their visibility through internal involvement in the organization and external involvement within the field. This credibility will benefit not only the CSO professionally but the value and reputation of the department within the organization.

- Manage relationships—Finally, the CSO should understand the decision makers in the organization and cultivate professional relationships with them. Having a relationship with other decision makers will enable the CSO to understand better how someone who evaluates alternatives and provides or recommends resource distribution is important.[13]

CSOs, like all cybersecurity professionals, should consider their education as a continuous process of life-long learning. They should expect to be constantly looking for sources of information on new cybersecurity threats, methodologies, approaches, and technologies, regardless of whether such a process is required for a professional certification.

Convergence and the Rise of the True CSO   Some organizations use the title chief cybersecurity officer to differentiate it from a role that might integrate cybersecurity with physical or corporate security. They might reserve the title of CSO for the leader of a converged security operation. Depending on the maturity of the organization, there can be differences in approach regarding cybersecurity and processes. The more mature (and often larger) organizations use the CSO title to identify a role that is responsible for the convergence of physical and IT risks into one complete program to control all those risks. Some, however, simply refer to the senior executive for physical cybersecurity as the CSO and define a role for the CSO that is not integrated into a holistic risk management program. As discussed earlier in this book, convergence of the physical and digital cybersecurity roles is a widely reported and debated consideration in larger organizations around the world.

Cybersecurity Managers

Cybersecurity managers, who report directly to the CSO or may be the CSO in smaller organizations, are responsible for the day-to-day operations of a cybersecurity program. They accomplish objectives identified by the chief cybersecurity officer (as shown in Figure 7-10) and resolve issues identified by the technicians, administrators, analysts, or staffers they supervise. Managing cybersecurity requires an understanding of technology but not necessarily technical mastery—configuration, operation, fault resolution, and so on. Some team leaders or project managers within the cybersecurity community may be responsible for management-like functions, such as planning, scheduling, setting priorities, or administering any number of procedural tasks, but they are not necessarily held accountable for making a particular technology function. Accountability for the actions of others is the hallmark of a true manager and is the criterion that distinguishes actual managers from those whose job titles merely include the word "manager."

Figure 7-10 Cybersecurity roles

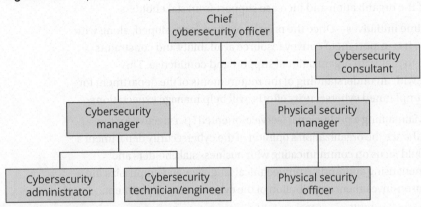

The following list of duties articulates the competencies that organizations usually expect from a cybersecurity manager:

- Providing the organization with cybersecurity oversight:
  - Maintain the current and appropriate body of knowledge necessary to perform the cybersecurity management function.
  - Effectively apply cybersecurity management knowledge to enhance the cybersecurity of networks and associated systems and services.
  - Maintain working knowledge of applicable legislative and regulatory initiatives. Interpret and translate requirements for implementation.
  - Develop appropriate cybersecurity policies, standards, guidelines, and procedures.
  - Work with other organization cybersecurity personnel, committees, and executive management in the governance process.
  - Provide meaningful reports for higher management, prepare effective presentations, and communicate cybersecurity objectives.
  - Participate in short-term and long-term planning.
  - Monitor the cybersecurity program measurement process and evaluate compliance effectiveness.
  - Oversee and conduct cybersecurity reviews and liaise with the broader organization.
  - Coordinate and perform reviews of contracts, projects, and proposals.
  - Assist information units with standards compliance.
  - Oversee the conduct of investigations of cybersecurity violations and computer crimes and work with management and external law enforcement to resolve these issues.
  - Review instances of noncompliance and work tactfully to correct deficiencies.
- Managing the cybersecurity office personnel:
  - Determine positions and personnel necessary to accomplish cybersecurity goals. Request staffing positions, screen personnel, and take the lead in the interviewing and hiring process.

- Develop meaningful job descriptions. Communicate expectations and actively coach personnel for success.

- Prioritize and assign tasks. Review performed work. Challenge staff to better themselves and advance the level of service provided.

- Provide meaningful feedback to staff on an ongoing basis and formally appraise performance annually.

Qualifications and Position Requirements It has become common for a cybersecurity manager to have a CISSP or CISM. These managers must have experience in traditional business activities, including budgeting, project management, personnel management, and hiring and firing, and they must be able to draft middle-level and lower-level policies as well as standards and guidelines. Experience with business continuity planning is usually considered a plus. There are several types of cybersecurity managers, and the people who fill these roles tend to be much more specialized than CSOs. For instance, a risk manager performs a different role than a manager hired to administer the SETA program. A careful reading of the job description can identify exactly what a particular employer is looking for.

Cybersecurity Administrators and Analysts

The cybersecurity administrator—a hybrid position comprising the responsibilities of both a cybersecurity technician and a cybersecurity manager—has technical knowledge and managerial skill. The cybersecurity administrator's role is similar to a systems administrator's or database administrator's role in the IT department. They are frequently called on to manage the day-to-day operations of cybersecurity technology and assist in the development and conduct of training programs, policy, and the like.

The cybersecurity analyst—a specialized cybersecurity administrator responsible for performing systems development life cycle (SDLC) activities in the development of a cybersecurity system or technology—corresponds to a systems analyst in IT. In addition to cybersecurity administration duties, the analyst must examine and design cybersecurity solutions within a specific domain, such as firewalls, intrusion detection systems (IDSs), and antimalware programs. Cybersecurity analysts must be able to identify users' needs and understand the technological complexities and capabilities of the cybersecurity systems they design.

Cybersecurity Technicians and Engineers

A cybersecurity technician—a technical specialist responsible for the selection or development, implementation, and administration of cybersecurity-related technology—is sometimes referred to as a cybersecurity engineer. The cybersecurity technician may configure firewalls and IDPSs, implement cybersecurity applications, diagnose and troubleshoot problems, and coordinate with systems and network administrators to ensure that cybersecurity technical controls are properly implemented. The role of cybersecurity technician can be a typical cybersecurity entry-level position, albeit a technical one. One dilemma for those seeking employment in the field is that it does require a certain level of technical skill, which can be difficult to obtain without experience. As a result, cybersecurity technicians are likely to be IT technicians who have migrated from a different career path.

Like network technicians, cybersecurity technicians tend to be specialized, focusing on one major cybersecurity technology group (e.g., firewalls, IDPSs, servers, routers, and applications) and then further specializing in a particular software or hardware package within the group (such as Palo Alto firewalls, Check Point advanced cybersecurity appliances, or Tripwire IDPSs). These areas are sufficiently complex to warrant this level of specialization. Cybersecurity technicians who want to move up in the corporate hierarchy must expand their technical knowledge horizontally and obtain an understanding of the organizational side of cybersecurity as well as all technical areas.

Qualifications and Position Requirements The technical qualifications and position requirements for a cybersecurity technician vary from one organization to another. Organizations typically prefer expert, certified, proficient technicians. Job requirements usually include some level of experience and possibly certification in a particular hardware or software package. Sometimes, familiarity with a particular technology is enough to secure an applicant an interview; however, experience using the technology is usually required. Wood's *Information Security Roles and Responsibilities Made Easy, Version 3* defines and describes the cybersecurity engineer position, as adapted here. Note that author observations are included in brackets ([ ]).

Job Title   Cybersecurity Engineer

Department: Cybersecurity
Reports to: Cybersecurity Manager
Summary: A cybersecurity engineer provides technical assistance with the design, installation, operation, service, and maintenance of a variety of multiuser cybersecurity systems, such as virtual private networks (VPNs) and cloud-based data replication systems. A hands-on technical specialist, an engineer handles the complex and detailed technical work necessary to establish cybersecurity systems such as firewalls and encryption-based digital signature software. An engineer configures and sets up cybersecurity systems such as IDSs, or trains others, such as access control system administrators, systems administrators, network administrators, and/or database administrators, to do these tasks themselves.

Responsibilities and Duties:

- Provides hands-on cybersecurity technical consulting services to teams of technical specialists working on the integration of shared, centralized, and networked systems. [Examples of such systems include an active data dictionary, a data warehouse, a data mart, and a storage area network (SAN).]

- Provides technical assistance with the initial setup, secure deployment, and proper management of systems that support cybersecurity, including virus detection systems, spyware and adware detection systems, spam filtering systems, content control software systems, website blocking systems, IDSs, intrusion prevention systems (IPSs), and software license management systems. [Other systems of this nature include single sign-on systems, centralized multiplatform access control databases, and enterprise cybersecurity management systems.]

- Offers technical cybersecurity consulting services to distributed personnel who are responsible for one or more cybersecurity systems; these people include network administrators, systems administrators, and database administrators.

- Evaluates IT bug reports, cybersecurity exploit reports, and other cybersecurity notices issued by IT vendors, government agencies, universities, professional associations, and other organizations; makes recommendations as needed to internal management and technical staff to take precautionary steps. [An example of these notices is the periodic reports issued by the Computer Emergency Response Team (CERT) at Carnegie-Mellon University.]

- Acts as the primary technical support liaison in charge of distributing and loading updates to antivirus systems, IDSs, firewalls, data loss prevention systems, and other deployed cybersecurity systems within Company X.

- Configures and tunes one or more IDSs and IPSs to ensure that only authorized personnel have access to Company X systems and networks and that only authorized activity is taking place on Company X systems and networks. [The monitoring of an IDS could be done by computer operations staff, network operations staff, or a monitoring system specialist. Note that a systems administrator may manage a host-based IDS and IPS while the engineer, a monitoring systems specialist, or another technical staff person in the cybersecurity department may manage a network-based IDS and IPS.]

- Runs, or works with others who periodically run, vulnerability identification software packages and related tools to immediately highlight errors in systems configuration, the need for the update of software with fixes and patches, and other cybersecurity-related changes. [Leaving this task solely to systems administrators introduces a conflict of interest because the results of such software will often indicate that systems administrators need to perform additional work. Internal audit staff should also check the status of software updates, patches, and fixes to make sure everything is up to date.]

- Runs, or works with others who periodically run, fixed password-auditing and evaluation software, unauthorized software for wireless network access point detection, and similar tools, and then informs those responsible about the need to change their systems to improve cybersecurity. [The first part of this task may not be necessary if an organization has gotten away from user-chosen fixed passwords and user-chosen encryption keys, perhaps through the use of dynamic passwords along with digital certificates.]

- With management authorization, collects, securely stores, and utilizes software that can perform penetration testing, encryption assessment, and software copyright assessment and attempt to otherwise circumvent cybersecurity measures. [These tools may be critical to off-site recovery efforts, successful cybersecurity incident investigations, and other special-situation cybersecurity-related tasks.]

- Compiles, maintains, and documents a collection of software that can trace the source of and otherwise investigate attacks on Company X systems. [Forensic tools are an example of this software.]

- Acts as a technical consultant on cybersecurity incident investigations and forensic technical analyses. [An example of such a forensic analysis would be determining whether a certain user had been downloading pornography with Company X computers and then deleting these files from their desktop computer.]

- Conducts selected tests of cybersecurity measures in accordance with specific instructions provided by the cybersecurity department manager. [This effort usually includes white-hat penetration tests.]

- Interprets cybersecurity policies, standards, and other requirements as they relate to a specific internal information system and assists with the implementation of these and other cybersecurity requirements.

- Redesigns and reengineers internal information-handling processes so that information is appropriately protected from a variety of problems, including unauthorized disclosure, unauthorized use, inappropriate modification, premature deletion, and unavailability.

- Serves as an active member of the CERT and participates in cybersecurity incident response by having an in-depth knowledge of common cybersecurity exploits, vulnerabilities, and countermeasures.

- Develops technical documentation describing the deployment, configuration, and management of shared, networked, and multiuser cybersecurity systems.

- Regularly attends conferences, professional association meetings, and technical symposia to remain aware of the latest cybersecurity technological developments. [An example would be digital rights management systems.][14]

Cybersecurity Staffers and Watchstanders

A **cybersecurity watchstander**—an entry-level cybersecurity professional responsible for the routine monitoring and operation of a particular cybersecurity technology—is also known as a cybersecurity staffer. The title includes individuals who monitor technical controls and systems and perform other routine administrative roles that support the mission of the cybersecurity department. They may be assigned to an IT service desk or to a security operations center. The role of the watchstander continues to evolve as cybersecurity operations centers become more common in larger organizations. They assist with the research and development of cybersecurity policy, plans, or risk management efforts. In this position, new cybersecurity professionals can learn more about the organization's cybersecurity program before becoming accountable for its administration.

Cybersecurity Consultants

The cybersecurity consultant is typically an independent expert in some aspect of cybersecurity, such as a technical specialty, disaster recovery, business continuity planning, cybersecurity architecture, policy development, or strategic planning. The consultant is usually brought in when the organization decides to outsource one or more aspects of its cybersecurity program. Larger organizations often outsource specific elements of their cybersecurity program to a managed cybersecurity service (MSS) provider. While it is usually preferable to involve a formal cybersecurity services company, qualified individual consultants are available for hire to organizations that do not choose to use an MSS company.

Security Officers and Investigators

Occasionally, the physical (or corporate) security and cybersecurity programs are blended into a single, converged functional unit. When that occurs, several roles are added to the pure IT cybersecurity program, including physical security officers and investigators. Sometimes referred to as the guards, gates, and guns (GGG, or 3G) aspect of security, these roles are often closely related to law enforcement and may rely on employing people trained in law enforcement or criminal justice. Physical security professionals comprise a vital component of cybersecurity; it is a truism that physical access trumps logical cybersecurity in most settings. The aspect of physical security cybersecurity professionals would be most unfamiliar with is the area of personal protection details, which provide executives with "bodyguard" protection, much like the Secret Service does for top politicians.

Help-Desk Personnel

An important part of the cybersecurity team is the help desk, which enhances the team's ability to identify potential problems. When a user calls the help desk with a complaint about their computer, the network, or an Internet connection, the user's problem may turn out to be an indicator of a bigger problem, such as a hacker, a DoS attack, or malware. Because help-desk technicians perform a specialized role in cybersecurity, they may need specialized training. These staff members must be prepared to identify and diagnose both traditional technical problems and threats to cybersecurity. Their ability to do so may cut precious hours off of incident response.

Cybersecurity Professional Credentials

Many organizations rely to some extent on professional certifications to ascertain the level of knowledge and experience possessed by a given candidate. Because some certification programs are relatively new, their precise value may not be fully understood by hiring organizations. The certifying organizations work diligently to educate the cybersecurity community on the value and qualifications of their respective credential holders. Employers struggle to match certifications to position requirements, while potential cybersecurity workers try to determine which certifications will help them in the job market. This section presents several widely recognized cybersecurity certification programs and describes their knowledge domains. A summary of the more managerial certifications is listed in Table 7-3.

Table 7-3 Managerial cybersecurity certifications

(ISC)²		
CISSP	Certified Information Systems Security Professional	
	ISSAP	Information Systems Security Architecture Professional
	ISSEP	Information Systems Security Engineering Professional
	ISSMP	Information Systems Security Management Professional
CGRC	Certified in Governance, Risk, and Compliance	
HCISPP	Health Care Information Security and Privacy Practitioner	

(Continues)

Table 7-3 Managerial cybersecurity certifications (*Continued*)

SSCP	Systems Security Certified Practitioner
Associate of (ISC)²	A professional that has passed one of the previously listed certifications but lacks the experience to receive the credential
ISACA	
CISM	Certified Information Security Manager
CGEIT	Certified in the Governance of Enterprise IT
CRISC	Certified in Risk and Information Systems Control
CISA	Certified Information Systems Auditor
GIAC (SANS Institute)	
GSP	GIAC Security Professional—Any three GIAC Practitioner Certifications plus any two GIAC Applied Knowledge Certifications
GSE	GIAC Security Expert—Any six GIAC Practitioner Certifications plus any four GIAC Applied Knowledge Certifications
EC-Council	
C|CISO	Certified Chief Information Security Officer
E|ISM	Information Security Manager Certification

Sources: isc2.org, isaca.org, giac.org, eccouncil.org

(ISC)² Certifications

The International Information System Security Certification Consortium, or (ISC)², offers several managerial cybersecurity-related certifications, including the widely respected and renowned CISSP. The organization's website is at www.isc2.org.

CISSP The vendor-neutral CISSP certification, considered to be one of the most valuable certifications for cybersecurity professionals, including managers and CSOs, recognizes mastery of an internationally identified common body of knowledge (CBK) in cybersecurity. To sit for the CISSP exam, the candidate must have at least five years of direct, full-time cybersecurity professional work experience in two or more of its eight domains, or four years of direct cybersecurity work experience in two or more domains in addition to a four-year college degree, regional equivalent, or additional (ISC)² credential. Table 7-4 lists the domains of cybersecurity knowledge and their weights on the exam.

Table 7-4 CISSP domains and weights

CISSP Domains	Weight
Asset cybersecurity	10%
Communications and network cybersecurity	13%
Identity and access management	13%
Security and risk management	15%
Security assessment and testing	12%

(Continues)

Table 7-4   CISSP domains and weights (*Continued*)

CISSP Domains	Weight
Security architecture and engineering	13%
Security operations	13%
Software development cybersecurity	11%

Source: (ISC)²[15]

CISSP certification requires both successful completion of the exam and attestation to submitted information, as described in the "The Ultimate Guide to the CISSP." The breadth and depth covered in each of the domains makes CISSP certification one of the most challenging cybersecurity certifications to obtain. Holders of the CISSP must earn continuing education credits every three years, with a minimum annual requirement, to retain the certification. Once candidates successfully complete the exam, they may be required to submit an endorsement by an actively credentialed CISSP or by their employer to validate their professional experience.

CISSP Concentrations   In addition to the major certifications that (ISC)² offers, three concentrations are available for CISSPs to demonstrate advanced knowledge beyond the CISSP CBK. Each concentration requires that the applicant be a CISSP in good standing, pass a separate examination, and maintain the certification in good standing through continuing professional education. These concentrations and their respective areas of knowledge are:

- ISSAP: Information Systems Security Architecture Professional—The CISSP-ISSAP is an appropriate credential if you're a chief security architect or analyst. Typically, you work as an independent consultant or in a similar capacity.[. . .] As the architect, you play a key role in the information security department. Your responsibilities fall between the C-suite and upper managerial level and the implementation of the security program. Although your role is tied closely to technology, it may be closer to the consultative and analytical process of information security. This security architect certification proves your expertise in developing, designing, and analyzing security solutions. It also shows you excel at giving risk-based guidance to senior management in order to meet organizational goals.[16]

- ISSEP: Information Systems Security Engineering Professional—The CISSP-ISSEP is an ideal credential for proving you know how to incorporate security into all facets of business operations.[. . .] This security engineering certification recognizes your keen ability to practically apply systems engineering principles and processes to develop secure systems. You have the knowledge and skills to incorporate security into projects, applications, business processes, and all information systems. The CISSP-ISSEP was developed in conjunction with the U.S. National Security Agency (NSA). It offers an invaluable tool for any systems security engineering professional.[17]

- ISSMP: Information Systems Security Management Professional—You are vital to your organization's success. Prove your knowledge and leadership skills with the CISSP-ISSMP.[. . .] This cybersecurity management certification shows you excel at establishing, presenting, and governing information security programs. You also demonstrate deep management and leadership skills whether you're leading incident handling or a breach mitigation team.[18]

SSCP   Because it is difficult to master all the domains and document the experience requirement of the CISSP certification, many cybersecurity professionals seek other less rigorous certifications, such as (ISC)²'s SSCP certification. Considered more applied than the CISSP, the SSCP questions focus on the operational nature of cybersecurity. The SSCP focuses on practices, roles, and responsibilities as defined by experts from major cybersecurity industries.[19] The SSCP exam covers seven domains: access controls; security operations and administration; risk identification, monitoring, and analysis; incident response and recovery; cryptography; network and communications security; and systems and application security.[20] The seven SSCP domains are not a subset of the CISSP domains, as they contain slightly more technical content. As with the CISSP, SSCP holders must earn continuing education credits to retain their certification.

Other (ISC)² Certifications   In addition to the CISSP, its concentrations, and the SSCP, (ISC)² offers specialized certifications, many of which are discussed elsewhere in the book:

- Certified in Cybersecurity—A first cybersecurity certification covering the foundational knowledge, skills, and abilities expected of an entry-level or junior cybersecurity professional
- Certified Governance, Risk, and Compliance (GRC)—For those with expertise and responsibilities in risk management, risk management framework security governance, and cybersecurity policy
- Certified Cloud Security Professional (CCSP)—For individuals with responsibility for cloud-based systems cybersecurity
- Certified Secure Software Lifecycle Professional (CSSLP)—For individuals with responsibility for the development and implementation of secure software
- Health Care Information Security and Privacy Practitioner (HCISPP)—For individuals working in the healthcare cybersecurity field or with responsibilities to manage, audit, or secure healthcare systems

Associate of (ISC)²   (ISC)² has an innovative approach to the experience requirement in its certification program. The Associate of (ISC)² program is geared toward individuals who want to take any of its certification exams before obtaining the requisite experience for certification. Those who successfully complete an (ISC)² certification examination may promote themselves as an Associate of (ISC)² and may petition (ISC)² for the full certification as soon as they complete the experience requirements.

Note 3 | For more information on (ISC)² and its certification offerings, visit www.isc2.org and www.isc2.org/Certifications/.

ISACA Certifications

Formerly known as the Information Systems Audit and Control Association, ISACA promotes five cybersecurity certifications with managerial content: CISM, Certified in the Governance of Enterprise IT (CGEIT), Certified in Risk and Information Systems Control (CRISC), Certified Data Privacy Solutions Engineer (CDPSE), and Certified Information Systems Auditor (CISA).

CISM   The CISM credential is geared toward experienced cybersecurity managers and others who may have cybersecurity management responsibilities. The CISM can assure executive management that a candidate has the required background needed for effective cybersecurity management and consulting. The CISM examination covers the following practice domains, as described in the "ISACA Exam Candidate Information Guide" and on the ISACA website:

1. Information security governance (17 percent)—This domain will provide you with a thorough insight into the culture, regulations, and structure involved in enterprise governance, as well as enabling you to analyze, plan, and develop information security strategies. Together, this will affirm high-level credibility in information security governance to stakeholders.
2. Information security risk management (20 percent)—This domain empowers you to analyze and identify potential information security risks, threats, and vulnerabilities as well as giving you all the information about identifying and countering information security risks you will require to perform at management level.
3. Information security program (33 percent)—This domain covers the resources, asset classifications, and frameworks for information security as well as empowering you to manage information security programs, including security control, testing, communications, and reporting and implementation.
4. Incident management (30 percent)—This domain provides in-depth training in risk management and preparedness, including how to prepare a business to respond to incidents and guiding recovery. The second module covers the tools, evaluation, and containment methods for incident management.[21]

To be certified, the applicant must:

- Pass the examination.
- Adhere to a code of ethics promulgated by ISACA.
- Pursue continuing education as specified.
- Document five years of cybersecurity work experience with at least three years in cybersecurity management in three of the four defined areas of practice.

CGEIT   Also available from ISACA is the CGEIT certification. The exam is targeted at upper-level executives, including CSOs and CIOs, directors, and consultants with knowledge and experience in IT governance. The CGEIT areas of knowledge include risk management components, making it of interest to upper-level cybersecurity managers. The exam covers the following areas, as described in the "ISACA Exam Candidate Information Guide" and on the ISACA CGEIT website:

1. Framework for the governance of enterprise IT (25 percent)—Ensure the definition, establishment, and management of a framework for the governance of enterprise IT in alignment with the mission, vision, and values of the enterprise.

2. Strategic management (20 percent)—Ensure that IT enables and supports the achievement of enterprise objectives through the integration and alignment of IT strategic plans with enterprise strategic plans.

3. Benefits realization (16 percent)—Ensure that IT-enabled investments are managed to deliver optimized business benefits, that benefit realization outcome and performance measures are established and evaluated, and that progress is reported to key stakeholders.

4. Risk optimization (24 percent)—Ensure that an IT risk management framework exists to identify, analyze, mitigate, manage, monitor, and communicate IT-related business risk, and that the framework for IT risk management is in alignment with the enterprise risk management (ERM) framework.

5. Resource optimization (15 percent)—Ensure the optimization of IT resources, including information, services, infrastructure, applications, and people, to support the achievement of enterprise objectives.[22]

The certification requirements are like those of other ISACA certifications, with a minimum of one year of experience in IT governance and additional experience in at least two of the domains listed.

CRISC   The next ISACA certification is CRISC. The certification positions IT and cybersecurity professionals for careers that link IT risk management with enterprise risk management. The CRISC areas of knowledge include risk management components, making it of interest to upper-level cybersecurity managers. The exam covers the following areas, as described in the "ISACA Exam Candidate Information Guide" and on the ISACA CRISC website:

1. Governance (26 percent)—The governance domain interrogates your knowledge of information about an organization's business and IT environments, organizational strategy, goals, and objectives, and examines potential or realized impacts of IT risk to the organization's business objectives and operations, including enterprise risk management and the Risk Management Framework.

2. IT risk assessment (20 percent)—This domain will certify your knowledge of threats and vulnerabilities to the organization's people, processes, and technology as well as the likelihood and impact of threats, vulnerabilities, and risk scenarios.

3. Risk response and reporting (32 percent)—This domain deals with the development and management of risk treatment plans among key stakeholders, the evaluation of existing controls and improving effectiveness for IT risk mitigation, and the assessment of relevant risk and control information to applicable stakeholders.

4. Information technology and security (22 percent)—In this domain, we interrogate the alignment of business practices with risk management and information security frameworks and standards, as well as the development of a risk-aware culture and implementation of security awareness training.[23]

For a list of supporting tasks expected of a CRISC, visit https://www.isaca.org/credentialing/crisc/crisc-exam-content-outline.

The certification requires the candidate to have a minimum of three years of experience in risk management and IT controls across at least three of the stated domains, although the candidate may elect to take the exam before having the experience. This practice is accepted and encouraged by ISACA, but the candidate will not receive the certification until the experience requirement is met.

CISA The CISA certification, while not specifically a cybersecurity certification, does include many cybersecurity components. ISACA promotes the certification as being appropriate for auditing, networking, and cybersecurity professionals. CISA requirements are as follows:

- Successful completion of the CISA examination
- Experience as a cybersecurity auditor, with a minimum of five years' professional experience in information systems auditing, control, or cybersecurity
- Agreement to the Code of Professional Ethics
- Payment of maintenance fees, a minimum of 20 contact hours of continuing education annually, and a minimum of 120 contact hours during a fixed three-year period
- Adherence to the Information Systems Auditing Standards

GIAC Certifications

The SANS Institute (www.sans.org) sponsors a series of cybersecurity training courses for which a professional can obtain certification from a partner organization—the Global Information Assurance Certification (GIAC; www.giac.org). The SANS Institute offers formal training while GIAC offers certifications. SANS is an acronym for SysAdmin, Audit, Network, and Security.

> GIAC offers two categories of stackable certifications to meet the needs of different professionals: Practitioner Certifications and Applied Knowledge Certifications. Candidates can choose from a wide range of certifications to create a unique portfolio of credentials that demonstrate their expertise in a specific field or across multiple focus areas. Those who build portfolios to become GIAC Security Professionals (GSPs) may choose to advance to the highest level of GIAC certification, the GIAC Security Expert (GSE).
>
> GIAC's Security Professional (GSP) Portfolio Certification is achieved by successfully completing any three Practitioner Certifications and any two Applied Knowledge Certifications. Select your certifications depending on your focus. Your portfolio can be built over any period of time as long as your certifications remain active.
>
> [The] GIAC's Security Expert (GSE) Portfolio Certification is [. . .] achieved by successfully completing any six Practitioner Certifications and any four Applied Knowledge Certifications. Like the GSP, you can take as long as you want to complete your GSE as long as your certifications remain active.[24]

The more than 40 GIAC certifications that comprise these two categories can be pursued with SANS training or without it; the latter option is known as challenge certification. Unlike other certifications, some GIAC certifications require the applicant to complete a written practical assignment that tests the applicant's ability to apply skills and knowledge. These assignments are submitted to the SANS Reading Room for review by cybersecurity practitioners, potential certificate applicants, and others with an interest in cybersecurity. Only when the practical assignment is complete is the candidate allowed to take the online exam.

Note 4 | For more information on GIAC cybersecurity-related certifications, visit www.giac.org/certifications/.

EC-Council Certifications

EC-Council currently offers 25 certifications focusing on ethical hacking, executive management, computer forensics, network security, encryption, penetration testing, incident handling, cloud security, development

security operations, cyber technicians, blockchains, business continuity and disaster recovery, security funda-
mentals, essentials, and application security. Their top cybersecurity management certification is the C|CISO.
See www.eccouncil.org for more information.

The C|CISO   EC-Council's C|CISO certification tests not only cybersecurity domain knowledge but execu-
tive business management knowledge. The C|CISO domains are as follows:

- Governance, Risk, Compliance
- Information Security Controls and Audit Management
- Security Program Management and Operations
- Information Security Core Competencies
- Strategic Planning, Finance, Procurement, and Third-Party Management[25]

Candidates must also have at least five years' experience in at least three of the domains.

Information Security Manager   Individuals who are interested in the C|CISO certification but have
not yet met the experience requirements can consider the Information Security Manager (E|ISM) certification.
The training and courseware content is the same as the C|CISO but allows candidates to take a scaled-down
version of the C|CISO to earn some recognition early in their careers.

CompTIA Certifications

The Computing Technology Industry Association (CompTIA) offered the first vendor-neutral professional IT
certifications—the A+ series. They offer several cybersecurity-related certifications:

- Security+—"Security+ is the first cybersecurity certification a candidate should earn. It establishes
  the core knowledge required in the field and provides a springboard to intermediate-level cybersecurity jobs. Security+ incorporates best practices in hands-on troubleshooting, ensuring you have the
  practical security problem-solving skills required to:
    - Assess the security of an organization and recommend and implement appropriate solutions.
    - Monitor and secure hybrid environments, including cloud, mobile, and IoT.
    - Operate with an awareness of applicable laws and policies, including principles of governance,
      risk, and compliance.
    - Identify, analyze, and respond to security events and incidents."[26]
- Cybersecurity Analyst+ (CySA+)—"Cybersecurity Analyst (CySA+) is a certification for cyber professionals tasked with incident detection, prevention, and response through continuous security monitoring.[. . .] The CompTIA Cybersecurity Analyst (CySA+) certification verifies that successful candidates
  have the knowledge and skills required to leverage intelligence and threat detection techniques, analyze and interpret data, identify and address vulnerabilities, suggest preventative measures, and effectively respond to and recover from incidents."[27]
- CompTIA Advanced Security Practitioner (CASP)—CASP "is an advanced-level cybersecurity certification for security architects and senior security engineers charged with leading and improving an
  enterprise's cybersecurity readiness.[. . .] CASP+ covers the technical knowledge and skills required to
  architect, engineer, integrate, and implement secure solutions across complex environments to support
  a resilient enterprise while considering the impact of governance, risk, and compliance requirements."[28]

Certification Costs

Certifications cost money, and the preferred certifications can be expensive. Individual certification exams can
cost from a few hundred to a few thousand dollars. Certifications that require multiple exams can end up costing several thousand dollars. In addition, the cost for formal training to prepare for the certification exams can
be even more substantial, running into the tens of thousands of dollars. While you should not wholly rely on
certification preparation courses as groundwork for a cybersecurity job, they can help you round out your knowledge and fill in gaps. Some certification exams, such as the CISSP, are very broad; others, such as some of the
GIAC certifications, are detailed and can be very technical. Given the nature of the knowledge needed to pass

the examinations, most experienced professionals find it difficult to do well without at least some review. Many prospective certificate holders engage in individual or group study sessions and purchase an exam study guide.

Certifications are designed to recognize experts in their respective fields, and the cost of certification deters those who might otherwise take the exam just to see if they can pass. Most examinations require that candidates document certain minimum experience requirements before they are permitted to sit for the exams, or before they can receive the certification. Before attempting a certification exam, do your homework. Look into the exam's published body of knowledge as well as its purpose and requirements to ensure that the time and energy needed to pursue the certification are well spent.

Entering the Cybersecurity Profession

Many cybersecurity professionals enter the field after having prior careers in law enforcement or the military, or after careers in other IT areas, such as networking, programming, database administration, or systems administration. Recently, college graduates who have tailored their degree programs to specialize in cybersecurity have begun to enter the field in significant numbers. Figure 7-11 illustrates these possible career paths.

Figure 7-11 Pathways to a cybersecurity career

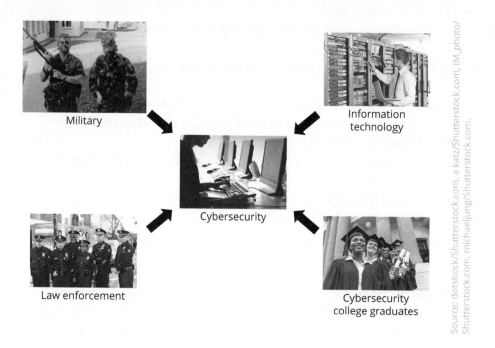

Source: dotshock/Shutterstock.com, a_katz/Shutterstock.com, IM_photo/Shutterstock.com, michaeljung/Shutterstock.com.

Because of a national increase in interest and demand for cybersecurity education, an increasing number of academic programs have cybersecurity content. The NSA's National Cryptologic School and its federal government partners, including the Cybersecurity and Infrastructure Security Agency (CISA), the Federal Bureau of Investigation (FBI), the NIST National Initiative for Cybersecurity Education (NICE), the National Science Foundation (NSF), the Department of Defense (DoD) Office of the Chief Information Officer, and U.S. Cyber Command, jointly sponsor a program to recognize some of the best institutions through the Centers of Academic Excellence (CAE) program.[29] The program was founded by the NSA in 1998. This program has three categories of institutions recognized for meeting formal designation criteria:

- Cyber Defense—The CAE-CD designation is awarded to regionally accredited academic institutions offering cybersecurity degrees and/or certificates at the associate, bachelor's, and graduate levels.
- Cyber Research—The CAE-R designation is awarded to DoD schools, PhD-producing military academies, or regionally accredited, degree-granting four-year institutions rated by the Carnegie Foundation Basic Classification system as either a Doctoral University, Highest Research Activity; Doctoral University, Higher Research Activity; or Doctoral University, Moderate Research Activity.

- Cyber Operations—The CAE-CO program is a deeply technical, interdisciplinary higher education program firmly grounded in the computer science, computer engineering, and/or electrical engineering disciplines, with extensive opportunities for hands-on applications via labs and exercises."[30]

Note 5 | For listings of CAE schools, see the CAE Community Institution Map at www.caecommunity. org/cae-map.

NIST NICE Cyber Workforce Framework

Institutions across the United States are also considering adopting the NICE program promoted by NIST. The NICE Cybersecurity Workforce Framework at www.nist.gov/itl/applied-cybersecurity/nice/resources/ nice-cybersecurity-workforce-framework focuses on seven cybersecurity work domains, some of which are unique to the government and intelligence communities:

- Securely provision—Conceptualizes, designs, and builds secure IT systems, with responsibility for aspects of systems and/or networks development
- Operate and maintain—Provides the support, administration, and maintenance necessary to ensure effective and efficient IT system performance and cybersecurity
- Investigate—Investigates cybersecurity events or crimes related to IT systems, networks, and digital evidence
- Protect and defend—Identifies, analyzes, and mitigates threats to internal IT systems and/or networks
- Collect and operate—Provides specialized denial and deception operations and collection of cybersecurity information that may be used to develop intelligence
- Analyze—Performs highly specialized review and evaluation of incoming cybersecurity information to determine its usefulness for intelligence
- Oversee and govern—Provides leadership, management, direction, or development and advocacy so the organization may effectively conduct cybersecurity work[31]

Many IT professionals believe that cybersecurity professionals must have expertise and experience in some other area of IT. However, IT professionals who move into cybersecurity tend to focus on technical problems and solutions to the exclusion of managerial cybersecurity issues, or they focus on the issue of efficiency over security. Organizations can foster greater professionalism in the cybersecurity discipline by clearly defining their expectations and establishing explicit position descriptions.

Self-Check

7. NIST provides no guidance for developing a cybersecurity program.

   a. True   **b.** False

8. Cybersecurity programs should be tailored to fit the unique needs and characteristics of the organization they are designed to protect.

   a. True   **b.** False

9. The cybersecurity field is experiencing a surplus of professionals, making it easy for organizations to meet their staffing needs.

   a. True   **b.** False

☐ Check your answers at the end of this chapter.

Implementing Security Education, Training, and Awareness Programs

Once the cybersecurity program's place in the organization is established, the next step is planning for a security education, training, and awareness (SETA) program—a program designed to improve the protection of information assets by providing targeted knowledge, skills, and guidance activities for an organization's employees. The SETA program is the responsibility of the CSO and is designed to reduce the incidence of accidental cybersecurity breaches by members of the organization, including employees, contractors, consultants, vendors, and business partners who interact with its information assets. Acts of "human error or failure" (known generally as "errors") are among the top threats to information assets. SETA programs offer three major benefits:

- They can improve employee behavior.
- They can inform members of the organization about where to report violations of policy.
- They enable the organization to hold employees accountable for their actions.

Employee accountability is necessary to ensure that the acts of an individual do not threaten the long-term viability of the entire organization. When employees recognize that the organization protects itself by enforcing accountability, they will be less likely to view these programs as punitive. In fact, when an organization does not enforce accountability, it increases the risk of incurring a substantial loss that might cause it to fail, costing the entire workforce their jobs.

SETA programs enhance cybersecurity behavior from internal and external stakeholders by focusing on cybersecurity policy and best practices. For example, if an organization finds that many employees are using email attachments in an unsafe manner, then email users must be trained or retrained. As a matter of good practice, all SDLC-type projects include user training during both the implementation and maintenance phases. Cybersecurity projects are no different; they require initial training programs as systems are deployed and occasional retraining as needs arise.

A SETA program consists of three elements: cybersecurity education, cybersecurity training, and cybersecurity awareness. An organization may not be able or willing to undertake the development of these components in-house and may therefore outsource them to local educational institutions. Cybersecurity education—the formal delivery of knowledge of cybersecurity issues and operations, usually through institutions of higher learning—is best provided by academic campuses. However, with preparation, an organization can design and deliver its own cybersecurity training, providing users with the knowledge, skill, and ability to use their assigned resources wisely and avoid creating additional risk to information assets. Educational programs can also increase cybersecurity awareness, the process of keeping users conscious of key cybersecurity issues through the use of newsletters, posters, trinkets, and other methods. The purpose of SETA is to enhance cybersecurity in three ways:

- By building in-depth knowledge as needed to design, implement, or operate cybersecurity programs for organizations and their information assets
- By developing skills and knowledge so that computer users can perform their jobs while using information assets more securely
- By improving awareness of the need for methods to protect information assets

Table 7-5 shows some of the features of SETA within the organization, how they are delivered, and how outcomes are assessed.

Table 7-5 Framework of cybersecurity education, training, and awareness

	Awareness	Training	Education
Attribute	Seeks to teach members of the organization what cybersecurity is and what the employee should do in some situations	Seeks to train members of the organization how they should react and respond when threats are encountered in specified situations	Seeks to tell members of the organization why it prepared in the way it has and why it reacts in the ways it does

(Continues)

Table 7-5 Framework of cybersecurity education, training, and awareness (*Continued*)

	Awareness	Training	Education
Level	Offers basic information about threats and responses	Offers more detailed knowledge about detecting threats and teaches skills needed for effective reaction	Offers the background and depth of knowledge to gain insight into how processes are developed and enables ongoing improvement
Objective	Members of the organization can recognize threats and formulate simple responses	Members of the organization can mount effective responses using learned skills	Members of the organization can engage in active defense and use understanding of the organization's objectives to make continuous improvement
Teaching methods	• Media videos • Newsletters • Posters • Informal training	• Formal training • Workshops • Hands-on practice	• Theoretical instruction • Discussions/seminars • Background reading
Assessment	True/false or multiple choice (identify learning)	Problem solving (apply learning)	Essay (interpret learning)
Impact time frame	Short-term	Intermediate	Long-term

Source: NIST SP 800-12

Security Education

Some organizations may have employees within the cybersecurity department who are not prepared by their background or experience for the cybersecurity roles they are supposed to perform. When tactical circumstances allow or strategic imperatives dictate, these employees may be encouraged to obtain formal education. Most organizations defer to institutions of higher education to provide this type of knowledge. Local and regional resources might provide information and services in educational areas.

Cybersecurity education programs must address the following issues:

- The educational components required of all cybersecurity professionals
- The general educational requirements that all IT professionals must have
- General foundational knowledge that all business professionals must understand

Many colleges and universities provide formal coursework in cybersecurity or related fields; see the list of CAE-designated institutions referenced earlier for examples. Unfortunately, most cybersecurity-related degrees (bachelor's or master's) are actually computer science or information systems degrees that include a concentration in cybersecurity. While some programs do offer depth and breadth in cybersecurity education, prospective students must carefully examine the curriculum before enrolling. Students planning for careers in cybersecurity should review the number of courses offered as well as the content of those courses.

Any cybersecurity curriculum needs to include coursework that prepares students to work in a secure and ethical computing environment. As noted by Irvine, Chin, and Frincke in their article "Integrating Security into the Curriculum":

> An educational system that cultivates an appropriate knowledge of computer security will increase the likelihood that the next generation of IT workers will have the background needed to design and develop systems that are engineered to be reliable and secure.[32]

To better define what security professionals should know and do, "The concept for the NICE Framework began before the establishment of NICE in 2010 and grew out of the recognition that the cybersecurity workforce had not been defined and assessed. In 2007, the Department of Homeland Security formed the IT

Security Essential Body of Knowledge (EBK): A Competency and Functional Framework for IT Security Workforce Development. The EBK sought to establish a national baseline representing the essential knowledge and skills that IT security practitioners should possess. The Federal Chief Information Officers Council took on the task in 2008 to build on this and provide a standard framework to understand the cybersecurity roles within the federal government. The first version was posted in September 2012."[33]

Because many institutions have no frame of reference for the knowledge and skills required for a particular job area, they frequently refer to the certifications offered in that field. A managerial program would examine certifications like the CISSP, CISM, or C|CISO described earlier. These certifications would tend to be more "educational" in nature, whereas a technical program would examine the specific GIAC or other technical certifications, which would focus more on training. See the next section, "Education versus Training?", for a delineation between the two topics. As more and more job candidates with formal cybersecurity education apply for security positions, the expectations for such credentials will decrease.

As more institutions of higher education expand their curriculum in cybersecurity-related disciplines, several U.S. and international efforts are underway to classify and document the knowledge areas included in educational programs that identify themselves as being in the realm of cybersecurity. This includes efforts for disciplines that are closely related to cybersecurity topics, such as IT and networking, along with both technical and managerial segments of the cybersecurity disciplines. These efforts should result in a better definition of the knowledge areas included in the many subdisciplines of cybersecurity. Unfortunately, many of the groups that establish these classifications, or even groups like ABET—the Accreditation Board for Engineering and Technology—may be influenced by a biased mindset that prefers one subdomain of security, such as software assurance, over GRC, policy, risk management, and other areas. Students should strive to fully understand the programs they are interested in before enrolling.

Education versus Training?

The lines between education and training are sometimes blurred, meaning that a common question remains: "What is the difference between education and training?" Traditionally, education-related instruction focuses on theoretical foundations, principles, and knowledge-based approaches. Educational instruction tends to emphasize understanding of the *what* much more than the *how* of the concepts in cybersecurity. Training-related instruction tends to be more practical, working to transfer skills and the processes of how certain activities are performed. However, even this explanation tends to leave some people confused. There is an ancient joke in academia that seeks to end some of this confusion: "If you're unclear about the difference between education and training, simply ask yourself this question: Would you rather your 14-year-old daughter receive sex education in school? Or sex training?"

Modern instruction in higher education tends to try to blend theoretical foundation and advanced learning of concepts with some experiential exposure to the subject. This is one reason many textbooks include laboratory exercises. We begin by learning about the theory and then move on to apply that learning to practice.

Within the organization, many activities conducted to introduce and then reinforce key cybersecurity behavior may do the same thing. First, we educate employees on desired behavior through policy, and then we reinforce how they comply with policy through training classes on the technology they use. The better employees master the technology and the better they understand the intent, the less likely they are to make mistakes, and the less likely they are to put the organization's information at risk.

Security Training

Security training involves providing members of the organization with detailed information and hands-on instruction to enable them to perform their duties securely. The organization can develop customized in-house training or outsource all or part of the training program. Alternatively, organizations can subsidize or underwrite industry training conferences and programs offered through professional agencies such as SANS, EC-Council, (ISC)², and the Information Systems Security Association (ISSA; www.issa.org). Many of these programs are too technical for the average employee, but they may be ideal for the continuing education requirements of cybersecurity professionals. Several commercial organizations offer cybersecurity-related training; some provide stand-alone training and awareness materials, while others bundle them with incident management applications or disaster recovery support tools.

Among the most useful documents for cybersecurity practitioners and those developing training programs is NIST SP 800-16, Rev. 1, "A Role-Based Model for Federal Information Technology/Cybersecurity Training." With extensive appendices, this document emphasizes training criteria and standards rather than specific curricula or content. The training criteria are established according to trainees' roles within their organizations and are measured by their on-the-job performance. This emphasis on roles and results rather than on fixed content gives the training requirements flexibility, adaptability, and longevity.[34] This approach makes the document a durable and useful guide. Although it was originally directed toward federal agencies and organizations, its overall approach applies to all types of organizations:

> Federal agencies and organizations cannot protect the integrity, confidentiality, and availability of information in today's highly networked systems environment without ensuring that each person involved understands their roles and responsibilities and is adequately trained to perform them.[35]

SP 800-16, Rev. 1 has been listed as "draft" since 2014 but still provides valuable information on developing and implementing security training.

The Computer Security Act of 1987 requires federal agencies to provide mandatory periodic training in computer cybersecurity awareness and accepted computer practices to all employees involved with the management, use, or operation of the agencies' computer systems. Specific federal requirements for computer cybersecurity training are contained in other federal documents.

Note 6 | For more information on U.S. government employee cybersecurity training, visit the GSA portal at www.gsa.gov/reference/gsa-privacy-program/training-requirements.

The more closely the training is designed to match specific needs, the more effective it is. Training includes teaching users not only what they should or should not do, but also how they should do it. There are many ways to customize training for users. The most common method involves customizing by functional background: general user, managerial user, and technical user.

- Training for general users—General users require training on how to do their jobs securely, including good cybersecurity practices, password management, specialized access controls, and violation reporting. A convenient time to conduct this type of training is during employee orientation. Because employees should have no preconceived notions or established methods of behavior at that point, they are more likely to be receptive to this instruction. This openness is balanced against their lack of familiarity with the systems and their jobs, so any specific issues that they might have questions about will not have arisen yet.

- Training for managerial users—Managers may have the same training requirements as general users, but managers typically expect a more personal form of training characterized by smaller groups and more interaction and discussion. In fact, managers often resist organized training of any kind. This is an area in which a champion can and should exert influence. Support at the executive level can convince managers to attend training events, which in turn reinforces the entire cybersecurity program.

- Training for technical users—Technical training for IT staff, cybersecurity staff, and technically competent general users is more detailed than general user or managerial training, and it may therefore require the use of consultants or outside training organizations. The same categorization methods discussed previously for structuring training can be used for technical users.

Other ways to categorize and specify training include those based on the following:

- Level of awareness—Dividing individuals into groups according to level of awareness may require research to determine how well employees follow computer cybersecurity procedures or understand how computer cybersecurity fits into their jobs.

- General job task or function—Individuals may be grouped as data providers, data processors, or data users.

- Specific job category—Many organizations assign individuals to job categories. As each job category generally has different job responsibilities, training for each will necessarily be different. Examples of job categories are general management, technology management, applications development, and cybersecurity.

- Level of computer knowledge or skill—Computer experts may find a program containing highly technical information more valuable than one covering management issues in computer cybersecurity. Conversely, a novice would benefit more from a training program that presents fundamentals and provides more direct supervision.

- Type of technology or system used—Security techniques used for each off-the-shelf product or application system usually vary. The users of major applications normally require training specific to that application.

The detailed discussion that follows focuses on the development of training by functional area.

Training Techniques

Good training techniques are as essential to successful training as thorough knowledge of the subject area. As explained by Charles Trepper in his article "Training Developers More Efficiently":

> Using the wrong method can actually hinder the transfer of knowledge and lead to unnecessary expense and frustrated, poorly trained employees. Good training programs, regardless of delivery method, take advantage of the latest learning technologies and best practices. Recent developments include less use of centralized public courses and more on-site training. Training is often needed for one or a few individuals, not necessarily for a large group. Waiting until there is a large enough group for a class can cost companies lost productivity. Other best practices include the increased use of short, task-oriented modules and training sessions, available during the normal work week, that are immediate and consistent. Newer concepts in training also provide students with the training they need when they need it—a practice often called just-in-time training.[36]

Delivery Methods

Selection of the training delivery method is not always based on the best outcome for the trainee. Often, other factors like budget, scheduling, and needs of the organization take priority. Table 7-6 lists the most common delivery methods.

Table 7-6   Training delivery methods

Method	Advantages	Disadvantages
One-on-one: A dedicated trainer works with each trainee on the areas specified.	- Informal - Personal - Customized to the needs of the trainee - Can be scheduled to fit the needs of the trainee	- Resource-intensive to the point of being inefficient
Formal class: A single trainer works with multiple trainees in a formal setting.	- Formal training plan, efficient - Trainees able to learn from each other - Interaction possible with trainer - Usually considered cost-effective	- Relatively inflexible - May not be sufficiently responsive to the needs of all trainees - Difficult to schedule, especially if more than one session is needed

(Continues)

Table 7-6   Training delivery methods (*Continued*)

Method	Advantages	Disadvantages
Computer-based training: Prepackaged software provides training at the trainee's workstation.	• Flexible, no special scheduling requirements • Self-paced, can go as fast or as slow as the trainee needs • Can be very cost-effective	• Software can be very expensive • Content may not be customized to the needs of the organization
Distance learning/web seminars: Trainees receive a seminar presentation at their computers. Some models allow teleconferencing for voice feedback; others have text questions and feedback.	• Can be live or can be archived and viewed at the trainee's convenience • Can be inexpensive or free	• If archived, can be very inflexible, with no mechanism for trainee feedback • If live, can be difficult to schedule
User support group: Support from a community of users is commonly facilitated by a particular vendor as a mechanism to augment the support for products or software.	• Allows users to learn from each other • Usually conducted in an informal social setting	• Does not use a formal training model • Centered on a specific topic or product
On-the-job training: Trainees learn the specifics of their jobs while working with the software, hardware, and procedures they will continue to use.	• Very applied to the task at hand • Inexpensive	• A sink-or-swim approach • Can result in substandard work performance until trainee gets up to speed
Self-study: Trainees study materials on their own, usually when not actively performing their jobs.	• Lowest cost to the organization • Places materials in the hands of the trainee • Trainees can select the material they need to focus on the most • Self-paced	• Shifts responsibility for training onto the trainee, with little formal support

Selecting the Training Staff

To provide employee training, an organization can use a local training program, the continuing education department at a local college or university, or another external training agency. Alternatively, it can hire a professional trainer, a consultant, or someone from an academic institution to conduct on-site training. It can also organize and conduct training in-house using its own employees. This last option should not be undertaken without careful consideration. Effective training requires a special set of skills and abilities. Teaching a class of five or more coworkers is very different from offering friendly advice to colleagues.

Implementing Training

While each organization can develop its own strategy based on the techniques discussed previously, the following seven-step methodology generally applies:

- Step 1—Identify program scope, goals, and objectives.
- Step 2—Identify training staff.
- Step 3—Identify target audiences.
- Step 4—Motivate management and employees.
- Step 5—Administer the program.
- Step 6—Maintain the program.
- Step 7—Evaluate the program.[37]

Identify Program Scope, Goals, and Objectives   The scope of the cybersecurity training program should encompass all personnel who interact with information assets and the systems that interact with them. Because users need training that relates directly to their use of particular systems, an organization-wide training program may need to be supplemented by more specific programs targeted at specific groups. Generally, the goal of a cybersecurity training program is to sustain an appropriate level of protection for computer resources by increasing employees' awareness of computer cybersecurity responsibilities and their ability to fulfill them. More specific goals may need to be established as well. Objectives should be defined to meet the organization's specific goals.

Identify Training Staff   Whether the trainer is an in-house expert or a hired professional, the organization should carefully match the capabilities of the training to the needs of the class. It is also vital that the trainer knows how to communicate information and ideas effectively.

Identify Target Audiences   A cybersecurity training program that distinguishes between groups of people, presents only the information needed by the audience, and omits irrelevant information yields the best results. In larger organizations, some individuals will fit into more than one group. In smaller organizations, it may not be necessary to draw distinctions between groups. As discussed previously, employees can also be divided into groups for training according to their characteristics, abilities, or needs.

Motivate Management and Employees   To successfully implement an awareness and training program, it is important to gain the support of both management and employees. For this reason, SETA program designers should consider incorporating motivational techniques. Motivational techniques should demonstrate to management and employees how participation in the cybersecurity training program benefits the organization. To motivate managers, for example, make them aware of the potential for losses and the role of training in computer cybersecurity. Employees must understand how computer cybersecurity benefits them and the organization.

Administer the Program   There are several important things to consider when administering a cybersecurity training program:

- Visibility—The visibility of a cybersecurity training program plays a key role in its success. Efforts to achieve a highly prominent place in the organization should begin during the early stages of developing the cybersecurity training program.
- Methods—The methods used in the cybersecurity training program should be consistent with the material presented and should be tailored to the specific audience's needs. Some training and awareness methods and techniques were listed earlier in the "Training Techniques" section.
- Topics—Topics should be selected based on the audience's requirements.
- Materials—In general, higher-quality training materials are more favorably received but are more expensive. To reduce costs, you can obtain training materials from other organizations. Modifying existing materials is usually cheaper than developing them from scratch.
- Presentation—Presentation issues to consider include the frequency of training (e.g., annually or as needed), the length of presentations (e.g., 20 minutes for general presentations, 1 hour for updates, or 1 business week for an off-site class), and the style of presentation (e.g., formal, informal, computer-based, humorous).

Maintain the Program   Efforts should be made to keep abreast of changes in computer technology and cybersecurity requirements. A training program that meets an organization's needs today may become ineffective if the organization begins using a new application or changes its environment. Likewise, an awareness program can become obsolete if laws, organizational policies, or common usage practices change. For example, if an awareness program uses Thunderbird (a popular email client program) to train employees about a new email usage policy even though the organization currently uses Microsoft Outlook for email, employees may discount the cybersecurity training program and, by association, the importance of cybersecurity.

Evaluate the Program   Organizations can evaluate their training programs by ascertaining how much information is retained, to what extent computer cybersecurity procedures are being followed, and attitudes toward computer cybersecurity. The results of such an evaluation should help identify and correct problems. Some popular evaluation methods are listed here; they can be used in conjunction with one another:

- Using trainee evaluations as feedback
- Observing how well employees follow recommended cybersecurity procedures after being trained
- Testing employees on material after it has been covered in training
- Monitoring the number and kind of computer cybersecurity incidents reported before and after the training program is implemented

Security Awareness

One of the least frequently implemented but most effective cybersecurity methods is the cybersecurity awareness program. As noted in NIST SP 800-12, Rev. 1:

> Often, it is the user community that is recognized as being the weakest link in securing systems. This is due to users not being aware of how their actions may impact the cybersecurity of a system. Making system users aware of their cybersecurity responsibilities and teaching them correct practices helps change their behavior. It also supports individual accountability, which is one of the most important ways to improve cybersecurity. Without knowing the necessary cybersecurity measures or how to use them, users cannot be truly accountable for their actions.[38]

A cybersecurity awareness program strives to keep key cybersecurity issues at the forefront of users' minds daily. This is accomplished by constantly reminding users about the importance of cybersecurity, the consequences of a loss, and how users are responsible for complying with organizational policy and procedures. Awareness serves to instill a sense of responsibility and purpose in employees who handle and manage information, and it leads employees to care more about their work environment. When developing an awareness program, be sure to do the following:

- Focus on people both as part of the problem and as part of the solution.
- Refrain from using technical jargon; speak the language the users understand.
- Use every available venue to access all users.
- Define at least one key learning objective, state it clearly, and provide sufficient detail and coverage to reinforce the learning of it.
- Keep things light; refrain from "preaching" to users.
- Do not overload users with too much detail or too great a volume of information.
- Help users understand their roles in cybersecurity and how a security breach can affect their jobs.
- Take advantage of in-house communications media to deliver messages.
- Make the awareness program formal; plan and document all actions.
- Provide good information early rather than perfect information late.

Susan Hansche, in an article titled "Designing a Security Awareness Program," has this to say about such programs:

> [They should be] supported and led by example from management, simple and straightforward, a continuous effort. They should repeat important messages to ensure they get delivered. They should be entertaining, holding the users' interest and humorous where appropriate in order to make slogans easy to remember. They should tell employees what the dangers are (threats) and how they can help protect the information vital to their jobs.[39]

Employee Behavior and Awareness

Security training and awareness are designed to modify any employee behavior that endangers the security of the organization's information assets. By teaching employees how to properly handle information, use applications, and operate within the organization, the risk of accidental compromise, damage, or destruction of information is reduced. Making employees aware of threats to cybersecurity, the potential damage that can result from these threats, and the ways that these threats can occur increases the probability that employees will take such threats seriously. By making employees aware of policy, the penalties for failure to comply with policy, and the mechanism by which policy violations are discovered, the probability that an employee will intentionally or unintentionally misuse or abuse information is reduced.

Effective training and awareness programs make employees accountable for their actions. As discussed earlier in the book, the legal principle "ignorantia juris non excusat" ("ignorance of the law is not an excuse") applies in a criminal courtroom, but ignorance does excuse employees involved in policy violation penalties in labor disputes, administrative law hearings, or civil court cases. Policy compliance and enforcement become easier when training and awareness programs are in place and effective.

Awareness Techniques

The NIST publication SP 800-12: "An Introduction to Computer Security: The NIST Handbook" describes the essentials of developing effective awareness techniques as follows:

> Awareness can take on different forms for particular audiences. Appropriate awareness for management officials might stress management's pivotal role in establishing organizational attitudes toward cybersecurity. Appropriate awareness for other groups, such as system programmers or information analysts, should address the need for cybersecurity as it relates to their job. In today's systems environment, almost everyone in an organization may have access to system resources and therefore may have the potential to cause harm.[. . .] Effective cybersecurity awareness programs need to be designed with the recognition that people tend to practice a tuning-out process (also known as acclimation). For example, after a while, a cybersecurity poster, no matter how well designed, will be ignored; it will, in effect, simply blend into the environment. For this reason, awareness techniques should be creative and frequently changed.[40]

Developing Security Awareness Components

Many cybersecurity awareness components are available at low cost or virtually no cost, except for the time and energy of the developer. Others can be very expensive if purchased externally. Cybersecurity awareness components include the following:

- Videos
- Posters and banners
- Presentations and conferences
- Computer-based training
- Newsletters
- Brochures and flyers
- Trinkets, such as coffee cups, pens, pencils, and T-shirts
- Bulletin boards

Several of these options are discussed in detail in the following sections.

Cybersecurity Newsletter   A cybersecurity newsletter is the most cost-effective method of disseminating cybersecurity information and news to employees. Newsletters can be disseminated via hard copy, email, or intranet. Newsworthy topics can include new threats to the organization's information assets, the schedule for upcoming cybersecurity classes, and the addition of new cybersecurity personnel. The goal is to keep cybersecurity prominent in users' minds and to stimulate them to be concerned about it. The newsletter could contain articles of interest gleaned from cybersecurity publications and local publications, summaries of policies, and cybersecurity-related activities. It might also include these items:

- Summaries of key policies (one per issue to avoid overloading the reader)
- Summaries of key news articles (one or two each at the national, state, and local levels)
- A calendar of cybersecurity events, including training sessions, presentations, and other activities
- Announcements relevant to cybersecurity, such as planned installations, upgrades, or deployment of new technologies or policies
- How-to articles, such as:

  - How to make sure virus definitions are current
  - How to report an incident
  - How to properly classify, label, and store information
  - How to determine whether email is dangerous
  - How to secure the office before leaving (clean-desk policies)
  - How to avoid tailgaters—those who follow other people closely through controlled entry gates or doors to avoid presenting credentials of their own

The form in which the newsletter is published could vary according to organizational needs. Hard copies, especially in color, may be considered unnecessarily expensive, even if the institution has its own reproduction equipment. Larger organizations may prefer to distribute color Portable Document Format (PDF) copies or even HTML documents via email or intranet. Some companies may choose to create a website and simply email links to users rather than distribute hard copy or send attachments. Figure 7-12 shows a cybersecurity newsletter created as a student project.

Figure 7-12 SETA awareness newsletter

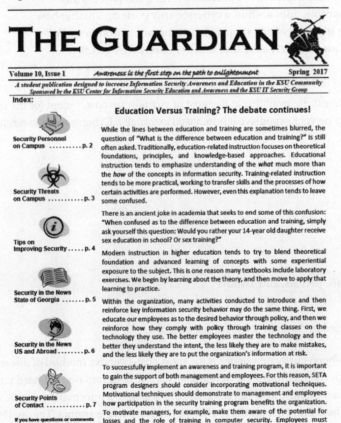

Security Poster   A cybersecurity poster series—which can be displayed in common areas, especially where technology is used—is a simple and inexpensive way to keep cybersecurity on people's minds. The examples shown in Figure 7-13, along with eight others, were developed in one long afternoon, with the bulk of the time spent looking for the right clip art. Professionally developed graphic posters can be quite expensive, so in-house development may be the best solution, especially if the organization has the ability to print on poster-sized paper. (Don't simply copy someone else's work.) If not, most copy shops can enlarge letter-sized copies to poster size.

Figure 7-13   SETA awareness posters

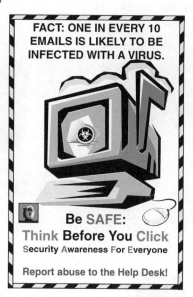

Several keys to a good poster series are:

- Varying the content and keeping posters updated
- Keeping them simple but visually interesting
- Making the message clear
- Providing information on reporting violations

A variation on the poster series is the screen saver slideshow. Many modern operating systems allow you to create a rotating slideshow that you can configure as a screen saver.

Trinket Program   Trinket programs are one of the more expensive options in a cybersecurity awareness program. Trinkets may not cost much on a per-unit basis, but they can be expensive to distribute throughout an organization. Trinkets are everyday items with specialized messages and slogans printed on them, as shown in Figure 7-14. Commonly used trinkets include pens, drink bottles, coffee mugs, hats, T-shirts, and mouse pads. Trinket programs can get people's attention at first, but the messages they impart will eventually be lost unless reinforced by other means.

Figure 7-14   SETA awareness trinkets

Cybersecurity Awareness Website   Organizations can develop webpages or sites dedicated to promoting cybersecurity awareness. As with other SETA awareness methods, the challenge lies in updating the messages frequently enough to keep them fresh. When new information is posted, employees can be informed via email. Newsletters and archived content can reside on the website, along with notices, press releases, awards, and recognitions. As an example, here are some tips from Scott Plous on creating and maintaining an educational website:

1. See what's already out there—Look at what other organizations have done with their cybersecurity awareness websites, but don't infringe on someone else's intellectual property.
2. Plan ahead—Design the website offline before placing it on the Internet or intranet.
3. Keep page loading time to a minimum—Avoid large images and complex, long pages.
4. Appearance matters—Create a themed look and feel for the pages, using templates and visually attractive formats.
5. Seek feedback—Ask others to review your work and accept the best suggestions for improvement.

6. Assume nothing and check everything—Verify your standards by using other computers to view the documents.

7. Spend time promoting your site—Let everyone at the company know it is there. Send notifications when new content is posted.[41]

One final recommendation is to place your website on the organization's intranet. You can then include phone numbers and information not generally released to the public, such as notices of breaches and violations as well as company policies and procedures for handling problems.

Security Awareness Conferences and Presentations Another means of renewing the cybersecurity message is to have a guest speaker or even a mini-conference dedicated to the topic—perhaps in association with International Computer Security Day! Never heard of it? That's not surprising. Even though it's been around since 1988, International Computer Security Day (November 30) is an underpromoted event. If this date does not suit your organization's calendar, you can always choose National Cybersecurity Awareness Month (every October since 2004) or the semiannual National Cybersecurity Days—October 31 and April 4. These dates are aligned with the changes to daylight savings time and are used to raise awareness in the United States on cybersecurity topics and practices. Guest speakers at this event could discuss vital industry-specific cybersecurity issues. Keep in mind the potential drawbacks to using speakers: they seldom speak for free, and few organizations are willing to suspend work for such an event, even a half-day conference.

Note 7 | The SANS Institute has published a useful report that describes how to develop an effective cybersecurity awareness program. You can get the latest version for free by using a search tool to look for "SANS cybersecurity awareness report" and downloading the report.

Self-Check

10. The SETA program is solely the responsibility of the IT department.

   a. True b. False

11. SETA programs only focus on improving employee behavior about cybersecurity.

   a. True b. False

12. Employee training for cybersecurity is customized based on the functional background of the employees.

   a. True b. False

☐ Check your answers at the end of this chapter.

Project Management in Cybersecurity

Another critical component of a cybersecurity manager's skill set is the use of project management—the process of identifying and controlling the resources applied to a project as well as measuring progress and adjusting the process as progress is made toward the goal. Whether the task is to roll out a new cybersecurity training program or to select and implement a new firewall, it is important that the process be managed as a project.

The need for project management skills within cybersecurity may not be evident at first. In fact, this very book emphasizes that cybersecurity is a process, not a project. However, each element of a cybersecurity program must be managed as a project, even if the overall program is perpetually ongoing.

Projects versus Processes

How can cybersecurity be both a process and a project? Cybersecurity is, in fact, a continuous series or chain of projects that comprise a process. As shown in Figure 7-15, each link in this chain of projects could be a specific project. Like a physical chain, it is only as strong as its weakest link. This means cybersecurity professionals should try to acquire and maintain strong project management skills and to sustain high quality in every part of the overall process. Note that each project should be guided by an SDLC methodology, as you will learn in later chapters.

Figure 7-15 A cybersecurity program process chain

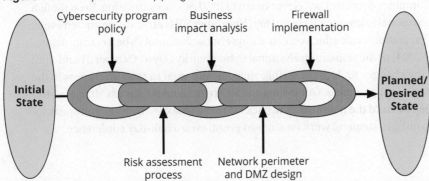

To be sure, some aspects of cybersecurity are not project-based; rather, they are managed processes. These managed processes include the monitoring of the external and internal environments during incident response, ongoing risk assessments of routine operations, and continuous vulnerability assessment and vulnerability repair. These activities are called operations and are ongoing. Projects, on the other hand, are discrete sequences of activities with starting points and defined completion points. A project is different from a process in that it is a temporary activity that is used to create a specific product, service, or end result.[42] Although each individual cybersecurity project may have an end point, larger organizations never completely finish the cybersecurity improvement process. That's why most improvement projects are called continuous improvement. These efforts periodically review progress and realign planning to meet business and IT objectives. This realignment can lead to new goals and projects as well as the modification, cancellation, or reprioritization of existing projects.

Originally developed by W. R. Duncan, the Project Management Institute's "A Guide to the Project Management Body of Knowledge" (PMBOK) defines project management as follows:

> [Project management is] the application of knowledge, skills, tools, and techniques to project activities to meet project requirements. Project management refers to guiding the project work to deliver the intended outcomes. Project teams can achieve the outcomes using a broad range of approaches (e.g., predictive, hybrid, and adaptive)."[43]

In other words, project management, which uses many of the approaches discussed earlier in this chapter, is focused on achieving the objectives of the project. Unlike ongoing operations, project management involves the temporary assembling of a group to complete the project, after which its members are released and perhaps assigned to other projects. Projects are sometimes seen as opportunities for employees and managers to extend their skills toward earning promotions. In organizations that have operations groups and project teams, this can lead to a common pitfall: the "prima donna effect," in which certain groups are perceived as "better" or more skilled than others, and certain projects are perceived as more desirable or beneficial to be involved with. An example is when workers in operations-support roles or software maintenance are seen as less dynamic or capable than their project-focused peers.

Although project management is focused on projects that have end points, this does not mean that these projects are one-time occurrences. Some are iterative and occur regularly. Budgeting processes, for example, are iterative projects—commonly referred to as cyclic projects. Each year, the budget committee meets, designs a proposed budget for the following year, and then presents it to the appropriate manager. The committee may not meet again until six or nine months later, when the next budget cycle begins. Another common practice is the creation of a sequence of projects, with periodic submission of grouped deliverables. Each project phase has a defined set of objectives and deliverables, and the authorization to progress to future phases is tied to the success of the preceding phase as well as availability of funding or other critical resources.

Organizational Support for Project Management

Some organizational cultures have a long record of relying on project management and have put in place training programs and reward structures to develop a cadre of highly skilled project managers and a corresponding group of trained technical personnel. Other organizations implement each project from scratch and define the process as they go. Organizations that make project management skills a priority benefit in the following ways:

- Implementing a methodology—such as the SDLC—ensures that no steps are missed.
- Creating a detailed blueprint of project activities provides a common reference tool and makes all project team members more productive by shortening the learning curve when getting projects underway.
- Identifying specific responsibilities for all involved personnel reduces ambiguity and reduces confusion when individuals are assigned to new or different projects.
- Clearly defining project constraints (including time frame and budget) and minimum quality requirements increases the likelihood that the project will stay within them.
- Establishing performance measures and creating project milestones simplifies project monitoring.
- Identifying deviations in quality, time, or budget early on enables early correction of the problems.

Successful project management relies on careful and realistic project planning coupled with aggressive, proactive control. Project success may be defined differently in each organization, but in general a project is deemed a success when:

- It is completed on time or early.
- It is completed at or below its budgeted amount.
- It meets all specifications outlined in the approved project definition, and the deliverables are accepted by the end user or assigning entity.

To lead effective cybersecurity projects, organizations should assign both technically skilled subject-matter experts and experienced project managers. The goal is to have all elements of the cybersecurity program completed with high-quality deliverables on a timely basis and within budget.

The job posting in Figure 7-16 shows the typical requirements for a cybersecurity analyst. Note that this posting requires project management experience, as do many such positions. Although project management and organizational skills are not included in every job description of a cybersecurity analyst position, many employers seek candidates who couple their cybersecurity focus and skills with strong project management skills. Many consulting firms now offer cybersecurity services in conjunction with, or in the context of, project management.

PMBOK Knowledge Areas

To apply project management to cybersecurity, you must first select an established project management methodology. Cybersecurity project managers often follow methodologies based on the PMBOK discussed earlier, a methodology promoted by the Project Management Institute. Although other project management approaches exist, the PMBOK is considered the industry best practice. This section examines the PMBOK in the context of cybersecurity project management.

Figure 7-16   Example cybersecurity analyst position posting

Cybersecurity Analyst

Reporting to the Manager of Cybersecurity Policy and Compliance, the Cybersecurity Analyst is responsible for cybersecurity policy development and maintenance; design of security policy education, training, and awareness activities; monitoring compliance with organizational IT security policy and applicable law; and coordinating investigation and reporting of security incidents. Working with the Information Technology Systems (ITS) team, monitor, assess, and fine-tune the business continuity and disaster recovery program, perform network vulnerability assessments, application vulnerability assessments, and other risk assessment reviews as assigned.

Responsibilities:

- Monitor and advise on cybersecurity issues related to the systems and workflow to ensure the internal security controls are appropriate and operating as intended.
- Coordinate and execute IT security projects.
- Coordinate response to cybersecurity incidents.
- Develop and publish cybersecurity policies, procedures, standards and guidelines based on knowledge of best practices and compliance requirements.
- Conduct organization-wide data classification assessment and security audits and manage remediation plans.
- Collaborate with IT management, the legal department, safety and security, and law enforcement agencies to manage security vulnerabilities.
- Create, manage, and maintain user security awareness.
- Conduct ongoing security intelligence gathering so as to keep abreast of current security issues.
- Assist ITS in the preparation of documentation, including department policies and procedures, notifications, web content, and ITS alerts
- Actively participate in at least some professional activities and professional societies
- Perform other related duties as assigned.

Requirements:

- BA or BS in Cybersecurity and Assurance, Computer Science, Management Information Systems, or a related field. Advanced degree desirable.
- Five+ years of progressive experience in computing and cybersecurity, including experience with Internet technology and security issues.
- Experience should include security policy development, security education, network penetration testing, application vulnerability assessments, risk analysis and compliance testing.
- CISSP, GIAC, or other security certifications desired.
- Strong project management and organization skills are required.
- Knowledge of cybersecurity standards (ISO 17799/27002, etc.), rules and regulations related to cybersecurity and data confidentiality (FERPA, HIPAA, etc.) and desktop, server, application, database, network security principles for risk identification and analysis.
- Strong analytical and problem solving skills.
- Excellent communication (oral, written, presentation), interpersonal, and consultative skills.

This position requires some weekend and evening assignments as well as availability during off-hours for participation in scheduled and unscheduled activities.

Effective with the seventh edition of the PMBOK, the focus shifts from the knowledge areas to a "tailoring" framework, which reflects the concept that one size may not fit all, allowing the project manager to adapt their project management methodology to the target environment. Under PMBOK 7, the methodology replaces the traditional knowledge areas with eight performance domains. A performance domain is "a group of related activities that are critical for the effective delivery of project outcomes."[44]

The eight performance domains according to the Project Management Institute are as follows:

1. Team—Activities and functions associated with the people who are responsible for producing project deliverables that realize business outcomes
2. Stakeholder—Addresses activities and functions associated with stakeholders
3. Development approach and life cycle—Activities and functions associated with the development approach, cadence, and life-cycle phases of the project
4. Planning—Activities and functions associated with the initial, ongoing, and evolving organization and coordination necessary for delivering project deliverables and outcomes
5. Uncertainty—Activities and functions associated with risk and uncertainty
6. Delivery—Activities and functions associated with delivering the scope and quality that the project was undertaken to achieve
7. Measurement—Activities and functions associated with assessing project performance and taking appropriate actions to maintain acceptable performance

8. Project work—Activities and functions associated with establishing project processes, managing physical resources, and fostering a learning environment[45]

In addition, PMBOK 7 provides 12 project management standards:

1. Be a diligent, respectful, and caring steward.
2. Create a collaborative project team environment.
3. Effectively engage with stakeholders.
4. Focus on value.
5. Recognize, evaluate, and respond to system interactions.
6. Demonstrate leadership behaviors.
7. Tailor based on context.
8. Build quality into processes and deliverables.
9. Navigate complexity.
10. Optimize risk responses.
11. Embrace adaptability and resiliency.
12. Enable change to achieve the envisioned future state.[46]

Dealing with Project Management Issues

When integrating the disparate elements of a complex cybersecurity project, complications are likely to arise. This will require resolving conflict and managing the impact of change. Note that the following issues require clear communication from the project manager to the various stakeholders to raise awareness, get and maintain buy-in, and escalate issues as needed.

When business units do not perceive the need or purpose of a cybersecurity project, they may not fully support it. When IT staff are not completely aligned with the objectives of the project or do not fully understand its impact or criticality, they may be less than fully supportive and may make less than a complete effort to ensure its success. They may even try to sabotage the project. The cybersecurity community must educate, inform, and include the other communities of interest so that cybersecurity projects are afforded the same support as other organizational projects.

Cybersecurity projects often introduce new technologies. Depending on an organization's appetite for risk, a project may execute technology-based controls that are new to the industry as well as the organization. Sometimes, the disparate members of the communities of interest that are needed to make a project successful are not open to new or different technologies, and the project manager becomes engaged in debates about technology selections or is required to build consensus around technology choices. Project team members as well as other workers in the organization may require special training when new technologies are introduced. This increases the risk of turnover because personnel trained in a new, high-demand skill are more likely to leave the organization for opportunities elsewhere. Proactive steps, such as retention bonuses or gain-sharing arrangements, may help mitigate this risk, but the project plan should include contingency standards for personnel turnover.

Project Scope Management   Project scope management ensures that the project plan includes only those activities that are necessary to complete it. Scope creep, the expansion of project deliverables from the original project plan, can undermine many projects once they are underway. Stopping scope creep can pose a challenge to many project managers, who seek to meet the objectives expressed to them by project sponsors. Experienced project managers who have been exposed to scope creep in the past are prepared to ask for a corresponding expansion of project work time, project resources, or both.

Note 8 | For more information about project management, the PMBOK standards, and certification, visit the Project Management Institute website at www.pmi.org.

Self-Check

13. Cybersecurity is solely a project-based activity.
    a. True   b. False

14. Project management skills are unnecessary for cybersecurity professionals.
    a. True   b. False

15. Organizational cultures that prioritize project management skills are likely to have more successful cybersecurity projects.
    a. True   b. False

☐ Check your answers at the end of this chapter.

Closing Case

"Thanks, that was very helpful," Mike Edwards said to the attorney from the corporate legal office, who'd just given a presentation on the SETA requirements of a newly enacted state computer crime and privacy law. "So, when does this law take effect, and how should we comply?"

The attorney gave a full analysis of the company's responsibilities, laying out in concrete terms what the law required of them for a SETA program. Mike then turned to his staff of department managers and said, "It's important that we comply with the new law. Part of this compliance will be to develop a cybersecurity education, training, and awareness program. I need your help to plan our new SETA program."

Case Discussion Questions

1. What elements would you recommend be included in this program?
2. What are the advantages and disadvantages of preparing the SETA program in-house or in hiring a consulting firm to develop it?

Case Ethical Decision Making

Assume that the costs for the proposed SETA program are far greater than the available budget for the current year. Is Mike ethically required to deploy a complete SETA program, as required by law? If Mike is not ethically bound to comply with the law, where does this ethical responsibility lie within the organization?

Summary

A cybersecurity program describes the structure and organization of the effort to contain risks to the information assets of an organization.

In the largest organizations, specific cybersecurity functions are likely to be performed by specialized groups of staff members; in smaller organizations, these functions may be carried out by all members of the department. These functions should be separated into four areas:

- Functions performed by nontechnical areas of the organization outside the IT area of management control
- Functions performed by IT groups outside the cybersecurity area of management control
- Functions performed within the cybersecurity department as a customer service to the organization and its external partners
- Functions performed within the cybersecurity department as a compliance enforcement obligation

Full-time cybersecurity personnel deployment will vary depending on the organization's size:

- Very large organizations may have more than 20 full-time cybersecurity personnel and 40 or more individuals with part-time responsibilities.
- Large organizations will have an average of one to two full-time managers, three to four full-time technicians/administrators, and as many as 16 part-time staff members.
- Medium-sized organizations may have only one full-time cybersecurity person and as many as three individuals with part-time responsibilities.
- Smaller organizations may have either one individual with full-time duties in cybersecurity or one individual who is a part-time manager.

The cybersecurity needs of an organization are unique to its culture, size, and budget and include personnel and the procedures to be integrated into all human resources activities, including hiring, training, promotion, and termination practices.

Selecting an effective mix of cybersecurity personnel for your organization requires that you consider a number of criteria, including standardizing job descriptions using standard roles and titles. These titles include CSO, cybersecurity managers, cybersecurity administrators and analysts, cybersecurity technicians and engineers, cybersecurity staffers and watchstanders, cybersecurity consultants, cybersecurity officers and investigators, and help-desk personnel.

Many organizations rely to some extent on professional certifications to ascertain the level of proficiency possessed by a given candidate. The more salient certifications include those from (ISC)², ISACA, the SANS Institute, EC-Council, and CompTIA.

Many cybersecurity professionals enter the field after prior careers in law enforcement or the military, after careers in other IT areas, or as college graduates who have tailored their degree programs to specialize in cybersecurity.

The NICE Cybersecurity Workforce Framework defines a common means of classifying roles in the discipline of cybersecurity.

The SETA program is the responsibility of the CSO and is designed to reduce the incidence of accidental cybersecurity breaches. SETA programs improve employee behavior and enable the organization to hold employees accountable for their actions.

Training is most effective when it is designed for a specific category of users. Training includes teaching users not only what they should or should not do but also how they should do it.

A cybersecurity awareness program can deliver its message via videos, newsletters, posters, bulletin boards, flyers, demonstrations, briefings, short reminder notices at log-on, talks, or lectures.

Project management is the application of knowledge, skills, tools, and techniques to project activities to meet project requirements. Project management is accomplished through the use of processes that include initiation, planning, execution, controlling, and closing.

Key Terms

chief cybersecurity officer
chief information officer (CIO)
chief security officer (CSO)
cybersecurity administrator
cybersecurity analyst

cybersecurity manager
cybersecurity program
cybersecurity technician
cybersecurity watchstander
project management

scope creep
security education, training, and awareness (SETA) program

Review Questions

1. What is the primary purpose of a cybersecurity program within an organization?

2. How does an organization's culture influence the structure and support of a cybersecurity program?

3. Describe the relationship between organization size and cybersecurity staffing.

4. What are the critical success functions of a cybersecurity program?

5. How does an organization's budget impact a cybersecurity program?

6. What is the strategic importance of aligning cybersecurity programs with organizational culture?

7. What role does training play in a cybersecurity program?

8. How do smaller organizations typically manage cybersecurity?

9. What are some common locations within an organization where the cybersecurity department is positioned?

10. Why might there be a conflict of interest when the cybersecurity department is placed within the IT division?

11. What are the advantages of having the cybersecurity department report directly to the CEO?

12. How does positioning the cybersecurity department outside the IT division benefit an organization?

13. What is the role of a cybersecurity management committee within an organization?

14. Describe an organizational structure where the cybersecurity department reports to an administrative services division.

15. What are some challenges associated with having the cybersecurity department report to a division that handles physical security?

16. Why is it recommended to separate cybersecurity management from IT management in larger organizations?

17. What could be the potential drawbacks of a cybersecurity department reporting to a strategy and planning division?

18. What are some of the elements included in a comprehensive cybersecurity program, according to NIST?

19. What role do the organization's vision and mission statements play in formulating a cybersecurity program?

20. How does a well-structured cybersecurity program incorporate human resources activities?

21. Why do some organizations choose to outsource parts of their cybersecurity program?

22. What are the implications of having cybersecurity requirements defined by government regulations for certain industries?

23. How should cybersecurity programs be tailored to fit an organization?

24. What factors contribute to the shortfall in the cybersecurity workforce?

25. How does the cybersecurity function support an organization's strategic objectives?

26. What is the main purpose of implementing a SETA program in an organization?

27. How does a SETA program enhance employee accountability?

28. What are the three elements of a SETA program, as mentioned in the text?

29. Why might an organization choose to outsource the components of a SETA program?

30. How do cybersecurity education, training, and awareness differ in their approach and objectives?

31. What teaching methods are used in SETA programs to engage different types of learners?

32. What assessment methods are employed in SETA programs to measure the effectiveness of cybersecurity education, training, and awareness?

33. How does continuous retraining in cybersecurity contribute to an organization's security posture?

34. What role does cybersecurity awareness play in the overall security strategy of an organization?

35. What is the role of project management in cybersecurity?

36. What is the importance of project management skills for cybersecurity professionals?

37. How do organizations benefit from prioritizing project management skills?

38. What are some characteristics of project success?

39. What challenges might arise in managing cybersecurity projects, and how should they be addressed?

40. Describe how new technologies impact cybersecurity.

Exercises

1. Assume a smaller organization has a plan to implement a cybersecurity program with three full-time staff and two or three groups of part-time roles from other parts of the business. What titles and roles do you recommend for the three full-time staff? What groups would commonly supply the part-time staff?

2. Assume that you are asked to recommend professional credentials for certain roles in cybersecurity at a larger organization. What is your recommendation for the credential to be held by the CSO? How about for a cybersecurity manager? What would be your recommended certifications for the senior technical

staff? For the last question, pick three technical roles and note the job title and recommended credentials for each.

3. Search the term "security awareness" on the Internet. Choose two or three sites that offer materials and services and describe what they offer.

4. Design three cybersecurity posters on various aspects of cybersecurity using a graphics presentation program and clip art. Bring the posters to class and discuss the methods you used to develop your materials.

5. Examine your institution's website and identify full- and part-time cybersecurity jobs. Create an organizational chart showing the reporting structures for these positions.

Solutions to Self-Check Questions

Organizing for Cybersecurity

1. The term "cybersecurity program" refers specifically to the activities, resources, personnel, and technologies used by an organization to manage its information security risks.
   Answer: a. True.
   Explanation: A cybersecurity program includes the complete set of activities, resources, personnel, and technologies used by an organization to manage risks to its information assets.

2. A strong organizational culture for cybersecurity often results in a smaller, less supported cybersecurity program.
   Answer: b. False.
   Explanation: A strong, positive view of cybersecurity within an organization typically results in a larger and well-supported cybersecurity program.

3. Large organizations spend a greater percentage of their IT budget on cybersecurity compared to smaller organizations.
   Answer: b. False.
   Explanation: Smaller organizations spend a larger proportion of their IT budget on cybersecurity compared to larger organizations, where the cybersecurity budget is a smaller fraction of the total IT budget.

Placing Cybersecurity within an Organization

4. In large organizations, cybersecurity is typically a part of the IT division.
   Answer: a. True.
   Explanation: In large organizations, cybersecurity is often located within an IT division, reflecting a common organizational structure.

5. The CSO typically reports directly to the CEO in most organizational structures.
   Answer: b. False.
   Explanation: It is more common for the CSO to report to the CIO or another executive, rather than directly to the CEO, except in certain high-profile or highly mature organizations.

6. Cybersecurity staff should report to the legal department due to the synergies in compliance and documentation.
   Answer: b. False.
   Explanation: While there are advantages to reporting to the legal department because of compliance and documentation concerns, it is not generally recommended as the primary reporting relationship because other strategic needs are more important.

Components of the Cybersecurity Program

7.   NIST provides no guidance for developing a cybersecurity program.

     Answer: b. False.

     Explanation: NIST's repository offers several guidance documents for developing cybersecurity programs, such as SP 800-12, Rev. 1: "An Introduction to Information Security."

8.   Cybersecurity programs should be tailored to fit the unique needs and characteristics of the organization they are designed to protect.

     Answer: a. True.

     Explanation: Cybersecurity programs need to fit their owners and conform to the objectives and activities of the owner, suggesting customization to the organization's needs.

9.   The cybersecurity field is experiencing a surplus of professionals, making it easy for organizations to meet their staffing needs.

     Answer: b. False.

     Explanation: The chapter notes a significant shortfall in the cybersecurity workforce, with an estimated gap of approximately 3.4 million workers despite nearly 4.7 million people being employed in the field.

Implementing Security Education, Training, and Awareness Programs

10. The SETA program is solely the responsibility of the IT department.

     Answer: b. False.

     Explanation: The SETA program is the responsibility of the CSO, and it involves multiple members of the organization, including employees, contractors, and business partners.

11. SETA programs only focus on improving employee behavior about cybersecurity.

     Answer: b. False.

     Explanation: While improving employee behavior is a major benefit of SETA programs, they also inform members about policy violation reporting and enhance accountability for employee actions.

12. Employee training for cybersecurity is customized based on the functional background of the employees.

     Answer: a. True.

     Explanation: The training is often customized to match specific needs, including the functional background of the employees, making it more effective.

Project Management in Cybersecurity

13. Cybersecurity is solely a project-based activity.

     Answer: b. False.

     Explanation: Cybersecurity is a continuous series or chain of projects, meaning it comprises both project-based and ongoing process activities.

14. Project management skills are unnecessary for cybersecurity professionals.

     Answer: b. False.

     Explanation: Cybersecurity professionals should acquire and maintain strong project management skills to ensure the high quality of each aspect of cybersecurity.

15. Organizational cultures that prioritize project management skills are likely to have more successful cybersecurity projects.

     Answer: a. True.

     Explanation: Organizations that make project management skills a priority benefit in several ways, such as implementing methodologies that ensure no steps are missed and creating detailed project plans that improve productivity.

Cybersecurity Management Models

Chapter Objectives

After reading this chapter and completing the exercises, you should be able to:

1   Describe the dominant cybersecurity management models, including national and international standards-based models.

2   Differentiate cybersecurity architecture models.

3   Explain why access control is an essential element of cybersecurity management.

4   Identify characteristics of the academic access control models.

> Security can only be achieved through constant change, through discarding old ideas that have outlived their usefulness and adapting others to current facts.
>
> —William O. Douglas, U.S. Supreme Court Justice (1898–1980)

Case Opener

Iris looked at the mound of documents on her desk. Each one was neatly labeled with its own number and acronym: NIST, ISO, COBIT, and so on. Her head was swimming. She had not imagined that it would be quite so difficult to choose a cybersecurity management model for her review of the ongoing cybersecurity program at Random Widget Works (RWW). She wanted an independent framework that would allow her to perform a thorough analysis of RWW's program. Iris had known that networking with her colleagues was important, but this set of references was a concrete example of the benefits of staying professionally engaged.

She was almost finished skimming the stack when she found what she was looking for: a document that contained a self-assessment checklist with page after page of key items in the management of cybersecurity. In fact, there were 18 *categories* of control elements to be considered, each with several individual items to be evaluated. Iris found the full document on the web and downloaded it. After making some changes, she created copies for the managers who worked for her and then scheduled a meeting.

At the meeting, the risk assessment and policy manager seemed surprised. "Gee, Iris," he said, "when did you have time to design this checklist?"

"I didn't," Iris replied. "I was lucky enough to find one that was close enough for us. I just changed a few items to make it specific to our needs."

Iris then quickly outlined her plan. Using the checklist, each manager would indicate the progress that RWW had made in that area—specifically, whether policy had been created and, if so, whether it had been integrated into the company culture. Iris explained how to use the forms and noted when she expected the assessment to be complete.

"What happens once we're done?" one manager asked.

"That's when the real work begins," Iris said. "We'll establish priorities for improving the areas that need revision and sustaining the areas that are satisfactory. Then we'll determine whether we have the resources to accomplish that work; if not, I'll go to the CIO and request more resources."

Introduction to Cybersecurity Blueprints, Frameworks, and Models

In this chapter, you will learn about the various cybersecurity management models, including access control models and cybersecurity architecture models. Cybersecurity models are standards that are used for reference or comparison and often serve as the stepping-off point for emulation and adoption. A methodology is simply a formal way of accomplishing a task, and it is usually recommended or endorsed by an organization or group of experts in a particular field. One way to select a cybersecurity methodology is to adapt an existing cybersecurity management model or set of practices. Several published cybersecurity models and frameworks exist, including options from government agencies and standards organizations that are presented later in this chapter. Because each cybersecurity environment is unique, you may need to adapt portions of different frameworks; what works well for one organization may not precisely fit another.

The communities of interest accountable for cybersecurity in an organization must design a working cybersecurity plan and then select and use a management model to execute and maintain that plan. This effort usually begins with the creation or selection of a cybersecurity framework, followed by the development of a cybersecurity blueprint that describes existing controls and identifies other necessary cybersecurity controls. The terms "framework," "model," and "blueprint" are closely related. A cybersecurity framework or model is a specification to be followed during the design, selection, and initial and ongoing implementation of a cybersecurity program, including cybersecurity policies, cybersecurity education and training programs, and technological controls. This specification is a generic outline of a more thorough cybersecurity blueprint—a framework or model customized to an organization, including implementation details. In some organizations, all three terms are used interchangeably, but here we distinguish the terms predominantly on the level of detail provided. As shown in the case opener, a chief security officer may review several cybersecurity models before selecting one for the organization and then add sufficient implementation details to create a blueprint. The framework or model describes what the end product should look like, while the blueprint includes information on how to get there and is customized to a specific organization. Think of it like building a house or other structure. First you select a model you like, and then you modify and customize it into a blueprint for the building you want.

To generate a usable cybersecurity blueprint, most organizations draw on established cybersecurity frameworks, models, and practices. Some of these models are proprietary and are only available for a fee; others are relatively inexpensive, such as standards from the International Organization for Standardization (ISO) and the Information Systems Audit and Control Association (ISACA). Others are free, like those from the National Institute of Standards and Technology (NIST) and a variety of other sources. The model you choose must be flexible, scalable, robust, and sufficiently detailed.

Another way to create a blueprint is to look at the paths taken by other organizations. In this kind of benchmarking, you follow the recommended practices or industry standards. Benchmarking, as discussed in detail in the next chapter, is the comparison of two related measurements—for example, comparing how many hours of unscheduled downtime your company had last year with the average hours of unscheduled downtime in all the companies in your industry. Is your performance better or worse than the average? Benchmarking can be used for both internal and external comparisons. Internal benchmarking, known as baselining, involves comparing an organization's performance at some defined point against current or expected performance.

External benchmarking involves comparing one's organizational results against similar organizations. Benchmarking can provide details on how controls are working or which new controls should be considered, but it does not provide implementation details for how controls should be put into action.

Cybersecurity Management Models

It sometimes seems that there are as many cybersecurity management models as there are consultants who offer them. Among the most accessible places to find a high-quality cybersecurity management model are federal agencies and international standard-setting organizations.

Some of the documents discussed in detail in the following sections are proprietary. Organizations that want to adopt proprietary models must purchase the right to do so. Alternatively, some public domain sources for cybersecurity management models offer free documentation. In the forefront of this category are documents provided by NIST's Computer Security Resource Center (http://csrc.nist.gov). This resource houses many publications, including cybersecurity management models and practices. Several chapters of this book refer to these publications. Other organizations provide freely accessible documentation for review to their memberships or for a fee to the public. Open and proprietary sources are described in the rest of this chapter.

The ISO 27000 Series

One of the most widely referenced cybersecurity management models is the Information Technology–Code of Practice for Information Security Management, which was originally published as British Standard BS7799. In 2000, the Code of Practice was adopted as an international standard framework for cybersecurity by the ISO and the International Electrotechnical Commission (IEC) as ISO/IEC 17799. The document was revised in 2005 (becoming ISO 17799:2005), and in 2007, it was renamed ISO 27002 to align it with the ISO 27001 document, which is discussed later in this chapter. While the details of ISO/IEC 27002:2022 (the most recent version) are only available to those who purchase the standard, its structure and general organization are well known. The 27002:2022 table of contents is shown in Table 8-1.

Table 8-1   ISO/IEC 27002:2022 table of contents

Foreword
0. Introduction
1. Scope
2. Normative references
3. Terms and definitions
4. Structure of this standard
5. Organizational controls
6. People controls
7. Physical controls
8. Technological controls
Annex A Using attributes
A.1 General
A.2 Organizational views
Annex B Correspondence of ISO/IEC 27002:2022 with ISO/IEC 27002: 2013
Bibliography

Source: ISO 27002:2022

The original purpose of ISO/IEC 17799 was to offer guidance for the management of cybersecurity to individuals responsible for their organizations' cybersecurity programs. According to 27000.org, the standard was "intended to provide a common basis for developing organizational cybersecurity standards and effective cybersecurity management practice and to provide confidence in interorganizational dealings."[1] ISO 27002, the successor to 17799, continues that focus. Where ISO/IEC 27002 is focused on a broad overview of the various areas of cybersecurity, providing information on 127 controls over 10 areas, ISO/IEC 27001 provides information on how to implement ISO/IEC 27002 and how to set up an information security management system (ISMS). As shown in Figure 8-1, ISO 27001 has moved from its previous Plan-Do-Check-Act format to a more formal and comprehensive approach to implementing the ISO 27002 control structure.

Figure 8-1   ISO/IEC 27001:2022 major process steps

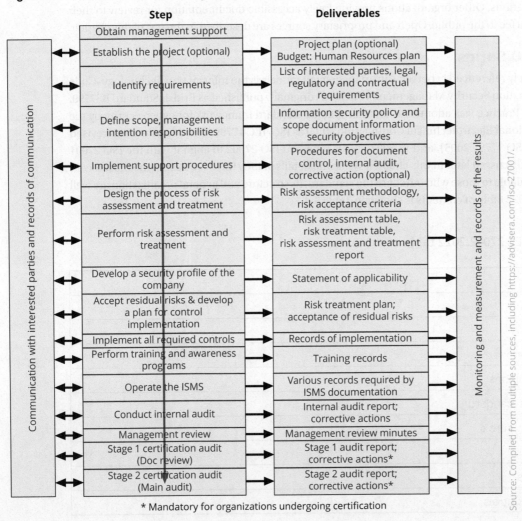

Source: Compiled from multiple sources, including https://advisera.com/iso-27001/.

* Mandatory for organizations undergoing certification

The ISO/IEC 27000 series of standards forms an increasingly important framework for the management of cybersecurity. It is rapidly becoming more significant to U.S. organizations, especially large to very large organizations obligated to follow industry standards that leverage the ISO/IEC 27000 series of standards and organizations that operate in the European Union or are otherwise obliged to meet its terms. Table 8-2 illustrates the sections of ISO 27001:2022.

The stated purpose of ISO/IEC 27002, as derived from its ISO/IEC 17799 origins, is to:

> offer guidelines and voluntary directions for cybersecurity management. It is meant to provide a high-level, general description of the areas currently considered important when initiating, implementing, or maintaining cybersecurity in an organization. . . . The document specifically identifies itself as "a starting point for developing organization-specific guidance." It states that not all of the guidance and controls it contains may be applicable and that additional controls not contained may be required. It is not intended to give definitive details or "how-to's."[2]

Table 8-2   ISO 27001:2022 table of contents

Foreword
0. Introduction
1. Scope
2. Normative references
3. Terms and definitions
4. Context of the organization
5. Leadership
6. Planning
7. Support
8. Operation
9. Performance evaluation
10. Improvement
Annex A (normative) information security controls reference
Bibliography

Source: ISO 27001 toolkit

ISO/IEC 27002:2022 is a broad overview of the various areas of cybersecurity. It provides information on four general control categories (organizational, people, physical, and technological) and addresses 93 individual controls. Its companion document, ISO/IEC 27001:2022, provides information for how to implement ISO/IEC 27002 and set up an ISMS. ISO/IEC 27001's primary purpose is to be used as a standard so organizations can adopt it to obtain certification demonstrating the implementation of a good cybersecurity program; ISO 27001 serves better as an assessment tool than as an implementation framework. ISO 27002 provides more detailed information about implementing these cybersecurity controls.

Note 1 | For a free guide to ISO 27001, download the ISO27k Toolkit from www.iso27001security.com/html/toolkit.html.

In 2007, the ISO announced plans for the numbering of current and impending standards related to cybersecurity issues and topics. Table 8-3 provides a list of ISO 27000 documents that are currently issued or planned.

Table 8-3   ISO 27000 series current and planned standards[3]

ISO/IEC 27000 Series Standard	Title or Topic	Comment
27000:2018	Series Overview and Terminology	Defines terminology and vocabulary for the standard series; this publication is free to download
27001:2022	Security Management System Specification	Draws from BS7799:2
27002:2022	Code of Practice for Security Management	Renumbered from ISO/IEC 17799; draws from BS7799:1
27003:2017	Security Management Systems Implementation Guidance	Guidelines for project planning requirements for implementing an ISMS
27004:2016	Security Measurements	Performance measure for cybersecurity management decisions
27005:2022	ISMS Risk Management	Supports 27001 but doesn't recommend any specific risk method
27006:2015	Requirements for Bodies Providing Audit and Certification of an ISMS	Largely intended to support the accreditation of certification bodies providing ISMS certification
27007:2020	Guidelines for ISMS Auditing	Focuses on management systems
27008:2019	Guidelines for Security Auditing	Focuses on cybersecurity controls
27010:2015	Guidelines for Inter-sector and Inter-organizational Communications	Focuses on communications about cybersecurity controls between industries, especially critical infrastructure
27011:2016	Guidelines for Telecomm Organizations	Focuses on cybersecurity practices of telecommunications-based organizations–both internal cybersecurity and cybersecurity of client data
27013:2021	Guideline on the Integrated Implementation of ISO/IEC 20000-1 and ISO/IEC 27001	Support for implementing an integrated dual management system
27014:2020	Security Governance Framework	ISO's approach to cybersecurity governance–guidance on evaluating, directing, monitoring, and communicating cybersecurity
27015:2012	Security Management Guidelines for Financial Services	Guidance for financial services organizations
27016:2014	Security and Organizational Economics	Provides insight into the financial justification of cybersecurity activities and services
27017:2015	Code of practice for cybersecurity controls for cloud computing services based on ISO/IEC 27002	Focuses on cybersecurity safeguards and practices for vendors offering cloud services
27018:2019	Code of practice for protection of personal identifiable information (PII) in public clouds acting as PII processors	Aimed at ensuring that cloud service providers are protecting client information stored in their clouds
27019:2017	Security management guidelines for process control systems specific to the energy industry	Focused on helping organizations in the energy industry implement ISO standards

(Continues)

Table 8-3 ISO 27000 series current and planned standards *(Continued)*

ISO/IEC 27000 Series Standard	Title or Topic	Comment
27021:2017	Competency requirements for ISMS professionals	Describes the knowledge and skills expected of ISMS professionals
27022:2021	Guidance on ISMS processes	Defines a process reference model for use in establishing a "process-oriented" approach to ISMSs
27023:2015	Mapping the revised editions of ISO/IEC 27001 and 27002	Provides a transition guide for organizations familiar with older versions of these documents

Note 2 | For a complete listing of the ISO 27000 standards currently available and planned for future publication, visit www.iso27001security.com/html/iso27000.html or go to the ISO catalog at www.iso.org/committee/45306/x/catalogue/.

NIST Cybersecurity Publications

Other approaches to structuring cybersecurity management are found in the many documents available from NIST's Computer Security Resource Center. These documents enjoy two notable advantages over many other sources of cybersecurity information: (1) They are publicly available at no charge and (2) they have been available for some time; thus, they have been broadly reviewed by government and industry professionals. You can use the NIST special publication (SP) documents discussed earlier in this book to help design a custom cybersecurity framework for your organization's cybersecurity program. The most relevant NIST SPs relative to cybersecurity management are listed here.

SP 800-12, Rev. 1: An Introduction to Information Security (2017) This document serves as a starting point for those with little or no background in cybersecurity. It provides the following:

1. Introduction to the special publication
2. Elements of cybersecurity:
    2.1 Cybersecurity supports the mission of the organization.
    2.2 Cybersecurity is an integral element of sound management.
    2.3 Cybersecurity protections are implemented to be commensurate with risk.
    2.4 Cybersecurity roles and responsibilities are made explicit.
    2.5 Cybersecurity responsibilities for system owners go beyond their own organization.
    2.6 Cybersecurity requires a comprehensive and integrated approach.
        2.6.1 Interdependencies of cybersecurity controls
        2.6.2 Other interdependencies
    2.7 Cybersecurity is assessed and monitored regularly.
    2.8 Cybersecurity is constrained by societal and cultural factors.
3. Key roles and responsibilities for both industry and government sectors
4. An overview of threats and vulnerabilities, including sources and events (attacks)
5. The three NIST cybersecurity policy categories: program policy (EISP), issue-specific policy (ISSP), and system-specific policy (SysSP)

6. An overview of the NIST Risk Management Framework and its use in risk management
7. Discussion of systems assurance, including authorization, engineering, and operations assurance
8. Cybersecurity considerations in systems support and operations
9. A discussion of the foundations and application of cryptography
10. The NIST control "families" that form the foundation of the NIST cybersecurity model:

    10.1 Access Control (AC)

    10.2 Awareness and Training (AT)

    10.3 Audit and Accountability (AU)

    10.4 Security Assessment and Authorization (CA)

    10.5 Configuration Management (CM)

    10.6 Contingency Planning (CP)

    10.7 Identification and Authentication (IA)

    10.8 Incident Response (IR)

    10.9 Maintenance (MA)

    10.10 Media Protection (MP)

    10.11 Physical and Environmental Security (PE)

    10.12 Planning (PL)

    10.13 Personnel Security (PS)

    10.14 Risk Assessment (RA)

    10.15 System and Services Acquisition (SA)

    10.16 System and Communication Protection (SC)

    10.17 System and Information Integrity (SI)

    10.18 Program Management (PM)

SP 800-18, Rev. 1: Guide for Developing Security Plans for Federal Information Systems (2006)

This guide provides detailed methods for assessing, designing, and implementing controls and plans for applications of various sizes. It serves as a guide for the cybersecurity planning activities described later and for the overall cybersecurity planning process. In addition, this document includes templates for major application cybersecurity plans. As with any publication of this scope and magnitude, SP 800-18 must be customized to fit the particular needs of the organization.

SP 800-30, Rev. 1: Guide for Conducting Risk Assessments (2012)

This guide provides a foundation for the development of an effective risk management program, and it contains both the definitions and the practical guidance necessary for assessing and mitigating risks identified within information technology (IT) systems. The ultimate goal is to help organizations better manage IT-related mission risks. The document is organized into three modules that explain the overall risk management process as well as preparing for, conducting, and communicating a risk assessment. The original document, SP 800-30, was functionally replaced by SP 800-53, Rev. 5. The document was substantially revised, and SP 800-30, Rev. 1 became a process document for the subtask of conducting risk assessment.

SP 800-34, Rev. 1: Contingency Planning Guide for Federal Information Systems (2010)

This guide defines the seven-stage methodology for responding to an event requiring disaster recovery operations. The guide also provides an overview of business continuity strategies and methods.

1. Develop the contingency planning policy statement. A formal policy provides the authority and guidance necessary to develop an effective contingency plan.
2. Conduct the business impact analysis (BIA). The BIA helps identify and prioritize information systems and components critical to supporting the organization's mission and business processes. A template for developing the BIA is provided to assist the user.

3. Identify preventive controls. Measures taken to reduce the effects of system disruptions can increase system availability and reduce contingency life cycle costs.

4. Create contingency strategies. Thorough recovery strategies ensure that the system may be recovered quickly and effectively following a disruption.

5. Develop an information system contingency plan. The contingency plan should contain detailed guidance and procedures for restoring a damaged system; it should be unique to the system's cybersecurity impact level and recovery requirements.

6. Ensure plan testing, training, and exercises. Testing validates recovery capabilities, whereas training prepares recovery personnel for plan activation and exercising the plan identifies planning gaps; combined, the activities improve plan effectiveness and overall organization preparedness.

7. Ensure plan maintenance. The plan should be a living document that is updated regularly to remain current with system enhancements and organizational changes.[4]

This document, when combined with NIST SP 800-61 (discussed later in this section), forms the basis for all incident response, disaster recovery, and business continuity discussions in this text.

SP 800-37, Rev. 2: Risk Management Framework for Information Systems and Organizations: A System Life Cycle Approach for Security and Privacy (2018)

As discussed in an earlier chapter, this document continues the NIST Risk Management Framework (RMF) program and provides additional guidance for its use.

SP 800-39: Managing Information Security Risk: Organization, Mission, and Information System View (2011)

This SP provides additional discussion on the higher-level functions associated with risk management, as discussed in a previous chapter.

SP 800-53, Rev. 5: Security and Privacy Controls for Information Systems and Organizations (2020)

This SP provides detailed information on the NIST family of cybersecurity controls and "a more holistic approach to cybersecurity and risk management by providing organizations with the breadth and depth of cybersecurity controls necessary to fundamentally strengthen their information systems and the environments in which those systems operate—contributing to systems that are more resilient in the face of cyberattacks and other threats. This 'Build It Right' strategy is coupled with a variety of cybersecurity controls for 'Continuous Monitoring' to give organizations near real-time information that is essential for senior leaders making ongoing risk-based decisions affecting their critical missions and business functions."[5]

This SP also discusses the use of controls as part of planned baselines of varying rigor (low, moderate, and high cybersecurity).

SP 800-53A, Rev. 5: Assessing Security and Privacy Controls in Information Systems and Organizations (2022)

The companion guide to SP 800-53, Rev. 5 and the functional successor to SP 800-26: "Security Self-Assessment Guide for Information Technology Systems," this SP provides a systems development life cycle approach to cybersecurity assessment of information systems. It takes the controls of SP 800-53 and "provides guidance for implementing specific steps in the Risk Management Framework (RMF). Special Publication 800-53 covers Step 2 in the RMF, cybersecurity, and privacy control selection (i.e., determining what controls are needed to manage risks to organizational operations and assets, individuals, other organizations, and the nation). Special Publication 800-53A covers RMF Step 4, Assess, and RMF Step 6, Monitor, and provides guidance on the cybersecurity assessment and privacy assessment processes. This guidance includes how to build effective assessment plans and how to analyze and manage assessment results."[6]

SP 800-55, Rev. 1: Performance Measurement Guide for Security (2008)

This SP provides guidance on the development and implementation of a performance measurement program, including the selection of key performance measures related to cybersecurity, to support an organization's continuous improvement program. As discussed in the following chapter, performance measures are used to assess the relative performance of the cybersecurity program and to report the successes and shortfalls to senior management as part of a governance program. In 2024, NIST published draft updates to SP 800-55, Rev. 1 titled SP 800-55, Vol. 1: "Measurement Guide for Information Security—Identifying and Selecting Measures" and SP 800-55, Vol. 2: "Measurement Guide for Information Security—Developing an Information Security Measurement Program." Once finalized, these documents will functionally replace SP 800-55, Rev. 1.

SP 800-61, Rev. 2: Computer Security Incident Handling Guide (2012)   This SP provides a methodology and specific measures for responding to computer incidents. This SP also provides guidance on the development of policy and plans for designing and implementing an incident response (IR) program. This text merges the methodology in SP 800-61 with that of NIST SP 800-34, Rev. 1, resulting in a comprehensive contingency planning program for an organization that also includes disaster recovery, business continuity, and crisis management. In 2024, NIST published a draft of SP 800-61, Rev. 3: "Incident Response Recommendations and Considerations for Cybersecurity Risk Management: A CSF 2.0 Community Profile" as the planned successor to Rev. 2.

SP 800-100: Information Security Handbook: A Guide for Managers (2007)   This SP serves as the managerial tutorial equivalent of SP 800-12, providing overviews of the roles and responsibilities of a cybersecurity manager in the development, administration, and improvement of a cybersecurity program. Topics covered include:

1. Cybersecurity governance
2. Systems development life cycles and the cybersecurity activities therein
3. Security education, training, and awareness (SETA)
4. Capital planning and investment controls for cybersecurity
5. Interconnecting systems and the cybersecurity issues therein
6. Performance measures, as described in NIST SP 800-55, Rev. 1
7. Cybersecurity planning
8. IT contingency planning, as described in NIST SP 800-34, Rev. 1
9. Risk management, as described in multiple SPs
10. Certification, accreditation, and cybersecurity assessments
11. Cybersecurity services and products acquisition
12. Incident response
13. Configuration management[7]

NIST has released a pre-draft (call for comments) version of SP 800-100, Rev. 1, which is available from the NIST publications site.

SP 800-184: Guide for Cybersecurity Event Recovery (2016)   This guide provides a significant update and extension to NIST SP 800-61 both in terms of methodology and approach. This SP extends the roles and responsibilities of those involved in incident response to include a tactical-to-strategic approach on the latter stages of IR—recovery and program improvement—involving management in the performance measures and continuous improvement administration of the IR program as well as technicians responsible for the recovery of technology and information assets from cybersecurity-related incidents.

SP 800-221: Enterprise Impact of Information and Communications Technology Risk: Governing and Managing ICT Risk Programs within an Enterprise Risk Portfolio (2023)   This SP is focused on supporting the management of risk to information and communications technologies (ICT) as part of an overall risk management program. It includes discussion of aggregating risks

Figure 8-2 NIST cybersecurity control assessment process overview

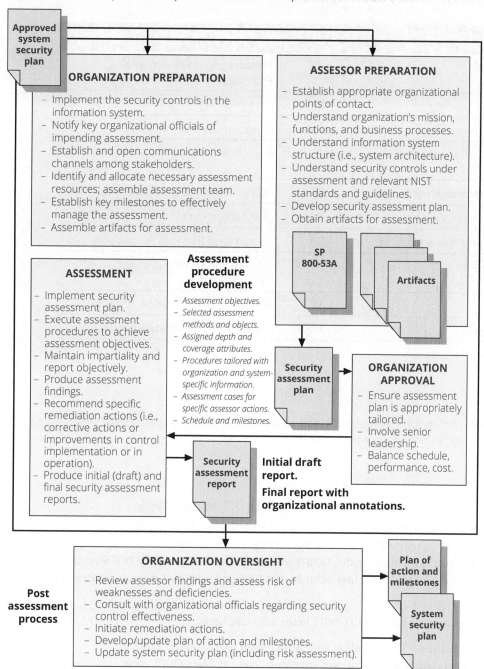

and resources to facilitate risk assessment and the creation and administration of "risk registers" as part of the RM program.

As shown in Figure 8-2, NIST has a comprehensive cybersecurity control assessment program that guides organizations through the preparation for, assessment of, and remediation of critical cybersecurity controls.

The controls recommended by NIST in this family of SPs are organized into "families" of controls, as mentioned earlier. These families, along with a managerial family called "Program Management," are used to structure the protection of information and are part of the NIST cybersecurity control assessment methodology. The controls are classified according to the three-category system used by NIST and are presented in Table 8-4.

Table 8-4   Cybersecurity and privacy control families[8]

ID	Family	ID	Family
AC	Access Control	PE	Physical and Environmental Protection
AT	Awareness and Training	PL	Planning
AU	Audit and Accountability	PM	Program Management
CA	Assessment, Authorization, and Monitoring	PS	Personnel Security
CM	Configuration Management	PT	PII Processing and Transparency
CP	Contingency Planning	RA	Risk Assessment
IA	Identification and Authentication	SA	System and Services Acquisition
IR	Incident Response	SC	System and Communications Protection
MA	Maintenance	SI	System and Information Integrity
MP	Media Protection	SR	Supply Chain Risk Management

Source: NIST 800-53, Rev. 5

Note 3 | The NIST special publications referenced in this chapter can be accessed along with many others at the NIST Computer Security Resource Center (https://csrc.nist.gov).

Control Objectives for Information and Related Technology

Control Objectives for Information and Related Technology (COBIT) provides advice about the implementation of sound controls and control objectives for cybersecurity. This document can be used not only as a planning tool for cybersecurity but also as a control model. COBIT was created by ISACA and the IT Governance Institute in 1992. Documentation on COBIT was first published in 1996 and was most recently updated in 2019. According to ISACA:

> COBIT 2019 improves on prior versions of COBIT in the following areas:
>
> - Flexibility and openness—The definition and use of design factors allow COBIT to be tailored for better alignment with a user's particular context. The COBIT open architecture enables adding new focus areas (see section 4.4) or modifying existing ones, without direct implications for the structure and content of the COBIT core model.
> - Currency and relevance—The COBIT model supports referencing and alignment to concepts originating in other sources (e.g., the latest IT standards and compliance regulations).
> - Prescriptive application—Models such as COBIT can be descriptive and prescriptive. The COBIT conceptual model is constructed and presented such that its instantiation (i.e., the application of tailored COBIT governance components) is perceived as a prescription for a tailored IT governance system.

- Performance management of IT—The structure of the COBIT performance management model is integrated into the conceptual model. The maturity and capability concepts are introduced for better alignment with Capability Maturity Model Integration. COBIT guidance uses the terms "governance of enterprise information and technology," "enterprise governance of information and technology," "governance of IT," and "IT governance" interchangeably.[9]

In COBIT 2019, ISACA uses an approach based on six principles for a governance system and three principles for a governance framework.

1. Each enterprise needs a governance system to satisfy stakeholder needs and to generate value from the use of information and technology (I&T). Value reflects a balance among benefits, risk, and resources, and enterprises need an actionable strategy and governance system to realize this value.

2. A governance system for enterprise I&T is built from a number of components that can be of different types and that work together in a holistic way.

3. A governance system should be dynamic. This means that each time one or more of the design factors are changed (e.g., a change in strategy or technology), the impact of these changes on the Enterprise Governance of Information and Technology (EGIT) system must be considered. A dynamic view of EGIT will lead toward a viable and future-proof EGIT system.

4. A governance system should clearly distinguish between governance and management activities and structures.

5. A governance system should be tailored to the enterprise's needs, using a set of design factors as parameters to customize and prioritize the governance system components.

6. A governance system should cover the enterprise end to end, focusing not only on the IT function but on all technology and information processing the enterprise puts in place to achieve its goals, regardless of where the processing is located in the enterprise.[10]

The COBIT 2019 principles for a governance framework are:

1. A governance framework should be based on a conceptual model, identifying the key components and relationships among components, to maximize consistency and allow automation.

2. A governance framework should be open and flexible. It should allow the addition of new content and the ability to address new issues in the most flexible way while maintaining integrity and consistency.

3. A governance framework should align to relevant major related standards, frameworks, and regulations.[11]

The principles and enablers of this governance framework are dependent on employees' skills and abilities within their organization. The primary enabler, "principles, policies, and frameworks," is depicted as guiding and affecting the others.

Although COBIT was designed to be an IT governance and management structure, it includes a framework to support cybersecurity requirements and assessment needs. Organizations that incorporate COBIT assessments into their IT management are better prepared for general cybersecurity risk management operations.

Note 4 | ISACA has developed a complete library of resources to support the COBIT 5 framework. It is available from ISACA at www.isaca.org/resources/cobit.

Committee of Sponsoring Organizations

Another control-based model is that of the Committee of Sponsoring Organizations (COSO) of the Treadway Commission, a private-sector initiative formed in 1985. Its major objective is to identify the factors that cause fraudulent financial reporting and to make recommendations to reduce its incidence. COSO has established a common definition of internal controls, standards, and criteria against which companies and organizations can assess their control systems.[12] COSO also helps organizations comply with critical regulations like the Sarbanes-Oxley Act of 2002. This framework was issued in 1992 and updated in 2013, with supplemental guidance published in 2023.

COSO Definitions and Key Concepts   According to COSO:

> [I]nternal control is a process, effected by an entity's board of directors, management, and other personnel, designed to provide reasonable assurance regarding the achievement of objectives in the following categories:
>
> - Effectiveness and efficiency of operations
> - Reliability of financial reporting
> - Compliance with applicable laws and regulations[13]

COSO describes its key concepts as follows:

> The COSO Internal Control–Integrated Framework (the Framework) outlines the components, principles, and factors necessary for an organization to effectively manage its risks through the implementation of internal control. There should be neither "gaps" in addressing risk and control nor unnecessary or unintentional duplication of effort.
>
> The Three Lines of Defense (the Model) addresses how specific duties related to risk and control could be assigned and coordinated within an organization, regardless of its size or complexity. In particular, the Model clarifies the difference and relationship between the organizations' assurance and other monitoring activities—activities that can be misunderstood if not clearly defined.[14]

COSO Framework   The COSO framework is built on five interrelated components. Again, while COSO is designed to serve as a framework that can describe and analyze internal control systems, some of those internal control systems are on IT systems that incorporate cybersecurity controls. COSO's five components are as follows:

- Control environment—This is the foundation of all internal control components. The environmental factors include integrity, ethical values, management's operating style, delegation of authority systems, and the processes for managing and developing people in the organization.
- Risk assessment—This assists in the identification and examination of valid risks to the organization's defined objectives. It can also include assessment of risks to information assets.
- Control activities—This includes policies and procedures that support management directives. These activities occur throughout the organization and include approvals, authorizations, verifications, reconciliations, reviews of operating performance, cybersecurity of assets, and segregation of duties.
- Information and communication—This encompasses the delivery of reports—regulatory, financial, and otherwise. Effective communications should also include those made to third parties and other stakeholders.
- Monitoring—This set of continuous or discrete activities ensures that internal control systems are functioning as expected; internal control deficiencies detected during these monitoring activities should be reported upstream, and corrective actions should be taken to ensure continuous improvement of the system.[15]

Note 5 | For free guidance from COSO on fraud deterrence, enterprise risk management, internal controls, and governance, visit www.coso.org and select a topic from the Guidance menu.

Information Technology Infrastructure Library

The Information Technology Infrastructure Library (ITIL) is a collection of methods and practices for managing the development and operation of IT infrastructures. It has been produced as a series of books, each of which covers an IT management topic. The names "ITIL" and "IT Infrastructure Library" are registered trademarks of the United Kingdom's Office of Government Commerce. Because ITIL includes a detailed description of many significant IT-related practices, it can be tailored to many IT organizations. You can see how the major elements of ITIL fit together in Figure 8-3.

Figure 8-3   Major elements of ITIL

Information Security Governance Framework

The Information Security Governance Framework is a managerial model provided by the National Cyber Security Partnership, an industry working group, and was the result of developmental efforts by the National Cyber Security Summit Task Force.[16] The framework, discussed in an earlier chapter, provides guidance in the development and implementation of an organization's cybersecurity governance structure and recommends the responsibilities that various members should have in an organization, including the following:

- Board of directors/trustees—Provide strategic oversight for cybersecurity.
- Senior executives—Provide oversight of a comprehensive cybersecurity program for the entire organization.
- Executive team members who report to a senior executive—Oversee the organization's cybersecurity policies and practices.
- Senior managers—Provide cybersecurity for the information and information systems that support the operations and assets under their control.
- All employees and users—Maintain cybersecurity of information and information systems accessible to them.

The framework specifies that each independent organizational unit should develop, document, and implement a cybersecurity program consistent with the guidance of accepted cybersecurity practices such as ISO/IEC 27001. This program should provide cybersecurity for the information and information systems that support the operations and assets of the organizational unit, including those provided or managed by another organizational unit, contractor, or other source. The document also recommends that each organization establish clear, effective, and periodic reporting about its cybersecurity program from each organizational unit and that each unit perform a regular evaluation to validate the effectiveness of its cybersecurity program.[17]

Verizon Cybersecurity Management Canvas

The Verizon cybersecurity consulting group publishes a periodic report on payment security focused on the successful implementation and management of Payment Card Industry Data Security Standard (PCI DSS) programs. The content can provide additional insight into management of cybersecurity as well. In the 2023 edition, Verizon outlines The Security Management Canvas (TSMC):

> The Security Management Canvas provides a single view of the entire security and compliance management process. It presents the foundational blocks of an effective management system. The design and implementation of a program based on TSMC structure can produce highly valuable, essential documents and produce the exact input needed to make important decisions throughout the program life cycle.[18]

The TSMC promotes five pillars with supporting documentation to facilitate security management:

1. Security business model (SBM): "An overarching model that ties all the elements together. It facilitates obtaining support for investment in security and compliance. The business model defines objectives and the structure of core processes to deliver maximum value to stakeholders. It supports the alignment between the strategy operations, security frameworks, and security program."[19]

   Key SBM documents: Business model, Value proposition, Stakeholders, Goals and objectives, Core processes architecture, Resources, Culture, Regulations, Risk management, Governance

2. Security strategy: "Defines the approach and determines the careful selection and prioritization of security compliance objectives—guiding the allocation of resources. The strategy defines the what and the why but not the how-to. To be successful, the security strategy must be aligned with the security business model."[20]

   Key strategy documents: Strategy, Stakeholders, Priorities (goals, objectives), Scope (focus, in-scope, excluded), Resources (in-house, third-party)

3. Security operating model (SOM): "A collection of documents that presents the functional components within your security and compliance operations. It aligns resources and core processes and visually presents how value is created for the organization from the security and compliance operations. It's great for diagnosing performance issues, such as understanding how your control environment functions and where improvements are needed. You have a current operating model but also need a target operating model to define how your operations should improve."[21]

   Key SOM documents: Operations (value chains, visual representation), Stakeholder relationships, Organizational charts, Geographic maps (facilities and operations), Organizational processes (core processes, supporting processes), Security processes, Network architecture, Functional responsibilities, Capabilities map, Constraints map

4. Frameworks and standards (F&A): "Act as support guides for your security and compliance management system. They drive the structure of your program and projects. Their success is determined by how well you implement them."[22]

   Key F&A documents: Integration of security frameworks and standards, PCI DSS, PCI PIN, PCI P2PE, PCI 3DS, CIS CSC, NIST CSF, SWIFT CSP, Coverage of standards and framework elements (partial implementation/full implementation), Scope of implementation across the environment (partial implementation/full implementation)

5. Security program: "Delivers outcomes by designing and managing a collection of projects to achieve long-term objectives. The program success depends on its interaction with and support from the preceding four pillars—the business model, strategy, operating model, and frameworks."[23]

Key program documents: Program management, Program office, Program charter, Program design, Life cycle management, Program scope, Resources (4 Ls), Constraints (7 Cs), Sustainability (9 Fs), Project management, Maturity (process, capability), Performance (metrics, reporting)

In addition, the Verizon report clarifies other available frameworks:

The four main types of security frameworks are:

1. Control frameworks, such as NIST 800-53; CIS Controls (CSCs); PCI DSS with a catalog set of baseline security controls

2. Program management frameworks, such as ISO 27001; NIST CSF

3. Risk management frameworks, such as NIST 800-39, 800-37, 800-30; ISO 27005; FAIR

4. Governance frameworks, such as ISO/IEC 27002, COBIT, COSO[24]

Verizon's insights include additional introspection into security management and security governance as it relates to PCI.

Note 6 | For more information on the Verizon Payment Security Report, go to www.verizon.com/business/reports/payment-security-report/.

View Point   Selecting the Appropriate Framework for an Organization

By Mark Reardon, CISO for Ernst & Young's (EY) U.S. Government and Public Sector Enclave; former CISO for the state of Georgia

It is important to view frameworks in two ways. Most frameworks have a compliance reporting component, and those reports are required with most organizations. However, the IT and information security departments also require a framework to implement. Attempting to implement separate frameworks across an organization is confusing and expensive.

When selecting the framework to implement, it is often best to start by gathering the requirements. Some organizations have many: HIPAA for healthcare, SOC 1 for financial reporting, PCI for payment card acceptance, and so on. It is often difficult to identify all such requirements, so it is important to speak with all of the relevant stakeholders. Some requirements are common for an industry and others may be included in various contracts.

Once the requirements are gathered, a theme often emerges because one particular framework supports the majority of the requirements. It then becomes the obvious choice. However, each oversight organization still expects compliance reports to use their terminology and comply with their requirements. When an organization has many requirements, the easiest solution is to invest in a governance, risk, and compliance system that can harmonize requirements and assist in creating controls that support all requirements. It can also help with reporting and supporting new requirements as they emerge.

For example, the state of Georgia has approximately 100 agencies, many of which have different oversight requirements. Most of these requirements are from the state's federal partners and are required for information sharing. Examples of federal requirements include HIPAA, FERPA, and IRC 6103. Federal agencies must translate these requirements to NIST's Risk Management Framework, which supports the requirements of the Federal Information Security Management Act (FISMA) and its updates. This became the obvious framework for Georgia. However, the state still needed to develop industry-specific compliance reports for PCI and SOC 1 terminology and requirements.

Sometimes, a portion of an organization has unique reporting or assessment requirements that the rest of the organization doesn't want to support. This is common with PCI or other requirements. In many healthcare settings, the IT that must follow PCI can be reduced to a small number of systems that can be isolated from the rest of the IT environment through network segmentation. This can be tricky, but it can also save an organization a great deal of money while simultaneously improving security.

Another option is to create an enclave of people and IT that supports unique requirements. At EY, the global firm adopted ISO 27001 for the protection of client information. While this satisfies most clients, U.S. government clients require their information to be safeguarded by following FISMA. The solution was for EY to create an enclave of people and systems that follow both ISO 27001 and FISMA.

With all the talk about which framework to report against and which one to implement, it is also important to remember that compliance is a by-product of good security. There are several good frameworks to choose from, but the best choice is one that supports securing your information and information systems appropriately.

Self-Check

1. Cybersecurity models serve as definitive guides that provide all necessary implementation details for organizations.

    a. True

    b. False

2. Benchmarking involves comparing an organization's performance against its own historical data as well as against similar organizations.

    a. True

    b. False

3. Proprietary cybersecurity models are always more effective than those available for free.

    a. True

    b. False

☐ Check your answers at the end of this chapter.

Cybersecurity Architecture Models

Cybersecurity architecture models illustrate cybersecurity implementations and can help organizations quickly make improvements through adaptation. Formal models do not usually find their way directly into usable implementations; instead, they form the basic approach that an implementation uses. These formal models are discussed here so that you can become familiar with them and see how they are used in various cybersecurity architectures. When a specific implementation is put into place, noting that it is based on a formal model may lend credibility, improve its reliability, and lead to improved results. Some models are implemented into computer hardware and software, some are implemented as policies and practices, and some are implemented in both. Some models focus on the confidentiality of information, whereas others focus on the integrity of the information as it is being processed.

The first models discussed here—specifically, the trusted computing base, Trusted Computer System Evaluation Criteria, the Information Technology System Evaluation Criteria, and the Common Criteria—are used as evaluation models and are also used to demonstrate the evolution of trusted system assessment. The academic models—Bell-LaPadula, Biba, and so forth—are used as demonstrations of models implemented in some computer cybersecurity systems to ensure that the confidentiality, integrity, and availability of information is protected.

TCSEC and the Trusted Computing Base

The Trusted Computer System Evaluation Criteria (TCSEC), an outdated system certification and accreditation standard from the U.S. Department of Defense (DoD) that defined the criteria for assessing the access controls in a computer system, was part of a larger series of standards collectively referred to as the "Rainbow Series" because of the color-coding used to uniquely identify each document. TCSEC was also known as the "Orange Book" and was considered the cornerstone of the series. As described later in this chapter, this series was replaced in 2005 with a set of standards known as the "Common Criteria," but cybersecurity professionals should be familiar with the terminology and concepts of this legacy approach because it is still sometimes referenced in older documentation and is part of some certification programs. TCSEC defined a trusted computing base (TCB) as the combination of all hardware, firmware, and software responsible for enforcing the cybersecurity policy. In this context, "cybersecurity policy" refers to the rules of configuration for a system rather than a managerial guidance document. TCB is only as effective as its internal control mechanisms and the administration of the systems being configured. TCB includes the hardware and software that has been implemented to provide cybersecurity for a particular information system, and it includes the operating system kernel and a specified set of cybersecurity utilities, such as the user login subsystem.

The term "trusted" can be misleading—in this context, it means that a component is part of TCB's cybersecurity system, not that it is necessarily trustworthy. The frequent discovery of flaws and the delivery of patches by software vendors to remedy cybersecurity vulnerabilities attest to the relative level of trust you can place in current generations of software.

Within TCB is an object known as the reference monitor—a conceptual piece of the system that manages access controls—to mediate access to objects by subjects. Systems administrators must be able to audit or periodically review the reference monitor to ensure it is functioning effectively without unauthorized modification.

One of the biggest challenges in TCB is the existence of covert channels, which are unauthorized or unintended methods of communications hidden inside a computer system. For example, researchers have discovered in some cases that the indicator lights blinking on the face of network routers were flashing in sync with the content of the data bits being transmitted, thus unintentionally displaying the contents of the data. TCSEC defined two kinds of covert channels:

- Storage channel—A TCSEC-defined covert channel that communicates by modifying a stored object, such as in steganography, which is described in a later chapter.
- Timing channel—A TCSEC-defined covert channel that communicates by managing the relative timing of events. An example is the flashing light described previously.

Products evaluated under TCSEC were assigned one of the following levels of protection:

- D: Minimal protection—A default evaluation when a product fails to meet any of the other requirements
- C: Discretionary protection
    - C1: Discretionary cybersecurity protection—Product includes discretionary access control (DAC) with standard identification and authentication functions, among other requirements
    - C2: Controlled access protection—Product includes improved DAC with accountability and auditability, among other requirements
- B: Mandatory protection
    - B1: Labeled cybersecurity protection—Product includes mandatory access control (MAC) over some subjects and objects, among other requirements

- B2: Structured protection—Product includes MAC and DAC over all subjects and objects, among other requirements
- B3: Security domains—The highest mandatory protection level; meets reference monitory requirements and clear auditability of cybersecurity events, with automated intrusion detection functions, among other requirements
- A: Verified protection
  - A1: Verified design—B3 level certification plus formalized design and verification techniques, among other requirements
  - Beyond A1—Highest possible protection level; reserved only for systems that demonstrate self-protection and completeness of the reference monitor, with formal top-level specifications and a verified TCB down to the source code level, among other requirements[25]

Note 7 | For more information on TCSEC, visit the NIST DoD Rainbow Series website at https://csrc .nist.gov/pubs/other/1985/12/26/dod-rainbow-series/final or the Federation of American Scientists website at https://irp.fas.org/nsa/rainbow.htm.

Information Technology System Evaluation Criteria

Under another standard called Information Technology System Evaluation Criteria (ITSEC)—an international set of criteria for evaluating computer systems that is very similar to TCSEC—targets of evaluation are compared to detailed cybersecurity function specifications, resulting in an assessment of systems functionality and comprehensive penetration testing. Like TCSEC, ITSEC was functionally replaced for the most part by the Common Criteria, as described in the following section. ITSEC rates products on a scale of E1 (lowest level) to E6 (highest level), in much the same way that TCSEC and the Common Criteria do, with E1 roughly equivalent to EAL2 evaluation of the Common Criteria and E6 roughly equivalent to EAL7.

The Common Criteria

The Common Criteria for Information Technology Security Evaluation, often called the Common Criteria or simply CC, is an international standard (ISO/IEC 15408) for computer security certification. It is widely considered the successor to both TCSEC and ITSEC in that it reconciles some of the differences between the various other standards. Most governments have discontinued their use of the other standards. CC is a combined effort of contributors from Australia, New Zealand, Canada, France, Germany, Japan, the Netherlands, Spain, the United Kingdom, and the United States. In the United States, the National Security Agency and NIST were the primary contributors. CC and its companion, the Common Methodology for Information Technology Security Evaluation (CEM), are the technical basis for an international agreement, the Common Criteria Recognition Agreement (CCRA), which ensures that products can be evaluated to determine their cybersecurity properties. CC seeks the widest possible mutual recognition of secure IT products.[26] The CC process ensures that the specification, implementation, and evaluation of computer cybersecurity products are performed in a rigorous and standard manner.[27]

CC terminology includes the following:

- Target of evaluation (ToE)—The system being evaluated
- Protection profile—A user-generated specification for cybersecurity requirements
- Security target—A document describing the ToE's cybersecurity properties
- Security functional requirements—A catalog of a product's cybersecurity functions
- Evaluation assurance level (EAL)—The rating or grading of a ToE after evaluation

EAL is typically rated on the following scale:

- EAL1: Functionally tested—Confidence in operation against nonserious threats
- EAL2: Structurally tested—More confidence required but comparable with good business practices
- EAL3: Methodically tested and checked—Moderate level of cybersecurity assurance
- EAL4: Methodically designed, tested, and reviewed—Rigorous level of cybersecurity assurance but still economically feasible without specialized development
- EAL5: Semiformally designed and tested—Certification requires specialized development above standard commercial products
- EAL6: Semiformally verified design and tested—Specifically designed cybersecurity ToE
- EAL7: Formally verified design and tested—Developed for extremely high-risk situations or for high-value systems[28]

The Common Criteria's companion methodology, CEM, describes how to evaluate a system to assess the CC level to which it is secure. This is restricted to routine cybersecurity systems but is mainly focused on getting systems certified to a specific CC level for use in achieving the CCRA. Much like the ISO standards, achieving this recognition is of value to organizations that want to demonstrate their competence in managing secure systems as a competitive business advantage or to meet the requirements to bid on certain government contracts.

Note 8 | For more information on the Common Criteria, visit the Common Criteria Portal at www.commoncriteriaportal.org.

Self-Check

4. Cybersecurity architecture models are directly implemented into usable systems without any modifications.

   a. True   b. False

5. The Common Criteria are an international standard that has replaced both TCSEC and ITSEC for computer security certification.

   a. True   b. False

6. Evaluation assurance level (EAL) 7 in the Common Criteria framework represents the highest level of cybersecurity assurance.

   a. True   b. False

☐ Check your answers at the end of this chapter.

Access Control Models

Access control—the selective method by which systems specify who may use a particular resource and how they may use it—regulates the admission of users into trusted areas of the organization. This control includes both logical access to information systems and physical access to the organization's facilities. Access control is maintained by means of a collection of policies, programs to carry out those policies, and technologies that enforce policies. You will learn the specifics of physical access controls and technology-based access controls later in this text. The general application of access control comprises four processes: obtaining the identity of the entity requesting access to a logical or physical area (identification); confirming the identity of the entity seeking access to a logical or physical area (authentication); determining which actions an authenticated entity can perform in that physical or logical area (authorization); and finally, documenting the activities of the authorized individual and systems (accountability).

Access control enables organizations to restrict access to information, information assets, and other tangible assets to users with a bona fide business need. Access control is built on several key principles, including the following:

- **Least privilege** is the data access principle that ensures no unnecessary access to data exists by regulating members so they can perform only the minimum data manipulation necessary. Least privilege presumes a need-to-know and implies restricted access to the level required for assigned duties. For example, if a task requires only the reading of data, the user is given read-only access, which does not allow the creation, updating, or deletion of data.

- **Need-to-know** is the principle of limiting users' access privileges to only the specific information required to perform their assigned tasks. It is focused on necessary access and not simply access based on the category of data or data classification required for a general work function. For example, a manager who needs to change a specific employee's pay rate is granted access to read and update that data but is restricted from accessing pay data for other employees. This principle is most frequently associated with data classification, which assigns a specific level of access to an information asset and a security clearance to a user. Just because an individual has a sufficient clearance level to review a classified document doesn't mean they have the need-to-know.

- **Separation of duties** is the principle that requires significant tasks to be split up so that more than one individual is needed to complete them. It is designed to ensure that no misuse can be committed by an individual in the organization. For example, in accounts payable situations, one person may set up a vendor account, another may request payment to the vendor, and a third person may authorize the payment. Separation of duties reduces the chance of an individual violating cybersecurity policy and breaching the confidentiality, integrity, and availability of information.

Categories of Access Controls

Several approaches are used to categorize access control methodologies. One approach depicts the controls by their inherent characteristics and classifies each control as one of the following:

- Directive—Employs administrative controls such as policy and training designed to proscribe certain user behavior in the organization; an example would be an appropriate-use policy that prohibits personal use of company assets for personal business purposes

- Deterrent—Discourages or deters an incipient incident; an example would be signs that indicate video monitoring

- Preventative—Helps an organization avoid an incident; an example would be the requirement for strong authentication in access controls

- Detective—Detects or identifies an incident or threat when it occurs (for example, antimalware software)

- Corrective—Remedies a circumstance or mitigates damage done during an incident—for example, changes to a firewall to block the recurrence of a diagnosed attack

- Recovery—Restores operating conditions back to normal; data backup and recovery software are examples

- Compensating—Resolves shortcomings, such as requiring the use of encryption for transmission of classified data over unsecured networks[29]

A second approach, described in the NIST special publication series, categorizes controls based on their operational impact on the organization:

- Managerial—Controls that cover cybersecurity processes designed by strategic planners, integrated into the organization's management practices, and routinely used by cybersecurity administrators to design, implement, and monitor other control systems
- Operational (or administrative)—Controls that deal with the operational functions of cybersecurity that have been integrated into the repeatable processes of the organization
- Technical—Controls that support the tactical portion of a cybersecurity program and that have been implemented as reactive mechanisms to deal with the immediate needs of the organization as it responds to the realities of the technical environment[30]

Table 8-5 shows examples of controls categorized by their characteristics as well as by operational impact.[31]

Table 8-5   Categories of access controls[32]

	Deterrent	Preventative	Detective	Corrective	Recovery	Compensating
Management	Policies	Registration procedures	Periodic violation report reviews	Employee or account termination	Disaster recovery plan	Separation of duties, job rotation
Operational	Warning signs	Gates, fences, and guards	Sentries, closed-circuit television	Fire suppression systems	Disaster recovery procedures	Defense in depth
Technical	Warning banners	Login systems, Kerberos	Log monitors and intrusion detection and prevention systems	Forensics procedures	Data backups	Key logging and keystroke monitoring

Source: © NIST SP 800 Series

A third approach describes the degree of authority under which the controls are applied. They can be mandatory, nondiscretionary, or discretionary. Each of these categories of controls regulates access to a particular type or collection of information, as explained in the following sections.

Mandatory Access Controls

As the name indicates, a mandatory access control (MAC) is a required, structured data classification scheme that rates each collection of information as well as each user; these ratings are often referred to as sensitivity or classification levels. A MAC mandates the information a user can access by classifying the information into tiered levels. For example, in the U.S. government and military, an individual with a Secret security clearance can view Secret and Confidential classified materials, subject to need-to-know, but cannot view Top Secret material. When MACs are implemented, users and data owners have limited control over access to information resources.

Data Classification Model   As mentioned in an earlier chapter, corporate and military organizations use a variety of classification schemes. As you might expect, the U.S. government classification scheme is a more complex categorization system than the schemes of most corporations. The military forces of the government are perhaps the best-known users of data classification schemes. The military has invested heavily in cybersecurity, operations security (OpSec), and communications security (ComSec). In fact, many developments in communications and cybersecurity are the result of DoD and military-sponsored research and development.

The U.S. government uses a three-level classification scheme for information deemed to be National Security Information (NSI), as defined in Executive Order 13526 in 2009. Here are the classifications along with descriptions from the document:

Sec. 1.2. Classification Levels.

(a) Information may be classified at one of the following three levels:

1. "Top Secret" shall be applied to information, the unauthorized disclosure of which reasonably could be expected to cause exceptionally grave damage to the national cybersecurity that the original classification authority is able to identify or describe.

2. "Secret" shall be applied to information, the unauthorized disclosure of which reasonably could be expected to cause serious damage to the national cybersecurity that the original classification authority is able to identify or describe.

3. "Confidential" shall be applied to information, the unauthorized disclosure of which reasonably could be expected to cause damage to the national cybersecurity that the original classification authority is able to identify or describe.

(b) Except as otherwise provided by statute, no other terms shall be used to identify United States classified information.

(c) If there is significant doubt about the appropriate level of classification, it shall be classified at the lower level.[33]

The U.S. government uses the term "Controlled Unclassified Information" (CUI) to categorize restricted information not covered under the three categories listed previously.

In addition, federal agencies such as the FBI and CIA use specialty classification schemes, such as Need-to-Know and Named Projects. Obviously, Need-to-Know authorization allows access to information by individuals who need the information to perform their work. The use of such specialty classification schemes is also commonly referred to as compartmentalization, which is the restriction of information to the fewest people possible—those with a need-to-know—to prevent compromise or disclosure to unauthorized individuals. For example, compartmentalization might be necessary for a secret military operation or corporate research project. Named Projects are clearance levels based on a scheme like Need-to-Know. When an operation, project, or set of classified data is created, the project is assigned a code name. Next, a list of authorized individuals is created and assigned to either the Need-to-Know or the Named Projects category.

For information that is not part of NSI, the federal government recently went from a simplistic approach of "For Official Use Only," "Sensitive But Unclassified," and "Law Enforcement Sensitive" categories to a complex collection of 23 specialized categories, many with multiple subcategories, in spite of the declaration of the executive order that it was simplifying and standardizing the process.

Note 9 | For more information on governmental cybersecurity classifications, read Executive Order 13526 (for NSI) at www.archives.gov/isoo/policy-documents/cnsi-eo.html or Executive Order 13556 for CUI (www.gpo.gov/fdsys/pkg/FR-2010-11-09/pdf/2010-28360.pdf).

Most organizations working outside the realm of national cybersecurity do not need the detailed level of classification used by government agencies. Nevertheless, they may find it necessary to classify data to provide protection. A general data classification scheme suitable for these organizations might have three categories: confidential, internal, and external (or public). Data owners must classify the information assets for which they are responsible, reviewing these classifications to ensure that the data is still classified correctly and the appropriate access controls are in place. Organizations should have procedures that call for this review to be done at least annually. With a simple scheme like the following, an organization can protect its sensitive information, such as marketing or research data, personnel data, customer data, and general internal communications:

- Public—For general public dissemination, such as web content, an advertisement, or a press release
- For internal (or official) use only—Not for public release but not particularly sensitive, such as internal communications
- Confidential (or sensitive)—Essential and protected information, the disclosure of which could severely damage the financial well-being or reputation of the organization

These categories may need more careful consideration than you might think. Many items that seem to deserve classification at a level of "For internal use" might actually belong at the higher Confidential level, and vice versa. What may seem to be routine internal communications might be embarrassing to their authors, their subjects, and the organization if there is a breach. For example, many internal emails from Sony Corporation were released to the public in the breach of 2014, causing the firm consternation and embarrassment. What we may generically consider "not particularly sensitive" is rooted both in time and context.

Security Clearances   Another component of a data classification scheme is the personnel security clearance structure, a personnel classification system in which users of an organization's information assets are assigned an authorization level that identifies the level of classified information they are "cleared" to access. This is usually accomplished by assigning each employee to a named role, such as data entry clerk, development programmer, cybersecurity analyst, or even chief information officer. Most organizations have developed a set of roles and corresponding security clearances so that individuals are assigned authorization levels correlating with the classifications of the information assets.

Beyond a simple reliance on the security clearance is the incorporation of the need-to-know principle, based on the requirement that people are not allowed to view data simply because it falls within their level of clearance; they must also have a business-related need-to-know. This extra requirement ensures that the confidentiality of information is properly maintained.

Managing Classified Information Assets   Managing an information asset includes all aspects of its life cycle—from specification to design, acquisition, implementation, use, storage, distribution, backup, recovery, retirement, and destruction. An information asset such as a report that has a classification designation other than unclassified or public must be clearly marked as such. The U.S. government, for example, uses color-coordinated cover sheets to protect classified information from the casual observer, as shown in Figure 8-4. Every classified document should also contain the appropriate cybersecurity designation at the top and bottom of each page. Classified documents must be accessible only to authorized individuals, which usually requires locking file cabinets, safes, or other such protective devices for hard copies and physical systems. When someone carries a classified report, it should be concealed, kept in a locked briefcase or portfolio, and in compliance with appropriate policies, such as requirements for double-sealed envelopes and tamper-proof seals. Operational controls need to consider these classification systems and their associated control mechanisms, which, despite their simplicity, can have significant impact. For example, a British military operation was compromised when a press photographer took a picture of a secret document that was not properly covered.[34]

Among the many controls that managers can use to maintain the confidentiality of classified documents is a risk management control known as the "clean desk policy." This policy requires each employee to secure all information in its appropriate storage container at the end of every business day.

When copies of classified information are no longer valuable or too many copies exist, care should be taken to destroy them properly, usually after double-signature verification. Documents should be destroyed by means of shredding, burning, or transfer to a service offering authorized document destruction. Policy should ensure that no classified information is inappropriately disposed of in trash or recycling areas. Otherwise, people who engage in dumpster diving—an information attack that involves

Figure 8-4 U.S. government data classification cover sheets

searching through a target organization's trash and recycling bins for sensitive information—may compromise the cybersecurity of the organization's information assets. If dumpster bins are located on public property, such as a public street or alley, individuals may not be violating the law to search through these receptacles. However, if the bin is located on private property, individuals may be charged with trespassing, although prosecution is unlikely. In a landmark 1998 decision, *California v. Greenwood*, the U.S. Supreme Court ruled that there is no expectation of privacy for items thrown away in trash or refuse containers.[35]

An access control commonly implemented in organizations is lattice-based access control—a variation on MAC access control that assigns users a matrix of authorizations for specific areas of access, incorporating the information assets of subjects such as users and objects. The level of authorization may vary depending on the authorizations that individuals possess for each group of information assets or resources. The lattice structure contains subjects (i.e., users) and objects (e.g., resources like computers and data files), and the boundaries associated with each subject/object pair are clearly demarcated. Lattice-based access control then specifies the level of access each subject has to each object, if any. With this type of control, the column of attributes associated with a particular object (such as a printer) is referred to as an access control list (ACL) and contains a subset of attributes referred to as a capabilities table—the row of attributes associated with a particular user or subject that describes what the user is permitted to do with the asset.

Nondiscretionary Controls

Nondiscretionary controls are access controls that are implemented by a central authority. If these controls are based on roles, they are called role-based access controls (RBACs). If the controls are based on a specified set of tasks, they are called task-based controls. Task-based access controls (TBACs) can, in turn, be based on lists maintained on subjects or objects. Role-based controls are tied to the role that a particular user performs in an organization, whereas task-based controls are tied to a particular assignment, project, or responsibility. RBACs tend to have longer durations because individuals can work in particular roles for a long time. Role-based and task-based controls make it easier to maintain controls and restrictions, especially if the person performing the role or task changes often. Instead of constantly assigning and revoking the privileges of people who come and go, the administrator simply assigns the associated access rights to the role or task. The person assigned to that role or task automatically receives the corresponding access. The administrator can easily remove people's associations with roles and tasks, thereby revoking their access.

Discretionary Access Controls

Discretionary access controls (DACs)—access controls that are implemented at the discretion or option of the data user—allow users to control and possibly provide access to information or resources at their disposal, such as a shared drive folder, individual file, or printer. Users can allow general unrestricted access or they can allow specific individuals or sets of individuals to access these resources. For example, suppose a user has a hard drive containing information to be shared with office coworkers. This user can allow specific individuals to access this drive by listing their names in the share control function. Most personal computer operating systems are designed based on the DAC model.

One discretionary model is rule-based access controls, in which access is granted based on a set of rules specified by a central authority. This is a DAC model because the individual user is the one who creates the rules. Role-based models, described in the previous section, can also be implemented under DAC if an individual system owner wants to create the rules for other users of the system or its data.

Other Forms of Access Control

Access control is an area that is developing rapidly in both its principles and technologies. Other models of access control include the following:

- Content-dependent access controls—As the name suggests, access to a specific set of information may be dependent on its content. For example, the marketing department needs access to marketing data, the accounting department needs access to accounting data, and so forth.
- Constrained user interfaces—Some systems are designed specifically to restrict what information an individual user can access. The most common example is a bank automated teller machine, which restricts authorized users to simple account queries, transfers, deposits, and withdrawals.
- Temporal (time-based) isolation—In some cases, access to information is limited by a time-of-day constraint. A physical example is a time-release safe, which is found in most convenience and fast-food establishments. The safe can only be opened during a specific time frame, even by an authorized user (e.g., the store manager).

One area of discussion among practitioners is whether access controls should be centralized or decentralized. A collection of users with access to the same data typically has a centralized access control authority, even under a DAC model. The appropriate level of centralization varies by organization and the type of information protected. The less critical the protected information, the more controls tend to be decentralized. When critical information assets are being protected, the use of a highly centralized access control toolset is indicated. These specialized tools, including Kerberos, are described in more detail in a later chapter.

Note 10 | For information on assessing access control systems, read NIST Report 7316, which is available from https://csrc.nist.gov/pubs/ir/7316/final.

Self-Check

7. Access control regulates both logical access to information systems and physical access to an organization's facilities.

   a. True   **b.** False

8. The principle of least privilege ensures that users have unrestricted access to all data in an organization.

   a. True   **b.** False

9. Nondiscretionary access controls can be based on roles or tasks and are implemented by a central authority.

   a. True   **b.** False

☐ Check your answers at the end of this chapter.

Academic Access Control Models

Some access control models were initially designed to teach system designers to create operating systems with cybersecurity built in by controlling the confidentiality or integrity of data within the software. Some of these academic models were built into actual operating systems, but most were used simply to better understand how systems *should* or could function.

Bell-LaPadula Confidentiality Model

The Bell-LaPadula (BLP) confidentiality model—a "state machine reference model" that ensures the confidentiality of the modeled system by using MACs, data classification, and information security clearances—is a model of an automated system that can manipulate its state or status over time. The intent of any state machine model is to devise a conceptual approach wherein the system being modeled can always be in a known secure condition; in other words, this kind of model is provably secure. A system that serves as a reference monitor compares the level of classification of the data with the clearance of the entity requesting access; it allows access only if the clearance is equal to or higher than the classification. BLP security rules prevent information from being moved from a level of higher security to a level of lower security. Access modes can be one of two types: simple security and the * (star) property.

Simple security (also called the "read property") prohibits a subject of lower clearance from reading an object of higher clearance but allows a subject with a higher clearance level to read an object at a lower level (read down).

The * property (the "write property"), on the other hand, prohibits a high-level subject from sending messages to a lower-level object. In short, subjects can "read down" and objects "can write or append up." BLP uses access permission matrices and a cybersecurity lattice for access control.[36]

This model can be understood by imagining a fictional interaction between General Bell, whose thoughts and actions are classified at the highest possible level, and Private LaPadula, who has the lowest security clearance in the military. It is prohibited for Private LaPadula to read anything written by General Bell and for General Bell to write in any document that Private LaPadula could read. In short, the principle is "no read up, no write down."

Biba Integrity Model

The Biba integrity model—an access control model that is similar to BLP based on the premise that higher levels of integrity are more worthy of trust than lower levels—is a state machine model that focuses on providing access controls to ensure that objects or subjects cannot have less integrity as a result of read/write operations. The Biba model assigns integrity levels to subjects and objects using two properties: the simple integrity (read) property and the integrity * property (write).

The simple integrity property permits a subject to have read access to an object only if the security level of the subject is either lower or equal to the level of the object. The integrity * property permits a subject to have write access to an object only if the security level of the subject is equal to or higher than that of the object. The Biba model ensures that no information from a subject can be passed on to an object in a higher security level. This prevents contaminating data of higher integrity with data of lower integrity.[37]

This model can be illustrated by imagining fictional interactions among a priest, a monk named Biba, and some parishioners of the Middle Ages. Priests are considered holier (i.e., to have greater integrity) than monks, who are holier (i.e., have greater integrity) than parishioners. A priest cannot read (or offer) Masses or prayers written by monks, who in turn cannot read items written by their parishioners. The parishioners are also prohibited from writing in Biba's books and notes, and he in turn is prohibited from writing in the works of the priests. This prevents the lower integrity of the lower level from corrupting the higher integrity of the upper level. On the other hand, higher-level entities can share their writings with the lower levels without compromising the integrity of the information. This illustrates the "no write up, no read down" principle behind the Biba model.

Clark-Wilson Integrity Model

The Clark-Wilson integrity model, which is built on principles of change control rather than integrity levels, was designed for the commercial environment. The change control principles on which it operates are as follows:

- No changes by unauthorized subjects
- No unauthorized changes by authorized subjects
- The maintenance of internal and external consistency

Internal consistency means that the system does what it is expected to do every time, without exception. External consistency means that the data in the system is consistent with similar data in the outside world. This model establishes a system of subject–program–object relationships so that the subject has no direct access to the object. Instead, the subject is required to access the object using a well-formed transaction via a validated program. The intent is to provide an environment where cybersecurity can be proven using separate activities, each of which is provably secure. The following controls are part of the Clark-Wilson model:

- Subject authentication and identification
- Access to objects by means of well-formed transactions
- Execution by subjects on a restricted set of programs

The elements of the Clark-Wilson model are:

- Constrained data item—A data item with protected integrity
- Unconstrained data item—Data not controlled by Clark-Wilson; nonvalidated input or any output
- Integrity verification procedure (IVP)—A procedure that scans data and confirms its integrity
- Transformation procedure (TP)—A procedure that only allows changes to a constrained data item

All subjects and objects are labeled with TPs. The TPs operate as the intermediate layer between subjects and objects. Each data item has a set of access operations that can be performed on it. Each subject is assigned a set of access operations that it can perform. The system then compares these two parameters and either permits or denies access by the subject to the object.[38]

Graham-Denning Access Control Model

The Graham-Denning access control model has three parts: a set of objects, a set of subjects, and a set of rights. The subjects are composed of two things: a process and a domain. The domain is the set of constraints controlling how subjects may access objects. The set of rights governs how subjects may manipulate the passive objects. This model describes eight primitive protection rights, called commands, that subjects can execute to interact with other subjects or objects. These rights are like the rights a user can assign to an entity in modern operating systems.[39]

The eight primitive protection rights are as follows:

1. Create object
2. Create subject
3. Delete object
4. Delete subject
5. Read access right
6. Grant access right
7. Delete access right
8. Transfer access right

Harrison-Ruzzo-Ullman Model

The Harrison-Ruzzo-Ullman (HRU) model defines a method to allow changes to access rights and the addition and removal of subjects and objects, a process that the BLP model does not have. Because systems change over time, their protective states need to change. HRU is built on an access control matrix and includes a set of generic rights and a specific set of commands. These include:

- Create subject/create object
- Enter right X into
- Delete right X from
- Destroy subject/destroy object

By implementing this set of rights and commands and restricting the commands to a single operation each, it is possible to determine when a specific subject can obtain a particular right to an object.[40]

Brewer-Nash Model (Chinese Wall)

The Brewer-Nash model, commonly known as a "Chinese Wall," is designed to prevent a conflict of interest between two parties. Imagine that a law firm represents two individuals who are involved in a car accident. One sues the other, and the firm must represent both. To prevent a conflict of interest, the individual attorneys should not be able to access the private information of both litigants. The Brewer-Nash model requires users to select one of two conflicting sets of data, after which they cannot access the conflicting data.[41]

Self-Check

10. The Bell-LaPadula (BLP) model allows a subject with a lower security clearance to read data at a higher classification level.

    a. True   **b.** False

11. The Brewer-Nash model, also known as the Chinese Wall, is designed to prevent conflicts of interest by restricting access to conflicting sets of data.

    a. True   **b.** False

12. The Biba integrity model prevents higher integrity level subjects from writing to lower integrity level objects.

    a. True   **b.** False

☐ Check your answers at the end of this chapter.

Closing Case

Iris sighed as she completed her initial review of her staff's checklist results. She pulled out a notepad and began outlining the projects she foresaw, based on the shortcomings identified via the checklist. She had decided to use the NIST approach for her cybersecurity management planning and felt fortunate to have found a useful model for a cybersecurity review of her program.

Case Discussion Questions

1. Based on your understanding of the chapter, from which NIST special publication did Iris draw her initial checklist?
2. Will the use of the special publication that Iris has identified to create a "to-do" list lead to a customized and repeatable cybersecurity program for the company? What else is needed to make a cybersecurity management model into a working cybersecurity program?
3. What did Iris mean by her final remark at the beginning of this chapter?
4. If the company intended to develop its own plan based on an unlicensed but copyrighted document, and if detection and prosecution for violating the copyright was unlikely, would it be unethical to take that approach?

Case Ethical Decision Making

Iris had gathered her planning team and announced the choice for the model on which they would base their approach, and now one of the more senior employees was asking why she had not chosen the ISO/IEC 27000 series as a model.

"Since the 27000 series is mostly complete these days, why wouldn't we use that?" he asked.

"Well, I looked at the details of that approach," Iris said, "and I decided that the expense of purchasing a copy of the standard for our use was not worth the few extra benefits it would provide us."

"But why do we have to pay a license fee?" the senior analyst asked. "I have a copy of the standard that I got from a friend of mine. It's a PDF file and we can use it right away."

Iris sighed, then paused. "It's a copyright-protected document," she finally said.

Is Iris correct in her decision to forgo the model with the best fit because the company does not have the budget to pay the licensing fee? What is the risk of using the model without a license?

Summary

A framework is the outline of a more thorough blueprint used in the creation of the cybersecurity environment. A cybersecurity model is a generic blueprint offered by a service organization.

One of the most widely referenced cybersecurity models is ISO/IEC 27001: 2005, Information Technology—Code of Practice for Information Security Management, which is designed to give recommendations for cybersecurity management. Other approaches to structuring cybersecurity management are found in the many documents available from NIST's Computer Security Resource Center.

Control Objectives for Information and Related Technology provides advice about the implementation of sound controls and control objectives for cybersecurity.

The Committee of Sponsoring Organizations of the Treadway Commission has established a common definition of internal controls, standards, and criteria against which companies and organizations can assess their control systems. The Information Technology Infrastructure Library is a collection of methods and practices for managing the development and operation of IT infrastructures.

The Information Security Governance Framework is a managerial model provided by an industry working group that can guide the development and implementation of an organization's cybersecurity governance structure.

Cybersecurity architecture models illustrate cybersecurity implementations and can help organizations make quick improvements through adaptation. The most common model is the Trusted Computer System Evaluation Criteria.

Access controls regulate the admission of users into trusted areas of the organization. Access control comprises four elements: identification, authentication, authorization, and accountability.

Access control is built on the principles of least privilege, need-to-know, and separation of duties.

Approaches to access control include directive, deterrent, preventative, detective, corrective, recovery, and compensating. Access controls may be classified as management, operational (or administrative), or technical.

Mandatory access controls are controls required by a system that operate within a data classification and personnel clearance scheme.

Nondiscretionary controls are determined by a central authority in the organization and can be based on roles or a specified set of tasks.

Discretionary access controls are implemented at the discretion or option of the data user.

Common academic access control models include the Bell-LaPadula confidentiality model, the Biba integrity model, the Clark-Wilson integrity model, the Graham-Denning access control model, the Harrison-Ruzzo-Ullman model for access rights, and the Brewer-Nash model.

Key Terms

access control
Bell-LaPadula (BLP) confidentiality
   model
Biba integrity model
blueprint
capabilities table
Common Criteria for Information
   Technology Security Evaluation
covert channel

discretionary access controls
   (DACs)
dumpster diving
framework
Information Technology System
   Evaluation Criteria (ITSEC)
lattice-based access control
least privilege
mandatory access control (MAC)
model

need-to-know
nondiscretionary controls
reference monitor
security clearance
separation of duties
storage channel
timing channel
Trusted Computer System
   Evaluation Criteria (TCSEC)
trusted computing base (TCB)

Review Questions

1. What are the primary functions of a cybersecurity framework or model within an organization?

2. How do the terms "framework," "model," and "blueprint" differ in the context of cybersecurity?

3. Why might an organization choose to adapt portions of different cybersecurity frameworks?

4. What role does benchmarking play in the development of a cybersecurity blueprint?

5. What are the four general control categories provided by ISO/IEC 27002:2022?

6. How does ISO/IEC 27001 differ from ISO/IEC 27002 in terms of their content and purpose?

7. What is the importance of the COSO framework in cybersecurity?

8. What advantages do NIST special publications offer compared to other cybersecurity documentation sources?

9. What is the role of cybersecurity architecture models in an organization?

10. How does the trusted computing base contribute to a computer system's security?

11. What is the primary purpose of the Trusted Computer System Evaluation Criteria?

12. What are covert channels, and how do they pose a challenge to cybersecurity?

13. What is the significance of the evaluation assurance level in the Common Criteria framework?

14. How do the concepts of a protection profile and security target function within the Common Criteria?

15. What are the two types of covert channels defined by TCSEC, and how do they differ?

16. Why is the concept of a reference monitor important in the context of the trusted computing base?

17. What are the four general processes involved in access control?

18. How does the principle of least privilege contribute to cybersecurity?

19. What is the purpose of the separation of duties in an organization's access control policy?

20. How do directive access controls differ from deterrent access controls?

21. What are the three main categories of access controls based on their operational impact, as described in the NIST special publication series?

22. What is a mandatory access control and how does it function?

23. What are the three classification levels used by the U.S. government for National Security Information, as defined in Executive Order 13526?

24. How does a lattice-based access control model work in regulating access?

25. What are discretionary access controls and how are they typically implemented in personal computer operating systems?

26. What is the primary focus of the Bell-LaPadula (BLP) confidentiality model?

27. How does the simple security property function in the BLP model?

28. What is the primary difference between the BLP model and the Biba integrity model?

29. What are the two main properties of the Biba integrity model?

30. What is the purpose of the Clark-Wilson integrity model in a commercial environment?

31. How does the Graham-Denning access control model structure its components?

32. What is the significance of the eight primitive protection rights in the Graham-Denning model?

33. How does the Harrison-Ruzzo-Ullman model address changes to access rights and system states?

34. What problem does the Brewer-Nash model, also known as the Chinese Wall, aim to solve?

Exercises

1. Visit the U.S. Postal Service webpage for Handbook 805 at http://about.usps.com/handbooks/as805.pdf. Review the contents page of this extensive manual. Compare this program to the NIST documents outlined in this chapter. Which areas are similar to those covered in the NIST documents? Which areas are different?

2. Compare the ISO/IEC 27001 outline with the NIST documents discussed in this chapter. Which areas, if any, are missing from the NIST documents? Identify the strengths and weaknesses of the NIST programs compared to the ISO standard.

3. Search the Internet for "cybersecurity best practices." Compare your findings to the recommended practices outlined in the NIST documents.

4. Search the Internet for "data classification model." Identify two such models and then compare and contrast the categories those models use for the various levels of classification.

5. Search the Internet for information on the Treadway Commission. What was it, and what is its major legacy in the field of cybersecurity?

Solutions to Self-Check Questions

Introduction to Cybersecurity Blueprints, Frameworks, and Models

1. Cybersecurity models serve as definitive guides that provide all necessary implementation details for organizations.

   Answer: b. False.

   Explanation: Cybersecurity models provide a general outline of what the end product should look like, but they do not provide detailed implementation instructions. Organizations often need to customize these models to fit their specific needs.

2. Benchmarking involves comparing an organization's performance against its own historical data as well as against similar organizations.

   Answer: a. True.

   Explanation: Benchmarking includes both internal benchmarking (baselining) and external benchmarking, comparing an organization's performance against its historical data and similar organizations.

3. Proprietary cybersecurity models are always more effective than those available for free.

   Answer: b. False.

   Explanation: The effectiveness of a cybersecurity model depends on the specific needs and context of the organization. Proprietary models and those available for free, such as those from NIST, can be effective if appropriately applied.

Cybersecurity Architecture Models

4. Cybersecurity architecture models are directly implemented into usable systems without any modifications.

   Answer: b. False.

   Explanation: Cybersecurity architecture models typically form the basic approach for implementations and do not usually find their way directly into usable systems without modifications.

5. The Common Criteria are an international standard that has replaced both TCSEC and ITSEC for computer security certification.

   Answer: a. True.

   Explanation: The Common Criteria are an international standard (ISO/IEC 15408) that has largely replaced both TCSEC and ITSEC by reconciling their differences.

6. Evaluation assurance level (EAL) 7 in the Common Criteria framework represents the highest level of cybersecurity assurance.

   Answer: a. True.

   Explanation: EAL 7 in the Common Criteria framework represents the highest level of cybersecurity assurance, indicating a formally verified design and tested system.

Access Control Models

7. Access control regulates both logical access to information systems and physical access to an organization's facilities.

   Answer: a. True.

   Explanation: Access control encompasses both logical access to information systems and physical access to an organization's facilities to ensure comprehensive security.

8. The principle of least privilege ensures that users have unrestricted access to all data in an organization.

   Answer: b. False.

   Explanation: The principle of least privilege ensures that users have no unnecessary access to data, allowing them only the minimum access necessary to perform their duties.

9. Nondiscretionary access controls can be based on roles or tasks and are implemented by a central authority.

   Answer: a. True.

   Explanation: Nondiscretionary access controls are implemented by a central authority and can be based on roles (role-based access controls) or tasks (task-based controls).

Academic Access Control Models

10. The Bell-LaPadula (BLP) model allows a subject with a lower security clearance to read data at a higher classification level.

    Answer: b. False.

    Explanation: To ensure confidentiality, the BLP model prohibits a subject with a lower security clearance from reading data at a higher classification level.

11. The Brewer-Nash model, also known as the Chinese Wall, is designed to prevent conflicts of interest by restricting access to conflicting sets of data.

    Answer: a. True.

    Explanation: The Brewer-Nash model prevents conflicts of interest by requiring users to select one set of conflicting data and then restricting access to the other.

12. The Biba integrity model prevents higher integrity level subjects from writing to lower integrity level objects.

    Answer: a. True.

    Explanation: To maintain data integrity, the Biba integrity model ensures that higher integrity level subjects cannot write to lower integrity level objects.

Cybersecurity Management Practices

Chapter Objectives

After reading this chapter and completing the exercises, you should be able to:

1   List the elements of key cybersecurity management practices.

2   Explain the role cybersecurity plays in recruiting, hiring, firing, and managing employees.

3   Describe the key components and suitable strategies for the implementation of a cybersecurity performance measurement program.

4   Differentiate the use of various types of benchmarking in security planning.

> In theory there is no difference between theory and practice, but in practice there is.
>
> —Attributed to multiple sources, including Yogi Berra and Jan L. A. Van de Snepscheut

Case Opener

"Come in," Iris said to Maria Rodriguez, one of the managers in the cybersecurity department. "Have a seat, please."

As Iris closed her office door, Maria sat down at a small table by the window.

"Maria," Iris said, "we've been working together since I joined RWW. I've been very happy with your work as the manager of the policy compliance team. You and your team have done a good job helping our business partners fix vulnerabilities across the company. I know how much collaboration and teamwork goes into that process. Now I'm ready to offer you another opportunity in a different part of the cybersecurity group. Are you ready for some new challenges?"

"Yes, I think I am," Maria said.

"Good," Iris said. "Would you be interested in taking over as the project manager for our new cybersecurity performance measures effort? It's technically a lateral move within our department, but due to the increased visibility of the program, it will come with a bump in salary and the opportunity to learn something new and vital to the future of RWW."

"Well, I don't have much experience with managing performance measures," Maria said, "but I'm willing to learn."

Iris smiled. "Maria, you have a great track record as a manager and as a technician before that, here at RWW," she said. "Plus, you've got the right attitude for this new role. I'll be here to help you, and I'll supplement your training budget to see that you get the skills to do this right. I'd like you to take next week to work out the transition of your team lead role, and we'll arrange for you to spend the following week in a performance measures training program."

Maria thought about it for a second, and then said, "I'm ready."

"Great," Iris said. "Who do you think is the best choice to take over as the policy compliance team lead?"

Maria thought for a moment. "I think Linda would be the best candidate for that role," she finally said.

Iris nodded. She had come to the same conclusion after seeing the last succession planning report Maria had prepared.

"Great," Iris said. "After I check with her, you can start her transition to policy compliance team leader while we get you started as the project manager for our cybersecurity performance measures effort. I'm counting on you to give me your best!"

"Will do!" Maria replied with a smile.

Introduction to Cybersecurity Practices

Organizations strive to deliver the most value with a given level of resources; this is known as the "value proposition." The development and use of sound and repeatable cybersecurity management practices brings organizations closer to meeting this objective. One of the challenges seldom considered in organizations is the need for a close working relationship between cybersecurity staff, the human resources (HR) department, and every department or division that is engaged in personnel management—specifically, hiring, evaluating, transitioning, and terminating employees. Part of each phase of the personnel management life cycle could potentially result in a risk to the organization's information assets, so cybersecurity staff should share the responsibility of educating the organization on how to avoid accidental information losses. This responsibility also extends to contract employees, such as temporary employees, employees of organizations that provide critical contract services (e.g., managed cybersecurity services or outsourced information technology services), and individuals and other organizations that work with the organization under various contracts and partnerships.

Executives and governance groups want assurance that organizations are working toward the value proposition and measuring the quality of management practices, either by comparing their programs to those of other organizations or by measuring compliance according to established standards. This chapter explores various methods of program comparison, including using benchmarks, baselines, and compliance measurement as a means of verifying that processes can be certified and validated as meeting required or recognized levels of maturity.

A significant cybersecurity incident occurred in July 2024. A faulty update released by the CrowdStrike software company for its Falcon cybersecurity platform led to global crashes of Microsoft Windows systems. The problem stemmed from a sensor configuration update that introduced a logic error in a critical system file. This error caused an out-of-bounds memory read, leading to "blue screens of death" on affected Windows machines. The update was quickly rolled back, but not before an estimated 8.5 million Windows systems had been affected, according to Microsoft.

To prevent similar problems in the future, CrowdStrike implemented several measures, including enhancing their internal update validation processes and adopting new testing methods such as fault injection to detect potential errors before updates are widely deployed. They also announced plans to roll out updates more gradually and to a smaller group of devices in order to catch issues early.

The CrowdStrike incident drew extensive attention from cybersecurity organizations, including the U.S. Cybersecurity and Infrastructure Security Agency (CISA), which warned about the potential for threat actors to exploit the situation, particularly through phishing attempts that targeted users affected by the outage. The impact on affected organizations was severe in some cases. News reports indicated that Delta Airlines alone was expected to suffer losses of up to $500 million and that the total cost of the incident was expected to be in the billions of dollars.

The CrowdStrike update failure was expected to lead to significant changes in cybersecurity practices from many organizations:

- Enhanced validation processes for planned updates
- Staggered rollouts, including pilot rollouts for critical updates
- Improvement in incident response and crisis communication practices
- Increased focus on recovery mechanisms
- Stronger vendor management and accountability

Overall, the CrowdStrike incident serves as a critical reminder of the importance of rigorous testing, phased deployment strategies, and effective communication in cybersecurity practices. It is likely to influence future industry standards and individual company practices.

Cybersecurity Employment Practices

The general management community of interest should integrate solid cybersecurity concepts across the organization's employment policies and practices. The following sections examine important concepts associated with recruiting, hiring, firing, managing, and releasing personnel. Including cybersecurity responsibilities in every employee's job description and subsequent performance reviews can make everyone in the organization take cybersecurity more seriously.

Hiring

From a cybersecurity perspective, the hiring of employees is laden with potential cybersecurity pitfalls. The chief security officer (CSO), in cooperation with the chief information officer (CIO) and relevant cybersecurity managers, should establish a dialogue with HR personnel and the departments or divisions requesting new personnel so that cybersecurity considerations become part of the hiring process. Figure 9-1 highlights some of the hiring concerns.

Figure 9-1 Cybersecurity hiring issues

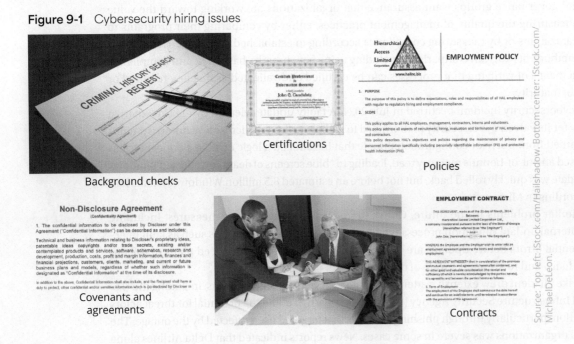

Background checks

Certifications

Policies

Covenants and agreements

Contracts

Job Descriptions

Integrating cybersecurity into the hiring process begins with reviewing and updating job descriptions to include cybersecurity responsibilities and screening for unwanted disclosures. Organizations that provide complete job descriptions when advertising open positions should omit elements of the job description that describe access privileges or the type and sensitivity of information to which the position would have access. Individuals who want to gain access to an organization's information may seek positions within it based on the description of access. Job descriptions should be focused on the skills and abilities needed by the candidate rather than describing the organization's systems, its cybersecurity, and details of the access or responsibilities the new hire will have.

Interviews

Some organizations use members of the HR staff to perform hiring interviews, whereas others prefer to include members of the department that the employee will eventually join. When a position within the cybersecurity department opens, the cybersecurity manager can take the opportunity to educate HR personnel on various relevant certifications, the specific experience each credential requires, and the qualifications of a good candidate. In general, the cybersecurity department should advise HR to limit the information provided to the candidates during the interview when it comes to the cybersecurity and systems details of the position. When an interview includes a site visit, the tour should avoid secure and restricted sites, as the job candidate is not yet bound by organizational policy or an employment contract and could observe enough information about the organization's operations or cybersecurity functions to represent a potential threat.

Background Checks

A background check should be conducted before the organization extends an offer to any candidate, regardless of job level. A background check can uncover past criminal behavior or other information that suggests a potential for future misconduct or a vulnerability that might make a candidate susceptible to coercion or blackmail. There are privacy regulations that govern which areas organizations are permitted to investigate and how the information gathered can influence the hiring decision. The cybersecurity and HR managers should discuss these matters with legal counsel to determine which regulations apply.

Background checks differ in their levels of detail and depth. In the government and military, background checks are used to help determine an individual's security clearance. In the business world, the thoroughness of a background check can vary with the level of trust required for the position being filled. Candidates for cybersecurity positions should expect to undergo a reasonably detailed and thorough background check. Those applying for jobs in law enforcement or high-trust positions may be required to submit to polygraph tests. Some of the common types of background checks are as follows:

- Identity checks—Personal identity validation; is the person who they claim to be?
- Education and credential checks—Institutions attended, degrees and certifications earned, and certification status
- Previous employment verification—Where candidates worked, why they left, what they did, and for how long
- Reference checks—Validity of references and integrity of reference sources
- Worker's compensation history—Claims from worker's compensation
- Motor vehicle records—Driving records, suspensions, and other items noted in the applicant's public record
- Drug history—Drug screening and drug usage, past and present
- Medical history—Current and previous medical conditions, usually associated with physical capability to perform the work in the specified position
- Credit history—Credit problems, financial problems, and bankruptcy

- Civil court history—Involvement as the plaintiff or defendant in civil suits
- Criminal court history—Criminal background, arrests, convictions, and time served[1]

Organizations must comply with regulations regarding the use of personal information in employment practices. Among the relevant federal regulations is the Fair Credit Reporting Act (FCRA), enacted in 1970, which governs the activities of consumer credit reporting agencies as well as the uses of the information procured from these agencies. Credit reports contain information on a job candidate's credit history, employment history, and other personal data.[2]

Among other things, FCRA prohibits employers from obtaining a credit report unless the candidate gives written permission for such a report to be released. This regulation also allows the candidate to request information on the nature and type of reporting used in making the employment decision, to know the content of these reports, and to know how they were used in making the hiring decision. FCRA restricts the time frame that these reports can cover. Unless the candidate earns more than $75,000 per year, the reports can contain only adverse information from the last seven years.[3]

Note 1 | For more information on background checks, including restrictions on the collection, use, and disposition of background information, visit the Federal Trade Commission's website at www.ftc.gov/business-guidance/resources/background-checks-what-employers-need-know.

Contracts and Employment

Once a candidate has accepted a job offer, the employment contract becomes an important cybersecurity instrument. Many of the policies discussed earlier in the book require an employee to agree to compliance in writing. It is important to have these contracts and agreements in place at the time of hire, as job offers can stipulate "employment contingent upon agreement," meaning people are not formally hired into a position unless they agree to the binding organizational policies. While such a policy may seem harsh, it is a necessary component of the cybersecurity process. Once a candidate signs the cybersecurity agreements, the remainder of the employment contract may be executed.

New Hire Orientation

As part of their orientation, new employees should receive an extensive cybersecurity briefing. This should cover policies, cybersecurity procedures, access levels, and training on the secure use of information technology (IT) systems. By the time new employees are ready to report to their supervisors, they should be thoroughly briefed on the cybersecurity component of their new positions as well as the rights and responsibilities of all personnel in the organization.

On-the-Job Cybersecurity Training

As described in earlier chapters, organizations should conduct periodic security education, training, and awareness (SETA) activities to keep cybersecurity at the forefront of employees' minds and minimize employee mistakes. SETA seminars also increase the level of cybersecurity awareness for all employees, especially cybersecurity employees.

Cybersecurity Expectations in the Performance Evaluation

To heighten cybersecurity awareness and change workplace behavior, organizations should incorporate cybersecurity components into employee performance evaluations. Employees tend to pay close attention to job performance evaluations. Including cybersecurity tasks in the employees' periodic evaluations will motivate them to take more care when performing these tasks.

For example, adding assessment areas and evaluation criteria for frequently encountered cybersecurity accountabilities might be reflected in review comments like these:

- Jane is meticulous in her management of classified documents.
- Tom continually emphasizes cybersecurity to coworkers.
- Tsu Ling led her department in the acquisition of new mobile devices with enhanced cybersecurity.
- Bob worked tirelessly to safeguard the newly developed intellectual property his team was responsible for.

Termination Issues

An organization can downsize, be bought out, be taken over, shut down, go out of business, or simply lay off, fire, or relocate its workforce. In any event, when an employee leaves an organization, many cybersecurity-related concerns arise. Chief among these is the continuity of protection of all information to which the employee had access. When an employee leaves an organization, the following tasks must be performed:

- The former employee's access to the organization's systems must be disabled.
- The former employee must return all organizational property, including any issued removable media, technology, and data.
- The former employee's hard drives must be secured.
- File cabinet locks must be changed or rekeyed.
- Office door locks must be changed or rekeyed.
- The former employee's keycard access must be revoked.
- The former employee's personal effects must be removed from the premises.
- The former employee should be escorted from the premises once keys, keycards, identification credentials, and any remaining organizational property have been turned over.

In addition to performing these tasks, organizations should conduct an exit interview to remind the employee of any contractual obligations, such as nondisclosure agreements, and to obtain feedback on the employee's tenure in the organization. At this time, the employee should be reminded that failure to comply with contractual obligations could lead to civil or criminal action.

Of course, depending on the type of departure, most employees are allowed to clean out their own offices, collect their personal belongings, and return their keys. From a cybersecurity standpoint, however, regardless of the level of trust in the employee or the level of cordiality in the office environment, voluntary or involuntary termination inevitably brings a risk of exposure of organizational information.

Some organizations adopt a policy of immediate severance for all employees, or for employees in certain positions or areas of trust. These organizations have examined the risks of the customary two-week notice model and instead opt to pay two weeks' severance while asking the employee to leave the facility immediately.

Two methods for processing departing employees, depending on the employee's reasons for leaving, are as follows:

- Hostile departure (usually involuntary), including termination, downsizing, layoff, or resignation—The security staff cuts off all logical and keycard access before the employee is terminated. As soon as the employee reports for work, they are escorted into their supervisor's office to receive the bad news. The individual is then escorted to their office, cubicle, or personal area to collect personal effects under supervision. No organizational property is allowed to leave the premises, including digital or hard-copy information. Once personal property has been gathered, the employee is asked to surrender all keys, keycards, other organizational identification and access devices, mobile phones and computing devices, and all other company property, and is then escorted from the building.

- Friendly departure (voluntary) for retirement, promotion, or relocation—The employee may tender notice well in advance of the actual departure date, but if the employee gives notice at the last minute, it can be much more difficult for cybersecurity staff to maintain positive control over the employee's access and information usage. Employee accounts are usually allowed to continue with a new expiration date. The employee can come and go at will and usually collects any belongings and leaves without an escort. The employee is asked to drop off all organizational property before departing.

In either circumstance, the offices and information used by departing employees must be inventoried, their files stored or destroyed, and all property returned to organizational stores. It is possible in either situation that departing employees have collected organizational information and taken home files, reports, data, and other items that could be valuable in their future employment. This outcome may be impossible to prevent. If the departing employee worked in the IT or cybersecurity department, the situation could become much more difficult to manage. For example, the employee may have set up alternate access methods or credentials, allowing indirect access to information even after their access has been revoked. Only by scrutinizing system logs during and after the employee's departure and distinguishing authorized actions from system misuse or information theft can the organization determine whether a breach of policy or a loss of information has occurred. If information has been illegally copied or stolen, it should be treated as an incident and the appropriate policy and plan must be followed.

Personnel Cybersecurity Practices

There are various ways of monitoring and controlling employees to minimize their opportunities to misuse information. Separation of duties (also known as segregation of duties) makes it difficult for an individual to violate cybersecurity and breach the confidentiality, integrity, or availability of information. This control is particularly important in financial matters. For example, banks typically require two employees to issue a cashier's check. The first is authorized to prepare the check for signature. The second, usually a supervisor, is authorized to sign the check. If one person has the authority to do both tasks, that person can prepare checks made out to co-conspirators, sign them, and steal large sums from the bank.

Separation of duties can also be applied to critical information and IT systems. For example, one programmer might update systems software and a supervisor or coworker might then apply the tested update to the production system following the procedures of the change management process. Alternatively, one employee might be authorized to initiate backups to the system, while another mounts and dismounts the physical media. Defeating this method of checks and balances requires collusion—a conspiracy or cooperation between two or more individuals or groups to commit illegal or unethical actions. The odds that two people will be able to collaborate successfully to misuse the system are much lower than the odds of one person doing so. A practice like separation of duties is two-person control or dual control, the organization of a task or process so that it requires at least two individuals to perform. Such a control requires that multiple individuals work on a task together and in some cases review and approve each other's work before the task is considered complete. Figure 9-2 illustrates the separation of duties and two-person control.

Other controls used to prevent personnel from misusing information assets are job rotation, the requirement that every employee be able to perform the work of at least one other employee, and task rotation, the requirement that all critical tasks can be performed by multiple individuals. Both job rotation and task rotation ensure that no one employee is performing actions that cannot be reviewed by another employee. In general, this overlap of knowledge is just good business sense. Among the many threats to an organization's information, a major concern is the inability to perform the tasks of a key employee who is suddenly unable or unwilling to perform them. If everyone knows at least part of another person's job, the organization can survive the loss of any single employee.

For similar reasons, many organizations implement a mandatory vacation policy—a requirement that all employees take time off from work, which allows the organization to audit the individual's areas of responsibility. This policy gives the organization a chance to perform a detailed review of everyone's work and work area. Employees who are stealing from an organization or otherwise misusing information or systems are reluctant to take vacations for fear that their actions will be detected if they are not present to conceal them. In order for such a policy to have a reliable effect, employees designated for mandatory vacations will have to be fully disconnected from the workplace with enforced rules mandating complete disengagement over all channels—remote connections, phone, and email.

Figure 9-2 Personnel cybersecurity controls

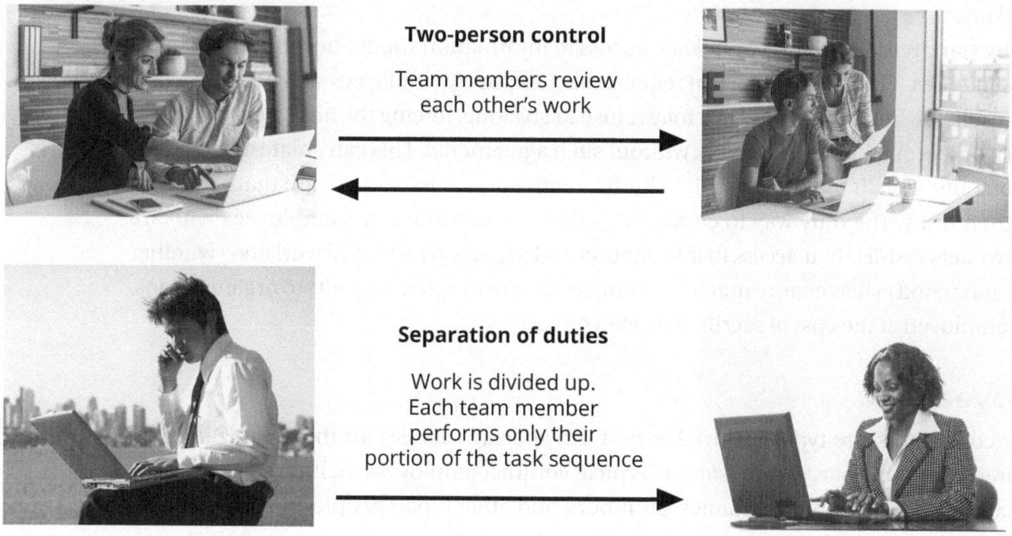

Source: Top left: Stock Rocket/Shutterstock.com. Bottom left: arek_malang/Shutterstock.com. Top right: Stock Rocket/Shutterstock.com. Bottom right: iofoto/Shutterstock.com.

Finally, another important way to minimize opportunities for employee misuse of information is to limit access to it through need-to-know and least privilege. These concepts were discussed in previous chapters.

Personnel and Personal Data Cybersecurity

Organizations are required by law to protect sensitive or personal employee information, including personal identifiable information such as employee addresses, phone numbers, Social Security numbers, medical conditions, other protected health information, and even names and addresses of family members. This responsibility also extends to customers, patients, and anyone with whom the organization has business relationships. While personnel data is, in principle, no different from other data that cybersecurity is expected to protect, certainly more regulations cover its protection. As a result, cybersecurity procedures should ensure that this data receives at least the same level of protection as the other important data in the organization.

Cybersecurity Considerations for Temporary Employees, Consultants, and Other Workers

People who are not regular employees of an organization often have access to sensitive organizational information. Relationships with people in this category should be carefully managed to prevent threats to information assets from materializing. Some of the workers in this category, and the cybersecurity considerations specific to them, are discussed in the sections that follow.

Temporary Workers

Temporary workers, or temps, are brought in by organizations to fill positions temporarily or to supplement the existing workforce. In many cases, they are employed and paid by a "temp agency," a company under contract to supply specially qualified individuals to an organization. Temps frequently provide secretarial or administrative support but can be used to fill almost any position in an organization, including executive positions. These workers are often exposed to a wide range of information as they perform their assigned duties. Because they are not employed by the organization for which they are working, however, they may not be subject to the contractual obligations or general policies that govern other employees. Therefore, if a temp violates a policy or causes a problem, the strongest action that the host organization can take is to terminate the relationship with the individual and request that they be censured by their employer. The employing agency is under no contractual obligation to do so but may want to accommodate a powerful or lucrative client. Unless specified in its contract with the organization, the temp agency may not be liable for losses caused by its workers.

From a cybersecurity standpoint, temporary workers' access to information should be limited to what is necessary to perform their duties. The organization can request that temporary employees sign nondisclosure agreements and fair-use policies, but the temp agency may refuse to go along, forcing the host organization to either dismiss the temp workers or allow them to work without such agreements. This can create an awkward and potentially dangerous situation. It may be difficult to limit a temp's access to information that is beyond the scope of their assigned tasks. The only way to combat this threat is to ensure that employees who are supervising temporary workers restrict their access to information and to make sure that all workers—whether employees or temps—follow good cybersecurity practices. Temps can provide great benefits to organizations, but they should not be employed at the cost of sacrificing cybersecurity.

Contract Employees

Contract employees, or contractors, are typically hired to perform specific services for the organization. In many cases, they are hired via a third-party organization. Typical contract employees include groundskeepers, maintenance services staff, electricians, mechanics, plumbers, and other repair people, but they can also include professionals such as attorneys, business consultants, and IT specialists.

While some contractors may require access to virtually all areas of the organization to do their jobs, most only need access to specific facilities and should not be allowed to wander freely in and out of buildings. In a secure facility, all contractors are escorted into and out of the facility and from room to room. When these contractors report to perform or provide services, someone must verify that those services were scheduled or requested. As mentioned earlier in this text, attackers have been known to dress up as telephone repairers, maintenance technicians, or janitors to gain physical access to a building. Any service agreements or contracts should contain the following stipulations: (1) The facility requires at least a 24-hour advance notice of a maintenance visit; (2) the facility requires all on-site personnel to undergo background checks; and (3) the facility requires advance notice for cancellation or rescheduling of a maintenance visit.

Consultants

Organizations sometimes hire self-employed or agent consultants for specific tasks or projects. Consultants have their own cybersecurity requirements and contractual obligations. The consultant contract should specify all necessary restrictions to information and facilities. Cybersecurity and IT consultants must be pre-screened, escorted at all times while on the organization's premises, and required to sign nondisclosure agreements to protect against intentional or accidental breaches.

Consultants seeking to engage a potential client might tend to call attention to the complexity of a particular job or previous services provided to a particularly prestigious client. If the organization does not want a consultant to make the relationship public or to disclose any details about its IT systems or cybersecurity configurations, the organization must write these restrictions into the contract. Although these professionals typically request permission to include the business relationship on their résumés or promotional materials, the hiring organization is not obligated to grant this permission and can explicitly deny it.

Just because you pay cybersecurity consultants does not mean that protecting your information is their top priority. Always remember to apply the principle of least privilege when working with consultants.

Business Partners

Businesses sometimes engage in strategic alliances with other organizations to exchange information, integrate systems, or enjoy some other mutual advantage. In these situations, a data use agreement or data transfer agreement is used to specify the levels of exposure that both organizations are willing to tolerate. Sometimes, one division of an organization enters a strategic partnership with an organization that also partners with the organization's competition. If the strategic partnership evolves into an integration of the systems of all companies involved, competing groups may be provided with information that neither organization expected. For this reason, there must be a meticulous, deliberate process of determining what information is to be exchanged, in which format, and with whom. Nondisclosure agreements are an important part of any such collaborative effort. The level of cybersecurity of all interconnected systems must be examined before any integration takes place; once the systems are connected, a vulnerability on one system becomes a vulnerability for all linked systems.

Self-Check

1. Job descriptions for cybersecurity positions should detail the specific access privileges the positions will have.

   a. True   **b.** False

2. Background checks for a cybersecurity position should include a thorough review of the candidate's educational and credential background.

   a. True   **b.** False

3. Temporary workers should have unrestricted access to all organizational information to perform their duties effectively.

   a. True   **b.** False

☐ Check your answers at the end of this chapter.

Cybersecurity Performance Measurement

Executives often ask the CSO questions like "What will this cybersecurity control cost?" or "Is it working?," or the even more ominous "Why did our cybersecurity fail?" As noted by chief information security officer and author Gerald Kovacich, "This last question often comes right after a successful attack."[4] While CSOs sometimes claim that the costs, benefits, and performance of cybersecurity are almost impossible to measure, in fact they are measurable; doing so requires the design and ongoing use of a cybersecurity performance management program based on effective performance measures.

Note 2 | Special Publication (SP) 800-55, Rev. 2 is currently in its initial working draft. It can be viewed at https://nvlpubs.nist.gov/nistpubs/SpecialPublications/NIST.SP.800-55r2.iwd.pdf. This publication is available from the National Institute of Standards and Technology (NIST).

Cybersecurity Performance Management

Organizations can use a program of cybersecurity performance management—the process of designing, implementing, and managing the use of specific measurements to determine the effectiveness of a cybersecurity program and its components. Performance measurements (or performance measures) are the data or trends in data that may indicate the effectiveness of cybersecurity efforts and programs implemented in the organization. All cybersecurity efforts and programs require some method of assessing the results of their use. Activities that are not effective should be modified or replaced, while those that are effective should be supported and continued. Measurement supports managerial decision making, increasing accountability and improving the effectiveness of the cybersecurity function. It also can help the organization align cybersecurity performance and objectives with the organization's overall mission.[5]

Measures, Metrics, and Key Performance Indicators

Many organizations use the terms "measures," "metrics," and "key performance indicators (KPIs)" interchangeably. The terms "metrics" and "measures," while originally different, have come to mean the same thing in use. A KPI is a measure of strategic interest to the organization. So, all KPIs are measures, but not all measures are KPIs. The governance team may identify a set of measures to classify as KPIs, which become a priority for collection, analysis, and reporting and will influence future cybersecurity efforts. This text adopts the NIST approach and uses the term "measures" to describe the results (the data that is collected, analyzed, and reported) of a measurement program (the process).[6]

Organizations typically use three types of measures:

- Those that determine the effectiveness of the execution of cybersecurity policy, most commonly issue-specific policies
- Those that determine the effectiveness and efficiency of delivering cybersecurity services
- Those that assess the impact of an incident or other cybersecurity event on the organization or its mission[7]

Performance measures are increasingly required in today's regulated cybersecurity environment. It is no longer sufficient simply to assert effective cybersecurity; to document due diligence, an organization must show that it is taking effective steps to control risk. According to NIST's SP 800-55, Rev. 1: "Performance Measurement Guide for Information Security," the following factors must be considered during development and implementation of a cybersecurity performance management program:

- Measures must yield quantifiable information (percentages, averages, and other numbers).
- Data that supports the measures needs to be readily obtainable.
- Only repeatable cybersecurity processes should be considered for measurement.
- Measures must be useful for tracking performance and directing resources.[8]

SP 800-55, Rev. 1 also identifies four factors as critical to the success of a cybersecurity performance measurement program:

- Strong upper-level management support—This is critical not only for the success of the measurement program but for the program's implementation.
- Practical cybersecurity policies and procedures—These should specify the cybersecurity management structure, identify key responsibilities, and lay the foundation to reliably measure progress and compliance.
- Quantifiable performance measures—These should be designed to capture and provide meaningful performance data. Based on cybersecurity performance goals and objectives, performance measures should be easily obtainable and feasible to implement.
- Results-oriented measures analyses—These should be used to apply lessons learned, improve effectiveness of existing cybersecurity controls, and plan for the implementation of future cybersecurity controls to meet new requirements as they occur.[9]

Managing cybersecurity performance measurement programs requires commitment from the cybersecurity management team. This effort will consume resources, including people's time, hardware cycles, and perhaps an investment in specialty software. The results of the effort must be periodically and consistently reviewed to make sure they remain relevant and useful. Before beginning the process of designing, collecting, and using measures, the CSO should be prepared to answer the following questions posed by Gerald Kovacich in *The Information Systems Security Officer's Guide*[10]:

- Why should these measures be collected?
- What specific measures will be collected?
- How will these measures be collected?
- When will these measures be collected?
- Who will collect these measures?
- Where (at what point in the function's process) will these measures be collected?

Building the Performance Measurement Program

Even with strong management support, a cybersecurity performance measurement program must be able to demonstrate value to the organization. The CSO, who is a key participant in the measurement program's development, must assist in building the case for the program.

The benefits of using a cybersecurity performance measurement program, according to SP 800-55, Rev. 1, include "increasing accountability for cybersecurity performance; improving effectiveness of cybersecurity activities; demonstrating compliance with laws, rules, and regulations; and providing quantifiable inputs for resource allocation decisions."[11]

A popular reference that supports the development of process improvement and performance measurement is *CMMI Distilled*, which is available from the CMMI Institute of ISACA (https://cmmiinstitute.com).

> Originally created for the U.S. Department of Defense to assess the quality and capability of their software contractors, CMMI models have expanded beyond software engineering to help any organization in any industry build, improve, and measure their capabilities and improve performance.
>
> CMMI best practices focus on what needs to be done to improve performance and align operations to business goals.
>
> ISACA's CMMI models help organizations understand their current level of capability and performance and offer a guide to optimize business results.[12]

Another popular approach, the one upon which this chapter is based, is that of NIST's SP 800-55, Rev. 1. The cybersecurity measurement development process recommended by NIST is shown in Figure 9-3. It is divided into two major activities:

- Identification and definition of the current cybersecurity program
- Development and selection of specific measures to gauge the implementation, effectiveness, efficiency, and impact of cybersecurity controls

Figure 9-3 Cybersecurity measurement program development

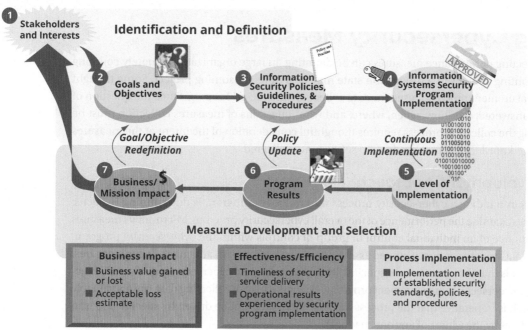

Phase 1 of the performance measurement development process identifies relevant stakeholders and their interests in cybersecurity measurement. The primary stakeholders are those with key cybersecurity responsibilities or data ownership. Secondary stakeholders, such as training and HR personnel, may not be primarily responsible for cybersecurity but have relevant tasks in some aspect of their jobs.

Phase 2 of the process is to identify and document the cybersecurity performance goals and objectives that would guide the implementation of controls for the cybersecurity program of a specific IT system.

Phase 3 focuses on organization-specific cybersecurity practices. Details of how cybersecurity controls should be implemented are usually provided in organization-specific policies and procedures that define a baseline of cybersecurity practices for its systems.

In Phase 4, any existing measures and data repositories that can be used to derive measurement data are reviewed. Following the review, applicable information is extracted and used to identify appropriate evidence of implementation that supports measurement development and data collection.

Phases 5, 6, and 7 involve developing measures that track process implementation, efficiency, effectiveness, and mission impact.[13]

Specifying Cybersecurity Measures

One critical task in the measurement process is to assess and quantify what will be measured. Cybersecurity planning and organizing activities may only require time estimates, but you must obtain more detailed measures when assessing the effort spent to complete production and project tasks. This usually means some form of time reporting system, either a paper-based or automated time accounting mechanism.

Measures collected from production statistics depend greatly on the number of systems and the number of users of those systems. As these two values change, the effort to maintain the same level of service will vary. Some organizations simply track these two values to measure the service being delivered. Other organizations need more detailed measures, perhaps including the number of new users added, number of access control changes, number of users removed or deauthorized, number of access control violations, number of awareness briefings, number of systems by type, number of incidents by category (such as virus or worm outbreaks), number of malicious code instances blocked by filters, and many other possible measures.

Collecting measures about project activities may be even more challenging. Unless the organization is satisfied with a simple tally of who spent how many hours doing what tasks (which is more project management than performance measurement), it needs some mechanism to link the outcome of each project, in terms of loss control or risk reduction, to the resources consumed. This is not a trivial process; most organizations rely on narrative explanations rather than measure-driven calculations to justify project expenditures.

Collecting Cybersecurity Measures

The prospect of collecting performance measures can be daunting. In large organizations, merely counting the number of computing systems in a production state may be a time-consuming project. Some thought must go into the measurement processes used for data collection and record keeping. Once the question of what to measure is answered, the "how, when, where, and who" questions of measures collection must be addressed. Designing the collection process requires thoughtful consideration of the intent of the measures along with a thorough knowledge of how production services are delivered.

Measures Development Approach

One of the priorities in building a cybersecurity process measurement program is determining its focus. Macro-focus measures examine the performance of the overall cybersecurity program. Micro-focus measures examine the performance of an individual control or group of controls within the cybersecurity program. Some organizations may want to conduct a limited assessment using both macro- and micro-focus measures.

What is important is that the measures are specifically tied to individual cybersecurity goals and objectives. Implementing a cybersecurity measurement program just for the sake of collecting data wastes valuable resources. Therefore, it is imperative that the process measurement program be driven by specific needs in the organization and not by the whims of any one manager.

Measures Prioritization and Selection

Because organizations seem to better manage what they measure (and incentivize), it is important to ensure that individual metrics are prioritized in the same manner as the processes that they measure. This can be achieved with a simple low-, medium-, or high-priority ranking system or a weighted scale approach, which would involve assigning values to each measure based on its importance in the context of the overall cybersecurity program and in the overall risk mitigation goals and criticality of the systems. While literally hundreds of measures could be used, only those associated with higher-priority activities should be incorporated. After all, the personnel resources needed to develop, implement, collect, analyze, and report the data are most likely limited, and other activities will inevitably compete for the use of those resources.

Establishing Performance Targets

Performance targets make it possible to define success in the cybersecurity program. For example, a goal of 100 percent employee cybersecurity training as an objective for the training program validates the continued collection of training measures. A periodic report indicating the status of employee training represents progress toward the goal. Many targets of cybersecurity performance measures are represented by a 100 percent target goal. Other types of performance measures, such as those used to determine the relative effectiveness, efficiency, or impact of cybersecurity on the organization's goals, tend to be more subjective and will require management to assess the purpose and value of such measures. For example, the increase in relative or perceived cybersecurity of the organization's information after the installation of a firewall requires a completely different perspective than that required from assessing personnel training performance through empirical measurement of attendance at training sessions or the evaluation of post-training quiz scores.

This example highlights one of the fundamental challenges in cybersecurity performance measurement—namely, defining effective cybersecurity. When is cybersecurity effective? Researchers who study cybersecurity success continue to grapple with this question. There is little agreement about how to define a successful program; some argue that simply avoiding losses is the best measurement, while others argue that any valid measure must be provable. The avoidance of losses may be attributed to luck or other factors unrelated to the program. This dilemma remains unresolved.

Measures Development Template

NIST recommends the documentation of performance measures in a standardized format to ensure the repeatability of their development, customization, collection, and reporting activities. One way to accomplish this is to develop a custom template that an organization can use to document its performance measures. Instructions for the development and format of such a template are provided in Table 9-1.

Table 9-1 Performance measures template and instructions

Field	Data
Measurement ID	Unique identifier used to measure tracking and sorting. The unique identifier can be from an organization-specific naming convention or directly reference another source. It should be meaningful to the source and use of the measure.
Goal	Statement of strategic goal or cybersecurity goal. For system-level cybersecurity control measures, the goal would guide cybersecurity control implementation for that information system.
	For program-level measures, both strategic goals and cybersecurity goals can be included. For example, cybersecurity goals can be derived from enterprise-level goals in support of the organization's mission. These goals are usually articulated in strategic and performance plans. When possible, include both the enterprise-level goal and the specific cybersecurity goal extracted from agency documentation, or identify a cybersecurity program goal that would contribute to the selected strategic goal.

(Continues)

Table 9-1   Performance measures template and instructions (*Continued*)

Field	Data
Measure	Statement of measure. Precisely identify the element to be measured; start with a percentage, number, frequency, average, or a similar term. If applicable, list the NIST SP 800-53 cybersecurity control(s) being measured. Any related cybersecurity controls providing supporting data should be identified. If the measures are applicable to a specific FIPS 199 impact level (high, moderate, or low), provide that means of evaluation.
Measure type	Statement of whether the measure is of implementation, effectiveness/efficiency, or impact.
Formula	Calculation to be performed that results in a numeric expression of a measure. The information gathered through listing implementation evidence serves as an input to the formula for calculating the measure.
Target	Threshold for a satisfactory rating for the measure, such as milestone completion or a statistical measure. The target can be expressed in percentages, time, dollars, or other appropriate units of measure. The target may be tied to a time frame for required completion. Select a final and interim target to enable tracking of progress toward the stated goal.
Implementation evidence	Use of implementation evidence to compute the measure, validate that the activity is performed, and identify probable causes of unsatisfactory results for a specific measure. 1. For manual data collection, identify questions and data elements that would provide data inputs necessary to calculate the measure's formula, qualify the measure for acceptance, and validate provided information. 2. For each question or query, list the status cybersecurity control number from NIST SP 800-53 that provides information, if applicable. 3. If the measure is applicable to a specific FIPS 199 impact level, questions should state the impact level. 4. For automated data collection, identify data elements that would be required for the formula, to qualify the measure for acceptance, and to validate the information provided.
Frequency	Indication of how often the data is collected and analyzed and how often the data is reported. State the frequency of data collection based on a rate of change in a particular cybersecurity control that is being evaluated. State the frequency of data reporting based on external reporting requirements and internal customer preferences.
Responsible parties	Indication of the following key stakeholders: • Information owner: Identify the organizational component and an individual who owns required pieces of information. • Information collector: Identify the organizational component and individual responsible for collecting the data. If possible, the information collector should not be the information owner or should even be a representative of a different organizational unit to avoid the possibility of conflict of interest and ensure separation of duties. Smaller organizations will need to determine whether it is feasible to separate these two responsibilities. • Information customer: Identify the organizational component and individual who will receive the data.
Data source	Location of the data to be used in calculating the measure. Include databases, tracking tools, organizations, or specific roles within organizations that can provide required information.
Reporting format	Indication of how the measure will be reported, such as pie charts, line charts, bar graphs, or another format. State the type of format or provide a sample.

Source: NIST SP 800-55, Rev. 1

An example of how one measure might be documented using the preceding template is provided in Table 9-2.

Table 9-2 Performance measure example

Field	Example Data
Measurement ID	Cybersecurity training coverage
Goal	Strategic goal: Ensure a high-quality workforce supported by modern and secure infrastructure and operational capabilities Cybersecurity goal: Ensure that the organization's personnel are adequately trained to carry out their assigned cybersecurity-related duties and responsibilities
Measure	The percentage of cybersecurity personnel who have received cybersecurity training
Measure type	Implementation
Formula	Number of cybersecurity personnel who have completed cybersecurity training within the past year divided by the total number of cybersecurity personnel, then multiplied by 100
Target	100 percent

Implementation evidence	1. Are significant cybersecurity responsibilities defined with qualifications criteria and documented in policy? Yes/No
	2. Are records kept for which employees have significant cybersecurity responsibilities? Yes/No
	3. How many employees in your department have significant cybersecurity responsibilities?
	4. Are training records maintained? Yes/No
	5. How many of those with significant cybersecurity responsibilities have received the required training?
	6. If all personnel have not received training, document all reasons that apply:
	   a. Insufficient funding
	   b. Insufficient time
	   c. Courses unavailable
	   d. Employee not registered
	   e. Other (specify)

Frequency	Collected as training is delivered Reported annually
Responsible parties	Information owner: training division Information collector: training division Information customer: CIO
Data source	Training and awareness tracking records
Reporting format	Pie chart illustrating the percentage of cybersecurity personnel who have received training versus those who have not received training If performance is below target, pie chart illustrating causes of the shortfall

Candidate Measures

A few example candidate measurements are provided in Table 9-3. Additional details on these measurements, including how they are calculated and used, are provided in NIST SP 800-55, Rev. 1.

Table 9-3   Examples of possible cybersecurity performance measurements

Percentage of the organization's information systems budget devoted to cybersecurity
Percentage of important vulnerabilities mitigated within organizationally defined time periods after discovery
Percentage space of remote access points used to gain unauthorized access
Percentage of information systems personnel who have received cybersecurity training
Average frequency of audit records review and analysis for inappropriate activity
Percentage of new systems that have completed operational risk assessment prior to their implementation
Percentage of approved and implemented configuration changes identified in the latest automated baseline configuration
Percentage of information systems that have conducted annual contingency plan testing
Percentage of users with access to shared accounts
Percentage of incidents reported within required time frame per applicable incident category
Percentage of system components that undergo maintenance in accordance with formal maintenance schedules
Percentage of media that passes sanitization procedures testing
Percentage of physical cybersecurity incidents allowing unauthorized entry into facilities containing information assets
Percentage of employees who are authorized access to information systems only after they sign an acknowledgment that they have read and understood the appropriate policies
Percentage of individuals screened before being granted access to organizational information and information systems
Percentage of vulnerabilities remediated within organizationally specified time frames
Percentage of system and service acquisition contracts that include recognized cybersecurity requirements and specifications
Percentage of mobile computers and devices that perform all cryptographic operations using organizationally specified cryptographic modules in approved modes of operation
Percentage of operating system vulnerabilities for which patches have been applied or that have been otherwise mitigated

Source: NIST SP 800-55, Rev. 1

Implementing Cybersecurity Performance Measurement

Once developed, cybersecurity performance measurements must be implemented and integrated into ongoing cybersecurity management operations. For the most part, it is insufficient simply to collect these measures once, although some activities only require the collection of data for one particular purpose, such as those that might occur when identifying costs in a formal cost–benefit analysis. Performance measurement is an ongoing, continuous improvement operation. The collection of all measurement data should be part of standard operating procedures across the organization.

The process for performance measurement implementation recommended in NIST SP 800-55, Rev. 1 involves six subordinate tasks, as shown in Figure 9-4:

- Phase 1—Prepare for data collection; identify, define, develop, and select cybersecurity measures.
- Phase 2—Collect data and analyze results; collect, aggregate, and consolidate measurement data collection and compare measures with targets (gap analysis).
- Phase 3—Identify corrective actions; develop a plan to serve as the road map for closing the gap identified in Phase 2. This includes determining the range of corrective actions, prioritizing corrective actions based on overall risk mitigation goals, and selecting the most appropriate corrective actions.
- Phase 4—Develop the business case.
- Phase 5—Obtain resources; address the budgeting cycle for acquiring resources needed to implement the remediation actions identified in Phase 3.
- Phase 6—Apply corrective actions; close the gap by implementing the recommended corrective actions in the cybersecurity program or in the cybersecurity controls.[14]

Figure 9-4   Implementing the cybersecurity measurement program

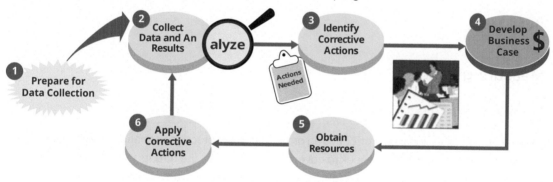

Reporting Cybersecurity Performance Measures

In most cases, simply listing the measurements collected does not adequately convey their meaning. For example, a line chart that shows the number of malicious code attacks occurring per day may communicate a basic fact, but unless the reporting mechanism can provide the context—for example, the number of new malicious code variants on the Internet in that time frame—the measure will not serve its intended purpose. In addition, you must make decisions about how to present correlated metrics—whether to use pie, line, scatter, or bar charts, and which colors to denote which kinds of results.

The CSO must also consider who should receive the results of the performance measurement program and how they should be delivered. The CSO often presents these types of reports in meetings with other key executives. It is seldom advisable to broadcast complex and nuanced metrics-based reports to large groups unless the key points are well established and embedded in a more complete context, such as a newsletter or press release.

Many organizations choose to implement a consolidated summary of key performance measures using a dashboard of cybersecurity indicators, as illustrated in Figure 9-5.

Figure 9-5   Cybersecurity dashboard

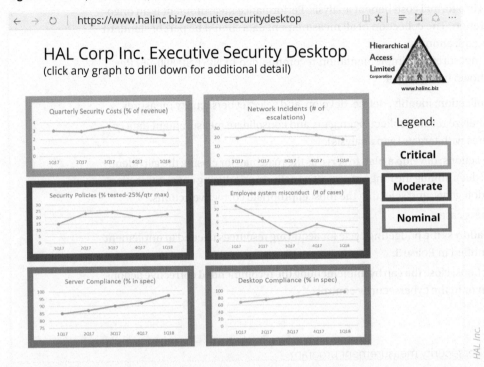

View Point   Measuring Success

By Martin Lee, Information Security Practitioner

Metrics tell the cybersecurity professional how effective an organization's protections are and if the situation is getting better or worse. These metrics should seek to cover measurement of the threats that the organization faces and the effectiveness of the mitigation strategies. Used judiciously, metrics illustrate the state of cybersecurity to specialists and nonspecialists alike.

The modern organization is not short of data from which to select metrics. Often, the answer to any question that a cybersecurity practitioner may wish to ask can be found in the data and logs generated by cybersecurity systems. A good metric simplifies this data to provide a concise answer to a pertinent question.

The adage "Not everything that can be counted counts, not everything that counts can be counted" ought to be remembered. Professionals should determine the figures that best illustrate how the organization is attaining its cybersecurity policy goals without overly expending effort. If a metric is computed from a scan of attached network devices to identify what percentage of them are patched against a suite of known vulnerabilities, that measure may provide a meaningful metric in its own right and may also represent the view that an attacker might have of internal systems.

In many safety-critical environments, statistics relating to events in which major incidents were only narrowly averted must be collected and reported. These can be taken as evidence of both the effectiveness of mitigations in averting a disaster and as evidence of failings in the overall mitigation regime because the threat was only neutralized at the last line of defense. The amount of missed spam or the detection of malware by endpoint protection systems similarly provide clear warnings of near misses and may illustrate weaknesses in protection.

Analyzing metrics by business unit identifies the departments that require attention to remedy cybersecurity weaknesses. For instance, a metric demonstrating that the entire organization meets the policy requirements for cybersecurity awareness may actually show that most business units exceed policy requirements but that a few fall below the required standard. Devoting resources to resolve these local problems can be an effective means of improving the levels of protection in the organization.

The collection of metrics should not be seen as an end in itself but as a means by which cybersecurity professionals identify weaknesses in protection and demonstrate progress toward cybersecurity goals.

Self-Check

4. The cost and effectiveness of cybersecurity controls are generally considered measurable.

   a. True   b. False

5. Only qualitative data should be considered when developing cybersecurity performance measures.

   a. True   b. False

6. Strong upper-level management support is not necessary for the success of a cybersecurity performance measurement program.

   a. True   b. False

□ Check your answers at the end of this chapter.

Benchmarking

As you learned earlier, organizations usually generate a cybersecurity blueprint by drawing from established cybersecurity models and frameworks. Another way to create such a blueprint is to look at the paths taken by organizations similar to the one whose plan you are developing. Using this method, which is called benchmarking (or external benchmarking), you improve practices by comparing an organization's efforts against the practices of a similar organization or an industry-developed standard to produce results you would like to duplicate. These organizations should be similar in size, structure, or industry. If the practices of similar organizations or industry standards appear to offer better results, the organization may choose to adopt all or portions of them. Because each organization is unique, you may need to modify or adapt portions of several recognized practices, as what works well for one organization may not precisely fit another. Benchmarking can help to determine which controls should be considered, but it cannot determine how those controls should be implemented in your organization or how successful they will be.

Benchmarking can also be used as an internal tool to compare current performance against past performance or a desired target value and to look for trends of improvement or areas that need additional work. This practice is known as internal benchmarking (or baselining); the comparisons improve practices by identifying progress or trends in performance, areas of excellence, and areas in need of improvement.

In cybersecurity, two categories of terms describing cybersecurity practices are commonly used: (1) standards of due care and due diligence and (2) recommended practices or best cybersecurity practices. The very best recommended practices are referred to as the gold standard.

Standards of Due Care and Due Diligence

For legal reasons, certain organizations may be compelled to adopt a stipulated minimum level of cybersecurity. Organizations that do so to establish a future legal defense may need to verify that they have done what any prudent organization would do in a comparable scenario. This is known as a standard of due care or simply *due care*—the legal standard that requires an organization and its employees to act as a "reasonable and prudent" individual or organization would under similar circumstances.

Implementing controls at this minimum standard—and maintaining them—demonstrates that an organization has performed due diligence. Although some argue that the two terms are interchangeable, the term "due diligence" (as in a standard of due diligence) encompasses a requirement that the implemented standards continue to provide the required level of protection; in other words, the organization has implemented a formal process to ensure continued compliance with the standards of due care. Failure to establish and maintain standards of due care and due diligence can expose an organization to legal liability if it can be shown that the organization was negligent in its application of information protection. This is especially important in organizations that maintain customer or client information, including medical, legal, or other personal data.

The cybersecurity environment that an organization must maintain is often large and complex. It may therefore be impossible to implement recommended practices in all categories at once. It may also be financially impossible for some organizations to provide cybersecurity levels on a par with those maintained by organizations that can spend more money on cybersecurity. Cybersecurity practices are often viewed relatively; as noted by F. M. Avolio, "Good cybersecurity now is better than perfect cybersecurity never," which is an applied version of the aphorism "The better is the enemy of the good [enough]." This adage dates to French and Italian sayings from the 1600s.[15]

Some organizations might want to implement the best, most technologically advanced controls available but cannot do so for financial, personnel, or other reasons. Ultimately, it is counterproductive to establish costly, state-of-the-art cybersecurity in one area, only to leave other areas exposed. Instead, organizations must make sure that they have met a reasonable level of cybersecurity in all areas and that they have adequately protected all information assets before making efforts to improve individual areas to meet the highest standards.

Recommended Cybersecurity Practices

Cybersecurity efforts to provide a superior level of performance in the protection of information are called recommended practices. In a similar vein, best practices are efforts that are considered among the best in the industry, although the terms are sometimes used interchangeably. These practices balance the need for information access with the need for adequate protection while demonstrating fiscal responsibility. Of course, companies with best practices may not have practices that are the best in every area; they may establish an extremely high-quality or successful cybersecurity effort in only one area. Yet, well-managed cybersecurity programs recognize the requirement that minimum quality standards are needed for the protection of all information assets.

> **Note 3** | To view several papers on best practices, visit the SANS White Paper website at sans.org/white-papers and search for "best practices."

Selecting Recommended Practices

Industries that are regulated by laws and standards and subject to government or industry oversight are required to meet regulatory or industry guidelines in their cybersecurity practices. For other organizations, government and industry guidelines can serve as excellent sources of information about what is required to control cybersecurity risks. These standards of performance can inform the selection of recommended practices.

When choosing recommended practices for your organization, consider the following questions:

- Does your organization resemble the target organization of the recommended practice? A recommended practice is only relevant if your organization is like the one from which the practice comes, at least in the area in which the practice will be applied.

- Are you in a similar industry as the target of the recommended practice? A strategy that works well in the manufacturing sector might have little relevance to a nonprofit organization or a retail enterprise.
- Do you face similar challenges as the target of the recommended practice? If your organization lacks a specific cybersecurity program, a recommended practice that assumes such a program is in place is not likely to be applicable.
- Is your organizational structure like the target of the recommended practice? A recommended practice proposed for an organization with a well-developed risk management infrastructure is not appropriate for an organization that is still developing its program.
- Can your organization expend resources at the level required by the recommended practice? A recommended practice that demands funding beyond what your organization can afford is of limited value.
- Is your threat environment like the one assumed by the recommended practice? Recommended practices that are years or even months old may not adequately address the current threat environment. Consider how many of the recommended practices for Internet connectivity and protection over the past 10 years have become obsolete.

Many resources are available from public and private organizations that promote sound recommended cybersecurity practices. A good source of information on recommended practices is the CISA site "Cybersecurity Best Practices," which can be found at www.cisa.gov/topics/cybersecurity-best-practices. This site presents various cybersecurity improvement practices that could be useful. Similarly, many vendors such as Microsoft, Oracle, and Cisco publish recommended practices for cybersecurity on their websites.

Note 4 | For other documents on best practices, visit the Carnegie Mellon University Software Engineering Institute digital library at http://resources.sei.cmu.edu/library and search on "best practice."

Investing a few hours in web research will reveal many sources that may align with your specific circumstances. However, finding information on cybersecurity design is the easy part; sorting through all the information can require a substantial investment in time and effort. The goal is to obtain a methodology for creating or adapting a framework that meets your situation, which in turn leads to a blueprint that sets out the specifics of a cybersecurity system that contains all the necessary components—policy, education and training programs, and technical controls.

Limitations to Benchmarking and Recommended Practices

The biggest barrier to benchmarking in cybersecurity is the fact that many organizations do not share results with other organizations. A successful attack is often perceived as an organizational failure and is kept secret, if possible. Sometimes, these events (especially the details) may have negative consequences for the organization in the marketplace or among various stakeholders. As a result, the entire industry suffers because valuable lessons are not recorded, disseminated, and evaluated. Today, however, an increasing number of cybersecurity administrators are joining professional associations and societies, such as the Information Systems Security Association (www.issa.org) or the Information Systems Audit and Control Association (ISACA; www.isaca.org), and they are sharing their stories and the lessons they have learned. Some industry groups sponsor information-sharing opportunities where peers can share experiences without some of the negative consequences that come from public dissemination. Other groups publish in cybersecurity journals, sharing information about attacks on their organizations while leaving out the identifying details.

Another barrier to benchmarking is that no two organizations are identical. Organizations that offer products or services in the same market may differ dramatically in size, composition, management philosophy, organizational culture, technological infrastructure, and expenditures for cybersecurity. What organizations seek most are lessons that can help them strategically rather than information about specific technologies they should adopt. If cybersecurity were a technical problem, then implementing the technology that has succeeded elsewhere would solve the problem regardless of industry or organizational composition. Because it is predominantly a managerial and personnel problem, however, the number and types of variables that affect the cybersecurity of the organization are likely to differ radically between any two organizations.

A third problem with benchmarking is that recommended practices are a moving target. Knowing what happened even a few years ago, which is typical in benchmarking, does not necessarily tell you what to do next. While it is true that in cybersecurity, those who do not prepare for the attacks of the past will see them again, it is also true that preparing for past threats does not necessarily protect you from what lies ahead. Cybersecurity programs must keep abreast of new threats as well as the methods, techniques, policies, guidelines, training, and technologies to combat them.

Baselining

A specific subset of benchmarking is baselining, also known as internal benchmarking—an assessment of the performance of some action or process against which future performance is assessed. Baselining is also the first measure in benchmarking, in which the organization conducts an initial assessment of its own current performance (known as a baseline). At some point in the future after a baseline has been recorded, the organization can compare its current performance against the historical baseline value for that action or process as a means of assessing progress toward a desired end state or for general improvement. An example of a performance measure incorporating a baseline might be the number of external attacks per week that an organization experiences. An organization might establish a baseline by counting the instances of that activity over time to derive an average observed weekly value. This value serves as a reference for future comparison. Later, the organization could compare the observed number of attacks per week against the initial baseline to see if the number is increasing or decreasing and what effect (if any) their cybersecurity efforts are having on that measure. The value of baselines is realized in organizations that implement thoughtful performance measurement practices. A gap analysis is used when comparing current performance to a desired future state. This technique is also used in strategic planning, as described previously.

Support for Benchmarks and Baselines

Simply researching baselining and benchmarking processes and procedures found in recommended practices will provide less design and implementation detail for a cybersecurity program than use of a complete methodology. Nevertheless, by benchmarking based on recommended practices, you can piece together the desired outcome of the cybersecurity process, then work backward to achieve an effective design of a methodology. For example, NIST offers several publications specifically written to support baselining activities, including:

- SP 800-27, Rev. A: "Engineering Principles for Information Technology Security (A Baseline for Achieving Security)," June 2004
- SP 800-53, Rev. 5: "Security and Privacy Controls for Information Systems and Organizations," December 2020
- SP 800-53A, Rev. 5: "Assessing Security and Privacy Controls in Information Systems and Organizations," January 2022

These documents are available at csrc.nist.gov under the Special Publications link.

Many organizations sponsor seminars and classes on recommended practices for implementing cybersecurity. For example, ISACA (www.isaca.org) hosts such seminars on a regular basis. Similarly, the International Association of Professional Security Consultants (www.iapsc.org) has a listing of recommended practices. You can also review web portals for posted cybersecurity recommended practices. Several free portals dedicated to cybersecurity maintain collections of practices, such as TechTarget's SearchSecurity site at www.techtarget.com/searchsecurity and NIST's Computer Security Resources Center at csrc.nist.gov.

A third example drawn from the many available is the Gartner Group, which has published 12 questions that can be used as a self-assessment for recommended cybersecurity practices. The questions are organized into three categories—people, processes, and technology—that loosely map to the managerial, operational, and technical areas of the NIST methodology:

People

1. Do you perform background checks on all employees with access to sensitive data, areas, or access points?
2. Would the typical employee recognize a cybersecurity issue?
3. Would the typical employee choose to report it?
4. Would the typical employee know how to report it to the right people?

Processes

5. Are enterprise cybersecurity policies updated on at least an annual basis, employees educated on changes, and policies consistently enforced?
6. Does your enterprise follow a patch/update management and evaluation process to prioritize and mediate new cybersecurity vulnerabilities?
7. Are the user accounts of former employees immediately removed on termination?
8. Are cybersecurity group representatives involved in all stages of the project life cycle for new projects?

Technology

9. Is every possible network route to the Internet protected by a properly configured firewall?
10. Is sensitive data on laptops and remote systems secured with functional encryption practices?
11. Are your information assets and the systems they use regularly assessed for cybersecurity exposures using a vulnerability analysis methodology?
12. Are systems and networks regularly reviewed for malicious software and telltale signs from prior attacks?[16]

The Payment Card Industry Data Security Standard (PCI DSS) is considered the recommended or best practice for organizations using payment cards. Examples of these cards include MasterCard, Visa, American Express, Discover, debit cards, and gift cards. While adhered to by organizations that require the certification to process these cards, the list also serves as a generic set of recommended practices for any organization.

As mentioned previously, PCI DSS addresses the following six areas with 12 requirements:

Area 1: Build and maintain a secure network and systems.

1. Install and maintain a firewall configuration to protect cardholder data.
2. Do not use vendor-supplied defaults for system passwords and other cybersecurity parameters.

Area 2: Protect cardholder data.

3. Protect stored cardholder data.
4. Encrypt transmission of cardholder data across open, public networks.

Area 3: Maintain a vulnerability management program.

5. Protect all systems against malware and regularly update antivirus software or programs.
6. Develop and maintain secure systems and applications.

Area 4: Implement strong access control measures.

7. Restrict access to cardholder data by a business's need to know.
8. Identify and authenticate access to system components.
9. Restrict physical access to cardholder data.

Area 5: Regularly monitor and test networks.

10. Track and monitor all access to network resources and cardholder data.
11. Regularly test cybersecurity systems and processes.

Area 6: Maintain a cybersecurity policy.

12. Maintain a policy that addresses cybersecurity for all personnel.[17]

The Council has also issued requirements called the Payment Application Data Security Standard (PA DSS) and PCI PIN Transaction Security (PCI PTS), which provide additional specifications for components of payment card processing.

While the standards are published through the PCI Security Standards Council, they are enforced through individual card vendors. To be qualified to collect payment for a particular card, an organization should coordinate closely with a particular merchant bank or card processing center to determine what requirements are mandated for that card. In most cases, if the organization is simply using a card-swipe device at a point-of-sale terminal, the requirements are minimal; these devices typically are provided by a credit-card processing service and only communicate with that center for approval and with the point-of-sale terminal to provide an approval code.

Note 5 | For more information on PCI DSS, visit https://www.pcisecuritystandards.org/.

ISO Certification

Organizations that do not do business with the federal government and would not be concerned with NIST certification and accreditation procedures may still desire to seek a recognized level of certification of their cybersecurity management systems. Those doing business internationally, or those just seeking to influence potential customers with their level of cybersecurity, could seek ISO 27000 certification. While ISO does not directly conduct certification assessments or issue certificates, it does authorize third parties to perform these tasks. "Like other ISO management system standards, certification to ISO/IEC 27001 is possible but not obligatory. Some organizations choose to implement the standard in order to benefit from the best practice it contains while others decide they also want to get certified to reassure customers and clients that its recommendations have been followed."[18]

The ISO certification process takes approximately six to eight weeks and involves three steps:

1. Initial assessment—The certification organization reviews the candidate organization's cybersecurity management systems, procedures, policies, and plans and then identifies areas where the candidate organization is not in compliance. Rather than simply rejecting the certification application, the certification organization makes recommendations for improvements in areas where the candidate organization falls short of the standard. The candidate organization is then allowed to demonstrate compliance or remediation of shortfalls.

2. Writing of the certification manual—The certification organization then creates a certification "manual" documenting all procedural compliance. Once the manual is complete, the organization verifies the contents against its business procedures.

3. Presentation of certification—Once the documentation has been reviewed and all requirements have been met, the certification organization issues the certificate and the organization is considered "certified."

Reported benefits of ISO 27001 certification to the organization include the following:

- Reduced costs associated with incidents
- Smoother operations resulting from more clearly defined processes and responsibilities
- Improved public image of the organization, as certification infers increased trustworthiness

Benefits to the organization's customers and stakeholders include the following:

- Increased sense of the organization's integrity and trustworthiness in the protection of information
- Increased confidence with customers and suppliers in the value chain

Benefits to the organization's employees include the following:

- Lower risk of employee accidents and incidents associated with critical or sensitive information
- Employee confidence in organizational cybersecurity practices
- More clearly defined cybersecurity roles and responsibilities, which increases employee productivity and job satisfaction[19]

Note 6 | As noted in this chapter, a solid reference for measuring performance in cybersecurity management settings can be found in NIST Special Publication 800-55, Rev. 1: "Performance Measurement Guide for Information Security," which is available from https://csrc.nist.gov/publications/sp800" available from https://csrc.nist.gov/publications/sp800.

Self-Check

7. Benchmarking can determine how controls should be implemented in an organization.
   a. True   **b.** False

8. One of the limitations of benchmarking is that no two organizations are identical.
   a. True   **b.** False

9. Baselining involves comparing an organization's current performance against the past performance of other organizations.
   a. True   **b.** False

☐ Check your answers at the end of this chapter.

Closing Case

Maria sighed as she considered her new assignment. It had seemed like a great idea when Iris offered her the role, but now she wondered if she could get her arms around the complex process of getting RWW certified as an ISO 27000-compliant organization. After reviewing the outline of the training class she would soon attend, she pulled out a notepad and began outlining the RWW compliance project. She hoped she could find a useful set of documents to prepare her for this project.

Case Discussion Questions

1. Which documents should Maria read before her class?
2. Based on what you know about ISO 27000 program certification, what are the major steps of the process Maria will have to oversee?

Case Ethical Decision Making

Maria was reconsidering her recent recommendation of Linda to supervise the policy compliance team. As she considered the nature of the job and some of the personal issues that Linda faced, she wondered if she should go back to Iris and revise her recommendation.

Linda was a single mother with three children; she also had a history of substance abuse, although she was in recovery. Maria found her to be good at her work and felt she had made remarkable progress during the time Maria had supervised her. However, Linda had taken numerous sick days due to her complex and busy home life. Although Maria had no concrete evidence that Linda was struggling with her recovery, there were some indications that everything was not as it should be.

1. Should Linda's history of past troubles lead Maria to withdraw her support and replace her without giving detailed reasons to Iris?
2. Should Maria's ethical responsibility to the company lead her to give a full report of her concerns to Iris?
3. Should Maria's ethical responsibility to Linda lead her to keep these concerns to herself and allow the recommendation to stand?

Summary

Management should integrate cybersecurity concepts and practices into an organization's employment activities, in accordance with the value proposition.

The CSO should work with the CIO and HR to integrate cybersecurity concerns into the hiring process. During the hiring process, applying regulated and constrained job descriptions can increase the degree of professionalism in the cybersecurity field and improve the consistency of roles and responsibilities among organizations.

When a job interview includes a site visit, the tour should avoid secure and restricted sites.

A background check should be conducted before the organization extends an offer to any candidate, regardless of job level, to uncover past criminal behavior or other information. Background checks differ in their levels of detail and depth.

Once a candidate has accepted a job offer, the employment contract becomes an important cybersecurity instrument. Many of the policies discussed in earlier chapters require an employee to agree to compliance in writing.

As part of their orientation, new employees should receive an extensive cybersecurity briefing that covers policies, cybersecurity procedures, access levels, and training on the secure use of information systems.

When an employee leaves an organization, a number of cybersecurity-related concerns arise, including the continuity of protection for all information to which the employee had access. These concerns can differ depending on whether the departure was friendly or hostile.

Separation of duties, two-person control, job and task rotation, mandatory vacations, and least privilege are among the practices and methods recommended to minimize employees' opportunities to misuse information.

Government-mandated requirements for the privacy and cybersecurity of personnel and personal data must be met by the organization's hiring program.

Organizations often need the special services of temporary employees, contractors, and consultants. These relationships must be carefully managed to prevent cybersecurity breaches.

Cybersecurity performance management is the process of designing, implementing, and managing the use of collected data elements called measurements to determine the effectiveness of the overall cybersecurity program.

There are three types of cybersecurity performance measurements: those that determine the effectiveness of the execution of cybersecurity policy, those that determine the effectiveness and efficiency of the delivery of cybersecurity services, and those that assess the impact of an incident or other cybersecurity event on the organization or its mission.

A critical task in the measurement process is to assess and quantify what will be measured and how it is measured.

Benchmarking is a process of following the recommended or existing practices of a similar organization or industry-developed standards. Two categories of benchmarks are used: standards of due care and due diligence and recommended practices.

Organizations may be compelled to adopt a stipulated minimum level of cybersecurity (that which any prudent organization would do), which is known as a standard of due care. Implementing controls at this minimum standard is deemed due diligence.

Cybersecurity efforts that seek to provide a superior level of performance in the protection of information are called recommended business practices or best practices. Security efforts that are among the best in the industry are termed best cybersecurity practices.

A practice related to benchmarking is baselining—a level of internal performance against which changes can be usefully compared. Baselining can provide the foundation for internal benchmarking.

ISO 27000 certification is a form of external recognition that is useful for the following types of organizations: those that do not do business with the federal government, those that do business internationally, and those just seeking to influence potential customers with their level of cybersecurity. ISO 27000 certification allows an organization to demonstrate an externally reviewed competence in cybersecurity management practices.

Key Terms

baseline

baselining

benchmarking

best practices

collusion

cybersecurity performance
management

external benchmarking

internal benchmarking

job rotation

mandatory vacation policy

performance
measurements

performance measures

recommended practices

standard of due care

task rotation

two-person control

Review Questions

1. Why is it important to include cybersecurity responsibilities in every employee's job description and performance reviews?

2. What should organizations avoid including in job descriptions for cybersecurity positions, and why?

3. How can the cybersecurity department support HR personnel during the hiring process?

4. What is the purpose of conducting background checks before extending a job offer to a candidate?

5. What should a new employee's cybersecurity orientation cover?

6. How can periodic SETA activities benefit an organization's cybersecurity?

7. Why might an organization incorporate cybersecurity expectations into employee performance evaluations?

8. What are some cybersecurity concerns when an employee leaves an organization?

9. How can the practice of separation of duties enhance an organization's cybersecurity?

10. What is the primary purpose of a cybersecurity performance management program?

11. How does NIST SP 800-55, Rev. 1 contribute to the development of a cybersecurity performance measurement program?

12. Why is it important for measures to yield quantifiable information in a cybersecurity performance measurement program?

13. What are the three types of measures commonly used to assess cybersecurity performance?

14. How can an organization ensure that its cybersecurity performance measures are aligned with its overall mission?

15. What are some of the critical factors for the success of a cybersecurity performance measurement program, as identified by NIST SP 800-55, Rev. 1?

16. Why is it necessary to periodically review the results of a cybersecurity performance measurement program?

17. What is the role of the CSO in the development of a cybersecurity performance measurement program?

18. How does the concept of key performance indicators (KPIs) differ from general performance measures in the context of cybersecurity?

19. What is benchmarking in the context of cybersecurity, and how can it be used by organizations?

20. What is the difference between due care and due diligence in cybersecurity?

21. Why might some organizations be unable to implement the best, most technologically advanced cybersecurity controls?

22. How do recommended practices differ from best practices in cybersecurity?

23. What are some key considerations when selecting recommended practices for an organization's cybersecurity program?

24. What are the limitations of benchmarking in cybersecurity?

25. What is baselining, and how does it support cybersecurity management?

26. How does the ISO 27001 certification process benefit organizations, and what are its steps?

27. Why is it important for cybersecurity programs to keep abreast of new threats, and how can organizations achieve this?

Exercises

1. Search the web for the term "cybersecurity best practices." Compare your findings to the recommended practices outlined in the NIST special publications on cybersecurity documents.

2. Search the web for several cybersecurity-related job postings. Do the postings align with the concerns outlined in this chapter? Why or why not?

3. Visit the websites of three major technology organizations: Microsoft, Oracle, and Cisco. Also, go to two more sites of technology organizations that you choose on your own. Search the websites for best cybersecurity practices. What do you find?

4. Download and review NIST SP 800-55, Rev. 1: "Performance Measurement Guide for Information Security." Using this document, identify five measures for your home computing systems and network that could yield interesting results.

5. Using the template provided in Table 9-1, develop documentation for one of the performance measurements you selected in Exercise 4.

Solutions to Self-Check Questions

Cybersecurity Employment Practices

1. Job descriptions for cybersecurity positions should detail the specific access privileges the positions will have.
   Answer: b. False.
   Explanation: Organizations should not include details of access privileges in job descriptions to avoid potential security risks from individuals seeking to exploit such information.

2. Background checks for a cybersecurity position should include a thorough review of the candidate's educational and credential background.
   Answer: a. True.
   Explanation: Education and credential checks are key components of background checks for cybersecurity positions.

3. Temporary workers should have unrestricted access to all organizational information to perform their duties effectively.
   Answer: b. False.
   Explanation: To prevent security risks, temporary workers' access to information should be limited to what is necessary for them to perform their duties.

Cybersecurity Performance Measurement

4. The cost and effectiveness of cybersecurity controls are generally considered measurable.
   Answer: a. True.

Explanation: While CSOs sometimes claim that the costs, benefits, and performance of cybersecurity are almost impossible to measure, in fact they are measurable.

5. Only qualitative data should be considered when developing cybersecurity performance measures.

   Answer: b. False.

   Explanation: Measures must yield quantifiable information, such as percentages, averages, and other numbers. This is a critical factor for a successful cybersecurity performance measurement program.

6. Strong upper-level management support is not necessary for the success of a cybersecurity performance measurement program.

   Answer: b. False.

   Explanation: Strong upper-level management support is a critical factor for the success of a cybersecurity performance measurement program.

Benchmarking

7. Benchmarking can determine how controls should be implemented in an organization.

   Answer: b. False.

   Explanation: Benchmarking can help determine which controls should be considered, but it cannot determine how those controls should be implemented in an organization.

8. One of the limitations of benchmarking is that no two organizations are identical.

   Answer: a. True.

   Explanation: A barrier to benchmarking is that organizations differ dramatically in size, composition, management philosophy, and other factors, making direct comparisons challenging.

9. Baselining involves comparing an organization's current performance against the past performance of other organizations.

   Answer: b. False.

   Explanation: Baselining, or internal benchmarking, involves comparing an organization's current performance against its past performance or a desired target value to assess progress or identify areas needing improvement.

10

Planning for Contingencies

Chapter Objectives

After reading this chapter and completing the exercises, you should be able to:

1 Discuss the need for contingency planning.

2 Describe the major components of incident response.

3 Outline a disaster recovery plan.

4 Explain the components and strategies of a business continuity plan.

5 Discuss how an organization would prepare and execute a test of contingency plans.

> Anything that can go wrong will go wrong.
>
> –Murphy's Law

Case Opener

A week after the strategic planning meeting, Iris was just finishing a draft of the cybersecurity strategic plan. Satisfied with her progress thus far, she opened her calendar and began reviewing her schedule, hoping to find an appointment time to meet with Mike Edwards to discuss contingency planning. During their last luncheon, her friend Charley had warned Iris not to wait too long before addressing the issue again. She knew he had a point. It simply was not a good idea to put off discussing such an important project until the end of the month, as Mike had suggested during last week's strategic planning meeting. Having plans in place in case of an emergency just made good business sense, even if it was not perceived as a high priority by many of her management peers.

Suddenly, the building's fire alarm went off. Heart pumping, Iris left her office. With or without a contingency plan, it was her responsibility to assess this situation as quickly and as safely as possible. Was this an incident? A disaster? Or was it simply a false alarm? As she quickly moved down the line of cubicles, Iris called for everyone who had not yet left the floor to leave by way of the nearest exit. Then she rushed to the floor's fire control panel located in the elevator lobby. A blinking light showed that one heat-sensitive sprinkler head had been activated. Iris waited a moment to see whether any other lights began to blink. None did, but the existing light stayed on. It seemed that she was dealing with an isolated incident and not a disaster.

Iris headed down the hall to the location shown on the fire panel where the sprinkler had been triggered. She turned the corner and saw Harry and Joel from the accounting department in the break room, which was across the hall from their offices. Harry was inspecting what had once been the coffeepot, while Joel held a fire extinguisher. Both were wet and irritated. The room was filled with smoke and smelled of scorched coffee. To Iris's relief, there was no fire.

"Is everyone all right?" she asked.

"Yeah," Harry replied, "but our offices are a mess. There's water everywhere."

Joel shook his head in disgust. "What a time for this to happen. We were just finishing the quarterly reports, too."

"Never mind that," Iris said. "The important thing is that you're both okay. Do you guys need to make a trip home so you can get changed?"

Before they could answer, Mike ran over to join them.

"What happened?" he asked.

Iris shrugged. "It's a minor incident, Mike, everything's under control. The fire department will be here any minute."

"Incident? Incident?" Joel said in dismay as he pointed at his desk, where steam rose from his soaked computer and a pile of drenched reports littered the floor. "This isn't an incident. This is a disaster!"

Introduction to Contingency Planning

You were introduced to planning earlier in the text, but this chapter focuses on another type of planning—plans that are made for adverse events and non-normal operations—when the use of technology is disrupted and business operations come to a standstill. Because technology drives business, planning for adverse events usually involves managers from all three communities of interest. They collectively analyze and assess the entire information technology (IT) infrastructure of the organization using the mission statement and current organizational objectives to drive their planning activities. For any plan to gain the support of all members of the organization, it must also be sanctioned and actively supported by the general business community of interest. It must also be carefully monitored and coordinated with the cybersecurity department to ensure that information is protected during and after an adverse event, whether an incident or a disaster. Critical information must be made securely available to the organization when it may not be operating under normal circumstances or in its normal location.

The need to have a plan in place that systematically addresses how to identify, contain, and resolve any possible adverse event was identified in the earliest days of IT. Professional practice in contingency planning continues to evolve, as reflected in Special Publication (SP) 800-34, Rev. 1, "Contingency Planning Guide for Federal Information Systems," issued by the National Institute of Standards and Technology (NIST). NIST is a nonregulatory federal agency within the U.S. Department of Commerce that serves to enhance innovation and competitiveness by acting as a clearinghouse for standards related to technology.[1] The Computer Security Division of NIST facilitates sharing of information about practices that can be used to secure information systems.[2] NIST advises the following:

> Because information system resources are essential to an organization's success, it is critical that identified services provided by these systems are able to operate effectively without excessive interruption. Contingency planning supports this requirement by establishing thorough plans, procedures, and technical measures that can enable a system to be recovered as quickly and effectively as possible following a service disruption.[3]

Many organizations, especially federal agencies, are charged by law or other mandate to always have such plans and procedures in place. Organizations of every size and purpose should prepare for the unexpected. In general, an organization's ability to survive losses caused by an adverse event depends on proper planning and execution of such a plan; without a workable plan, an adverse event can cause severe damage to an organization's information resources and assets from which it may never recover. The Hartford insurance company estimates that more than 40 percent of businesses that don't have a disaster plan go out of business after a major loss like a fire, a break-in, or a storm.[4]

The development of a plan for handling unexpected events should be a high priority for all managers. The plan should account for the possibility that key members of the organization will not be available to assist in the recovery process. In fact, many organizations expect that some key members may not be accessible when an unexpected event occurs. To keep the consequences of adverse events less catastrophic, the concept of a designated survivor has become more common in government and businesses—a certain number of executives or other specialized personnel are kept away from group events in case of adverse unexpected events. More organizations now understand that preparations against the threat of attack remain an urgent and important activity but that defenses will fail as attackers acquire new capabilities and systems reveal latent flaws. When—not if—defenses are compromised, prudent cybersecurity managers have prepared the organization to minimize losses and reduce the time and effort needed to recover. Sound risk management practices dictate that organizations must be ready for anything.

Fundamentals of Contingency Planning

The overall process of preparing for adverse events—events with negative consequences that could threaten an organization's information assets or operations—is called contingency planning (CP). CP is the set of actions taken by senior management to specify the organization's priorities and actions if an adverse event becomes an incident or disaster. During CP, the IT and cybersecurity communities of interest prepare their respective units to prepare for, detect, respond to, and recover from events that threaten the organization's resources and assets, including human, information, and capital. The main goal of CP is to restore normal modes of operation with minimal cost and disruption to business activities after an adverse event—in other words, to make sure things get back to the way they were as quickly as possible. Ideally, CP should ensure the continuous availability of information systems to the organization even in the face of the unexpected.

CP consists of four major components:

- Business impact analysis (BIA)
- Incident response (IR) plan
- Disaster recovery (DR) plan
- Business continuity (BC) plan

The BIA is a key preparatory activity for all CP components. It helps determine which business processes and IT systems are critical to the success of the organization. The IR plan focuses on the immediate response to an incident. Any unexpected adverse event is treated as an incident until a response team deems it to be a disaster. Then the DR plan, which focuses on restoring operations at the primary site, is invoked. If operations at the primary site cannot be restored quickly—for example, when the damage is significant enough to affect the organization's ability to function normally—the BC plan is implemented concurrently with the DR plan, enabling the business to set up and conduct operations at an alternate site until it can resume operations at its primary site or select and occupy a new primary location.

Depending on the organization's size and business philosophy, IT and cybersecurity managers can either create and develop the four CP components as one unified plan or create the four plans separately, in conjunction with a set of interlocking procedures that enable continuity. Typically, larger, more complex organizations create and develop the CP components separately, as each component differs in scope, applicability, and design. Smaller organizations tend to adopt a one-plan method consisting of a straightforward set of recovery strategies.

Ideally, managers from all three communities of interest should be actively involved in the creation and development of all CP components. The elements required to begin the CP process include a planning methodology, a policy environment to enable the planning process, an understanding of the causes and effects of core precursor activities (the BIA), and access to financial and other resources, as articulated and outlined by the planning budget. Each of these is explained in the sections that follow. Once formed, the contingency planning management team (CPMT) begins developing CP documents. NIST recommends using the following steps:

1. Develop the CP policy statement. A formal policy provides the authority and guidance necessary to develop effective contingency plans.

2. Conduct the BIA. The BIA helps identify and prioritize information systems and components critical to supporting the organization's business processes. A template for developing the BIA is provided to assist the user.

3. Identify preventive controls. Measures taken to reduce the effects of system disruptions can increase system availability and reduce contingency life cycle costs.

4. Create contingency strategies. Thorough recovery strategies ensure that the system may be recovered quickly and effectively following a disruption.

5. Develop contingency plans. Contingency plans should contain detailed guidance and procedures for restoring damaged facilities unique to each business unit's impact level and recovery requirements.

6. Ensure plan testing, training, and exercises. Testing validates recovery capabilities, whereas training prepares recovery personnel for plan activation and exercising the plan identifies planning gaps; combined, the activities improve plan effectiveness and overall organization preparedness.

7. Ensure plan maintenance. The plans should be living documents that are updated regularly to remain current with system enhancements and organizational changes.[5]

Even though NIST methodologies are used extensively in this chapter, NIST treats incident response separately from contingency planning, with the latter focused on disaster recovery and business continuity. This chapter integrates the approach to contingency planning from NIST SP 800-34, Rev. 1 with the guide to incident handling from NIST SP 800-61, Rev. 2, and it incorporates material from NIST SP 800-184, "Guide for Cybersecurity Event Recovery."

Effective CP begins with an effective CP policy. Before the CPMT can fully develop the planning documents, the team must receive guidance from executive management, as described earlier, through formal CP policy. This policy defines the scope of the CP operations and establishes managerial intent regarding timetables for response to incidents, recovery from disasters, and reestablishment of operations for continuity. It also stipulates responsibility for the development and operations of the CPMT in general and may provide specifics on the constituencies of all CP-related teams. It is recommended that the CP policy contain the following sections at a minimum:

- An introductory statement of philosophical perspective by senior management emphasizing the importance of CP to the strategic, long-term operations of the organization

- A statement of the scope and purpose of the CP operations, stipulating the requirement to cover all critical business processes and activities

- A call for periodic (e.g., yearly) risk assessment and BIA by the CPMT; it should include identification and prioritization of critical business processes (while the need for such studies is well understood by the CPMT, the formal inclusion in policy reinforces that need to the rest of the organization)

- A description of the major components of CP to be designed by the CPMT, as described earlier

- A call for and guidance on selecting recovery options and continuity strategies

- A requirement to test the various plans on a regular basis (e.g., semiannually, annually, or more often as needed)

- Identification of key regulations and standards that impact CP planning and a brief overview of their relevance

- Identification of key individuals responsible for CP operations—for example, the appointment of the chief operations officer (COO) as CPMT lead, the chief security officer (CSO) as IR team lead, two managers of business operations as DR and BC team leads, and legal counsel as crisis management team lead

- An appeal to the individual members of the organization, asking for their support and reinforcing their importance as part of the overall CP process
- Additional administrative information, including the policy date, revision dates, and a schedule for periodic review and maintenance

Several individuals and teams are involved in CP and contingency operations:

- CPMT—This team collects information about the organization and the threats it faces, conducts the BIA, and then coordinates the development of contingency plans for incident response, disaster recovery, and business continuity. The CPMT often consists of a coordinating executive, representatives from major business units, and the managers responsible for each of the other three teams. It should include the following personnel:
  - Champion—A high-level manager to support, promote, and endorse the findings of the project, typically the COO or (ideally) the CEO/president
  - Project manager—A senior operations manager who leads the project, putting in place a sound project planning process, guiding the development of the project, and prudently managing resources
  - Team members—Managers or their representatives from the various communities of interest: business, IT, and cybersecurity, each providing details of their activities and insight into processes critical to running the business. A representative from legal affairs can help keep all planning steps within legal and contractual boundaries. A member of the communications department can make sure the crisis management and communications plan elements are appropriate. Supplemental team members should also include representatives of supplemental planning teams: the incident response planning team (IRPT), disaster recovery planning team (DRPT), and business continuity planning team (BCPT). For organizations that decide to separate crisis management from disaster recovery, there may also be representatives from the crisis management planning team (CMPT).

As indicated earlier, in larger organizations these teams are distinct entities with memberships that do not overlap, although all teams should have representatives on the CPMT. In smaller organizations, the four planning teams may include overlapping groups of people. However, including overlapping individuals on the *response* teams should be discouraged because the three planning teams (IR, DR, BC) may have different responsibilities in different locations at the same time. It is virtually impossible to establish operations at an alternate site if team members are busy managing the recovery at the primary site, some distance away.

As illustrated in the opening case, contingency planning often fails to receive the high priority necessary for the efficient and timely recovery of business operations during and after an unexpected event. Here is how NIST describes the need for this type of planning:

> These procedures (contingency plans, business interruption plans, and continuity of operations plans) should be coordinated with the backup, contingency, and recovery plans of any general support systems, including networks used by the application. The contingency plans should ensure that interfacing systems are identified and contingency/disaster planning coordinated.[6]

As you learn more about CP, you may notice that it shares certain characteristics with risk management and the systems development life cycle. Because many IT and cybersecurity managers are already familiar with these processes, they can readily adapt their existing knowledge to the CP process.

Components of Contingency Planning

Whether an organization adopts the one-plan method or the multiple-plan method with interlocking procedures, each of the CP components (the BIA and the IR, DR, and BC plans) must be addressed and developed in their entirety. The following sections describe each component in detail, including when and how each should be used. They also explain how to determine which plan is best suited for the identification, containment, and resolution of any given unexpected event. Figure 10-1 depicts the major project modules performed during CP efforts. Figure 10-2 shows the overall stages of the CP process, which are derived from the NIST IR and CP methodologies presented earlier.

Figure 10-1   Contingency planning hierarchies

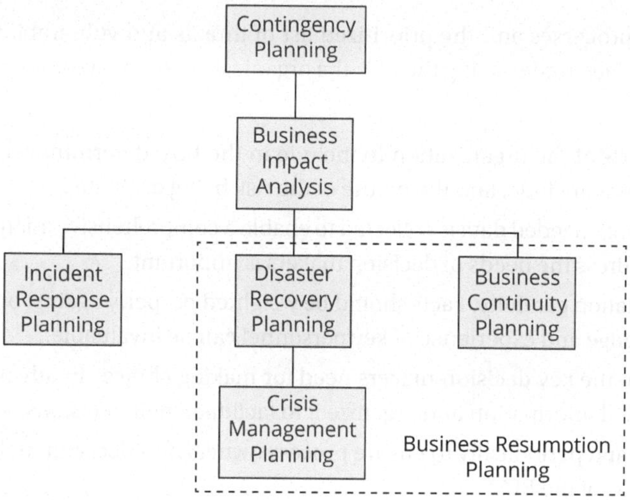

Figure 10-2   Contingency planning life cycle

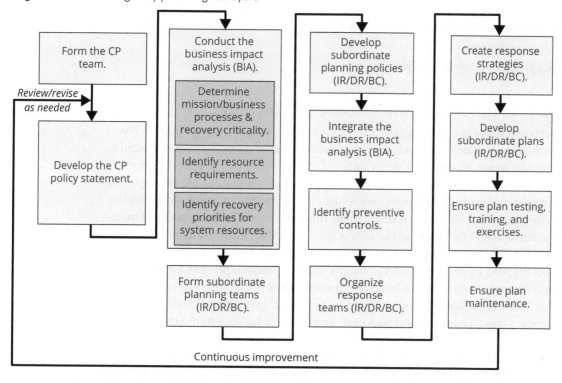

Business Impact Analysis

The first major component of the CP process is the business impact analysis (BIA), an investigation and assessment of adverse events that can affect the organization. It is conducted as a preliminary phase of the contingency planning process, which includes a determination of how critical a system or set of information is to the organization's core processes and its recovery priorities. One of the fundamental differences between a BIA and risk management processes is that risk management focuses on identifying the threats, vulnerabilities, and attacks to determine which controls can protect the information, but the BIA assumes that these controls have been bypassed, have failed, or have otherwise proved ineffective, that the attack succeeded, and that the adversity being defended against has been successful. By assuming the worst has happened, then assessing how it will impact the organization, insight is gained for how the organization must respond, minimize damage, recover from the effects, and return to normal operations.

The BIA begins with a list of business processes and the prioritized list of threats and vulnerabilities identified in the risk management process. When undertaking the BIA, the organization should consider the following:

- Scope—Carefully consider which parts of the organization to include in the BIA; determine which business units to cover, which systems to include, and the nature of the risk being evaluated.
- Plan—Work from a careful plan to ensure needed data is collected to enable a comprehensive analysis. Getting the correct information to address the needs of decision makers is important.
- Balance—Weigh the available information carefully. Facts should be weighted properly against opinions; however, sometimes the knowledge and experience of key personnel can be invaluable.
- Objective—Identify what information the key decision makers need for making choices in advance. Structure the BIA to provide the needed information and organize it to facilitate their decisions.
- Follow-up—Communicate regularly and periodically to ensure process owners and decision makers will support the process and the results of the BIA.[7]

According to NIST's SP 800-34, Rev. 1, the CPMT conducts the BIA in three stages, as described in the sections that follow:[8]

1. Determine business processes and recovery criticality.
2. Identify resource requirements.
3. Identify recovery priorities for system resources.

Determine Business Processes and Recovery Criticality

The first major BIA task is the analysis and prioritization of business processes within the organization, based on their relationship to the organization's mission. Each business unit must be independently evaluated to determine how important its processes are to the survivability of the organization. For example, recovery operations would probably focus on the IT department and network operation before turning to the hiring activities of the human resources department. Likewise, recovering a manufacturing company's assembly line is more urgent than recovering its maintenance tracking system. This is not to say that personnel and maintenance activities are unimportant to the business, but unless the organization's main revenue-producing operations can be restored quickly, other processes are irrelevant.

Note that throughout the NIST references provided, the term "mission/business process" is used. Do not let the term confuse you. Government agencies like NIST have missions, while nongovernment organizations have business processes. This text has standardized on "business processes" to describe all such activities.

It is important to collect critical information about each business unit before prioritizing their processes. It is also important to avoid turf wars and instead focus on the selection of processes that must be sustained to ensure the organization's survival. While a manager or executive might feel that their processes are critical to the organization, those processes might be less critical in the event of an incident or disaster. It is the role of senior management to arbitrate these inevitable conflicts about priority. The weighted table or weighted factor analysis described previously can be useful in resolving the issue of which business process is the most critical. The CPMT can use this tool to prioritize business processes based on developed criteria.

A BIA questionnaire can be used to collect relevant business impact information for this analysis. It can also be used to allow managers to enter information about the business processes within their area of control, their impacts on the organization's strategic mission, and any dependencies that exist for the processes from resources and outside service providers.

Note 1 | For more information on BIA questionnaires or to download samples, visit the following web-sites: csrc.nist.gov/publications/nistpubs/800-34-rev1/sp800-34-rev1_bia_template.docx, www.ready.gov/business/planning/impact-analysis, and www.cms.gov/Research-Statistics-Data-and-Systems/CMS-Information-Technology/InformationSecurity/Downloads/Business-Impact-Analysis-BIA-Process-and-Template.docx.

NIST's SP 800-34, Rev. 1 recommends that organizations use simple qualitative categories like "low impact," "moderate impact," or "high impact" for the cybersecurity objectives of confidentiality, integrity, and availability. Note that large quantities of information may be needed, so a formal data collection process is essential if all meaningful and useful information collected for the BIA is to be made available for use in CP development.

When organizations consider recovery criticality, key recovery measures are usually described in terms of how much of the asset they must recover within a specified time frame. The terms most commonly used to describe this are:

- **Recovery point objective (RPO)**—The point in time to which systems will be recovered; the maximum amount of data loss the organization will accept, given the most recent backup copy of the data. The RPO answers the question "How much recent data can we afford to lose? 20 minutes? An hour?"

- **Recovery time objective (RTO)**—The maximum amount of time that a critical system can remain unavailable before there is an unacceptable impact on other system resources, supported business processes, and the MTD. The RTO answers the question "How long can our systems be offline?"

- **Maximum tolerable downtime (MTD)**—The total amount of time the system owner or authorizing official is willing to accept for a business process outage or disruption, including all impact consider-ations. The sum of the RTO and WRT. The MTD asserts, "We can't be offline more than. . . ."

- **Work recovery time (WRT)**—The amount of effort (expressed as elapsed time) needed to make busi-ness processes work again after the technology element is recovered, as identified by the RTO. The WRT asserts, "As soon as the data is recovered, we'll be operational in. . . ."

The difference between RTO and RPO is illustrated in Figure 10-3. WRT typically involves the addition of nontechnical tasks required for the organization to make the information asset usable again for its intended function. The WRT can be added to the RTO to determine the realistic amount of elapsed time required before a business process is back in service, as illustrated in Figure 10-4.

Figure 10-3 RTO versus RPO

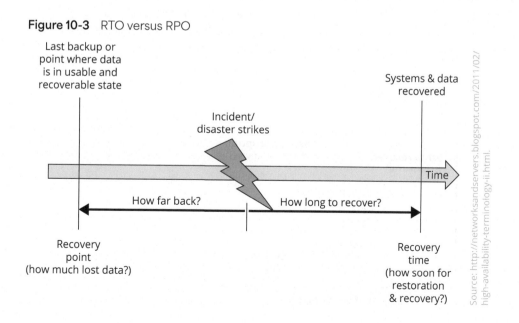

Figure 10-4   RTO, RPO, MTD, and WRT

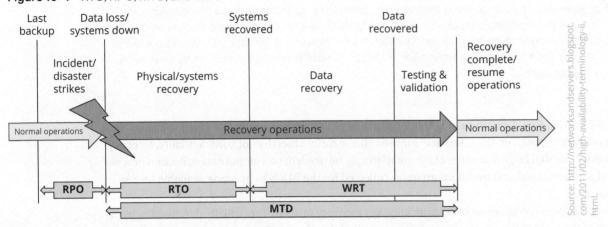

Source: http://networksandservers.blogspot.com/2011/02/high-availability-terminology-ii.html.

NIST states that failing to determine MTD "could leave contingency planners with imprecise direction on (1) selection of an appropriate recovery method and (2) the depth of detail that will be required when developing recovery procedures, including their scope and content."[9] Determining the information system resource's RTO, NIST adds, "is important for selecting appropriate technologies that are best suited for meeting the MTD."[10] As for reducing RTO, that requires mechanisms to shorten the start-up time or provisions to make data available online at a failover site. Unlike RTO, NIST adds, "RPO is not considered as part of MTD. Rather, it is a factor of how much data loss the business process can tolerate during the recovery process."[11] Reducing RPO requires mechanisms to increase the speed of data replication between production systems and backup systems.

Because of the critical need to recover business functionality, the total time needed to restore the business process to operation must be shorter than the MTD. Planners should determine the optimal point to recover the information system to meet BIA-mandated recovery needs while balancing the cost of system inoperability against the cost of the resources required for restoring systems. This must be done in the context of the BIA-identified critical business processes and can be illustrated with a simple chart, such as the one in Figure 10-5.

The longer an interruption to system availability remains, the more impact and cost it will have for the organization and its operations. When plans require a short RTO, the solutions are usually more expensive to design and use. For example, if a system must be recovered immediately, it will have an RTO of 0. These types of solutions will require fully redundant alternative processing sites and will therefore have much higher costs. On the other hand, a longer RTO would allow a less expensive recovery system. Plotting the cost balance points will show an optimal point between disruption and recovery costs, as shown in Figure 10-5. This point will be different for every organization and system, based on the financial constraints and operating requirements.[12]

Figure 10-5   Cost balancing

Cost to recover
(system mirror)

Cost of disruption
(business downtime)

Cost

Cost Balance Point

Cost to recover
(tape backup)

Length of disruption time

Information Asset Prioritization   As the CPMT conducts the BIA, it will be assessing priorities and relative impacts of business processes on the organization's mission. To do so, it needs to understand the resources needed by those processes. If a particular business process needs high-value information assets, that may influence its priority. Normally, this task would be performed as part of risk-assessment activities within the risk management process. If the organization has not performed this task, the BIA process is the appropriate time to do so.

Identify Recovery Resource Requirements

Once the organization has created a prioritized list of its business processes, it needs to determine what resources would be required to recover those processes and the assets associated with them. Some processes are resource-intensive—like IT processes. Supporting customer data, production data, and other organizational information requires extensive quantities of information processing, storage, and transmission (through networking). Other business production-oriented processes require complex or expensive components to operate. For each process identified in the previous BIA stage, the organization should identify and describe the relevant resources, IT or other, needed to provide or support that process. A simplified method for organizing this information is to put it into a resource/component table, like the example shown in Table 10-1. Note how one business process may have multiple components, each of which must be documented separately.

Table 10-1   Example resource/component table

Business Process	Required Resource Components	Additional Resource Details	Description and Estimated Costs
Provide customer support (help desk)	Trouble ticket and resolution application	Application server with Linux OS, Apache server, and SQL database	Each help-desk technician requires access to the organization's trouble ticket and resolution software application, which is hosted on a dedicated server. See current cost recovery statement for valuation.
Provide customer support (help desk)	Help desk network segment	25 Cat5e network drops, gigabit network hub	The help-desk applications are networked and require a network segment to access. See current cost recovery statement for valuation.
Provide customer support (help desk)	Help desk access terminals	One laptop/PC per technician, with web-browsing software	The help-desk applications require a web interface on a laptop/PC to access. See current cost recovery statement for valuation.
Provide customer billing	Customized accounts receivable application	Application server with Linux OS, Apache server, and SQL database	Accounts Receivable requires access to its customized software and customer database to process customer billing. See current cost recovery statement for valuation.

Identify System Resource Recovery Priorities

The last stage of the BIA is prioritizing the resources associated with the business processes, which provides a better understanding of what must be recovered first, even within the most critical processes. With the information from previous steps in hand, the organization can create additional weighted tables for the resources needed to support each process. By assigning values to each resource, the organization will have a custom-designed "to-do" list available once the recovery phase commences. Whether it is an IR- or DR-focused recovery or the implementation of critical processes in an alternate site during business continuity, these lists will prove invaluable to those tasked to establish or reestablish critical processes quickly.

In addition to the weighted tables described earlier, a simple valuation and classification scale, such as Primary/Secondary/Tertiary or Critical/Very Important/Important/Routine, can be used to provide a quicker method of valuating the supporting resources. What is most important is not to get so bogged down in the process that you lose sight of the objective. Teams that spend too much time developing and completing weighted tables may find a simple classification scheme more suited for their task. However, in a complex process with many resources, a more sophisticated valuation method like the weighted tables may be necessary. While preparing to conduct the BIA, one of the jobs of the CPMT is to determine what method should be used to valuate processes and their supporting resources.

Contingency Planning Policies

Prior to the development of each of the CP documents outlined in this chapter, the CP team should work to develop the policies that will enable the BIA process and should provide guidance for the creation of each of the planning components (IR, DR, and BC) and the structure of the subordinate teams. The CP team should also assist in the structuring of each plan. Each of the CP components will need a policy to define the related roles and responsibilities for that element of the overall CP environment within the organization.

Self-Check

1. Contingency planning involves only the cybersecurity community of interest within an organization.
   a. True   **b.** False

2. A business impact analysis helps identify and prioritize information systems critical to supporting the organization's business processes.
   a. True   **b.** False

3. A comprehensive contingency plan must include the disaster recovery plan and the business continuity plan.
   a. True   **b.** False

   ☐ Check your answers at the end of this chapter.

Incident Response

Most organizations have experience dealing with attacks, employee mistakes, service outages, and other small-scale adverse events. While they may not have formally labeled such efforts, they are performing incident response (IR)—an organization's set of planning and preparation efforts for detecting, responding to, and recovering from an incident. Organizations depend heavily on the quick and efficient containment and resolution of incidents. Incident response planning is performed by the IRPT. Note that the term "incident response" could be used either to describe the entire set of activities or a specific phase in the overall reaction. However, to minimize confusion, this text uses the term "IR" to describe the overall process, and it uses "reaction" rather than "response" to describe the organization's performance after it detects an incident.

In business, unexpected events happen. When those events represent the potential for loss or damage, they are referred to as adverse events or incident candidates. When an adverse event becomes a real threat to information, it becomes an incident—an event that could result in loss or damage to information assets but does not threaten the viability of the entire organization. The IR plan is usually activated when the organization detects an incident that affects it, regardless of how minor the effect is.

Getting Started

As mentioned previously, an early task for the CPMT is to form the IRPT, which will begin by developing a policy to define the team's operations. The IRPT then forms the **cybersecurity incident response team (CIRT or CSIRT)—** an IR team composed of IT and cybersecurity professionals who are prepared to detect, respond to, and recover from an incident. This team is referred to in NIST literature as the computer security incident response team. Figure 10-6 illustrates the NIST incident response life cycle. Some members of the IRPT may be part of the CIRT.

Figure 10-6 NIST incident response life cycle

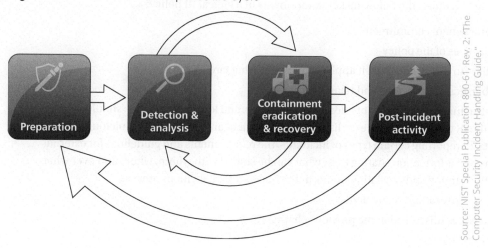

Source: NIST Special Publication 800-61, Rev. 2: "The Computer Security Incident Handling Guide."

As part of an increased focus on cybersecurity infrastructure protection, NIST has developed a Framework for Improving Critical Infrastructure Security, also referred to as the NIST Cybersecurity Framework (CSF). The CSF includes, and is designed to be complementary to, the existing IR methodologies and SPs. In fact, the documents described in this chapter are the foundation of the new CSF. Figure 10-7 shows the phases in the CSF, including those of event recovery, the subject of NIST SP 800-184, "Guide for Cybersecurity Event Recovery." Within the CSF, the six stages shown in Figure 10-7 include:

- Govern—Relates to the executive development and oversight of the organization's cybersecurity strategies, programs, and policies
- Identify—Relates to the understanding of the organization's current cybersecurity risks
- Protect—Relates to implementation of effective cybersecurity controls (policy, education, training and awareness, and technology)
- Detect—Relates to the identification of adverse events
- Respond—Relates to reacting to an incident
- Recover—Relates to putting things "as they were before" the incident

The Detect, Respond, and Recover stages directly relate to NIST's IR strategy, as described in detail in SP 800-61, Rev. 2.

Figure 10-7 NIST Cybersecurity Framework

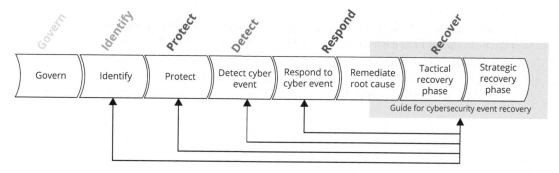

Incident Response Policy

An important early step for the IRPT is to develop an IR policy. NIST's SP 800-61, Rev. 2, "Computer Security Incident Handling Guide," identifies the following key components of a typical IR policy:

- Statement of management commitment
- Purpose and objectives of the policy
- Scope of the policy (to whom and what it applies and under what circumstances)
- Definition of cybersecurity incidents and related terms
- Organizational structure and definition of roles, responsibilities, and levels of authority; should include the authority of the IR team to confiscate or disconnect equipment and to monitor suspicious activity, the requirements for reporting certain types of incidents, the requirements and guidelines for external communications and information sharing (e.g., what can be shared with whom, when, and over what channels), and the handoff and escalation points in the incident management process
- Prioritization or severity ratings of incidents
- Performance measures (discussed in the previous chapter)
- Reporting and contact forms[13]

IR policy, like all policies, must gain the full support of top management and be clearly understood by all affected parties. It is especially important to gain the support of communities of interest that will be required to alter business practices or make changes to their IT infrastructures. For example, if the CIRT determines that the only way to stop a massive denial-of-service attack is to sever the organization's connection to the Internet, it should have that action preauthorized. This ensures that the CIRT is performing authorized actions and protects both the CIRT members and the organization from misunderstanding and potential liability.

Incident Response Planning

When one of the threats identified in earlier chapters is made manifest in an actual adverse event, it is classified as a cybersecurity incident, but only if it has the following characteristics:

- It could impact the organization's information assets.
- It has a realistic probability of success.
- A successful attack threatens the confidentiality, integrity, or availability of information resources and assets.

The prevention of attacks has been intentionally omitted from this discussion because guarding against such possibilities is primarily the responsibility of the cybersecurity department, which works with the rest of the organization to implement sound policy, effective risk controls, and ongoing training and awareness programs. It is important to understand that IR is a reactive measure, not a preventive one, although most IR plans include preventative recommendations.

The responsibility for creating an organization's IR plan usually falls to the chief information officer or the CSO. The IRPT leader should select representatives from each community of interest to form the IRPT. The roles and responsibilities of IRPT members should be clearly documented and communicated throughout the organization.

Using the multistep CP process discussed in the previous section as a model, the IRPT can create the IR plan with the assistance of the CPMT. According to NIST SP 800-61, Rev. 2, the IR plan should include the following elements:

- Mission
- Strategies and goals

- Senior management approval
- Organizational approach to incident response
- How the IR team will communicate with the rest of the organization and with other organizations
- Metrics for measuring IR capability and its effectiveness
- Roadmap for maturing IR capability
- How the program fits into the overall organization[14]

During this planning process, the IR procedures, commonly referred to as standard operating procedures (SOPs), take shape. For every incident scenario, the IRPT creates three sets of incident-handling procedures:

1. **During the incident**—The planners develop and document the procedures that must be performed during the incident. These procedures are grouped and assigned to individuals. Systems administrators' tasks differ from managerial tasks, so members of the planning committee must draft a set of specific procedures.

2. **After the incident**—Once the procedures for handling an incident are drafted, the planners develop and document the procedures that must be performed immediately after the incident has ceased. Again, separate functional areas may require different procedures.

3. **Before the incident**—The planners draft a third set of procedures: tasks that must be performed to prepare for the incident, including actions that could mitigate any damage from the incident. These procedures include details of the data backup schedules, disaster recovery preparation, training schedules, testing plans, copies of service agreements, and BC plans, if any.

Figure 10-8 presents an example of pages from an IR plan that support each of these phases. Once these sets of procedures are clearly documented, the IR portion of the IR plan is assembled.

Figure 10-8 Example of IR plan incident-handling procedures

Before an Attack

Users
1. Don't put suspicious media in your co
   Check your system before booting for
   suspicious USB drives.
2. Don't download free games or utilities
   system without authorization from the
   services department.
3. Don't click on links or open attachmer
   in unsolicited e-mail. Make sure all att
   are from the sending party by confirm
4. Don't forward messages that ask you t
   warn others of a virus or threat.

Technology Services
1. Ensure virus/malware protection softv
   is installed, properly configured, and u
2. Automate whenever possible.
3. Provide awareness and training to all
   users on proper use of the e-mail syst
   antivirus software.

After an Attack

Users
1. Scan your computer regularly and
   thoroughly for additional viruses/m
2. Review e-mail (TITLES ONLY, DO NC
   REOPEN attachments) for suspiciou
   content.
3. Write down everything you were do
   before you detected the virus/malw
4. Verify that your antivirus/antimalwa
   software and definitions are up to c

Technology Services
1. Conduct an incident recovery invest
2. Interview all users detecting the viru
3. Verify that all systems antivirus/mal
   software and definitions are up to c
4. Reconnect quarantined users to the
5. Brief all infected users on proper ar
   procedures.
6. File the incident recovery investigat
7. Notify all users that this particular s
   of virus/malware has been detected
   antivirus/antimalware software and

During an Attack

Users
1. If your antivirus/antimalware software detects an attack, it will delete the virus/malware or quarantine the file that carries it. Record any messages that your software displays and notify IT Services immediately.
2. If your computer begins behaving unusually or you suspect that you have contracted a virus or other malware, turn off your computer immediately by pulling the plug. Notify IT Services immediately.

Technology Services
1. If users begin reporting virus attacks, record the information provided by the users.
2. Temporarily disconnect those users from the network at the switch.
3. Begin scanning all active systems for that strain of virus.
4. Deploy a response team to inspect the users' systems.

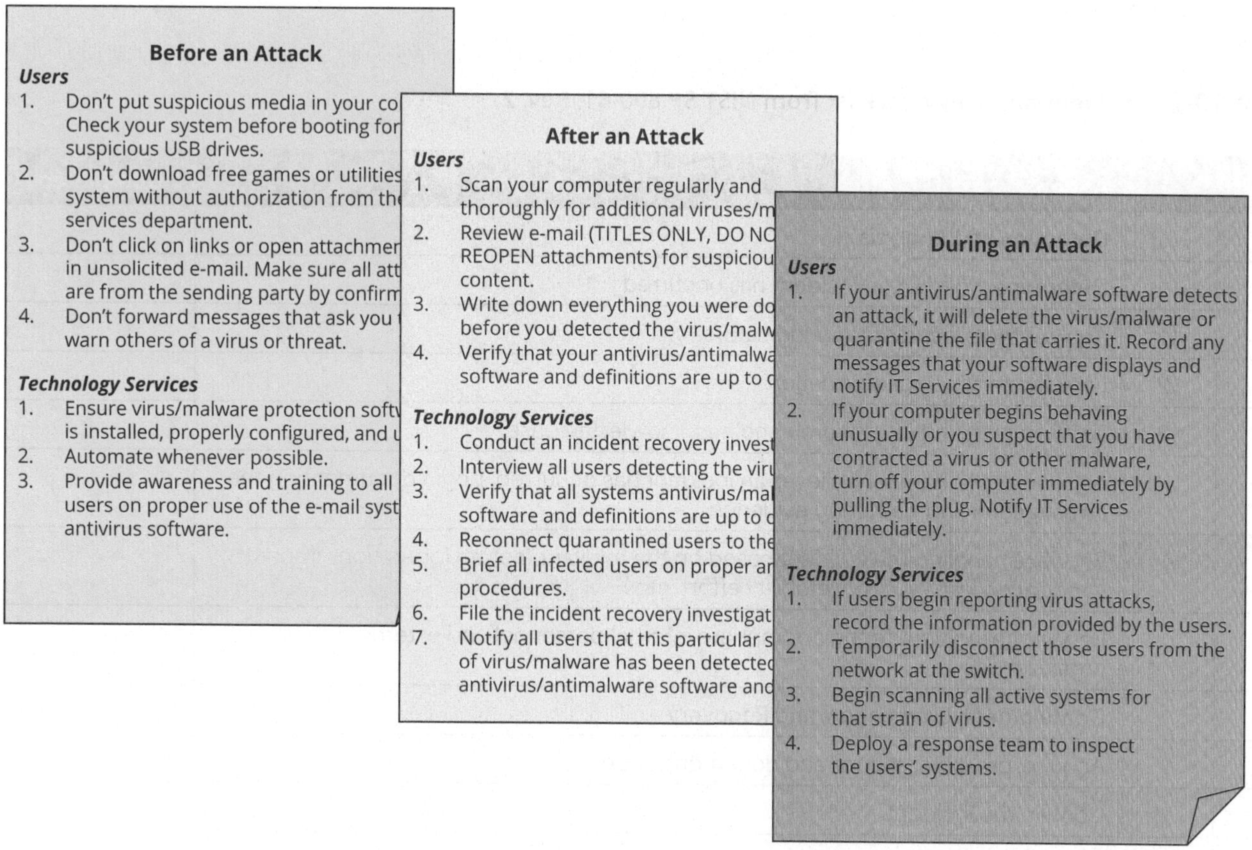

The IRPT seeks to develop a series of predefined responses that will guide the CIRT and cybersecurity staff through the IR process. Predefining incident responses enables the organization to respond to a detected incident quickly and effectively, without confusion or wasted time and effort. The execution of the IR plan typically falls to the CIRT. As noted previously, the CIRT is a separate group from the IRPT, although some overlap may occur; it is composed of IT and cybersecurity professionals prepared to diagnose and respond to an incident.

In smaller organizations, the CIRT may simply be a loose or informal association of IT and cybersecurity staffers who would be called if an attack was detected on the organization's information assets. In larger organizations, the CIRT is usually a more formal group that works and trains together. This is like the difference between a volunteer fire department, whose members have other "day jobs," and a professional fire department with dedicated firefighters working in shifts day and night.

Any employee who discovers or suspects that an incident has occurred should be able to contact the CIRT. One or more CIRT members, depending on the magnitude of the incident and availability of personnel, then handle the incident. The incident handlers analyze the incident data, determine the impact of the incident, and act appropriately to limit the damage to the organization and restore normal services. Although the CIRT may have only a few members, the team's success depends on the cooperation and support of individuals throughout the organization. Within the CIRT, each team member has a specific role to perform so that the team acts as a unified body that assesses the situation, determines the appropriate response, and coordinates the response. Each CIRT member must know their role, work in concert with other team members, and execute the procedures of the IR plan.

IR actions can be organized into three basic phases:

- Detect—Recognition that an incident is under way
- Respond—Reacting to the incident in a predetermined fashion to contain and mitigate its potential damage
- Recover—Returning all systems and data to their state before the incident

Table 10-2 shows the incident handling checklist from NIST SP 800-61, Rev 2.

Table 10-2   Incident handling checklist from NIST SP 800-61, Rev. 2

		Action	Completed
		Detection and Analysis	
1.		Determine whether an incident has occurred	
	1.1	Analyze the precursors and indicators	
	1.2	Look for correlating information	
	1.3	Perform research (e.g., search engines, knowledge base)	
	1.4	As soon as the handler believes an incident has occurred, begin documenting the investigation and gathering evidence	
2.		Prioritize handling the incident based on the relevant factors (operations impact, information impact, recoverability effort, etc.)	
3.		Report the incident to the appropriate internal personnel and external organizations	
		Containment, Eradication, and Recovery	
4.		Acquire, preserve, secure, and document evidence	
5.		Contain the incident	

(Continues)

Table 10-2 Incident handling checklist from NIST SP 800-61, Rev. 2 *(Continued)*

		Action	Completed
6.		Eradicate the incident	
	6.1	Identify and mitigate all vulnerabilities that were exploited	
	6.2	Remove malware, inappropriate materials, and other components	
	6.3	If more affected hosts are discovered (e.g., new malware infections), repeat the Detection and Analysis steps (1.1, 1.2) to identify all other affected hosts, then contain (5) and eradicate (6) the incident for them	
7.		Recover from the incident	
	7.1	Return affected systems to an operationally ready state	
	7.2	Confirm that the affected systems are functioning normally	
	7.3	If necessary, implement additional monitoring to look for future related activity	
		Post-Incident Activity	
8.		Create a follow-up report	
9.		Hold a lessons-learned meeting (mandatory for major incidents, optional otherwise)*	

*While not explicitly mentioned in the NIST document, most organizations will document the findings from this activity and use them to update relevant plans, policies, and procedures.

Source: NIST SP 800-61, Rev. 2

Data Protection in Preparation for Incidents

An organization has several options for protecting its data and restoring it quickly after an incident:

- Traditional data backups—The organization can use a combination of on-site and off-site backup methods; because the backup point is some time in the past, recent data is potentially lost, as mentioned in the previous discussion of RPO
- Electronic vaulting—A backup method that uses bulk transfer of data to an off-site facility
- Remote journaling—A backup method that transfers transaction data to an off-site facility as the backups occur, with the receiving server archiving the data as it is received
- Database shadowing—A backup strategy to store duplicate online transaction data along with duplicate databases at the remote site on a redundant server, combining electronic vaulting with remote journaling

For off-site or cloud storage, these options may use leased lines or secure Internet connections. Recent advances in cloud storage have resulted in most backups being stored in the cloud, with multiple, dated copies accessible.

Detecting Incidents

The challenge for every CIRT is determining whether an event is a by-product of routine systems use or an actual incident. Incident classification, the process of examining an adverse event that has the potential to escalate into an incident and determining whether it constitutes an actual incident, is the responsibility of the incident commander (IC), the on-duty manager of the CIRT. When an adverse event is detected and reported by end users, host- and network-based intrusion detection systems, virus detection software, or systems administrators, the IC is responsible for classifying it as an incident and activating the IR plan. Then the CIRT can execute the corresponding procedures. This is the primary purpose of the first phase of IR: incident detection—the identification and classification of an adverse event as an incident, accompanied by the CIRT's notification and the implementation of the IR Respond phase.

Several events can signal the presence of an incident. Unfortunately, these same events can result from an overloaded network or computer. Other incidents resemble the actions of a misbehaving computing system, software application, or other less serious event. To help make incident detection more effective, cybersecurity consultant and author Donald Pipkin has identified three categories of incident indicators: possible, probable, and definite.[15]

Possible Indicators

The following events are considered possible indicators of an incident:

- Presence of unfamiliar files
- Presence or execution of unknown programs or processes
- Unusual consumption of computing resources
- Unusual system crashes

Probable Indicators

The following events are considered probable indicators of an incident:

- Activities at unexpected times
- Presence of new accounts
- Reported attacks
- Notification from an intrusion detection and prevention system (IDPS)

Definite Indicators

The following events are definite indicators of an incident, signaling that an incident is in progress or has occurred. If these events are detected, the IR plan should be activated immediately.

- Use of dormant accounts
- Unexpected or unauthorized changes to logs
- Presence of hacker tools on systems or servers
- Notifications by business partners or peers
- Notification by hacker

Reacting to Incidents

Once an incident has been confirmed and classified, the IR plan moves from the Detect phase to the Respond phase. NIST SP 800-61, Rev. 2 combines the Reaction and Recovery phases into a Containment, Eradication, and Recovery phase, but they are treated separately as Respond and Recover under the new CSF.[16]

The steps in IR are designed to contain an incident, mitigate its effects, and support recovery. In the Respond phase, the steps taken by the CIRT and others must occur quickly and may take place concurrently. To allow for efficient reference during an incident, an effective IR plan prioritizes and documents steps involving the notification of key personnel, assignment of tasks, and documentation of the incident.

Notification of Key Personnel

As soon as the CIRT determines that an incident is in progress, the right people must be notified in the right order. Most "response" organizations, such as firefighters or the military, use an alert roster—a list of contact information for personnel to be notified in the event of an incident or disaster—for just such a situation. An effective IR plan would include such a roster and keep it updated. Historically, alert rosters relied on employees calling by phone to warn others of an incident or disaster. Fortunately, many automated systems are now available to facilitate this emergency notification, with the ability to program different lists for different emergencies.

> **Note 3** | For more information on selecting an emergency notification system, read the article on AlertMedia's website at www.alertmedia.com/blog/finding-the-best-emergency-notification-vendor-8-tips-for-approaching-the-evaluation-process.

The alert roster delivers an **alert message**—a description of the incident or disaster that usually contains just enough information so that each person knows what portion of the IR or DR plan to implement without slowing down the notification process. It is important to recognize that not everyone is on the IR alert roster; it only lists people who must respond to a specific incident. As with any part of the IR plan, the alert roster must be regularly maintained, tested, and rehearsed if it is to remain effective.

During this phase, upper management and other key personnel must be notified of the incident as well. This notification should occur only after the incident has been confirmed but before the media or other external sources learn of it. Among those likely to be included in the notification process are members of the legal, communications, and human resources departments. Some incidents are disclosed to all employees either as part of the reaction to the incident or afterward as a lesson in cybersecurity. Other incidents may not be revealed to all employees. In general, IR planners should determine in advance whom to notify and when and offer guidance about additional notification steps to take as needed.

Documenting an Incident

As soon as an incident has been confirmed and the notification process is under way, the team should begin to document the incident. The documentation should record the "who, what, when, where, why, and how" of each action taken while the incident is occurring. This documentation serves as a case study after the fact to determine whether the right actions were taken and if they were effective. It can also serve to prove that the organization did everything possible to prevent the spread of the incident, as needed for legal purposes. Incident documentation can also be used as a training tool for CIRT teams.

Incident Containment Strategies

One of the most critical components of IR is stopping the incident and containing its impact. Incident containment strategies vary depending on the incident and the amount of damage caused. Before an incident can be stopped or contained, however, the affected areas must be identified. Incident containment strategies focus on two tasks: stopping the incident and recovering control of the affected systems.

If the incident originates outside the organization, the simplest and most straightforward approach the CIRT can employ is to disconnect the affected communication circuits. Of course, if the organization needs those circuits to remain operational, this step may be too drastic. If the incident does not threaten critical areas, it may be more feasible to monitor the incident and contain it another way. One approach used by some organizations is to dynamically apply filtering rules to limit network access. For example, if a threat agent is attacking a network by exploiting a vulnerability in the Simple Network Management Protocol (SNMP), then applying a blocking filter for SNMP's IP ports will stop the attack without compromising other services. Depending on the nature of the attack, temporary controls can sometimes give an organization valuable time to devise a more permanent strategy. Typical containment strategies include the following:

- Disabling compromised user accounts
- Reconfiguring a firewall to block the problem traffic
- Temporarily disabling the compromised process or service
- Taking down the affected application or server
- Disconnecting systems from the affected network
- Shutting down all computers and network devices

Obviously, the final strategy is used only when all system control has been lost and the only hope is to preserve the data stored on the computers so that operations can resume normally once the incident is resolved. The CIRT, following the procedures outlined in the IR plan, determines the length of the interruption.

Consider the chapter-opening scenario again. What if, instead of a fire, the event had been a malware attack? What if the key incident response personnel had been on sick leave, on vacation, or otherwise not there? Think how many people in your class or office are not there on a regular basis. Many businesses require travel, with employees going off-site to meetings, seminars, or training or to fulfill other diverse requirements. In addition, "life happens"—employees are sometimes absent due to illness, injury, routine medical activities, and other unexpected events. In considering these possibilities, the importance of preparedness becomes clear. Everyone should know how to respond to an incident, not just the CIRT team.

Incident Escalation

An incident may increase in scope or severity to the point that the IR plan can no longer adequately handle it. An important part of knowing how to handle an incident is knowing at what point to escalate it to a disaster or transfer the incident to an outside authority such as law enforcement or another public response unit. During the BIA, each organization will have to determine the point at which an incident is deemed a disaster. These criteria must be included in the IR plan. The organization must also document when to involve outside responders.

Recovering from Incidents

Once the incident has been contained and system control has been regained, incident recovery can begin. As in the incident reaction phase, the first task is to inform the appropriate human resources. Almost simultaneously, the CIRT must assess the full extent of the damage to determine what must be done to restore the systems. Everyone involved should begin recovery operations based on the appropriate incident recovery section of the IR plan. NIST SP 800-184, "Guide for Cybersecurity Event Recovery," contains a detailed methodology for responding to and recovering from cybersecurity incidents.

Immediate determination of the incident's impact is referred to as incident damage assessment. Incident damage assessment can take days or weeks, depending on the extent of the damage, which can range from minor (a curious hacker snooping around) to severe (hundreds of computer systems infected by ransomware). System logs, IDPS logs, configuration logs, and other documents, as well as direct assessment by the CIRT, can provide information on the type, scope, and extent of damage. Using this information, the CIRT determines the current state of the information and systems and uses it to begin the recovery process. The CIRT must be trained to collect and preserve potential evidence in case the incident results in some form of legal action.

Once the extent of the damage has been determined, the recovery process begins. According to Pipkin, this process involves the following steps:[17]

- Identify the vulnerabilities that allowed the incident to occur and spread. Resolve them.
- Address the safeguards that failed to stop or limit the incident or were missing from the system in the first place. Install, replace, or upgrade them.
- Evaluate monitoring capabilities (if present). Improve detection and reporting methods or install new monitoring capabilities.
- Restore the data from backups, as needed. The CIRT must understand the backup strategy used by the organization, restore the data contained in backups, and then use the appropriate recovery processes to re-create any data that was created or modified since the last backup.
- Restore the services and processes in use. Compromised services and processes must be examined and then restored. If services or processes were disabled while regaining control of the systems, they need to be enabled again.
- Continuously monitor the system to prevent reoccurrence. Hackers frequently post their successes and methods online. If word gets out, others may be tempted to try the same or different attacks on your systems. It is important to maintain vigilance during the entire IR process.

- Restore the organization's confidence. Management or the CIRT may want to notify the organization of the incident and assure everyone that it was handled and the damage was fixed. If the incident was minor, say so. If the incident was major or severely damaged systems or data, reassure users that they can expect operations to return to normal as soon as possible. This serves to minimize panic and prevent confusion from further disrupting the operations of the organization.

Before returning to its routine duties, the CIRT must conduct an after-action review (AAR), a detailed examination and discussion of the events that occurred during an incident or disaster, from first detection to final recovery. The AAR provides an opportunity for everyone who was involved in an incident or disaster to sit down and discuss what happened. In an AAR, a designated moderator encourages everyone to share what happened from their perspective while ensuring there is no blame. All involved personnel review their actions and identify areas where the IR plan worked or not or could be improved. Once completed, the AAR is written up and archived to serve as a training case for future staff or as an account of the event. The AAR brings the reaction team's actions to a close.

According to McAfee, the most common mistakes an organization can make in IR are failing to do the following:

- Appoint a clear chain of command with a specified individual in charge.
- Establish a central operations center.
- "Know their enemy," as described in earlier chapters.
- Develop a comprehensive IR plan with containment strategies.
- Record IR activities at all phases, especially help-desk tickets, to detect incidents.
- Document the events as they occur in a timeline.
- Distinguish incident containment from incident remediation (as part of reaction).
- Secure and monitor networks and network devices.
- Establish and manage system and network logging.
- Establish and support effective antivirus and antimalware solutions.[18]

NIST SP 800-61, Rev. 2 makes the following recommendations for handling incidents:

- Acquire tools and resources that may be of value during incident handling.
- Prevent incidents from occurring by ensuring that networks, systems, and applications are sufficiently secure.
- Identify precursors and indicators through alerts generated by several types of cybersecurity software.
- Establish mechanisms for outside parties to report incidents.
- Require a baseline level of logging and auditing on all systems and a higher baseline level on all critical systems.
- Profile networks and systems.
- Understand the normal behaviors of networks, systems, and applications.
- Create a log retention policy.
- Perform event correlation.
- Keep all host clocks synchronized.
- Maintain and use a knowledge base of information.
- Start recording all information as soon as the team suspects that an incident has occurred.
- Safeguard incident data.
- Prioritize handling of incidents based on the relevant factors.
- Include provisions for incident reporting in the organization's IR policy.
- Establish strategies and procedures for containing incidents.
- Follow established procedures for evidence gathering and handling.
- Capture volatile data from systems as evidence.
- Obtain system snapshots through full forensic disk images, not file system backups.
- Hold lessons-learned meetings (AARs) after major incidents.[19]

CIRT members should be very familiar with these recommendations prior to an incident. Trying to use unfamiliar procedures in the middle of an incident could prove very costly to the organization and cause more harm than good.

Note 4 | For more information on incident handling, read the "Incident Handlers Handbook" by Patrick Kral, which is available from the SANS reading room at www.sans.org/white-papers/33901/, or search for other incident handling papers at www.sans.org/white-papers.

Organizational Philosophy on Incident and Disaster Handling

Eventually the organization will encounter incidents and disasters that stem from an intentional attack on its information assets as opposed to one from an unintentional source, such as a service outage, employee mistake, or natural disaster. Before reaching that point, the organization must define its philosophy with regard to the root cause of incidents and disasters and for the expected involvement of digital forensics and law enforcement:

- **Protect and forget**—The organizational CP philosophy that focuses on the defense of information assets and preventing reoccurrence rather than the attacker's identification and prosecution. This philosophy is also known as "patch and proceed." An investigation that takes this approach focuses exclusively on the resolution of an incident and recovery of operations. Once the current event is over, the questions of who caused it and why are immaterial.

- **Apprehend and prosecute**—The organizational CP philosophy that focuses on the identification and prosecution of the attacker in addition to asset defense and preventing reoccurrence. This philosophy is also known as "pursue and prosecute." In this approach, significant attention is paid to the collection and preservation of potential evidentiary material that might support legal proceedings and prosecution of the source of the attack.

An organization should certainly adopt the latter approach if it wants to punish an employee suspected of illegal or unethical behavior, especially if the employee is likely to challenge these penalties. The use of digital forensics to aid in IR and DR is key to this approach.

View Point   The Causes of Incidents and Disasters

By Karen Scarfone, Principal Consultant, Scarfone Cybersecurity

The term "incident" has somewhat different meanings in the contexts of incident response and disaster recovery. People in the incident response community generally think of an incident as being caused by a malicious attack and a disaster as being generated by natural causes (fire, flood, earthquake, etc.). Meanwhile, people in the disaster recovery community tend to use the term "incident" in a cause-free manner, with the cause of the incident or disaster generally being irrelevant and the difference between the two being based solely on the scope of the event's impact. An incident is a milder event and a disaster is a more serious event.

The result is that people who are deeply embedded in the incident response community often think of incident response as being largely unrelated to disaster recovery because they think of a disaster as being caused by a natural event, not an attack. Incident responders also often think of operational problems, such as major service failures, as being neither incidents nor disasters. Meanwhile, people who are deeply embedded in the disaster recovery community see incident response and disaster recovery as being much more similar and covering a much more comprehensive range of problems.

So where does the truth lie? Well, it depends on the organization. Some organizations take a more integrated approach to business continuity and have their incident response, disaster recovery, and other business continuity components closely integrated so that they work together fairly seamlessly. Other organizations treat these business continuity components as more discrete elements and focus on making each element strong rather than establishing strong commonalities and linkages among the components. There are pluses and minuses to each of these approaches.

Personally, I find that the most important thing is to avoid turf wars between the business continuity component teams. There is nothing more frustrating than delaying the response to an incident or disaster because people disagree on its cause. The cybersecurity folks say it is an operational problem, the operational folks say it is a disaster, and the disaster folks say it is a cybersecurity incident. So, like a hot potato, the event gets passed from team to team while people argue about its cause. In reality, for some problems, the cause is not immediately apparent.

What is important to any organization is that each adverse event, regardless of the cause, be assessed and prioritized as quickly as possible. That means teams need to be willing to step up and address adverse events, regardless of whether the event is clearly their responsibility. The impact of the incident is largely unrelated to the cause. If later information shows there is a particular cause that better fits a different team, the handling of the event can be transferred to the other team. Teams should be prepared to transfer events and to receive transferred events from other teams at any time.

Responding as quickly as possible to incidents has become even more important with the increasing integration between the cyber world and the physical world. Operational technology, cyber-physical systems, and the Internet of Things are all driving this integration. Now an attacker can exploit cyber vulnerabilities to cause physical impacts, including overriding a building's card readers and other physical cybersecurity systems to gain unauthorized access and feeding crafted malicious data into a factory's power system in order to start a fire or cause an explosion. Delaying the response to an incident may put human lives at unnecessary risk and ultimately lead to deaths that should have been prevented.

Digital Forensics and Incident Response

When an organization finds itself having to deal with a suspected policy or law violation, it must appoint an individual who investigates. How the internal investigation proceeds will dictate whether the organization can act against the suspect if evidence is found that supports the accusation. To protect the organization and assist law enforcement in the conduct of an investigation, the appointed investigator must document what happened and how by examining computer systems for digital proof. This investigation of what happened and how is called digital forensics.

Digital forensics is a set of investigations involving the preservation, identification, extraction, documentation, and interpretation of computer media for evidentiary and root cause analysis. Like traditional forensics, it follows clear, well-defined methodologies and allows investigators to determine *what* happened by examining the results of an event. It also allows them to determine *how* the event happened by examining system information, individual actions, physical evidence, and testimony related to the event. What it may never do is figure out the *why*.

Digital forensics focuses on finding information stored in an electronic format on any of the myriad devices available, even if the information is partially overwritten or hidden. The skill of the investigator plays a key role in discovering potential evidentiary material (EM), also known as items of potential evidentiary value. An item does not become evidence until it is formally admitted in a legal proceeding by a judge or other ruling official.

Related to the field of digital forensics is e-discovery—the identification and preservation of evidentiary material related to a specific legal action. While digital forensics concentrates on the collection, preservation, and presentation of digital content, e-discovery is focused on the identification and location of potential evidence, usually after it was collected through digital forensics. Digital forensics focuses on file extraction, drive imaging, and memory analysis to find data, often at very technical levels, while e-discovery uses search and analysis tools to quickly locate specific data that has already been extracted from the media. E-discovery may simply focus on extensive email and database searches to identify information related to specific key terms. Both are used in investigations, but usually at opposite ends of the process. First you collect and organize data using digital forensics, and then you find the specific item (potential evidence) you need with e-discovery.

Digital forensics is typically used for two purposes:

- To investigate allegations of digital malfeasance—To find digital proof of misuse or illegal activity. Investigating digital malfeasance indicates that the process is intended to end in some form of legal proceeding. As such, the data is collected more to "apprehend and prosecute."

- To perform root cause analysis—To find out why an attack was successful and what damage resulted from it. If the organization suspects an attack was successful, digital forensics can be used to examine the path and methodology used to gain unauthorized access as well as determine how pervasive and successful the attack was. Performing root cause analysis is directly related to IR; the IR team will use root cause analysis when examining systems after an incident. Here, the primary intent goes to "protect and forget," which may result in the contamination of potential evidence because the focus is almost exclusively on organizational protection of information assets.

Some investigations can be undertaken by an organization's personnel, whereas others require immediate involvement of law enforcement. In general, whenever investigators discover evidence of the commission of a crime, they should immediately notify management and recommend contacting law enforcement. Failure to do so could result in unfavorable legal action against the investigator or organization.

Digital Forensics Team

Most organizations cannot sustain a permanent digital forensics team. In most organizations, such expertise is so rarely used that it may be better to seize the equipment under investigation and then outsource data collection and analysis to an expert. The organization can then maintain distance from the situation and have additional expertise to call upon if the process ends in legal proceedings. Even so, there should be people in the cybersecurity group trained to understand and manage the forensics process. Should a report of suspected misuse arise from an internal or external party, the person or group must be familiar enough with digital forensics procedures to avoid contaminating potential EM. This expertise can be obtained by sending employees to a cybersecurity conference with digital forensics content or to dedicated digital forensics training.

Affidavits and Search Warrants

Many investigations begin with an allegation or an indication of an incident. Whether via the help desk, the organization's sexual harassment reporting channels, or direct report, someone alleges that an employee is performing actions that are illegal, prohibited by the organization, or the cause of a hostile work environment. The organization must then either hire an investigator or deploy a team to investigate internally. This team will need permission to examine digital media for potential EM. In law enforcement, the investigating agent creates an affidavit requesting a search warrant. When an approving authority signs the affidavit or creates a synopsis form based on this document, it becomes a search warrant and grants permission to search for EM of a certain type at the specified location or to seize items to return to the investigator's lab for examination. In corporate environments, the names of these documents may be different or may be verbal in nature, but the process should be the same. Formal permission is obtained before an investigation begins.

Digital Forensics Methodology

In digital forensics, all investigations follow the same basic methodology once permission to search and seize is received:

- Identify relevant items of evidentiary value (EM).
- Acquire (seize) the evidence without alteration or damage, usually by extracting the hard drive and imaging (copying) it.
- Take steps to ensure that the EM is verifiably authentic at every stage and is unchanged from the time it was seized, usually by calculating hash values of the original drive and its images.

- Analyze the data without risking modification or unauthorized access; only analyze the image in the forensic application.
- Report the findings to the proper authority.

This general process is illustrated in Figure 10-9.

Figure 10-9   Digital forensics process

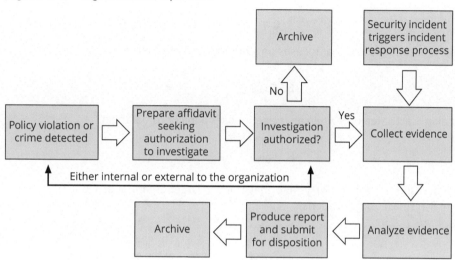

To support the selection and implementation of a methodology, the organization may want to seek legal advice or consult with local or state law enforcement. Publications that should become part of the organization team's library include the following:

- "Electronic Crime Scene Investigation: A Guide for First Responders," 2nd edition (www.ojp.gov/pdf-files1/nij/219941.pdf)
- "First Responders Guide to Computer Forensics" (http://resources.sei.cmu.edu/library/asset-view.cfm?assetID=7251)
- "Searching and Seizing Computers and Obtaining Electronic Evidence in Criminal Investigations" (www.justice.gov/file/442111/download)
- "Digital Evidence Guide for First Responders" (www.iacpcybercenter.org/wp-content/uploads/2015/04/digitalevidence-booklet-051215.pdf)

Law Enforcement Involvement

When an incident or disaster violates civil or criminal law, it is the organization's responsibility to notify the proper authorities. Selecting the appropriate law enforcement agency depends on the type of crime committed. Involving law enforcement agencies has both advantages and disadvantages; for example, such agencies are usually much better equipped to process evidence than a business. Unless the security forces in the organization have been trained in processing evidence and computer forensics, they may do more harm than good when attempting to extract information that can lead to the legal conviction of a suspected criminal. Law enforcement agencies are also prepared to handle the warrants and subpoenas necessary when documenting a case. They are adept at obtaining statements from witnesses, affidavits, and other required documents. For all these reasons, law enforcement personnel can be a security administrator's greatest ally in investigating and prosecuting a digital crime.

The disadvantages of law enforcement involvement include possible loss of control over the chain of events following an incident, including the collection of potential evidence and the prosecution of suspects. An organization that simply wants to reprimand or dismiss an employee for system misuse will normally not involve law enforcement in the resolution of an incident. The organization may not hear about the case for weeks or even months due to heavy law enforcement caseloads or resource shortages. A very real issue for commercial organizations is the potential confiscation of vital equipment as EM. Despite these difficulties, if the organization detects a criminal act, it has the legal obligation to notify appropriate law enforcement officials. It is up to the CSO, in consultation with upper management and legal counsel, to determine when law enforcement should be involved.

Self-Check

4. Incident response is a preventive measure that focuses on stopping incidents before they happen.
   a. True   b. False

5. The incident response plan is activated only when an incident poses a major threat to an organization's viability.
   a. True   b. False

6. The cybersecurity incident response team is always a formal group in larger organizations, but the team may be informal in smaller organizations.
   a. True   b. False

☐ Check your answers at the end of this chapter.

Disaster Recovery

The next vital part of CP focuses on disaster recovery (DR)—an organization's planning and preparation efforts for detecting, reacting to, and recovering from a disaster. Disaster recovery planning (DRP) entails the preparation for and recovery from a disaster, whether natural or man-made. In some cases, incidents detected by the IR team may escalate to the level of disaster, and the IR plan may no longer be able to contain the incident or help recover from the loss. For example, if a ransomware program evades detection and infects an organization's systems, interrupting its ability to function, the DR plan is activated. Sometimes, events are by their nature immediately classified as disasters, such as an extensive fire, flood, tornado, or earthquake.

As you learned earlier in this chapter, the CP team creates the DRPT. The DRPT in turn organizes and prepares the DR response teams (DRRTs) to implement the DR plan in the event of a disaster. An organization may need different DRRTs, each tasked with a different aspect of recovery. These teams may have multiple responsibilities in the recovery of the primary site and the reestablishment of operations, including:

- Recovering information assets that are salvageable from the primary facility after the disaster
- Purchasing or otherwise acquiring replacement IT assets from appropriate sources
- Reestablishing necessary IT and information assets at the primary site or a new location, if necessary

Some common DRRTs include:

- DR management team—Coordinates the on-site efforts of all other DRRTs
- Communications team—Provides feedback to anyone who wants additional information about the organization's efforts in recovering from the disaster; this team may include representatives from the public relations and legal departments
- Computer recovery (hardware) team—Works to recover any physical computing assets that might be usable after the disaster and acquire and install replacement assets as needed

- Systems recovery (OS) team—Works to recover operating systems and may be combined with the applications recovery team as a "software recovery team" or with the hardware team as a "systems recovery team"
- Network recovery team—Works to recover or install network wiring and hardware (hubs, switches, and routers), reestablish connectivity, and acquire and install replacement assets as needed
- Storage recovery team—Works with the other teams to recover storage-related information assets and may be combined with hardware or software teams
- Applications recovery team—Works to recover critical applications
- Data management team—Works on data restoration and recovery, whether from on-site, off-site, or online transactional data
- Vendor contact team—Works as an intermediary between teams, suppliers, and vendors to replace damaged or destroyed materials, equipment, or services
- Damage assessment and salvage team—Provides initial assessments of the extent of damage to materials, inventory, equipment, and systems on-site to assist other teams' efforts
- Business interface team—Works with the remainder of the organization to assist in the recovery of nontechnology assets and functions
- Logistics team—Responsible for providing any needed supplies, space, materials, food, services, or facilities at the primary site; it may be combined with the vendor contact team
- Other teams as needed

Smaller organizations may combine many of these teams into a simpler structure, such as a hardware team, a software team, a data team, and a network team. The number and names of these teams are only constrained by the ability of the organization to staff and operate them after a disaster.

Disaster Recovery Process

In general, a disaster has occurred when either of two criteria is met: (1) The organization is unable to contain or control the impact of an incident or (2) the level of damage or destruction from an incident is so severe that the organization cannot quickly recover from it.

The distinction between an incident and a disaster may be subtle. However, this distinction is critical because it determines which plan is activated. The key role of the DR plan is to prepare to reestablish operations at the organization's primary location after a disaster or to establish operations at a new location if the primary site is no longer viable.

You learned earlier in this chapter about the CP process recommended by NIST, which uses seven steps. These steps can be adapted and applied here within the narrower context of DRP, resulting in an eight-step DR process.

1. Organize the DR teams.
2. Develop the DR policy.
3. Review the BIA for relevant information.
4. Identify and review preventive controls (if any).
5. Develop or select DR strategies.
6. Develop the DR plan.
7. Ensure DR plan testing, training, and exercises.
8. Ensure DR plan maintenance.

Disaster Recovery Policy

As noted in step 2 of the preceding list, the DRPT, led by the team leader, begins developing the DR policy soon after the teams are formed. The policy presents an overview of the organization's philosophy on the conduct of DR operations and serves as the guide for developing the DR plan. The DR policy itself may be created by the organization's CPMT, with the team leader as a member. Alternatively, the DR team may be assigned the role of developing the DR policy. In either case, the DR policy contains the following key elements:

- Purpose—The purpose of the DR program is to provide direction and guidance for all DR operations. In addition, the program provides for the development and support of the DR plan.
- Scope—This section of the policy identifies the organizational units and groups of employees to which the policy applies; this is especially important if the organization has multiple locations.
- Roles and responsibilities—This section of the policy identifies the roles and responsibilities of the key individuals in the DR operation and teams.
- Resource requirements—This section specifies resources provided for the development and execution of DR plans.
- Training requirements—This section defines and highlights the training requirements for the business units within the organization and their employees.
- Exercise and testing schedules—This section stipulates the testing specification for the DR plan, including type, frequency, and participants.
- Plan maintenance schedule—This section states the required review and update schedule for the plan and specifies the review process and responsible individuals.
- Special considerations—This section includes such items as information storage and maintenance as well as references to any laws, regulations, or other policies.

Disaster Classification

A DR plan can classify disasters in several ways. The most common method of disaster classification is to evaluate the amount of damage that could be caused—usually on a scale of Moderate, Severe, or Critical, for example. Disasters could also be classified by their origin, such as natural or man-made. Most incidents fall into the man-made category (like hacker intrusions or ransomware), but some could be tied to natural origins, such as fires or floods.

Many disasters begin as incidents; only when they reach a specified threshold are they escalated from incident to disaster. A denial-of-service attack that affects a single system for a short time may be an incident, but when it escalates to affect an entire organization for a much longer time, it may be reclassified as a disaster. Who makes this classification? It is most commonly done by a senior IT or cybersecurity manager working closely with the CIRT and DRRT leads. When the CIRT reports that an incident or collection of incidents has begun to exceed the capability to respond, the team may request that the incident(s) be reclassified as a disaster for the organization to better handle the expected damage or loss.

Disasters may also be classified by their rate of occurrence. Slow-onset disasters build up gradually over time before they can degrade the ability of the organization to withstand their effect. Hazards that cause these disaster conditions typically include natural causes such as droughts, famines, environmental degradation, desertification, deforestation, and pest infestation. Man-made causes include malware, hackers, disgruntled employees, and service provider issues.

Usually, disasters that strike quickly are instantly classified as disasters. These disasters are commonly referred to as rapid-onset disasters because they occur suddenly with little warning, taking people's lives and destroying means of production. Rapid-onset disasters may be caused by natural effects like earthquakes, floods, storm winds, tornadoes, and mud flows or by man-made effects like massively distributed denial-of-service attacks or acts of terrorism, including cyberterrorism or hacktivism and acts of war. Table 10-3 presents a list of natural disasters, their effects, and recommendations for mitigation.

Table 10-3   Natural disasters and their effects on information systems

Natural Disaster	Effects and Mitigation
Fire	Damages the building that houses the computing equipment that constitutes all or part of the information system. Also encompasses smoke damage from the fire and water damage from sprinkler systems or firefighters. Can usually be mitigated with fire casualty insurance or business interruption insurance.
Flood	Can cause direct damage to all or part of the information system or to the building that houses all or part of the information system. May also disrupt operations by interrupting access to the buildings that house all or part of the information system. Can sometimes be mitigated with flood insurance or business interruption insurance.
Earthquake	Can cause direct damage to all or part of the information system or, more often, to the building that houses it. May also disrupt operations by interrupting access to the buildings that house all or part of the information system. Can sometimes be mitigated with specific casualty insurance or business interruption insurance but is usually a specific and separate policy.
Lightning	Can directly damage all or part of the information system or its power distribution components. Can also cause fires or other damage to the building that houses all or part of the information system. May also disrupt operations by interrupting access to the buildings that house all or part of the information system as well as the routine delivery of electrical power. Can usually be mitigated with multipurpose casualty insurance or business interruption insurance.
Landslide or mudslide	Can damage all or part of the information system or, more likely, the building that houses it. May also disrupt operations by interrupting access to the buildings that house all or part of the information system as well as the routine delivery of electrical power. Can sometimes be mitigated with casualty insurance or business interruption insurance.
Tornado or severe windstorm	Can directly damage all or part of the information system or, more likely, the building that houses it. May also disrupt operations by interrupting access to the buildings that house all or part of the information system as well as the routine delivery of electrical power. Can sometimes be mitigated with casualty insurance or business interruption insurance.
Hurricane or typhoon	Can directly damage all or part of the information system or, more likely, the building that houses it. Organizations located in coastal or low-lying areas may experience flooding. May also disrupt operations by interrupting access to the buildings that house all or part of the information system as well as the routine delivery of electrical power. Can sometimes be mitigated with casualty insurance or business interruption insurance.
Tsunami	Can directly damage all or part of the information system or, more likely, the building that houses it. Organizations located in coastal areas may experience tsunamis. May also cause disruption to operations by interrupting access or electrical power to the buildings that house all or part of the information system. Can sometimes be mitigated with casualty insurance or business interruption insurance.
Electrostatic discharge (ESD)	Can be costly or dangerous when it ignites flammable mixtures and damages costly electronic components. Static electricity can draw dust into clean-room environments or cause products to stick together. The cost of servicing ESD-damaged electronic devices and interruptions can range from a few cents to millions of dollars for critical systems. Loss of production time in information processing due to the effects of ESD is significant. While not usually viewed as a threat, ESD can disrupt information systems but is not usually an insurable loss unless covered by business interruption insurance. ESD can be mitigated with special static discharge equipment and by managing HVAC temperature and humidity levels.
Dust contamination	Can shorten the life of information systems or cause unplanned downtime. Can usually be mitigated with an effective HVAC filtration system and simple procedures, such as efficient housekeeping, placing tacky floor mats at entrances, and prohibiting the use of paper and cardboard in the data center.

Planning to Recover

To plan for disasters, the CPMT and DRPT jointly engage in scenario development and impact analysis while categorizing the level of threat that each potential disaster poses. When generating a DR scenario, start with the most important asset: people. Do you have the human resources with the appropriate organizational knowledge to restore business operations? Organizations must cross-train their employees to ensure that operations and a sense of normalcy can be restored. In addition, the DR plan must be tested regularly so that the DR team can lead the recovery effort quickly and efficiently. Key elements that the DRPT must build into the DR plan include the following:

- Clear delegation of roles and responsibilities—Everyone assigned to the DR team should be aware of their duties during a disaster. Some team members may be responsible for coordinating with local services, such as fire, police, and medical personnel. Some may be responsible for the evacuation of company personnel, if required. Others may be assigned to simply pack up and leave.

- Execution of the alert roster and notification of key personnel—These notifications may extend outside the organization to include the fire, police, or medical services mentioned earlier. They may also include insurance agencies, disaster teams such as those of the Red Cross, and management teams.

- Clear establishment of priorities—During a disaster response, the top priority is always the preservation of human life. Data and systems protection is subordinate when the disaster threatens the lives, health, or welfare of employees or members of the community. Only after all employees and neighbors have been safeguarded can the DR team attend to protecting other organizational assets.

- Procedures for documentation of the disaster—Just as in an incident response, the disaster must be carefully recorded from the onset. This documentation is used later to determine how and why the disaster occurred.

- Action steps to mitigate the impact of the disaster on the operations of the organization—The DR plan should specify the responsibilities of each DR team member, such as the evacuation of physical assets or making sure that all systems are securely shut down to prevent further loss of data.

- Alternative implementations for various system components if primary versions are unavailable—These components include stand-by equipment that is either purchased, leased, or under contract with a DR service agency. Developing systems with excess capacity, fault tolerance, auto-recovery, and fail-safe features facilitates a quick recovery. Data recovery requires effective backup strategies as well as flexible hardware configurations.

As part of DR plan readiness, each employee should always have two emergency information cards in their possession. The first lists personal emergency information—the person to notify in case of an emergency (next of kin), medical conditions, and a form of identification. The second contains a set of instructions for what to do in the event of an emergency. This snapshot of the DR plan should contain a contact number or hotline for calling the organization during an emergency, emergency services numbers (fire, police, medical), evacuation and assembly locations (e.g., storm shelters), the name and number of the DR coordinator, and any other needed information.

Responding to the Disaster

When a disaster strikes, events can overwhelm even the best of DR plans. To be prepared, the DRPT should incorporate flexibility into the plan. If an organization's physical facilities are intact, the DR team should begin the restoration of systems and data to work toward full operational capability. If the organization's facilities are damaged or destroyed beyond recovery, alternative actions must be taken until new facilities can be acquired. When a disaster threatens the viability of an organization at the primary site, the DR process becomes a business continuity process, which is described next.

A Simple Disaster Recovery Plan

Figure 10-10 shows an outline of what may be found in a simple DR plan. Such an outline would serve as a means of collecting the information needed to construct an effective DR plan. The plan has nine major sections, each of which is outlined here. Many organizations—particularly ones with multiple locations and hundreds of employees—would find this outline of a plan too simple. Nevertheless, the basic structure provides a solid starting point for any organization.

1. Name and location of company or branch—The first section identifies the department, division, or organization to which this plan applies. The location must also be listed. This identification is especially important in organizations that are large enough to require more than one plan.

2. Dates of completion and update of the plan.

3. Staff to be called in the event of a disaster—This roster should be kept current to ensure the list includes employees who are still in their DR roles. This section should also identify key support personnel, such as building maintenance supervisors, physical security directors, legal counsel, and the starting points on the alert roster. A copy of the alert roster (also known as the telephone tree) should be attached.

4. Emergency services to be called (if needed) in the event of a disaster—While dialing 911 will certainly bring police, fire, and ambulance services, the organization may have equally pressing needs for emergency teams from the gas, plumbing, electric, and water companies as well as key software and hardware vendors.

5. Locations of in-house emergency equipment and supplies—This section should include maps and floor plans with directions to all critical in-house emergency materials, including shut-off switches and valves for gas, electricity, and water. Directions to key supplies, including first aid kits, fire extinguishers, flashlights, batteries, and a stash of office supplies, should also be provided. It is a good idea to place a disaster pack on every floor in an unlocked closet or readily accessible location. These items should be regularly inventoried and updated as needed.

6. Sources of off-site equipment and supplies—These items include contact sources for mobile phones, dehumidifiers, industrial equipment (such as forklifts and portable generators), and other safety and recovery components.

7. Salvage priority list—While the IT director may have just enough time to grab the last on-site backup before darting out the door in the event of a fire, additional materials can most likely be salvaged if recovery efforts permit. In this event, recovery teams should know what has priority. The plan should include the locations and priorities of all items of value to the organization. When determining priorities, ask questions such as: Are these records archived elsewhere (i.e., off-site), or is this the only copy? Can these records be reproduced if lost, and if so, at what cost? Is the cost of replacement more or less than the value of the materials? It may be useful to create a simple rating scheme for materials, such as "First-priority salvage," "Second-priority salvage," and "Do not salvage."

8. Disaster recovery procedures—This very important section outlines the specific assignments given to key personnel, including the DR team, to be performed in the event of a disaster. If these duties differ by type of disaster, it may be useful to create multiple scenarios, each listing the duties and responsibilities of the parties involved. It is equally important to make sure that all personnel identified in this section have a copy of the DR plan stored where they can easily access it and that they are familiar with their responsibilities.

9. Follow-up assessment—The final section details what is to be accomplished after disaster strikes—specifically, what documentation is required for recovery efforts, including mandatory insurance reports and the AAR format.

Figure 10-10   Disaster recovery plan outline

Disaster Recovery Plan Outline

1. Name of Company_____

2. Date of completion or update of the plan _____

3. Staff to be called in the event of a disaster:
   Name: Numbers: Position:
   ...

   Note below who is to call whom upon the discovery of a disaster (Telephone Tree):
   ...

4. Emergency services to be called (if needed) in event of a disaster:
   Service: Contact Person: Number:
   ...

5. Locations of in-house emergency equipment and supplies (attach map or floor plan with locations marked):
   ...

6. Sources of off-site equipment and supplies (if maintained on-site, note location):
   Item: Contact/Company: Number:
   ...

7. Salvage Priority List:

   Attach a copy of the records retention schedule identifying all vital/essential records series. The location and record medium of the preservation duplicate for each vital records series should be noted.

   It is also very helpful if other records series are reviewed to determine their priority for salvage should a disaster occur. The following questions can be helpful in determining priorities:

       1) Can the records be replaced? At what cost?
       2) Would the cost of replacement be less or more than restoration of the records?
       3) How important are the records to the organization?
       4) Are the records duplicated elsewhere?

   To simplify this process, priorities may be assigned as follows:
       1) Salvage at all costs.
       (for example, records that are historically valuable or non-vital records that are important to operations and very difficult to re-create)

       2) Salvage if time and resources permit.
       (for example, records that are less important to the agency or somewhat easier to re-create)

       3) Dispose of as part of general cleanup.
       (for example, records that do not need to be salvaged because they are convenience copies and the record copy is at another location)

8. Disaster Recovery Procedures:
   Attach a list of specific procedures to be followed in the event of a disaster in your organization, including responsibilities of in-house recovery team members.

9. Follow-up Assessment:
   A written report, including photographs, should be prepared after recovery and attached to a copy of the disaster plan. The report should note the effectiveness of the plan, and should include an evaluation of the sources of supplies and equipment, and of any off-site facilities used.

Self-Check

7. The disaster recovery planning process includes developing strategies to recover both information and physical IT assets.

   a. True   **b.** False

8. Rapid-onset disasters usually provide significant warning before they occur.

   a. True   **b.** False

9. Disaster classification can be based on the origin of the disaster, such as natural or man-made.

   a. True   **b.** False

☐ Check your answers at the end of this chapter.

Business Continuity and Crisis Management

Sometimes, disasters have such a profound effect on the organization that it cannot continue operations at its primary site until it fully completes all DR efforts. To deal with such events, the organization implements its strategies for **business continuity (BC)**—efforts to ensure long-term viability when a disaster precludes operations at the primary site—by temporarily establishing critical operations at an alternate site until it can resume operations at the primary site or select and occupy a new one.

Business continuity planning (BCP) ensures that critical business processes can continue if a disaster occurs, enabling the organization to stay in business. Like the DR plan, the BC plan is usually managed by the COO or CEO of an organization. It is activated and executed concurrently with the DR plan when the disaster is major or long-term and requires a more intensive restoration of information and IT resources. While the DR plan focuses on the reestablishment of technical infrastructure and business operations at the primary site, the BC plan reestablishes critical business processes at an alternate site. Not every business needs such a plan or such facilities, as small companies or fiscally sound organizations may be able to simply cease operations or work from home until the primary facilities are restored.

During the recent COVID-19 pandemic, many organizations faced the need to quickly implement virtual operations or other alternatives. Many service organizations like restaurants had to implement delivery and no-contact pickup options. Many academic institutions had to shift to all online classes. While there was no physical damage to facilities, the impact of the pandemic was more significant than a natural disaster in preventing organizations from working in their primary facilities.

BC is an element of CP, and it is best accomplished using a repeatable process or methodology. NIST's SP 800-34, Rev. 1, "Contingency Planning Guide for Federal Information Systems," includes guidance for planning for incidents, disasters, and situations that require BC.

The first step in all contingency efforts is the development of policy; thus, the BCPT creates the BC policy first, closely followed by the BC plan. The same seven-step approach that NIST recommends for CP can be adapted to an eight-step model that can be used to develop and maintain a viable BC program:

1. Form the BC teams—As was done with DRP, the initial assignments to the BCPT, including the team lead, are performed by the CPMT. The BCPT will then assign additional personnel as necessary to the BC response teams and define and assign their roles and responsibilities.

2. Develop the BC policy.

3. Review the BIA—The critical organizational processes and systems identified and prioritized in the BIA will be needed for the BP plan to facilitate establishing operations in an alternate site in the event of a disaster.

4. Identify preventive controls—Little is done here exclusively for BC. Most of the steps taken in the CP and DRP processes will provide the necessary foundation for BCP.

5. Create relocation strategies—Thorough relocation strategies are critical to BC to ensure key business processes will be reestablished quickly and effectively at an alternate location following a disruption.

6. Develop the BC plan—The BC plan should contain detailed guidance and procedures for implementing BC strategies at predetermined locations in accordance with management's guidance.

7. Ensure BC plan testing, training, and exercises.

8. Ensure BC plan maintenance.

Business Continuity Policy

BCP begins with the development of the BC policy, which reflects the organization's philosophy on the conduct of BC operations and serves as the guiding document for the development of BCP. The BC team leader might receive the BC policy from the CP team or the BCPT may be directed to develop it. The BC policy contains the following key sections:

- Purpose—The purpose of the BC program is to provide the necessary planning and coordination to help relocate critical business processes if a disaster prohibits continued operations at the primary site.

- Scope—This section identifies the organizational units and groups of employees to which the policy applies; it is especially useful for geographically dispersed organizations or those with multiple divisions.

- Roles and responsibilities—This section identifies the roles and responsibilities of key players and teams involved in BC operations.

- Resource requirements—Organizations can allocate specific resources to the development and implementation of BC plans.

- Training requirements—This section specifies the training requirements for various employee groups.

- Exercise and testing schedules—This section stipulates the frequency of BC plan testing and can specify both the type of exercise or testing required and the individuals involved.

- Plan maintenance schedule—This section specifies the procedures and frequency of BC plan reviews and identifies the personnel who will be involved in the review.

- Special considerations—In extreme situations, the DR and BC plans overlap, as described earlier. Thus, this section provides an overview of the organization's information storage and retrieval plans. At a minimum, the plan should identify where detailed documentation is kept, which individuals are responsible, and any other information needed to implement the strategy.

You may have noticed that this structure is virtually identical to that of the disaster recovery policy and plans. The processes are generally the same, with minor differences in implementation.

The cornerstone of the BC plan is the identification and prioritization of critical business processes and the resources to support them from the BIA. When a disaster strikes, these processes are the first to be reestablished at the alternate site. The BCPT, in cooperation with the CPMT, will evaluate and compare the various alternatives and recommend which strategy should be selected and implemented. The strategy selected usually involves an off-site facility, which should be inspected, configured, secured, and tested on a periodic basis. The selection should be reviewed periodically to determine whether the current solution is still viable, a better alternative has emerged, or the organization needs a different solution.

Many organizations with operations in New York City had their BC efforts (or lack thereof) tested critically on September 11, 2001. Similarly, organizations on the U.S. Gulf Coast had their BC plans' effectiveness tested during the aftermath of Hurricane Katrina in 2005 and the series of hurricanes that affected Texas and Florida in 2017. The entire world faced a worst-case scenario when governments implemented stay-at-home lockdowns during the recent COVID-19 pandemic. Some organizations never recovered; however, many organizations have retained the lessons learned during the pandemic, allowing remote and virtual work options.

Continuity Strategies

The BCPT can choose from several strategies in its plan, but the determining factor is usually cost. The options that follow are some of the most common. Also, many organizations now use cloud-based production systems, which preclude many of the following approaches because the cloud often has integral continuity strategies built into the architecture.

In general, there are three types of BC usage strategies in which the organization has the right to the exclusive use of a facility and access is not shared with other organizations:

- **Hot site**—A fully configured computing facility that includes all services, communications links, and physical plant operations. A hot site duplicates computing resources, peripherals, phone systems, applications, and workstations. A hot site needs only the latest data backups and personnel to resume operations. Depending on design choices and the level of contingency preparation, a hot site can be fully functional within minutes. Not surprisingly, near real-time cutover is the most expensive alternative. Disadvantages include the need to provide maintenance and protection for all the systems and equipment at the hot site. A hot site is the optimal strategy if the organization requires immediate and continuous capabilities for near real-time recovery.

- **Warm site**—A facility that provides many of the same services and options as a hot site, but typically without installed and configured software applications. A warm site may include computing equipment and peripherals with servers but not client workstations. It offers many of the advantages of a hot site at a lower cost. The disadvantage is that hours or days may be required to make the warm site fully operational.

- **Cold site**—A facility that provides only rudimentary services, with no computer hardware, peripherals, or active communications services. A cold site is essentially an empty facility with standard heating, air conditioning, and electrical service, which may need to be activated on occupancy. Everything else is an added-cost option. Despite these disadvantages, a cold site may be better than nothing. Its primary advantage is its low cost. The most useful feature of this approach is that it ensures an organization has floor space if a widespread disaster strikes.

If the preceding three options are not suitable or affordable for an organization, there are three sharing strategies an organization can use when needed for BC operations:

- **Timeshare**—A continuity strategy in which an organization co-leases facilities with a business partner or sister organization. A timeshare allows the organization to provide a DR/BC option while reducing its overall costs. The primary disadvantage is the possibility that multiple organizations will need the facility simultaneously. Other disadvantages include the need to stock the facility with the equipment and data from all organizations involved, the complexity of negotiating the timeshare with the sharing organizations, and the possibility that one or more sharing organizations might exit the agreement or sublease their options. Operating under a timeshare is much like agreeing to co-lease an apartment with a group of friends.

- **Service bureau**—A continuity strategy in which an organization contracts with a service agency to provide a BC facility for a fee. In the case of DR/BC planning, the service is the provision of physical facilities in the event of a disaster. Contracts with service bureaus can specify exactly what the organization needs under certain circumstances. A service agreement usually guarantees space when needed and possibly requires the service bureau to acquire additional space in the event of a widespread disaster. In this sense, it resembles the rental car provision in a car insurance policy. The disadvantages are that service contracts must be renegotiated periodically, rates can change, and the service can be quite expensive, depending on the needs of the organization.

- **Mutual agreement**—A continuity strategy in which two organizations sign a contract to assist the other in a disaster by providing BC facilities, resources, and services until the organization in need can recover from the disaster. This arrangement can be a lot like moving in with relatives or friends; it may not take long for an organization to wear out its welcome. Many organizations balk at the idea of having to fund duplicate services and resources, even in the short term. Still, mutual agreements between divisions of the same parent company, between subordinate and senior organizations, or between business partners may be a cost-effective solution when both parties to the agreement have a mutual interest in the other's continued operations and both have similar capabilities and capacities.

In addition to the basic strategies just described, there are specialized alternatives:

- **Rolling mobile site**—A continuity strategy that involves contracting with an organization to provide specialized facilities configured in the payload area of a tractor-trailer. An organization might arrange with a prefabricated building contractor or specialized DR/BC service for immediate, temporary facilities (mobile offices) on-site in the event of a disaster. With the recent expansion in cloud-based provisioning, like Amazon Web Services, the need to have systems or data stored locally has dwindled. As long as the individual employees have laptop or desktop systems, this service can be both a potential continuity option for production systems and a mechanism to manage recovery from disrupted operations. Because this option is mobile by definition, the site can even be set up in the parking lot of a facility undergoing DR, providing close and convenient access for both DR and BC team members and other employees.

- **Work-from-home**—A continuity strategy in which the entire organization works remotely, usually at home or while traveling, using virtual meetings and remote access to critical systems. Developed by necessity during the COVID-19 pandemic, the work-from-home approach forced many organizations to rethink how they operate. Organizations that never considered remote work were forced to implement hasty operations using employees working from home and conducting business via teleconferencing and video streaming. In many cases, additional risk was introduced when work-from-home approaches were implemented with poor planning.

Timing and Sequence of CP Elements

As indicated earlier, the IR plan focuses on immediate response. Still, if the incident escalates into a disaster, the IR plan may give way to the DR plan and possibly the BC plan, as illustrated in Figure 10-11. The BC plan could be implemented concurrently with the DR plan when the damage is major or long-term and requires more than simple restoration of information and information resources, as illustrated in Figure 10-12.

Figure 10-11 Incident response and disaster recovery

Incident: Ransomware attack on
a single system/user

Disaster: Ransomware attack on
all organizational systems/users

Attack occurs: Depending on scope, may be
classified as an incident or a disaster

Some experts argue that the three planning components of CP (IR, DR, and BC) are so closely linked that they are indistinguishable, even if each has a distinct place, role, and planning requirement. Furthermore, each component comes into play at a specific time in the life of an incident. Figure 10-13 illustrates this sequence and shows the overlap that may occur. How the plans interact and the ways in which they are brought into action are discussed in the following sections.

Figure 10-12 Disaster recovery and business continuity planning

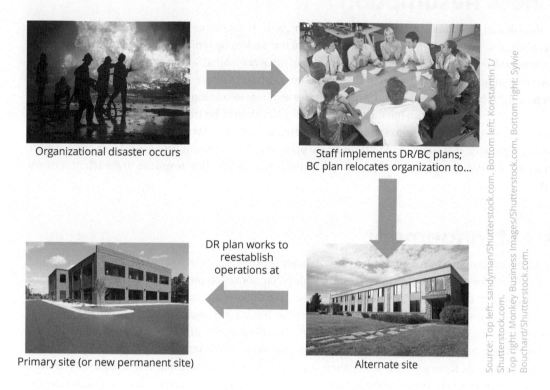

Organizational disaster occurs

Staff implements DR/BC plans;
BC plan relocates organization to...

DR plan works to
reestablish
operations at

Primary site (or new permanent site)

Alternate site

Figure 10-13 Contingency planning implementation timeline

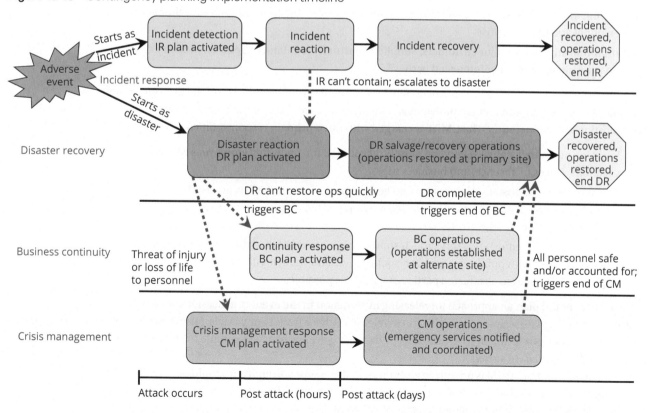

Business Resumption

Because the DR and BC plans are closely related, most organizations merge the two processes into a single function called business resumption planning (BRP)—actions taken by senior management to develop and implement a combined DR and BC policy, plan, and set of recovery teams. Such a comprehensive plan must be able to support both DR and BC operations. Therefore, although a single planning team can develop the business resumption plan, execution of the plan requires separate execution teams.

The planning process for the business resumption plan should be tied to, but distinct from, the IR plan. As noted earlier in the chapter, an incident may escalate into a disaster when it grows dramatically in scope and intensity. It is important that the three planning development processes be so tightly integrated that the reaction teams can easily make the transition from incident response to disaster recovery and BCP.

Crisis Management

Another process that organizations may plan for separately is crisis management (CM)—the planning and preparation efforts for dealing with potential human injury, emotional trauma, loss of life from a disaster, or an adverse event that dramatically and negatively impacts the organization's image or that of its employees. CM focuses almost exclusively on the effects that a disaster has on the organization's people. While some organizations include crisis management as a subset of the DR plan, the protection of human life and the organization's image is such a high priority that it may deserve its own committee, policy, and plan. Thus, the organization should form a CMPT, which then organizes a crisis management response team (CMRT). The appropriate DRRT works closely with the CMRT to ensure complete and timely communication during a disaster. According to Gartner Research, the crisis management team is responsible for managing the event from an enterprise perspective and performs the following roles:

- Supporting personnel and their loved ones during the crisis
- Keeping the public informed about the event and the actions being taken to ensure the recovery of personnel and the enterprise
- Communicating with major customers, suppliers, partners, regulatory agencies, industry organizations, the media, and other interested parties[20]

The CMRT should establish a base of operations or command center near the site of the disaster as soon as possible. The CMRT should include individuals from all functional areas of the organization to facilitate communication and cooperation. The CMRT is charged with three primary responsibilities:

1. Verifying personnel status—Everyone must be accounted for, including employees who are on vacations, leaves of absence, and business trips.
2. Activating the alert roster—Alert rosters and general personnel phone lists are used to notify individuals whose assistance may be needed or simply to tell employees not to report to work until the disaster is over.
3. Coordinating with emergency services—If someone is injured or killed during a disaster, the CMRT will work closely with public emergency response units and agencies like the Red Cross to provide appropriate services to all affected parties as quickly as possible.

The CMPT should plan an approach for releasing information in the event of a disaster and should perhaps even have boilerplate scripts prepared for press releases. Advice from Lanny Davis, former counselor to President Bill Clinton, is relevant here. When beset by damaging events, heed the subtitle to Davis's memoir: *Tell It Early, Tell It All, Tell It Yourself.*[21]

As with IR, DR, and BC, if CM is organized and conducted as a separate entity, it should have a CM policy and a CM plan. The methodologies for CM policies and planning can follow the same basic models as DR policies and plans, but they should include specialized content focused on personnel safety, such as shelter areas, evacuation plans, and contact information for emergency services.

Note 5 | For more information, including crisis management materials, visit the National Science Foundation's website "Creating a Successful Crisis Management Plan" at www.nsf.org/knowledge-library/creating-successful-crisis-management-plan.

Self-Check

10. Business continuity planning ensures that critical business processes can continue if a disaster occurs, enabling the organization to stay in business.
    a. True   **b.** False

11. A hot site is a fully configured computing facility that includes all services, communications links, and physical plant operations used for business continuity.
    a. True   **b.** False

12. The business continuity plan is usually managed by the chief information officer of an organization.
    a. True   **b.** False

☐ Check your answers at the end of this chapter.

Testing Contingency Plans

Few plans are executable as initially written; instead, they must be tested to identify vulnerabilities, faults, and inefficient processes. Once problems are identified during testing, improvements can be made and the resulting plan can be relied on in times of need. The following strategies can be used to test contingency plans:

- Desk check—A CP testing strategy in which copies of the appropriate plans are distributed to all individuals who will be assigned roles during an actual incident or disaster, with everyone reviewing the plan and validating its components. While not a true test, this strategy is a good way to review the perceived feasibility and effectiveness of the plan and ensure at least a nominal update.

- Structured walk-through—A CP testing strategy in which all involved individuals walk through the organization or alternate site and discuss the steps they would take during an actual CP event. A walk-through can also be conducted as a conference room talk-through. This exercise can consist of an on-site walk-through, in which everyone discusses their actions at each location and juncture, or it may be more of a talk-through—a form of structured walk-through in which individuals meet in a conference room and discuss CP rather than walking around the organization.

- Simulation—A CP testing strategy in which the organization conducts a role-playing exercise as if an actual incident or disaster had occurred. In a simulation, the CP team is presented with a scenario of an incident or disaster and expected to respond as if it had occurred. The simulation usually involves performing the communications that should occur and specifying the required physical tasks, but it stops short of performing the actual tasks required. The major difference between a walk-through and a simulation is that in simulations, the discussion is driven by a scenario, whereas walk-throughs focus on simply discussing the plan. Simulations tend to be much more structured, with time limits, planned AARs, and moderators to manage the scenarios.

- Full-interruption testing—A CP testing strategy in which all team members follow each IR, DR, or BC procedure, including those for interruption of service, restoration of data from backups, and notification of appropriate individuals. This exercise is often performed after normal business hours in organizations that cannot afford to disrupt or simulate the disruption of business processes. Although full-interruption testing is the most rigorous testing strategy, it is too intrusive for most businesses.

At a minimum, organizations should conduct periodic talk-throughs or walk-throughs of each of the CP components on a regular basis. Failure to update these plans as the organization changes can erode the team's ability to respond to an incident or possibly cause greater damage than the incident itself. If this sounds like a major training effort, consider what the author Richard Marcinko, a former Navy SEAL, has to say about motivating a team:[22]

- The more you sweat in training, the less you bleed in combat.
- Training and preparation can hurt.
- Lead from the front, not the rear.
- You don't have to like it; you just have to do it.
- Keep it simple.
- Never assume.
- You are paid for your results, not your methods.

One often-neglected aspect of training is cross-training. In a real incident or disaster, some employees may not be available, requiring alternates to perform their duties. The testing process should train people to take over if a team leader or other member of the team is unavailable.

Final Thoughts on CP

As in all organizational efforts, practice makes perfect, and iteration results in improvement. A critical component of the NIST-based methodologies presented in this chapter is continuous process improvement. Each time the organization rehearses its plans, it should learn from the process, improve the plans, and then rehearse again. Each time an incident or disaster occurs, the organization should review what went right and what went wrong. The actual results should be so thoroughly analyzed that any changes to the plans that could have resulted in an improved outcome will be implemented into a revised set of plans. Through ongoing evaluation and improvement, the organization continues to move forward and continually improves upon the process so that it can strive for an even better outcome.

Several key lessons can be learned from the recent COVID-19 pandemic regarding CP operations:

- Physical meetings aren't necessarily as important as they seem. They are typically viewed as a managerial control mechanism, but employees have proven they can be effective without physical meetings.
- Virtual meetings allow individuals to quickly move from meeting to meeting without the hassle and delay of travel. In larger organizations or with individuals who work in the field, time and money are saved when employees don't have to physically move between internal meetings with coworkers or external meetings with suppliers and clients.
- A lot of activities that were seen as critical before the pandemic don't seem quite as important now. An organization can develop a lot of bad habits or institutionalized processes, and not all support efficient or effective operations. During the pandemic, many organizations found that they can trim less essential activities and still be competitive in the marketplace.

A University of California, Berkeley study found that organizational culture fundamentally shifted during and after the pandemic:

> Three patterns emerged from our study. First, the COVID-19 pandemic led organizations to emphasize certain cultural elements and to downplay others. In particular, the five cultural elements that organizations placed greater emphasis on were: flexibility, transparency, supportiveness, decisiveness, and confronting conflict. At the same time, the five cultural elements that organizations deemphasized in response to the pandemic were: customer orientation, individualism, detail orientation, results orientation, and collaboration. In short, organizational cultures in the pandemic era have generally shifted away from a high performance orientation to one that prizes empathy, understanding, and mutual support.[23]

No matter how you look at it, life as we know it has changed and may never revert to the pre-COVID standard.

Note 6 | A complete treatment of the contingency planning process is presented in *Principles of Incident Response and Disaster Recovery*, 3rd edition, by Michael Whitman and Herbert Mattord, published by Cengage.

Self-Check

13. The desk-check strategy involves physically walking through an organization to discuss the contingency plan.

    a. True

    b. False

14. Full-interruption testing is the most rigorous form of contingency plan testing but is often too intrusive for most businesses.

    a. True

    b. False

15. Simulations are driven by scenarios and tend to be more structured than walk-throughs.

    a. True

    b. False

☐ Check your answers at the end of this chapter.

Closing Case

Iris tried not to smile. "Of course, it isn't technically a disaster," she explained, "but I understand what you mean. How much information is lost?"

Joel looked at her in dismay. "Lost? All of it! We had just saved the report and sent it to the department print server!"

"Where did you save it?" Iris asked. "To your local drive or to the department share?"

Joel tried to remember. "I think it was to the OneDrive," he said. "Why?"

"Well, OneDrive is a cloud storage service, which wasn't affected by this incident," Iris replied. "It's probably fine. And if you did save it to your local drive, there's a high probability we can get it anyway, one way or another. I doubt the water damaged the hard drive itself."

Iris paused for a moment, then continued: "We were lucky this time. No one was hurt, and if the fire had spread to the server room next door, things could have been much worse."

Case Discussion Questions

1. Extrapolate on the case. At what point could this incident have been declared a disaster?
2. What would Iris have done differently if this adverse event had been much worse and had been declared a disaster?
3. Identify the procedures that Joel could have taken to minimize the potential loss in this incident. What would he need to do differently in the event of a disaster, if anything?

Case Ethical Decision Making

Imagine that the fire in the break room was caused by Joel, who accidentally started it while microwaving a bag of popcorn and then forgetting it. In that case, would Joel have been responsible for the damage caused to the break room and adjoining office? What if no one knew who the culprit had been? Would it then be unethical for Joel to deny that the fire was his fault if Iris asked him about it? How would your answer differ if the organization did not have a formal break room policy and the area did not have signs posted regarding the use of the microwave oven?

Summary

Planning for unexpected events is usually the responsibility of managers from both the IT and cybersecurity communities of interest. For a plan to be seen as valid by all members of the organization, it must be sanctioned and actively supported by the general business community of interest. Some organizations are required by law or other mandate to have contingency planning procedures in place at all times, but all business organizations should prepare for the unexpected.

Contingency planning (CP) is the process by which the information technology and cybersecurity communities of interest position their organizations to prepare for, detect, respond to, and recover from events that threaten the cybersecurity of information resources and assets. CP is made up of four major components: the data collection and documentation process known as the business impact analysis (BIA), the incident response (IR) plan, the disaster recovery (DR) plan, and the business continuity (BC) plan.

Organizations can either create and develop the three planning elements of the CP process (the IR, DR, and BC plans) as one unified plan or they can create the three elements separately in conjunction with a set of interlocking procedures that enable continuity.

To ensure continuity during the creation of the CP components, a seven-step CP process is used:

1. Develop the CP policy statement.
2. Conduct the BIA.
3. Identify preventive controls.
4. Create contingency strategies.
5. Develop a contingency plan.
6. Ensure plan testing, training, and exercises.
7. Ensure plan maintenance.

Four teams are involved in CP and contingency operations: the CP team, the IR team, the DR team, and the BC team. The IR team ensures that the cybersecurity incident response team is formed.

The IR plan is a detailed set of processes and procedures that plan for, detect, and resolve the effects of an unexpected event on information resources and assets. For every scenario identified, the CP team creates three sets of procedures—for before, during, and after the incident—to detect, contain, and resolve the incident. Incident classification is the process by which the IR team examines an incident candidate and determines whether it constitutes an actual incident. Three categories of incident indicators are used: possible, probable, and definite. When any one of the following happens, an actual incident is in progress: loss of availability of information, loss of integrity of information, loss of confidentiality of information, violation of policy, or violation of law.

Digital forensics involves identifying, preserving, extracting, documenting, and interpreting computer data to determine what occurred and how it happened. This is essential both for legal proceedings and organizational protection. The methodology includes acquiring evidence without alteration, ensuring its authenticity, and analyzing it to report findings. Digital forensics can be used for investigating digital malfeasance or performing root cause analysis. Organizations may outsource these tasks to experts due to their complexity, but having trained internal personnel is also crucial to avoid contamination of potential evidence.

DR planning encompasses preparation for handling and recovering from a disaster, whether natural or man-made. The DR plan must include crisis management, the action steps taken during and after a disaster.

BC planning ensures that critical business processes continue if a catastrophic incident or disaster occurs. BC plans can include provisions for hot sites, warm sites, cold sites, timeshares, service bureaus, and mutual agreements.

Because the DR and BC plans are closely related, most organizations prepare the two at the same time and may combine them into a single planning document called the business resumption plan.

All plans must be tested to identify vulnerabilities, faults, and inefficient processes. Several testing strategies can be used to test contingency plans, including desk checks, structured walk-throughs, simulations, and full-interruption.

Key Terms

adverse events
after-action review (AAR)
alert message
alert roster
apprehend and prosecute
business continuity (BC)
business impact analysis (BIA)
business resumption planning
   (BRP)
cold site
contingency planning (CP)
crisis management (CM)
cybersecurity incident response
   team (CIRT or CSIRT)
database shadowing

desk check
digital forensics
disaster recovery (DR)
e-discovery
electronic vaulting
full-interruption testing
hot site
incident
incident classification
incident commander
incident detection
incident response (IR)
maximum tolerable downtime
   (MTD)
mutual agreement

protect and forget
recovery point objective (RPO)
recovery time objective (RTO)
remote journaling
rolling mobile site
service bureau
simulation
structured walk-through
talk-through
timeshare
warm site
work-from-home
work recovery time (WRT)

Review Questions

1. What is the primary goal of contingency planning in an organization?

2. How does a business impact analysis assist in contingency planning?

3. What are the four major components of contingency planning mentioned in the text?

4. Why is the involvement of the general business community of interest important in contingency planning?

5. What is the function of the recovery point objective in contingency planning?

6. Describe the role of the contingency planning management team in the contingency planning process.

7. How does NIST SP 800-34, Rev. 1 influence contingency planning practices?

8. What is the importance of the disaster recovery plan in contingency planning?

9. Why is it essential to regularly update contingency plans?

10. What is the primary goal of an incident response plan within an organization?

11. How does NIST SP 800-61, Rev. 2 contribute to the development of an organization's incident response plan?

12. What are the three phases of incident response actions, as outlined in the chapter?

13. What is the purpose of having a cybersecurity incident response team in an organization?

14. Why is it important for an incident response policy to have the full support of top management?

15. What are the key components of a typical incident response policy, as identified by NIST SP 800-61, Rev. 2?

16. What steps should be taken during the incident containment phase?

17. How does digital forensics assist in the incident response process?

18. What is the difference between the "protect and forget" and "apprehend and prosecute" philosophies in incident and disaster handling?

19. What is the role of the disaster recovery planning process in an organization?

20. How does an organization determine when to escalate an incident to a disaster?

21. What are the primary responsibilities of the disaster recovery planning team?

22. What is the importance of the business impact analysis in the DRP process?

23. Describe the purpose of the disaster recovery policy within an organization.

24. How are disasters classified based on their rate of occurrence?

25. What steps should be included in a simple disaster recovery plan outline?

26. Why is cross-training employees important in disaster recovery planning?

27. What key elements should the disaster recovery planning team incorporate into the disaster recovery plan to ensure readiness?

28. What is the purpose of business continuity planning, and why is it important for an organization?

29. Describe the difference between a hot site, a warm site, and a cold site in the context of business continuity.

30. How did the COVID-19 pandemic impact the way organizations approached business continuity?

31. What are the key sections of a business continuity policy, and what is their significance?

32. Explain the concept of business resumption planning and how it relates to disaster recovery and business continuity.

33. What role does the crisis management planning team play during a disaster, and what are its primary responsibilities?

34. How does a timeshare strategy differ from a service bureau strategy in the context of business continuity?

35. What are the benefits and disadvantages of using a rolling mobile site as a business continuity strategy?

36. Why is plan maintenance a critical part of the business continuity plan, and what does it typically involve?

37. What is the purpose of testing contingency plans, and what can be done once vulnerabilities are identified during the testing process?

38. Describe the desk-check strategy and its primary benefit.

39. How does a structured walk-through differ from a desk check in testing contingency plans?

40. What makes simulations more structured compared to walk-throughs, and what do they typically involve?

41. Why is full-interruption testing considered the most rigorous strategy, and what are the challenges associated with it?

42. What are the benefits of conducting periodic talk-throughs or walk-throughs of contingency planning component plans?

43. According to the text, why is cross-training important in the context of contingency planning?

44. How has the COVID-19 pandemic influenced organizational culture, according to a University of California, Berkeley study?

45. What are some key lessons learned from the COVID-19 pandemic regarding contingency planning and organizational operations?

Exercises

1. Using a web search engine, search for "disaster recovery" and "business continuity." How many responses do you get for each term? Note how many companies do not distinguish between the two.

2. Go to http://csrc.nist.gov. Click the plus sign (+) next to Publications, select NIST Special Publications (SPs), and then locate SP 800-34, "Contingency Planning Guide for Federal Information Systems." Download and review this document. Summarize the key points for an in-class discussion.

3. Using a web search engine, visit one of the popular disaster recovery or business continuity sites, such as www.disasterrecoveryworld.com, www.drj.com, www.drie.org, www.drii.org, or csrc.nist.gov. Search for "hot site," "warm site," and "cold site." Do the provided descriptions match those in this chapter? Why or why not?

4. Using the format provided in the text, design an incident response plan for your home computer. Include actions to be taken if each of the following events occur:

- Virus attack
- Power failure
- Fire
- Burst water pipe
- Internet service provider (ISP) failure

What other scenarios do you think are important to plan for?

5. Look for information on incident response on your institution's website. Does your institution have a published plan? Identify the areas in an academic institution's contingency planning that might differ from those of a for-profit institution.

Solutions to Self-Check Questions

Introduction to Contingency Planning

1. Contingency planning involves only the cybersecurity community of interest within an organization.
   Answer: b. False.
   Explanation: Contingency planning involves managers from the business, IT, and cybersecurity communities of interest.

2. A business impact analysis helps identify and prioritize information systems critical to supporting the organization's business processes.
   Answer: a. True.
   Explanation: A business impact analysis is crucial for determining which information systems are essential for business continuity.

3. A comprehensive contingency plan must include the disaster recovery plan and the business continuity plan.
   Answer: a. True.
   Explanation: A complete contingency plan encompasses both the disaster recovery plan and the business continuity plan.

Incident Response

4. Incident response is a preventive measure that focuses on stopping incidents before they happen.
   Answer: b. False.
   Explanation: Incident response is a reactive measure, not a preventive one, although incident response plans may include preventative recommendations.

5. The incident response plan is activated only when an incident poses a major threat to an organization's viability.
   Answer: b. False.
   Explanation: The plan is activated when the organization detects an incident that affects it, regardless of how minor the effect is.

6. The cybersecurity incident response team is always a formal group in larger organizations, but the team may be informal in smaller organizations.
   Answer: a. True.
   Explanation: In larger organizations, the team is usually a more formal group that works and trains together. In smaller organizations, the team may be a loose association of IT and cybersecurity staffers.

Disaster Recovery

7. The disaster recovery planning process includes developing strategies to recover both information and physical IT assets.

    Answer: a. True.

    Explanation: The process involves recovering information assets and acquiring replacement IT assets as well as reestablishing necessary IT and information assets at the primary site or a new location if necessary.

8. Rapid-onset disasters usually provide significant warning before they occur.

    Answer: b. False.

    Explanation: Rapid-onset disasters occur suddenly with little warning, taking people's lives and destroying means of production.

9. Disaster classification can be based on the origin of the disaster, such as natural or man-made.

    Answer: a. True.

    Explanation: Disasters can be classified by their origin. For example, a flood is a natural disaster and a hacker intrusion is a man-made disaster.

Business Continuity and Crisis Management

10. Business continuity planning ensures that critical business processes can continue if a disaster occurs, enabling the organization to stay in business.

    Answer: a. True.

    Explanation: Business continuity planning is designed to ensure that critical business processes can continue during a disaster, allowing the organization to maintain operations.

11. A hot site is a fully configured computing facility that includes all services, communications links, and physical plant operations used for business continuity.

    Answer: a. True.

    Explanation: A hot site is a fully equipped facility ready for immediate use in business continuity operations, requiring only the latest data backups and personnel to resume operations.

12. The business continuity plan is usually managed by the chief information officer of an organization.

    Answer: b. False.

    Explanation: The plan is typically managed by the chief operations officer or chief executive officer.

Testing Contingency Plans

13. The desk-check strategy involves physically walking through an organization to discuss the contingency plan.

    Answer: b. False.

    Explanation: A desk check is a strategy in which copies of the plan are reviewed by individuals. A desk check is not the same thing as a physical walk-through.

14. Full-interruption testing is the most rigorous form of contingency plan testing but is often too intrusive for most businesses.

    Answer: a. True.

    Explanation: Full-interruption testing involves following all procedures, including those for interruption of service, making it very rigorous but often too intrusive.

15. Simulations are driven by scenarios and tend to be more structured than walk-throughs.

    Answer: a. True.

    Explanation: Simulations involve a role-playing exercise driven by a scenario and are more structured than walk-throughs.

Cybersecurity Maintenance

Chapter Objectives

After reading this chapter and completing the exercises, you should be able to:

1. Identify the 13 monitoring activities for a cybersecurity program in NIST SP 800-100.

2. Summarize the cybersecurity maintenance models.

> We want a fresh start only because we didn't sufficiently care for the last fresh start.
>
> —Craig D. Lounsbrough

Case Opener

Iris leaned back in her chair. It was Monday morning, the first workday after the biggest conversion weekend of the Random Widget Works cybersecurity upgrade. Iris had just reviewed the results. So far, everything had gone according to plan. The initial penetration tests run on Sunday afternoon were clean, and every change request processed over the past three months had gone through without any issues. Iris was eager to return to the routine she had begun to enjoy since her promotion to chief security officer (CSO).

Kelvin Urich, the lead cybersecurity analyst, tapped on the open door of Iris's office. "Hey, Iris," he said, "Have you seen the email I just sent? There's a new CVE on cve.org about an HTTP vulnerability in our Apache server. It's called request smuggling, and it could allow an attacker to bypass security controls and compromise system data. The open-source community just released a critical patch, and they recommend that it be applied immediately. Should I get the system programming team started on it?"

"Absolutely! Ask them to pull the download from the distribution site as soon as possible," said Iris. "But remember, we must follow our maintenance plan and each quality assurance step carefully. Before they install it on a single production system, I was hoping you could review the test results and QA report yourself. After you sign off on the test results, have them patch the servers for the HQ development team. Oh, and don't forget you need to get change orders into change control ASAP if we go forward on the patch and you plan to hit the next critical systems change window."

"I'll get right on it," Kelvin said.

After Kelvin left, Iris pulled up www.cve.org on her computer. She was reading about the vulnerability when she heard another knock on the door. It was Linda Simpson, the new compliance team lead.

"Hi, Iris," Linda said. "Got a second?"

"Sure, Linda. How have you been? Settling in okay?"

She smiled and nodded. "Yeah, this is a good group. Everyone pitched in and helped round up the documentation I needed. I have been studying the documentation trail since before the cybersecurity program was implemented. I came to see you because I am reassessing the information asset inventory and the threat vulnerability update you requested."

Iris was confused for a second, but then she remembered the task she had assigned to Linda. "Oh, right," she said, with a slight grimace. "Sorry—I had put the quarterly asset and threat review out of my mind while we were busy implementing the new change program. I suppose it's time to start planning for the regular reviews, isn't it?"

Linda handed her a folder and said, "Here's the first draft of the plan for the review project. Maria and Kelvin have already seen it, and they suggested I review it with you. Could you review it and let me know when you would like to go over it in detail?"

Introduction to Cybersecurity Maintenance

After successfully implementing and testing changes to the cybersecurity program, an organization may feel more confident about the level of protection it provides for its information assets. But it shouldn't, really. In all likelihood, a good deal of time has passed since the organization began the process. In that time, the dynamic aspects of the organization's environment will have changed. Almost all aspects of a company's environment are dynamic, meaning threats that were originally assessed in the early stages of the organization's risk management program have probably changed and new priorities have emerged. New types of attacks have been developed, and new variants of existing attacks have probably emerged as well. In addition, many other items outside and inside the organization have most likely changed.

Developing a comprehensive list of dynamic factors in an organization's environment is beyond the scope of this text. However, the following changes may affect an organization's cybersecurity environment:

- The acquisition or installation of new assets and the divestiture or decommissioning of old assets
- The emergence of vulnerabilities associated with new or existing assets
- The emergence of new threats and exploits or the evolution of current threats and exploits
- Shifting business priorities
- Changes in the business environment or legal landscape
- The formation of new partnerships or the dissolution of old ones
- The hiring of new personnel and departure of personnel who were knowledgeable about the organization's information and cybersecurity strategies, tactics, and tools

As this list shows, by the time a cycle of the risk management program is completed, the organization's cybersecurity, information technology (IT), and business environments have probably changed considerably. A cybersecurity team needs to be able to assure management that the program is resilient and capable of accommodating these changes. If the program is not adjusting adequately to change, it may be necessary to begin the risk management cycle again. If an organization deals successfully with change and has created procedures and systems that can be adjusted to the environment, the existing cybersecurity improvement program can continue to work well. Deciding whether to continue with the current improvement program or to renew the investigation, analysis, and design phases depends on how much change has occurred and how well the organization and its program for cybersecurity maintenance is adapting to its evolving environment.

Before learning about the maintenance model described here, you need some background on the management and operation of a cybersecurity program. In this chapter, you will learn about the methods organizations use to monitor the three primary aspects of cybersecurity risk management, which are commonly referred to as the TVA triplet: threats, vulnerabilities, and assets.

To manage and operate the ongoing cybersecurity program, the cybersecurity community must select and adapt a management maintenance model. In general, management models are frameworks that structure the tasks of managing a particular set of activities or business functions. A maintenance model is a specialized management model designed to ensure continuous monitoring and improvement of a particular program or operation.

NIST SP 800-100, "Information Security Handbook: A Guide for Managers"

Special Publication (SP) 800-100, "Information Security Handbook: A Guide for Managers," provides managerial guidance for the establishment and implementation of a cybersecurity program. In particular, this handbook from the National Institute of Standards and Technology (NIST) addresses the ongoing tasks expected of a cybersecurity manager once the program is working and day-to-day operations are established.

For each of the 13 areas of cybersecurity management presented in SP 800-100, there are specific monitoring activities—tasks that cybersecurity managers should perform on an ongoing basis to monitor the function of the cybersecurity program and take corrective actions when issues arise. Not all issues are negative, like the situation described in the chapter case opener. Some are normal changes in the business environment, while others are changes in the technology environment—for example, the emergence of new technologies that could improve cybersecurity or new cybersecurity standards and regulations with which the organization should comply. The following sections describe monitoring actions for the 13 cybersecurity areas, as adapted from SP 800-100.

Note 1 | For more information on NIST SP 800-100 and other NIST special publications, visit https://csrc.nist.gov/publications/sp800.

Cybersecurity Governance

As described in previous chapters, an effective cybersecurity governance program requires constant review. Organizations should monitor the status of their programs to ensure the following:

- Ongoing cybersecurity activities are providing appropriate support to the organization's mission.
- Policies and procedures are current and aligned with evolving technologies, if appropriate.
- Controls are accomplishing their intended purpose.
- The cybersecurity leadership is reporting on the status of the cybersecurity program and its projects to the governance group on a regular basis and incorporating its feedback and priorities into the program.

Over time, policies and procedures may become inadequate because of changes in the organization's mission and operational requirements, threats, or the environment; deterioration in the degree of compliance; or changes in technology, infrastructure, or business processes. Periodic assessments and reports on activities can identify areas of noncompliance, remind users of their responsibilities, and demonstrate management's commitment to the cybersecurity program. While an organization's mission does not frequently change, the organization may expand its mission or operations, requiring it to adjust its efforts to secure its programs and assets and to modify its cybersecurity requirements and practices.

Table 11-1 provides a broad overview of key ongoing activities that can assist in monitoring and improving an organization's information governance activities.

Table 11-1 Ongoing monitoring activities of cybersecurity governance[1]

Activities	Description of Activities
Plans of action and milestones (POA&Ms)	POA&Ms assist in identifying, assessing, prioritizing, and monitoring the progress of corrective efforts for cybersecurity weaknesses found in programs and systems. The POA&M tracks the measures implemented to correct deficiencies and to reduce or eliminate known vulnerabilities. POA&Ms can also assist in identifying performance gaps, evaluating an organization's cybersecurity performance and efficiency, and conducting oversight.
Measurement and measures	Measures are tools designed to improve performance and accountability through the collection, analysis, and reporting (measurement) of relevant performance data. Cybersecurity measures monitor the accomplishment of goals and objectives by quantifying the implementation level of cybersecurity controls and their efficiency and effectiveness, by analyzing the adequacy of cybersecurity activities, and by identifying possible improvements. The terms "measures" and "measurement" seem to have some overlap in their meanings. A measure is a question asked or statement of data collected as part of a measurement program, whereas a measurement is the process of collecting measures.
Continuous assessment (CA)	The CA process monitors the initial cybersecurity implementation of an IT system to track changes to it, analyzes the cybersecurity impact of those changes, makes appropriate adjustments to the cybersecurity controls and the system's cybersecurity plan, and reports the system's cybersecurity status to appropriate organization officials.
Configuration management (CM)	CM is an essential component of monitoring the status of cybersecurity controls and identifying potential cybersecurity problems in IT systems. This information can help cybersecurity managers understand and monitor the evolving nature of vulnerabilities that appear in a system under their responsibility, thus enabling managers to direct appropriate changes as required.
Network monitoring	Information about network performance and user behavior on the network helps cybersecurity program managers identify areas in need of improvement and point out potential performance improvements. This information can be correlated with other sources of information, such as the POA&M and CM, to create a comprehensive picture of the cybersecurity program.
Incident and event statistics	Incident statistics are valuable in determining the effectiveness of implemented cybersecurity policies and procedures. Incident statistics provide cybersecurity program managers with further insights into the status of cybersecurity programs under their purview, help them observe performance trends in program activities, and inform them about the need to change policies and procedures. These statistics may also be associated with the measurement program.

Systems Development Life Cycle

As you learned in earlier chapters, the systems development life cycle (SDLC) is the overall process of developing, implementing, and maintaining IT systems through a multistep approach—initiation, analysis, design, implementation, and maintenance to disposal. Each phase of the SDLC includes a minimum set of activities required to effectively incorporate cybersecurity into a system. During each phase, the organization should continuously monitor system performance to ensure that it is consistent with established user and cybersecurity requirements and that needed system modifications are incorporated.

For **configuration and change management (CCM)**, also known as **configuration management (CM)**—an approach to implementing system change that uses policies, procedures, techniques, and tools to manage and evaluate proposed changes, track changes through completion, and maintain systems inventory and supporting documentation—it is important to document proposed or actual changes in the system cybersecurity plan. Information systems are typically in a constant state of evolution with upgrades to hardware, software, and firmware and possible modifications to the system's environment. Documenting IT system changes and assessing their potential impact on the system's cybersecurity is an essential part of continuous monitoring and key to avoiding a lapse in cybersecurity. Monitoring cybersecurity controls helps to identify potential problems in the IT system that are not identified during a cybersecurity impact analysis. This analysis is conducted as part of the CM and control process.

Awareness and Training

As discussed earlier in the text, once the cybersecurity program has been implemented, processes must be put in place to monitor compliance and effectiveness. An automated tracking system could be implemented to capture key information about program activity, such as content, dates, audience, costs, and sources. A tracking system like this should capture data at an organization level so it can be used to provide enterprise-wide analysis and reporting about awareness, training, and education initiatives.

Tracking compliance involves assessing the status of the program and mapping it to standards established by the organization. Reports can be generated and used to identify gaps or problems. Corrective action and necessary follow-up can then be taken. This follow-up may take the form of formal notifications to management; additional awareness, training, or education offerings; and the establishment of a corrective plan with scheduled completion dates. As the organization's environment changes, cybersecurity policies must evolve, and all awareness and training material should reflect these changes.

Capital Planning and Investment Control

Increased competition for limited resources requires that departments allocate available funding toward their highest-priority cybersecurity investments to afford the organization the appropriate degree of cybersecurity for its needs. This goal can be achieved through a formal enterprise capital planning and investment control process designed to facilitate the organization's expenditures.

NIST SP 800-65, "Integrating IT Security into the Capital Planning and Investment Control Process," provides a seven-step process for prioritizing cybersecurity activities and corrective actions for funding purposes:

1. Identify the baseline. Use cybersecurity measures or other available data to baseline the current cybersecurity posture.
2. Identify prioritization requirements. Evaluate the cybersecurity posture against legislative requirements, other requirements from the chief information officer (CIO), and the organization's mission.
3. Conduct enterprise-level prioritization. Establish the priority of potential cybersecurity investments at the enterprise level against the organization's mission and prioritize the financial impact of implementing appropriate cybersecurity controls.
4. Once enterprise-level priorities are established, conduct system-level prioritization. Establish the priority of potential system-level corrective actions, considering the system categories and the needed corrective action impacts.
5. Develop supporting materials. Develop an initial business plan and business case analysis for enterprise-level investments. For system-level investments, request additional funding as needed to mitigate prioritized weaknesses.
6. Implement an investment review board and portfolio management. Prioritize organization-wide business cases against requirements and CIO priorities and determine the investment portfolio.
7. Submit any required budget approval paperwork.[2]

Interconnecting Systems

System interconnection is the connection of two or more IT systems for the purpose of sharing data and other resources. Organizations choose to interconnect their systems for a variety of reasons based on their needs. For example, they may interconnect systems to exchange data, collaborate on joint projects, or securely store data and backup archives.

Interconnecting IT systems can expose the participating organizations to risk. For instance, if the interconnection is not properly designed, cybersecurity vulnerabilities could compromise the connected systems and their data. Similarly, if one of the connected systems is compromised, the interconnection could be used as a conduit to compromise the other system and its data.

NIST SP 800-47, Rev. 1, details a four-phase life cycle management approach for information exchange between IT systems that emphasizes cybersecurity:

1. Planning the information exchange: The participating organizations perform preliminary activities; examine all relevant technical, security, and administrative issues; and develop an appropriate agreement to govern the management and use of the information and how it is to be exchanged (for example, via a dedicated circuit or virtual private network, database sharing, cloud- or web-based services, or simple file exchange).

2. Establishing the information exchange: The organizations develop and execute a plan for establishing the information exchange, including implementing or configuring appropriate security controls and developing and signing appropriate agreements.

3. Maintaining the exchange and associated agreements: The organizations actively maintain the security of the information exchange after it is established and ensure that the terms of the associated agreements are met and remain relevant, including reviewing and renewing the agreements at an agreed-upon frequency.

4. Discontinuing the information exchange: Information exchange may be temporary, or at some point the organizations may need to discontinue the information exchange. Whether the exchange was temporary or long-term, the conclusion of an information exchange is conducted in a manner that avoids disrupting any other party's system. In response to an incident or other emergency, however, the organizations may decide to discontinue the information exchange immediately.[3]

Performance Measurement

As described in a previous chapter, a performance measurement program provides many financial and administrative benefits to organizations. Organizations can develop cybersecurity measures that assess the effectiveness of their cybersecurity program and can provide data to be analyzed and used by program managers and system owners to isolate problems, justify investment requests, and target funds to the areas that need improvement. By using specific measures to target cybersecurity investments, organizations can get the best value from available resources. The typical performance management program consists of four interdependent components: senior management support, cybersecurity policies and procedures, quantifiable performance measures, and analyses.

Cybersecurity measurement programs should be used for monitoring the performance of cybersecurity controls and initiating performance improvements. A constraint to these improvements is the reality of the organization's budget, which may preclude the implementation of all desired or even recommended changes.

Control Performance Baselines and Measurements

Because many technical controls for cybersecurity are implemented on common IT systems, it is important to monitor the performance of cybersecurity systems and their underlying IT infrastructure to determine if they are working effectively. This type of performance monitoring is especially important for network appliances such as firewalls and content filters that look for inappropriate use of Internet resources and operate as bypass devices. When these appliances are not able to handle the level of traffic or are not properly tuned for sufficient performance, they do not stop the actions they are designed to block. Some common system and network measurements used in performance management are also applicable for cybersecurity, especially when the components being managed involve the ebb and flow of network traffic. Based on the "60 percent rule," there are a few guidelines that cybersecurity personnel can use when exploring the issues of system and network performance. For example, when any IT-based resource (processor, hard drive, or network device) regularly exceeds 60 percent capacity, it's time to consider an upgrade.

To evaluate the performance of a cybersecurity system, administrators must establish system performance baselines, as described in a previous chapter. Organizations should establish baselines for different criteria and for various periods of time, such as days of the week, weeks of the year, months of the year, and times of the day. For example, network traffic levels are deemed high when traffic reaches or surpasses the level of the performance baseline. To put it another way, the planning of capacity upgrades should begin before users complain about issues such as slow webpages or downloads.

Cybersecurity Planning

As discussed in an earlier chapter, planning is one of the most crucial ongoing responsibilities in cybersecurity management. This section of SP 800-100 focuses on the controls available to address shortfalls identified in the planning process. Federal Information Processing Standard (FIPS) 200, "Minimum Security Requirements for Federal Information and Information Systems," specifies federal cybersecurity requirements in 17 areas. In addition to reviewing the minimum cybersecurity requirements in FIPS 200, private organizations would benefit from studying the controls in NIST SP 800-53, Rev. 5, "Security and Privacy Controls for Information Systems and Organizations." NIST SP 800-18, Rev. 1, "Guide for Developing Security Plans for Federal Information Systems," provides a template for a systems cybersecurity plan in Appendix A of the document.

IT Contingency Planning

Contingency planning focuses on the development of plans for non-normal operations resulting from incidents or disasters. The ongoing responsibilities of cybersecurity management involve the maintenance of the contingency plan. Periodic reviews of the plan must be conducted to ensure currency of key personnel and vendor information, system components and dependencies, the recovery strategy, vital records, and operating requirements. While some changes may be obvious, such as personnel turnover or vendor changes, others require analysis. The business impact analysis should be reviewed periodically and updated with new information to identify new contingency requirements and priorities. Changes to the plan are noted in a record of changes, with revised plans or plan sections circulated to those with planning responsibilities. Because of the impact that plan changes may have on interdependent business processes or IT systems, the changes must be clearly communicated and properly annotated at the beginning of the document.

Risk Management

Risk management is an ongoing effort as well. Risk identification, analysis, and management are a cyclic and fundamental part of continuous improvement in cybersecurity. The principal goal of risk management is to protect the organization and its ability to perform its mission, not just protect its information assets. Because risk cannot be eliminated entirely, the risk management process allows cybersecurity program managers to balance operating and economic costs of protective measures and achieve gains in mission capability. By employing practices and procedures designed to foster informed decision making, organizations help protect the IT systems and data that support their mission.

Many risk management activities are conducted during a snapshot in time—a static representation of a dynamic environment. All the changes that occur to systems during normal, daily operations have the potential to adversely affect system cybersecurity in some fashion. The goal of the risk management evaluation and assessment process is to ensure that the system continues to operate efficiently, effectively, and securely. This goal can be facilitated by implementing a strong configuration management program. In addition to monitoring the cybersecurity of an IT system on a continuous basis, organizations must track findings from cybersecurity control assessments to ensure they are addressed appropriately and do not pose risks to the system or introduce new vulnerabilities.

The process of managing risk permeates the SDLC, from the early stages of project inception through the retirement of the system and its data. From inception forward, organizations should consider possible threats, vulnerabilities, and risks to the system so they can better prepare it to operate securely and effectively in its intended environment. During a cybersecurity assessment process like risk management, the organization should determine whether its systems are operating within the organization's risk appetite.

Certification, Accreditation, and Cybersecurity Assessments

Certification and accreditation for federal systems has radically changed for systems not designated as national security information systems. Some organizations need to review their own systems against the national certification and accreditation standards to comply with banking, healthcare, international, or other regulations. Others may want the recognition offered by certifications like the ISO 27000 series. Cybersecurity certification and accreditation is designed to ensure that an IT system operates with the appropriate management review, that there is ongoing monitoring of cybersecurity controls, and that reaccreditation occurs periodically. Even organizations that are not required to follow these standards could benefit from reviewing the standards and evaluating their systems against them.

Continuous monitoring of cybersecurity assessment programs, as a function of certification and accreditation, is an essential component of any cybersecurity program. During this phase, the status of cybersecurity controls in the information system is checked on an ongoing basis. An effective continuous monitoring program can be used to support the annual requirement specified in the Federal Information Security Management Act of 2002 (FISMA) for assessing cybersecurity controls in information systems. At a minimum, an effective monitoring program requires the following:

- Configuration management and configuration control processes for the system
- Security impact analyses on changes to the system
- Assessment of selected cybersecurity controls in the system and reporting of the system's cybersecurity status to appropriate organization managers

Note 2 | For more information on updated FISMA legislation, visit the U.S. Cybersecurity and Infrastructure Security Agency (CISA) site at www.cisa.gov/topics/cyber-threats-and-advisories/federal-information-security-modernization-act.

Organizations should identify all cybersecurity controls that are continuously monitored as annual testing and evaluation activities. Once this is complete, organizations should look at remaining controls that have not been tested that year and decide whether to conduct further testing based on risk, the importance of the control, and the date of the last test. The results of continuous monitoring should be reviewed regularly by senior management and any necessary updates should be made to the system cybersecurity plan. An example reporting form for continuous monitoring is provided in NIST SP 800-53A, Rev. 5.

Part of the ongoing cybersecurity assessment is auditing, the review of a system's use to determine if misuse or malfeasance has occurred. Most computer-based systems used in cybersecurity can create logs of their activity, recording non-normal events in some and normal activities in others. These logs are a vital part of the detective functions associated with determining what happened, when it happened, and how. Managing systems logs in large organizations is a complex process. Fortunately, automated tools known as log analyzers can simplify this process by consolidating systems logs, performing comparative analysis, and detecting unusual events or behaviors of interest. Behaviors of interest may include port scanning and other anomalous network activity, malware signatures, hacking attempts, and illicit use of controlled network resources or computer systems. Logs are invaluable records of events and should be archived and stored for future review as needed. System intruders have been known to attempt to cover their tracks by deleting logs or erasing entries in logs, so wise administrators configure their systems to create duplicate copies of the logs and store the copies on sources that cannot be easily modified. Many vendors offer log consolidation and analysis features that allow for integration of log files from multiple products, such as firewalls, network equipment, and even products from other vendors.

To assist organizations in meeting their reporting requirements, NIST SP 800-100 provides a cybersecurity assessment survey that covers many of the areas typically required for inclusion in reports. The questionnaire can be customized for an organization or program and can be completed by the CIO, the chief information security officer (CISO), or an independent assessor of the organization's cybersecurity program.

Cybersecurity Services and Products Acquisition

Cybersecurity services and products are essential elements of an organization's cybersecurity program. Cybersecurity products and services may be selected and used to support the organization's overall program to manage the design, development, and maintenance of its cybersecurity infrastructure and to protect its mission-critical information. Organizations should use their risk management program to help identify and mitigate risks associated with product acquisition.

When acquiring cybersecurity products, organizations are encouraged to conduct a cost–benefit analysis—one that also includes the "total cost of ownership" associated with the product. This analysis should include a life cycle cost estimate for current products and one for each identified alternative while highlighting the benefits associated with each alternative. NIST SP 800-36, "Guide to Selecting Information Technology Security Products," defines broad cybersecurity product categories and then specifies product types, product characteristics, and environment considerations within those categories. The guide also provides a list of pertinent questions that organizations should ask when selecting products. While this SP is officially listed as "withdrawn" due to the rapid changes in the security technology market, the questions listed are still applicable to newer technologies. Each person or group involved in product or service acquisition should understand the cybersecurity impacts of their decisions.

Just as the SDLC supports the development of products, the security services life cycle (SSLC) provides a framework to help decision makers organize and coordinate their cybersecurity efforts from initiation to completion. Figure 11-1 depicts the SSLC for obtaining cybersecurity services at a high level. Table 11-2 provides a summary of each phase, adapted from SP 800-36.

Figure 11-1 The security services life cycle

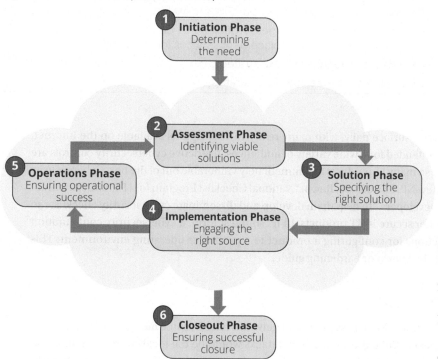

Source: Adapted from NIST SP 800-36.

Table 11-2　The security services life cycle[4]

Phase	Activity
Phase 1–Initiation	• Begin when the need to initiate the services life cycle is recognized. • This phase consists of needs determination, cybersecurity categorization, and the preliminary risk assessment.
Phase 2–Assessment	• Develop an accurate portrait of the current environment before identifying possible solutions for decision makers to consider. • Baseline the existing environment; measure creation, gathering, and analysis; and establish the total cost of ownership. • Analyze opportunities and barriers. • Identify options and risks.
Phase 3–Solution	• Develop an appropriate solution from the viable options identified during the selected assessment phase. • Develop the business case. • Develop the service arrangement. • Develop the implementation plan.
Phase 4–Implementation	• Service providers are implemented during this phase. • Identify the service provider and develop the service agreement. • Finalize and execute the implementation plan. • Manage expectations.
Phase 5–Operations	• The service's life cycle becomes iterative; the service is working, the service provided is fully installed, and a constant assessment must be made of the service level and source performance. • Monitor and measure organization performance. • Evaluate current operations and direct actions for continuous improvement.
Phase 6–Closeout	• Because of the iterative nature of the life cycle, the service and service provider could continue indefinitely, but this is unlikely. • If the environment changes, cybersecurity program managers will identify triggers that initiate new and replacement services for cybersecurity. • Select the appropriate exit strategy. • Implement the selected exit strategy.

Vulnerabilities in IT products surface daily, with many ready-to-use exploits available on the Internet. Because IT products are often intended for a wide variety of audiences, restrictive cybersecurity controls are usually not enabled by default, so many IT products are immediately vulnerable out of the box. Cybersecurity program managers should review NIST SP 800-70, Rev. 4, "National Checklist Program for IT Products: Guidelines for Checklist Users and Developers," to help them develop and disseminate cybersecurity checklists so that their organization can better secure its IT products. In its simplest form, a cybersecurity configuration checklist is a series of instructions for configuring a product to a particular operating environment. This checklist is sometimes called a lockdown or hardening guide.

Incident Response

As illustrated throughout this text, attacks on IT systems and networks have become more numerous, sophisticated, and severe in recent years. While preventing such attacks would be the ideal course of action, not all cybersecurity incidents can be prevented. Every organization that depends on IT systems and networks should identify and assess the risks to its systems and reduce those risks to an acceptable level. An important component of this risk management process is the analysis of past computer cybersecurity incidents and the identification of effective ways to deal with them. A well-defined incident response capability helps the organization detect incidents rapidly, minimize loss and destruction, identify weaknesses, and restore IT operations quickly.

Help-desk personnel must be trained to distinguish a cybersecurity problem from other system problems. As help-desk personnel screen problems, they must also track the activities involved in resolving each complaint in the help-desk system. One key advantage to having formal help-desk software is the ability to create and develop a knowledge base of common problems and solutions. This knowledge base can be searched when a user problem comes up; if it is like a problem that was already reported and resolved, the complaint can be resolved more quickly. This knowledge base can also generate statistics about the frequency of problems by type, by user, or by application, and thus can detect trends and patterns in the data. Incidentally, some user problems may be created or influenced by a cybersecurity program because of modifications to firewalls, implementations of rules for intrusion detection and prevention systems (IDPSs), or new systems policies in the network that can directly affect how users interact with the systems.

The Help Desk

With a relatively small investment in an IT help desk, an organization can improve the quality of its IT support and cybersecurity function. A small help desk with only a few call agents can provide service for an organization of several hundred users. Large organizations can also improve customer service using a help desk, if it receives adequate funding and effective management. Although it may function differently depending on the organization, a help desk commonly provides the following services:

- A single point of contact for service requests from users
- Initial screening of requests, answering common questions, solving common problems, and dispatching other types of calls to other units
- Entering all calls into a tracking system
- Dispatching service providers to respond to calls
- Reporting and analysis of call volumes, patterns, and process improvement
- Early detection of adverse events, which could escalate to incidents or foreshadow disasters

Other services that may be integrated into the help desk include:

- Desk-side support for common IT applications such as Windows and end-user computing tools
- Managing new users
- Timely removal of users who no longer need system access
- Password management
- Smart card management
- Knowledge management for service requests and optimum resolutions
- Server configuration
- Network monitoring
- Server capacity monitoring
- Virus activity monitoring and virus pattern management

While each organization has its own approach to creating and developing a help-desk solution, many help desks evolve and alter their mix of services over time.[5]

To resolve a problem, a support technician may need to visit a user's office to examine equipment or observe the user's procedures or interact with other departments or workgroups. The help-desk team could include a dedicated cybersecurity technician. In any case, the person working to resolve the trouble ticket must document both the diagnosis and the resolution, as they are invaluable components of the knowledge base and are useful in detecting larger issues like cybersecurity incidents.

Configuration and Change Management

The purpose of configuration and change management is to manage the effects of changes or differences in configurations on an IT system or network. In some organizations, configuration management is the identification, inventory, and documentation of the current IT systems, including hardware, software, and networking configurations. Change management is sometimes described as a separate function that only addresses modifications to this base configuration. Here, the two concepts are combined to address the current and proposed states of the systems and the management of any needed modifications.

> **Note 3** | For additional discussion and details on configuration and change management, download the CRR Supplemental Resource Guide from www.cisa.gov/sites/default/files/c3vp/crr_resources_guides/CRR_Resource_Guide-CCM.pdf.

Just as documents should have version numbers, revision dates, and other features designated to monitor and administer changes made to them, so should technical components of systems, such as software, hardware, and firmware. Several key phrases are used in the management of configuration and change in technical components, as shown in quotation marks in the following hypothetical example.

Let's assume that XYZ Cybersecurity Solutions Corporation has developed a new software application called Panacea, the Ultimate Cybersecurity Solution. Panacea is the "configuration item." Panacea's "configuration" consists of three major software components: See-all, Know-all, and Protect-all. Thus, Panacea is "version" 1.0, and it is built from its three components. The "build list" is See-all 1.0, Know-all 1.0, and Protect-all 1.0, as this is the first "major release" of the complete application and its components. The "revision date" is the date associated with the first "build." To create Panacea, the programmers at XYZ Cybersecurity Solutions pulled information from their "software library." Suppose that while the application is being used in the field, the programmers discover a minor flaw in a component or related element. When they correct this flaw, they issue a "minor release," Panacea 1.1. If at some point they need to make a major revision to the software to meet changing market needs or fix more substantial problems with the subcomponents, they would issue a major release, Panacea 2.0. In addition to the challenge of keeping applications at the current version level, administrators face the release of newer versions of operating systems and ongoing rollouts of newer hardware versions. The combination of updated hardware, operating systems, and applications is further complicated by the constant need for bug fixes and cybersecurity updates to these elements.

CCM assists in streamlining change management processes and prevents changes that could adversely affect the cybersecurity of a system. In its entirety, the CCM process reduces the risk that any changes to a system will compromise its confidentiality, integrity, or availability because the process provides a repeatable mechanism for effecting system modifications in a controlled environment. In accordance with the CCM process, system changes must be tested prior to implementation to observe the effects of the change and minimize the risk of adverse results. NIST SP 800-64, Rev. 2, "Security Considerations in the System Development Life Cycle," states:

> Configuration management and control procedures are critical to establishing an initial baseline of hardware, software, and firmware components for the information system and subsequently to controlling and maintaining an accurate inventory of any changes to the system. Changes to the hardware, software, or firmware of a system can have a significant impact on the cybersecurity of the system . . . changes should be documented, and their potential impact on cybersecurity should be assessed regularly.[6]

NIST SP 800-53, Rev. 5, "Assessing Security and Privacy Controls in Information Systems and Organizations," defines seven CM controls that organizations are required to implement based on an information system's cybersecurity categorization. The required CM controls are defined in Table 11-3.

Table 11-3 NIST SP 800-53, Rev. 5, Configuration Management Control Family[7]

Identifier	Title	Control
CM-1	Policies and Procedures	The organization: a. Develops, documents, and disseminates a CM policy that addresses purpose, scope, roles, responsibilities, management commitment, coordination among organizational entities, and compliance; it also develops, documents, and disseminates procedures to facilitate the implementation of the CM policy and associated CM controls. b. Designates an employee to manage the CM policy and associated CM controls. c. Reviews and updates the current CM policy and procedures.
CM-2	Baseline Configuration	The organization: a. Develops, documents, and maintains a current baseline configuration of the information system. b. Reviews and updates the baseline configuration periodically and as needed.
CM-3	Configuration Change Control	The organization: a. Determines the types of changes to the information system that are configuration-controlled. b. Reviews proposed configuration-controlled changes to the information system and approves or disapproves such changes with explicit consideration for cybersecurity impact analyses. c. Documents configuration change decisions associated with the information system. d. Implements approved configuration-controlled changes to the information system. e. Retains records of configuration-controlled changes to the information system for a specified time. f. Monitors and reviews activities associated with configuration-controlled changes to the information system. g. Coordinates and provides oversight for configuration change control activities through the organization's configuration change control committee or board.
CM-4	Impact Analyses	The organization analyzes changes to the information system to determine potential cybersecurity impacts prior to change implementation.
CM-5	Access Restrictions for Change	The organization defines, documents, approves, and enforces physical and logical access restrictions associated with changes to the IT system.
CM-6	Configuration Settings	The organization: a. Establishes and documents configuration settings for IT products employed within the information system, using cybersecurity configuration checklists that reflect the most restrictive mode consistent with operating requirements. b. Implements the configuration settings. c. Identifies, documents, and approves any deviations from established configuration settings for the organization's information system components based on operating requirements. d. Monitors and controls changes to the configuration settings in accordance with the organization's policies and procedures.
CM-7	Least Functionality	The organization: a. Configures the IT system to provide only essential capabilities. b. Prohibits or restricts the use of certain functions, ports, protocols, and services.

The CM process identifies the steps required to ensure that all changes are properly requested, evaluated, and authorized. The CM process also provides a detailed, step-by-step procedure for identifying, processing, tracking, and documenting changes. An example CM process is described in the following sections.

Step 1: Identify Change

The first step of the CM process begins when a person or process associated with the information system identifies the need for a change. The change can be initiated by users, system owners, or IT or cybersecurity teams, or it can be identified during audits or other reviews. Once the need for a change has been identified, a change request should be submitted to the appropriate decision-making body.

Step 2: Evaluate Change Request

After initiating a change request, the organization must evaluate possible effects that the change may have on the system or other interrelated systems. An impact analysis of the change should be conducted using the following guidelines:

- Whether the change is viable and improves the performance or cybersecurity of the system
- Whether the change is technically correct, necessary, and feasible within the system constraints
- Whether system cybersecurity will be affected by the change
- Whether associated costs for implementing the change were considered
- Whether cybersecurity components are affected by the change

Step 3: Make Implementation Decision

Once the change has been evaluated and tested, one of the following actions should be taken:

- Approve: Implementation is authorized and may occur at any time after the appropriate authorization signature has been documented.
- Deny: The request is immediately denied regardless of circumstances and the information provided.
- Defer: The immediate decision is postponed until further notice. In this situation, additional testing or analysis may be needed before a final decision can be made.

Step 4: Implement Approved Change Request

Once the decision has been made to implement the change, it should be moved from the test environment into production. The personnel who update the production environment may not be the same people who developed the change; this provides greater assurance that unapproved changes are not implemented into production.

Step 5: Conduct Continuous Monitoring

The CCM process calls for continuous system monitoring to ensure that it is operating as intended and that implemented changes do not adversely affect the system's performance or cybersecurity posture. Organizations can achieve the goals of continuous system monitoring by performing configuration verification tests to ensure that the selected configuration for a given system has not been altered outside the established CCM process. In addition to configuration verification tests, organizations can perform system audits. Both require an examination of system characteristics and supporting documentation to verify that the configuration meets user needs and ensure that the current configuration is the approved system configuration baseline.

As part of the overall CCM process, organizations should also perform patch management during this step. Patch management helps lower the potential risk to systems and networks by "patching" or repairing known vulnerabilities in any of the software, firmware, or hardware environments. Increasingly, vendors are proactive in developing fixes or antidotes to known vulnerabilities and releasing them to the public. Organizations must remain vigilant to ensure that they capture all relevant fixes as they are released, test their implementation for adverse effects, and implement the fixes after testing is concluded. Patching is associated with phases 2, 3, and 4 of the life cycle. In phase 2, patch management relates to risk management to prevent any vulnerability from being exploited and compromised. Phase 3 contains the testing to ensure that patching and any other changes do not negatively affect the system.

In general, configuration and change management should not interfere with the use of the technology. One person on the IT or cybersecurity team should be appointed as the configuration or change manager and made responsible for maintaining appropriate data elements in the organization's cataloging mechanism, such as the specific version, revision date, and build associated with each piece of implemented hardware and software. In some cases, someone outside the implementation process might be better suited to this role because they would not be distracted by the installation, configuration, and troubleshooting of the new implementation. In the case of minor revisions, it may be simpler to have a procedure that requires documenting the machines on which a revision is installed, the date and time of the installation, and the name of the installer. While the documentation procedures required for CCM may seem inconvenient, they enable cybersecurity teams to quickly and accurately determine which systems are affected when a new vulnerability arises. When stored in a comprehensive database with risk, threat, and attack information, configuration information enables organizations to respond quickly to new and rapidly changing threats and attacks.

Self-Check

1. A cybersecurity governance program does not need to be reviewed constantly once it is implemented.

   a. True
   b. False

2. Configuration management is unnecessary once an IT system is initially implemented.

   a. True
   b. False

3. Incident statistics can help determine the effectiveness of cybersecurity policies and procedures.

   a. True
   b. False

   ☐ Check your answers at the end of this chapter.

The Cybersecurity Maintenance Model

While management models such as the ISO 27000 series and NIST special publications deal with methods to manage and operate systems, a maintenance model is designed to focus the organization's effort on maintaining systems. Figure 11-2 illustrates an approach recommended for dealing with change caused by cybersecurity maintenance. The figure diagrams a full maintenance program and serves as a framework for the discussion that follows.

The recommended maintenance model is based on five subject areas or domains:

- External monitoring
- Internal monitoring
- Planning and risk assessment
- Vulnerability assessment and remediation
- Readiness and review

The following sections explore each of these domains and their interactions.

Monitoring the External Environment

The objective of the external monitoring domain—the component of the maintenance model that focuses on evaluating external threats to the organization's information assets—is to provide early awareness of new and emerging threats, threat agents, vulnerabilities, and attacks so the organization can mount an effective

Figure 11-2   The cybersecurity maintenance model

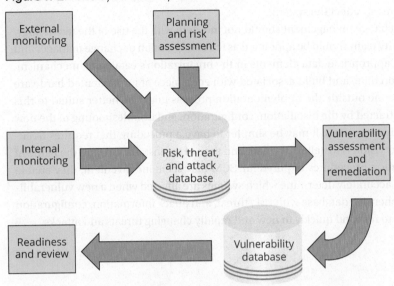

and timely defense. Figure 11-3 shows the primary components of the external monitoring process. External monitoring entails forming intelligence from various data sources and giving that intelligence context and meaning for use by decision makers within the organization.

Data Sources

Acquiring data about threats, threat agents, vulnerabilities, and attacks is not difficult. There are many sources of raw intelligence and relatively few costs associated with gathering it. The challenge is turning this flood of data into information that decision makers can use. For this reason, many organizations outsource this component of the maintenance model. Service providers can provide a tailored supply of processed intelligence to organizations that can afford their fees.

Figure 11-3   External monitoring

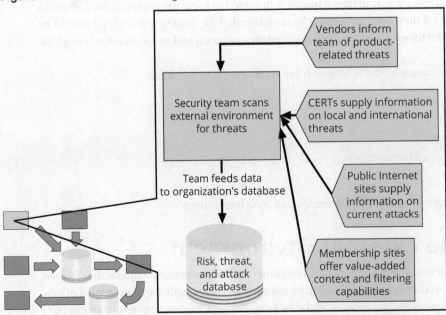

As shown in Figure 11-3, external intelligence can come from these classes of sources:

- Vendors—When an organization uses specific hardware and software as part of its cybersecurity program, the vendor often provides either direct support or indirect tools that allow user communities to support each other. This support often includes intelligence on emerging threats. This can be more complex if the organization uses outsourcing vendors and managed service providers.

- CERT organizations—Computer emergency response teams (CERTs) exist in varying forms around the world. CISA (www.cisa.gov) is often viewed as the definitive authority. CISA and the Department of Homeland Security (DHS) work with other agencies and institutions to provide information and support for the general public.

- Public network sources—Many publicly accessible information sources, including mailing lists and websites, are freely available to organizations and people who have the time and expertise to use them. Table 11-4 lists some of these cybersecurity intelligence sources.

- Membership sites—Various groups and organizations provide value to subscribers by adding contextual detail to publicly reported events and offering filtering capabilities that allow subscribers to quickly pinpoint the possible impact to their own organizations.

Table 11-4 External intelligence sources

Source Name	Type	Comments
CISA	Website, mailing list, news	"In 2023, CISA retired US-CERT and ICS-CERT, integrating CISA's operational content into a new cisa.gov website that unifies CISA's mission. CISA will be responsible for coordinating cybersecurity programs within the U.S. government to protect against malicious cyber activity, including activity related to industrial control systems. In keeping with this responsibility, CISA will continue responding to incidents, providing technical assistance, and disseminating timely notifications of cyber threats and vulnerabilities." For more details, see www.cisa.gov.[8]
National Vulnerability Database (NVD)	Website, news, data feeds	The U.S. government repository, hosted by NIST and sponsored by DHS, CISA, and the National Cybersecurity and Communications Integration Center, is an online repository for vulnerability management data. The content of the site can be used to support automation of vulnerability detection. NVD includes several databases of cybersecurity-related software flaws, information on misconfigurations, checklists for assessment of vulnerabilities, and other related content like impact measures. The contents of this database are synchronized with the cve.mitre.org database. For details, see nvd.nist.gov.
CERT Coordination Center (CERT/CC)	Website, blogs, news	CERT/CC is a center of Internet cybersecurity expertise at the Software Engineering Institute, a federally funded research and development center operated by Carnegie Mellon University. CERT/CC and DHS support the website, which is usually considered the definitive authority to be consulted when emerging threats become demonstrated vulnerabilities. See CERT/CC's home page at www.sei.cmu.edu/about/divisions/cert/index.cfm.

(Continues)

Table 11-4 External intelligence sources (*Continued*)

Source Name	Type	Comments
InfraGard	Membership website, mailing list	InfraGard is a partnership between the Federal Bureau of Investigation and members of the private sector. The InfraGard program provides a vehicle for seamless public or private collaboration with government that expedites the timely exchange of information and promotes learning opportunities for protecting critical infrastructure. With thousands of vetted members nationally, InfraGard's membership includes business executives, entrepreneurs, military and government officials, computer professionals, academics, and state and local law enforcement; all are dedicated to contributing industry-specific insight and advancing national cybersecurity. Today, there are tens of thousands of members nationwide in more than 77 local member alliances. For more details, go to www.infragard.org.
IBM's Cybersecurity Services	Website, news	A commercial site with a focus on the vendor's own commercial IDPS and other cybersecurity products. The site also provides breaking news about emerging threats and allows individuals to subscribe to alerts. See www.ibm.com/services/security.
Insecure.org	Website, mailing lists, blog	Insecure.org is the creation of the well-known "white-hat hacker" Fyodor. The site provides the Internet community with software (for example, Nmap) and information about vulnerabilities. Many topics are covered in the available lists at seclists.org.
Mitre	Website, news	The dictionary of Common Vulnerabilities and Exploits (see cve.mitre.org) is an online database managed by the Mitre Corporation. Available from the site is information and news on current vulnerabilities and related exploitation methods.
Packet Storm	News	A commercial site that provides news and discussion focusing on current cybersecurity events and tools. See packetstormsecurity.com.
SecurityFocus	Website, mailing lists	A commercial site providing general coverage and commentary on cybersecurity. See www.securityfocus.com.
Snort	Mailing list and blogs	Includes announcements and discussion about Snort, an open-source IDPS. The available lists (Users, SIGs, Developers, and OpenAppId) include discussions and information about the program and its rule sets and signatures. This site can be a useful source for information about detecting emerging threats. You can view these lists and blogs at www.snort.org/community.
SourceForge	Blogs	Maintains a large number of blogs and downloadable products for open-source software with integral comments. To search for a particular topic, visit https://sourceforge.net.
Tenable	Web blog	A website dedicated to the Nessus vulnerability scanner. It has information about emerging threats and how to test for them. The blog is at www.tenable.com/blog.

Regardless of where or how external monitoring data is collected, it is not useful unless it is analyzed in the context of the organization's cybersecurity environment. To perform this evaluation and take appropriate actions in a timely fashion, the CSO must:

- Staff the program with people who understand the technical aspects of cybersecurity, have a comprehensive understanding of the organization's complete IT infrastructure, and have a thorough grounding in the organization's business operations.

- Provide documented and repeatable procedures.

- Train the primary and backup staff assigned to perform the monitoring tasks.

- Equip the assigned staff with proper access and tools to perform the monitoring function.

- Cultivate expertise among monitoring analysts so they can cull meaningful summaries and actionable alerts from the vast flow of raw intelligence.

- Develop suitable communications methods for moving processed intelligence to designated internal decision makers in all three communities of interest—IT, cybersecurity, and general management.

- Integrate the incident response plan with the results of the external monitoring process to produce appropriate, timely responses.

- Clearly identify in corporate policy whether managed services are monitored by the organization or by the vendor providing the services.

- Specify how embedded systems (for example, Internet of Things) are monitored for vulnerabilities.

Monitoring, Escalation, and Incident Response

The purpose of the external monitoring process is to monitor activity, report results, and escalate warnings. The best approach for escalation is based on a thorough integration of the monitoring process into the incident response plan. The monitoring process has three primary deliverables:

- Specific warning bulletins issued when developing threats and specific attacks pose a measurable risk to the organization

- Periodic summaries of external information

- Detailed intelligence on the highest risk warnings

Data Collection and Management

Over time, the external monitoring processes should capture information about the external environment in a format that can be referenced throughout the organization as threats emerge and then can be archived for historical use. In the final analysis, external monitoring collects raw intelligence, filters it for relevance to the organization, assigns it a relative risk impact, and communicates these findings to decision makers in time to make a difference.

Monitoring the Internal Environment

The primary goal of the internal monitoring domain—the component of the maintenance model that focuses on identifying, assessing, and managing the configuration and status of information assets in an organization—is an informed awareness of the state of the organization's IT systems and cybersecurity defenses. Internal monitoring is accomplished by:

- Building and maintaining an inventory of network devices and channels, IT infrastructure and applications, and elements of cybersecurity infrastructure

- Leading the IT governance process within the organization to integrate the inevitable changes found in all IT and cybersecurity systems and programs

- Monitoring IT activity in real time using IDPSs to detect and respond to actions or events that introduce risk to the organization's information assets

- Monitoring the internal state of the organization's networks and systems; the review should cover all active services but focus extra scrutiny on newer services offered on the network, and it can be accomplished through automated difference-detection methods that identify variances introduced to the network or system hardware and software

The value of internal monitoring is increased when knowledge gained from networks and systems is fed into the vulnerability assessment and remediation domain. However, this knowledge becomes invaluable when incident response is fully integrated with the monitoring processes. Figure 11-4 shows the component processes of the internal monitoring domain, which are discussed in the sections that follow.

Figure 11-4   Internal monitoring

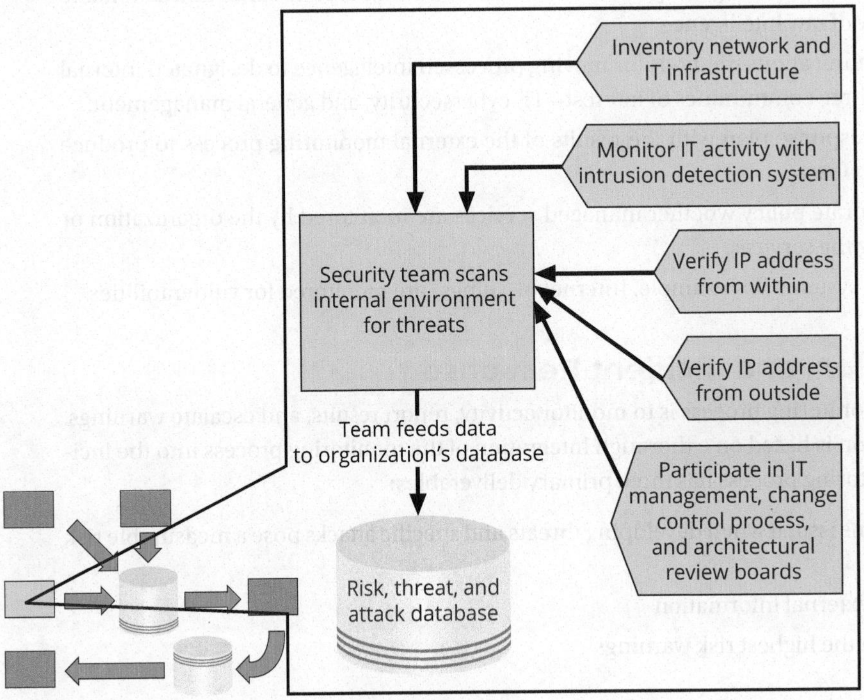

Network Characterization and Inventory

Organizations should have and maintain a carefully planned and fully populated inventory of all their network devices, communication infrastructure, and computing devices. This inventory should include all hardware and software, including operating systems and applications. The inventory should also include partner interconnections—network devices, communications channels, and applications that may not be owned by the organization but are essential to its partnership with another company. The process of collecting this information is often referred to as characterization.

Note 4 | As reported by journalist Brian Krebs, a high-profile data breach at Target stores was traced back to network credentials that were stolen from a refrigeration, heating, and air conditioning subcontractor. Read more at https://krebsonsecurity.com/?s=target+breach.

Once the characteristics of the network environment have been identified and documented as data, they must be carefully organized and stored using a mechanism that allows for timely retrieval and rapid integration of disparate facts. For all but the smallest network environments, this requires a relational database. In contrast to the attributes collected for risk management, which are important for economic and business value, the characteristics collected here, such as manufacturer and software versions, relate to technical functionality and so should be kept accurate and up to date. Also, the technology needed to store this data should be stand-alone and portable because if the data is needed to support incident response and disaster recovery, server or network access may be unavailable.

Making IDPSs Work

To be used most effectively, the information that comes from an IDPS must be integrated into the maintenance process. An IDPS can generate a seemingly endless flow of alert messages that often have little bearing on the immediate effectiveness of the cybersecurity program. Except for an occasional real-time alert that is not a false positive, the IDPS reports events that have already occurred. Given this, the most important value of raw intelligence provided by the IDPS is that it can be used to prevent future attacks by indicating current or imminent vulnerabilities. Whether the organization outsources IDPS monitoring, staffs IDPS monitoring around the clock, staffs IDPS monitoring during business hours, or merely ignores the real-time alerts from the IDPS, the log files from the IDPS engines can be mined for information that can be added to the internal monitoring knowledge base.

Another element of IDPS monitoring is traffic analysis. Analyzing the traffic that flows through a system and its associated devices can often be critically important because the traffic identifies the most frequently used devices. An example of the type of vulnerability exposed by traffic analysis occurs when an organization tries to determine if all its device signatures have been adequately masked. In general, the default configuration setting of many network devices allows them to respond to any request with a device signature message that identifies the device's make and model and perhaps even its software version. In the interest of better cybersecurity, many organizations require that all devices be reconfigured to conceal their device signatures.

Detecting Differences

One approach that can improve the awareness of the cybersecurity function uses a process known as difference analysis—a procedure that compares the current state of a network segment against a known previous state of the same network segment, known as the baseline—to quickly identify changes to the internal environment. Table 11-5 shows how several kinds of difference analyses can be used. Note that the table lists suggestions for possible difference analyses; each organization should identify the differences it wants to measure and its criteria for action.

Table 11-5 Types of difference analysis

Suggested Frequency	Method of Analysis	Data Source	Purpose
Quarterly	Manual	Firewall rules and logs	To verify that new rules follow all risk assessment and procedural approvals, identify illicit rules, ensure removal of expired rules, and detect tampering
Quarterly	Manual	Edge router rules and logs	To verify that new rules follow all risk assessment and procedural approvals, identify illicit rules, ensure removal of expired rules, and detect tampering
Quarterly	Manual	Internet footprint	To verify that public Internet addresses registered to the organization are accurate and complete

(Continues)

Table 11-5   Types of difference analysis (*Continued*)

Suggested Frequency	Method of Analysis	Data Source	Purpose
Monthly	Automated	Fingerprinting of all IP addresses	To verify that only known and authorized devices offering critical services can be reached from the internal network
Weekly	Automated	Fingerprint services on critical servers on the internal network	To verify that only known and approved services are offered from critical servers in the internal network
Daily	Automated	Fingerprinting of all IP addresses from the outside	To verify that only known and approved servers and other devices can be reached from the public network
Hourly	Automated	Fingerprint services on critical servers exposed to the Internet	To enable email notification of administrators if unexpected services become available on critical servers exposed to the Internet

The value of difference analysis depends on the quality of the baseline, which is the initial snapshot portion of the difference comparison. The value of the analysis also depends on the degree to which the notification of discovered differences can induce action.

Planning and Risk Assessment

The primary objective of the planning and risk assessment domain—the component of the maintenance model that focuses on identifying and planning ongoing cybersecurity activities and managing risks introduced through IT and cybersecurity projects—is to keep lookout over the entire cybersecurity program. In fact, the bulk of the cybersecurity management maintenance model could fit in this domain. The primary objectives of this domain are as follows:

- Establishing a formal review process for the cybersecurity program that complements and supports both IT planning and strategic planning
- Instituting formal project identification, selection, planning, and management processes for follow-up activities that augment the current cybersecurity program
- Coordinating with IT project teams to introduce risk assessment and review for all IT projects so that risks introduced by the launches of new projects are identified, documented, and factored into decisions about the projects
- Integrating a mindset of risk assessment throughout the organization encouraging other departments to perform risk assessment activities when any technology system is implemented or modified

Figure 11-5 illustrates the relationships between the components of this maintenance domain. Note that there are two pivotal processes: the planning needed for cybersecurity programs and evaluation of current risks using operational risk assessment.

Figure 11-5   Planning and risk assessment

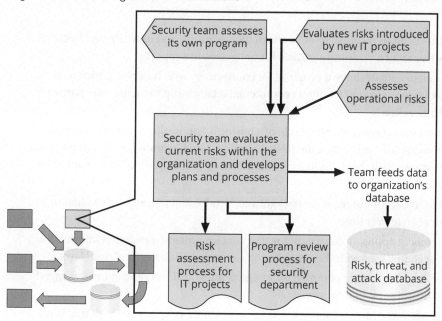

Cybersecurity Program Planning and Review

An organization should periodically review its ongoing cybersecurity program and any planning for enhancements and extensions. The strategic planning process should include examination of the organization's future IT needs and their impact on cybersecurity. A recommended approach is to take advantage of the fact that most larger organizations have annual capital budget planning cycles. Thus, the IT group can develop an annual list of project ideas for planning and then prepare an estimate for the effort needed to complete them, the estimated amount of capital required, and a preliminary assessment of the risks associated with performing each project or not. These assessments become part of the organization's project-planning process.

When capital and expense budgets are made final, the projects to be funded are chosen using the planning information on hand. This allows executives to make informed decisions about which projects to fund. The IT group then follows up with quarterly reviews of progress, which include an updated project risk assessment. As each project nears completion, an operational risk assessment group reviews the impact of the project on the organization's risk profile. The sponsors of the project and other executives can then determine if the risk level is acceptable, the project requires additional risk remediation, or the project must be aborted.

Projects that organizations might fund to maintain, extend, or enhance the cybersecurity program will arise in almost every planning cycle. Larger cybersecurity projects should be broken into smaller, incremental projects, which is important for several reasons:

- Smaller projects tend to have more manageable impacts on networks and users. Larger projects tend to complicate the change control process in the implementation phase.

- Shorter planning, development, and implementation schedules reduce uncertainty for IT planners and financial sponsors.

- Most large projects can easily be broken into smaller projects, giving the cybersecurity team more opportunities to change direction and gain flexibility as events occur and circumstances change.

Security Risk Assessments

A key component in the engine that drives change in the cybersecurity program is a relatively straightforward process called a risk assessment (RA). The RA is a method of identifying and documenting the risk that a project, process, or action introduces to the organization, and it may also offer suggestions for controls that can reduce the risk. The cybersecurity group coordinates the preparation of many types of RA documents, including:

- Network connectivity RA—Used to respond to network change requests and network architectural design proposals; it may be part of a business partner's RA or be used to support it
- Business partner RA—Used to help evaluate a proposal for connectivity with business partners; note that business partner risks extend beyond the direct contractual relationship to include the partner's vendors, landlords, and other clients
- Application RA—Used at various stages in the life cycle of a business application; its content depends on the project's position in the life cycle when the RA is prepared. Usually, multiple RA documents are prepared at different stages, with the definitive version prepared as the application is readied for conversion to production.
- Vulnerability RA—Used to help communicate the background, details, and proposed remediation as vulnerabilities emerge or change over time
- Privacy RA—Used to document applications or systems that contain protected personal information that must be evaluated for compliance with the organization's privacy policies and relevant laws
- Acquisition or divestiture RA—Used when planning for reorganization as the organization is engaged in mergers, acquisitions, divestitures, or relocations
- Other RA—Used when a statement about risk is needed for any project, proposal, or fault that is not contained in the preceding list

The RA process identifies risks and proposes controls. Most training programs on cybersecurity include training sessions for the preparation of RA documents.

A risk assessment's identification of systemic or latent vulnerabilities that introduce risk to the organization can provide the opportunity to create a proposal for a cybersecurity project. When used as part of a complete risk management maintenance process, the RA can be a powerful and flexible tool that helps identify and document risk and remediate the underlying vulnerabilities that expose the organization to risks of loss.

Vulnerability Assessment and Remediation

The vulnerability assessment and remediation domain is the component of the maintenance model focused on identifying documented vulnerabilities and remediating them in a timely fashion. These activities are accomplished by:

- Using documented vulnerability assessment procedures to safely collect intelligence about internal and public networks; platforms, including servers, desktops, and process control; and wireless network systems
- Documenting background information and providing tested remediation procedures for reported vulnerabilities
- Tracking vulnerabilities from the time they are identified until they are remediated or the risk of loss has been accepted by an authorized member of management
- Communicating vulnerability information, including an estimate of the risk and detailed remediation plans to the owners of vulnerable systems
- Reporting on the status of vulnerabilities that have been identified
- Ensuring that the proper level of management is involved in deciding to accept the risk of loss associated with unrepaired vulnerabilities

Figure 11-6 illustrates the process flow of the vulnerability assessment and remediation domain. Using the inventory of environment characteristics stored in the risk, threat, and attack database, the organization performs vulnerability assessment, the process of identifying and documenting provable flaws in the organization's information asset environment. They are stored, tracked, and reported in the vulnerability database to make sure that they are successfully remediated in a timely fashion.

Figure 11-6 Vulnerability assessment and remediation

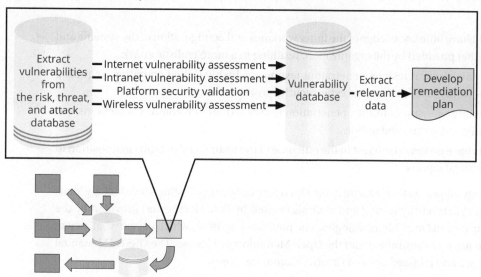

As shown in Figure 11-6, there are four common vulnerability assessment processes: Internet, intranet, platform cybersecurity validation, and wireless. While the exact procedures associated with each can vary, these four processes can help many organizations balance the intrusiveness of vulnerability assessment with the need for a stable and effective production environment. Some organizations pursue a strategy of monthly vulnerability assessments that involves all four processes. Others perform an Internet vulnerability assessment every week and rotate the other three processes on a monthly or quarterly basis. These choices depend on the quantity and quality of resources dedicated to vulnerability assessments.

Note 5 | For a list of the "top 125 network security tools," including vulnerability assessment tools, visit sectools.org, a website hosted by insecure.org.

Penetration Testing

Penetration testing (or pen testing)—the investigation, assessment, and evaluation of a system by authorized individuals emulating an attack—is a level of sophistication beyond vulnerability testing. A penetration test, or pen test, is usually performed periodically as part of a full cybersecurity audit. In most cybersecurity tests, such as vulnerability assessments, great care is taken not to disrupt normal business operations, but in pen testing, the analyst tries to get as far as possible by simulating the actions of an attacker. Unlike the attacker, however, the pen tester's ultimate responsibility is to identify weaknesses in the cybersecurity of the organization's systems and networks and then present findings to the system's owners in a detailed report.

While vulnerability testing is usually performed inside the organization's cybersecurity perimeter with complete knowledge of the networks' configuration and operations, pen testing can be conducted in one of two ways: black-box pen testing and white-box pen testing. In black-box pen testing, or blind testing, the "attacker" has no prior knowledge of the systems or network configurations and thus must investigate the organization's information infrastructure from scratch. In white-box testing, also known as full-disclosure testing, the organization provides information about the systems to be examined, allowing for a faster, more focused test. White-box pen testing is typically used when a specific system or network segment is suspect and the organization wants the pen tester to focus on a particular aspect of the target. Variations of black-box and white-box testing, known as gray-box or partial-disclosure tests, involve partial knowledge of the organization's infrastructure.

Organizations often hire private cybersecurity firms or consultants to perform penetration testing for several reasons, including:

- The "attacker" would have little knowledge of the inner workings and configuration of the systems and network other than that provided by the organization, resulting in a more realistic attack.
- Unlike vulnerability assessment testing, penetration testing is a highly skilled operation, requiring levels of expertise beyond that of the average cybersecurity professional.
- Also unlike vulnerability assessment testing, penetration testing requires customized attacks instead of standard, preconfigured scripts and utilities.
- External consultants have no vested interest in the outcome of the testing and are thus in a position to offer more honest, critical reports.

A common methodology for pen testing is found in the Open Source Security Testing Methodology Manual (OSSTMM), a guide to cybersecurity testing and analysis created by Pete Herzog and provided by the nonprofit Institute for Security and Open Methodologies. The methodology itself, which covers what, when, and where to test, is free to use and distribute under the Open Methodology License. The OSSTMM manual is free for noncommercial use and released under a Creative Commons license.

Note 6 | For more information on OSSTMM, including manual and software downloads, visit www.isecom.org/research.html.

Penetration testing certifications are available for people who are interested in this aspect of cybersecurity. For example, CompTIA offers the PenTest+ training and certification, GIAC offers multiple penetration tester certifications, and EC-Council offers the Licensed Penetration Tester certification. Other penetration testing certifications and approaches use the term "ethical hacking." While these certifications and efforts are valid, the use of the term is a problem for some because hacking is often defined as unauthorized and illegal attempts to circumvent cybersecurity controls.

View Point   Planning Against Attacks

By Donald McCarthy, independent security researcher

Sometimes it can be useful to imagine what could happen when things go wrong.

Let's imagine you were promoted to the CISO role of a healthcare company 90 days ago. Within the first month of your tenure, an intrusion was detected. Today you presented to the board a report on a set of cascading failures that could cost the company more than $1 million.

The digital forensics/incident response (DFIR) firm you hired found the source of the breach 52 days ago, along with the persistence mechanism the attackers used. A senior executive's assistant opened an email that contained a malicious payload and was detected as suspicious by the antivirus (AV) software. During the software's decision-making process, the payload was parsed in the kernel with system-level privileges. A flaw in the AV engine led to remote code execution (RCE). From there, the attacker had full control of the system and began post-exploitation tasks.

The attacker's first pivot was to a file server. The same payload from the executive assistant's machine was copied onto the file server, yielding the same result: RCE on the file server. Loose firewall controls caused by complaints to the help desk about connectivity issues allowed systems in the executive group to talk to all systems in the network.

The second pivot was to the vulnerability scanner, which had unfettered access to every piece of critical infrastructure for the entire corporate network. This machine also held credentials for every machine on the network.

Once the attacker had credentials to all systems, there was a methodical scan of all file shares and databases. The next series of movements gathered and exfiltrated the most sensitive data the company possessed: patient data, payment card data, and plans for three upcoming hospital acquisitions.

This intrusion was preventable and a failure of policy, design, and risk assessment. The initial deployment of the company's new email client had the reading pane disabled. This generated so many calls to the help desk about email problems that an emergency change was implemented to turn on the reading pane. The RCE in the AV software had been disclosed for more than a year. The patch required a license upgrade to the AV management server and client. Because the AV clients were receiving definition updates, this expense was not viewed as critical. The vulnerability scanner had an uptime of 710 days and was not configured to check itself. The cybersecurity operations center (SOC) silenced the alerts from the vulnerability scanner because it generated numerous false positives. Data was moved from database servers, file servers, and application servers to a company web server. From there, the attacker used a rate-limited download to exfiltrate files without attracting attention. The risk assessment the company used was modeled on keeping attackers out; there were no controls in place to keep data from leaving the internal network. The risk assessment also never listed any of the cybersecurity appliances or tools in a column other than mitigating controls.

The extensive report prepared later by the DFIR firm could be condensed to two main truths. First, the very tools meant to protect your company had been the critical enablers of the attacker. Second, the DFIR company fees for the past 60 days were enough to pay for 10 vulnerability servers, the salaries of four SOC analysts, the AV license upgrade, and salaries for 20 full-time help-desk employees.

This story could have happened. This story could be you at work. With a bit of creative thinking, we can look at networks like attackers do. It is not popular with executives to plan network defense from the perspective of "when we will be breached," but it might well be the only way to keep data in the network and out of the hands of attackers.

Internet Vulnerability Assessment

The Internet vulnerability assessment—an assessment approach designed to find and document vulnerabilities that may be present in the organization's public network—is usually performed against all public addresses using every possible penetration testing approach because attackers from this direction can take advantage of any flaw. The steps in the process are as follows:

- Planning, scheduling, and notification of penetration testing—To execute the data collection phase of this assessment, large organizations often need long periods when changes are not allowed on the organization's systems or networks in order to obtain the results needed for analysis. Scanning times should be spread out so that analysis is performed on fresh scanning results over the course of the assessment period. IT and cybersecurity technical support teams should be given the details of the plan so they know when each device is scheduled for testing and what tests are used, making any disruptions caused by invasive penetration testing easier to diagnose and recover from.

- Target selection—Working from the network characterization elements stored in the risk, threat, and attack database, the organization selects its penetration targets. As previously noted, most organizations choose to test every device that is exposed to the Internet.

- Test selection—This step involves using external monitoring intelligence to configure a test engine, such as Nessus, for the tests to be performed. Selecting the test library to employ is usually a process that evolves over time and matches the evolution of the threat environment. After the ground rules are established, there is usually little debate about the risk level of the tests used. After all, if a device is placed in a public role, it must be able to take everything the Internet can send its way, including the most aggressive penetration test scripts.

- Scanning—The penetration test engine is unleashed at the scheduled time using the planned target list and test selection. The results of the test run are logged for analysis. This process should be monitored so that if an invasive penetration test causes a disruption to a targeted system, the outage can be reported immediately and recovery activities can be initiated. Note that the log files generated by this scanning, along with all data generated in the rest of this maintenance domain, must be treated as confidential.

- Analysis—A knowledgeable and experienced vulnerability analyst screens the test results for possible vulnerabilities logged during scanning. During this step, the analyst must perform three tasks:

  - Classify the risk level of the possible vulnerability as needing attention or as acceptable.

  - Validate the vulnerability when it is deemed to be a significant risk—for example, when the risk is higher than the risk appetite of the organization. This task is important because it validates the presence and significance of the risk; the analyst must therefore use manual testing, human judgment, and a large dose of discretion. The goal of this step is to tread lightly and cause as little disruption and damage as possible while removing false positives from further investigation. Proven cases of real vulnerabilities can now be considered vulnerability instances.

  - Document the results of the verification by saving a "trophy" (usually a screenshot) that can be used to convince skeptical systems administrators that the vulnerability is real.

- Record keeping—In this phase, the organization must record the details of the documented vulnerability in the vulnerability database, identifying logical and physical characteristics and assigning a response risk level to differentiate the truly urgent vulnerability from the merely important. When coupled with the criticality level from the characteristics in the risk, threat, and attack database, these records can help systems administrators decide which items they need to remediate first.

As the list of documented vulnerabilities is identified for Internet information assets, confirmed items are moved to the remediation stage.

Intranet Vulnerability Assessment

The next assessment area is the intranet vulnerability assessment, an approach designed to find and document selected vulnerabilities that are likely to be present on the organization's internal network. Intranet attackers are often employees, business partners, or automated attack vectors, such as viruses and worms, moving from compromised system to system. This assessment is usually performed against critical internal devices with a known, high value and thus requires the use of selective penetration testing.

Many employees and others are now allowed to access an organization's networks using their own devices. This type of environment is often referred to as "bring your own device" (BYOD). BYOD implies that all devices connected to the network, whether owned by the organization or individual workers within it, are in scope for vulnerability assessment. The steps in the assessment process are almost identical to those in the Internet vulnerability assessment, except as noted here:

- Planning, scheduling, and notification of penetration testing—Most organizations are amazed at how many devices exist inside even a moderately sized network. As in Internet scanning, the IT and cybersecurity technical support teams should be notified to support diagnosis and recovery of issues resulting from the testing. In contrast to Internet systems administrators, who prefer penetration testing to be performed during periods of low demand, such as nights and weekends for commercial operations, intranet administrators often prefer that penetration testing be performed during high-demand, working hours.

- Target selection—Like the Internet vulnerability assessment, the intranet scan starts with the network characterization elements stored in the risk, threat, and attack database. Intranet testing has so many target possibilities, however, that a more selective approach is required. At first, penetration test scanning and analysis should focus on the most valuable and critical systems. As the configuration of these systems is improved and fewer possible vulnerabilities are found in the scanning step, the target list can be expanded. The list of targeted intranet systems should eventually reach equilibrium so that it scans and analyzes as many systems as possible, given the resources dedicated to the process.

- Test selection—The testing for intranet vulnerability assessment typically uses less stringent criteria than those for Internet scanning. Test selection usually evolves over time and matches the evolution of the perceived intranet threat environment. Most organizations focus their intranet scanning efforts on a few critical vulnerabilities at first and then expand the test pool to include more test scripts and detect more vulnerabilities. The degree to which an organization is willing to accept risk while scanning and analyzing also affects the selection of test scripts. If the organization is unwilling to risk disruptions to critical internal systems, test scripts that pose such risks should be avoided in favor of alternate means that confirm safety from suspected vulnerabilities.

- Scanning—Intranet scanning is the same process used for Internet scanning. The process should be monitored so that if an invasive penetration test causes disruption, it can be reported for repair.

- Analysis—Despite the differences in targets and tested vulnerabilities, the intranet scan analysis is essentially identical to the Internet analysis. It follows the same three steps: classify, validate, and document.

- Record keeping—This step is identical to the one followed in Internet vulnerability analysis. Organizations should use similarities between the processes to their advantage by sharing the database, reports, and procedures used for record keeping, reporting, and follow-up.

By leveraging the common assessment processes and using difference analysis on the data collected during the vulnerability assessment, an organization can identify a list of documented internal vulnerabilities, which is the essential information needed for the remediation stage.

Platform Security Validation

The next assessment area is platform security validation (PSV), an assessment approach designed to find and document vulnerabilities that may be present because misconfigured systems are used within the organization. These systems fail to comply with company policy or standards that are adopted by the IT governance groups and communicated in the cybersecurity and awareness program. Fortunately, automated measurement systems are available to help with the intensive process of validating the compliance of platform configuration with policy.

- Product selection—Typically, an organization implements a PSV solution when deploying the cybersecurity program. If a product has not yet been selected, a separate cybersecurity project selects and deploys a PSV solution.

- Policy configuration—As organizational policy and standards evolve, the policy templates of the PSV tool must be changed to match. After all, the goal of any selected approach is to be able to measure how well the systems comply with policy.

- Deployment—At a minimum, mission-critical systems should be enrolled in PSV measurement, with additional systems added as funding permits. Cybersecurity personnel should remember that attackers often enter a network using the weakest link, which may not be a critical system itself but a device connected to critical systems.

- Measurement—Using the PSV tools, the organization should measure the compliance of each enrolled system against the policy templates, reporting deficiencies as vulnerabilities.

- Exclusion handling—Some provision should be made for the exclusion of specific policy or standard exceptions. For instance, one measurement identifies user accounts that never expire. Some organizations assume the risk of having service accounts that do not expire or that have longer change intervals than standard user accounts. If the proper decision makers have made an informed choice to assume such risks in an organization, the automated PSV tool should be able to exclude the assumed risk factor from the compliance report.

- Reporting—Using the standard reporting components in the PSV tool, most organizations can inform systems administrators of deficiencies that need remediation.

- Remediation—Noncompliant systems need to be updated with configurations that comply with policy. When the PSV process shows an outstanding configuration fault that has not been promptly remedied, the information should be recorded in the vulnerability database to assure remediation.

The ability of PSV software products to integrate with custom vulnerability databases is not a standard feature, but most PSV products can export data in a format that an organization can import into its vulnerability database for integrated use in the remediation phase. If this degree of integration is not needed or cannot be justified, the stand-alone reporting capabilities of the products can generate sufficient reports for remediation functions.

Wireless Vulnerability Assessment

The next assessment area is wireless vulnerability assessment, an approach designed to find and document vulnerabilities that may be present in the organization's wireless local area networks. Because attackers from this direction are likely to take advantage of any flaw, this assessment is usually performed against all publicly accessible areas using every possible approach to wireless penetration testing. The steps in the process are as follows:

- Planning, scheduling, and notification of wireless penetration testing—This is a noninvasive scanning process that can be done almost any time without notifying systems administrators. Testing times and days should be rotated over time to detect wireless devices that are used for intermittent projects.
- Target selection—All areas on the organization's premises should be scanned with a portable wireless network scanner, with special attention to the following: all areas that are publicly accessible; all areas in range of commonly available products, such as 802.11 Wi-Fi; and areas where visitors might linger without attracting attention. Because the radio emissions of wireless network equipment can act in surprising ways, all locations should be tested periodically.
- Test selection—Wireless scanning tools should look for all wireless signals that do not meet the organization's minimum level of encryption strength.
- Scanning—The walking scan should survey the entire target area and identify all wireless access points that are not cryptographically secure.
- Analysis—A knowledgeable and experienced vulnerability analyst should screen the test results for wireless networks that have been logged, as previously described. During this step, the analyst should do the following:
  - Remove false-positive candidates from further consideration as vulnerabilities while causing as little disruption or damage as possible.
  - Document the results of the verification, as described previously.
- Record keeping—Good reporting makes the effort to communicate and follow up much easier. As in other phases of the vulnerability assessment, effective reporting maximizes results.

At this stage in the process, wireless vulnerabilities are documented and ready for remediation.

In previous sections, we discussed the importance of scanning and analysis tools in cybersecurity. While these tools are essential for maintaining and improving security, they also exemplify the dual-use nature of many technologies in the field. Cybersecurity professionals must remain knowledgeable about both the defensive and offensive applications of these tools in order to effectively protect systems from potential attacks. Additionally, professionals must be aware of the inherent risks associated with using these tools because improper use can introduce new vulnerabilities or cause unintended harm both to internal and external systems.

Once each group of vulnerability assessments has been described, a discussion of the record-keeping process is in order.

Documenting Vulnerabilities

The vulnerability database, like the risk, threat, and attack database, both stores and tracks information. It should provide details about the vulnerability being reported and link to the information assets characterized in the risk, threat, and attack database. While this can be done through manual data storage, the low cost and ease of use associated with relational databases makes them a more realistic choice. The data stored in the vulnerability database should include the following:

- A unique vulnerability ID number for reporting and tracking remediation actions
- Linkage to the risk, threat, and attack database based on the physical information asset underlying the vulnerability; the IP address is a good choice for this linkage
- Vulnerability details, which are usually based on the test script used during the scanning step of the process; if the Nessus scanner is used, each test script has an assigned code (NASL, or Nessus attack scripting language) that can identify the vulnerability effectively
- Dates and times of notification and remediation activities
- Status of the vulnerability, such as found, reported, or repaired
- Comments, which give analysts the opportunity to provide systems administrators with detailed information for fixing the vulnerability
- Other fields as needed to manage the reporting and tracking processes in the remediation phase

The vulnerability database is an essential part of effective remediation because it helps organizations keep track of vulnerabilities as they are reported and remediated.

Remediating Vulnerabilities

The final process in the vulnerability assessment and remediation domain is the remediation phase. The objective of remediation is to repair the flaw that caused a vulnerability or remove the risk associated with the vulnerability. Alternatively, informed decision makers with the proper authority may decide to accept the risk as a last resort.

When approaching the remediation process, it is important to recognize that the key to success is building relationships with those who control the information assets. In other words, success depends on the organization adopting a team approach to remediation in place of the push and pull between departments or divisions. Vulnerabilities can be remediated by accepting or transferring the risk, removing the threat, or repairing the vulnerability.

Acceptance or Transference of Risk   In some instances, risk must either simply be acknowledged as part of an organization's business process or the organization should buy insurance to transfer the risk to another entity, like a managed security services organization. The cybersecurity professional must assure the general management community that the decision to accept or transfer the risk was made by properly informed decision makers. Furthermore, these decision makers must have the proper level of authority within the organization to assume the risk. Many situations in which risk is assumed violate the preceding conditions:

- Decisions are made at the wrong level of the organization. For example, systems administrators should not be allowed to skip using passwords on a critical application server just because it creates more work for them.
- Decisions are made by uninformed decision makers. For example, a project manager should not convince an application sponsor that database-level cybersecurity is not needed in an application and that all users need unlimited access to all data.

In the final analysis, the cybersecurity group must make sure the right people make risk assumption decisions and that they are aware of the potential impact of those decisions and the cost of the available cybersecurity controls.

Threat Removal   In some circumstances, threats can be removed without requiring a repair of the vulnerability. For example, if an application can only run on an older desktop system that cannot support passwords, the system can be removed from the network and stored in a locked room or equipment rack for use as a stand-alone device. Other vulnerabilities may be mitigated by inexpensive controls—for example, disabling web services on a server that provides other important services instead of taking the time to update the web software on the server.

Vulnerability Repair   The best solution in most cases is to repair the vulnerability, often by applying patch software or implementing a workaround. Many recent vulnerabilities have exploited web servers on Windows operating systems, so simply updating the version of the installed web server removes the vulnerability. Simple repairs are possible in other cases, too. For instance, if an account is flagged as a vulnerability because it has a password that has not been changed within the specified time interval, changing the password removes the vulnerability. Of course, the most common repair is the application of a software patch; this usually makes the system function in the expected fashion and removes the vulnerability.

Readiness and Review

The primary goal of the readiness and review domain is to keep the cybersecurity program functioning as designed and improve it continuously over time. This goal can be accomplished by doing the following:

- Policy review—Policy needs to be reviewed and refreshed from time to time to ensure its soundness—in other words, it must provide a current foundation for the cybersecurity program.
- Program review—Major planning components should be reviewed on a periodic basis to ensure that they are current, accurate, and appropriate.
- Rehearsals—When possible, major plan elements should be rehearsed.

The relationships among the sectors of the readiness and review domain are shown in Figure 11-7. As the diagram indicates, policy review is the primary initiator of this domain. As policy is revised or current policy is confirmed, the planning elements are reviewed for compliance, the cybersecurity program is reviewed, and rehearsals are held to make sure all participants can respond as needed.

Figure 11-7   Readiness and review

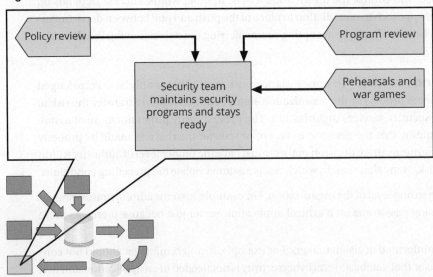

Policy Review and Planning Review

As you learned earlier, policy needs to be reviewed periodically. The planning and review process for contingency planning and its domains were covered in the prior chapter.

Program Review

As business needs shift, a thorough and independent review of the entire cybersecurity program is needed. While an exact timetable for review is not proposed here, many organizations find that the CSO should conduct a formal review annually. Earlier in this chapter, you learned about the role of the CSO in the maintenance process. The CSO uses the results of maintenance activities and the review of the cybersecurity program to determine if the status quo is adequate against the threats at hand. If the current cybersecurity program is not up to the challenges, the CSO must determine if incremental improvements are possible or if it is time to reorganize the entire cybersecurity program within the organization.

Rehearsals

Whenever possible, major planning elements should be rehearsed. Rehearsal adds value by exercising procedures, identifying shortcomings, and providing cybersecurity personnel with the opportunity to improve a plan before it is needed. In addition, rehearsals make people more effective when an event occurs. A type of rehearsal known as a war game or simulation exercise puts a subset of plans in place to create a realistic test environment. This adds to the value of the rehearsal and can enhance training.

> **Note 7** | Although the Information Technology Infrastructure Library (ITIL) is not discussed at length in this text, there is a lot of overlap between what it takes to maintain IT systems in general and the maintenance of cybersecurity management systems. We recommend the book *ITIL For Beginners: The Complete Beginner's Guide to ITIL* (available in paperback), published by ClydeBank Technology.

Self-Check

4. The primary goal of the external monitoring domain is to provide awareness of internal system vulnerabilities.
   a. True   b. False

5. Internal monitoring involves maintaining an inventory of network devices and IT infrastructure.
   a. True   b. False

6. Penetration testing is typically less invasive than vulnerability assessments.
   a. True   b. False

□ Check your answers at the end of this chapter.

Closing Case

Linda completed the note she was adding to the list of assets, threats, and vulnerabilities, which was the reason for the two-hour meeting that was now wrapping up.

Iris cleared her throat and said, "Okay. Good meeting, folks. Everyone happy with the updates to the risk assessments of our risk treatment strategies? The next step is to develop our plans for the coming year to update our controls."

Kelvin and Maria nodded and Linda started gathering her notes. She said, "I'll update these documents and post them to the team share."

All of them stood and headed for the door, happy to have the tedious meeting behind them.

Case Discussion Questions

1. As the team prepares to plan for upgrades to the cybersecurity controls in use at the company, describe how each subject area of the cybersecurity maintenance model will be used as they make these plans, based on the revised risk assessments just completed.

2. Describe how ongoing events and risk reviews should be integrated into the readiness and review domain of the cybersecurity maintenance model.

Case Ethical Decision Making

Referring back to the case opener of this chapter, suppose Iris had just finished a search for a new job and knew that she would soon be leaving the company. When Linda came in to talk about the tedious and time-consuming review process, suppose Iris had put Linda off and asked her to schedule another meeting "in two or three weeks," knowing full well that she would be gone by then.

Do you think this kind of action would be unethical if Iris knew she was leaving soon?

Summary

Change is inevitable, so organizations should have procedures to deal with changes in the operation and maintenance of the cybersecurity program.

The organization decides whether the cybersecurity program can adapt to change as it is implemented or the macroscopic process of the risk management program must be started anew.

To stay current, the cybersecurity community of interest and the CSO must constantly monitor the three components of the cybersecurity triplet—threats, assets, and vulnerabilities.

To assist the cybersecurity community in managing and operating the ongoing cybersecurity program, the organization should adopt a cybersecurity management maintenance model. These models are frameworks that are structured by the tasks of managing a particular set of activities or business functions.

NIST SP 800-100, "Information Security Handbook: A Guide for Managers," outlines managerial tasks performed after the program is operational. For each of the 13 areas of cybersecurity management presented in SP 800-100, there are specific monitoring activities.

The maintenance model recommended in this chapter is made up of five subject areas or domains: external monitoring, internal monitoring, planning and risk assessment, vulnerability assessment and remediation, and readiness and review.

The objective of the external monitoring domain in the maintenance model is to provide early awareness of new and emerging threats, threat agents, vulnerabilities, and attacks so that an effective and timely defense can be mounted.

The objective of the internal monitoring domain is an informed awareness of the state of the organization's networks, information systems, and cybersecurity defenses. The cybersecurity team documents and communicates this awareness, particularly when it concerns system components that face the external network.

The primary objective of the planning and risk assessment domain is to keep an eye on the entire cybersecurity program.

The primary objectives of the vulnerability assessment and remediation domain are to identify documented vulnerabilities and remediate them in a timely fashion.

The primary objectives of the readiness and review domain are to keep the cybersecurity program functioning as designed and keep improving it over time.

Key Terms

auditing	Internet vulnerability assessment	vulnerability assessment
configuration and change management (CCM)	intranet vulnerability assessment	vulnerability assessment and remediation domain
configuration management (CM)	pen testing	wireless vulnerability assessment
difference analysis	penetration testing	
external monitoring domain	planning and risk assessment domain	
internal monitoring domain	platform security validation (PSV)	

Review Questions

1. What is the purpose of a maintenance model in cybersecurity?

2. What managerial guidance does NIST SP 800-100 provide for cybersecurity managers?

3. Why is continuous review important in a cybersecurity governance program?

4. What are plans of action and milestones used for in cybersecurity governance?

5. How does continuous assessment contribute to cybersecurity?

6. What role does configuration management play in monitoring IT systems?

7. How do incident and event statistics help cybersecurity managers?

8. What is the importance of documenting changes in the systems development life cycle?

9. What should a tracking system capture in cybersecurity awareness and training programs?

10. What does capital planning and investment control aim to achieve in cybersecurity?

11. How can performance measurement programs benefit cybersecurity?

12. What is the help desk's role in managing cybersecurity incidents?

13. What is the primary objective of the external monitoring domain in a cybersecurity maintenance model?

14. Why do many organizations choose to outsource the external monitoring component of their cybersecurity maintenance model?

15. What are some of the sources of external intelligence used for monitoring cybersecurity threats?

16. How does the internal monitoring domain contribute to an organization's cybersecurity maintenance model?

17. What is the significance of maintaining an inventory of network devices and IT infrastructure within the internal monitoring domain?

18. What is difference analysis, and how is it used in internal monitoring?

19. What are the primary objectives of the planning and risk assessment domain in cybersecurity maintenance?

20. What role does a risk assessment play in a cybersecurity maintenance model?

21. Describe the process of vulnerability assessment and remediation.

22. What is the difference between penetration testing and vulnerability assessment?

23. Why is policy review an important part of the readiness and review domain?

24. What benefits do rehearsals offer in the context of cybersecurity readiness and review?

Exercises

1. Search the web for information on the Forum of Incident Response and Security Teams. In your own words, what is the forum's mission?

2. Search the web for two or more sites that discuss the ongoing responsibilities of a cybersecurity manager. What other components of cybersecurity management can be adapted for use in the cybersecurity management model?

3. This chapter mentions several tools that can be used by cybersecurity administrators, network administrators, and attackers alike. Search the web for three to five other tools that fit this description. What are the risks of using such tools?

4. Using a web browser and the names of the tools from Exercise 3, find a site that claims to be dedicated to supporting hackers. Do you find any references to other hacker tools? If you do, create a list of the tools along with a short description of what they do and how they work.

5. Using the components of risk assessment documentation presented in the chapter, draft a tentative risk assessment of a lab, department, or office at your university. Outline the critical risks you found and discuss them with your class.

Solutions to Self-Check Questions

NIST SP 800-100, "Information Security Handbook: A Guide for Managers"

1. A cybersecurity governance program does not need to be reviewed constantly once it is implemented.

   Answer: b. False.

   Explanation: An effective cybersecurity governance program requires constant review to ensure policies and procedures are current and controls are effective.

2. Configuration management is unnecessary once an IT system is initially implemented.

   Answer: b. False.

   Explanation: Configuration management is essential for continuously monitoring the status of cybersecurity controls and identifying potential problems in IT systems.

3. Incident statistics can help determine the effectiveness of cybersecurity policies and procedures.

   Answer: a. True.

   Explanation: Incident statistics provide insights into the status of cybersecurity programs and help managers observe performance trends and the need for policy changes.

The Cybersecurity Maintenance Model

4. The primary goal of the external monitoring domain is to provide awareness of internal system vulnerabilities.

   Answer: b. False.

   Explanation: The primary goal of the external monitoring domain is to provide early awareness of new and emerging threats, threat agents, vulnerabilities, and attacks from outside the organization.

5. Internal monitoring involves maintaining an inventory of network devices and IT infrastructure.

   Answer: a. True.

   Explanation: Internal monitoring includes building and maintaining an inventory of network devices, IT infrastructure, and applications to monitor the state of the organization's systems.

6. Penetration testing is typically less invasive than vulnerability assessments.

   Answer: b. False.

   Explanation: Penetration testing is more invasive than vulnerability assessments because it simulates the actions of an attacker and tries to identify weaknesses through active testing.

Cybersecurity Protection Mechanisms

Chapter Objectives

After reading this chapter and completing the exercises, you should be able to:

1 Describe the various access control approaches, including authentication, authorization, and biometric access controls.

2 Summarize the technologies used to manage network security.

3 Identify the cryptographic tools needed to protect sensitive information.

> If you think technology can solve your security problems, then you don't understand the problems and you don't understand the technology.
>
> —Bruce Schneier

Case Opener

One night toward the end of his shift, Drew Brown, a technician at Random Widget Works, Inc. (RWW), received a call from his wife. One of their children was ill, and she wanted Drew to pick up some medicine on his way home from work. He decided to leave a few minutes early.

Like all watchstanding employees in the security operations center, Drew had a procedures manual that was organized sequentially. He used the checklists for everyday purposes and had an index to look up anything else he needed. Only one box remained unchecked on the list when Drew snapped the binder closed and hurriedly secured his workstation. That oversight would cause the whole company grief in the next few hours.

Because he was the second-shift operator and RWW did not have a third shift in its data center, Drew carefully reviewed the room shutdown checklist next to the door, making sure all the room's environmental, safety, and physical security systems were set correctly. One of those settings activated the burglar alarm, so Drew quickly exited the room and the building and was soon on his way to the drugstore.

At about the same time, a high school student in San Diego was up late and working at her computer. Her parents assumed she was doing homework with school friends online. In fact, she had become bored and discovered some new friends on the Internet—friends who shared her interest in programming. One of these new friends sent her a link to a new *warez* site for illegally copied software.

The girl downloaded a program called EZMailz from the warez site. Blendo is a tool built into the program to help novice hackers create attack programs that combine a mass emailer with a worm, a macro virus, and a network scanner. The girl clicked her way through the configuration options, clicked a button labeled "custom scripts," and pasted in a script that one of her new friends had emailed to her. This script was built to exploit a brand-new vulnerability announced only a few days before. Although she didn't know it, the high schooler had just created new malware that would soon overload thousands of email servers in organizations across the United States.

She compiled the attack script, attached it to an email from her anonymous web-based account, and sent it through a remailer service to be forwarded to as many email accounts as possible. Thirty minutes later, she checked her email account and saw that she had more than 100,000 new messages; the only reason there were not even more was that her mailbox was full.

Back at RWW, the email gateway was sorting and forwarding all the incoming email. RWW's sales email account always received a lot of traffic, as did the account for support services. Tonight was no exception. Unfortunately for RWW, and for the second-shift operator who had failed to download and install the patch that fixed the new vulnerability just announced by the vendor, the young hacker's attack script tricked the RWW mail server into running the program. The mail server, with its high-performance processors, large RAM storage, and high-speed Internet connection, began to do three things at once: It sent an infected email to everyone with whom RWW had ever exchanged email, it infected every RWW server that the email server could reach, and it started randomly deleting files on each infected server.

Within a fraction of a second, the network intrusion detection system determined that something was afoot. By then, it was too late to stop the massive denial-of-service attack, but just before the system was overwhelmed, it sent a message to Iris's smartphone.

Protection Mechanisms

You should know by now that technical controls alone cannot secure an information technology (IT) environment, but they are an essential part of the cybersecurity program. Managing the development and use of technical controls to treat risks requires knowledge and familiarity with the technology that enables those controls. In this chapter, you will learn about firewalls, intrusion detection and prevention systems, encryption systems, and some other widely used cybersecurity technologies. The chapter is designed to help you understand how to evaluate and manage the technical controls used by cybersecurity programs.

Technical controls can enable and enforce policies where human behavior is difficult to regulate. A password policy that specifies the strength of the password (its length and the types of characters it uses), regulates how often passwords must change, and prohibits the reuse of passwords would be impossible to enforce by simply asking employees if they had complied. This type of requirement is best enforced by the implementation of a policy (rule) in the operating system.

Figure 12-1 illustrates how technical controls can be implemented at several points in a technical infrastructure. The technical controls that defend against threats from outside the organization are shown on the left side of the diagram. The controls that defend against threats from within the organization are shown on the right side of the diagram; these controls were covered in previous chapters. Because individuals inside an organization often have direct access to information, they can circumvent many of the most potent technical controls. Controls that can be applied to this human element are also shown on the right side of the diagram.

Access Controls and Biometrics

As explained in an earlier chapter, access controls regulate the admission of users into trusted areas of the organization—both logical access to information and systems and physical access to the organization's facilities. Access control is maintained by means of a collection of policies, programs to carry out those policies, and technologies that enforce policies.

Access control approaches involve four functions, as defined earlier: obtaining the identity of the person requesting access to a logical or physical area (identification), confirming the identity of the person seeking access to a logical or physical area (authentication), determining which actions the person can perform in that logical or physical area (authorization), and documenting the activities of the authorized individual and systems (accountability). A successful access control approach, whether intended to control logical or physical access, always incorporates all four of these elements, known collectively as IAAA (I triple-A).

Figure 12-1 Spheres of cybersecurity

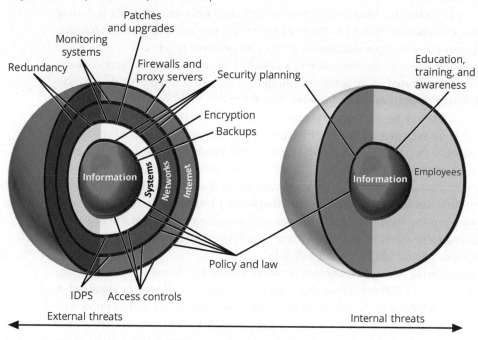

There are three types of authentication mechanisms:

- Something a person knows—for example, a password or passphrase
- Something a person has—for example, a cryptographic token or smart card
- Something a person can produce, such as fingerprints, palm prints, hand topography, hand geometry, retinal and iris scans, or a voice or signature that is analyzed using pattern recognition. These characteristics can be assessed with biometrics, the use of physiology to provide authentication for a person's identification and validate that they are who they claim to be.

The following sections describe each of these authentication mechanisms.

Something a Person Knows

This authentication mechanism verifies the user's identity by means of a password, a secret combination of characters that only the user should know; a passphrase, a plain-language phrase that is typically longer than a password, from which a virtual password is derived; or some other unique authentication code, such as a personal identification number (PIN).

One of the biggest cybersecurity debates focuses on password complexity, the degree of variation or complication in a password or passphrase. The industry standard for password complexity is "10.4," which means the password is at least 10 characters and includes at least one uppercase letter, one lowercase letter, a special character, and a number. A password should be difficult to guess, which means it cannot be easily associated with the user, such as the name of a spouse, child, or pet. A password also should not be a number easily associated with the user, such as a phone number, Social Security number, or birthdate. At the same time, the password must be something the user can easily remember, which means it should be short and have an association with the user that is not accessible to others. The current industry best practice is for all passwords to conform to the 10.4 rule and be case-sensitive.

As passwords get more complex, they become increasingly difficult to remember, which can lead to employees recording them in unauthorized locations and defeating the whole purpose of having passwords. The greatest challenge of complex password usage comes from employees who allow the local web browser to remember passwords for them; anyone who can access the system then will have access to any online resources commonly used from that system. Many users incorporate simple access controls into their home systems but are then required to use complex passwords for online applications. This issue creates a huge cybersecurity problem for organizations that allow employees to work from home on their personal equipment, as was often the case during the COVID-19 pandemic. Organizations must enforce access control requirements, including strong passwords on in-house systems, restrictions on allowing systems to retain access control credentials, and restrictions on allowing users to access organizational resources with personal systems.

The passphrase and virtual password, the derivative of a passphrase, are an improvement over the standard password because they are based on an easily memorable phrase. For example, while a typical password might be 23_$K1d00>, a passphrase could be "May_The_Force_Be_With_You!," from which the virtual password Ma1T4sBwU! is derived. Another way to create a virtual password is to use a set of construction rules applied to facts you know very well, such as the first three letters of your last name, a hyphen, the first two letters of your first name, a special character, the first two letters of a female relative's maiden name, another special character, and the first four letters of the city in which you were born, went to school, or lived for a long period of time. This may sound complicated, but once memorized, the construction rules are easy to use. If you add another rule to substitute numbers for certain letters—1 for L or I, 0 for O, and 3 for E—and capitalize the first letter of each section, then you have a very powerful virtual password that you can easily reconstruct. Using the preceding rules would create a very strong virtual password for Charlie Moody (born in Atlanta, mother's maiden name Meredith) of "M00-Ch_M3-At1a".

Another method for remembering strong passwords is to use an encryption-based password storage application such as eWallet from Ilium Software (www.iliumsoft.com/ewallet), as shown in Figure 12-2. This application and others like it are available for smartphones, tablets, laptops, and PCs; they provide an encrypted database to store the system name (or URL), username, and password for hundreds of systems. You can also use such applications to store credit card information, frequent flyer information, loyalty shopper rewards numbers, and any portable data that needs protection. Most systems like this use strong encryption, such as 256-bit AES, which is described later in this chapter.

Figure 12-2   eWallet password management

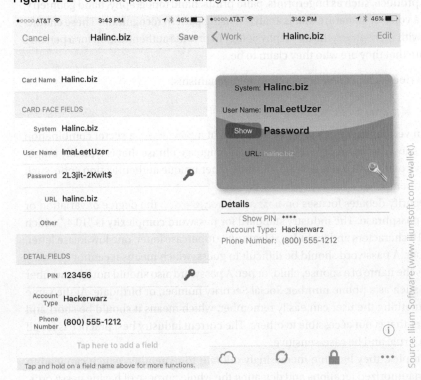

How important is it to have a strong password that is not obvious to others? As shown in Table 12-1, the longer the password, the lower the odds of it being guessed in a brute-force attack using random bit combinations. If a particular system does *not* require case-sensitive passwords, the user should adopt a standard password length of at least 12 characters, incorporating at least one letter, one number, and one special character to create a reasonable delay in the attacker's effort to crack a password with a brute-force attack. This delay causes the attacker's work effort to exceed their reward. If the system does require case-sensitive passwords, which is the much-preferred alternative, then the average password length need only follow the 10.4 password complexity requirements described earlier to result in an acceptable delay against brute-force attacks. Fortunately, few systems allow passwords to be incorrectly guessed more than a few times before deploying a timeout or lockout, so most brute-force attacks can only be used on captured password files. Of course, if you give your password away in a phishing or spear-phishing attack, the strength of your password is irrelevant. Multifactor authentication can help in that case, but complexity does not.

Table 12-1 Password power

Case-Insensitive Passwords Using a Standard Alphabet Set (No Numbers or Special Characters)		
Password Length	Odds of Cracking: 1 in (based on number of characters ^ password length):	Estimated Time to Crack*
8	208,827,064,576	0.25 seconds
9	5,429,503,678,976	6.4 seconds
10	141,167,095,653,376	2.77 minutes
11	3,670,344,486,987,780	1.2 hours
12	95,428,956,661,682,200	1.3 days
13	2,481,152,873,203,740,000	33.9 days
14	64,509,974,703,297,200,000	2.4 years
15	1,677,259,342,285,730,000,000	62.7 years
16	43,608,742,899,428,900,000,000	1,630.7 years
Case-Sensitive Passwords Using a Standard Alphabet Set with Numbers and 20 Special Characters		
Password Length	Odds of Cracking: 1 in (based on number of characters ^ password length):	Estimated Time to Crack*
8	2,044,140,858,654,980	40.2 minutes
9	167,619,550,409,708,000	2.3 days
10	13,744,803,133,596,100,000	187.6 days
11	1,127,073,856,954,880,000,000	42.1 years
12	92,420,056,270,299,900,000,000	3,455.9 years
13	7,578,444,614,164,590,000,000,000	283,385.5 years
14	621,432,458,361,496,000,000,000,000	23,237,610.8 years
15	50,957,461,585,642,700,000,000,000,000	1,905,484,088.3 years
16	4,178,511,850,022,700,000,000,000,000,000	156,249,695,242.8 years

*Estimated Time to Crack is based on a 2024-era Intel Core i9-13900 with 8 P-Cores and 16 E-Cores (24 cores) and 32 threads, running at clock speeds of 3.7 GHz (P-Cores) and 2.76 GHz (E-Cores) and performing 848 Dhrystone GFLOPS (giga/billion floating point operations per second).[1]

Note: Modern workstations are capable of using multiple CPUs, further decreasing time to crack or simply splitting the workload among multiple systems.

Something a Person Has

This authentication mechanism makes use of an item (a card, key, or token) that the user or system has. One example of this mechanism is a dumb card, an authentication card that contains digital user data such as a PIN against which user input is compared. A card used to access an automatic teller machine is an example of a dumb card. A more capable object is the smart card, an authentication component similar to a dumb card that contains a computer chip to verify and validate several pieces of information instead of just a PIN. Another device is the cryptographic token, a computer chip in a card that has a display. This device contains a built-in seed number that uses a formula or a clock to calculate a number that can be used to perform a remote login authentication.

Tokens may be synchronous or asynchronous. Synchronous tokens are an authentication component in the form of a card or key fob that contains a computer chip and a display and shows a time-based, computer-generated number used to support remote login authentication. This token must be calibrated with the corresponding software on the central authentication server. Asynchronous tokens are an authentication component in the form of a card or key fob that contains a computer chip and a display and shows a computer-generated number that is activated to support remote login authentication. This token does not require calibration of the central authentication server; instead, it uses a challenge/response system.

The rise of smartphones has led to the increasing use of communication of authentication code using out-of-band transmission. This is often combined with something a person knows to create multifactor authentication. The use of text messages and custom applications is quickly replacing the use of dedicated tokens. Figure 12-3 shows two SecurID tokens, a PayPal authentication token, Google Authenticator software, and Duo—a two-factor authentication application.

Figure 12-3   Multifactor access control

Source: RSA, Google, and Cisco Duo.

Something a Person Can Produce

This authentication mechanism takes advantage of something inherent in the user that is evaluated using biometrics. Biometric authentication methods include the following:

- Comparison of a person's fingerprint to a stored image or value
- Comparison of a person's palm print to a stored image or value
- Hand geometry comparison of a person's hand to a stored measurement
- Facial recognition using a photographic ID card, in which a human security guard compares the person's face to a photo; this is the most widely used form of identification today
- Facial recognition using a digital camera, in which a person's face is compared to a stored image or measurement
- Comparison of the person's retinal print to a stored image or measurement
- Comparison of the person's voice print to a recorded voice
- Comparison of the person's iris pattern to a stored image or measurement

Most of the technologies that scan human characteristics convert these images to data based on some form of minutiae—unique points of reference that are digitized and stored. Some technologies encrypt the minutiae to make them more resistant to tampering. Each subsequent scan is also digitized and then compared with the encoded value to determine whether users are who they claim to be. One limitation of this technique is that some human characteristics can change over time due to normal development, injury, or illness. Among all possible biometrics, only three human characteristics are usually considered truly unique and suitable for use:

- Fingerprints
- Retina of the eye (blood vessel pattern)
- Iris of the eye (random pattern of features found in the iris, including freckles, pits, striations, vasculature, coronas, and crypts)

DNA or genetic authentication will be included in this category if it ever becomes a cost-effective, time-efficient, and socially accepted technology.

For items a person can produce, signature recognition is commonplace. Retailers historically have used signature capture as part of the authentication process at a point-of-sale purchase, although it is falling out of favor. Customers sign a special pad using a stylus; the signatures are then digitized and saved for use should the transaction be challenged. Signature capture is much more widely used than signature comparison because signatures can vary due to several factors, including age, fatigue, and the speed with which they are written. Signature capture and comparison is being replaced rapidly by chip and PIN technology because it is much more time-efficient at the point of sale.

Voice recognition for authentication captures the analog waveforms of a person's speech and compares a digitized version of these waveforms to a stored version. Voice recognition systems provide users with a phrase they must read—for example, "My voice is my password, please verify me. Thank you." Figure 12-4 depicts some biometric and other human recognition characteristics.

Figure 12-4 Biometric recognition characteristics

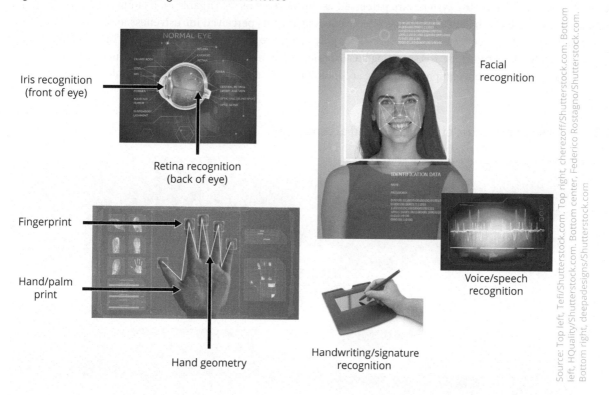

Evaluating Biometrics

Biometric technologies are generally evaluated according to three basic criteria based on sensitivity levels:

- False reject rate—The percentage of authorized users who are denied access
- False accept rate—The percentage of unauthorized users who are allowed access
- Crossover error rate—The point at which the number of false rejections equals the number of false acceptances

False Reject Rate   The false reject rate is the rate at which authentic users are denied or prevented access to authorized areas because of a failure in the biometric device. Such a failure is known as a Type I error or a false negative. Rejection of an authorized individual represents more of a hindrance to legitimate use than a threat to cybersecurity. Consequently, it is often not seen as a serious problem until the rate increase is high enough to affect productivity and disrupt work.

False Accept Rate   The false accept rate is the rate at which fraudulent users or nonusers are allowed access to systems or areas as a result of a failure in the biometric device. Such a failure is known as a Type II error or a false positive, and it represents a serious cybersecurity breach. Often, multiple authentication measures must be used to back up a device whose failure would otherwise result in erroneous authorization. The false accept rate is obviously more serious than the false reject rate. However, adjusting the sensitivity levels of most biometrics to reduce the false accept rate could dramatically increase the false reject rate and significantly hamper normal operations.

Crossover Error Rate   The crossover error rate (CER), also called the equal error rate, is the point at which the rate of false rejections equals the rate of false acceptances. The CER is considered the optimal outcome for biometric systems because it represents balance between the two error rates. CERs are commonly used to compare various biometrics but may vary by manufacturer. A biometric device that provides a CER of 1 percent is considered superior to one with a CER of 5 percent, for example.

Acceptability of Biometrics

A balance must be struck between the acceptability of a system to its users and the effectiveness of the system. Many of the reliable, effective biometric systems are perceived as intrusive by users. Organizations implementing biometrics must carefully balance a system's effectiveness against its perceived intrusiveness and acceptability to users. The rated effectiveness of a system is roughly inverse to its acceptability, as shown in Table 12-2. Since the technology came out, iris scanning has experienced a rapid growth in popularity due mainly to its use of inexpensive camera equipment and the acceptability of the technology. Iris scanners only

Table 12-2   Ranking of biometric effectiveness and acceptance[2]

Biometrics	Universality	Uniqueness	Permanence	Collectability	Performance	Acceptability	Circumvention
Face	H	L	M	H	L	H	L
Face Thermogram	H	H	L	H	M	H	H
Fingerprint	M	H	H	M	H	M	H
Hand Geometry	M	M	M	H	M	M	M
Hand Vein	M	M	M	M	M	M	H
Eye: Iris	H	H	H	M	H	H	H
Eye: Retina	H	H	M	L	H	L	H
DNA	H	H	H	L	H	L	L
Odor & Scent	H	H	H	L	L	M	L
Voice	M	L	L	M	L	H	L
Signature	L	L	L	H	L	H	L
Keystroke	L	L	L	M	L	M	M
Gait	M	L	L	H	L	H	M

need a snapshot of the eye rather than an intrusive scan. Even though iris scanning is ranked slightly lower than retinal scanning in terms of accuracy and effectiveness (as iris scanning results in more false negatives), it is believed to be the most generally accepted biometric.

Note 1 | For more information on using biometrics for identification and authentication, read Special Publication (SP) 800-76-2 by going to the website of the National Institute of Standards and Technology (NIST; https://csrc.nist.gov/publications/sp800) and clicking the document's link. You can also visit the Department of Homeland Security's Office of Biometric Identity Management site at www.dhs.gov/biometrics.

Self-Check

1. Technical controls alone can secure an IT environment.
   a. True
   b. False

2. Biometric authentication mechanisms use physiological characteristics to validate a person's identity.
   a. True
   b. False

3. The false accept rate is more serious than the false reject rate in biometric systems.
   a. True
   b. False

☐ Check your answers at the end of this chapter.

Managing Network Security

Typically, a large portion of the organization's information assets are accessible from its networks and possibly by users across the Internet. With the never-ending push to have information where you want it, when you want it, and how you want it, cybersecurity professionals are under increasing pressure to provide global access to information assets without sacrificing cybersecurity. Fortunately, many technologies support the protection of information assets across networks and the Internet, including firewalls, virtual private networks (VPNs), intrusion detection and prevention systems (IDPSs), wireless access points, network security protocols, and system scanning tools. Each of these is examined in this chapter.

Firewalls

In construction, a physical firewall is a concrete or masonry wall running from the basement through the roof to prevent fire from spreading. In the aircraft and automotive industries, a firewall is an insulated metal barrier that keeps the hot and dangerous moving parts of the engine separate from the passenger cabin. In cybersecurity, a firewall is the combination of hardware and software that filters or prevents specific information from moving between the outside network, known as the untrusted network (for example, the Internet), and the inside network, known as the trusted network. The firewall may be a separate computer system, a service running on an existing router or server, or a separate network segment containing several supporting devices.

Categories of Firewalls

Firewalls have made significant advances since their earliest implementations. While most firewalls are an amalgamation of various options, services, and capabilities, most are associated with one of the basic categories or types of firewalls. The most common types are packet filtering firewalls, application layer proxy firewalls, stateful packet inspection firewalls, and Unified Threat Management devices. Each of these is examined in turn.

Packet Filtering Firewalls   The first category of firewalls is the packet filtering firewall, a networking device that examines the header information of data packets that come into a network and determines whether to drop them (deny) or forward them to the next network connection (allow), based on its configuration rules. By examining every incoming and outgoing packet, the firewall can selectively filter (accepting or rejecting packets) based on the packet header fields, such as Internet Protocol (IP) address, type of packet, port request, and other elements present in the packet. Originally deployed as a router function, filtering examines packets for compliance with or violation of rules configured in the device's rule base. The rules most commonly implemented in packet filtering are based on a combination of IP source and destination address, direction (inbound or outbound), and source and destination port requests. Figure 12-5 shows how such a firewall typically works.

Figure 12-5   Packet filtering firewall

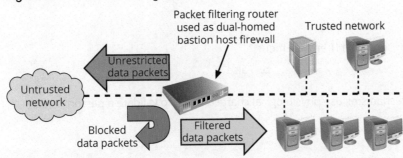

A network configured with the rules shown in Table 12-3 blocks inbound connection attempts by all computers or network devices in the 10.10.x.x address range. This first rule blocks traffic that is attempting to spoof an internal address and thus bypasses the firewall filters. Unfortunately, attackers can change the source (from) field and try to make it look like the packet is from the internal network (spoofing). The second rule is an example of a specific block, perhaps on traffic from an objectionable location; the rule effectively blacklists that external network from connecting to the network. The third rule could be used to allow an off-site administrator to directly access an internal system by the Secure File Transfer Protocol (SFTP). If the organization does not want to manage its devices from outside the perimeter (if, for example, it prefers to use a VPN), it can change this rule to explicitly deny any direct connection requests to the firewall itself from the outside. The next two rules would allow outside systems to access email and web servers, but only if using the appropriate protocols. The final rule, known as the cleanup rule, enforces an exclusionary policy that blocks all access that is not specifically allowed. This rule is sometimes implicitly included in a device and thus is not needed; in other systems, it should be included in the firewall rule set.

Table 12-3   Example of a packet filtering rule set

Source Address	Destination Address	Service Port	Action
10.10.x.x	Any	Any	Deny
192.168.x.x	10.10.x.x	Any	Deny
172.16.121.1	10.10.10.22	SFTP	Allow
Any	10.10.10.24	SMTP	Allow
Any	10.10.10.25	HTTP	Allow
Any	10.10.10.x	Any	Deny

Note: These rules apply to a network at 10.10.x.x. The table uses special, nonroutable IP addresses in the rules for this example. An actual firewall that connects to a public network would use real address ranges, at least on its externally focused rule sets.

Application Layer Proxy Firewalls The next category of firewalls is the application layer proxy firewall, a device capable of functioning both as a firewall and an application layer proxy server. The exact name and function of these devices can be confusing, as multiple terms have commonly been associated with them. An application layer proxy server is distinct from an application layer proxy firewall, which is different from an application layer firewall. What a particular device is capable of most commonly boils down to the implementation of technologies by the vendor. In the strictest sense, an application layer firewall or application-level firewall is a device capable of examining the application layer of network traffic (for example, HTTP, SMTP, and FTP) and filtering based on its header content rather than the traffic IP headers. It works like a packet filtering firewall but at the application layer of the Transmission Control Protocol/Internet Protocol (TCP/IP). A proxy server acts as an intermediary, intercepting requests for information from external users and providing the requested information by retrieving it from an internal server, thus protecting and minimizing the demand on internal servers. If such a server stores the most recently or most commonly accessed information in its internal cache to provide content to others accessing the same information, it may also be called a cache server. Many people consider a cache server to be a form of firewall, but a cache server does not filter; it only stores and provides requested content by obtaining it from the source on behalf of the client and archiving it for future needs. A proxy firewall, on the other hand, is a device that provides both firewall and proxy services. By extension, an application layer proxy server works between a client and the data server and focuses on one application or a small set of them, like webpages. It is now common in the market to refer to a firewall that provides application layer proxy services and packet filtering firewall services as an application layer proxy firewall.

When the firewall is configured with a network segment to intercept and direct filtered traffic to servers placed in the network segment and not inside the trusted network, it is considered deployed with a demilitarized zone, or DMZ—an intermediate area between a trusted network and an untrusted network that restricts access to internal systems. See Figure 12-8 later in this chapter for an example. Using this model, additional filtering devices are placed between the proxy server and internal systems, thereby restricting access to internal systems only to those connections that are made through the proxy server.

The primary disadvantage of application layer firewalls is that they are designed for a specific application layer protocol and cannot easily be reconfigured to work with other protocols. This requires additional application layer firewalls for each protocol set employed or an advanced model capable of multiprotocol filtering.

Stateful Packet Inspection Firewalls The third category of firewalls is a stateful packet inspection (SPI) firewall (also known as a dynamic packet filtering firewall), which keeps track of each network connection between internal and external systems using a state table and expedites the filtering of those communications. This device is also capable of dynamically changing its rule base to filter suspicious or malicious traffic. A state table is a record of the state and context of each packet in a conversation between an internal and external user or system; the state table records which station sent which packet and when. It is used to expedite traffic filtering. SPI firewalls perform packet filtering; however, unlike simple packet filtering firewalls, which merely allow or deny certain packets based on their addresses, an SPI firewall can speed up responses to internal requests. If the SPI firewall receives an incoming packet that does not match an entry in its state table, it defaults to performing traditional packet filtering against its rule base. If the traffic is allowed and becomes a conversation, the device updates its state table with the information.

Whereas static packet filtering firewalls are only able to interpret traffic based on manually configured rule sets, SPI firewalls can react to network traffic, adjusting their rule base content and sequence. They do so by understanding how the protocol functions and by opening and closing "holes" or "doors" in the firewall based on the information contained in the packet header, which allows specially screened packets to bypass the normal packet filtering rule set. Both SPI firewalls and application-level proxy firewalls are considered examples of dynamic packet filtering firewalls.

Unified Threat Management Devices One of the newest generations of firewalls isn't truly new at all, but a hybrid built from the capabilities of modern networking equipment that can perform a variety of tasks according to the organization's needs. These Unified Threat Management (UTM) devices are categorized by the ability to perform the work of multiple devices, such as stateful packet inspection firewalls, network intrusion detection and prevention systems, content filters, spam filters, and malware scanners and filters. UTM systems take advantage of increasing memory capacity and processor capability and can reduce the complexity associated with deploying, configuring, and integrating multiple networking devices. With the proper configuration, deep packet inspection (DPI) devices are able to examine multiple protocol headers and even the content of network traffic, all the way through the TCP/IP layers and including encrypted, compressed, or encoded data. The primary disadvantage of UTM systems is the creation of a single point of failure should the device experience technical issues or become the subject of an attack.[3]

Next-Generation (NextGen) Firewalls　Another recent development in firewall approaches is the Next-Generation Firewall, also known as NextGen or NGFW. Like UTM devices, NextGen firewalls combine traditional firewall functions with other network cybersecurity functions such as deep packet inspection, IDPSs, and the ability to decrypt encrypted traffic. The functions are so similar to those of UTM devices that the difference may lie only in the vendor's description. According to Kevin Beaver of Principle Logic, LLC, the difference may be only one of scope: "Unified Threat Management systems do a good job at a lot of things, while next-generation firewalls do an excellent job at just a handful of things."[4] Again, careful review of the solution's capabilities against the organization's needs will facilitate selection of the best equipment. Organizations with limited budgets may benefit from these "all-in-one" devices, while larger organizations with more staff and funding may prefer separate devices that can be managed independently and function more efficiently on their own platforms.

Firewall Implementation Architectures

Each of the firewall categories described here can be implemented in multiple architectural configurations. These configurations are sometimes mutually exclusive but sometimes can be combined. The configuration that works best for an organization depends on the uses of its network, the organization's ability to develop and implement the architectures, and the available budget. Although hundreds of variations exist, three architectural implementations of firewalls are especially common: single bastion hosts, screened-host firewalls, and screened-subnet firewalls.

Single Bastion Host Architecture　Most organizations with an Internet connection use some form of device between their internal networks and the external service provider. The single bastion host architecture is a firewall architecture in which a single device performing firewall duties, such as packet filtering, serves as the only perimeter protection between an organization's networks and the external network. As shown in Figure 12-5 earlier in this chapter, the single bastion host architecture can be implemented as a packet filtering router or it could be a firewall behind a router that is not configured for packet filtering.

Any network system, router, or firewall placed between an external untrusted network and an internal trusted network that is exposed to the untrusted network can be referred to as a bastion host. Also known as a sacrificial host, it serves as the sole target for attack and should therefore be thoroughly secured.

The bastion host is usually implemented as a dual-homed host, a network configuration in which a device contains two network interfaces: one that is connected to the external network and one that is connected to the internal network. All traffic must go through the device to move between the internal and external networks. Such an architecture lacks defense in depth, and the complexity of the access control lists used to filter the packets can grow and degrade network performance. An attacker who infiltrates the bastion host can discover the configuration of internal networks and possibly provide external sources with internal information.

A technology known as network-address translation (NAT) is often implemented with this architecture. NAT is a method of converting multiple, routable external IP addresses to special ranges of internal IP addresses, usually on a one-to-one basis; that is, one external valid address directly maps to one assigned internal address. A related approach, called port-address translation (PAT), converts a single external IP address to special ranges of internal IP addresses—that is, a one-to-many approach in which one address is mapped dynamically to a range of internal addresses by adding a unique port number when traffic leaves the private network and is placed on the public network. This unique number serves to identify which internal host is engaged in the specific network connection. The combination of the TCP/IP address and service port (known as a socket) is then easily mapped to the internal address. The socket is important because it helps allow packets to be delivered to the proper service location on a packet-switched network. Both NAT and PAT create a barrier to intrusion from outside the local network because the addresses that are then being used for the internal network cannot be used for traffic to be routed over the public network. These special, nonroutable addresses can be selected from three possible sets:

- Organizations that need very large numbers of local addresses can use the 10.x.x.x range, which has more than 16.5 million usable addresses.
- Organizations that need a moderate number of addresses can use the 192.168.x.x range, which has more than 65,500 addresses.
- Organizations with smaller needs can use the 172.16.0.0—172.16.15.0 range, which has approximately 4,000 usable addresses.

This approach has two disadvantages: If the dual-homed host is compromised, it can take out the connection to the external network, and as traffic volume increases, the dual-homed host can become overloaded. Compared to more complex solutions, though, this architecture provides strong protection with minimal expense. Figure 12-6 shows a typical configuration of a dual-homed host firewall that uses NAT or PAT and proxy access to protect the internal network.

Figure 12-6   Dual-homed bastion host firewall

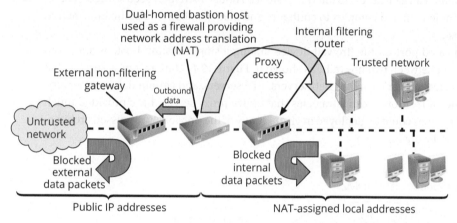

Screened-Host Architecture   The screened-host architecture combines the packet filtering router with a second, dedicated device, such as a proxy server or proxy firewall. This approach allows the router to screen packets to minimize the network traffic and load on the proxy, while the proxy examines an application layer protocol such as HTTP and performs the proxy services. To its advantage, a dual-homed screened host requires an external attack to compromise two separate systems before the attack can access internal data. Consequently, this configuration protects data more fully than a packet filtering router alone. Figure 12-7 shows a typical configuration of a screened-host architectural approach. Note that the bastion host could also be placed immediately behind the firewall in a dual-homed configuration.

Screened-Subnet Architecture   The screened-subnet architecture is a firewall model that consists of one or more internal bastion hosts located behind a packet filtering router on a dedicated network segment, with each host performing a role in protecting the trusted network. Many variants of the screened-subnet architecture exist. The first general model uses two filtering routers with one or more dual-homed bastion hosts between them, as was shown in Figure 12-6. In the second general model, illustrated in Figure 12-8, connections are routed as follows:

- Connections from the outside or untrusted network are routed through an external filtering router.
- Connections from the outside or untrusted network are routed into—and then out of—a routing firewall to the separate network segment known as the DMZ.
- Connections into the trusted internal network are allowed only from the DMZ bastion host servers.

Figure 12-7   Screened-host firewall

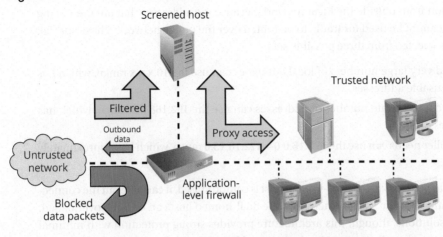

As depicted in Figure 12-8, the screened subnet is an entire network segment that performs two functions: It protects the DMZ systems and information from outside threats, and it protects the internal networks by limiting how external connections can gain access to internal systems. Though extremely secure, the screened subnet can be expensive to implement and complex to configure and manage; the value of the information it protects must justify the cost.

The DMZ can be a dedicated port on the firewall device linking a single bastion host, as shown in Figure 12-7, or it can be an area between two firewalls, as shown in Figure 12-8. Until recently, servers that provide services via the untrusted network, such as web servers, FTP servers, and certain database servers, were commonly placed in the DMZ. More recent strategies that utilize proxy servers have provided much more secure solutions. UTM systems could be deployed in virtually any of the previously discussed architectures according to the needs of the organization.

Figure 12-8   Screened subnet (DMZ)

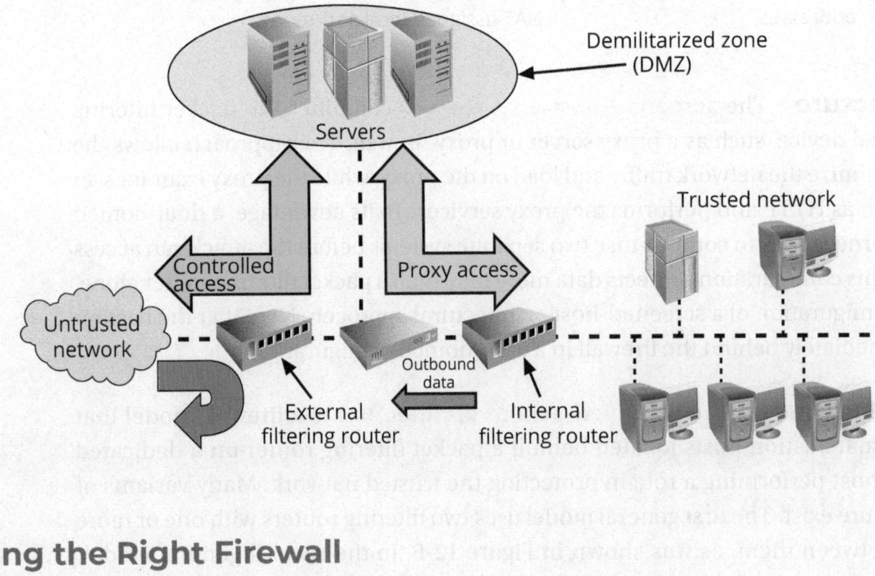

Selecting the Right Firewall

When evaluating a firewall for your networks, ask the following questions:

- What type of firewall technology offers the right balance between protection and cost for the needs of the organization?
- What features are included in the base price? What features are available at extra cost? Are all cost factors known?

- How easy is it to set up and configure the firewall? How accessible are the staff technicians who can competently configure the firewall?
- Can the candidate firewall adapt to the growing network in the organization?

The second question addresses an important issue: cost. A firewall's cost may put a certain make, model, or type out of reach for a particular cybersecurity solution. As with all cybersecurity decisions, the budgetary constraints stipulated by management must be considered. It is important to remember that the total cost of ownership for any piece of technology, including firewalls, will almost always greatly exceed the initial purchase price. The total cost of ownership (TCO) is a measurement of the true cost of a device or application, which includes not only the purchase price but annual maintenance or service agreements, upgrade fees, subscriptions, the cost to train personnel to manage the device or application, the cost of systems administrators, and the cost to protect it.

Content Filters

Another type of tool that effectively protects the organization's systems from misuse and unintentional denial-of-service (DoS) conditions across networks is the content filter. Although technically not a firewall, a content filter (or Internet filter) is a software program or hardware/software appliance that allows administrators to restrict content that comes into or leaves a network—for example, restricting user access to websites with material that is not related to business, such as pornography or entertainment. Another application is the restriction of spam email from outside sources. Content filters ensure that employees are not using network resources inappropriately. Unfortunately, these systems require extensive configuration and constant updating of the list of unacceptable destinations or restricted incoming email source addresses.

Managing Firewalls

Any firewall device—whether a packet filtering router, bastion host, or other firewall implementation—must have its own set of configuration rules that regulate its actions. With packet filtering firewalls, these rules may be simple statements regulating source and destination addresses, specific protocol or port usage requests, or decisions to allow or deny certain types of requests. In all cases, a policy for the implementation and configuration of a firewall should be developed and forwarded to the firewall team before it is made operable.

In practice, configuring firewall rule sets can be something of a nightmare. Logic errors in the preparation of the rules can cause unintended behavior, such as allowing access instead of denying it, specifying the wrong port or service type, or causing the network to misroute traffic. These and myriad other mistakes can turn a device designed to protect communications into a choke point. For example, a novice firewall administrator might improperly configure a virus-screening email gateway (think of it as a type of email firewall), resulting in the blocking of all incoming email instead of screening only email that contains malicious code. Each firewall rule must be carefully crafted, placed into the list in the proper sequence, debugged, and tested. A proper rule sequence ensures that the most resource-intensive actions are performed after the most restrictive ones, thereby reducing the number of packets that undergo intense scrutiny. Because of the complexity of the process, the impact of incorrect configuration, and the need to conform to organizational practices, all firewall rule changes must be subject to an organization's usual change control procedures. In addition, most organizations that need load balancing and high availability will use multiple independent devices for firewall rule application. These devices must be kept in synch.

The ever-present need to balance performance against restrictions imposed by cybersecurity practices is obvious in the use of firewalls. If users cannot work due to a cybersecurity restriction, then the cybersecurity administration will most likely be told by management to remove it. Organizations are much more willing to live with a potential risk than a failure to operate.

Using a computer to protect another computer is fraught with problems that must be managed by careful preparation and continuous evaluation. For the most part, automated control systems, including firewalls, cannot learn from mistakes or adapt to changing situations. They are limited by the constraints of their programming and rule sets in the following ways:

- Firewalls are not creative and cannot make sense of human actions outside the range of their programmed responses.

- They deal strictly with defined patterns of measured observation. These patterns are known to possible attackers and can be used to their benefit in an attack.
- Firewalls are computers themselves and are thus prone to programming errors, flaws in rule sets, and inherent vulnerabilities.
- They are designed to function within limits of hardware capacity and thus can only respond to patterns of events that happen in an expected and reasonably simultaneous sequence.
- Firewalls are designed, implemented, configured, and operated by people and are subject to the expected series of mistakes from human error.[5]

There are also several administrative challenges to the operation of firewalls:

- Training—Most managers think of a firewall as just another device, more or less like the computers already installed in the organization. If administrators get time to read manuals, they are lucky.
- Uniqueness—Suppose you have mastered your firewall, and now every new configuration requirement is just a matter of a few clicks in the Telnet window; however, each brand of firewall is different, so a new e-commerce project might require a new firewall running on a different operating system.
- Responsibility—Because you are the firewall guy, suddenly everyone assumes that anything to do with computer cybersecurity is your responsibility.
- Administration—Being a firewall administrator for a medium-sized or large organization should be a full-time job; however, that's hardly ever the case.[6]

Laura Taylor, chief technology officer and founder of Relevant Technologies, recommends the following practices for firewall use:

- All traffic from the trusted network is allowed out. This way, members of the organization can access the services they need. Filtering and logging outbound traffic is possible when indicated by specific organizational policy goals.
- The firewall device is never accessible directly from the public network. Almost all access to the firewall device is denied to internal users as well. Only authorized firewall administrators can access the device via secure authentication mechanisms, with preference for a method based on cryptographically strong authentication using two-factor access control techniques.
- Simple Mail Transport Protocol (SMTP) data is allowed to pass through the firewall, but all of it is routed to a well-configured SMTP gateway to filter and route messaging traffic securely.
- All Internet Control Message Protocol (ICMP) data is denied. Known as the ping service, this is a common method for hacker reconnaissance and should be turned off to prevent snooping.
- Telnet/terminal emulation access to all internal servers from the public networks is blocked. At the very least, Telnet access to the organization's Domain Name Service (DNS) server should be blocked to prevent illegal zone transfers and to prevent hackers from taking down the organization's entire network. If internal users need to reach an organization's network from outside the firewall, use a VPN client or other secure authentication system to allow this kind of access.
- When web services are offered outside the firewall, HTTP traffic is prevented from reaching your internal networks via the implementation of some form of proxy access or DMZ architecture. That way, if any employees are running web servers for internal use on their desktops, the services will be invisible to the outside Internet. If your web server is located behind the firewall, you need to allow HTTP or HTTPS (SHTTP) data through for the Internet at large to view it. The best solution is to place the web servers containing critical data inside the network and to use proxy services from a DMZ (screened network segment). It is also advisable to restrict incoming HTTP traffic to internal network addresses so that the traffic must be responding to requests originating at internal addresses. This restriction can be accomplished through NAT or firewalls that can support stateful inspection or are directed at the proxy server itself. All other incoming HTTP traffic should be blocked. If the web servers contain only advertising, they should be placed in the DMZ and rebuilt when (not if) they are compromised.[7]

Note 2 | For additional reading on firewalls and firewall management, visit https://www.sans.org/white-papers/ and search their white papers for articles on the subject.

Self-Check

4. Firewalls can only be implemented as separate computer systems.

   a. True
   b. False

5. Packet filtering firewalls examine the header information of data packets to determine whether to drop or forward them.

   a. True
   b. False

6. Unified Threat Management devices are limited to performing only firewall functions.

   a. True
   b. False

☐ Check your answers at the end of this chapter.

Intrusion Detection and Prevention Systems

Intrusion detection and prevention system (IDPS) is the general term for a system with the capability to detect intrusions and modify its configuration and environment to prevent intrusions. An IDPS encompasses the functions of both intrusion detection systems and intrusion prevention technology, and it works like a burglar alarm. When the system detects a violation—the IT equivalent of an opened or broken window or door—it activates the alarm. This alarm can be audible and visible (sound and lights), or it can be a silent alarm that sends a message to an administrator or a monitoring company. With almost all IDPSs, administrators can choose the configuration and alarm levels. Many IDPSs can be configured to notify administrators via email, phone, or text. The systems can also be configured to notify an external cybersecurity service organization, just as burglar alarms do. IDPSs combine tried-and-true detection methods from intrusion *detection* systems (IDSs) with the capability to react to changes in the environment, which is available in intrusion *prevention* technology. Because most modern technology in this category has the capability both to detect and prevent, the term "IDPS" is generally used to describe the devices or applications.

Systems that include intrusion prevention technology attempt to prevent an attack from succeeding by one of the following means:

- Stopping the attack by terminating the network connection or the attacker's user session
- Changing the cybersecurity environment by reconfiguring network devices (firewalls, routers, and switches) to block access to the targeted system
- Changing the attack's content to make it benign—for example, by removing an infected file attachment from an email before the email reaches the recipient

Intrusion prevention technologies can include a mechanism that severs the communications circuit, an extreme measure that may be justified when the organization is hit with a massive distributed DoS or malware-laden attack.

All IDPSs require complex configurations to provide the appropriate level of detection and response. These systems are either network-based to protect network information assets or host-based to protect server or client information assets. IDPSs use one of two basic detection methods: signature-based or anomaly-based. Figure 12-9 depicts two typical approaches to intrusion detection and prevention where IDPSs are used to monitor both network connection activity and current information states on host systems.

Host-Based IDPS

A host-based IDPS (HIDPS) resides on a particular computer or server known as the host and monitors activity only on that system. It is also known as a system integrity verifier, as it works by configuring and classifying various categories of systems and data files. In many cases, IDPSs provide only a few general levels of alert notification. For example, an administrator might configure an IDPS to report changes to certain folders, such as system folders (C:\Windows, perhaps), cybersecurity-related applications (C:\Tripwire), or critical data folders; at the same time, the IDPS might be instructed to ignore changes to other files (such as C:\Program Files\Office). Administrators might configure the system to instantly text or email them for high-priority alerts but to simply record lower-priority activity in a log. Most administrators are concerned only if unauthorized changes occur in sensitive areas. After all, applications frequently modify their internal files, such as dictionaries and configuration templates, and users constantly create, update, and delete their own data files. Unless the IDPS is precisely configured, these actions can generate a large volume of false alarms. Some organizations use a variable degree of reporting and recording detail. During times of routine operation, the system will alert for only urgent reasons and record for exceptions. During periods of increased threat, however, it may send alerts on suspicious activity and record all activity for later analysis.

Figure 12-9   Intrusion detection and prevention systems

Host IDPS: Examines the data in files stored on the host and alerts systems administrators to any changes

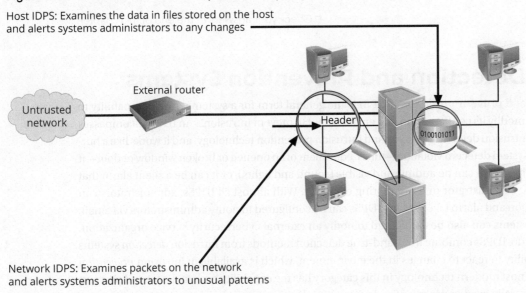

Network IDPS: Examines packets on the network and alerts systems administrators to unusual patterns

Host-based IDPSs can monitor multiple computers simultaneously. They do so by storing an agent on each monitored system (host) and then making that agent report back to the master console, which is usually located on the system administrator's computer or a special server. This master console monitors the information from the managed systems and notifies the administrator when predetermined attack conditions occur.

Network-Based IDPS

In contrast to host-based IDPSs, which reside on a host (or hosts) and monitor only activities on that host, a network-based IDPS (NIDPS) resides on a computer or appliance connected to a segment of an organization's network and monitors traffic on that segment for indications of attacks. When a predefined condition occurs, the network-based IDPS notifies the appropriate administrator. Whereas host-based IDPSs look for changes in file attributes (create, modify, delete), the network-based IDPS looks for patterns in network traffic, such as large collections of related traffic that can indicate a DoS attack, a series of related packets that could indicate a port scan in progress, or files with a specific header or attachment that could signal a malware attack. Consequently, network IDPSs require a much more complex configuration and maintenance program than host-based IDPSs. Network IDPSs must match network traffic against their knowledge base to determine whether an attack is under way. These systems yield many more false-positive readings than do host-based IDPSs because they are attempting to read the network activity pattern to determine whether it is "normal" or not.

Most organizations that implement an IDPS solution install data collection sensors that are both host-based and network-based. A system of this type is called a hybrid IDPS, and it usually includes a provision to concentrate event notifications from all sensors into a central repository for analysis. The analysis makes use of signature-based or anomaly-based detection techniques, or it might use both.

Signature-Based IDPS

IDPSs that use signature-based methods work like antivirus software. In fact, antivirus software can be classified as a form of signature-based IDPS. A signature-based IDPS, also known as a knowledge-based IDPS, examines data traffic for something that matches the signatures of preconfigured, predetermined attack patterns. The problem with this approach is that the signatures must be continually updated as new attack strategies emerge. Failure to stay current allows attacks using new strategies to succeed. Another weakness of this method is the time frame over which attacks occur. If attackers are slow and methodical, they may slip undetected through the IDPS because their actions may not match a signature that includes factors based on duration of the events. The only way to resolve this dilemma is to collect and analyze data over longer periods of time, which requires substantially larger data storage ability and additional processing capacity.

Anomaly-Based IDPS

Another popular type of IDPS is the anomaly-based IDPS (formerly called a statistical anomaly-based IDPS), which is also known as a behavior-based IDPS. The anomaly-based IDPS first collects data from normal traffic and establishes a baseline. It then periodically samples network activity using statistical methods and compares the samples to the baseline. When the activity falls outside the baseline parameters (known as the clipping level, a predefined assessment level that triggers a predetermined response when surpassed), the IDPS notifies the administrator, records the event in a log file, or performs additional actions. The baseline variables can include a host's memory or CPU usage, network packet types, and packet quantities.

The advantage of this approach is that the system can detect new types of attacks because it looks for abnormal activity of any type. Unfortunately, these IDPSs require much more overhead and processing capacity than signature-based versions because they must constantly attempt to match the pattern of activity to the baseline. In addition, they may not detect minor changes to system variables and may generate many false-positive warnings. If the actions of users or systems on the network vary widely, with unpredictable periods of low-level and high-level activity, this type of IDPS may not be suitable because it will almost certainly generate false alarms. As a result, it is more difficult to configure than the signature-based approach.

Managing Intrusion Detection and Prevention Systems

As with any alarm system, if there is no response to an IDPS alert, it does no good. An IDPS does not remove or deny access to a system by default; unless it is programmed to take action, it merely records the events that trigger it. IDPSs must be configured using adequate technical, business, and cybersecurity knowledge to differentiate between routine operations or traffic and low, moderate, or severe threats to the organization's information assets.

A properly configured IDPS can translate a cybersecurity alert into different types of notification—for example, log entries for low-level alerts, emails for moderate-level alerts, and text messages or system banners or pop-ups for severe alerts. Some organizations may configure systems to automatically act in response to IDPS alerts, although this technique should be carefully considered and undertaken only by organizations with experienced staff and well-constructed cybersecurity procedures. A poorly configured IDPS may yield information overload, causing the IDPS administrator to mute or ignore a continuous stream of alert messages or to fail to detect an actual attack. This can be called alert fatigue. When a system is configured to take unsupervised action without obtaining human approval, the organization must be prepared to take accountability for the IDPS's actions.

Alert fatigue and other human responses to false alarms can lead to behavior that could be exploited by attackers. For example, consider the following tactic—a car theft strategy that exploits people's intolerance for technological glitches that cause false alarms. In the early-morning hours—say, 2:00 a.m.—a thief deliberately sets off the target car's alarm and then retreats a safe distance. The owner comes out, resets the alarm, and goes back to bed. A half-hour later, the thief does it again, and then again. After the third or fourth time, the owner assumes that the alarm is faulty and turns it off, leaving the vehicle unprotected. The thief is then free to steal the car without having to deal with the now-disabled alarm.

Most IDPSs monitor systems by means of agents. An **agent** (sometimes called a **sensor**) is a piece of software that resides on a system and reports back to a management application or server. If this piece of software is not properly configured and does not use a secure transmission channel to communicate with its manager, an attacker could compromise and subsequently exploit the agent or the information from the agent.

A valuable tool in managing an IDPS is the consolidated enterprise management service. This software allows the cybersecurity professional to collect data from multiple host-based and network-based IDPSs and look for patterns across systems and network segments. An attacker might potentially probe one network segment or computer host and then move on to another target before the first system's IDPS has caught on. The consolidated management service not only collects responses from all IDPSs, providing a central monitoring station, it can identify these cross-system probes and intrusions.

Note 3 | For more information on IDPSs, read NIST SP 800-94, "Guide to Intrusion Detection and Prevention Systems," which is available at https://csrc.nist.gov/publications/sp800.

Self-Check

7. An IDPS can only notify administrators via email.

   a. True   **b.** False

8. A host-based IDPS can monitor multiple computers simultaneously.

   a. True   **b.** False

9. An anomaly-based IDPS requires more overhead and processing capacity than a signature-based IDPS.

   a. True   **b.** False

☐ Check your answers at the end of this chapter.

Wireless Networking Protection

The use of wireless network technology is an area of concern for cybersecurity professionals. Most organizations that have wireless networks use an implementation based on the 802.11 protocol from the Institute of Electrical and Electronics Engineers (IEEE). A wireless network provides a low-cost alternative to a wired network because it does not require the difficult and often expensive installation of cable in an existing structure. The downside is the management of the wireless network **footprint**—the geographic area in which there is sufficient signal strength to make a network connection. The size of the footprint depends on the amount of power emitted by the transmitter/receiver's **wireless access point (WAP)**—the device used to connect wireless networking users and their devices to the rest of the organization's networks. A WAP is also known as a Wi-Fi router. Sufficient power must exist to ensure high-quality connections within the intended area, but users outside the organization should not be able to receive the connections.

War driving is an attacker technique of moving through a geographic area or building while actively scanning for open or unsecured WAPs. In some cities, groups of war-drivers move through an area and mark locations of unsecured wireless access with chalk (a practice called war-chalking). There are specific encryption protocols that can be used to secure wireless networks; the most common is the Wi-Fi Protected Access family of protocols. Its predecessor, unfortunately still in use, is Wired Equivalent Privacy, which is considered by most observers to be insecure and easily breached.

Wired Equivalent Privacy

Wired Equivalent Privacy (WEP) is a set of protocols designed to provide a basic level of cybersecurity protection to wireless networks and to prevent unauthorized access or eavesdropping. WEP is part of the IEEE 802.11 wireless networking standard. However, WEP does not protect users from each other; it only protects the network from unauthorized users. In the early 2000s, cryptologists found several fundamental flaws in WEP, resulting in vulnerabilities that could be exploited to gain access. These vulnerabilities ultimately led to the replacement of WEP with WPA as the industry standard.

Wi-Fi Protected Access

Created by an industry group called the Wi-Fi Alliance, Wi-Fi Protected Access (WPA) is a set of protocols used to secure wireless networks. It was developed as an intermediate solution until the IEEE 802.11i standards were fully developed. IEEE 802.11i has been implemented in products such as WPA2 and WPA3. It is an amendment to the 802.11 standard published in June 2004, specifying cybersecurity protocols for wireless networks. While WPA works with virtually all wireless network cards, it is not compatible with some older WAPs. WPA2 and WPA3, on the other hand, may have compatibility issues with older wireless network cards. Compared to WEP, WPA systems provide increased capabilities for authentication and encryption as well as increased throughput.

Unlike WEP, WPA systems can use an IEEE 802.1X authentication server. This type of authentication server can issue keys to users who have been authenticated by the local system. The alternative is to allow all users to share a predefined password or passphrase known as a preshared key. Use of these keys is convenient but not as secure as other authentication techniques. WPA also uses a message integrity code (a type of message authentication code) to prevent certain types of attacks. Before being officially replaced by WPA2 in 2006, WPA was the strongest possible mechanism that was backward-compatible with older systems, as implemented using the Temporal Key Integrity Protocol. WPA2 introduced newer, more robust cybersecurity protocols based on the Advanced Encryption Standard, which is discussed later in this chapter.

WPA3 is the current generation of Wi-Fi security; it was announced by the Wi-Fi Alliance in 2018 with the requirement that all devices support WPA3 by 2020. The WPA3 standard is currently incorporated in virtually all Wi-Fi devices and should be used when available because it permits the use of improved encryption protocols. WPA3 offers the following enhancements over WPA and WPA2:

- Increased protection for passwords. Attackers are no longer able to record wireless traffic and then attempt to break passwords offline. The new WPA3 systems require direct interaction for password submission (and guessing).
- Increased data protection. Using a process called forward secrecy, WPA3 provides additional protection for encrypted data, preventing attackers from using a newly discovered password to crack older recorded and encrypted data.
- Wi-Fi Easy Connect. This feature simplifies the connection process by providing a QR code to support device registration.
- Increased security for public Wi-Fi. WPA3's Wi-Fi Certified Enhanced Open certification will provide encryption for open networks, improving security and confidentiality.
- Enhanced enterprise mode. Organizations using WPA3 can employ stronger encryption for their wireless networks, including an enhanced mode that employs minimum-strength security protocols and cryptographic protection.

Next-Generation Wireless Protocols

Robust Secure Network (RSN) is a protocol for establishing secure communications over an 802.11 wireless network. It is a part of the 802.Hi standard. RSN uses the Advanced Encryption Standard (AES) along with 802.1x and Extensible Authentication Protocol. RSN extends AES with the Counter Mode CBC MAC Protocol. AES supports key lengths of up to 256 bits, but it is not compatible with older hardware.

A specification called Transitional Security Network allows RSN and WEP to coexist on the same wireless local area network (WLAN). Note, however, that a WLAN on which devices still use WEP is not optimally secured. The RSN protocol functions as follows:

1. The wireless network interface card (NIC) sends a probe request.
2. The wireless access point sends a probe response with an RSN Information Exchange (IE) frame.
3. The wireless NIC requests authentication via one of the approved methods.
4. The wireless access point provides authentication for the wireless NIC.
5. The wireless NIC sends an association request with an RSN IE frame.
6. The wireless access point sends an association response.[8]

Bluetooth

Bluetooth is a de facto industry standard for short-range wireless communications between a wide range of computers, mobile devices, and accessories. Bluetooth's wireless communications can be exploited by anyone within its approximately 30-foot range unless suitable cybersecurity controls are implemented. The standard continues to increase in popularity; it has been estimated that almost 1 billion Bluetooth-enabled devices will be in use by the end of the decade. In discoverable mode—which allows other Bluetooth systems to detect and connect—devices can easily be accessed. Even in nondiscoverable mode, a device is susceptible to access by other devices that have connected with it in the past.

By default, Bluetooth does not authenticate connections; however, it does implement some degree of cybersecurity when devices access certain services, such as dial-up accounts and local area file transfers. Paired devices—usually a computer or a phone and a peripheral that a user plans to connect to it—require that the same passkey be entered on both devices. This key is used to generate a session key for all future communications. The only way to secure Bluetooth-enabled devices is to incorporate a twofold approach: (1) turn off Bluetooth when you do not intend to use it and (2) do not accept an incoming pairing request unless you know who the requester is.

Managing Wireless Connections

Users and organizations can use a variety of measures to implement a secure wireless network. These safeguards include the wireless cybersecurity protocols mentioned earlier, VPNs, and firewalls. It is also possible to restrict network access to a preapproved set of media access control addresses on a wireless network card. This is especially easy in small or personal networks where all possible users are known.

One of the first management requirements for wireless networks is to regulate the size of the network footprint. The initial step is to determine the best locations for placement of the WAPs. In addition, by using radio-strength meters, network administrators can adjust the power of the broadcast antennae to provide sufficient but not excessive coverage. This is especially important in areas where public access is possible.

WEP used to be the first choice in network installation and is still available as an option on many technologies, but WPA3 is preferred.

Note 4 | For more information on wireless networking and cybersecurity, visit the Wi-Fi Alliance website at www.wi-fi.org.

Self-Check

10. Wireless networks that use the IEEE 802.11 protocol are generally more expensive to install than wired networks.

    a. True   **b.** False

11. Wired Equivalent Privacy protects users on a wireless network from unauthorized access and each other.

    a. True   **b.** False

12. WPA3 offers increased data protection by using forward secrecy, which prevents attackers from using a newly discovered password to crack older recorded and encrypted data.

    a. True   **b.** False

☐ Check your answers at the end of this chapter.

Scanning and Analysis Tools

The previous section covered wireless network controls. Now we return to the technology and tools that are useful in all networks. Although they are not always perceived as defensive tools, scanners, sniffers, and other analysis tools enable cybersecurity administrators to see what an attacker sees. Scanner and analysis tools can find vulnerabilities in systems, in their cybersecurity components, and in unsecured points on the network. Unfortunately, they cannot detect the unpredictable behavior of people.

Some of these devices are extremely complex; others are very simple. Some are expensive commercial products; others are available for free from their creators. Conscientious administrators will have several hacking websites bookmarked and will frequently browse for discussions about new vulnerabilities, recent conquests, and favorite assault techniques. There is nothing wrong with cybersecurity administrators taking advantage of tools used by hackers to examine their own defenses and search out areas of vulnerability. A word of caution, however: Many of these tools have distinct signatures, and some service providers scan for these signatures. If a service provider discovers someone using hacker tools across their service, they may choose to deny access to that customer and discontinue the service. It is best to establish a working relationship with service providers and notify them before using such tools on networks and systems outside your organization's control.

Scanning tools collect the information that an attacker needs to succeed. Collecting information about a potential target is done through a research process known as footprinting—the organized investigation of Internet addresses owned or controlled by a target organization (not to be confused with the wireless footprint described earlier). Attackers may use public Internet data sources to perform keyword searches and identify the network addresses of an organization. They may also use the organization's webpage to find information that can be used in social engineering attacks. For example, the Reveal Source option on most popular web browsers allows users to see the source code behind a webpage.

The next phase of the pre-attack data-gathering process is fingerprinting, the systematic survey of a targeted organization's Internet addresses collected during the footprinting phase to identify the network services offered by the hosts in that range. The discussions of these tools are necessarily brief; to attain true expertise in the use and configuration of these tools, you will need more advanced education and training.

Port Scanners

Port scanners are tools used both by attackers and defenders to identify or fingerprint active computers on a network, the active ports and services on those computers, the functions and roles of the machines, and other useful information. These tools can scan for specific types of computers, protocols, or resources or perform generic scans. It is helpful to understand your network environment so that you can select the best tool for the job. The more specific the scanner is, the more detailed and useful the information it provides. However, you should keep a broadly focused scanner in your toolbox as well to help locate and identify rogue nodes on the network that administrators may not be aware of.

The first step in securing a system is to secure open ports. Why? Simply put, an open port can be used to send commands to a computer, gain access to a server, and exert control over a networking device. As a rule, you should secure all ports and remove from service any ports not required for essential functions. For instance, if an organization does not host web services, there is no need for ports 80, 443, or 8443 to be available in its network or on its servers.

Vulnerability Scanners

A vulnerability scanner is an application that examines systems connected to networks and their network traffic to identify exposed usernames and groups, open network shares, configuration problems, and other vulnerabilities in servers. One well-known and respected vulnerability scanner is Nmap, a professional freeware utility available from www.insecure.org/nmap. Nmap identifies the systems available on a network, the services (ports) each system is offering, the operating system and version they are running, the type of packet filters and firewalls in use, and dozens of other characteristics. Several commercial vulnerability scanners are available as well, including products from Tenable (Nessus), Rapid7 (Metasploit and Nexpose), and Invicti Security (Invicti).

Packet Sniffers

A packet sniffer can provide a network administrator with valuable information to help diagnose and resolve networking issues. In the wrong hands, it can be used to eavesdrop on network traffic. Commercially available and open-source sniffers include Sniffer, Snort, and Wireshark. Wireshark is an excellent, free network protocol analyzer that allows administrators to examine both live network traffic and previously captured data. This application offers a variety of features, including language filters and a TCP session reconstruction utility.

To use a packet sniffer effectively, you must be connected directly to a local network from an internal location. Simply tapping into any public Internet connection will flood you with more data than you can process, and technically it constitutes a violation of wiretapping laws. To use a packet sniffer legally, you must satisfy the following criteria:

1. Be on a network that the organization owns, not leases.
2. Be under the direct authorization of the network's owners.
3. Have the knowledge and consent of the content creators (users).
4. Have a justifiable business reason for doing so.

If all four conditions are met, you can look at anything you want captured on the network. If not, you can only selectively collect and analyze packets using packet header information to identify and diagnose network problems. Conditions 1, 2, and 4 are self-explanatory, and condition 3 is usually a stipulation for using the company network. Incidentally, these conditions are the same as for employee monitoring in general.

Trap and Trace

Trap and trace applications are another set of technologies that combine the function of honey pots or honey nets with the capability to track an attacker back through the network. Trap function software entices attackers to illegally access the internal areas of a network and determine who they are. While perusing, these attackers discover indicators of particularly rich content areas on the network, but these areas are set up specifically to attract attackers. The software distracts the attacker while notifying the administrator of the intrusion.

The accompaniment to the trap is the trace. Similar in concept to telephone caller ID service, the trace is a process by which the organization attempts to determine the identity of someone discovered in unauthorized areas of the network or systems. However, you must understand that it is a violation of the Electronic Communications Protection Act to trace communications *outside* of networks owned by the organization. Use of any trap and trace functions requires compliance with the same four rules as packet sniffers.

The U.S. government defines a trap and trace device as a pen register in U.S. Code Title 18, Section 3127:

> The term "pen register" means a device or process which records or decodes dialing, routing, addressing, or signaling information transmitted by an instrument or facility

from which a wire or electronic communication is transmitted, provided, however, that such information shall not include the contents of any communication, but such term does not include any device or process used by a provider or customer of a wire or electronic communication service for billing, or recording as an incident to billing, for communications services provided by such provider or any device or process used by a provider or customer of a wire communication service for cost accounting or other like purposes in the ordinary course of its business.

The term "trap and trace device" means a device or process which captures the incoming electronic or other impulses which identify the originating number or other dialing, routing, addressing, and signaling information reasonably likely to identify the source of a wire or electronic communication, provided, however, that such information shall not include the contents of any communication."[9]

Note that these definitions explicitly exclude the content of communications and only focus on the header information to trace the origins of communications. Unlike packet sniffers, trap and trace devices are mainly used by law enforcement to identify the origin of communications for legal and prosecution purposes.

Managing Scanning and Analysis Tools

It is vitally important that the cybersecurity manager be able to see the organization's systems and networks from the viewpoint of potential attackers. Therefore, the cybersecurity manager should develop a program, using in-house resources, contractors, or an outsourced service provider, to periodically scan the organization's systems and networks for vulnerabilities using the same tools a hacker might use.

There are several drawbacks to using scanners and analysis tools, content filters, and trap and trace tools:

- These tools are not human and thus cannot simulate the more creative behavior of a human attacker.

- Most tools function by pattern recognition, so only previously known issues can be detected. New approaches, modifications to well-known attack patterns, and the randomness of human behavior can cause misdiagnoses, thereby allowing vulnerabilities to go undetected or threats to go unchallenged.

- Most of these tools are computer-based software or hardware and so are prone to errors, flaws, and vulnerabilities of their own.

- All these tools are designed, configured, and operated by humans and are subject to human errors.

- You get what you pay for. The use of "hackerware" may infect a system with a virus or open the system to outside attacks or other unintended consequences. Always view a hacker kit skeptically before using it and especially before connecting it to the Internet. Never put anything valuable on the computer that houses the hacker tools. Consider segregating it from other network segments and disconnect it from the network when not in use.

- Specifically for content filters, some governments, agencies, institutions, and universities have established policies or laws that protect the individual user's right to access content, especially if it is necessary for the conduct of their job. There are also situations in which an entire class of content has been proscribed and mere possession of that content is a criminal act—for example, child pornography.

- Tool usage and configuration must comply with an explicitly articulated policy as well as the law, and the policy must provide for valid exceptions. This mandate prevents administrators from becoming arbiters of morality as they create a filter rule set.[10]

Note 5 | For lists and reviews of scanning and analysis tools, perform web searches for the "Open Source Network Security Tools," the "Open Source Security and Risk Analysis Report," and "Top network and scanning tools" for the current year.

Self-Check

13. Port scanners are used exclusively by attackers to identify active computers and services on a network.

 a. True   **b.** False

14. A vulnerability scanner can only identify configuration problems in servers.

 a. True   **b.** False

15. Using hacker tools to examine an organization's defenses is acceptable if done responsibly.

 a. True   **b.** False

               ☐ Check your answers at the end of this chapter.

Managing Server-Based Systems with Logging

Some systems are configured to record a common set of data by default; other systems must be configured to have logging activated. Log files, or logs, are collections of data stored by a system and used by administrators to audit system performance. This data is used both by authorized and unauthorized users. Table 12-4 illustrates log data categories and types of data normally collected during logging. To protect the log data, you must ensure that the servers that create and store the logs are secure.

Table 12-4 Log data categories and types of data

Category	Data Type
Network performance	• Total traffic load in and out over time (packet, byte, and connection counts) and by event (new product or service release) • Traffic load (percentage of packets, bytes, connections) in and out over time sorted by protocol, source address, destination address, and other packet header data • Error counts on all network interfaces
Other network data	• Service initiation requests • Name of the user or host requesting the service • Network traffic (packet headers) • Successful connections and connection attempts (protocol, port, source, destination, time) • Connection duration • Connection flow (sequence of packets from initiation to termination) • States associated with network interfaces (up, down) • Network sockets currently open • Mode of network interface card (promiscuous or not) • Network probes and scans • Results of administrator probes
System performance	• Total resource use over time (CPU, memory used and free, percentage of disk used and free) • Status and errors reported by systems and hardware devices • Changes in system status, including shutdowns and restarts • File system status (where mounted, free space by partition, open files, biggest file) over time and at specific times

(Continues)

Table 12-4   Log data categories and types of data (*Continued*)

Category	Data Type
	• File system warnings (low free space, too many open files, file exceeding allocated size) • Disk counters (input/output, queue lengths) over time and at specific times • Hardware availability (modems, network interface cards, memory)
Other system data	• Actions requiring special privileges • Successful and failed logins • Modem activities • Presence of new services and devices • Configuration of resources and devices
Process performance	• Amount of resources used (CPU, memory, disk, time) by specific processes over time • Top resource-consuming processes • System and user processes and services executing at any given time
Other process data	• User executing the process • Process start-up time, arguments, filenames • Process exit status, time, duration, resources consumed • Means by which each process is normally initiated (by an administrator, other users, or other programs or processes) and with what authorization and privileges • Devices used by specific processes • Files currently open by specific processes
Files and directories	• List of files, directories, and attributes • Cryptographic checksums for all files and directories • Information about file access operations (open, create, modify, execute, delete) as well as their time and date • Changes to file sizes, contents, protections, types, and locations • Changes to access control lists on system tools • Additions and deletions of files and directories • Results of virus scanners
Users	• Login and logout information (location, time): successful attempts, failed attempts, attempted logins to privileged accounts • Login and logout information on remote access servers that appears in modem logs • Changes in user identity • Changes in authentication status (such as enabling privileges) • Failed attempts to access restricted information (such as password files) • Keystroke monitoring logs • Violations of user quotas
Applications and services	• Application information, such as network traffic (packet content), mail logs, FTP logs, web server logs, modem logs, firewall logs, SNMP logs, DNS logs, intrusion detection system logs, and database management system logs • FTP file transfers and connection statistics • Web connection statistics, including pages accessed, credentials of the requester, user requests over time, most requested pages, and identities of requesters • Mail sender, receiver, size, and tracing information for mail requests • Mail server statistics, including number of messages over time and number of queued messages • DNS questions, answers, and zone transfers • File server transfers over time • Database server transactions over time

According to NIST, log management infrastructure involves two tiers, each with its own subtasks: log generation and log analysis and storage.[11]

Log Generation

Log generation involves the configuration of systems to create logs as well as configuration changes needed to consolidate the logs. This typically requires activating logging on the various servers and defining where to store logging data, either locally on the system that generates the logs or on an alternative such as a centralized log analysis system. Issues in log generation include the following:

- Multiple log sources—The diversity of systems that generate logs can result in issues. For example, some servers generate multiple logs, such as Microsoft's application, system, security, and setup logs that are prevalent in most Windows operating systems. Some logs consist of pieces of information collected from multiple sources, such as from network monitoring agents. The reintegration of the data collected from these logs can also cause issues in log consolidation.

- Inconsistent log content—What gets stored in a log may depend on options chosen by the operating system developer or the systems administrator. Some systems allow the administrator to specify what gets logged, but this content is predefined in other systems.

- Inconsistent timestamps—In addition to the fact that dates and times in logs may be formatted differently, servers that are not associated with a central time server or service may result in different times recorded for events that are simultaneous. If an incident hits multiple servers in a particular sequence but the timestamps on those machines are off by a few seconds or even fractions of a second, it becomes much more difficult to analyze the incident.

- Inconsistent log format—Because many different systems create logs, the structure and content of those logs may differ dramatically. Even a simple data element such as a date can be stored in different formats. For example, the standard for storing dates in the United States is Month, Day, Year (MMDDYYYY), but the standard used in many European countries is Day, Month, Year (DDMMYYYY). Some systems store ports by number, others by name.

To interpret data from the log generation tier of log management infrastructure, the following functions must be addressed:

- Log parsing—The division of data within logs into specific values, as some logs may consist of a solid stream of data

- Event filtering—The separation of "items of interest" from the rest of the data that the log collects

- Event aggregation—The consolidation of similar entries or related events within a log; aggregation is critical for the organization to be able to handle the thousands of data points multiple servers will generate[12]

Log Analysis and Storage

Log analysis and storage is the transference of log data to an analysis system that may or may not be separate from the system that collects the log data. Collectively, systems of this type are known as security event information management (SEIM) systems. SEIM systems are log management systems specifically tasked to collect log data from multiple servers or other network devices for the purpose of interpreting, filtering, correlating, analyzing, storing, and reporting the data.

Important management functions within log storage include the following:

- Log rotation—The file-level management of logs (for example, when a single log file is closed and another started), usually done on a set schedule

- Log archival—The backup and storage of logs based on policy or legal and regulatory requirements; this function includes log retention (the routine storage of all logs for a specified duration) and log preservation (the saving of logs of particular interest based on content)

- Log compression—The reduction in file size of logs to save drive space, using compression formats like zip, tar, or RAR

- Log reduction—The removal of unimportant or uneventful log entries to reduce the size of a log file, also known as "event reduction"
- Log conversion—The modification of the format or structure of a log file to allow it to be accessed by another application, such as an analysis tool
- Log normalization—The standardization of log file structures and formats using log conversion
- Log file integrity—The determination of whether the log files have been modified, usually through the message digest or hashes

Important management functions within log analysis include the following:

- Event correlation—The association of multiple log file entries according to a predefined event or activity
- Log viewing—The display of log data in a form that is easily understandable by humans; usually it involves adding field data
- Log reporting—The display of the results of log analysis

Managing Logs

The final responsibility within this tier is the management of the logs once they are moved to storage. Log disposal or log clearing is the specification of when logs may be deleted or overwritten within a system, whether you are referring to the system that generated the logs or the system that stores and analyzes them.[13] General suggestions for managing logs include:

- Make sure that data stores can handle the amount of data generated by the configured logging activities. Some systems may generate multiple gigabytes of data for each hour of operation.
- Rotate logs when unlimited data storage is not possible. Some systems overwrite older log entries with newer entries to accommodate space limitations. Log rotation settings must be configured for your system, which may require modifying the default settings.
- Archive the logs. Log systems can copy logs periodically to remote storage locations. There is no set requirement for how long log files should be retained. Some argue that log files may be subpoenaed during legal proceedings and thus should be routinely destroyed as soon as possible to prevent unwanted disclosure. Others argue that the information gained from analyzing legacy and archival logs outweighs the risk. Still others propose aggregating the log information and then destroying the individual entries. Regardless of the method employed, policies and plans must be in place to handle these files.
- Secure the logs. Archived logs should be encrypted to prevent unwanted disclosure if the log data store is compromised. This should also protect the integrity of the log data, as many attackers will seek to delete or obfuscate log data to cover the tracks of the attack.
- Destroy logs. Once log data has outlived its usefulness, it should be securely destroyed.[14]

Self-Check

16. Logs can only be generated by systems that are specifically configured to do so.
    - **a.** True
    - **b.** False

17. Log archival involves reducing the file size of logs to save drive space.
    - **a.** True
    - **b.** False

18. Event aggregation is the process of consolidating similar entries or related events within a log.
    - **a.** True
    - **b.** False

☐ Check your answers at the end of this chapter.

Managing Cybersecurity for Emerging Technologies

IT is subject to ongoing evolution as organizations implement information systems to remain competitive. Cybersecurity professionals are expected to understand innovations in the field and take the actions necessary to implement new technologies in secure ways. This can be quite challenging, as there will be expectations for flexible and rapid deployment with little time to study the vulnerabilities and exposures introduced by the new technologies.

When a cybersecurity team is faced with a new technology, whether it is an advance in IT, cybernetics, or cybersecurity-related controls, they should adopt a supportive approach that asks one fundamental question: Do the benefits of the proposed technology justify the expected costs of implementing that technology? The team should take a holistic approach and look at all possible benefits (financial and other) as well as examine the TCO of the new technology, including acquisition, implementation, maintenance, and eventual retirement. Those costs must include any additional risk control requirements that are mandated by the new technology. The added cost of cybersecurity for any new technology should consider how the proposed solution will affect the organization's risk exposure and how that risk exposure will be treated.

Bring-Your-Own Devices (BYOD) Using Network Access Control

Recent trends in supplier collaboration and increasing user mobility have led companies to open their networks to third parties and employees. Using nonstandard smart devices to perform workplace activities has enabled organizations to move from a network used only by employees, with a single standard device per user, to a much more open network environment that can support multiple nonstandard devices per user and include vendors, event clients, and other third parties. In addition, these devices may or may not be issued and controlled by the company. To manage these trends, many organizations have turned to network access control (NAC) technology.

A properly deployed NAC will enable administrators to define and control how devices and users access resources from the organization's network. To be most effective, a NAC must offer scalable capacity, be vendor-neutral, support wired and wireless-enabled delivery, and offer multiple deployment options, including physical and virtual appliances as well as cloud services. More importantly, a NAC needs to communicate and exchange information with all network devices rather than require an access control solution for each network segment. Several vendors offer products to meet such needs in this relatively mature segment of cybersecurity tools.

Embedded Systems and the Internet of Things

Computing devices have become pervasive, long ago leaving the data center and now going beyond personal and laptop computers. Embedded systems are now found in a wide range of devices, and securing them has become a concern. When supervisory control and data acquisition (SCADA) solutions began to be used in manufacturing and facilities management, they were often deployed on separate, private networks. For reasons of economics and convenience, SCADA and other embedded systems have been merged into a common network infrastructure with information processing systems. As a result, many organizations are now struggling to manage a highly complex network infrastructure where IT systems, sensors, actuators, and business appliances interconnect. This environment is known as the Internet of Things (IOT).

When SCADA devices like programmable logic controllers were used in manufacturing settings on their own isolated networks, some semblance of perimeter cybersecurity enabled a degree of control for these relatively defenseless devices. Newer low-cost sensors and controllers, especially those that operate on Wi-Fi networks, have led to the dissolution of many perimeter boundaries. Most of today's computing applications and those of the next generation will involve embedded systems.

Some emerging cybersecurity needs for the IoT are managed in the usual course of risk treatments from traditional, general-purpose computing systems. However, ubiquitous embedded systems create new challenges where the combination of protocols and functions is complex and often difficult to control while still allowing functionality. As these challenges are considered, keep in mind the following points:

- Some IoT devices are brought to the market with insufficient cybersecurity and are themselves at risk of compromise.
- Once compromised, IoT devices can be used as a launching point for attacks against other assets on the same network.
- Compromised IoT devices can also be used as zombies or bots to launch distributed DoS attacks.

Blockchain and the New World of Distributed Ledgers

A new technology known as blockchain is revolutionizing the way business uses networks, including how cybersecurity management systems operate. This technology can allow automated systems to have higher levels of trust while increasing transparency and accountability. Blockchain solutions can also make networks and transactions more efficient, allowing operations at lower costs.

A blockchain is a decentralized method of storing data in a network of computers; within the network, a continuously growing linked list of records is stored using cryptographic techniques. The approach is resistant to modifications of past data and is especially well suited to the creation of a distributed ledger where transactions can be added to the sequence of transactions that came before.

A blockchain consists of two kinds of records: transactions and blocks. Blocks are batches of validated transactions; each block is hashed and includes a pointer to the previous block. These linked blocks form a chain—hence the name. Each block in the chain makes use of public key cryptography to secure the transactions' contents; data stored on a blockchain is generally considered incorruptible.

Blockchain infrastructure can be used to create distributed ledgers that enable high-performance, distributed record keeping for transactions. As cybersecurity control technologies begin to use blockchain approaches to communicate log transactions and event reporting, cybersecurity management systems will become increasingly more robust and efficient, enjoying greater reliability and effectiveness.

Artificial Intelligence

In the realm of cybersecurity, artificial intelligence (AI) has the opportunity to play a pivotal role on both the red and blue sides of the battlefield. On the red team, which focuses on offensive strategies, AI-driven tools can automate and enhance the efficiency of cyberattacks. These tools can conduct sophisticated phishing campaigns, exploit vulnerabilities at a scale and speed beyond human capabilities, and utilize machine learning to adapt tactics in real time based on the defenses as they are encountered. On the blue team, which is responsible for defense, AI can be used to bolster threat detection and response. Advanced AI systems can analyze vast amounts of network data to identify unusual patterns and potential threats, facilitating rapid incident response and reducing the time between detection and remediation. AI enhances the blue team's ability to predict and thwart potential attacks, providing a crucial edge in protecting digital assets.

However, the integration of AI into cybersecurity also introduces significant risks related to data misuse and leaks. The same AI technologies that empower defense mechanisms can be weaponized for unauthorized data extraction, creating new avenues for cybercriminals to exploit. AI systems can be used to sift through vast data sets and identify sensitive information, potentially leading to illegal data harvesting or privacy breaches. Moreover, the sophistication of AI-driven tools can make it easier for malicious actors to bypass traditional security measures, resulting in an increased risk of corporate data leaks. As organizations increasingly rely on AI for their cybersecurity needs, they must also implement robust safeguards and ethical guidelines to mitigate the risk of these technologies being used to compromise data integrity and privacy.

Cryptography

Although it is not a specific application or cybersecurity tool, cryptography represents a sophisticated element of control that is often included in other cybersecurity controls. **Cryptography** (from the Greek words *kryptos*, meaning "hidden," and *graphein*, meaning "to write") is the set of processes involved in using codes to secure information or make it unreadable to unauthorized users. Cryptography's parent discipline, **cryptology**, is the field of science that encompasses both cryptography and cryptanalysis (derived from *analyein*, meaning "to break up"). Cryptanalysis is the process of obtaining the plaintext message from a ciphertext message without knowing the keys used to perform the encryption.

Many cybersecurity-related tools use embedded cryptographic technologies to protect sensitive information. The use of the proper cryptographic tools can ensure confidentiality by keeping private information concealed from those who do not need to see it. Other cryptographic methods can provide increased information integrity via a mechanism to guarantee that a message in transit has not been altered—for example, a process that creates a secure message digest, or hash. In e-commerce situations, some cryptographic tools can be used to ensure that parties to a transaction are authentic so that they cannot later deny having participated in it. This feature is often called **nonrepudiation**, the process of reversing public key encryption to verify that a message was sent by a specific sender and thus cannot be refuted.

Cryptography Definitions

You can better understand the tools and functions popular in encryption cybersecurity solutions if you know some basic terminology:

- **Algorithm**—A mathematical formula or method used to convert an unencrypted message into an encrypted message
- **Cipher**—When used as a verb, the transformation of the individual components (characters, bytes, or bits) of an unencrypted message into encrypted components or vice versa; when used as a noun, the process of encryption or the algorithm used in encryption
- **Ciphertext** or **cryptogram**—The unintelligible encoded message resulting from an encryption
- **Cryptosystem**—The set of transformations necessary to convert an unencrypted message into an encrypted message
- **Decryption**—The process of converting an encoded or enciphered message (ciphertext) back to its original readable form (plaintext); also referred to as deciphering
- **Encryption**—The process of converting an original message (plaintext) into a form that cannot be used by unauthorized individuals (ciphertext); also referred to as enciphering

- Key—The information used in conjunction with an algorithm to create ciphertext from plaintext; it can be a series of bits used in a mathematical algorithm or the knowledge of how to manipulate the plaintext (sometimes called a cryptovariable)
- Keyspace—The entire range of values that can possibly be used to construct an individual key
- Plaintext—The original unencrypted message that is encrypted; also, the result of successful decryption
- Steganography—The process of hiding messages; for example, a message can be hidden within the digital encoding of a picture or graphic so that it is almost impossible to detect that the hidden message even exists
- Work factor—The amount of effort (usually expressed in units of time) required to perform cryptanalysis on an encoded message

Encryption Operations

Encryption is accomplished by using algorithms or techniques to manipulate plaintext into ciphertext and protect the confidentiality of information while it's in storage or transmission. Some widely used encryption operations are explained in the sections that follow.

Common Ciphers

In encryption, the most commonly used algorithms include the following three functions: substitution, transposition, and XOR. In a substitution cipher, you replace one value with another. For example, using the lines labeled "Input text" and "Output text" that are shown here, you can replace each character in the plaintext with the character that is three values to the right of that character in the alphabet:

```
Input text:   ABCDEFGHIJKLMNOPQRSTUVWXYZ
Output text: DEFGHIJKLMNOPQRSTUVWXYZABC
```

Thus, the plaintext of BERLIN becomes EHUOLQ in ciphertext.

This is a simple method, but it becomes very powerful if combined with other operations. Our example is based on a monoalphabetic substitution, as it uses only one alphabet, but more advanced substitution ciphers use two or more alphabets and are called polyalphabetic substitutions.

Like the substitution operation, transposition is simple to understand, but it can be complex to decipher if properly used. Unlike the substitution cipher, the transposition cipher (or permutation cipher) rearranges the values within a block based on an established pattern to create the ciphertext. This can be done at the bit or byte (character) level. For an example of how a transposition cipher works, consider the following plaintext and key:

```
Plaintext: 001001010101101011110010101010101100
Key: 1>3, 2>6, 3>8, 4>1, 5>4, 6>7, 7>5, 8>2
```

The key works like this: Bit 1 moves to position 3, bit 2 moves to position 6, and so on, with bit position 1 being the rightmost bit and position 2 being just to the left of position 1 (bit positions 87654321).

Applying this key, here is the plaintext (broken into 8-bit blocks for ease of discussion) and the corresponding ciphertext:

```
Plaintext 8-bit blocks: 00100101 01101011 10010101 01010100
Ciphertext:             11000100 01110101 10001110 10011000
```

Transposition ciphers and substitution ciphers can be used together in multiple combinations to create a very secure encryption process. To make the encryption stronger (more difficult to cryptanalyze), the keys and block sizes can be made much larger (128-, 256-, 512-, 1023-bit or even larger), resulting in substantially more complex substitutions or transpositions.

In the XOR cipher conversion, the bit stream is subjected to a Boolean XOR function against some other data stream, typically a key stream. The symbol commonly used to represent the XOR function is "^". Simply put, if two values are the same, you get 0; if not, you get 1. Suppose you have a data stream in which the first byte is 01000001. If you have a key stream in which the first "byte" is 0101 1010 and you XOR them:

```
Plaintext:   0100 0001
Key stream:  0101 1010
Ciphertext:  0001 1011
```

This process is reversible. That is, if you XOR the ciphertext with the key stream, you get the plaintext.

Symmetric Encryption

Each of the aforementioned cryptographic methods requires that the same key—a secret key—be used with the algorithm both to encipher and decipher the message. This is known as private key encryption or symmetric encryption. Symmetric encryption is efficient and easy to process as long as both the sender and the receiver possess the encryption key. Of course, if either copy of the key becomes compromised, the adversary can decrypt and read the messages. One challenge in symmetric key encryption is getting a copy of the key to the receiver, a process that must be conducted out-of-band (i.e., through a different channel or band than the one carrying the ciphertext) to avoid interception. Figure 12-10 illustrates the concept of symmetric encryption.

Figure 12-10   Symmetric encryption

Rachel at ABC Corp. generates a secret key. She must somehow get it to Alex at XYZ Corp. out-of-band. Once Alex has the key, Rachel can use it to encrypt messages and Alex can use it to decrypt and read them.

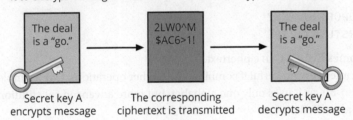

Several popular symmetric cryptosystems are available. One of the most familiar is Data Encryption Standard (DES). DES was developed in 1977 by IBM and is based on the Data Encryption Algorithm, which uses a 64-bit block size and a 56-bit key. With a 56-bit key, the algorithm has 2^{56} (more than 72 quadrillion) possible keys.

DES was a federally approved standard for nonclassified data, as explained in "Federal Information Processing Standards Publication 46-2" at www.itl.nist.gov/fipspubs/fip46-2.htm. It was cracked in 1997 when the developers of a competing algorithm called Rivest-Shamir-Adleman offered a $10,000 reward for the first person or team to do so. About 14,000 users collaborated over the Internet to break the encryption. Triple DES (3DES) was then developed as an improvement to DES. It is substantially more secure than DES, not only because it uses as many as three keys instead of one but because it performs three different encryption operations.

The current industry and government standard in symmetric encryption is AES. It is based on the Rijndael Block Cipher, which features a variable block length and a key length of 128, 192, or 256 bits.

Asymmetric Encryption

Another encryption technique is asymmetric encryption, also known as public key encryption, a cryptographic method that incorporates mathematical operations involving both a public key and a private key to encipher or decipher a message. Either key can be used to encrypt a message but the other key is required to decrypt it. So, if Key A is used to encrypt the message, then only Key B can decrypt it; conversely, if Key B is used to encrypt a message, then only Key A can decrypt it. This technique is most valuable when one of the keys is private and the other is public. The public key is stored in a public location where anyone can use it. The private key, as its name suggests, is a secret known only to the owner of the key pair. Figure 12-11 provides an illustration of how asymmetric encryption works.

The problem with asymmetric encryption is that it requires four keys to hold a single conversation between two parties. If four organizations want to exchange messages frequently, each must manage its private key and four public keys. It can be confusing to determine which public key is needed to encrypt a particular message. With more organizations in the loop, the problem grows geometrically. Also, asymmetric encryption is not as efficient in its use of CPU resources as symmetric encryptions when performing its mathematical calculations. As a result, the hybrid system described later in this chapter is more commonly used.

Figure 12-11 Asymmetric encryption

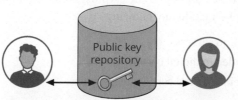

Alex at XYZ Corp. wants to send a message to Rachel at ABC Corp. Rachel stores her public key where it can be accessed by anyone. Alex retrieves her public key and uses it to create ciphertext that can only be decrypted by Rachel's private key, which she keeps secret. To respond, Rachel gets Alex's public key to encrypt her messages.

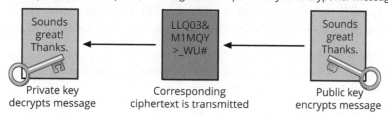

Digital Signatures

When the asymmetric process is reversed—the private key is used to encrypt a (usually short) message, and the corresponding public key is used to decrypt it—the fact that the message was sent by the organization that owns the private key cannot be refuted. This nonrepudiation is the foundation of digital signatures. Digital signatures are encrypted messages whose authenticity can be independently verified by a central facility (registry), but they can also be used to prove certain characteristics of the message or file with which they are associated. A pop-up window shows that the downloaded files came from the purported agency and thus can be trusted. A digital certificate is a public key container file that allows system components and end users to validate a public key and identify its owner. A digital certificate is like a digital signature and is commonly attached to a file to certify it is from the organization it claims to be from and has not been modified from the original format. Digital certificates are often used in Internet software updates (see Figure 12-12). A certificate authority (CA) is an entity that manages the issuance of certificates and serves as an electronic "notary public" to verify their origin and integrity.

Figure 12-12 Digital certificates in Windows

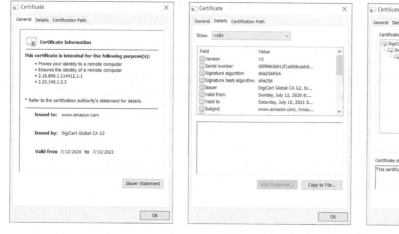

Source: Microsoft Corporation

RSA

One of the most popular public key cryptosystems is a proprietary model called Rivest-Shamir-Adleman (RSA), which is named after its developers. The first public key encryption algorithm developed for commercial use, RSA has been integrated into almost all web browsers.

Public Key Infrastructure

A public key infrastructure (PKI) is the entire set of hardware, software, and cryptosystems necessary to implement public key encryption. PKI systems are based on public key cryptosystems and include digital certificates and CAs. Common implementations of PKI include the following:

- Systems that issue digital certificates to users and servers
- Systems with computer key values to be included in digital certificates
- Tools for managing user enrollment, key generation, and certificate issuance
- Verification and return of certificates
- Key revocation services
- Other services associated with PKI that vendors bundle into their products

The use of cryptographic tools is made more manageable when using PKI. An organization can increase its cryptographic capabilities in protecting its information assets by using PKI to provide the following services:

- Authentication—Digital certificates in a PKI system permit individuals, organizations, and web servers to authenticate the identity of each of the parties in an Internet transaction.
- Integrity—Digital certificates assert that the content signed by the certificate has not been altered while in transit.
- Confidentiality—PKI keeps information confidential by ensuring that it is not intercepted during transmission over the Internet.
- Authorization—Digital certificates issued in a PKI environment can replace user IDs and passwords, enhance cybersecurity, and reduce some of the overhead for authorization processes and controlling access privileges for specific transactions.
- Nonrepudiation—Digital certificates can validate actions, making it less likely that customers or partners can later repudiate a digitally signed transaction, such as an online purchase.

Hybrid Systems

Purely asymmetric key encryption is not widely used except with certificates. For other purposes, it is typically employed in conjunction with symmetric key encryption, creating a hybrid encryption system. In a hybrid encryption system, asymmetric encryption is used to exchange symmetric keys so that two organizations can conduct quick, efficient, and secure communications based on symmetric encryption. The hybrid process in widespread use is based on the Diffie-Hellman key exchange method, which provides a way to exchange private keys without exposure to any third parties. Diffie-Hellman is the foundation for subsequent developments in public key encryption.

The process, which is illustrated in Figure 12-13, works like this: Because symmetric encryption is more efficient than asymmetric encryption for sending messages, and because asymmetric encryption does not require out-of-band key exchange, asymmetric encryption can be used to transmit symmetric keys in a hybrid approach. Suppose Alex at XYZ Corp. wants to communicate with Rachel at ABC Corp. First, Alex creates a session key—a symmetric key for limited-use, temporary communications. Alex encrypts a message with the session key and then gets Rachel's public key. He uses her public key to encrypt both the session key and the message that is already encrypted. Alex transmits the entire package to Rachel, who uses her private key to decrypt the package containing the session key and the encrypted message and then uses the session key to decrypt the message. Rachel can then continue the electronic conversation using only the more efficient symmetric session key.

Figure 12-13   Hybrid encryption

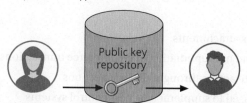

Rachel at ABC Corp. stores her public key where it can be accessed. Alex at XYZ
Corp. retrieves it and uses it to encrypt his private (symmetric) key. He sends it to
Rachel, who decrypts Alex's private key with her private key and then uses Alex's
private key for regular communications.

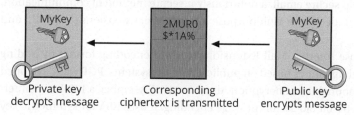

Private key   Corresponding   Public key
decrypts message   ciphertext is transmitted   encrypts message

Note 6 | For insight into the history of cryptology in the U.S. government, visit the National Security
Agency's website on cryptologic heritage, specifically the Center for Cryptologic History's listing of
historical publications, at www.nsa.gov/History/Cryptologic-History/Historical-Publications. For additional content on cryptography, visit the Coursera site at https://www.coursera.org/ and search on
"cryptography."

Self-Check

22. Cryptology solely focuses on the process of converting plaintext into ciphertext.

    a. True   **b.** False

23. Symmetric encryption is also known as public key encryption.

    a. True   **b.** False

24. In a hybrid encryption system, symmetric encryption is used to exchange private keys between
    two parties.

    a. True   **b.** False

▫ Check your answers at the end of this chapter.

Using Cryptographic Controls

Cryptographic controls are often misunderstood by those new to the area of cybersecurity. While modern
cryptosystems can certainly generate unbreakable ciphertext, it is possible only when the proper key management infrastructure has been constructed and when the cryptosystems are operated and managed correctly.
As in many cybersecurity endeavors, technical controls are valuable as long as they are founded on sound
policy and managed with an awareness of the organization's fundamental objectives.

Organizations with the need and the ability to have cryptographic controls can use them to support several aspects of the business:

- Confidentiality and integrity of email and its attachments
- Authentication, confidentiality, integrity, and nonrepudiation of e-commerce transactions
- Authentication and confidentiality of remote access through VPN connections
- A higher standard of authentication when used to supplement access control systems

Email Cybersecurity

Cryptosystems have been adapted to help secure email, a notoriously insecure method of communication. Two of the more popular adaptations include Secure Multipurpose Internet Mail Extensions (S/MIME) and Pretty Good Privacy (PGP).

S/MIME builds on the Multipurpose Internet Mail Extensions (MIME) encoding format by adding encryption and authentication via digital signatures based on public key cryptosystems. PGP was developed by Phil Zimmerman and uses the International Data Encryption Algorithm (IDEA) cipher, a 128-bit symmetric key block encryption algorithm with 64-bit blocks for message encoding. It uses RSA for symmetric key exchange and to support digital signatures.

Securing the Web

Just as S/MIME and PGP help secure email operations, cryptosystems help to secure web activity, especially transactions between customers' browsers and the web servers at e-commerce sites. Among the protocols used for this purpose are Secure Sockets Layer, Secure Hypertext Transfer Protocol, Secure Shell, and IP Security.

Secure Sockets Layer (SSL) was developed by Netscape in 1994 to provide cybersecurity for online e-commerce transactions. It uses a variety of algorithms but mainly relies on RSA for key transfer and IDEA, DES, or 3DES for encrypted symmetric key-based data transfer. Figure 12-12 shows the certificate and SSL information that is used to secure the transaction when you perform the check-out step on an e-commerce site. If the web connection does not automatically display the certificate, you can right-click in the window and select Properties to view the connection encryption and certificate properties.

Secure Hypertext Transfer Protocol (SHTTP) is an encrypted solution to the unsecured version of HTTP. It provides an alternative to the aforementioned protocols and can provide secure e-commerce transactions as well as encrypted webpages for secure data transfer over the web using a number of different algorithms.

Secure Shell (SSH) is a popular extension to the TCP/IP suite. Sponsored by the Internet Engineering Task Force (IETF), SSH provides cybersecurity for remote access connections over public networks by creating a secure and persistent connection. It provides authentication services between a client and a server and is used to secure replacement tools for terminal emulation, remote management, and file transfer applications.

IP Security (IPSec) is the primary and now dominant cryptographic authentication and encryption product of the IETF's IP Security Protocol Working Group. It supports a variety of applications, just as SSH does. A framework for cybersecurity development within the TCP/IP family of protocol standards, IPSec provides application support for all uses within TCP/IP. This protocol combines several different cryptosystems:

- Diffie-Hellman key exchange for deriving key material between peers on a public network
- Public key cryptography for signing the Diffie-Hellman exchanges to guarantee the identity of the two parties
- Bulk encryption algorithms, such as DES, for encrypting the data
- Digital certificates signed by a CA to act as digital ID cards

IPSec has two components: (1) the IP cybersecurity protocol itself, which specifies the information to be added to an IP packet and indicates how to encrypt packet data; and (2) the Internet Key Exchange, which uses asymmetric key exchange and negotiates the cybersecurity associations.

IPSec works in two modes of operation: transport and tunnel. In transport mode, only the IP data is encrypted—not the IP headers themselves. This allows intermediate nodes to read the source and destination addresses. In tunnel mode, the entire IP packet is encrypted and inserted as the payload in another IP packet. This requires other systems at the beginning and end of the tunnel to act as proxies to send and receive the encrypted packets. These systems then transmit the decrypted packets to their true destinations.

IPSec and other cryptographic extensions to TCP/IP are often used to support a virtual private network (VPN), which uses encryption to keep the contents of network messages hidden from observers who may have access to public traffic. Using the VPN tunneling approach just described, an individual or organization can set up a network connection on the Internet and send encrypted data back and forth, using the IP-packet-within-an-IP-packet method to deliver the data safely and securely. VPN support is built into most Microsoft Server software, including Windows Server 2003 and later versions, and client support for VPN services is included in most modern Windows clients (such as Windows 10 and 11). While true private network services can cost hundreds of thousands of dollars to lease, configure, and maintain, a VPN can be established for much less.

Securing Authentication

Cryptosystems can also be used to provide enhanced and secure authentication. One approach to this issue is provided by Kerberos, named after the three-headed dog of Greek mythology (*Cerberus* in Latin) that guarded the gates to the underworld. Kerberos is an authentication system that uses symmetric key encryption to validate an individual user's access to various network resources by keeping a database containing the private keys of clients and servers within the authentication domain it supervises. Network services running on the servers in the shared authentication domain register with Kerberos, as do clients that want to use those services.[15]

The Kerberos system recognizes these private keys and can authenticate one network node (client or server) to another. For example, it can authenticate a client to a print service. To understand Kerberos, think of a typical multiscreen cinema. You acquire your ticket at the box office, and the ticket-taker then admits you to the proper screening room based on the contents of your ticket. Kerberos also generates temporary session keys—that is, private keys given to the two parties in a conversation. The session key is used to encrypt all communications between these two parties. Typically, a user logs into the network, is authenticated to the Kerberos system, and is then authenticated by the Kerberos system to other resources on the network.

Kerberos consists of three interacting services, all of which rely on a database library:

- Authentication server (AS)—A Kerberos server that authenticates clients and servers
- Key distribution center (KDC)—Generates and issues session keys
- Kerberos ticket granting service (TGS)—Provides tickets to clients who request services. An authorization ticket is an identification card for a client that verifies to the server that the client is requesting services, is a valid member of the Kerberos system, and is therefore authorized to receive services. The ticket consists of the client's name and network address, a ticket validation starting and ending time, and the session key—all of which are encrypted in the private key of the target server.

Kerberos operates according to the following principles:

- The KDC knows the secret keys of all clients and servers on the network.
- The KDC initially exchanges information with the client and server by using the secret keys.
- Kerberos authenticates a client to a requested service on a server through TGS and by issuing temporary session keys for communications between the client and the KDC, the server and the KDC, and the client and the server.
- Communications take place between the client and server using the temporary session keys.[16]

People and organizations that decide to use Kerberos should be aware of some concerns. If the Kerberos servers are subjected to DoS attacks, no client can request (or receive) any services. If the Kerberos servers, service providers, or clients' machines become compromised, their private key information may also be compromised.

Managing Cryptographic Controls

Cryptographic controls require close management attention. Some of the more important managerial issues are as follows:

- Don't lose your keys. Any key-based system is contingent upon the physical cybersecurity of its keys. If the keys are compromised, so is all communication. If the keys are lost, any data encrypted with those keys may be lost as well. Unlike your car keys, which the dealer can replace, cryptographic keys are not known to software vendors and are usually not recoverable. The purpose of the encryption algorithm is to prevent unauthorized users from viewing the data. Unless your organization has made an investment in a key management solution that enables key recovery, losing your key means you may lose your data or the service being protected. Loss of unrecoverable keys will deny access to everyone. Given the current state of cryptographic technology, breaking the code is very likely impossible.

- Know who you are communicating with. One of the most popular encryption-based attacks is the man-in-the-middle attack, in which the attacker pretends to be the second party in a conversation and relays the traffic to the actual second party. The attacker collects, decrypts, reads, possibly modifies, reencrypts, and transmits the information. This type of operation is possible only if the attacker is involved in the initial key exchange. Always verify the public keys in a public key exchange.

- It may be illegal to use a specific encryption technique when communicating to some nations. Federal export regulation still restricts the countries with which you can share strong encryption. Check the U.S. Department of Commerce's frequently asked questions (www.bis.doc.gov/index.php/policy-guidance/encryption/6-faqs) for more information.

- Every cryptosystem has weaknesses. Make sure you can live with the weaknesses of any system you choose. Research your selection before trusting any cryptosystem.

- Give access only to users, systems, and servers with a business need, a principle known as least privilege. Do not load cryptosystems on systems that can be easily compromised.

- When placing trust in a CA, ask the following question: Quis custodiet ipsos custodes? That is, who watches the watchers? CAs do not assume any liability for the accuracy of their information, which is strange, given that their purpose is to validate the identity of a third party. However, if you read the fine print on the CA agreement, you will most likely find statements that absolve them of liability.

- There is no security in obscurity. Just because a system is secret does not mean it is safe. It is better to put your trust in a tried-and-true tested solution.

- Security protocols and the cryptosystems they use are subject to the same limitations as firewalls and IDPSs. They are all installed and configured by humans and are only as secure as their configuration allows. VPNs are particularly vulnerable to direct attacks; compromise of the remote client can directly result in compromise of a trusted system. Home-computing users frequently use the Windows "remember passwords" function, which could present a real problem if these systems are compromised. Don't let telecommuters use this option.

As with all other cybersecurity program components, make sure that your organization's use of cryptography is based on well-constructed policy and supported with sound management procedures. The tools themselves may work exactly as advertised, but if they are not used correctly and managed diligently, your organization's secrets may soon be public knowledge.

View Point Leveraging Protection Mechanisms to Provide Defense in Depth

By Todd E. Tucker, Managing Director, FAIR Institute for Cyber Risk Management

Defense in depth is a protection strategy with a long history. It is characterized by layers of protection that, while not impenetrable, provide the advantage of increasing the amount of time and resources necessary to penetrate every layer of defense. Perhaps the best-known physical example of defense in depth comes from the archetypal fortress built with high walls, manned by armed guards, and placed behind a protective moat. In cybersecurity, layered protection mechanisms are essential for providing defense in depth. Each mechanism, when considered alone, often provides limited protection against today's sophisticated attacks. However, cybersecurity architects build systems and networks by implementing layers of protection. For example, architects leverage a secured physical perimeter to protect media and hardware, implement firewalls to secure internal networks from untrusted ones, install endpoint security software to detect and respond to attacks on clients and servers, implement extended detection and response systems to identify and respond to attacks, and harden critical platforms to reduce vulnerabilities. These protection mechanisms become the walls, guards, and moats of today's electronic fortresses and effectively provide defense in depth.

Defense in depth provides several advantages to organizations. The obvious benefit is the added cybersecurity that results from requiring an attacker to spend more time and resources to break in. Another benefit is the flexibility it provides in responding to specific threats. For example, consider a worm that exploits databases via a specific TCP port. The options for responding to the threat include shutting down the port the worm uses, hardening the database directly, or perhaps setting intrusion detection rules to spot and terminate an attack. Flexibility is important in production environments, where one action may adversely impact mission-critical systems and require other actions to be considered.

Defense in depth provides a major disadvantage, too: complexity. Defense in depth increases the number of protection mechanisms implemented. It requires architects and administrators to consider the overall design of the network. Moreover, they must consider all protection mechanisms to ensure they adequately protect against threats and do not conflict with one another.

As you learn about protection mechanisms, think not just about their technical aspects and the cybersecurity they provide. Think about their ability to work with other mechanisms to provide defense in depth. How can they work together to increase the overall cybersecurity of the system? Also, consider the management implications of each mechanism. Remember that these mechanisms are often implemented on a large scale and that each one requires maintenance, administration, and monitoring. One of the greatest challenges in cybersecurity today is managing protection mechanisms on an enterprise scale and effectively leveraging them to provide defense in depth.

Note 8 | Technical cybersecurity controls are the most glamorous part of the cybersecurity field and the most rapidly evolving. Staying current requires that you read the latest on emerging vulnerabilities and how to control them. To help you get started, here is a list of what we consider some of the best technical cybersecurity control blogs and news feeds:

- Krebs on Security at krebsonsecurity.com—Krebs offers a keen business perspective balanced with a thorough technical understanding. Also, it is usually very timely.
- DARKReading at www.darkreading.com—Populated with thought leaders and technology specialists, this site offers lots of cybersecurity techniques and provides a comprehensive, thought-provoking gateway into the industry.

- ThreatPost at threatpost.com—This site provides leading information about IT and business cyber-security by highlighting high-impact, engaging articles with supervision from industry-leading cybersecurity journalists.
- Schneier on Security at www.schneier.com—Bruce Schneier is celebrating his 10th anniversary in IT thought leadership. Nicknamed the "security guru," he is an author of 13 books, detailed academic articles, essays, and papers. As a highly engaged individual in this sector, Schneier's blog is a must follow.
- Stay Safe Online guides and resources at staysafeonline.org/resources—This site offers a collection of information on online security and related topics.

Self-Check

25. Cryptography can only be used to ensure the confidentiality of information.
    a. True   **b.** False

26. The Internet Key Exchange component of IPSec is responsible for negotiating cybersecurity associations and using asymmetric key exchange.
    a. True   **b.** False

27. Losing cryptographic keys can result in the loss of encrypted data or the service being protected.
    a. True   **b.** False

☐ Check your answers at the end of this chapter.

Closing Case

Iris's smartphone beeped. Frowning, she glanced at the screen, expecting to see yet another junk email.

"We've really got to do something about the spam!" she muttered to herself. She scanned the header of the message.

"Uh-oh!" Iris glanced at her watch, looked at her incident response pocket card, and then dialed the home number of the on-call systems administrator (SA). When he answered, Iris asked, "Seen the alert yet? What's up?"

"Wish I knew—some sort of virus," the SA replied. "A user must have opened an infected attachment."

Iris made a mental note to remind the awareness program manager to restart the refresher training program for virus control. Her users should know better, but some new employees had not been trained yet.

"Why didn't the firewall catch it?" Iris asked.

"It must be a new one," the SA replied. "It slipped by the pattern filters. Somebody must have missed an update."

"What are we doing now?" Iris was growing more nervous by the minute.

"I'm ready to cut our Internet connection remotely, then drive down to the office and start our planned recovery operations—shut down infected systems, clean up any infected servers, recover data from backups, and notify our peers that they may receive this virus from us in our email. I just need your go-ahead."

The admin sounded uneasy. This was not a trivial operation, and he was facing a long night of intense work.

"Do it," Iris said. "I'll activate the incident response plan and start working the notification call list to get some extra hands in to help." Iris knew this situation would be the main topic at the weekly CIO's meeting. She just hoped her team would be able to restore the systems to safe operation quickly. She looked at her watch: 12:35 a.m.

Case Discussion Questions

1. What can be done to minimize the risk of this situation recurring? Can these types of situations be completely avoided?
2. Once the timeline of events has been established, how would you approach your interaction with the second-shift operator?
3. How should RWW go about notifying its peers? What other procedures should Iris have the technician perform?
4. When would be the appropriate time to begin forensic data collection to analyze the root cause of this incident? Why?

Case Ethical Decision Making

1. Regarding the actions taken by the San Diego student as described in this chapter's case opener, did she break the law? (You may want to review the discussions of applicable laws earlier in this book.) If she did not break any laws, was the purposeful damage via malware infection an unethical action? If not, why not?
2. Regarding the actions taken by the second-shift operator, was his oversight in running the routine update of the malware pattern file a violation of law? Was it a violation of policy? Was the mistake an ethical lapse?

Summary

Identification is a mechanism that provides basic information about an unknown entity to the known entity that it wants to communicate with.

Authentication is the validation of a user's identity. Authentication devices can depend on one or more of three factors: what you know, what you have, and what you can produce.

Authorization is the process of determining which actions an authenticated person can perform in a particular physical or logical area.

Accountability is the documentation of actions on a system and the tracing of those actions to a user who can then be held responsible for them. Accountability is performed using system logs and auditing.

To obtain strong authentication, a system must use two or more authentication methods.

Biometric technologies are evaluated on three criteria: false reject rate, false accept rate, and crossover error rate.

A firewall in a cybersecurity program is any device that prevents specific information from moving between the outside world (the untrusted network) and the inside world (the trusted network).

Types of firewalls include packet filtering firewalls, application layer proxy firewalls, stateful packet inspection firewalls, and Unified Threat Management devices. There are three common architectural implementations of firewalls: single bastion hosts, screened-host firewalls, and screened-subnet firewalls.

A host-based IDPS resides on a particular computer or server and monitors activity on that system. A network-based IDPS monitors network traffic; when a predefined condition occurs, it responds and notifies the appropriate administrator.

A signature-based IDPS, also known as a knowledge-based IDPS, examines data traffic for activity that matches signatures, which are preconfigured, predetermined attack patterns. An anomaly-based IDPS (also known as a behavior-based IDPS) collects data from normal traffic and establishes a baseline. When the activity is outside the baseline parameters (called the clipping level), the IDPS notifies the administrator.

The science of encryption, known as cryptology, encompasses cryptography and cryptanalysis. Cryptanalysis is the process of obtaining the original message from an encrypted code without the use of the original algorithms and keys.

In encryption, the most commonly used algorithms employ either substitution or transposition. A substitution cipher substitutes one value for another. A transposition cipher (or permutation cipher) rearranges the values within a block to create the ciphertext.

Symmetric encryption uses the same key, also known as a secret key, both to encrypt and decrypt a message. Asymmetric encryption (public key encryption) uses two different keys for these purposes.

A digital certificate is a block of data, similar to a digital signature, that is attached to a file to certify it is from the organization it claims to be from and has not been modified.

A public key infrastructure encompasses the entire set of hardware, software, and cryptosystems necessary to implement public key encryption.

A number of cryptosystems have been developed to make email more secure. Examples include Pretty Good Privacy and Secure Multipurpose Internet Mail Extensions.

A number of cryptosystems work to secure web browsers, including Secure Sockets Layer, Secure Hypertext Transfer Protocol, Secure Shell, and IP Security.

Key Terms

agent
algorithm
anomaly-based IDPS
application layer firewall
application layer proxy firewall
asymmetric encryption
asynchronous token
bastion host
behavior-based IDPS
biometrics
blockchain
Bluetooth
cache server
certificate authority (CA)
cipher
ciphertext
clipping level
content filter
crossover error rate (CER)
cryptogram
cryptography
cryptology
cryptosystem
decryption
deep packet inspection (DPI)
demilitarized zone (DMZ)
Diffie-Hellman key exchange
    method
digital certificates
digital signatures
dual-homed host

dumb card
dynamic packet filtering firewall
encryption
false accept rate
false reject rate
fingerprinting
firewall
footprint
footprinting
host-based IDPS (HIDPS)
hybrid encryption system
intrusion detection and
    prevention system (IDPS)
IP Security (IPSec)
Kerberos
key
keyspace
knowledge-based IDPS
log files
logs
monoalphabetic substitution
network-address translation (NAT)
network-based IDPS (NIDPS)
nonrepudiation
packet filtering firewall
passphrase
password
password complexity
permutation cipher
plaintext
polyalphabetic substitution

port-address translation (PAT)
port scanners
private key encryption
proxy firewall
proxy server
public key encryption
public key infrastructure (PKI)
sacrificial host
screened-host architecture
screened-subnet architecture
security event information
    management (SEIM)
sensor
signature-based IDPS
single bastion host architecture
smart card
stateful packet inspection (SPI)
    firewall
state table
steganography
substitution cipher
symmetric encryption
synchronous tokens
total cost of ownership (TCO)
transport mode
transposition cipher
trap and trace applications
tunnel mode
Unified Threat Management
    (UTM)
virtual password

virtual private network (VPN)
vulnerability scanner
war driving

Wi-Fi Protected Access (WPA)
Wired Equivalent Privacy (WEP)
wireless access point (WAP)

work factor
XOR cipher conversion

Review Questions

1. What role do technical controls play in a cybersecurity program?

2. Why is it difficult to enforce a password policy without technical controls?

3. What are the four functions involved in access control approaches?

4. How does biometric authentication verify a person's identity?

5. What are the three types of authentication mechanisms mentioned in the chapter?

6. Why is password complexity important in cybersecurity?

7. What is a virtual password, and how is it created?

8. How does a smart card differ from a dumb card in authentication mechanisms?

9. What is the false reject rate in biometric systems?

10. What is the false accept rate, and why is it significant?

11. What is the crossover error rate in biometric systems?

12. How has the rise of smartphones impacted multifactor authentication?

13. What are the primary functions of a firewall in cybersecurity?

14. How do packet filtering firewalls determine whether to drop or forward data packets?

15. What distinguishes an application layer proxy firewall from a standard packet filtering firewall?

16. What capabilities do Unified Threat Management devices provide beyond traditional firewall functions?

17. What is the primary disadvantage of using application layer firewalls?

18. How does a single bastion host architecture function, and what is a significant drawback of this approach?

19. How does an intrusion detection and prevention system (IDPS) respond when it detects a violation?

20. What are the two basic detection methods used by IDPSs?

21. What is the primary difference between a host-based IDPS and a network-based IDPS?

22. What is a key challenge associated with signature-based IDPS methods?

23. Why is proper configuration of an IDPS critical for effective cybersecurity management?

24. What are some common technologies that support the protection of information assets across networks and the Internet?

25. What is war driving, and how is it typically conducted?

26. Why is Wired Equivalent Privacy considered insecure, and what has replaced it as the industry standard?

27. How does WPA3 enhance security for public Wi-Fi networks, compared to its predecessors?

28. What measures can users and organizations take to manage wireless network security effectively?

29. What two key approaches can be taken to secure Bluetooth-enabled devices?

30. How do scanners and analysis tools help cybersecurity administrators?

31. What is the process of footprinting in the context of pre-attack data gathering?

32. What conditions must be met to legally use a packet sniffer on a network?

33. What is the primary purpose of using a port scanner in network security?

34. What are the potential drawbacks of using scanning and analysis tools?

35. What are the main categories of log data illustrated in Table 12-4?

36. Why is it important to secure the servers that create and store logs?

37. What are the primary issues involved in log generation?

38. What functions must be addressed to interpret data from the log generation tier of log management infrastructure?

39. What are some of the important management functions within log storage?

40. How should cybersecurity professionals approach the implementation of new technologies in an organization?

41. What are the key characteristics of an effective network access control solution?

42. Why has the integration of SCADA systems into common network infrastructures created challenges for organizations?

43. What are some of the risks associated with IoT devices in a networked environment?

44. How does blockchain technology enhance cybersecurity management systems?

45. What is the primary purpose of cryptography in cybersecurity?

46. How does symmetric encryption differ from asymmetric encryption?

47. What is a digital signature, and what role does it play in cybersecurity?

48. Explain the concept of a hybrid encryption system.

49. What is the significance of the work factor in cryptography?

50. Describe the process of encryption and decryption in the context of symmetric encryption.

51. What are the main functions of a public key infrastructure?

52. How does the XOR cipher work, and what is its key feature?

53. How does Secure Multipurpose Internet Mail Extensions enhance email security?

54. What is the primary purpose of the Secure Sockets Layer in online transactions?

55. How does Pretty Good Privacy secure email communication?

56. Describe the role of the key distribution center in the Kerberos authentication system.

57. What are the two modes of operation for IPSec, and how do they differ?

58. Why is key management crucial in cryptographic systems?

59. What are some common applications of cryptographic controls in organizations?

Exercises

1. Create a spreadsheet in which a user inputs eight values into eight different cells. Then create a row that transposes the cells to simulate a transposition cipher using the example from the text. Remember to work from right to left with the pattern 1 > 3, 2 > 6, 3 > 8, 4 > 1, 5 > 4, 6 > 7, 7 > 5, 8 > 2, where 1 is the rightmost of the eight cells. Input the text ABCDEFGH as single characters into the first row of cells. What is displayed at the end of the simulation?

2. Search the Internet for information about a technology called personal or home office firewalls. Examine the various alternatives, select three of the options, and compare their functionalities, cost, features, and types of protection.

3. Go to the website of VeriSign (part of Symantec), one of the market leaders in digital certificates. Determine whether VeriSign serves as a registration authority, certificate authority, or both. Download its free guide to PKI and summarize VeriSign's services.

4. Go to csrc.nist.gov and locate Federal Information Processing Standard (FIPS) 197. What encryption standard does it address? Examine the contents of this publication and describe the algorithm discussed. How strong is it? How does it encrypt plaintext?

5. Search the Internet for vendors of biometric products. Find one vendor with a product designed to examine each characteristic mentioned in Figure 12-4. What is the crossover error rate associated with each product? Which product would be more acceptable to users? Which would be preferred by cybersecurity administrators?

Solutions to Self-Check Questions

Protection Mechanisms

1. Technical controls alone can secure an IT environment.
   Answer: b. False.
   Explanation: Technical controls are essential but cannot secure an IT environment on their own; they must be part of a broader cybersecurity program.

2. Biometric authentication mechanisms use physiological characteristics to validate a person's identity.
   Answer: a. True.
   Explanation: Biometrics utilize unique physical traits such as fingerprints, retinal patterns, and voice recognition to authenticate individuals.

3. The false accept rate is more serious than the false reject rate in biometric systems.
   Answer: a. True.
   Explanation: A high false accept rate poses a greater security risk because it allows unauthorized access, whereas a high false reject rate primarily affects user convenience.

Managing Network Security

4. Firewalls can only be implemented as separate computer systems.
   Answer: b. False.
   Explanation: Firewalls can be implemented as separate computer systems, as services running on existing routers or servers, or as separate network segments containing several supporting devices.

5. Packet filtering firewalls examine the header information of data packets to determine whether to drop or forward them.
   Answer: a. True.
   Explanation: Packet filtering firewalls examine the header information of data packets and use configuration rules to decide whether to drop or forward them.

6. Unified Threat Management devices are limited to performing only firewall functions.
   Answer: b. False.
   Explanation: These devices are capable of performing multiple tasks, including stateful packet inspection, intrusion detection and prevention, content filtering, spam filtering, and malware scanning.

Intrusion Detection and Prevention Systems

7. An IDPS can only notify administrators via email.
   Answer: b. False.
   Explanation: An IDPS can notify administrators via email, phone, or text and can also notify an external cybersecurity service organization.

8. A host-based IDPS can monitor multiple computers simultaneously.
   Answer: a. True.
   Explanation: A host-based IDPS can monitor multiple computers by storing an agent on each monitored system and having them report back to a master console.

9. An anomaly-based IDPS requires more overhead and processing capacity than a signature-based IDPS.

Answer: a. True.

Explanation: An anomaly-based IDPS requires more overhead and processing capacity because it constantly matches activity patterns to a baseline.

Wireless Networking Protection

10. Wireless networks that use the IEEE 802.11 protocol are generally more expensive to install than wired networks.

    Answer: b. False.

    Explanation: Wireless networks provide a low-cost alternative to wired networks because they do not require the expensive and difficult installation of cables.

11. Wired Equivalent Privacy protects users on a wireless network from unauthorized access and each other.

    Answer: b. False.

    Explanation: It only protects the network from unauthorized users and does not protect users from each other.

12. WPA3 offers increased data protection by using forward secrecy, which prevents attackers from using a newly discovered password to crack older recorded and encrypted data.

    Answer: a. True.

    Explanation: WPA3 provides additional protection for encrypted data through a process called forward secrecy.

Scanning and Analysis Tools

13. Port scanners are used exclusively by attackers to identify active computers and services on a network.

    Answer: b. False.

    Explanation: Port scanners are used both by attackers and defenders to identify active computers and services on a network.

14. A vulnerability scanner can only identify configuration problems in servers.

    Answer: b. False.

    Explanation: A vulnerability scanner examines systems to identify various vulnerabilities, including exposed usernames, open network shares, and other issues besides just configuration problems.

15. Using hacker tools to examine an organization's defenses is acceptable if done responsibly.

    Answer: a. True.

    Explanation: Cybersecurity administrators can use hacker tools to examine their own defenses and identify vulnerabilities, provided they inform service providers and comply with policies.

Managing Server-Based Systems with Logging

16. Logs can only be generated by systems that are specifically configured to do so.

    Answer: b. False.

    Explanation: Some systems are configured to record a common set of data by default; others must be configured to activate logging.

17. Log archival involves reducing the file size of logs to save drive space.

    Answer: b. False.

    Explanation: Log archival refers to the backup and storage of logs based on policy or legal/regulatory requirements. Log compression is the process that reduces file size.

18. Event aggregation is the process of consolidating similar entries or related events within a log.

    Answer: a. True.

    Explanation: Event aggregation is critical for handling the thousands of data points multiple servers generate by consolidating similar entries.

Managing Cybersecurity for Emerging Technologies

19. A properly deployed network access control solution must be vendor-specific to ensure compatibility.

    Answer: b. False.

    Explanation: A properly deployed network access control must be vendor-neutral to effectively manage various devices and users accessing the organization's network.

20. Blockchain technology increases transparency and accountability in network transactions.

    Answer: a. True.

    Explanation: Blockchain technology allows for higher levels of trust, transparency, and accountability in network transactions due to its decentralized and cryptographic nature.

21. The integration of SCADA systems into common network infrastructures has simplified network management.

    Answer: b. False.

    Explanation: The integration of SCADA systems into common network infrastructures has led to complex network management challenges.

Cryptography

22. Cryptology solely focuses on the process of converting plaintext into ciphertext.

    Answer: b. False.

    Explanation: Cryptology involves not only converting plaintext into ciphertext but also encompasses cryptanalysis, which is the process of obtaining plaintext from ciphertext without knowing the keys.

23. Symmetric encryption is also known as public key encryption.

    Answer: b. False.

    Explanation: Symmetric encryption uses the same key for both encryption and decryption, whereas public key encryption involves a pair of keys (public and private) and is known as asymmetric encryption.

24. In a hybrid encryption system, symmetric encryption is used to exchange private keys between two parties.

    Answer: b. False.

    Explanation: In a hybrid encryption system, asymmetric encryption is used to exchange symmetric keys, which are then used for efficient communication between the parties.

Using Cryptography Controls

25. Cryptography can only be used to ensure the confidentiality of information.

    Answer: b. False.

    Explanation: Cryptography can ensure confidentiality, integrity, authentication, and nonrepudiation of information.

26. The Internet Key Exchange component of IPSec is responsible for negotiating cybersecurity associations and using asymmetric key exchange.

    Answer: a. True.

    Explanation: It uses asymmetric key exchange to negotiate cybersecurity associations for IPSec.

27. Losing cryptographic keys can result in the loss of encrypted data or the service being protected.

    Answer: a. True.

    Explanation: If cryptographic keys are lost, any data encrypted with those keys may become inaccessible or the service may be disrupted.

Glossary

4-1-9 fraud   A form of social engineering in which some third party offers an email recipient the promise of a large amount of money and requests a small advance fee or personal banking information to facilitate the transfer. Also known as advance-fee fraud.

A

acceptance risk treatment strategy   A risk treatment strategy that indicates an organization is willing to accept the current level of residual risk; as a result, the organization makes a conscious decision to do nothing else to protect an information asset from risk and to "live with" the outcome from any resulting exploitation. Also known as risk acceptance.

access control   The selective method by which systems specify who may use a particular resource and how they may use it.

access control lists (ACLs)   Specifications of authorization that govern the rights and privileges of users to a particular information asset.

accountability   The access control mechanism that ensures all actions on a system, whether authorized or unauthorized, can be attributed to an authenticated identity.

advanced persistent threat (APT)   A collection of processes, typically directed by a human threat agent, that targets a specific organization or individual.

advance-fee fraud (AFF)   A form of social engineering in which some third party offers an email recipient the promise of a large amount of money and requests a small advance fee or personal banking information to facilitate the transfer. Also known as 4-1-9 fraud.

adverse events   Events with negative consequences that could threaten an organization's information assets or operations.

after-action review (AAR)   A detailed examination and discussion of the events that occurred during an incident or disaster, from first detection to final recovery.

agent   A piece of software that resides on a system and reports back to a management application or server.

alert message   A description of the incident or disaster that usually contains just enough information so that each person knows what portion of the IR or DR plan to implement without slowing down the notification process.

alert roster   A list of contact information for personnel to be notified in the event of an incident or disaster.

algorithm   A mathematical formula or method used to convert an unencrypted message into an encrypted message.

annualized failure rate (AFR)   The probability of a failure of hardware based on the manufacturer's data of failures per year.

annualized loss expectancy (ALE)   In the context of a cost–benefit analysis, the product of the annualized rate of occurrence and single loss expectancy.

annualized rate of occurrence (ARO)   In a cost–benefit analysis, the probability or likelihood of an adverse event per year.

anomaly-based IDPS   An IDPS that first collects data from normal traffic and establishes a baseline. It then periodically samples network activity using statistical methods and compares the samples to the baseline.

application layer firewall   A device capable of examining the application layer of network traffic (for example, HTTP, SMTP, FTP) and filtering based on its header content rather than the traffic IP headers.

application layer proxy firewall   A device capable of functioning both as a firewall and an application layer proxy server.

apprehend and prosecute   An organizational CP philosophy that focuses on the identification and prosecution of the attacker in addition to asset defense and preventing reoccurrence. Also known as "pursue and prosecute."

asset   An organizational resource that is being protected. An asset can be logical, such as a website, software information, or data, or it can be physical, such as a person, computer system, hardware, or other tangible object. Assets, particularly information assets, are the focus of what security efforts are attempting to protect.

asset valuation   The process of assigning financial value or worth to each information asset.

asymmetric encryption   A cryptographic method that incorporates mathematical operations involving both a public key and a private key to encipher or decipher a message. Either key can be used to encrypt a message but the other key is required to decrypt it.

asynchronous token   An authentication component in the form of a card or key fob that contains a computer chip and a display and shows a computer-generated number that is activated to support remote login authentication.

attack   An intentional or unintentional act that can damage or otherwise compromise information and the systems that support it. Also known as a threat event.

auditing   The review of a system's use to determine if misuse or malfeasance has occurred.

authentication   The access control mechanism that requires the validation and verification of an entity's asserted identity.

authorization   The access control mechanism that represents the matching of an authenticated entity to a list of information assets and their corresponding access levels.

availability   The attribute of information that describes how data is accessible and correctly formatted for use without interference or obstruction.

availability disruption   An interruption in services that causes an adverse event within the organization.

B

back door   A malware payload that provides access to a system by bypassing normal access controls. Also known as a trap door or maintenance hook.

baseline   A measure of current performance.

baselining   A method of improving practices by comparing an organization's current efforts against its past efforts or a desired target value. Sometimes called internal benchmarking.

bastion host   Any network system, router, or firewall placed between an external untrusted network and an internal trusted network that is exposed to the untrusted network.

behavioral feasibility   An examination of how well a particular solution fits within an organization's culture and the extent to which users are expected to accept the solution. Also known as operational feasibility.

behavior-based IDPS   An IDPS that first collects data from normal traffic and establishes a baseline. It then periodically samples network activity using statistical methods and compares the samples to the baseline.

Bell-LaPadula (BLP) confidentiality model   A "state machine reference model" that ensures the confidentiality of the modeled system by using mandatory access controls, data classification, and information security clearances.

benchmarking   A method of improving practices by comparing an organization's efforts against the practices of a similar organization or an industry-developed standard to produce results you would like to duplicate.

best practices   Efforts that are considered among the best in the industry.

Biba integrity model   An access control model that is similar to BLP based on the premise that higher levels of integrity are more worthy of trust than lower levels.

biometrics   The use of physiological characteristics to provide authentication for a person's identification and validate that they are who they claim to be.

blackout   A long-term interruption (outage) in electrical power availability.

blockchain   A decentralized method of storing data in a network of computers; within the network, a continuously growing linked list of records is stored using cryptographic techniques.

blueprint   A framework or model customized to an organization, including implementation details.

Bluetooth   A de facto industry standard for short-range wireless communications between a wide range of computers, mobile devices, and accessories.

boot-sector virus   A type of virus that targets the boot sector or Master Boot Record (MBR) of a computer system's hard drive or removable storage media. Also known as a boot virus.

boot virus   A type of virus that targets the boot sector or Master Boot Record (MBR) of a computer system's hard drive or removable storage media. Also known as a boot-sector virus.

bot   An abbreviation of "robot," an automated software program that executes certain commands when it receives a specific input from a system that is directed remotely by the attacker (usually via a transmitted command) to participate in a DoS attack. Also known as a zombie.

brownout   A long-term decrease in the quality of electrical power availability.

brute-force password attack   An effort to guess a password by attempting every possible combination of characters and numbers.

business continuity (BC)   An organization's efforts to ensure its long-term viability when a disaster precludes operations at the primary site.

business email compromise (BEC)   A social engineering attack directed toward an employee by an individual posing as their supervisor or an organizational executive.

business impact analysis (BIA)   An investigation and assessment of adverse events that can affect an organization. It is conducted as a preliminary phase of the contingency planning process, which includes a determination of how critical a system or set of information is to the organization's core processes and its recovery priorities.

business resumption planning (BRP)   Actions taken by senior management to develop and implement a combined DR and BC policy, plan, and set of recovery teams.

C

cache server   A web server that only stores and provides requested content by obtaining it from the source on behalf of the client and archiving it for future needs.

capabilities table   In a lattice-based access control, the row of attributes associated with a particular user or subject.

certificate authority (CA)   An entity that manages the issuance of certificates and serves as an electronic "notary public" to verify their origin and integrity.

champion   A high-level executive who will provide support and influence for a project.

chief cybersecurity officer   A role that might integrate cybersecurity with physical or corporate security at some organizations.

chief information officer (CIO)   Typically the top information technology executive in an organization; the CIO usually reports directly to the CEO.

chief security officer (CSO)   The top cybersecurity manager in an organization.

cipher   When used as a verb, the transformation of the individual components (characters, bytes, or bits) of an unencrypted message into encrypted components or vice versa; when used as a noun, the process of encryption or the algorithm used in encryption.

ciphertext   The unintelligible encoded message resulting from an encryption.

clickbait   Content such as email attachments or embedded links crafted to convince unsuspecting users into clicking them, which results in more web traffic for the content provider or the installation of unwanted software or malware.

clipping level   A predefined assessment level that triggers a predetermined response when surpassed.

cold site   A facility that provides only rudimentary services, with no computer hardware, peripherals, or active communications services; it is used for BC operations.

collusion   A conspiracy or cooperation between two or more individuals or groups to commit illegal or unethical actions.

Common Criteria for Information Technology Security Evaluation   An international standard (ISO/IEC 15408) for computer security certification.

communications security   The protection of all communications media, technology, and content.

competitive intelligence   The collection and analysis of information about an organization's business competitors through legal and ethical means to gain business intelligence and competitive advantage.

Computer Fraud and Abuse (CFA) Act of 1986   The cornerstone of many computer-related federal laws and enforcement efforts.

computer security   The protection of computerized information processing systems and the data they contain and process.

Computer Security Act (CSA) of 1987   A U.S. law designed to improve the security of federal information systems.

confidentiality   An attribute of information that describes how data is protected from disclosure or exposure to unauthorized individuals or systems. It requires limiting access to information only to those who need it and preventing access by those who do not.

configuration and change management (CCM)   An approach to implementing system change that uses policies, procedures, techniques, and tools to manage and evaluate proposed changes, track changes through completion, and maintain systems inventory and supporting documentation.

configuration management (CM)   An approach to implementing system change that uses policies, procedures, techniques, and tools to manage and evaluate proposed changes, track changes through completion, and maintain systems inventory and supporting documentation.

configuration rules   Instructional codes or scripts that guide the execution of a system when information is passing through it.

consequence   The potential outcome of the successful exploitation of a specific asset's vulnerability by a threat. See also impact.

content filter   A software program or hardware/software appliance that allows administrators to restrict content that comes into or leaves a network.

contingency planning (CP)   The actions taken by senior management to specify an organization's priorities and actions if an adverse event becomes an incident or disaster.

controlling   The process of monitoring progress and making necessary adjustments to achieve desired goals or objectives.

controls and safeguards   Security mechanisms, policies, or procedures that can successfully counter attacks, reduce risk, resolve vulnerabilities, and otherwise improve security within an organization.

cost avoidance   The financial savings from using the defense risk treatment strategy to implement a control and eliminate the financial ramifications of an incident.

cost-benefit analysis (CBA)   The formal assessment and presentation of the economic expenditures needed for a particular cybersecurity control, contrasted with its projected value to an organization.

covert channel   An unauthorized or unintended method of communication hidden inside a computer system.

cracker   A hacker who intentionally removes or bypasses software copyright protection.

cracking   Attempting to reverse-engineer, remove, or bypass a password or other access control protection, such as the copyright protection on software.

crisis management (CM)   The planning and preparation efforts for dealing with potential human injury, emotional trauma, loss of life from a disaster, or an adverse event that dramatically and negatively impacts an organization's image or that of its employees.

crossover error rate (CER)   The point at which the rate of false rejections equals the rate of false acceptances; it is considered the optimal outcome for biometric systems because it represents balance between the two error rates. Also called the equal error rate.

cryptogram   The unintelligible encoded message resulting from an encryption.

cryptography   The set of processes involved in using codes to secure information or make it unreadable to unauthorized users.

cryptology   The field of science that encompasses both cryptography and cryptanalysis.

cryptosystem   The set of transformations necessary to convert an unencrypted message into an encrypted message.

cyberactivist   An attacker who seeks to interfere with or disrupt systems to protest the operations, policies, or actions of an organization or government agency. See also hacktivist.

cyber hygiene   The individual decisions made and practices used when interacting with computing technology.

cybersecurity   The protection of the confidentiality, integrity, and availability of information assets, whether in storage, processing, or transmission, via the application of policy, education, training and awareness, and technology. Cybersecurity overlaps with all other security areas.

cybersecurity administrator   A hybrid position comprising the responsibilities of both a cybersecurity technician and a cybersecurity manager.

cybersecurity analyst   A specialized cybersecurity administrator responsible for performing systems development life cycle activities in the development of a cybersecurity system or technology.

cybersecurity incident response team (CIRT or CSIRT)   An IR team composed of IT and cybersecurity professionals who are prepared to detect, respond to, and recover from an incident.

cybersecurity manager   A manager responsible for the day-to-day operations of a cybersecurity program; this manager may report directly to the CSO or may be the CSO in smaller organizations.

cybersecurity performance management   The process of designing, implementing, and managing the use of specific measurements to determine the effectiveness of cybersecurity efforts.

cybersecurity policy   A statement of managerial intent designed to direct and regulate employee and other stakeholder behavior regarding the authorized use of information assets and their technologies, including penalties for noncompliance.

cybersecurity program   The entire set of activities, resources, personnel, and technologies used by an organization to manage the risks to its information assets.

cybersecurity program policy (CPP)   A high-level cybersecurity directive that sets the strategic direction, scope, and tone for an organization's cybersecurity efforts.

cybersecurity risk management   The application of safeguards or controls to reduce the risks to an organization's information assets to an acceptable level.

cybersecurity technician   A technical specialist responsible for the selection or development, implementation, and administration of cybersecurity-related technology.

cybersecurity watchstander   An entry-level cybersecurity professional responsible for the routine monitoring and operation of a particular cybersecurity technology.

cyberterrorism   The conduct of terrorist activities by online attackers.

cyberwarfare   Formally sanctioned, offensive cyber operations conducted by one government or nation-state against another. See also information warfare.

D

data classification scheme   The assignment of levels of confidentiality to information assets as part of an access control methodology; the scheme is designed to restrict the number of people who can access it.

database shadowing   A backup strategy to store duplicate online transaction data along with duplicate databases at the remote site on a redundant server, combining electronic vaulting with remote journaling.

decryption   The process of converting an encoded or enciphered message (ciphertext) back to its original readable form (plaintext). Also referred to as deciphering.

deep packet inspection (DPI)   A type of device that can examine multiple protocol headers and even the content of network traffic, all the way through the TCP/IP layers and including encrypted, compressed, or encoded data.

defense risk treatment strategy   The preferred approach to risk treatment; it is accomplished by means of countering threats, removing vulnerabilities in assets, limiting access to assets, and adding or improving protective safeguards. Sometimes called risk mitigation.

demilitarized zone (DMZ)   An intermediate area between a trusted network and an untrusted network that restricts access to internal systems.

denial-of-service (DoS) attack   An attack that attempts to overwhelm a computer target's ability to handle incoming communications, prohibiting legitimate users from accessing those systems.

desk check   A CP testing strategy in which copies of the appropriate plans are distributed to all individuals who will be assigned roles during an actual incident or disaster, with everyone reviewing the plan and validating its components.

deterrence   The act of attempting to prevent an unwanted action by threatening punishment or retaliation on the instigator if they perform the action.

dictionary attack   A variation of the brute-force password attack that attempts to narrow the range of possible passwords guessed by using a dictionary of common passwords and possibly including attempts based on the target's personal information. Also known as a dictionary password attack.

dictionary password attack   A variation of the brute-force password attack that attempts to narrow the range of possible passwords guessed by using a dictionary of common passwords and possibly including attempts based on the target's personal information. Also known as a dictionary attack.

difference analysis   A procedure that compares the current state of a network segment against a known previous state of the same network segment (the baseline).

Diffie-Hellman key exchange method   A technique that provides a way to exchange private keys without exposure to any third parties. Diffie-Hellman is the foundation for subsequent developments in public key encryption.

digital certificates   Public key container files that allow PKI system components and end users to validate a public key and identify its owner.

digital forensics   Investigations involving the preservation, identification, extraction, documentation, and interpretation of computer media for evidentiary and root cause analysis.

digital signatures   Encrypted message components that can be mathematically proven to be authentic.

disaster recovery (DR)   An organization's planning and preparation efforts for detecting, reacting to, and recovering from a disaster.

disclosure   The intentional or unintentional exposure of an information asset to unauthorized parties.

discretionary access controls (DACs)   Access controls that are implemented at the discretion or option of the data user.

distributed denial-of-service (DDoS) attack   A DoS attack in which a coordinated stream of requests is launched against a target from many locations at the same time using other compromised systems.

Domain Name System (DNS) cache poisoning   The intentional hacking and modification of a DNS database to redirect legitimate traffic to illegitimate Internet locations.

dual-homed host   A network configuration in which a device contains two network interfaces: one that is connected to the external network and one that is connected to the internal network.

due diligence   The reasonable steps taken by people or organizations to meet the obligations imposed by laws or regulations.

dumb card   An authentication card that contains digital user data, such as a personal identification number (PIN), against which user input is compared. A card used to access an automatic teller machine is an example of a dumb card.

dumpster diving An information attack that involves searching through a target organization's trash and recycling bins for sensitive information.

dynamic packet filtering firewall A firewall type that keeps track of each network connection between internal and external systems using a state table and that expedites the filtering of those communications.

E

e-discovery The identification and preservation of evidentiary material related to a specific legal action.

Electronic Communications Privacy Act (ECPA) of 1986 A collection of U.S. statutes that regulate the interception of wire, electronic, and oral communications, commonly referred to as the "federal wiretapping acts."

electronic vaulting A backup method that uses bulk transfer of data to an off-site facility.

elite hacker A hacker who uses extensive knowledge of the inner workings of computer hardware and software to gain unauthorized access to systems and information. Also known as an expert hacker.

encryption The process of converting an original message (plaintext) into a form that cannot be used by unauthorized individuals (ciphertext). Also referred to as enciphering.

enterprise risk management (ERM) The evaluation and reaction to risk for the entire organization, not just the risk facing information assets.

ethics The branch of philosophy that considers the nature, criteria, logic, and validity of moral judgment.

expert hacker A hacker who uses extensive knowledge of the inner workings of computer hardware and software to gain unauthorized access to systems and information. Also known as an elite hacker.

exploit A technique used to compromise a system.

exposure factor (EF) In the context of a cost–benefit analysis, the percentage loss that would occur from a given vulnerability being exploited.

external benchmarking A method of improving practices by comparing an organization's efforts against the practices of a similar organization or an industry-developed standard to produce results you would like to duplicate.

external monitoring domain The component of the maintenance model that focuses on evaluating external threats to an organization's information assets.

F

false accept rate The rate at which fraudulent users or nonusers are allowed access to systems or areas as a result of a failure in a biometric device. Such a failure is known as a Type II error or a false positive and represents a serious cybersecurity breach.

false reject rate The rate at which authentic users are denied or prevented access to authorized areas because of a failure in a biometric device. Such a failure is known as a Type I error or a false negative.

fault A short-term interruption in electrical power availability.

fingerprinting The systematic survey of a targeted organization's Internet addresses collected during the footprinting phase to identify the network services offered by the hosts in that range.

firewall The combination of hardware and software that filters or prevents specific information from moving between the outside network, known as the untrusted network (for example, the Internet), and the inside network, known as the trusted network.

footprint The geographic area in which there is sufficient signal strength to make a network connection.

footprinting The organized research and investigation of Internet addresses owned or controlled by a target organization.

framework A specification to be followed during the design, selection, and initial and ongoing implementation of a cybersecurity program, including cybersecurity policies, cybersecurity education and training programs, and technological controls. See also model.

full-interruption testing A CP testing strategy in which all team members follow each IR, DR, or BC procedure, including those for interruption of service, restoration of data from backups, and notification of appropriate individuals.

G

gap analysis A comparison of actual versus planned or desired performance, outcomes, or achievements.

governance The set of responsibilities and practices exercised by the board and executive management with the goal of providing strategic direction, ensuring that objectives are achieved, ascertaining that risks are managed appropriately, and verifying that the enterprise's resources are used responsibly.

guidelines Nonmandatory recommendations the employee may use as a reference in complying with a policy.

H

hacker   A person who accesses systems and information without authorization and often illegally.

hacktivist   An attacker who seeks to interfere with or disrupt systems to protest the operations, policies, or actions of an organization or government agency. See also cyberactivist.

Health Insurance Portability and Accountability Act (HIPAA) of 1996   A law that attempts to protect the confidentiality and security of healthcare data by establishing and enforcing standards and by standardizing electronic data interchange. Also known as the Kennedy-Kassebaum Act.

host-based IDPS (HIDPS)   An IDPS that resides on a particular computer or server known as the host and monitors activity only on that system.

hot site   A fully configured computing facility that includes all services, communications links, and physical plant operations; it is used for BC operations.

hybrid asset valuation   An attempt to create a value for an information asset that reduces some of the ambiguity of qualitative measures without resorting to the unsubstantiated estimations used for quantitative measures. Also known as semi-qualitative asset valuation.

hybrid encryption system   An approach using asymmetric encryption to exchange symmetric keys so that two organizations can conduct quick, efficient, and secure communications based on symmetric encryption.

I

IAAA security framework   An architectural framework that is used to allow access to computer resources, enforce policies, and facilitate audits. It is essential for network and computer management and security. This process is mainly used so that network and software application resources are accessible to specific and legitimate users.

identification   The access control mechanism whereby unverified entities who seek access to a resource provide a credential by which they are known to the system.

impact   The potential outcome of the successful exploitation of a specific asset's vulnerability by a threat. See also consequence.

incident   An adverse event that could result in a loss of information assets but does not threaten the viability of the entire organization.

incident classification   The process of examining an adverse event that has the potential to escalate into an incident and determining whether it constitutes an actual incident.

incident commander   The on-duty manager of the CIRT.

incident detection   The identification and classification of an adverse event as an incident.

incident response (IR)   An organization's set of planning and preparation efforts for detecting, responding to, and recovering from an incident.

industrial espionage   The collection and analysis of information about an organization's business competitors, often through illegal or unethical means, to gain an unfair competitive advantage.

information aggregation   The collection and combination of pieces of nonprivate data, possibly resulting in information that violates privacy.

information assets   The focus of cybersecurity; information that has value to the organization, and the systems that store, process, and transmit the information.

information extortion   The theft of confidential information from an organization and subsequent demand for compensation for its return or for an agreement not to disclose it.

information media   System elements such as hardware, operating systems, applications, and utilities that collect, store, process, and transmit information. See also system components.

Information Technology System Evaluation Criteria (ITSEC)   An international set of criteria for evaluating computer systems that is very similar to TCSEC.

information warfare   Formally sanctioned, offensive cyber operations conducted by one government or nation-state against another. See also cyberwarfare.

InfraGard   A U.S. association consisting of regional chapters of the Federal Bureau of Investigation (FBI) and affiliations of public, private, and academic organizations that cooperate to exchange information on the protection of critical national information resources.

integrity   An attribute of information that describes how data is whole, complete, and uncorrupted.

intellectual property (IP)   The creation, ownership, and control of original ideas as well as the representation of those ideas.

internal benchmarking   A method of improving practices by comparing an organization's current efforts against its past efforts or a desired target value. Sometimes called baselining.

internal monitoring domain   The component of the maintenance model that focuses on identifying, assessing, and managing the configuration and status of information assets in an organization.

Internet vulnerability assessment   An assessment approach designed to find and document vulnerabilities that may be present in an organization's public network.

intranet vulnerability assessment   An assessment approach designed to find and document selected vulnerabilities that are likely to be present on an organization's internal network.

intrusion detection and prevention system (IDPS)   A system with the capability to detect intrusions and modify its configuration and environment to prevent intrusions.

IP Security (IPSec)   The primary and now dominant cryptographic authentication and encryption product of the IETF's IP Protocol Security Working Group.

IP spoofing   A technique for gaining unauthorized access to computers using a forged or modified source IP address to give the perception that messages are coming from a trusted host.

issue-specific policy   An organizational directive that provides detailed, targeted instructions for all members of an organization in the use of an issue or resource.

J

jailbreaking   A process of escalating privileges to gain administrator-level control over a smartphone operating system.

job rotation   The requirement that every employee be able to perform the work of at least one other employee.

jurisdiction   The area within which an entity such as a court or law enforcement agency is empowered to make legal decisions.

K

Kerberos   An authentication system that uses symmetric key encryption to validate an individual user's access to various network resources by keeping a database containing the private keys of clients and servers within the authentication domain it supervises.

key   The information used in conjunction with an algorithm to create ciphertext from plaintext; it can be a series of bits used in a mathematical algorithm or the knowledge of how to manipulate the plaintext. Sometimes called a cryptovariable.

keyspace   The entire range of values that can possibly be used to construct an individual key.

knowledge-based IDPS   An IDPS that examines data traffic for something that matches the signatures of preconfigured, predetermined attack patterns.

L

lattice-based access control   A variation on mandatory access control that assigns users a matrix of authorizations for specific areas of access, incorporating the information assets of subjects such as users and objects.

leadership   The ability to influence others and gain their willing cooperation to achieve an objective by providing purpose, direction, and motivation.

leading   The application of leadership to encourage the implementation of the planning and organizing functions.

least privilege   The data access principle that ensures no unnecessary access to data exists by regulating members so they can perform only the minimum data manipulation necessary.

liability   An entity's legal obligation or responsibility.

likelihood   The probability of the successful exploitation of a specific asset's vulnerability by a threat.

log files   Collections of data stored by a system and used by administrators to audit systems performance. This data is used both by authorized and unauthorized users.

logs   Collections of data stored by a system and used by administrators to audit systems performance. This data is used both by authorized and unauthorized users.

long-arm jurisdiction   The ability of a legal entity to exercise its influence beyond its normal boundaries by asserting a connection between an out-of-jurisdiction entity and a local legal case.

M

macro virus   A type of virus written in a specific macro language to target applications that use the language.

mail bomb   An attack designed to overwhelm the receiver with excessive quantities of email.

maintenance hook   A malware payload that provides access to a system by bypassing normal access controls. Also known as a back door or trap door.

malicious code   Computer software specifically designed to perform malicious or unwanted actions. Also known as malicious software or malware.

malicious software   Computer software specifically designed to perform malicious or unwanted actions. Also known as malicious code or malware.

malware   Computer software specifically designed to perform malicious or unwanted actions. Also known as malicious code or malicious software.

management   The process of achieving objectives by appropriately applying a given set of resources.

mandatory access control (MAC) A required, structured data classification scheme that rates each collection of information as well as each user; these ratings are often referred to as sensitivity or classification levels.

mandatory vacation policy A requirement that all employees take time off from work, which allows an organization to audit the individual's areas of responsibility.

man-in-the-middle attack Attacks whereby a person intercepts a communications stream and inserts themselves in the conversation to convince each of the legitimate parties that the attacker is the other communications partner.

maximum tolerable downtime (MTD) The total amount of time a system owner or authorizing official is willing to accept for a business process outage or disruption, including all impact considerations. The sum of the RTO and WRT.

mean time between failures (MTBF) The average amount of time between hardware failures, calculated as the total amount of operation time for a specified number of units divided by the total number of failures.

mean time to diagnose (MTTD) The average amount of time a computer repair technician needs to determine the cause of a failure.

mean time to failure (MTTF) The average amount of time until the next hardware failure is expected.

mean time to repair (MTTR) The average amount of time a computer repair technician needs to resolve the cause of a failure through replacement or repair of a faulty unit.

methodology A formal approach to solving a problem based on a structured sequence of procedures, the use of which ensures a rigorous process and increases the likelihood of achieving the desired final objective.

mitigation risk treatment strategy A risk treatment strategy that attempts to eliminate or reduce risk through the application of additional controls and safeguards.

model A specification to be followed during the design, selection, and initial and ongoing implementation of a cybersecurity program, including cybersecurity policies, cybersecurity education and training programs, and technological controls. See also framework.

monoalphabetic substitution A substitution cipher that incorporates only a single alphabet in the encryption process.

mutual agreement A continuity strategy in which two organizations sign a contract to assist the other in a disaster by providing BC facilities, resources, and services until the organization in need can recover from the disaster.

N

need-to-know The principle of limiting users' access privileges to only the specific information required to perform their assigned tasks.

network-address translation (NAT) A method of converting multiple real, routable external IP addresses to special ranges of internal IP addresses, usually on a one-to-one basis; that is, one external valid address directly maps to one assigned internal address.

network-based IDPS (NIDPS) An IDPS that resides on a computer or appliance connected to a segment of an organization's network and monitors traffic on that segment for indications of attacks.

network security A subset of communications security; the protection of voice and data networking components, connections, and content.

network sniffer A software program or hardware appliance that can intercept and interpret network traffic. Also known as a packet sniffer.

noise Additional, disruptive signals in network communications or electrical power delivery.

nondiscretionary controls Access controls that are implemented by a central authority and that can be based on roles.

nonrepudiation The process of reversing public key encryption to verify that a message was sent by a specific sender and thus cannot be refuted.

novice hacker A relatively unskilled hacker who uses the work of expert hackers to perform attacks.

O

operational feasibility An examination of how well a particular solution fits within an organization's culture and the extent to which users are expected to accept the solution. Also known as behavioral feasibility.

operations security The protection of the details of an organization's operations and activities.

organizational feasibility An examination of how well a particular solution fits within an organization's strategic planning objectives and goals.

organizing The structuring of resources to maximize their efficiency and ease of use.

P

packet filtering firewall A networking device that examines the header information of data packets that come into a network and determines whether to drop them (deny) or forward them to the next network connection (allow), based on its configuration rules.

packet monkey   A novice hacker who uses automated exploits to engage in denial-of-service attacks for no obvious reason.

packet sniffer   A software program or hardware appliance that can intercept and interpret network traffic. Also known as a network sniffer.

passphrase   A plain-language phrase, typically longer than a password, from which a virtual password is derived.

password   A secret combination of characters that only the user should know; it authenticates the user.

password complexity   The degree of variation or complication in a password or passphrase.

pen testing   The investigation, assessment, and evaluation of a system by authorized individuals emulating an attack.

penetration tester   A cybersecurity professional with authorization to attempt to gain system access in an effort to identify and recommend resolutions for vulnerabilities in those systems.

penetration testing   The investigation, assessment, and evaluation of a system by authorized individuals emulating an attack.

performance measurements   The data or trends in data that may indicate the effectiveness of cybersecurity efforts and programs implemented in an organization. See also performance measures.

performance measures   The data or trends in data that may indicate the effectiveness of cybersecurity efforts and programs implemented in an organization. See also performance measurements.

permutation cipher   A cryptographic operation that involves simply rearranging the values within a block based on an established pattern.

pharming   An attack using the redirection of legitimate user web traffic to illegitimate websites with the intent to collect personal information.

phishing   A form of social engineering in which the attacker provides what appears to be a legitimate communication, but it either contains hidden or embedded code that redirects the reply to a third-party site to extract personal or confidential information or asks the respondent to contact the sender directly.

physical security   The protection of physical items, objects, or areas from unauthorized access and misuse; known in industry as corporate security.

plaintext   The original unencrypted message that is encrypted; also, the result of successful decryption.

planning   The process of creating designs or schemes for future efforts or performance.

planning and risk assessment domain   The component of the maintenance model that focuses on identifying and planning ongoing cybersecurity activities and managing risks introduced through IT and cybersecurity projects.

platform security validation (PSV)   An assessment approach designed to find and document vulnerabilities that may be present because misconfigured systems are used within an organization.

policy   Managerial guidance that dictates certain behavior within the organization.

political feasibility   An examination of how well a particular solution fits within an organization's political environment.

polyalphabetic substitution   A substitution cipher that incorporates two or more alphabets in the encryption process.

polymorphic threat   A type of malware that evolves over time by changing the way it appears to antivirus software programs, making it undetectable by techniques that look for preconfigured signatures.

port-address translation (PAT)   A firewall architecture in which a single external IP address is mapped dynamically to a range of internal IP addresses by adding a unique port number when traffic leaves the private network and is placed on the public network.

port scanners   Tools used both by attackers and defenders to identify or fingerprint active computers on a network, the active ports and services on those computers, the functions and roles of the machines, and other useful information.

possession   An attribute of information that describes how the data's ownership or control is legitimate or authorized.

practices   Examples of actions that illustrate compliance with policies.

pretexting   A form of social engineering in which the attacker pretends to be an authority figure who needs information to confirm the target's identity, when their intent is to trick the target into revealing confidential information.

privacy   The right of individuals or groups to protect themselves and their information from unauthorized access, providing confidentiality.

Privacy Act of 1974   A U.S. law that regulates the government's collection, storage, use, and dissemination of individual personal information contained in records maintained by the federal government.

private key encryption A cryptographic method in which the same algorithm and secret key are used both to encipher and decipher the message.

privilege escalation The unauthorized modification of an authorized or unauthorized system user account to gain advanced access and control over system resources.

procedures Step-by-step instructions designed to assist employees in following policies, standards, and practices.

process communications The necessary information flow within and among the governance group, RM framework team, and RM process team during the implementation of RM.

process monitoring and review The data collection and feedback associated with performance measures used during the conduct of a process.

professional hacker A hacker who conducts attacks for personal financial benefit, for a crime organization, or for a foreign government.

project management The process of identifying and controlling the resources applied to a project as well as measuring progress and adjusting the process as progress is made toward the goal.

protect and forget The organizational CP philosophy that focuses on the defense of information assets and preventing reoccurrence rather than the attacker's identification and prosecution. Also known as "patch and proceed."

proxy firewall A device that provides both firewall and proxy services.

proxy server A server that acts as an intermediary, intercepting requests for information from external users and providing the requested information by retrieving it from an internal server, thus protecting and minimizing the demand on internal servers.

public key encryption A cryptographic method that incorporates mathematical operations involving both a public key and a private key to encipher or decipher a message. Either key can be used to encrypt a message but the other key is required to decrypt it.

public key infrastructure (PKI) The entire set of hardware, software, and cryptosystems necessary to implement public key encryption. PKI systems are based on public key cryptosystems and include digital certificates and certificate authorities.

R

rainbow table A database of hash values and their corresponding plaintext values that can be used to look up password values if an attacker possesses the hashed password.

ransomware A type of malware specifically designed to identify and encrypt valuable information in a victim's system to extort payment for the key needed to unlock the encryption.

recommended practices Efforts that seek to provide a superior level of performance in the protection of information.

recovery point objective (RPO) The point in time to which systems will be recovered; the maximum amount of data loss the organization will accept, given the most recent backup copy of the data.

recovery time objective (RTO) The maximum amount of time that a critical system can remain unavailable before there is an unacceptable impact on other system resources, supported business processes, and the MTD.

reference monitor A conceptual piece of a system that manages access controls.

remote journaling A backup method that transfers transaction data to an off-site facility as the backups occur, with the receiving server archiving the data as it is received.

residual risk The risk to information assets that remains even after current controls have been applied.

restitution A legal requirement to make compensation or payment resulting from a loss or injury.

risk acceptance A risk treatment strategy that indicates an organization is willing to accept the current level of residual risk; as a result, the organization makes a conscious decision to do nothing else to protect an information asset from risk and to "live with" the outcome from any resulting exploitation. Also known as the acceptance risk treatment strategy.

risk aggregation The merging or combining of groups of assets, threats, and their associated risks into more general categories to simplify risk assessment.

risk analysis A determination of the extent to which an organization's information assets are exposed to risk.

risk appetite The quantity and nature of risk that organizations are willing to accept as they evaluate the trade-offs between perfect cybersecurity and unlimited accessibility.

risk appetite statement A formal document developed by the organization that specifies its overall willingness to accept risk to its information assets, based on a synthesis of individual risk tolerances.

risk avoidance A risk treatment strategy that eliminates all risk associated with an information asset by removing it from service. Also known as risk termination or the termination risk treatment strategy.

risk control   The reduction of risk, including cybersecurity risk, to an acceptable level. See also risk treatment.

risk determination   The calculation of risk associated with a Threats–Vulnerabilities–Assets (TVA) triplet using a formula based on the methodology employed.

risk evaluation   The process of comparing an information asset's risk rating to the numerical representation of the organization's risk appetite or risk threshold to determine if risk treatment is required.

risk identification   The recognition, enumeration, and documentation of risks to an organization's information assets.

risk management   The process of discovering and assessing the risks to an organization's operations and determining how those risks can be controlled or mitigated.

risk management plan   A document that contains specifications for the implementation and conduct of RM efforts.

risk management policy   The managerial directive designed to regulate organizational efforts related to the identification, assessment, and treatment of risk to information assets.

risk mitigation   The preferred approach to risk treatment; it is accomplished by means of countering threats, removing vulnerabilities in assets, limiting access to assets, and adding or improving protective safeguards. Sometimes called the defense risk treatment strategy.

risk rating factor   The quantification of risk present in a Threats–Vulnerabilities–Assets (TVA) triplet, as derived in risk determination.

risk rating worksheet   An extension of the TVA spreadsheet that only includes assets and relevant vulnerabilities along with the risk determination.

risk sharing   A risk treatment strategy that attempts to shift risk to other assets, processes, or organizations. Also known as the transference risk treatment strategy or risk transfer.

risk termination   A risk treatment strategy that eliminates all risk associated with an information asset by removing it from service. Also known as risk avoidance or the termination risk treatment strategy.

risk threshold   The assessment of the amount of risk an organization is willing to accept for a particular information asset or set of assets. See also risk tolerance.

risk tolerance   The assessment of the amount of risk an organization is willing to accept for a particular information asset or set of assets, typically synthesized into the organization's overall risk appetite. See also risk threshold.

risk transfer   A risk treatment strategy that attempts to shift risk to other assets, processes, or organizations. Also known as risk sharing or the transference risk treatment strategy.

risk treatment   The reduction of risk, including cybersecurity risk, to an acceptable level. See also risk control.

RM framework   The overall structure of the strategic planning and design for the entirety of the organization's RM efforts.

RM process   The identification, analysis, evaluation, and treatment of risk to information assets, as specified in the RM framework.

rolling mobile site   A continuity strategy that involves contracting with an organization to provide specialized facilities configured in the payload area of a tractor-trailer.

rooting   A process of escalating privileges to gain administrator-level control over a computer system.

S

sacrificial host   Any network system, router, or firewall placed between an external untrusted network and an internal trusted network that is exposed to the untrusted network.

sag   A short-term decrease in electrical power availability.

scope creep   The expansion of project deliverables from the original project plan.

screened-host architecture   A firewall architecture that combines the packet filtering router with a second, dedicated device, such as a proxy server or proxy firewall.

screened-subnet architecture   A firewall architectural model that consists of one or more internal bastion hosts located behind a packet filtering router on a dedicated network segment, with each host performing a role in protecting the trusted network.

script kiddie   A novice hacker who uses software written by a commercial organization or expert hacker to attack a system. Also known as a skid, skiddie, or script bunny.

security   The state of being secure and free from danger or harm, or the actions taken to make someone or something secure.

security clearance   A personnel classification system in which users of an organization's information asset are assigned an authorization level that identifies the level of classified information they are "cleared" to access.

security education, training, and awareness (SETA) program   A program designed to improve the protection of information assets by providing targeted knowledge, skills, and guidance activities for an organization's employees.

security event information management (SEIM)   A log management system specifically tasked to collect log data from multiple servers or other network devices for the purpose of interpreting, filtering, correlating, analyzing, storing, and reporting the data.

semi-qualitative asset valuation   An attempt to create a value for an information asset that reduces some of the ambiguity of qualitative measures without resorting to the unsubstantiated estimations used for quantitative measures. Also known as hybrid asset valuation.

sensor   A piece of software that resides on a system and reports back to a management application or server.

separation of duties   The principle that requires significant tasks to be split up so that more than one individual is needed to complete them.

service bureau   A continuity strategy in which an organization contracts with a service agency to provide a BC facility for a fee.

service level agreement (SLA)   A document that specifies the expected level of service from a service provider and usually contains provisions for minimum acceptable availability and penalties or remediation procedures for downtime.

session hijacking   A form of man-in-the-middle attack whereby the attacker inserts themselves into TCP/IP-based communications. Also known as TCP hijacking.

shoulder surfing   The direct, covert observation of individual information or system use.

signature-based IDPS   An IDPS that examines data traffic for something that matches the signatures of preconfigured, predetermined attack patterns.

simulation   A CP testing strategy in which an organization conducts a role-playing exercise as if an actual incident or disaster had occurred.

single bastion host architecture   A firewall architecture in which a single device performing firewall duties, such as packet filtering, serves as the only perimeter protection between an organization's networks and the external network.

single loss expectancy (SLE)   In the context of a cost–benefit analysis, the calculated value associated with the most likely loss from an attack (impact); it is the product of the asset's value and the exposure factor.

smart card   An authentication component similar to a dumb card that contains a computer chip to verify and validate several pieces of information instead of just a PIN.

social engineering   The process of using social skills to convince people to reveal access credentials or other valuable information to an attacker.

software piracy   The unauthorized duplication, installation, or distribution of copyrighted computer software.

spam   Unsolicited commercial email, typically advertising transmitted in bulk.

spear phishing   A highly targeted phishing attack.

spike   A short-term increase in electrical power availability. Also known as a swell.

stakeholders   People or organizations that have a vested interest in a particular aspect of the planning or operation of an organization.

standard of due care   The legal standard that requires an organization and its employees to act as a "reasonable and prudent" individual or organization would under similar circumstances.

standards   Detailed statements of what must be done to comply with policy; sometimes viewed as the rules governing policy compliance.

state table   A record of the state and context of each packet in a conversation between an internal and external user or system.

stateful packet inspection (SPI) firewall   A firewall type that keeps track of each network connection between internal and external systems using a state table and that expedites the filtering of those communications.

steganography   The process of hiding messages; for example, a message can be hidden within the digital encoding of a picture or graphic so that it is almost impossible to detect that the hidden message even exists.

storage channel   A TCSEC-defined covert channel that communicates by modifying a stored object, such as in steganography.

strategic planning   The process of defining and specifying the long-term direction to be taken by an organization, and the acquisition and allocation of resources needed to pursue this effort.

structured walk-through   A CP testing strategy in which all involved individuals walk through an organization or alternate site and discuss the steps they would take during an actual CP event.

substitution cipher   An approach to encryption in which one value is replaced with another.

surge   A long-term increase in electrical power availability.

swell A short-term increase in electrical power availability. Also known as a spike.

symmetric encryption A cryptographic method in which the same algorithm and secret key are used both to encipher and decipher the message.

synchronous token An authentication component in the form of a card or key fob that contains a computer chip and a display and shows a time-based, computer-generated number used to support remote login authentication.

system components System elements such as hardware, operating systems, applications, and utilities that collect, store, process, and transmit information. See also information media.

system-specific policies Organizational directives that function as standards or procedures to be used when configuring or maintaining systems.

systems development life cycle (SDLC) A methodology for the design and implementation of an information system, generally containing phases that address the investigation, analysis, design, implementation, and maintenance of the system.

T

tactics, techniques, and procedures (TTP) The behavior of an actor. A tactic is the highest-level description of the behavior; techniques provide a more detailed description of the behavior in the context of a tactic; and procedures provide a lower-level, highly detailed description of the behavior in the context of a technique.

talk-through A form of structured walk-through in which individuals meet in a conference room and discuss CP rather than walking around the organization.

task rotation The requirement that all critical tasks can be performed by multiple individuals.

TCP hijacking A form of man-in-the-middle attack whereby the attacker inserts themselves into TCP/IP-based communications. Also known as session hijacking.

technical feasibility An examination of how well a particular solution can be supported given an organization's current technological infrastructure and resources, which include hardware, software, networking, and personnel.

termination risk treatment strategy A risk treatment strategy that eliminates all risk associated with an information asset by removing it from service. Also known as risk avoidance or risk termination.

theft The illegal taking of another's property, whether physical, electronic, or intellectual.

threat Any event or circumstance that has the potential to adversely affect operations and assets.

threat agent A specific instance or a component of a threat. Also known as a threat source.

threat assessment An evaluation of the threats to information assets, including a determination of their likelihood of occurrence and potential impact of an attack.

threat event An intentional or unintentional act that can damage or otherwise compromise information and the systems that support it. Also known as an attack.

threat source A specific instance or a component of a threat. Also known as a threat agent.

timeshare A continuity strategy in which an organization co-leases facilities with a business partner or sister organization.

timing channel A TCSEC-defined covert channel that communicates by managing the relative timing of events.

total cost of ownership (TCO) A measurement of the true cost of a device or application that includes not only the purchase price but annual maintenance or service agreements, upgrade fees and subscriptions, the cost to train personnel to manage the device or application, the cost of systems administrators, and the cost to protect it.

transference risk treatment strategy A risk treatment strategy that attempts to shift risk to other assets, processes, or organizations. Also known as risk sharing or risk transfer.

transport mode An operating mode of IPSec in which only the IP data is encrypted—not the IP headers themselves.

transposition cipher A cryptographic operation that involves simply rearranging values within a block based on an established pattern.

trap and trace applications A set of technologies that combine the function of honey pots or honey nets with the capability to track the attacker back through the network.

trap door A malware payload that provides access to a system by bypassing normal access controls. Also known as a back door or maintenance hook.

trespass The unauthorized entry into the real or virtual property of another party.

Trojan horse A malware program that hides its true nature and reveals its designed behavior only when activated.

Trusted Computer System Evaluation Criteria (TCSEC) An outdated system certification and accreditation standard from the U.S. Department of Defense that defined the criteria for assessing the access controls in a computer system.

trusted computing base (TCB)   The combination of all hardware, firmware, and software responsible for enforcing a cybersecurity policy.

tunnel mode   An operating mode of IPSec in which the entire IP packet is encrypted and inserted as the payload in another IP packet.

two-person control   The organization of a task or process so that it requires at least two individuals to perform.

U

uncertainty   The state of having limited or imperfect knowledge of a situation, making it less likely that organizations can successfully anticipate future events or outcomes.

Unified Threat Management (UTM)   A device categorized by the ability to perform the work of multiple devices, such as a stateful packet inspection firewall, network intrusion detection and prevention system, content filter, spam filter, and malware scanner and filter.

V

virtual password   A derivative of a passphrase that is an improvement over the standard password because it is based on an easily memorable phrase.

virtual private network (VPN)   A means to use encryption to keep the contents of network messages hidden from observers who may have access to public traffic.

virus   A type of malware that is attached to other executable programs.

vulnerability   A potential weakness in an asset or its defensive control systems.

vulnerability assessment   The process of identifying and documenting provable flaws in an organization's information asset environment.

vulnerability assessment and remediation domain   The component of the maintenance model focused on identifying documented vulnerabilities and remediating them in a timely fashion.

vulnerability scanner   A scanner application that examines systems connected to networks and their network traffic to identify exposed usernames and groups, open network shares, configuration problems, and other vulnerabilities in servers.

W

war driving   An attacker technique of moving through a geographic area or building, actively scanning for an open or unsecured WAP.

warm site   A facility that provides many of the same services and options as a hot site, but typically without

installed and configured software applications; it is used for BC operations.

Wi-Fi Protected Access (WPA)   A set of protocols used to secure wireless networks; it was developed as an intermediate solution until the IEEE 802.11i standards were fully developed.

Wired Equivalent Privacy (WEP)   A set of protocols designed to provide a basic level of cybersecurity protection to wireless networks and to prevent unauthorized access or eavesdropping.

wireless access point (WAP)   A device used to connect wireless networking users and their devices to the rest of an organization's network(s); also known as a Wi-Fi router.

wireless vulnerability assessment   An assessment approach designed to find and document vulnerabilities that may be present in an organization's wireless local area networks.

work factor   The amount of effort (usually expressed in units of time) required to perform cryptanalysis on an encoded message.

work-from-home   A continuity strategy in which an entire organization works from remote locations, usually home or travel locations, using virtual meetings and remote access to critical systems.

work recovery time (WRT)   The amount of effort (expressed as elapsed time) needed to make business processes work again after the technology element is recovered, as identified by the RTO.

worm   A type of malware that is capable of activation and replication without being attached to an existing program.

X

XOR cipher conversion   A cryptographic operation in which a bit stream is subjected to a Boolean XOR function against some other data stream, typically a key stream. The XOR function compares bits from each stream and replaces similar pairs with a 0 and dissimilar pairs with a 1.

Z

zero tolerance risk exposure   An extreme level of risk acceptance whereby the organization is unwilling to allow any successful attacks or suffer any loss to an information asset.

zombie   An automated software program that executes certain commands when it receives a specific input from a system that is directed remotely by the attacker (usually via a transmitted command) to participate in a DoS attack. Also known as a bot.

Endnotes

Chapter 1

1. Davis, J. H. "Hacking of Government Computers Exposed 21.5 Million People." *New York Times*. July 9, 2015.

2. Chin, K. "Biggest Data Breaches in US History [Updated 2022]." August 5, 2022. www.upguard.com/blog/biggest-data-breaches-us.

3. Sun-Tzu. "Sun Tzu's The Art of War." Translated by the Sonshi Group. www.sonshi.com/original-the-art-of-war-translation-not-giles.html.

4. Internet World Stats. "Internet Usage Statistics: The Internet Big Picture, World Internet Users and Population Stats." www.internetworldstats.com/stats.htm.

5. Whitman, M., and Mattord, H. "Threats to Cybersecurity Revisited." *Journal of Information Systems Security*. 8(1), 2012. www.jissec.org/.

6. Webopedia. "Static Electricity and Computers." www.webopedia.com/DidYouKnow/Computer_Science/static.asp.

7. Wlasuk, A. "Cyber-Extortion–Huge Profits, Low Risk." *Security Week*. July 13, 2012. www.securityweek.com/cyber-extortion-huge-profits-low-risk.

8. "FBI: Cryptowall Ransomware Cost US User $18 Million." *Information Week*. June 24, 2015. www.darkreading.com/endpoint/fbi-cryptowall-ransomware-cost-us-users-$18-million/d/d-id/1321030.

9. Dickson, F., and Kissel, C. "IDC's 2021 Ransomware Study: Where You Are Matters!" www.idc.com/getdoc.jsp?containerId=US48093721.

10. Osterman Research. "Understanding the Depth of the Global Ransomware Problem." August 2016. www.malwarebytes.com/pdf/white-papers/UnderstandingTheDepthOfRansomwareIntheUS.pdf.

11. Druva. "You've Got Ransomware. Now What?" http://comztech.com/wp-content/uploads/2017/03/After%20a%20Ransomware%20Attack%20Todo%20list.pdf.

12. Dossett, J. "A Timeline of the Biggest Ransomware Attacks." November 15, 2021. CNET. www.cnet.com/personal-finance/crypto/a-timeline-of-the-biggest-ransomware-attacks/.

13. Bridis, T. "British Authorities Arrest Hacker Wanted as 'Fluffi Bunni.'" April 29, 2003. www.securityfocus.com/news/4320.

14. Perlroth, N., and Sanger, D. "Cyberattacks Seem Meant to Destroy, Not Just Disrupt." *New York Times*. March 28, 2013. www.nytimes.com/2013/03/29/technology/corporate-cyberattackers-possibly-state-backed-now-seek-to-destroy-data.html.

15. Sanger, D. E. "Pentagon Announces New Strategy for Cyberwarfare." *New York Times*. www.nytimes.com/2015/04/24/us/politics/pentagon-announces-new-cyberwarfare-strategy.html.

16. Leyden, J. "Multiple New Flaws Uncovered in SolarWinds Software Just Weeks After High-Profile Supply Chain Attack." *The Daily Swig*. February 3, 2021. https://portswigger.net/daily-swig/multiple-new-flaws-uncovered-in-solarwinds-software-just-weeks-after-high-profile-supply-chain-attack.

17. Pearce, J. "Security Expert Warns of MP3 Danger." ZDNet News Online. March 18, 2002. www.zdnet.com/article/security-expert-warns-of-mp3-danger/.

18. "Murphy's Laws Site." www.murphys-laws.com.

19. Russ, K. "How To: Mean Time Between Failures (MTBF)." *ComputerWorld*. October 31, 2005. www.computerworld.com/article/2560019/computer-hardware/mtbf.html.

20. OWASP. "OWASP Top Ten." 2021. https://owasp.org/www-project-top-ten.

21. Austin, R. "Conversations on Deadly Sins of Software Security—Programming Flaws and How to Fix Them." June 23, 2017.

22. Ibid.

23. Wheeler, D. "Write It Secure: Format Strings and Locale Filtering." www.dwheeler.com/essays/write_it_secure_1.html.

24. Austin, R. "Conversations on Deadly Sins of Software Security—Programming Flaws and How to Fix Them." June 23, 2017.

25. Brumley, D., Tzi-cker, C., Johnson, R., Lin, H., and Song, D. "RICH: Automatically Protecting Against Integer-Based Vulnerabilities." www.isoc.org/isoc/conferences/ndss/07/papers/efficient_detection_integer-based_attacks.pdf.

26. Austin, R. "Conversations on Deadly Sins of Software Security—Programming Flaws and How to Fix Them." June 23, 2017.

27. Nguyen, C. "More PCs Are Running Windows XP Than Windows 11." Digital Trends. April 13, 2022. www.digitaltrends.com/computing/more-pcs-are-running-windows-xp-than-windows-11/.

28. Bencsáth, B., Pék, G., Buttyán, L., and Félegyházi, M. "Duqu: A Stuxnet-Like Malware Found in the Wild." Technical report, Budapest University of Technology and Economics, 2011. www.crysys.hu/publications/files/bencsathPBF11duqu.pdf.

29. Kaspersky Lab. "Duqu 2.0: Frequently Asked Questions." http://media.kaspersky.com/en/Duqu-2-0-Frequently-Asked-Questions.pdf.

30. Schneier, B. "Duqu 2.0." www.schneier.com/blog/archives/2017/06/duqu_20.html.

Chapter 2

1. Wood, Charles Cresson. *Information Security Roles and Responsibilities Made Easy*. Version 3. Houston, TX: Information Shield, Inc., 2012. 137.

2. National Institute of Standards and Technology (NIST). "About NIST." www.nist.gov/about-nist.

3. Ward, B. "Planning as Doing: Accelerating the Business Planning Process." www.Managerwise.com. Accessed from www.refresher.com/Archives/!bwplanning.html.

4. *Information Security Governance: A Call to Action*, 2nd ed., Rolling Meadows, IL: IT Governance Institute, 2006.

5. Ibid.

6. Ibid.

7. Ibid.

8. Corporate Governance Task Force. "Information Security Governance: A Call to Action." National Cyber Security Partnership, 2004.

9. Ibid.

10. *Information Security Governance: A Call to Action*, 2nd ed., Rolling Meadows, IL: IT Governance Institute, 2006.

11. Westby, J. R., and Allen, J. H. "Governing for Enterprise Security (GES) Implementation Guide." 2007. Carnegie Mellon University, Software Engineering Institute, CERT®. http://resources.sei.cmu.edu/asset_files/TechnicalNote/2007_004_001_14837.pdf.

12. Westby, J. R., and Allen, J. H. "Governing for Enterprise Security (GES) Implementation Guide, Article 1: Characteristics of Effective Security Governance." 2007. Carnegie Mellon University, Software Engineering Institute, CERT. http://resources.sei.cmu.edu/asset_files/WhitePaper/2007_019_001_54375.pdf.

13. Westby, J. R., and Allen, J. H. "Governing for Enterprise Security (GES) Implementation Guide, Article 2: Defining an Effective Enterprise Security Program (ESP)." 2007. Carnegie Mellon University, Software Engineering Institute, CERT. http://resources.sei.cmu.edu/asset_files/WhitePaper/2007_019_001_54378.pdf.

14. Ibid.

15. Ibid.

16. Westby, J. R., and Allen, J. H. "Governing for Enterprise Security (GES) Implementation Guide, Article 3: Enterprise Security Program Activities." 2007. Carnegie Mellon University, Software Engineering Institute, CERT. http://resources.sei.cmu.edu/asset_files/WhitePaper/2007_019_001_54388.pdf.

17. International Organization for Standardization. ISO/IEC 27014: 2020. "Information Security, Cybersecurity and Privacy Protection—Governance of Information Security."

18. CQI/IRCA. "Providing Good Governance for Information Security." February 8, 2021. www.quality.org/knowledge/providing-good-governance-for-information-security.

19. Mahncke, R. "The Applicability of ISO/IEC 27014:2013 for Use Within General Medical Practice." Australian eHealth Informatics and Security Conference. December 2–4, 2013, Edith Cowan University, Perth, Western Australia. http://ro.ecu.edu.au/aeis/12.

20. International Organization for Standardization. ISO/IEC 27014, "Information Security, Cybersecurity and Privacy Protection—Governance of Information Security." www.iso.org/obp/ui/#iso:std:iso-iec:27014:ed-2:v1:en.

21. Ibid.

22. Verizon. Payment Security Report 2022. www.verizon.com/about/news/2022-verizon-business-payment-security-report.

23. Booz Allen Hamilton. "Convergence of Enterprise Security Organizations." 2005. www.asisonline.eu/docs/Convergence-Enterprise-Security-Organizations.pdf.

24. Deloitte and Touche. "The Convergence of Physical and Information Security in the Context of Enterprise Risk Management." Alliance for Enterprise Security Risk Management (AESRM). 2007.

25. "Findings from the OCEG GRC Strategy Study: How We Develop, Manage, and Evaluate GRC Efforts." OECG, Deloitte and Touche, SAP, Cisco, 2007.

26. Whitman, M., and Mattord, H. "SEC/CISE Survey of Information Protection Threats." www.securityexecutivecouncil.com/common/download.html?PROD=743.

27. Mattord, H., Whitman, M., Kotwica, K., and Battaglia, E. "Organizational Perspectives on Converged Security Operations." *Information and Computer Security*. January 2023. doi:10.1108/ICS-03-2023-0029.

28. Wood, Charles Cresson. *Information Security Roles and Responsibilities Made Easy*. Version 3. Houston, TX: Information Shield, Inc., 2012. 174.

Chapter 3

1. "Sun Tzu's The Art of War." Translated by the Sonshi Group. www.sonshi.com/original-the-art-of-war-translation-not-giles.html.

2. Scheierman, L. "How to Define Risk Management Goals and Objectives in Your Organization." KnowledgeLeader Blog. February 13, 2017. http://info.knowledgeleader.com/bid/164011/how-to-define-risk-management-goals-and-objectives-in-your-organization.

3. KPMG. "Understanding and Articulating Risk Appetite." https://erm.ncsu.edu/library/article/articulating-risk-appetite.

4. "Special Publication 800-30, Revision 1: Guide for Conducting Risk Assessments." National Institute of Standards and Technology (NIST). 2012. http://nvlpubs.nist.gov/nistpubs/Legacy/SP/nistspecialpublication800-30r1.pdf.

5. "The President's Executive Order 13526." www.archives.gov/isoo/policy-documents/cnsi-eo.html.

6. Zetter, K. "Lifelock Once Again Failed at Its One Job: Protecting Data." *Wired*. July 21, 2015. www.wired.com/2015/07/lifelock-failed-one-job-protecting-data.

7. Krebs, B. "Krebs on Security." July 25, 2018. https://krebsonsecurity.com/2018/07/lifelock-bug-exposed-millions-of-customer-email-addresses/.

8. Whitman, M., and Mattord, H. "Threats to Information Security Revisited." *Journal of Information Systems*. 8(1), 2012.

9. Whitman, M. "Enemy at the Gates: Threats to Information Security." *Communications of the ACM*. 46(8), August 2003.

10. Embroker. "Top 10 Cybersecurity Threats in 2024." January 4, 2024. www.embroker.com/blog/top-cybersecurity-threats/.

11. Verizon. "Cybercrime Thrives During Pandemic: Verizon 2021 Data Breach Investigations Report." https://www.verizon.com/about/news/verizon-2021-data-breach-investigations-report.

12. Rapid7. "Under the Hoodie." www.rapid7.com/globalassets/_pdfs/research/rapid7-under-the-hoodie-2018-research-report.pdf.

13. Verizon. "2021 Data Breach Investigation Report." www.verizon.com/business/resources/reports/2021/2021-data-breach-investigations-report.pdf.

14. Check Point. "Mobile Security Trends in 2022." www.checkpoint.com/cyber-hub/threat-prevention/what-is-mobile-security/mobile-security-trends-in-2022.

15. Cyrus, C. "IoT Cyberattacks Escalate in 2021, According to Kaspersky." IOT World Today. www.iotworldtoday.com/security/iot-cyberattacks-escalate-in-2021-according-to-kaspersky#close-modal.

16. Cybereason. "Ransomware: The True Cost to Business." 2022. www.cybereason.com/hubfs/dam/collateral/ebooks/Cybereason_Ransomware_Research_2021.pdf.

17. Ibid.

18. Sanger, D. E., and Perlroth, N. "F.B.I. Identifies Group Behind Pipeline Hack." *New York Times*. May 10, 2021.

19. Schwirtz, M., and Perlroth, N. "DarkSide, Blamed for Gas Pipeline Attack, Says It Is Shutting Down." *New York Times*. May 14, 2021.

20. "Special Publication 800-30, Revision 1: Guide for Conducting Risk Assessments." National Institute of Standards and Technology (NIST). 2012. http://nvlpubs.nist.gov/nistpubs/Legacy/SP/nistspecialpublication800-30r1.pdf.
21. Ibid.
22. Ibid.
23. Ibid.

Chapter 4

1. Peters, T., and Waterman, R. *In Search of Excellence: Lessons from America's Best-Run Companies.* New York: Harper and Row, 2004.
2. FDIC. "Tools to Manage Technology Providers' Performance Risk: Service Level Agreements." 2014. www.fdic.gov/news/financial-institution-letters/2014/tools-to-manage-technology-providers.pdf.
3. Ibid.
4. Anderson, J. "Panel Comments at 2002 Garage Technology Venture's State of the Art Conference." 2002.
5. "Special Publication 800-30, Revision 1: Guide for Conducting Risk Assessments." National Institute of Standards and Technology (NIST). September 2012. http://csrc.nist.gov/publications/PubsSPs.html.
6. FEMA. "Ready Business Mentoring Guide: Working with Small Businesses to Prepare for Emergencies." www.fema.gov/media-library-data/1392217307183-56ed30008abd809cac1a3027488a4c24/2014_business_user_guide.pdf.
7. Avolio, F. "Best Practices in Network Security." *Network Computing.* 11(5), March 20, 2000, pp. 60, 72.
8. ENISA. "The Risk Management Process." www.enisa.europa.eu/activities/risk-management/current-risk/risk-management-inventory/rm-process.

Chapter 5

1. Noone, J. "Rousseau's Social Contract: A Conceptual Analysis." University of Georgia Press, 1981.
2. "The Ten Commandments of Computer Ethics." Computer Professionals for Social Responsibility. cpsr.org/issues/ethics/cei.
3. Harrington, S. "The Effects of Codes of Ethics and Personal Denial of Responsibility on Computer Abuse Judgment and Intentions." *MIS Quarterly.* September 1996, 257–278.
4. Foote Partners, LLC. Press release. New Canaan, CT. August 18, 2003.
5. "(ISC)² Code of Ethics." (ISC)². www.isc2.org/Ethics#.
6. "Code of Ethics." GIAC. www.giac.org/about/program-overview/ethics.
7. "ISACA Code of Ethics." ISACA. www.isaca.org/credentialing/code-of-professional-ethics.
8. "What Is ISSA?" ISSA. www.issa.org/?page=AboutISSA.
9. "Code of Ethics." ISSA. www.issa.org/?page=CodeofEthics.
10. Ibid.
11. "Computer Security Act of 1987." Epic. epic.org/crypto/csa/csa.html.
12. *The American Heritage Dictionary of the English Language,* 4th ed., 2000.
13. "The Bill of Rights: A Transcription." National Archives, Archives.gov. www.archives.gov/founding-docs/bill-of-rights-transcript.
14. "Annotation 1—Fourth Amendment." Findlaw. constitution.findlaw.com/amendment4/annotation01.html.
15. "USC Title 47, Chapter 5, Subchapter II, Part I, § 222. Privacy of customer information." Cornell Law School. www.law.cornell.edu/uscode/47/222.html.
16. "The Privacy Act of 1974." U.S. Department of Justice. www.justice.gov/opcl/privacy-act-1974.
17. "USC Title 18, Part I, Chapter 119." Cornell Law School. www.law.cornell.edu/uscode/text/18/part-I/chapter-119.
18. Kelley, H. "Butt-Calls Aren't Private If Someone Listens on the Other End, Court Finds." http://money.cnn.com/2015/07/23/technology/buttcall-pocket-dial-case/index.html.
19. "Health Information Privacy." HIPAA Advisory. www.hhs.gov/hipaa/index.html.
20. "The Security Rule." U.S. Department of Health and Human Services. www.hhs.gov/hipaa/for-professionals/security/index.html.
21. "The HIPAA Privacy Rule." U.S. Department of Health and Human Services. www.hhs.gov/hipaa/for-professionals/privacy/index.html.

22. "Select Portions of the HITECH Act and Relationship to ONS Work." U.S. Department of Health and Human Services. October 30, 2009. healthit.gov/policy-researchers-implementers/select-portions-hitech-act-and-relationship-onc-work.

23. "Breach Notification Rule." U.S. Department of Health and Human Services. www.hhs.gov/ocr/privacy/hipaa/administrative/breachnotificationrule/index.html.

24. "Enforcement." U.S. Federal Trade Commission. www.ftc.gov/enforcement.

25. "The Economic Espionage Act of 1996." www.gpo.gov/fdsys/pkg/PLAW-104publ294/pdf/PLAW-104publ294.pdf.

26. "Sarbanes-Oxley Act." en.wikipedia.org/wiki/Sarbanes-Oxley_Act.

27. Fair, L. "First FTC Health Breach Notification Rule Case Addresses GoodRx's Not-So-Good Privacy Practices." Federal Trade Commission. www.ftc.gov/business-guidance/blog/2023/02/first-ftc-health-breach-notification-rule-case-addresses-goodrxs-not-so-good-privacy-practices.

28. "Welcome to the Data Privacy Framework (DPF) Program." www.dataprivacyframework.gov/.

29. "High Tech Crime." Australian Federal Police. www.afp.gov.au/what-we-do/crime-types/cybercrime/high-tech-crime.

30. "Official Code of Georgia Annotated (OCGA) §10-15-1. Definitions." law.justia.com/codes/georgia/2010/title-10/chapter-15/10-15-1.

31. Official Code of Georgia Annotated (OCGA) §10-15-2. "Disposal of Business Records Containing Personal Information." law.justia.com/codes/georgia/2010/title-10/chapter-15/10-15-2/.

32. Olsen, K. and Newman, C. "NYS Cyber Regulation Countdown: Risk Assessment—Now or Later?" Data Security Law. https://datasecuritylaw.com/nys-cyber-regulation-countdown-risk-assessment-now-or-later/.

33. PCI DSS 4.0. https://docs-prv.pcisecuritystandards.org/PCI%20DSS/Standard/PCI-DSS-v4_0.pdf.

34. PCI Data Security Standard (PCI DSS) version 3.2. April 2016. www.pcisecuritystandards.org/document_library?category=pcidss&document=pci_dss.

35. Verizon 2019 Payment Security Report. www.verizon.com/business/resources/Td5e/reports/2019-payment-security-fullreport-bl.pdf.

36. Ibid.

37. Ibid.

38. PCI Security Standards Council. "Why Security Matters." www.pcisecuritystandards.org/pci_security/why_security_matters.

39. Verizon Cyber Security Consulting. "PSR: Payment Security Report 2022." www.verizon.com/business/reports/payment-security-report/.

40. Alberts, R., Townsend, A., and Whitman, M. "The Threat of Long-Arm Jurisdiction to Electronic Commerce." *Communications of the ACM*. December 1998, 41(12), 15–20.

41. "About the National Protection and Programs Directorate." Department of Homeland Security. www.dhs.gov/about-national-protection-and-programs-directorate.

42. "InfraGard: A Partnership That Works." U.S. Federal Bureau of Investigation. www.fbi.gov/news/stories/2010/march/infragard_030810.

43. "About NSA." U.S. National Security Agency. www.nsa.gov/about.

44. "Information Assurance." U.S. National Security Agency. www.nsa.gov/what-we-do/information-assurance/.

45. "The Investigative Mission." U.S. Secret Service. www.secretservice.gov/investigation/.

Chapter 6

1. Helsing, C., Swanson, N., and Todd, M. National Institute of Standards and Technology. Special Publication 500–169: "Executive Guide to the Protection of Information Resources." October 1989. http://nvlpubs.nist.gov/nistpubs/Legacy/SP/nistspecialpublication500-169.pdf.

2. Wood, Charles Cresson. *Information Security Policies Made Easy*, 12th ed. Information Shield, 2012: 1.

3. Bergeron, F., and Bérubé, C. "End Users Talk Computer Policy." *Journal of Systems Management*. December 1990, 41(12): 14–17.

4. Wood, Charles Cresson. *Information Security Policies Made Easy*, 12th ed. Information Shield, 2012: 1.

5. Washington University in St. Louis. Information Security Policy. https://informationsecurity.wustl.edu/policies/.

6. Ibid.

7. Whitman, M. E. "Security Policy: From Design to Maintenance." *Information Security Policies and Strategies*—An Advances in MIS Monograph. Goodman, S., Straub, D., & Zwass, V. (eds.). M. E. Sharp, 2008.

8. Highlights of the 2017 U.S. PIAAC Results Web Report (NCES 2020-777). U.S. Department of Education. Institute of Education Sciences, National Center for Education Statistics. https://nces.ed.gov/surveys/piaac/current_results.asp.

9. Institute of Education Sciences. "U.S. Adults with Low Literacy and Numeracy Skills: 2012/14 to 2017." U.S. Department of Education. https://nces.ed.gov/pubs2022/2022004.pdf.

10. Ricks, D. A. *Blunders in International Business*. Blackwell, 1993: 40.

11. "Can Your Employees Understand Your Policies? How Readability Impacts Your Ethics & Compliance Program Effectiveness." December 3, 2014. www.jdsupra.com/legalnews/can-your-employees-understand-your-polic-04000/.

12. Whitman, M. E. "Security Policy: From Design to Maintenance." *Information Security Policies and Strategies*—An Advances in MIS Monograph. Goodman, S., Straub, D., & Zwass, V. (eds). 2008. Armonk NY: M. E. Sharp, Inc.

13. Ibid.

14. Ibid.

15. Wood, Charles Cresson. *Information Security Policies Made Easy*, 12th ed. Information Shield, 2012: 9.

16. Ibid.

Chapter 7

1. "Organizational Culture." www.businessdictionary.com/definition/organizational-culture.html.

2. Briney, A., and Prince, F. "Does Size Matter?" *Information Security*. September 2002, 36–54.

3. Ibid.

4. Ibid.

5. Ibid.

6. Ibid.

7. Hayes, M. "Where the Chief Security Officer Belongs." *InformationWeek*. February 25, 2002. www.informationweek.com/where-the-chief-security-officer-belongs/d/d-id/1013832?.

8. Kosutic, D. "Chief Information Security Officer (CISO)—Where Does He Belong in an Org Chart?" The ISO 27001 & ISO 22301 Blog. September 11, 2012. https://advisera.com/27001academy/blog/2012/09/11/chief-information-security-officer-CSO-where-does-he-belong-in-an-org-chart/.

9. Ibid.

10. (ISC)². 2022 Cybersecurity Workforce Study. www.isc2.org//-/media/ISC2/Research/2022-WorkForce-Study/ISC2-Cybersecurity-Workforce-Study.ashx.

11. Wood, Charles Cresson. *Information Security Roles and Responsibilities Made Easy*, Version 3. Information Shield, 2012: 161–341.

12. Schwartz, E., Erwin, D., Weafer, V., and Briney, A. "Roundtable: Information Security Staffing Help Wanted!" *Cybersecurity Magazine Online*. April 2001.

13. Sehmbi, A. "What Makes a CSO Employable?" *Information Security*. www.cybersecurity-magazine.com/magazine-features/what-makes-a-CSO-employable/.

14. Wood, Charles Cresson. *Information Security Roles and Responsibilities Made Easy*, Version 3. Information Shield, 2012: 188.

15. (ISC)². The Ultimate Guide to the CISSP. https://cloud.connect.isc2.org/cissp-ultimate-guide.

16. (ISC)². CISSP-ISSAP: Information Systems Security Architecture Professional. www.isc2.org/Certifications/CISSP-Concentrations.

17. (ISC)². CISSP-ISSEP: Information Systems Security Engineering Professional. www.isc2.org/Certifications/CISSP-Concentrations.

18. (ISC)². CISSP-ISSMP: Information Systems Security Management Professional. www.isc2.org/Certifications/CISSP-Concentrations.

19. (ISC)². "SSCP®—Systems Security Certified Practitioner." www.isc2.org/sscp/default.aspx.

20. Ibid.

21. ISACA. "What is Covered on the CISM Exam?" www.isaca.org/credentialing/cism/cism-exam-content-outline.

22. ISACA. "What is Covered on the CGEIT Exam?" www.isaca.org/credentialing/cgeit/cgeit-exam-content-outline.

23. ISACA. CRISC Certification Job Practice—Effective 2015. www.isaca.org/credentialing/cgeit/cgeit-exam-content-outline.

24. GIAC. "Introducing GIAC's New Certification Journey." www.giac.org/blog/giacs-new-certification-journey/.

25. EC-Council. "C|CISO Domain Details." www.eccouncil.org/train-certify/certified-chief-information-security-officer-cciso/.

26. CompTIA. CompTIA Security+. www.comptia.org/certifications/security.

27. CompTIA. CompTIA CySA+. www.comptia.org/certifications/cybersecurity-analyst.

28. CompTIA. CompTIA Advanced Security Practitioner. www.comptia.org/certifications/comptia-advanced-security-practitioner.

29. National Security Agency. Centers of Academic Excellence. www.nsa.gov/Academics/Centers-of-Academic-Excellence/.

30. Ibid.

31. Newhouse, B., Keith, S., Scribner, B., and Witte, G. National Institute of Standards and Technology (NIST). Draft Special Publication 800-181, "NICE Cybersecurity Workforce Framework (NCWF)." 2017. http://csrc.nist.gov/publications/drafts/800-181/sp800_181_draft.pdf.

32. Irvine, C., Chin, S.-K., and Frincke, D. "Integrating Security into the Curriculum." *Electrical Engineering and Computer Science*. December 1998, 31(12), 25–30.

33. NIST NICE. "Cybersecurity Workforce Framework History." www.nist.gov/itl/applied-cybersecurity/nice/nice-framework-resource-center/nice-framework-history.

34. Toth, P., and Klein, P. NIST. Special Publication 800-16, Rev. 1, "A Role-Based Model for Federal Information Technology/Cybersecurity Training." 2014. https://csrc.nist.gov/pubs/sp/800/16/r1/3pd.

35. Ibid.

36. Trepper, C. "Training Developers More Efficiently." *InformationWeek*. June 14, 1999, 1A–10A.

37. Nieles, M., Dempsey, K., and Pillitteri, V. NIST. Special Publication 800-12, Rev. 1: "An Introduction to Information Security." June 2017. http://nvlpubs.nist.gov/nistpubs/SpecialPublications/NIST.SP.800-12r1.pdf.

38. Ibid.

39. Hansche, S. "Designing a Security Awareness Program: Part I." *Information Systems Security*. 9(6), January/February 2001, 14–23.

40. Guttman, B., and Roback, E. NIST. Special Publication 800-12: "An Introduction to Computer Security: The NIST Handbook." October 1995. http://nvlpubs.nist.gov/nistpubs/Legacy/SP/nistspecialpublication800-12.pdf.

41. Plous, S. "Tips on Creating and Maintaining an Educational Web Site." *Teaching of Psychology*, 27, 2000, 63–70.

42. Project Management Institute. "A Guide to the Project Management Body of Knowledge (PMBOK Guide)," 7th edition. 2021.

43. Ibid.

44. Project Management Institute. "PMBOX Project Performance Domains." www.pmi.org//media/pmi/documents/public/pdf/pmbok-standards/pmbok-project-performance-domains.pdf.

45. Ibid.

46. Project Management Institute. "A Guide to the Project Management Body of Knowledge (PMBOK Guide)," 7th edition. 2021.

Chapter 8

1. "Introduction to ISO 27002." International Organization for Standardization (ISO). www.27000.org/iso-27002.htm.

2. "International Standard ISO/IEC 17799:2000 Code of Practice for Information Security Management." ISO. November 2002. www.iso.org/standard/33441.html.

3. "About the ISO27k Standards." www.iso27001cybersecurity.com/html/iso27000.html.

4. Swanson, M., Bowen, P., Phillips, W., Gallup, D., and Lynes, D. Special Publication (SP) 800-34, Rev. 1: "Contingency Planning Guide for Federal Information Systems." National Institute of Standards and Technology. http://nvlpubs.nist.gov/nistpubs/Legacy/SP/nistspecialpublication800-34r1.pdf.

5. SP 800-53, Rev. 5: "Security and Privacy Controls for Information Systems and Organizations." National Institute of Standards and Technology. September 2020. https://nvlpubs.nist.gov/nistpubs/SpecialPublications/NIST.SP.800-53r5.pdf.

6.   SP 800-53A, Rev. 5: "Assessing Security and Privacy Controls in Information Systems and Organizations." National Institute of Standards and Technology. 2022. https://nvlpubs.nist.gov/nistpubs/SpecialPublications/NIST.SP.800-53Ar5.pdf.

7.   Bowen, P., Hash, J., and Wilson, M. SP 800-100: "Information Security Handbook: A Guide for Managers." National Institute of Standards and Technology. 2006. http://nvlpubs.nist.gov/nistpubs/Legacy/SP/nistspecialpublication800-100.pdf.

8.   SP 800-53, Rev. 5, "Security and Privacy Controls for Information Systems and Organizations." National Institute of Standards and Technology. September 2020. https://nvlpubs.nist.gov/nistpubs/SpecialPublications/NIST.SP.800-53r5.pdf.

9.   COBIT 2019 Framework: Introduction and Methodology. Information Systems Audit and Control Association (ISACA).

10. Ibid.

11. Ibid.

12. "Committee of Sponsoring Organizations of the Treadway Commission." Committee of Sponsoring Organizations (COSO). www.coso.org/SitePages/Internal-Control.aspx?web=1.

13. "Internal Control-Integrated Framework." COSO. www.coso.org/documents/internal%20control-integrated%20framework.pdf.

14. "Leveraging COSO Across the Three Lines of Defense." COSO. www.coso.org/default.htm.

15. Ibid.

16. Corporate Governance Task Force. "Information Security Governance: A Call to Action." April 2004. www.criminal-justice-careers.com/sites/default/files/resources/cybersecurityGov4_04.pdf.

17. Ibid.

18. Verizon. "2023 Payment Security Reports Insights." www.verizon.com/business/resources/T32d/whitepapers/2023-payment-security-report-insights.pdf.

19. Ibid.

20. Ibid.

21. Ibid.

22. Ibid.

23. Ibid.

24. Ibid.

25. "Department of Defense Trusted Computer System Evaluation Criteria." National Institute of Standards and Technology. https://csrc.nist.gov/csrc/media/publications/conference-paper/1998/10/08/proceedings-of-the-21st-nissc-1998/documents/early-cs-papers/dod85.pdf.

26. "The Common Criteria." Common Criteria. www.commoncriteriaportal.org.

27. Ibid.

28. Ibid.

29. "Access Control." Official (ISC)^2 Guide to the CISSP CBK. (ISC)^2. Tipton, H., and Hernandez, S. (eds.). CRC Press, 2012.

30. Special Publications (800 Series). National Institute of Standards and Technology. http://csrc.nist.gov/publications/PubsSPs.html.

31. Ibid.

32. Ibid.

33. The President Executive Order 13526–Classified National Security Information. www.archives.gov/isoo/policy-documents/cnsi-eo.html.

34. Evans, M., and Jenkins, R. "Major MI5 Operation Against al-Qaeda Endangered by Security Breach." *The Times.* April 9, 2009. www.thetimes.co.uk/tto/news/uk/crime/article1875995.ece.

35. "California v. Greenwood, 486 U.S. 35." Supreme Court of the United States. 1988. http://caselaw.findlaw.com/us-supreme-court/486/35.html.

36. "Security Architecture and Design." Official (ISC)^2 Guide to the CISSP CBK. (ISC)^2. Tipton, H., and Hernandez, S. (eds.). CRC Press, 2012.

37. Ibid.

38. Ibid.

39. Ibid.

40. Ibid.
41. Ibid.

Chapter 9

1. "What Do Background Checks Show?" BackgroundChecks.com. www.backgroundchecks.com/learningcenter.
2. "Fact Sheet 16b: Small Business Owner Background Check Guide." Privacy Rights Clearinghouse. www.privacyrights.org/small-business-owner-background-check-guide.
3. Ibid.
4. Kovacich, G. L. *The Information Systems Security Officer's Guide*, 2nd ed. Elsevier Science, 2003: 196.
5. Chew, E., Swanson, M., Stine, K., Bartol, N., Brown, A., and Robinson, W. Special Publication 800-55, Rev. 1: "Performance Measurement Guide for Information Security." National Institute of Standards and Technology. July 2008. csrc.nist.gov/publications/nistpubs/800-55-Rev1/SP800-55-rev1.pdf.
6. Ibid.
7. Ibid.
8. Ibid.
9. Ibid.
10. Kovacich, G. L. *The Information Systems Security Officer's Guide*, 2nd ed. Elsevier Science, 2003: 196.
11. Chew, E., Swanson, M., Stine, K., Bartol, N., Brown, A., and Robinson, W. Special Publication 800-55, Rev. 1: "Performance Measurement Guide for Information Security." National Institute of Standards and Technology. July 2008. csrc.nist.gov/publications/nistpubs/800-55-Rev1/SP800-55-rev1.pdf.
12. ISACA. "What is CMMI?" https://cmmiinstitute.com/cmmi/intro.
13. Chew, E., Swanson, M., Stine, K., Bartol, N., Brown, A., and Robinson, W. Special Publication 800-55, Rev. 1: "Performance Measurement Guide for Information Security." National Institute of Standards and Technology. July 2008. csrc.nist.gov/publications/nistpubs/800-55-Rev1/SP800-55-rev1.pdf.
14. Ibid.
15. Avolio, F. "Best Practices in Network Security." *Network Computing*. March 20, 2000.
16. Gartner Group. Enterprise Security Diagnostic: Best Practices. www.gartnerinfo.com/sec_diagnostic.
17. PCI Security Standards Council. "Payment Card Industry (PCI) Data Security Standard: Requirements and Security Assessment Procedures, V. 3.0." www.pcicybersecuritystandards.org/documents/PCI_DSS_v3.pdf.
18. ISO. "ISO/IEC 27000 Family—Cybersecurity Management Systems." www.iso.org/isoiec-27001-information-cybersecurity.html.
19. QSL. "ISO Certification Kept Simple." www.isoqsltd.com/flipbook/2016/files/assets/basic-html/index.html#11.

Chapter 10

1. "NIST General Information." National Institute of Standards and Technology. www.nist.gov/public_affairs/general_information.cfm.
2. "Computer Security Division." National Institute of Standards and Technology. https://csrc.nist.gov/about.
3. Swanson, M., Bowen, P., Phillips, A., Gallup, D., and Lynes, D. Special Publication 800-34, Rev. 1, "Contingency Planning Guide for Federal Information Systems." National Institute of Standards and Technology. csrc.nist.gov/publications/nistpubs/800-34-rev1/sp800-34-rev1_errata-Nov11-2010.pdf.
4. "Disaster Recovery Guide." The Hartford. www.thehartford.com/claims/business-disaster-recovery-guide.
5. Swanson, M., Bowen, P., Phillips, A., Gallup, D., and Lynes, D. Special Publication 800-34, Rev. 1, "Contingency Planning Guide for Federal Information Systems." National Institute of Standards and Technology. csrc.nist.gov/publications/nistpubs/800-34-rev1/sp800-34-rev1_errata-Nov11-2010.pdf.
6. Swanson, M., Hash, J., and Bowen, P. Special Publication 800-18, Rev. 1, "Guide for Developing Information Security Plans for Information Systems." National Institute of Standards and Technology. February 2006. csrc.nist.gov/publications/nistpubs/800-18-Rev1/sp800-18-Rev1-final.pdf.
7. Zawada, B., and Evans, L. "Creating a More Rigorous BIA." CPM Group. November/December 2002. www.contingencyplanning.com/archives/2002/novdec/4.aspx.

8. Swanson, M., Bowen, P., Phillips, A., Gallup, D., and Lynes, D. Special Publication 800-34, Rev. 1, "Contingency Planning Guide for Federal Information Systems." National Institute of Standards and Technology. csrc.nist.gov/publications/nistpubs/800-34-rev1/sp800-34-rev1_errata-Nov11-2010.pdf.

9. Ibid.

10. Ibid.

11. Ibid.

12. Ibid.

13. Cichonski, P., Millar, T., Grance, T., and Scarfone, K. Special Publication 800-61, Rev. 2, "Computer Security Incident Handling Guide." National Institute of Standards and Technology. nvlpubs.nist.gov/nistpubs/SpecialPublications/NIST.SP.800-61r2.pdf.

14. Ibid.

15. Pipkin, D. *Information Security: Protecting the Global Enterprise.* Prentice Hall PTR, 2000:285.

16. Cichonski, P., Millar, T., Grance, T., and Scarfone, K. Special Publication 800-61, Rev. 2, "Computer Security Incident Handling Guide." National Institute of Standards and Technology. nvlpubs.nist.gov/nistpubs/SpecialPublications/NIST.SP.800-61r2.pdf.

17. Pipkin, D. *Information Security: Protecting the Global Enterprise.* Prentice Hall PTR, 2000:285.

18. McAfee. "Emergency Incident Response: 10 Common Mistakes of Incident Responders." www.mcafee.com/us/resources/white-papers/foundstone/wp-10-common-mistakes-incident-responders.pdf.

19. Cichonski, P., Millar, T., Grance, T., and Scarfone, K. Special Publication 800-61, Rev. 2, "Computer Security Incident Handling Guide." National Institute of Standards and Technology. nvlpubs.nist.gov/nistpubs/SpecialPublications/NIST.SP.800-61r2.pdf.

20. Witty, R. "What Is Crisis Management?" Gartner Online. September 19, 2001. www.gartner.com/doc/340971.

21. Davis, L. *Truth to Tell: Tell It Early, Tell It All, Tell It Yourself: Notes from My White House Education.* Free Press, 1999.

22. Marcinko, R., and Weisman, J. *Designation Gold.* Pocket Books, 1998.

23. Brown, N. D., Chen, Y., Harrington, H., Vicinanza, P., Chatman, J. A., Goldberg, A., and Srivastava, S. "How Have Organization Cultures Shifted During the COVID-19 Pandemic." https://cmr.berkeley.edu/2021/07/how-have-organizational-cultures-shifted/.

Chapter 11

1. Bowen, P., Hash, J., and Wilson, M. Special Publication (SP) 800-100, "Information Security Handbook: A Guide for Managers." National Institute of Standards and Technology. October 2006. nvlpubs.nist.gov/nistpubs/Legacy/SP/nistspecialpublication800-100.pdf.

2. Hash, J., Bartol, N., Rollins, H., Robinson, W., Abeles, J., and Batdorff, S. SP 800-65, "Integrating IT Security into the Capital Planning and Investment Control Process." National Institute of Standards and Technology. January 2005. nvlpubs.nist.gov/nistpubs/Legacy/SP/nistspecialpublication800-65.pdf.

3. Dempsey, K., Pillitteri, V. Y., and Regenscheid, A. SP 800-47, Rev. 1, "Managing the Security of Information Exchanges." National Institute of Standards and Technology. 2021. https://nvlpubs.nist.gov/nistpubs/SpecialPublications/NIST.SP.800-47r1.pdf.

4. Grance, T., Stevens, M., and Myers, M. SP 800-36, "Guide to Selecting Information Technology Security Products." National Institute of Standards and Technology. October 2003. csrc.nist.gov/publications/nistpubs/800-36/NIST-SP800-36.pdf.

5. Cuff, J. "Grow Up: How Mature Is Your Help Desk?" Compass America, Inc. fsz.ifas.ufl.edu/HD/GrowUpWP.pdf.

6. Kissel, R., Stine, K., Scholl, M., Rossman, H., Fahlsing, J., and Gulick, J. SP 800-64, Rev. 2, "Security Considerations in the System Development Life Cycle." National Institute of Standards and Technology. October 2008. nvlpubs.nist.gov/nistpubs/Legacy/SP/nistspecialpublication800-64r2.pdf.

7. Joint Task Force Transformation Initiative. SP 800-53, Rev. 4, "Assessing Security and Privacy Controls in Information Systems and Organizations." National Institute of Standards and Technology. April 2013. nvlpubs.nist.gov/nistpubs/SpecialPublications/NIST.SP.800-53r4.pdf.

8. U.S. Cybersecurity and Infrastructure Security Agency. "US-CERT and ICS-CERT Transition to CISA." www.cisa.gov/news-events/alerts/2023/02/24/us-cert-and-ics-cert-transition-cisa.

Chapter 12

1. Mujtaba, H. "Intel Core i9-13900 'Raptor Lake' Early CPU Sample Tested, Up To 50% Faster Than Core i9-12900 'Alder Lake' at Just 3.7 GHz Clock Speeds." Wccftech. https://wccftech.com/intel-raptor-lake-core-i9-13900-es-cpu-up-to-50-percent-faster-than-alder-lake-core-i9-12900-leaked-benchmarks.

2. From multiple sources, including Jain, A., Ross, A., and Prabhakar, S. "An Introduction to Biometric Recognition." *IEEE Transactions on Circuits and Systems for Video Technology*, 14(1). January 2004; and Yun, W. "The '123' of Biometric Technology." 2003. www.newworldencyclopedia.org/entry/Biometrics.

3. Cobb, M. "What Are Common (and Uncommon) Unified Threat Management Features?" SearchMidmarketSecurity. searchmidmarketsecurity.techtarget.com/tip/What-are-common-and-uncommon-unified-threat-management-features.

4. Beaver, K. "Finding Clarity: Unified Threat Management Systems vs. Next-Gen Firewalls." searchsecurity.techtarget.com/tip/Finding-clarity-Unified-threat-management-systems-vs-next-gen-firewalls.

5. Day, K. *Inside the Security Mind: Making the Tough Decisions*. Prentice-Hall, 2003: 220.

6. Grigorof, A. "Challenges in Managing Firewalls." www.eventid.net/show.asp?DocId=18.

7. Taylor, L. "Guidelines for Configuring Your Firewall Rule-Set." ZDNet, April 12, 2001. www.zdnet.com/news/guidelines-for-configuring-your-firewall-rule-set/298790.

8. "What Is RSN (Robust Secure Network)?" Tech FAQ Online. www.tech-faq.com/rsn-robust-secure-network.html.

9. Title 18 U.S. Code, Section 3127. www.law.cornell.edu/uscode/text/18/3127.

10. Day, K. *Inside the Security Mind: Making the Tough Decisions*. Prentice-Hall, 2003: 225.

11. Kent, K., and Souppaya, M. Special Publication 800-92, "Guide to Computer Security Log Management." National Institute of Standards and Technology. 2006. csrc.nist.gov/publications/nistpubs/800-92/SP800-92.pdf.

12. Ibid.

13. Ibid.

14. Ibid.

15. Steiner, J., Neuman, C., and Schiller, J. "An Authentication Service for Open Network Systems." Paper presented for Project Athena, March 30, 1988. www.scs.stanford.edu/nyu/05sp/sched/readings/kerberos.pdf.

16. Krutz, R., and Vines, R. D. *The CISSP Prep Guide: Mastering the Ten Domains of Computer Security*. John Wiley and Sons, 2001: 40.

Index